HISTORICAL DICTIONARIES OF RELIGIONS,
PHILOSOPHIES, AND MOVEMENTS
Jon Woronoff, Series Editor

Historical Dictionary of Seventh-day Adventists

Gary Land

Historical Dictionaries of Religions, Philosophies, and Movements, No. 56

The Scarecrow Press, Inc.
Lanham, Maryland • Toronto • Oxford
2005

SCARECROW PRESS, INC.

Published in the United States of America
by Scarecrow Press, Inc.
A wholly owned subsidary of
The Rowman & Littlefield Publishing Group, Inc.
4501 Forbes Boulevard, Suite 200, Lanham, Maryland 20706
www.scarecrowpress.com

PO Box 317
Oxford
OX2 9RU, UK

British Library Cataloguing in Publication Information Available

Library of Congress Cataloging-in-Publication Data
Land, Gary, 1944–
  Historical dictionary of Seventh-Day Adventists / by Gary Land.
    p. cm. — (Historical dictionaries of religions, philosophies, and
movements ; no. 56)
  Includes bibliographical references.
  ISBN 0-8108-5345-0 (hardcover : alk. paper)
  1. Seventh-Day Adventists—History—Dictionaries. I. Title. II. Series.
BX6153.L36 2005
286.7'32'03—dc22

                                                                    2004022979

Contents

Editor's Foreword

The Seventh-day Adventists form one of the more recent Christian denominations, only reaching back less than two centuries to their occasionally tumultuous founding. In that relatively brief span they have created one of the most dynamic churches in nearly every respect. Most obvious has been the sheer growth in numbers, expanding at an exceptional pace and, most unusually, not even predominantly among older Christian groups or in their country of origin but abroad, often enough in what is called the "Third World." This alone has done much to reshape them in many ways. But they were also reshaped with regards to doctrine and theology as different ideas and theories contended and found greater or lesser acceptance, sometimes also resulting in breakaway or splinter groups. They have also periodically reinvented themselves organizationally, going from an almost total lack of structure to a fairly complex yet comparatively open and democratic one. Alongside the many religious currents, the Adventists have also been pioneers in secular areas such as health care and health reform, education, and use of the media. Still, despite their continuing efforts to be better known, they remain a mystery to sectors of the general public.

This *Historical Dictionary of the Seventh-day Adventists* will hopefully remove some of the mystery since, although compiled by someone who knows the denomination extremely well from inside, it is written in terms that can be readily understood by outsiders as well. This starts with a brief chronology, tracing the SDA's unexpected emergence and rapid expansion. It continues with a broad introduction covering most basic aspects of its history and functions. Then there are numerous dictionary entries on specific features of its history and development, its structure and organization, its theology and practical activities. These include brief biographies of key persons, since they shaped the denomination, and particularly helpful synopses of the situation in each country or region to which it has spread. The bibliography includes books with very different views on occasion and will certainly be useful for anyone who wants to explore further.

This volume was, as indicated, written by a member of the church, and one with particularly useful experience and a broad perspective. Among other things, since 1970 Gary Land has been teaching at Andrews University, a major SDA educational institution, with an emphasis but hardly exclusive interest in Seventh-day Adventist history. He has written widely on Adventism, including articles and papers, while also acting as editor and/or coauthor of three major works on the denomination's history. He has also contributed to several SDA journals and newsletters and has served as coeditor of *Adventist Heritage* and as a member of the board of *Spectrum*. Moreover, Dr. Land is a member of the Association of Seventh-day Adventist Historians. With this sort of background it was not surprising that he has done such a thorough job of providing both the big and little pictures which makes this encyclopedia such a useful tool.

Jon Woronoff
Series Editor

Acknowledgments

In addition to the many published and unpublished sources from which I have obtained information, several individuals have given information and/or have read various entries. These include Samuele Bacchiocchi, Greg Constantine, Delmer Davis, James Ford, Øystein LaBianca, Linda Mack, Scott Moncrieff, Dale Ratzlaff, Ciro Sepulveda, and Dan Shultz. Russell Staples, Floyd Greenleaf, Brian Strayer, and Michael Campbell kindly read the entire original manuscript. Although these individuals have saved me from making several mistakes and have made many helpful suggestions, any errors of fact or interpretation are, of course, my own responsibility. In addition, series editor Jon Woronoff has helpfully guided the development of this project, making many suggestions regarding both content and approach. Finallly, I am grateful to Debi Everhart for her help with formatting the book when my computer skills proved inadequate and to Terri Calkins, who entered a large portion of the bibliography into the manuscript.

Reader's Note

For consistency throughout this volume, I have based the national membership statistics on the *2003 Yearbook* of the Seventh-day Adventist Church. Individuals desiring historical statistics can find them in the *Yearbooks* published annually between 1883 and 1894 and since 1904. The *Review and Herald* often published statistics during those years when there was no *Yearbook*. Statistics for the period after 2003 may be found in future editions of the *Yearbook* and at www.adventiststatistics.org. I have chosen my entry selections through an analysis of the contents of both general and specialized works on Seventh-day Adventist history, entries in the *Seventh-day Adventist Encyclopedia*, and suggestions of those who read the original manuscript. The *Encyclopedia* was also often indispensable in providing information regarding the history of Adventism in individual countries. At this point in time, North American and European names and institutions dominate the entries, but with the dramatically changed membership patterns of the past half century, a work such as this written 50 years from now will show a much more international cast of characters. Readers should be aware that through the mid-20th century, most Adventist sources use initials in place of given names. I have provided first given names whenever I have been able to identify them. Finally, I have limited organizational abbreviations to a minimum, using them only to avoid unnecessary repetition of a name within an entry.

Cross references are indicated by bold face type. "See" references indicate entries of related interest.

Acronyms and Abbreviations

AAAF	Association of Adventist Forums
AAW	Association of Adventist Women
ADRA	Adventist Development and Relief Agency International
AFM	Adventist Frontier Missions
AHS	Adventist Health System
AIIAS	Adventist International Institute of Advanced Studies
AJY	Adventist Junior Youth
AMC	Adventist Media Center
ARLA	American Religious Liberty Association
ASI	Adventist-Laymen's Services and Industries
ASRS	Adventist Society for Religious Studies
ATS	American Temperance Society; Adventist Theological Society
AU	Andrews University
AUC	Atlantic Union College
AUP	Adventist Univeristy of the Philippines
AUSS	Andrews University Seminary Studies
AWI	Adventist Women's Institute
AWR	Adventist World Radio
AY	Adventist Youth
AY2Y	Adventist Youth to Youth
AYS	Adventist Youth Service
BRI	Biblical Research Institute
CME	College of Medical Evangelists
CUC	Columbia Union College; Canadian University College
ECD	East-Central Africa Division
EMC	Emmanuel Missionary College
ESD	Euro-Asia Division
EUD	Euro-Africa Division
GC	General Conference of Seventh-day Adventists
GRI	Geoscience Research Institute
HSI	Home Study International

IAD	Inter-American Division
JMV	Junior Missionary Volunteer Society
LLU	Loma Linda University
LSU	La Sierra University
MCC	Medical Cadet Corps
MMBA	Medical Missionary and Benevolent Association
MV	Missionary Volunteer Society
NAD	North American Division
NRLA	National Religious Liberty Association
NSD	Northern Asia-Pacific Division
NSO	National Service Organization
OC	Oakwood College
PARL	Department of Public Affairs and Religious Liberty
PPPA	Pacific Press Publishing Association
PUC	Pacific Union College; Philippine Union College
RHPA	Review and Herald Publishing Association
RLA	Religious Liberty Association of North America
SAD	South American Division
SAU	Southern Adventist University
SAWS	Seventh-day Adventist World Service, Inc.
SDA	Seventh-day Adventist
SID	Southern Africa-Indian Ocean Division
SMC	Southern Missionary College
SPA	Southern Publishing Association
SPD	South Pacific Division
SSD	Southern Asia-Pacific Division
SUD	Southern Asia Division
SWAU	Southwestern Adventist University
3ABN	Three Angels Broadcasting Network
T & M Soc.	Tract and Missionary Societies
TEAM	Time for Equality in Adventist Ministry
TED	Trans-European Division
UC	Union College
VOP	*Voice of Prophecy*
WAD	Western Africa Division
WMC	Washington Missionary College
WWC	Walla Walla College

Chronology

1818   From his study of the book of Daniel, William Miller concludes that the Second Coming of Jesus will occur about 1843

1831   William Miller begins publicly preaching his views

1840   Joshua V. Himes publishes the first issue of *The Signs of the Times*

1843   William Miller concludes that Jesus will return between March 21, 1843, and March 21, 1844, dates that he calculated as correlating with the Jewish calendar year

1844   Samuel S. Snow promotes the view that Jesus would return on the Day of Atonement, which according to his interpretation of the Jewish Karaite calendar, would take place on October 22, 1844

    Jesus does not return on October 22

    In December Ellen Harmon experiences her first vision

1845   Mutual Conference of Adventists meets at Albany, New York

    Joseph Bates adopts the seventh-day, Saturday, as the Sabbath

1846   O. R. L. Crosier publishes an article in the *Day Star Extra* arguing that on October 22, 1844, Jesus moved from the Holy Place to the Most Holy Place of the heavenly sanctuary

1847-48 A series of "Sabbath Conferences" brings together a group coalescing around beliefs in the seventh-day Sabbath, Christ's ministry in the heavenly sanctuary, and the divine inspiration of Ellen (Harmon) White

1849   James White publishes *Present Truth*

1850   James White publishes *Advent Review* and then combines it with *Present Truth* under the title *Second Advent Review and Sabbath Herald*

1855   Sabbatarian Adventist leaders move the *Review* office from Rochester, New York, to Battle Creek, Michigan

1859   Merritt G. Kellogg arrives in California

1860   Committee of sabbatarian Adventists choose the name "Seventh-day Adventist"

1861   The Seventh-day Adventist Publishing Association and the Michigan Conference of Seventh-day Adventists are organized

1863   The General Conference of Seventh-day Adventists is organized

Ellen G. White experiences her first health vision at Otsego, Michigan

1864   Michael B. Czechowski goes to Europe as an unofficial Seventh-day Adventist missionary

1866   Health Reform Institute opens in Battle Creek, Michigan

1868   First official camp meeting takes place at Wright, Michigan

1872   John G. Matteson begins the first Seventh-day Adventist foreign-language journal

1874   Battle Creek College is established in Battle Creek, Michigan

John Nevins Andrews goes to Europe as the first official Seventh-day Adventist missionary

Isaac and Adelia Van Horn begin evangelism in Pacific Northwest

1875   Pacific Seventh-day Adventist Publishing Association organizes in Oakland, California

1876   General Conference session adopts tithing

1877   General Conference sends John G. Matteson as a missionary to Scandinavia

1878   William Ings introduces Adventism to Great Britain

1881   Healdsburg College is established in California

1882   Uriah Smith's *Daniel and the Revelation* becomes the first significant subscription book

1884   Dr. Katherine Kindsay opens a nursing school in Battle Creek, Michigan

1885   Stephen N. Haskell and others arrive as missionaries in Australia

1886   *The American Sentinel*, journal of religious liberty, is first published

Gerhardt Perk and Louis R. Conradi preach Adventism in the Crimea

1887   D. A. Robinson and C. L. Boyd arrive in Cape Town, South Africa, as the first Adventist missionaries to the continent

1888   General Conference session at Minneapolis debates "righteousness by faith"

Abram La Rue establishes a seaman's mission in Hong Kong

1890   Mission schooner, *Pitcairn*, is launched to work in the South Pacific

1892   Z. G. Baharian and Theodore Anthony hold evangelistic meetings in Turkey

1894   Australia organizes the first union conference

Solusi Mission, the first Adventist mission for Black Africans, is established in Rhodesia

F. H. Westphal begins Seventh-day Adventist efforts in Argentina

1895   Georgia Burrus begins teaching in India

Edson White takes riverboat, *The Morning Star*, into the American South, spreading Adventism among African Americans

1896   Oakwood Industrial School for African Americans opens in Huntsville, Alabama

1897   Avondale School for Christian Workers opens in Australia

1901   General Conference session reorganizes denomination

Battle Creek College moves to Berrien Springs, Michigan; renamed Emmanuel Missionary College

1902   Battle Creek Sanitarium and Review and Herald Publishing Association buildings burn

George McCready Price publishes *Outlines of Modern Christianity and Modern Science*

1903   General Conference moves from Battle Creek, Michigan, to Takoma Park, Maryland, a suburb of Washington, D.C.

1904   Nashville Agricultural and Normal Institute established in Tennessee as first "self-supporting" institution

1907   Battle Creek Seventh-day Adventist Church terminates John Harvey Kellogg's membership

1908   Robert H. Habenicht founds River Plate Sanitarium, first Adventist health care institution in South America

1910   College of Medical Evangelists opens in Loma Linda, California

1911   Ferdinand and Ana Stahl begin missionary work in Lake Titicaca region of Peru

1915   Ellen G. White dies

1918   General Conference session adopts divisional organization

1921   The number of Seventh-day Adventists outside North America surpasses the number within the continent

1922   General Conference Ministerial Association established

1932   Pacific Union College becomes first Adventist college to receive accreditation

1937   Seventh-day Adventist Theological Seminary opens in Takoma Park, Maryland

Leo and Jessie Halliwell launch *Luzeiro* on the Amazon

1939   General Conference approves Medical Cadet Corps program

1942   The *Voice of Prophecy*, featuring H. M. S. Richards, Sr. broadcasts over a national radio network

1945   First Black regional conferences created in the United States

1947   Association of Seventh-day Adventist Self-Supporting Institutions formed

1950   *Faith for Today* television program airs in New York City

1953   First volume of *Seventh-day Adventist Bible Commentary* published

1956   Seventh-day Adventist Welfare Relief Service established

1957   General Conference establishes Geoscience Research Institute

Evangelical-Adventist dialogue leads to publication of *Seventh-day Adventists Answer Questions on Doctrine*

1960   Andrews University organized in Berrien Springs, Michigan

1962   General Conference sponsors "Five-day Plan to Stop Smoking"

1971   Adventist World Radio begun

1973   Merikay Silver sues Pacific Press Publishing Association for gender discrimination

Medical school opens at Montemorelos University in Mexico

1974   Black television program, *Breath of Life*, airs first broadcast

1977   North American Adventist Media Center established

1979   Inter-American Division becomes the largest world division

1987   Adventist International Institute of Advanced Studies opens in the Philippines

1989   Zaoksky Theological Seminary opens in Soviet Union

General Conference moves to Silver Spring, Maryland

1990   Independent North American Division established

Global Mission becomes an official program

1991   White South African Union and Black Southern Union merge

1995   Church begins satellite evangelism with 'Net '95

1996   Cuba Adventist Seminary dedicates new building

1999   Jan Paulsen becomes the first European to be elected General Conference president since Ole Oleson, an immigrant to America, in 1888

2000   Southeastern California Conference issues same credentials to both men and women

2002   First of three annual Faith and Science conferences takes place in Colorado

Introduction

Seventh-day Adventism has been something of an enigma to observers. Scholars have described it as a fundamentalist[1] or evangelical Christian sect or denomination[2] (although this is often qualified by a variant of the phrase "close to"), as a non- or sub-Christian cult,[3] and even as Gnostic.[4] One textbook author has stated that "other Americans, in the general structure of their beliefs and attitudes, were much like Seventh-day Adventists, while Seventh-day Adventists were much like other Americans."[5] It is not surprising, therefore, that the general public, at least in the United States, has had an equally difficult time identifying Adventists, frequently confusing them with the Church of Jesus Christ of Latter-Day Saints (Mormons) or with Jehovah's Witnesses.[6]

Despite this confusion regarding classification or definition, it is relatively easy to describe Adventism as a social phenomenon. Although born as a radical millenarian sect in 19th-century America, Adventism has spread across the world, achieving far more success in Latin America, Africa, and Asia than in its native land. In what seems a paradox to many observers, Adventist expectation of Christ's imminent return has led the denomination to develop extensive educational and health systems. Increasingly established within a variety of societies, Adventism over time has modified its views on many issues and accommodated itself to the "delay" of the Second Advent. In the process it has become a multicultural religion that nonetheless reflects the dominant influence of its American origins.

Adventism and the Second Great Awakening

Beginning around 1800 the United States experienced a religious revival that has come to be known as the Second Great Awakening. With its origins marked by the 1801 Cane Ridge camp meeting in Kentucky (attended by more than 10,000 people) and a religious awakening at Yale College in 1802 that students spread up and down the East Coast, the revival moved in waves throughout the Northeastern and Western (as it was called at the time) United States for nearly half a century. Upstate New York experienced such a succession of revivals that it became known as the "burned-over district." Emerging as the leading preacher of the awakening, Charles G. Finney (1792-1875) helped fashion a style of revivalism, involving such "new measures" as direct preaching and prayer, protracted meetings, and the anxious bench, that has shaped American evangelism down to our own time. Along with many other preachers of the awakening, he emphasized personal conversion and a form of perfectionism. As the popular revival hymn, "Rock of Ages," stated: "Be of sin the double cure, Save from wrath and make me pure."

This desire for personal perfection was also, for many revivalists and their converts, linked with a post-millennial expectation that the awakening was preparing the way for the establishment of God's kingdom. To help that kingdom along they formed voluntary societies to promote religion, including the American Bible Society (1816), the American Sunday School Union (1824), and the American Tract Society (1825). They also sought to attack society's ills through such organizations as the Society for the Promotion of Temperance (1826) and, most importantly, the American Anti-Slavery Society (1833).

While the Methodist and Baptist churches grew rapidly during the Second Great Awakening, more radical groups sought to restore primitive New Testament Christianity. The most prominent of these restorationists were Alexander Campbell and Barton W. Stone, who strongly objected to creeds and opposed the organization of denominations. Nonetheless, they established a new denomination, the Disciples of Christ. While Campbell and Stone preached restorationism in the West, a less prominent group, the Christian Connection (originally spelled Connexion), promoted similar ideas in New England. And in upstate New York, Joseph Smith took the restoration idea one step further when, with the *Book of Mormon*, he claimed to have received a new revelation, a third testament as it were.

William Miller, a farmer living in Low Hampton, New York, contributed to this Second Great Awakening mix of revivalism, millennialism, and restorationism with his startling prediction, first publicly presented in 1831, that Jesus would return about the year 1843. Miller, a former Deist turned Baptist, reflected the democratic Christianity developing in America[7] with his belief that any individual could properly interpret the Bible without dependence on scholarly authorities. Although he used other biblical evidence as well, Miller focused on Daniel 8:14, "Unto two thousand and three hundred days; then shall the sanctuary be cleansed." Understanding that a day in prophetic time referred to a year of actual time and that the term sanctuary meant the earth, Miller believed that this text foretold the time of Christ's second advent. While his premillennialist understanding of the Second Advent differed from the reigning postmillennialism of the Awakening, Miller's "lectures," as he called them, produced revivals, and ministers in his region called on him to speak to their churches. Miller had only regional impact in the 1830s, but his meeting with Boston's Christian Connection pastor Joshua V. Himes in 1839 brought him to national prominence.

Using the promotional tools forged by the various reform groups to which he belonged, Himes made Millerism a movement. As conferences and camp meetings were organized, papers published, and preachers sent throughout the Northeast and Old Northwest, the Adventist thrust moved far beyond Miller's control. Indeed, pressure from the movement forced Miller to more precisely state that Jesus would return between March 21, 1843, and March 21, 1844; and in 1843 Charles Fitch, in contrast with Miller's opposition to formation of a new sect, called on the Millerites to leave their home churches, for those denominations had become Babylon. Finally, in the summer of 1844, when Jesus had not come as expected, Samuel S. Snow, a minor Millerite preacher, predicted that Jesus would come that year on the Day of Atonement, October 22, an idea that spread like wildfire through the movement. While the masses of Millerites gathered around this new expectation, Miller and the other leaders did not accept it until late September and early October. When Jesus did not return, however, it was left to Himes, Miller, and other leaders to help their followers recover from the "Great Disappointment," an effort that they started almost immediately.

Despite the fact that the Millerite movement ended in disappointment, it should be recognized as a major religious development of the 1840s. While estimates of the number of adherents have run from 50,000 to 250,000, the movement had an impact far beyond its true believers. In the first serious historical study of the Millerites, for instance, Everett N. Dick found that local Baptist and Methodist churches experienced their greatest growth when Millerite preachers came into their territory.[8] Rather than being a strange movement outside the norms of 19th-century American society, several scholars have argued that the Millerites were very much a part of their culture.[9] And, as Richard Carwardine points out, the Millerite movement constituted the final thrust of the Second Great Awakening.[10]

The Emergence of Seventh-day Adventism

Out of the confusion following the "Great Disappointment," the Millerites went in several directions: some lost faith in Christianity, many returned to their original churches, and others eventually established such Adventist denominations as the Advent Christian Church and the Church of God of the Abrahamic Faith. But on the fringes of the movement between 1845 and 1849 emerged a radical group, the sabbatarian Adventists, who in time would become the largest of all the Adventist churches.

The sabbatarians regarded themselves as the true descendents of the Millerite faith, for they continued believing that the sanctuary had been cleansed beginning on October 22, 1844. Rather than identifying the sanctuary of Daniel 8:14 as the earth, as Miller had done, through the influence of Hiram Edson, a New York farmer, and his associate O. R. L. Crosier, they concluded that the sanctuary to be cleansed was the heavenly sanctuary referred to in Hebrews 8 and 9. On the day of the Great Disappointment, therefore, Jesus had begun his ministry as High Priest in the sanctuary not made with hands; when that work—which they later identified as one of judgment—was finished he would return for the saints.

Through this sanctuary doctrine, the sabbatarian Adventists maintained their Millerite millennial heritage but they also linked this millennialism with the restorationism that was an important part of the Second Great Awakening. As a result of the witness of Rachel Oakes Preston, a Seventh Day Baptist, a congregation of Adventists observing Saturday as the Sabbath formed in Washington, New Hampshire, in 1844. About the same time, perhaps influenced by this group, Millerite preacher Thomas M. Preble also began observing the Sabbath and the following year published an article and tract arguing that the fourth commandment was still binding on Christians. Although Preble later abandoned his Sabbath belief, his tract fell into the hands of Joseph Bates, a former sea captain and Millerite preacher, who adopted the Sabbath doctrine in 1845 and later that year met with Frederick Wheeler, pastor of the Washington, New Hampshire, congregation. Not simply seeing the Sabbath as the restoration of a doctrine long hidden by tradition and after learning of Edson's interpretation of October 22, 1844, Bates argued in a series of tracts that Christ's entrance into the Most Holy Place of the heavenly sanctuary opened a new emphasis on the Sabbath, for the Ten Commandments were in the ark located in the second apartment and that doctrine was now the symbol of true faith in God. As their thinking developed, the sabbatarian Adventists came to see themselves as fulfilling what the Protestant Reformation had begun, bringing Christianity full-circle back to true biblical belief and practice. Drawing identity from the three angels' messages of Revelation 14:6-11, these Adventists saw their task as one of warning the world against worshipping the beast and his image, which they identified as Roman Catholicism's and "apostate" Protestantism's observance of Sunday. In these last days, they believed, true Christians must join those who "keep the commandments of God, and the faith of Jesus" (Rev. 14:12).

In addition to this millennialist and restorationist combination of the sanctuary and Sabbath doctrines, the visions of Ellen G. White formed a third strand that shaped the sabbatarian Adventist movement. A 17-year-old Millerite, Ellen née Harmon experienced her first vision in December 1844 in Portland, Maine, and soon began speaking to small Millerite groups. Her travels brought her into contact with James White, a minor Millerite preacher, and in 1846 they married. In the autumn of that year they read one of Bates's pamphlets and began observing the Sabbath. About this same time Ellen started experiencing visions that confirmed their new doctrinal positions, something that continued as they adopted the sanctuary interpretation in 1847 and with Bates led out in a series of "Sabbath Conferences" in 1848 that codified the beliefs of the sabbatarian Adventist movement. In their thinking, Adventists understood Ellen White's visionary role as one that confirmed and clarified the results of their Bible study, rather than presenting new doctrinal revelations in the manner of Joseph Smith.

As their thought developed, the sabbatarian Adventists continued the democratic theology of the Second Great Awakening. None of them was a trained biblical scholar or theologian. Rather they were farmers, school teachers, a sea captain, and even—in Ellen White's case—a minimally educated young woman, yet they confidently believed that they could accurately interpret the Bible and correct centuries of Christian tradition. In fact, the Adventists concluded that they had discovered long neglected or misunderstood doctrines, particularly Christ's ministry in the heavenly sanctuary and the seventh-day Sabbath, that were "present truth" for their time. Called by God to awaken the world to these truths, they believed, the "great second Advent movement" would play the key role as earth's history moved toward its climax.

Adventism, Organization, and Institutions

Through the 1850s, however, most sabbatarian Adventists opposed organizing their movement as a denomination. The conflict that had developed between the Millerites and the established churches in the 1840s largely shaped the Adventist view that the temptations of power and control turned organized religion into "Babylon." As leaders such as Joseph Bates and James and Ellen White visited the scattered groups of Adventists, however, they increasingly recognized the need for some form of organization. Whether the issue was certification of bona fide Adventist ministers, financial support of the ministry, or ownership of the *Review and Herald* printing facilities, they concluded that the movement must develop a formalized structure. As early as 1851 James White began calling for "gospel order." Although some rudimentary steps toward organization were taken during the next few years, the question of ownership of the *Review* "office" pushed the Adventists to adopt the name "Seventh-day Adventist" in 1860 and organize the Seventh-day Adventist Publishing Association the following year. In 1862 the churches in Michigan organized the first Adventist conference, which was followed by the organization of six more conferences during the next several months. In 1863 delegates from six of these conferences formed the General Conference.

It appears that once Seventh-day Adventists decided to organize they embraced the concept wholeheartedly, for during the next several years they formed many entities. By 1874 they had created the Health Reform Institute and Battle Creek College in Battle Creek, Michigan, following the example of previous health reformers and evangelical revival movements. After expanding to California in the 1860s Adventists soon established publishing, educational, and health institutions similar to those in Battle Creek, and repeated this tripartite pattern again in Australia in the 1890s. By that point Adventists had concluded that their success depended to a considerable degree on establishing an institutional base. Although legal restrictions sometimes limited their institution building, nearly everywhere that Adventists went they soon created publishing, educational, and health institutions that became foundation stones for the denomination's growth.

In addition to institutions, the Seventh-day Adventists, again following the pattern of earlier reform and religious organizations, created societies to, among other things, publish and distribute tracts and books, organize Sabbath schools, promote temperance, advocate religious liberty, and establish missions. Although these organizations had their own separate legal charters, they were tied to the General Conference through interlocking directorates. When the denomination reorganized in 1901 it began dissolving these societies and replaced them with departments of the General Conference. By the time this process was completed in 1904, all of the denomination-wide activities were part of a single organizational structure. Furthermore, when the church reorganized in 1901 it established an additional organizational layer, the union conference, which was formed by the conferences in a given geographical area and became the constituent body of the General Conference. In time the conferences and union conferences developed departments similar to those in the General Conference.

Although in their early history Seventh-day Adventists opposed church organization, by the early 20th century they had created a highly structured organization and built institutions that became the geographical centers from which their membership spread. Further underlining their commitment to organization, denominational leaders were highly uncomfortable with the independent or "self-supporting" Adventist enterprises that had developed beginning in the 1890s and over which they had no control. Increasingly, Seventh-day Adventism was a religion whose success was identified with its organization and institutions.

Becoming a World Religion

Born in the United States and having only some 3,000 members at the time it organized the General Conference in 1863, the Seventh-day Adventist Church did not at first consider sending missionaries abroad. After Michael B. Czechowski, a former Roman Catholic priest who had converted to Adventism, failed in his effort to have the denomination send him as a missionary to Europe, he went anyway in 1864 under the auspices of the Advent Christian Church, although he preached Seventh-day Adventist doctrines. Czechowski's converts in Switzerland learned of the existence of the Seventh-day Adventist Church through papers that he had left in a room where he had stayed, and in 1869 they sent a representative to Battle Creek. As a result of this contact with believers in Switzerland, the General Conference sent John Nevins Andrews, its first official foreign missionary, to that country in 1874.

During the next two decades Adventists established mission work in several areas, most of them either English-speaking or having significant immigrant populations in the United States. They first introduced missions in Denmark (1877), England (1884), Australia (1885), and Germany (1888). In the 1890s they expanded their efforts to include the South Pacific, South Africa, Latin America, India, and Japan. Although by the beginning of the 20th century Adventists had established a presence on every continent and in most of the larger nations, they were still an American church, with 80 percent of their 67,000 members living in the United States.

That situation would change dramatically during the next two decades. The establishment of the Solusi Mission in Rhodesia in 1894, the first Adventist mission to Black Africans, had symbolized a shift in the denomination that would soon produce significant results. In Latin America, Asia, India, and elsewhere in Africa, Adventists by the early

20th century were moving beyond the European populations they had first evangelized to the native peoples who, in many cases, proved far more accepting of their teaching. This shift, combined with a strong emphasis on missions by two General Conference presidents, Arthur G. Daniells and William A. Spicer, dramatically changed the geographical distribution of Adventist membership. By 1921 membership outside North America exceeded that within. Although at that time Europe was second in membership to North America, by 1940 it was clear where the momentum of growth lay, for between 1920 and 1940, Africa had increased from 2,700 members to over 48,000, Asia from 7,000 to 60,000, and Latin America from 15,000 to 70,000. North America, meanwhile, had increased from 96,000 to 185,000 and Europe from 46,000 to 102,000. Total denominational membership had moved from 184,000 to 504,000.

This membership growth impacted the organizational structure of the church, for out of the General Conference sessions of 1913 and 1918 a new entity emerged. The division, unlike conferences and union conferences, was an administrative unit of the General Conference and attempted to provide direction and cohesion to the union conferences within particular geographical areas. By 2003 there were 13 divisions: East-Central Africa (2,012,030 members), Euro-Africa (169,690), Euro-Asia (145,591), Inter-American (2,279,608), North American (963,042), Northern Asia-Pacific (502,307), South American (1,980,526), South Pacific (359,944), Southern Africa-Indian Ocean (1,569,033), Southern Asia (630,957), Southern Asia-Pacific (1,124,134), Trans-European (92,991), and Western Africa (640,851). World membership at that time totaled 12,593,704.[11]

Clearly, by the early 21st century Seventh-day Adventism had become a world church. By creating divisions of the General Conference denominational leaders had hoped to preserve unity and central direction to the church, but it was apparent that the divisions were acquiring considerable independence, each having its own officers and budget, and increasing influence, as when representatives from Africa and Latin America successfully opposed the North American effort to gain authorization for the ordination of women at the 1990 and 1995 General Conference sessions. More significant, and at this point yet unclear, was the impact that world membership growth would have on Adventist beliefs and practices. As seminaries and graduate schools developed around the world to train ministers and educators, and as teachers and ministers sought to more effectively relate Adventism to their native cultures, only the future would tell how a theological understanding forged out of the experience of a small group of mid-19th century American Millerites would be transformed as it became a multicultural and international possession.

1. Sydney E. Ahlstrom, *A Religious History of the American People* (New Haven, CT: Yale University Press, 1972), 481.
2. Mark A. Noll, *A History of Christianity in the United States and Canada* (Grand Rapids, MI: Eerdmans, 1992), 466.
3. Anthony Hoekema, *The Four Major Cults: Christian Science, Jehovah's Witnesses, Mormonism, Seventh-day Adventism* (Grand Rapids, MI: Eerdmans, 1963), 89-169.
4. Harold Bloom, *The American Religion: The Emergence of the Post-Christian Nation* (New York: Simon & Schuster, 1992), 147-58.
5. Catherine L. Albanese, *America: Religions and Religion*, 2nd ed. (Belmont, CA: Wadsworth, 1992), 234.
6. Robert W. Nixon, "Public Opinion About Adventists," *Adventist Review*, 3 July 1986, 8-9; Monte Sahlin, Carole Luke Kilcher, and Paul Richardson, "What Does the Public Think of Us?," *Adventist Review*, February 1995, 18-20.
7. Nathan O. Hatch, *The Democratization of American Christianity* (New Haven, CT: Yale University Press, 1989).
8. Everett N. Dick, *William Miller and the Advent Crisis, 1831-1844*, with Foreword and Historiographical Essay by Gary Land (Berrien Springs, MI: Andrews University Press, 1994), 163-64.
9. For example, see Whitney R. Cross, *The Burned-Over District: The Social and Intellectual History of Enthusiastic Religion in Western New York, 1800-1850* (Ithaca: Cornell University Press, 1950), 287-321; David L. Rowe, *Thunder and Trumpets: Millerites and Dissenting Religion in Upstate New York, 1800-1850* (Chico, CA: Scholars Press, 1985); and Ruth Alden Doan, *The Miller Heresy, Millennialism, and American Culture* (Philadelphia, PA: Temple University Press, 1987).
10. Richard Carwardin, *Transatlantic Revivalism: Popular Evangelicalism in Britain and America, 1790-1865* (Westport, CT: Greenwood Press, 1978), 52.
11. *Seventh-day Adventist Church Yearbook 2003* (Silver Spring, MD: General Conference of Seventh-day Adventists, 2003), 4, 39, 65, 87, 107, 155, 223, 237, 279, 301, 323, 343, 385, 409. I have given the official names of the divisions, although they do not have consistent form. For example, both "Africa" and "African" appear in these titles.

The Dictionary

A

ACADEMY. Term used by Seventh-day Adventists to identify their secondary schools. Beginning with the incorporation in 1883 of **South Lancaster Academy** in Massachusetts, Seventh-day Adventists used the term "academy" to name several institutions established to train denominational workers. By the mid-1920s, however, academies had become well-defined secondary schools with an academic status similar to public high schools.

ACCREDITING ASSOCIATION OF SEVENTH-DAY ADVENT-IST SCHOOLS, COLLEGES AND UNIVERSITIES. *See* EDUCATION.

ADVANCED BIBLE SCHOOL. A summer program for secondary and college teachers and **ministers** that operated between 1934 and 1936 on the campus of **Pacific Union College.** Although it offered no degree program at the time it opened, the Advanced Bible School anticipated approval for offering the Master of Arts. In 1936 the **General Conference** decided to end the Bible School and organize the **Seventh-day Adventist Theological Seminary** at Takoma Park, Maryland.

ADVENT CHRISTIAN CHURCH. One of the principal churches that arose out of the **Millerite movement**. Coalescing in the New York-Connecticut area around the *Second Advent Watchman* (edited by Joseph Turner and W. S. Campbell) this group maintained **William Miller's** system of prophetic interpretation and adopted the doctrine of **conditional immortality**, among other beliefs. Another paper, *World's Crisis*, became the chief publication of the group in the mid-1850s and led a movement toward church organization, culminating in the formation of the Advent Christian

Association in 1860. The movement remained loosely organized, however, waiting until the 1890s to organize an Advent Christian General Conference, which in turn became an effective structure only after 1916. In 1964 the Life and Advent Union, which had separated from the Advent Christians in the early 1860s, merged with the Advent Christian Church. As of 2003, the General Conference headquarters are located in Charlotte, North Carolina and the denomination has a membership of about 20,000.

ADVENTIST BOOK CENTERS. *See* TRACT AND MISSIONARY SOCIETIES.

ADVENTIST DEVELOPMENT AND RELIEF AGENCY (ADRA). Seventh-day Adventist aid organization. At the end of World War II, Seventh-day Adventists provided clothing, food, and medical supplies to Europe. Local church **Dorcas Societies** collected much of the material; the **General Conference** (GC) through its Lay Activities Department organized distribution. Similar efforts continued through the mid-1950s in response to natural disasters in various parts of the world. In 1956 the GC organized the Seventh-day Adventist Welfare Relief Service, Inc., to coordinate the denomination's relief efforts, although it continued to operate under the Lay Activities Department. As the organization moved beyond emphasizing disaster relief to address such issues as malnutrition and agricultural productivity, it was renamed Seventh-day Adventist World Service (SAWS) and became a separate agency of the GC. Much of its funding came from the U.S. Agency for International Development. In 1983 SAWS reorganized as the Adventist Development and Relief Agency. Its activities in subsequent years included conservation projects in **Bolivia**, planting trees in the Democratic Republic of **Congo**, providing clean water in **China**, and supplying humanitarian aid during the **Serbian-Croatian** crisis of the 1990s. Because of its reliance on government funds and its policy of avoiding proselytizing and other sectarian activities, some Adventists questioned whether the ADRA was an appropriate denominational program.

ADVENTIST FRONTIER MISSIONS (AFM). Self-supporting Seventh-day Adventist missionary agency. Founded by Clyde and Cathy Morgan in 1985, Adventist Frontier Missions placed missionaries in areas with no Adventist presence. It sent its first missionaries to northern Luzon in the **Philippines** in 1987. Since that time, it has established missions in such places as **Cambodia, Albania,** and **Mongolia**. Once it had organized **churches** and trained local workers in a given area, it turned the project over to the local **mission** or **conference** of the Seventh-day Adventist Church. As of 2003 the organization published a monthly magazine, *Adventist Frontiers*.

ADVENTIST HEALTH SYSTEM (AHS). Organization of Seventh-day Adventist health care institutions in the **United States**. Although Seventh-day Adventist **sanitariums and hospitals** had begun in various ways, by the mid-20th century most were owned by local **conferences**. In the 1970s regional hospital systems were developed to manage these institutions until the early 1980s when five separate systems operated nearly 80 hospitals and an additional 40 other health care facilities. In 1982 these systems combined into the Adventist Health System/US. Changes in Medicare payment policies, among other things, created economic pressures that forced the system to reorganize in 1991 with the regional systems separating from the national corporation. As of 2003 there were five systems managing institutions in the United States: Adventist Health System Sunbelt Healthcare Corporation, Adventist Health System/West DBA Adventist Health, Atlantic Adventist Healthcare Corp., Kettering Adventist Healthcare, and **Loma Linda University** Adventist Health Sciences Center.

ADVENTIST INTERNATIONAL INSTITUTE OF ADVANCED STUDIES (AIIAS). Seventh-day Adventist graduate school located in Silang, Cavite, **Philippines**. Philippine Union College (PUC), now **Adventist University of the Philippines**, graduated its first master's students in religion in 1959. By 1972 this program had grown into the Seventh-day Adventist Theological Seminary, which was accredited by the Association of Theological Schools in South East Asia the following year. When the college moved to Silang in 1978, the seminary, though it also moved to the new campus and acquired responsibility for all graduate programs, became a separate organizational entity. At the same time, it took the name **Asia** Adventist Theological Seminary and passed from the ownership of the Philippine **Union Conference** to that of the Far Eastern **Division**. In 1987 the seminary adopted a new name, Adventist International Institute of Advanced Studies (AIIAS), and in 1991 moved to its own separate campus about 15 miles away from PUC. By this time it was offering master's and doctoral programs in a variety of fields and in 1996 became a **General Conference**

institution. As of 2003 the institution had two divisions: a Theological Seminary and a School of Graduate Studies, the latter offering programs in health, education, and business.

ADVENTIST MEDIA CENTER (AMC). Seventh-day Adventist organization that coordinates media programs for North America. Established in 1972 by the **General Conference** in Thousand Oaks, California, the Adventist Media Center became the production and broadcast facility for *Voice of Prophecy*, *It is Written*, and *Faith for Today*. It also produced audiovisual materials for evangelism and later added *Breath of Life* and *La Voz de la Esperanza*, a Hispanic version of the *Voice of Prophecy*. In 1996 ownership of the Media Center transferred from the General Conference to the North American **Division**.

ADVENTIST REVIEW. Official weekly paper of the Seventh-day Adventist church. In 1849 **James White** began publishing *Present Truth*, a paper that emphasized the doctrine of the seventh-day **Sabbath** and the following year started the *Advent Review*, which sought to demonstrate that the sabbatarian Adventists were the true descendents of the **Millerite movement**. In November 1850 White combined the two papers into the *Second Advent Review and Sabbath Herald*. In 1961 the name was shortened to *Review and Herald* and in 1978 was revised as *Adventist Review*. The paper now appears in several languages in addition to English.

ADVENTISTS AFFIRM. Independently published journal begun in 1987, which describes itself as "a publication affirming Adventist beliefs."

ADVENTIST SOCIETY FOR RELIGIOUS STUDIES (ASRS). Independent scholarly society. In 1972, sponsored by the **Biblical Research Institute** (BRI), Seventh-day Adventist religion scholars began meeting annually in conjunction with the American Academy of Religion and Society of Biblical Literature (AARS/SBL) sessions. After BRI ended its sponsorship, the scholars formed the Andrews Society for Religious Studies in 1979, naming their organization after **John Nevins Andrews**, an early Adventist scholar and missionary, because the AARS/SBL did not allow denominational names for its associated groups. After these restrictions were lifted in 1993, the organization changed its name to "Adventist Society for Religious Studies."

ADVENTIST THEOLOGICAL SOCIETY (ATS). Organization founded in 1988 for scholarly study of the Bible and theology. Members are required to give assent to a statement of belief, which includes such elements as **creation** in six 24-hour days and the **sanctuary doctrine**. It holds a variety of meetings each year, including an annual session for scholars in conjunction with the Evangelical Theological Society yearly meetings. In 1992 the organization began publishing the biannual *Journal of the Adventist Theological Society*.

ADVENTIST TODAY. An independently published bimonthly magazine of Adventist news and commentary, begun in 1993.

ADVENTIST UNIVERSITY OF THE PHILIPPINES (AUP). Seventh-day Adventist **educational** institution located in Putting Kahoy, Silang, Cavite. In 1917 the **Philippine** Seventh-day Adventist **Academy** opened near Manila. The school began offering college work in 1926 and took the name Philippine Junior College. As its enrollment grew, the college needed a new campus and moved to Baesa, Caloocan, Rizal, in 1932, at which time it became Philippine Union College and offered bachelor's programs, the first Adventist institution outside North America to do so. Although World War II put the missionary teachers into internment camps, throughout the 1930s the number of Filipinos on the faculty had steadily increased and the school was able to continue operations, except for 1944-45. The college introduced master's degrees in education (1954) and religion (1964), thereby becoming the first Adventist institution outside the **United States** to offer graduate degrees. Between 1978 and 1981 the institution moved to its present campus and achieved university status in 1996. As of 2003 the AUP enrolled over 2,500 students.

ADVENTIST WORLD RADIO (AWR). Seventh-day Adventist short-wave radio broadcasting project. Beginning by placing programming on Radio-Trans-**Europe** in 1971, the denomination was using four transmitters by 1980 to broadcast 80 hours of programming each week in 18 different languages. In 1985 the **General Conference** voted to establish its own radio station on **Guam** to broadcast to **Asia**. By the end of the 1990s, Adventist World Radio had built additional transmitting sites in **Latin America** and **Italy** and leased time on additional European stations. By that point it was presenting some 1,000 hours of weekly programming transmitted in 46 languages.

ADVENTIST YOUTH SERVICE (AYS). Seventh-day Adventist volunteer missionary program. **Columbia Union College** (CUC) at the suggestion of William Loveless, pastor of Takoma Park's Sligo **Church**, sent a student missionary in 1959 to work for a summer in **Mexico**. Other colleges soon followed CUC's lead and by 1975 more than 1,200 students had served in 83 different countries, many of the volunteers spending a year teaching or assisting pastors and **evangelists**. Those who went to such places as **Japan**, **Korea**, and **Taiwan** often worked in the English Language Schools that the Far Eastern **Division** had started in 1966. In 1982 the program was opened to all Adventists aged 18 to 30 and within two years seven of the denomination's divisions were participating.

AFRICA. *See* ANGOLA; BENIN; BOTSWANA; BURKINA FASO; BURUNDI; CAMEROON; CAPE VERDE; CENTRAL AFRICAN REPUBLIC; CHAD; CONGO, DEMOCRATIC REPUBLIC OF; CONGO, REPUBLIC OF; CÔTE D'IVOIRE; EQUATORIAL GUINEA; ETHIOPIA; GABON; GAMBIA, THE; GHANA; GUINEA; GUINEA-BISSAU; KENYA; LESOTHO; LIBERIA; MADAGASCAR; MALAWI; MOZAMBIQUE; NAMIBIA; NIGERIA; RWANDA; SENEGAL; SEYCHELLES; SIERRA LEONE; SOUTH AFRICA; SUDAN; SWAZILAND; TANZANIA; TOGO; UGANDA; ZAMBIA; ZIMBABWE.

AGE TO COME ADVENTISTS. *See* CHURCH OF GOD GENERAL CONFERENCE.

ALBANIA. In 1932 E. Hennecke, director of the Grecian **Mission**, was forced to leave **Greece** and settled in Tirana, Albania. He received permission to bring in two nurses from **Germany** to establish medical work. Although all foreign workers had to leave the country within a few months, one woman was baptized as a result of Hennecke's efforts. In 1938 D. C. Lewis, an Albanian who had learned about Seventh-day Adventism while in the **United States**, was baptized in Greece while returning to his native country. After arriving in Albania, he converted four individuals, who were baptized in 1940 by C. A. Christoforides, director of the Greek mission. Contact with Albania was largely lost during and after World War II until the collapse of Communism in the late 1980s. When Seventh-day Adventists reestablished contact with the country in 1991 they discovered that two practicing Adventists remained. In 1992 David Currie of the Trans-**European Division** began conducting **evangelistic** meetings and organized the first Adventist **church** late that year. The Albanian Mission of Seventh-day Adventists was established in 1992 as part of the Adriatic **Union Conference** of the Trans-European Division. As of 2003 there were three churches and a membership of 262.

ALBANY CONFERENCE. *See* MUTUAL CONFERENCE OF ADVENTISTS.

ALGERIA. Joseph Gomis, son of a Spanish Catholic family living in Algeria, converted to Seventh-day Adventism while visiting **Switzerland**. Returning to Algeria he became a baker in Relizane about 1886 and shared his faith with his family and associates. In 1889 Albert Vuilleumier baptized several of these individuals, many of whom later emigrated to South America. The next Adventist missionaries arrived after 1905 and in 1909 baptized four women. In 1910 Albert Guyot came to Algeria and reestablished contact with Gomis and found that four families were observing the **Sabbath**. When the Algerian **Mission** organized in 1921 it had 61 members. In 1933 Adventists opened their first medical clinic, which was located in Algiers. Probably about the same time they opened a school in the same city. Although by 1958 Algeria had 540 members, almost all **European**, when the country became independent in 1962 most of these people emigrated. The government soon closed the Adventist school and clinic. As of 2003 Algeria was part of an Attached **Field**, the Trans-Mediterranean Territories of the Euro-**Africa Division** which reported no membership statistics. *The Seventh-day Adventist Encyclopedia* (1996) stated that in 1993 there were 12 members in the country.

AMAZING FACTS. Independent Seventh-day Adventist radio and television ministry. Established by Adventist **minister** Joe Crews in Baltimore, Maryland, in 1966, the radio program was broadcast throughout the **United States** by the mid-1970s. As the ministry developed, Crews established a Bible study course, wrote many small books, and trained **evangelists**. A television program was added about 1986. After Crews's death in 1994, **Doug Batchelor** became director and principal speaker. As of 2003, *Amazing Facts*, located in Sacramento, California, produced television programs and a radio program entitled *Bible Answers Live*, conducted evangelistic meetings under the title "Bible Seminars," and trained evangelists through its "College of Evangelism."

AMERICAN EVANGELICAL ADVENT CONFERENCE. Initially, the largest group arising out of the **Millerite movement** and including prominent leaders such as **Joshua V. Himes**, I. C. Wellcome, **Josiah Litch**, and Sylvester Bliss. Coalescing around the *Advent Herald*, published by Himes, they opposed new doctrines, such as time setting for the **second advent** and **conditional immortality**. In 1853 they began organizing regional conferences, which they combined into the American Evangelical Advent Conference in 1858. These "Evangelical Adventists," as they were popularly known, held beliefs similar to other premillennial Christians and largely disappeared by the 20th century.

AMERICAN HEALTH AND TEMPERANCE ASSOCIATION. *See* TEMPERANCE.

AMERICAN MEDICAL MISSIONARY COLLEGE. A medical school sponsored by but separate from the **Battle Creek Sanitarium**. Founded by **John Harvey Kellogg**, the school opened with a coeducational class of 40 students in 1895. Located in both Battle Creek and Chicago, Illinois, the college's faculty came from the Sanitarium staff and physicians in the Chicago area, where its students worked at the **Chicago Medical Mission**. The medical curriculum was a four-year program that introduced students to clinical experience during their first year. By 1900 the school had gained admission to the Association of American Medical Colleges, thereby bringing its graduates recognition from state licensing boards. Lack of sufficient funding and problems between Kellogg and the Seventh-day Adventist Church contributed to closure of the school in 1910 and its merger with the Medical School of the University of Illinois. During its existence, the college graduated 187 doctors of medicine.

AMERICAN TEMPERANCE SOCIETY (ATS). *See* TEMPERANCE.

ANDERSON, HARRY (1906-1996). Seventh-day Adventist illustrator. After attending the University of Illinois and the Syracuse School of Art, Anderson established himself as an illustrator in the 1930s, providing pictures for advertising campaigns and to accompany stories in such magazines as

Colliers, Cosmopolitan, and the *Saturday Evening Post.* In the early 1940s he and his wife Ruth joined the Seventh-day Adventist Church and he soon began providing illustrations for denominational publications, one of which was **Arthur S. Maxwell's** *The Bible Story,* a multivolume children's work sold widely on a subscription basis. Perhaps his best-known single illustration was "What Happened to Your Hand," which first appeared in a 1945 children's book. In addition to his work for Adventists, Anderson continued to provide illustrations for other organizations, including the Exxon Oil Company and the Church of Jesus Christ of Latter-day Saints. In 1994 the Society of Illustrators elected him to membership in its Hall of Fame.

ANDERSON, ROY ALLAN (1895-1985). Seventh-day Adventist **minister** and evangelist. Anderson conducted large urban evangelistic campaigns in **Australia** and London in the 1920s and 1930s, experimenting with new advertising techniques and using a variety of venues. He communicated his knowledge of **evangelism** through institutes and field schools, having considerable impact on Adventist evangelism internationally. In 1938 he began teaching at La Sierra College and in 1941 joined the **Ministerial Association** of the **General Conference**. He wrote several books, of which *The Shepherd-Evangelist* (1950) was probably the most influential, and participated in the **evangelical-Adventist dialogues**.

ANDERSON, WILLIAM HARRISON (1870-1950). Seventh-day Adventist missionary to **Africa**. Subsequent to attending **Battle Creek College**, in 1895 Anderson went to Africa to work at the **Solusi Mission**, in present-day **Zimbabwe**. After several years developing this mission station, Anderson traveled by foot about 300 miles into what is now **Zambia**, where he established the Rusangu **Mission**. He later established new missions in present-day **Botswana**, **Angola**, and elsewhere in Africa. He wrote about his experiences in *On the Trail of Livingstone* (1919) and promoted missions on return trips to the **United States**.

ANDREASEN, MILIAN LAURITZ (1876-1962). Seventh-day Adventist church administrator, teacher, and author. Born in Denmark, Andreasen received his education at the University of Nebraska. He served as president of several **conferences** and Adventist colleges, as a professor at the **Seventh-day Adventist Theological Seminary**, and as a field secretary of the **General Conference**. He wrote several books, including *The Sanctuary*

Service (1937) and *The Book of Hebrews* (1948). In *Letters to the Churches* (1959), he criticized the church for allegedly revising some of its doctrinal positions in *Seventh-day Adventists Answer Questions on Doctrine* (1957).

ANDREWS, JOHN NEVINS (1829-1883). Seventh-day Adventist **minister**, writer, and missionary. Born in Portland, Maine, Andrews converted to sabbatarian Adventism at age 17 and began working as a minister in 1850. For the next three years he **evangelized** in the Northeastern **United States** and eastern **Canada**, and went as far west as Michigan. He also wrote extensively for sabbatarian Adventist publications. In 1853 Andrews received ministerial authorization (Adventists at this time had no formal **ordination** procedure) from **James White**, who in 1855 asked him to research the question of when to begin and end the **Sabbath**. In a *Review and Herald* article, Andrews presented his conclusion that the sabbath begins at Friday sundown and ends on Saturday sundown. This view became the established position among the sabbatarian Adventists.

Because of health problems, in 1855 Andrews joined his parents in Iowa and clerked in his uncle's store. He became an active minister again in 1859, working in both the Midwest and Northeast. In 1861 he published *History of the Sabbath and the First Day of the Week*, a work that appeared in several subsequent editions. Andrews actively participated in the formal organization of the Seventh-day Adventist Church, helping develop the organizational plan for the Seventh-day Adventist Publishing Association in 1860 and drafting the constitution and bylaws for the **General Conference** (GC) in 1863. Subsequently, he began holding administrative positions, serving as a member of the New York **Conference** committee in 1864 and the GC Executive Committee in 1865, prior to a term as president of the GC from 1867 to 1869. In 1864 he met with officials of the U.S. government in an unsuccessful effort to gain recognition of Adventists as **noncombatants**. In 1869-70 he served as editor of the *Review and Herald*.

In 1874 Andrews went to **Europe** as the first official Seventh-day Adventist **missionary**, locating in **Switzerland** where he worked first with small groups that had been converted to Adventism by **Michael Czechowski**. Two years later, with $10,000 from the GC, he established a printing house and began publishing *The Signs of the Times*. Although he spent much of his time in writing and publishing, Andrews pursued evangelism in both **Germany** and **Italy** but was plagued by ill-health until his death in Switzerland.

ANDREWS UNIVERSITY. Seventh-day Adventist university, located in Berrien Springs, Michigan. Andrews University was formed after Potomac University, which consisted of the **Seventh-day Adventist Theological Seminary** and a School of Graduate Studies, moved from Takoma Park, Maryland, to the campus of **Emmanuel Missionary College** in Berrien Springs, Michigan, in 1959. The following year the schools combined as Andrews University, named after **John Nevins Andrews**, the first official Seventh-day Adventist missionary. In 1974 the undergraduate programs were organized into two schools, the College of Arts and Sciences and the College of Technology. The School of Business was created in 1980, the School of Education in 1983, and the Division of Architecture in 1993. In addition to the masters programs inherited from Potomac University, Andrews continued to develop new graduate programs, including doctoral programs offered by the Seminary and the School of Education. Accredited by the North Central Association of Colleges and Schools, the university played an important role in international Adventist **education** through its various affiliation programs, which enabled students at schools in other parts of the world to earn an Andrews University degree while their local institutions worked toward their own independent accreditation. The university publishes *Andrews University Seminary Studies* and *Journal of Research on Christian Education*; it also sponsors Andrews University Press. As of 2003 the university had approximately 2,900 students, of whom some 20 percent came from outside the **United States**.

ANGOLA. In 1924 **William H. Anderson**, J. D. Baker, and O. O. Bredenkamp established the first Seventh-day Adventist **mission** in Angola at Bongo. They opened a school that eventually became the Bongo Mission Training School; the arrival of Dr. Archie N. Tonge in 1926 enabled the addition of the Bongo Mission Hospital. As mission work gradually expanded to other areas of the country, the denomination began broadcasting Adventist radio programs in 1953. First organized in 1925, the Angola **Union Mission** as of 2003 was part of the Euro-**Africa Division**. It had 797 **churches** with over 226,000 members. Bongo Adventist Seminary, Bongo Adventist Secondary School, Bongo Mission Hospital, three dispensaries, and the Angola Publishing House were located in Angola.

ANNIHILATIONISM. *See* CONDITIONAL IMMORTALITY.

ANTIGUA AND BARBUDA. *See* LEEWARD AND WINDWARD ISLANDS.

ANTITRINITARIANISM. *See* TRINITY.

ARCHAEOLOGY, BIBLICAL. Because of its interest in establishing the historical validity of the Old Testament, the Seventh-day Adventist Church has had a long-standing interest in biblical archaeology. Its professional involvement in the field began when Lynn H. Wood received a Ph.D. from the University of Chicago and served as an expedition surveyor in a 1936-37 excavation under the direction of Nelson Glueck, director of the American School of Oriental Research in Jerusalem. Subsequently Wood taught at the **Seventh-day Adventist Theological Seminary**, where he established a master's degree in archaeology and history of antiquity. After Wood's retirement, **Siegfried H. Horn**, who earned a Ph.D. in Egyptology from the University of Chicago, began teaching archaeology at the seminary. In 1968 he organized an archaeological expedition, sponsored by **Andrews University**, at Tell Hesban in Jordan, the first of a series of digs that continued into the 1980s, involving several schools and scholars from both inside and outside the Adventist Church, and produced numerous professional publications. Lawrence T. Geraty, who directed the Tell Hesban project after Horn's retirement, began the Madaba Plains Archaeological Project at Tell el-Umeiri, Jordan, in 1984. By the mid-1990s more than 100 individuals were participating in the summer digs.

ARCHBOLD, BENDER LAWTON (1908-). Seventh-day Adventist church administrator. Born on **Colombia's** Old Providence Island, Archbold received his B.A. from **Pacific Union College** in 1935. He served as a teacher and dean of men at West Indies College in **Jamaica** from 1935 to 1940 before entering into church administration as secretary of the **Panama Conference**, a position he held until 1947. Returning briefly to **education**, he was principal of Panama **Academy** from 1947 to 1949, and then became secretary of the Caribbean **Union Conference** in 1957. Between 1957 and 1962 Archbold was president of Caribbean Union College in **Trinidad**, before joining the Inter-American **Division**, first as secretary in 1966 and next as president in 1970. Archbold's career illustrated Adventism's increasing emphasis on leadership from outside North America, for he was the first Inter-American to hold most of these positions. More significantly, Archbold's emphasis on **evangelism** made Inter-America the largest division in the denomination at the time of his retirement in 1980.

ARCHITECTURE. There is no distinctive Seventh-day Adventist style of architecture. The denomination's early churches were simple rectangular wooden structures, following the model of the Washington, New Hampshire, church built by the Christian brethren in 1842 or 1843, where the first sabbatarian Adventist group worshipped. The first complex church building, erected in 1878-79, was Battle Creek's "Dime Tabernacle," so named because dime offerings were requested to pay for the structure. With a brick veneer over a frame structure, this church seated 3,200 people and included, in addition to the main auditorium, a belfry, balcony, and basement. It burned in 1922. Up to the 1930s most Adventist buildings in North America, including churches, hospitals, and educational institutions used wood construction; after that time such buildings were almost always made of brick or stone. In design, however, they tended to reflect both regional styles and the prevailing tastes of the period in which they were constructed, always within the constraints of available economic resources. Similarly, outside of North America denominational buildings were strongly influenced by their cultural settings and ranged from bamboo and thatch to brick and stone construction. The denomination began training professional designers in 1977 when **Andrews University** introduced an architectural program that as of 2003 offered both a B.S. and an M.Arch.

ARGENTINA. In 1890 four **German** farm families living in Kansas, who had converted to Seventh-day Adventism, moved to Argentina under the leadership of George Riffel to share their faith with Germans living there. Responding to requests from Riffel for a missionary, the **General Conference** in 1894 sent **Frank H. Westphal,** who that same year organized the first Adventist **church** in South America. In 1899 River Plate College opened and nine years later River Plate Sanitarium. The first radio **evangelism** took place in 1933. As of 2003 Argentina was part of the Austral Union Conference of the South American Division and had 414 churches with nearly 80,000 members. **River Plate Adventist University,** River Plate **Sanitarium and Hospital**, Northeast Argentine Sanitarium, Belgrano Adventist Clinic, Argentina Food

Factory, and Buenos Aires Publishing House, as well as 15 Adventist secondary schools were located in the country.

ARMENIA. After several Seventh-day Adventists from Stavropol were exiled to the Mt. Ararat region in 1886, interest in **Sabbath** observance developed among Molokans living in the area. By 1908 there were several Adventist congregations in existence. The *Seventh-day Adventist Encyclopedia* (1996) reported that in 1993 there were nine **churches** and four additional congregations with a total of 365 members in Armenia. As of 2003 the Armenian **Mission**, part of the Caucasus **Union Mission** of the Euro-**Asia Division**, had 13 **churches** with a membership of about 800.

ART. Beginning with the **Millerites**, Adventists have taken a largely utilitarian and didactic approach to visual art. In 1840 David Campbell published a critique of **William Miller's** prophetic interpretation, entitled *Illustrations of Prophecy*, which included wood engravings of elements from the biblical books of Daniel and Revelation. This work strongly shaped Millerite pictorial representation of the Bible prophecies, for the Adventists borrowed these same pictures to illustrate excerpts from Miller's lectures published in their papers in the early 1840s and drew upon them, both directly and indirectly, to create the images used in the prophetic chart (known as the "'43 chart" because it projected that Christ would come in that year) developed by **Charles Fitch** and Apollos Hale in 1842. This chart, which combined a chronological outline with representations of such things as the beasts in Daniel's visions, became a staple in Millerite preaching, for speakers could hang it easily and thereby attract a crowd of curious onlookers. By translating the prophecies into concrete visual form, the chart provided an orientation to time similar to the function of a map in relation to space.

In 1850 **James White**, one of the sabbatarian Adventist leaders, promoted a chart developed by Samuel Rhodes that drew much of its imagery from Millerite publications and was used almost exclusively by preachers. Rhodes also added some new elements, including the **three angels** of Revelation 14, the **sanctuary** of Hebrews 9, and the two-horned beast of Daniel 8, each of which represented distinctive sabbatarian interpretations. Probably because of its cost, White ceased publishing this chart in 1853. In 1858, however, he put out a smaller paper version of the chart, apparently for use as home decoration. Five years later White produced two new charts, "A Pictorial Illustration of the Visions of

Daniel & John" and "The Law of God." In contrast to earlier prophetic charts, the 1863 version eliminated nearly all text, emphasizing instead pictures and brief timelines; in 1864 **Uriah Smith** provided verbal explanation with his *Key to the Prophetic Chart*. The "Law of God" reprinted the Ten Commandments with illustrations of the Ark of the Covenant and a modernized representation of the original stone tablets on which the commandments were written. White advocated that these charts be used for both preaching and home decoration.

Meanwhile, in 1852 Uriah Smith produced a woodcut that portrayed a tree from whose branches hung the two tables of the law. With its appearance in the *Review and Herald* on March 23, 1852, this image became the first illustration to appear in a Sabbatarian paper; in August the *Youth's Instructor* used the same image. Although illustrations were appearing frequently in the *Youth's Instructor* (but not the *Review and Herald*) by the 1870s, the young denomination, organized in stages between 1860 and 1863, made its first major commitment to pictorial representation in 1873 with the publication of **Merritt G. Kellogg's** lithograph, "The Way of Life from Paradise Lost to Paradise Regained." Apparently developed as an Adventist alternative to Currier and Ives prints, this allegorical representation incorporated familiar Adventist symbols and was accompanied by the publication of Kellogg's *Key of Explanation*. As with the 1858 and 1863 charts, the denomination promoted the lithograph as an "ornament" for the home. Three years later, James White produced an extensively revised version of Kellogg's lithograph. In 1881 White engaged the American painter Thomas Moran to develop a new print based on a sketch prepared by the Adventist leader. Entitled "Christ, The Way of Life," this picture appeared in 1883 and, in contrast to the earlier lithographs, used the crucifixion as its central element. It seemed to represent a subtle shift in Adventist consciousness; whereas the previous prints had emphasized doctrinal instruction, Moran's image encouraged an emotional or devotional response.

As Adventists became more comfortable with pictures and as they sought to sell their books to the general public, they produced extensively illustrated works beginning with the 1882 edition of Uriah Smith's *Thoughts on Daniel and the Revelation*. Other illustrated volumes included *Bible Readings for the Home Circle* (1888), **James Edson White's** *The Coming King* (1898), and **Ellen G. White's** *Steps to Christ* (1892), *Thoughts from the Mount of Blessing* (1896), *The Desire of Ages* (1898), and *Christ's Object Lessons* (1900). Although Ellen White questioned the quality and expense of some of these illustrated editions, the denominational **publishing** houses found them to be attractive products for sale by the **literature evangelists**. In the 20th century, therefore, art continued to be an important element of the subscription books produced by denominational publishing houses. **Arthur S. Maxwell's** 10-volume *The Bible Story* (1953-57) was the first to use color illustrations exclusively and drew upon 21 illustrators, among them **Harry Anderson**, Harry Baerg, Vernon Nye, and Russell Harlan. Also, throughout the century Adventist magazines increasingly used illustrations, including drawings, paintings, and photographs; in the latter half of the century color appeared more frequently, particularly in publications, such as *Signs of the Times* and *Liberty*, produced for the public. In the late 20th century, Nathan Greene became the most prominent Adventist illustrator.

To train artists for the publishing houses, and later to prepare school-teachers, Adventist colleges began offering art courses. Healdsburg College (later **Pacific Union College**) in 1887 was the first to introduce a drawing and painting course, and by 1900 such courses were available at most of the denomination's colleges. Not until the early 1950s, however, did the schools start organizing art departments that over time encouraged students to pursue fine art that emphasized personal expression rather than a utilitarian purpose. The first significant denominationally-sponsored recognition of such artists took place when Greg Constantine, professor of art at **Andrews University**, organized an international exhibition at the 1985 **General Conference session** held in New Orleans, Louisiana. The show included 100 works of art from 61 painters, water colorists, and sculptors representing 23 countries. In the last half of the 20th century, Adventist institutional interest in art also appeared in the use of sculpture, including the work of Alan Collins for the Trans-**European Divison** headquarters, **Andrews University**, and **Loma Linda University**, among others, and that of Wayne Hazen at **Atlantic Union College**, Hinsdale Hospital, Andrews University, and elsewhere. In 2000 the School of Visual Art and Design at **Southern Adventist University** introduced a film production program that in 2003 released on DVD its first production, *Angel in Chains*.

ASIA. *See* AZERBAIJAN; BANGLADESH; CAMBODIA; CHINA, PEOPLE'S REPUBLIC OF; CHINA, REPUBLIC OF; HONG KONG; INDIA; INDONESIA; JAPAN; KAZAKHSTAN; KOREA; KYRGYZ REPUBLIC; LAOS; MACAO; MALAYSIA; MONGOLIA; MYANMAR; PAKISTAN; PHILIPPINES;

SINGAPORE; SRI LANKA; TAJIKISTAN; THAILAND; TIBET; TURKMENISTAN; UZBEKISTAN.

ASSOCIATION OF ADVENTIST FORUMS (AAF). Independent organization, founded in 1967, that examined issues of concern to Adventists. Directed primarily toward Adventist graduate students and professionals, the organization sponsored discussion forums in some of the larger Adventist **churches**, organized conferences, and published *Spectrum*, a quarterly journal begun in 1969.

ASSOCIATION OF ADVENTIST WOMEN (AAW). Independent **women's** organization. Formed in 1982, the organization has sought to provide support for and encourage communication among Adventist women and encourage the denominational organization to better understand and support them. It has focused on two principal activities, publication of a newsletter, *The Adventist Woman*, and the organization of an annual conference. As of 2003 its headquarters were located at **La Sierra University** in California.

ASSOCIATION OF SEVENTH-DAY ADVENTIST SELF-SUP- PORTING INSTITUTIONS (ASI). *See* SELF-SUPPORTING WORK.

ATLANTIC UNION COLLEGE (AUC). Seventh-day Adventist educational institution located in South Lancaster, Massachusetts. Atlantic Union College grew out of **South Lancaster Academy**, founded in 1882. Although the **academy** had previously offered some college-level work, it did not become a junior college until 1918, at which time it was renamed Lancaster Junior College. Four years later it began offering a four-year Bachelor of Theology degree and changed its name to Atlantic Union College. Its offerings gradually expanded when in 1926 it introduced the Bachelor of Religious Education and in 1933 the B.A. The school received accreditation from the New England Association of Schools and Colleges in 1945; it added the B.S. in 1954 and M.Ed. in 1990. By 2003 the school offered 25 bachelor's degree programs and had an enrollment of about 500 students.

ATONEMENT. Christian doctrine of reconciliation of humans to God through the sacrifice of Jesus on the cross. Early sabbatarian Adventists argued that rather than taking place at the crucifixion of Jesus, as Christians generally believed, atonement occurred in the heavenly **sanctuary** after Christ's ascension. Although **O. R. L. Crosier** introduced this concept in his 1846 exposition of the sanctuary doctrine, **Uriah Smith** developed the Seventh-day Adventist understanding of the atonement more fully in a series of *Review and Herald* articles in 1876. He asserted that if the atonement took place at the crucifixion, as most Christians understood, either universalism or Calvinism necessarily resulted. In contrast, Smith believed that although Christ's death on the cross met the demands of the law, individuals who personally accepted Jesus' sacrifice and began following God's law could receive atonement only after he had returned to heaven and ministered as High Priest on their behalf in the heavenly sanctuary. As early as the 1860s, however, **Ellen G. White** referred to Christ's death on the cross as involving atonement, and by the 1890s Adventists were placing much more emphasis on the crucifixion. The denomination's 1931 statement of **fundamental beliefs** did not use the term "atonement" but in article 3 said that Jesus "died for our sins on the cross, was raised from the dead, and ascended to the Father, where He ever lives to make intercession for us." Article 9 of the 1980 Fundamental Beliefs referred specifically to "atonement": "In Christ's life of perfect obedience to God's will, His suffering, death, and resurrection, God provided the only means of atonement for human sin, so that those who by faith accept this atonement may have eternal life." In article 23 on the sanctuary, the statement called Christ's work as High Priest "the second and last phase of His atoning ministry." As these statements of belief suggest, for most Seventh-day Adventists today, the term "atonement" includes both Christ's sacrifice at the crucifixion and his current work as High Priest in the heavenly sanctuary.

AUSTRALIA. At the urging of **Ellen G. White**, the **General Conference** in 1885 sent **Stephen N. Haskell** and several others to Australia. Selling books and holding **evangelistic** meetings, they organized the first Adventist **church** in 1886 in South Melbourne. That same year they began publishing *The Bible Echo and Signs of the Times*. As they organized additional churches, more workers from the **United States** arrived in 1887 to help them. In 1888 the Adventist group organized the Australian **Conference**, the Echo Publishing Company, and the Australian Tract and Missionary Society. Three years later Ellen G. White arrived, staying until 1900. With her encouragement, the Adventists opened a Bible training school in Melbourne, which was to become **Avondale**

College, and held their first camp meeting in Brighton, Victoria, in 1894. They opened medical treatment rooms in Ashfield in 1896, moving this effort to Summer Hill and ultimately to a suburb of Sydney, where Sydney Sanitarium opened in 1903. In 1898 they also began **Sanitarium Health Food Company** in Melbourne. With this institutional base, replicating the Adventist pattern begun in the **United States**, Adventism in Australia continued to grow. As of 2003 the Australian **Union Conference**, part of the **South Pacific Division**, had 410 churches and a membership of nearly 50,000. Avondale College, 14 secondary schools, Sanitarium Health Food Company, **Sydney Adventist Hospital**, Signs Publishing Company, and the South Pacific Adventist Media Center were among the major Adventist institutions in Australia.

AUSTRIA. Although there was at least one Seventh-day Adventist in Vienna as of 1896, the first organized Seventh-day Adventist work began with the organization of the Austrian **Mission**, which also included Prague, in 1902. In 1903 Elise Schütt arrived from **Germany** to work as a **Bible instructor** in Graz, where she stayed until 1908. After various organizational changes, by 1913 the mission included primarily the territory that is now Austria and had a membership of 242. In 1920 the mission reorganized as the Austrian **Conference** with a membership of 526 and, about the same time, the Hamburg Publishing House opened a branch in Vienna. In 1947 the Austrian **Union Conference** formed with a membership of about 2,000. In 1949 the Austrian Missionary Seminary, now known as Bogenhofen Seminary, opened near Salzburg. As of 2003 the Adventist church in Austria was organized as the Austrian Union of Churches, part of the Euro-**Africa Division**, with 48 churches and a membership of about 3,500. In addition to Bogenhofen Seminary, the Austrian Union of Churches operated the Austrian Publishing House.

AVONDALE COLLEGE. Seventh-day Adventist college in Cooranbong, New South Wales, **Australia**. Although a small Bible school had been established in Melbourne in 1892, **Ellen G. White** urged Australian Adventists in 1893 to find a more rural location for an educational facility. Church leaders found a 1450-acre estate about 75 miles north of Sydney and invited White to inspect the property. Through her urging and financial support, the denomination purchased the property and opened the Avondale School for Christian Workers in 1897, changing its name to Australasian Missionary College in 1911. The school strongly influenced subsequent Adventist **education**, particularly by showing the advantages of a rural location, a work-study program, and school industries that provided both opportunities for student labor and financial support for the institution. Until 1951 Avondale offered only two years of college study based on a 5-year secondary program; in that year it created a three-year ministerial program. Shortly thereafter it provided students the opportunity to earn the B.Sc. through a University of London external degree program and the B.A. through an affiliation with **Pacific Union College**, a Seventh-day Adventist institution in California. In 1964 the school adopted the name Avondale College and in 1974 began offering its own bachelors degrees after receiving New South Wales accreditation. Starting in the 1970s the masters degree became available through an affiliation with **Andrews University**, a Seventh-day Adventist school in Michigan; in the 1990s Avondale began offering its own M.A. programs. As of 2003 the school had approximately 850 students.

AZERBAIJAN. In 1894 Jacob Klein, a Seventh-day Adventist **minister,** visited Baku and the surrounding area, meeting with **German** families who were already observing the seventh-day **Sabbath.** After conducting some **baptisms** he was expelled from the country and those he had baptized were soon exiled. In 1906 Albert Ozel baptized several individuals in Koryazhno (present-day Fizuli) and another congregation formed in Novo-Vasiljevka. The *Seventh-day Adventist Encyclopedia* (1996) reported that in 1993 there were four **churches** and two other congregations with a membership of 259. As of 2003 the Azerbaijan **Mission**, part of the Caucasus **Union Mission** of the Euro-**Asia Division**, had four churches with a membership of about 500.

B

BACCHIOCCHI, SAMUELE (1938-). Seventh-day Adventist **educator** and theologian. Born in **Italy**, Bacchiocchi received a B.A. (1960) from **Newbold College** and an M.A. (1962) and B.D. (1964) from **Andrews University**. After teaching history and Bible at Adventist Ethiopian College from 1964 to 1969, he pursued doctoral study at the Pontifical Gregorian University. Upon completion of his Ph.D. in 1974, he joined the religion department at Andrews University, where he taught until his retirement in 2000. Starting with *From Sabbath to Sunday* (1977), Bacchiocchi wrote numerous books on a variety of topics, including *Divine Rest for*

Human Restlessness (1980), *The Advent Hope for Human Hopelessness* (1986), *Women in the Church* (1987), *Wine in the Bible* (1989), *God's Festivals in Scripture and History* (1995), *Immortality or Resurrection* (1997), and *The Christian and Rock Music* (2000). Beginning in the mid-1980s Bacchiocci traveled widely in both the **United States** and internationally to conduct seminars on issues in Adventist theology, often in conjunction with his publications. He also produced a newsletter, *Endtime Issues*, first published in 1998 and distributed widely by e-mail.

BAHAMAS. C. H. Richards, a **literature evangelist**, arrived with his wife in Nassau in 1893, followed by another colporteur, Charles F. Parmele, in 1895. The first conversions to Seventh-day Adventism appear to have occurred shortly after Parmele's arrival. In 1909 W. A. Sweany went to the Bahamas as a full-time missionary and organized the first **church** at Nassau in 1911. Two years later J. H. Smith replaced Sweany and began working on other islands. R. J. Sype organized the second Adventist church in the Bahamas in the early 1930s on the island of San Salvador. By 1940 the Bahamas **Mission** had 12 churches and 545 members. As of 2000 the Bahamas **Conference**, part of the West Indies **Union Conference** of the Inter-American **Division**, had 41 churches with a membership of over 11,000, and operated one secondary school.

BAHARIAN, ZADOUR G. (?-1915). Armenian Seventh-day Adventist **evangelist** and missionary. Baharian converted to Adventism in 1890 through contact in **Turkey** with Theodore Anthony, a shoemaker who had accepted the Seventh-day Adventist faith while living in the **United States** and who had then returned to his homeland. Zaharian then went to Basel, **Switzerland**, location of an Adventist publishing house, where for the next two years he studied Adventist beliefs. Returning to Turkey, Baharian worked for several years with Anthony, establishing small groups of Adventist believers in Turkey and elsewhere in Asia Minor. In 1894 he was **ordained** and later served as superintendent of the Armenian **Mission**. He was killed by his Kurdish driver while traveling to Constantinople.

BALLENGER, ALBION FOX (1861-1921). Seventh-day Adventist **minister** and later critic of the denomination. Born in Illinois, Ballenger began working in the Adventist ministry in 1885 and was **ordained** in 1893. He worked primarily in **religious liberty** affairs from 1889 to 1897. Attracted to Holiness themes, from late

1897 through 1899 he traveled throughout the **United States** on behalf of the **General Conference** preaching "Receive Ye the Holy Ghost." His book *Power for Witnessing* (1900) drew from his sermons. In 1901 he went to **Great Britain**, serving as an **evangelist** and church administrator until he expressed doubts about the **sanctuary doctrine.** He returned to the United States in 1905 and lost his ministerial credentials in that year. During the next few years he worked as a farmer in Virginia until moving to California in 1908. He published his criticisms of the sanctuary doctrine in *Cast Out for the Cross of Christ* (c. 1909) and, although for a time continuing to farm and do odd jobs, gradually developed a preaching and writing career. Between 1911 and 1919 he made six extended cross-country trips, speaking primarily to disaffected Adventists. He became editor of *The Gathering Call*, a magazine begun by a **Church of God** minister in 1915, and published two books, *Forty Fatal Errors Regarding the Atonement* (c. 1913) and *The Proclamation of Liberty and the Unpardonable Sin* (1915), in addition to various tracts.

BANGLADESH. Although Seventh-day Adventist **literature evangelists** had entered Bengal in the 1890s, **Lal Gopal Mookerjee** established the first Adventist mission station in the area in 1906. Adventists organized their first **church** at Barisal in 1910 and established a girl's school at Hooghly in 1916 and a boy's school at Gopalganj five years later. The schools eventually combined and moved to Jalirpar, becoming the Jalirpar Secondary Boarding School in 1939. In 1946 this institution became Kellogg-Mookerjee Memorial Seminary. Meanwhile, the territory that is now Bangladesh was part of the Bengali **Mission**, organized in 1910, and later operated under other missions. When independence came to the country in 1971, the Seventh-day Adventist organization took the name Bangladesh Section and in 1979 became the Bangladesh **Union Mission.** As of 2003 the Union Mission was part of the Southern **Asia**-Pacific **Division**, with 90 **churches** and a membership of about 27,000. It operated the Bangladesh Adventist Seminary and College, three secondary schools, Adventist Dental Clinic, and Bangladesh Adventist Publishing House.

BAPTISM. Ordinance of initiation into the Christian church. From their beginning, Seventh-day Adventists have practiced believers baptism by immersion, probably because many of their early members were drawn from the **Christian Connection** and Baptist churches. After lengthy discussion of whether converts who had been previously baptized should be baptized again, the **General Conference session** of 1886 voted that individuals who had been immersed by another denomination should decide for themselves whether to be rebaptized.

BARBADOS. Seventh-day Adventism began in Barbados when Anna Alleyne received Adventist **publications** in the 1880s from her sister in British **Guiana.** Over time more papers and books arrived and a small group began meeting together at Bridgetown. In 1891 D. A. Ball organized this group into a Seventh-day Adventist **church**. Other missionaries arrived over the next several years. During the first half of the 20th century, the Bahamas passed through a series of **conference** organizations. As of 2003, with Dominca, St. Vincent, and the Grenadines, Barbados was part of the East Caribbean Conference, which in turn was a member of the **Caribbean Union Conference** of the Inter-American **Division**. In 2003 the East Caribbean Conference had 101 churches, a membership of 32,000, and operated one secondary school.

BATCHELOR, DOUGLAS (1957-). Seventh-day Adventist radio and television **evangelist**. The son of a wealthy businessman, Batchelor was a drop-out from mainstream society and part of the Southern California counter-culture when he converted to Adventism in the mid-1970s. After attending **Southwestern Adventist College** for a short time, he worked in a variety of positions, including serving as a devotional speaker for the **Heritage Singers** and a missionary to the Navajo in New Mexico. He began working as a pastor in northern California in the 1980s and in 1994 became director and principal speaker of *Amazing Facts*, a television and radio ministry. Batchelor told his life story in *The Richest Caveman* (1991), written with Marilyn Tooker.

BATES, JOSEPH (1792-1872). Cofounder and **minister** of the Seventh-day Adventist Church. A seaman who was impressed by the British navy and held as a prisoner of war until the end of the War of 1812, Bates became a captain of a merchant ship in 1820. In 1821 he gave up drinking "ardent spirits" and the following year wine; shortly thereafter he discarded use of tobacco. He converted to Christianity in 1824, joining his wife's Fairhaven Christian Church, a **Christian Connection** group, in 1827. A short time later, Bates helped organize the Fairhaven **Temperance** Society and turned his ship into a temperance vessel, on which he allowed no alcoholic beverages, swearing, or washing of clothes on

Sunday. He retired from the sea in 1828 and over the next several years was active in several reform movements, including antislavery.

In 1839 Bates accepted **William Miller's** teaching that Christ would return about 1843 and became active in the movement. He served on the committee that planned the first Millerite general conference, held in Boston in 1840, became a Millerite preacher, and chaired the movement's sixth general conference, which took place in 1842. The following year Bates sold most of his property, including his home, to support the Millerite cause. About this time he also adopted various **health reform** practices, including vegetarianism.

Following the **Great Disappointment** in 1844 Bates held to his Millerite belief. After reading **Thomas M. Preble's** article advocating the seventh-day **Sabbath** in early 1845 and visiting with Frederick Wheeler, who led a Sabbath-keeping Adventist congregation in New Hampshire, Bates accepted the doctrine. In 1846 he wrote a tract, *The Seventh-day Sabbath.* The following year he revised this tract to argue that the Sabbath was a key element in the **third angel's message** of Revelation 14. He developed this point more fully in *A Seal of the Living God* (1849). Also in 1846 Bates accepted **Hiram Edson's** view that on October 22, 1844 Jesus had entered the Most Holy Place of the Heavenly Sanctuary; that same year Bates met with Edson and his associates in Port Gibson, New York. Meanwhile, Bates's first tract on the Sabbath came to the attention of **James** and **Ellen White**, who accepted the doctrine in late 1846. Soon thereafter Bates met the Whites and in early 1847 endorsed Ellen's visions as given by God in a joint publication with the Whites, *A Word to the "Little Flock."* Together with the Whites, Bates played a leading role in the Sabbath Conferences of 1848-49, where the beliefs of the sabbatarian Adventists coalesced.

Thereafter, Bates helped expand the sabbatarian Adventist movement. In 1849 he took its message to Michigan and again in 1852, establishing a small group of believers in Battle Creek. This group brought the Whites and the *Review and Herald* to their city in 1855; until the early 20th century Battle Creek would serve as the physical center of Adventism. In addition to preaching sabbatarian Adventism, Bates led in organizing the movement into a denomination. He chaired the committees that chose the name "Seventh-day Adventist" in 1860 and established the Michigan **Conference** of Seventh-day Adventists in 1861 and helped form the **General Conference of Seventh-day Adventists** in 1863.

BATTLE CREEK COLLEGE. First Seventh-day Adventist **educational** institution, located in Battle Creek, Michigan. In 1868 **Goodloe H. Bell** established a private school for Adventist students that he turned over to the **General Conference** (GC) of Seventh-day Adventists in 1872. Desiring to transform the school into a college, the following year the GC established the Seventh-day Adventist Educational Society to raise money for constructing a building. Although **Ellen White** strongly urged that the school be located outside the city, the society purchased a 12-acre plot of land within Battle Creek and near the **Health Reform Institute**. After the erection of a three-story building, Battle Creek College opened in 1874 with about 100 secondary and college students. Despite Ellen White's counsel that the curriculum include manual labor, the courses of studies were similar to those at other colleges of the time. Significantly, no Bible courses appeared in the curriculum. **James White** served as president until 1880, while **Sidney Brownsberger**, the principal, handled day-to-day operations and succeeded White as president.

The institution went through considerable turmoil after Brownsberger left in 1881, temporarily closing in 1881-82. After reopening in 1883, the school revised its curriculum, developed short courses of study to prepare denominational workers, and constructed residence halls, thereby addressing the long-standing problem of student housing. It also made some halting steps to establish manual labor. The curriculum continued to develop during the 1890s, with one year of Bible becoming mandatory and modern literature and history gradually replacing much of the classical curriculum. Denominational leaders, however, believed that the changes were inadequate; a group of reformers, led by **Alonzo T. Jones** and **John Harvey Kellogg**, in 1897 called **Edward A. Sutherland**, president of **Walla Walla College**, to serve as president. Sutherland began an extensive reform program that included, among other things, largely abolishing the classical curriculum, introducing industrial courses such as agriculture, printing, and cooking, replacing the playing fields with a garden, and purchasing an 80-acre farm outside of Battle Creek. He also advocated use of the Bible as a textbook and promoted religious revivals. In 1899 the administration announced that it would no longer award degrees because of their alleged papal origins, although it was unable to fully institute this policy through 1901. Many Adventists reacted negatively to these reforms, with the result that enrollment dropped from its high point of 768 students in 1893 to the mid-

300s between 1897 and 1901. The school became increasingly
burdened with debt.

Through a series of legal and financial decisions, control of
Battle Creek College passed from the hands of the Educational Society to a newly established Seventh-day Adventist Central Educational Association. The latter organization was incorporated under
a Charitable Societies law, which meant that it could not offer degrees, thereby fulfilling one of Sutherland's goals. In 1901 the
Michigan **Sanitarium** and Benevolent Association purchased the
college property for the use of the **American Medical Missionary
College**. In April the Educational Association voted to relocate the
school to a rural area and in July it purchased property near Berrien
Springs, Michigan, where it established **Emmanuel Missionary
College.**

BATTLE CREEK SANITARIUM. Former Seventh-day Adventist
medical institution located in Battle Creek, Michigan. In May 1866
Ellen G. White, who had recently taken her husband to Dr. James
Caleb Jackson's "Our Home on the Hillside," in Dansville, New
York, urged the **General Conference** to establish a health
institution in Battle Creek. Responding favorably, church leaders
raised money and purchased land, enabling the Health Reform
Institute to open in September, 1866. During its first 10 years of
operation, the institute had an inadequate medical staff and,
experiencing difficulty in attracting patients, came near to closing
its doors. When **John Harvey Kellogg**, a graduate of Bellevue
Hospital Medical College in New York, joined the staff in 1875
and became the medical superintendent the following year, the
institution became more successful. In 1877 Kellogg changed its
name to "Medical and Surgical **Sanitarium**," although it became
popularly known as the "Battle Creek Sanitarium." Kellogg also
constructed a new building, which came to be known as "Old
Main," completed in 1878 but with major additions in 1884 and
1891. He also developed the Sanitarium Food Company, which
marketed a variety of whole grain foods.

Kellogg stated that the term "sanitarium" meant "a place
where people learn to stay well." He worked to eliminate meat,
tea, and coffee from the dining room, something that took him 20
years to accomplish, and gave frequent lectures on "biologic
living." Combining elements of reform medicine, such as
hydrotherapy, with standard medical practice, the sanitarium
became internationally known.

Problems were developing, however. As it expanded, the institution acquired significant indebtedness, about which Ellen White publicly raised concern. Also, when the Health Reform Institute charter expired in 1897, the charter and bylaws of the new Michigan Sanitarium and Benevolent Association, the legal owner of the sanitarium, did not require that stockholders be Seventh-day Adventists or specify a quorum for association meetings; it also used the terms "undenominational" and "unsectarian" to describe the purposes of the institution. Denominational leaders soon raised questions regarding Kellog's intentions for what was supposed to be a church-related institution.

In February 1902 a fire destroyed the sanitarium's main building. Kellogg immediately laid plans to rebuild. Drawing largely on the profits of the Sanitarium Food Company and the Sanitas Food Company, a private food manufacturing business that Kellogg had begun in the 1890s, the new building—which had about seven acres of indoor space—reached completion in 1903 at a cost of approximately $1,000,000.

Meanwhile, Kellogg and Adventist leaders had come into increasing conflict over the purposes of the sanitarium, the doctor's effort to control the medical work of the denomination, and his alleged pantheistic theology. After the Battle Creek **church** dropped the doctor from membership in 1907, he adroitly used the 1897 charter and bylaws to remove most Adventist leaders from the association in 1908. After that time the sanitarium was independent of Adventist ownership and control. The institution continued to operate successfully through the 1920s, but control gradually passed from Kellogg to Dr. Charles Stewart. In 1927 the sanitarium issued $3 million in bonds to construct a 15-story addition, but the stock market crash of 1929 and subsequent Great Depression quickly reduced the number of patients. The sanitarium could not carry its debt load and went into receivership in 1933. In 1942 the United States Army bought the main buildings, which it operated as Percy Jones Hospital through World War II and the Korean War. The General Services Administration took over the building in 1954, using it as the Battle Creek Federal Center. At the time of the government purchase, the medical services of the sanitarium moved across the street to a building called the "Annex," where they continued to function until going into receivership in 1957. At that time a group of Seventh-day Adventist physicians took control; the institution operated under a variety of names until its sale in 1993. *See also* HEALTH CARE; HEALTH REFORM.

BEACH, BERT BEVERLY (1928-). Seventh-day Adventist **educator**, church administrator, and **religious liberty** leader. The son of **Walter R. Beach,** Beach received his B.A. from **Pacific Union College** in 1948 and attended Stanford University for one year before becoming an elementary school principal in northern California in 1949. Three years later he became principal of Italian Junior College in Florence, serving there until 1958. Receiving a Ph.D. from the University of Paris in 1958, he joined the history faculty at **Columbia Union College** where he taught for two years. He then became director of the education department of the Northern **Europe**-West **Africa Division,** where he worked until 1975. During this time he also adddressed religious liberty concerns, and helped arrange a series of annual discussions that took place from 1965 to 1972 between Adventist leaders and World Council of Churches representatives. *So Much in Common* (1973) collected documents from these discussions. In 1980 Beach joined the **General Conference** staff as director of the Public Affairs and Religious Liberty Department. Since his retirement in 1995 he has advised the General Conference on religious liberty and interchurch relations. Among his books are *Vatican II: Bridging the Abyss* (1968), *Ecumenism: Boon or Bane?* (1974), and *Bright Candle of Courage* (1989). With W. R. Beach he wrote *Pattern for Progress* (1985) and with John Graz, *101 Questions Adventists Ask* (2000).

BEACH, WALTER RAYMOND (1902-93). Seventh-day Adventist church administrator. Born in North Dakota, Beach received his B.A. from **Walla Walla College** in 1923, after which he served as a boy's dean and teacher at Auburn **Academy** from 1923-26. In 1926 he became secretary of the Latin **Union Conference,** which had its headquarters in **Switzerland,** at which time he received **ordination.** While in this position he earned an M.A. from the University of Paris in 1927 before becoming president of the **Belgian Conference** in 1928. In 1936 he joined the Southern **European Division** as secretary, becoming the division president in 1946. Elected general field secretary of the **General Conference** in 1954, he served in that capacity until his retirement in 1970. Beach developed a reputation as the denomination's foremost statesman, representing Adventism effectively to governments and other churches. His books included *Light from God's Lamp* (1960), *Dimensions in Salvation* (1963), *Focusing on Fundamentals* (1965), and *The Creed that Changed the World* (1970).

BEDIAKO, MATTHEW ANGO (1942-). Seventh-day Adventist **minister** and church administrator. Receiving his childhood education in Adventist schools in **Ghana**, Bediako attended the Adventist College of West **Africa**—now Babcock University—in **Nigeria**, from which he graduated in 1967. Returning to Ghana, he first served as a Bible teacher at the Bekwai Seventh-day Adventist Secondary School and then entered the ministry. In 1975 he was elected president of the Ghana **Conference**. In that position Bediako developed funding for **evangelism** and **education** and organized the South Ghana **Mission**. In 1980 he became president of the West African **Union Mission**, and subsequently was elected to several **General Conference** (GC) positions, including field secretary (1980), general vice president (1990), and executive secretary (2000), the first African to hold these positions. While vice president of the GC, Bediako presided over the meetings that led to the unification of the Black Southern **Union Conference** and the White **South African** Union Conference into the Southern Africa Union Conference in 1991.

BELDEN, FRANKLIN E. (1858-1945). Seventh-day Adventist musician and composer. A nephew of **Ellen G. White**, he compiled, with Edwin Barnes, *Hymns and Tunes* (1886), for many years the official Adventist **hymnal**. He worked as a superintendent at the **Review and Herald Publishing Association,** wrote many hymns and **Sabbath school** songs, and compiled *Christ in Song* (1900, 1908), the second edition of which became the denomination's unofficial hymnal for nearly half a century. He left the Seventh-day Adventist Church about 1907 following conflict with the publishing house over royalties from his songbooks. *The Seventh-day Adventist Hymnal* (1985) included 16 of Belden's songs.

BELGIUM. In 1897 C. Augsberger arrived in Belgium from **Switzerland**, joined a year later by C. Grin, and as a result of their work the first Seventh-day Adventist **church** organized in 1898. Until 1904, when Reinhold G. Klingbeil began to **evangelize** in Flemish, all Adventist efforts took place in the French-speaking part of the country. In 1919 the territory organized as the Belgian **Conference** and by 1940 had 15 churches with 624 members. As of 2003 Belgium was part of the Belgian-Luxembourg Conference, which belonged to the Euro-**Africa Division**. The conference had 25 churches and a membership of about 1,600.

BELIZE. Mrs. E. Gauterau, who introduced Seventh-day Adventism into **Honduras**, appears to have distributed denominational publications in British Honduras in 1885. Various Adventist missionaries visited the area briefly in the 1890s. Later James A. Morrow settled there and conducted **evangelistic** meetings, developing a congregation of about 50 members by 1902. After operating under a succession of **conferences** and **missions**, the area organized in 1918 as the Honduras Mission, including both Honduras and British Honduras with a total membership of 267. When British Honduras organized as its own mission in 1937 it had nearly 400 members. Belize Adventist College, a secondary school, opened in 1969. As of 2003 the Belize Mission was part of the Central American **Union Conference** of the Inter-American **Division**. It had 48 **churches** with a membership of nearly 25,000. The Union Conference operated Belize Adventist **Academy**.

BELL, GOODLOE HARPER (1832-1899). Seventh-day Adventist **educator** and author. After overworking himself as a schoolteacher, Bell came to the Health Reform Institute (later **Battle Creek Sanitarium**) in 1867. Formerly a Baptist and then a member of the Disciples of Christ, he converted to Adventism while convalescing. In 1868 he opened a private school for Adventist young people in Battle Creek, Michigan, that became known as the "Select School." From 1869 to 1871 he also edited *The Youth's Instructor*, the denomination's paper for young people. In 1872 the **General Conference** assumed administrative and financial responsibility for the Select School, which in 1874 it transformed into **Battle Creek College**. At that time Bell became head of the English department, in reality the secondary school. When the college closed temporarily, Bell left in 1882 to become principal of a new school in South Lancaster, Massachusetts, which soon was named **South Lancaster Academy**. Two years later he returned to Battle Creek where he taught private lessons and published a magazine, *The Fireside Educator*. His books included *Natural Method in English* (1881), *Familiar Talks on Language* (1885), and *Primary Language Lessons from Life, Nature, and Revelation* (1890).

BENIN. George Vaysse, a **literature evangelist** from **Europe**, sold Seventh-day Adventist books in what was then known as Dahomey for two years, beginning in 1957. Henri Kempf, president of the Ivory Coast **Mission**, visited the territory in 1964, made some converts, and organized the Togo-Dahomey Mission. As of 2003 the Benin Mission, part of the Sahel **Union Mission** of the Western **Africa Division**, had 12 **churches** with a membership of about 2,000.

BIBLE INSTRUCTOR. A Seventh-day Adventist term referring to an individual, usually a **woman**, who is assigned to a local **church**, a denominational institution, or an evangelist to direct individuals or small groups in the study of Adventist doctrines. Bible Instructors are also sometimes referred to as "Bible Workers." This approach to **evangelism** developed in the early 1880s when **city missions** began training women to conduct house-to-house evangelism and **Stephen N. Haskell** in 1883 introduced "Bible readings," in which series of texts were organized around various doctrinal subjects for the purpose of individual or small group study. By the early 20th century some women prepared to be Bible instructors by taking the undergraduate ministerial course. Later, Adventist colleges and the **Seventh-day Adventist Theological Seminary** offered courses for the training of Bible instructors.

BIBLE TRAINING SCHOOL. Seventh-day Adventist **evangelistic** journal. **Stephen N. Haskell** and his wife Hetty **published** the *Bible Training School* as a monthly magazine to be sold in city streets in conjunction with evangelistic campaigns. From 1902 to 1907 the denomination sponsored the journal; privately published after 1907, it ceased publication in 1913.

BIBLICAL RESEARCH INSTITUTE (BRI). Seventh-day Adventist organization for the study of theological issues. Concerned about both offshoot groups and other critics of Seventh-day Adventism, denominational leaders established a committee in 1943 to prepare replies and in 1952 named it the Defense Literature Committee. Recognizing that the church needed to do more than simply reply to critics, four years later the **General Conference** reorganized the committee into the Biblical Study and Research Group. In 1975 the organization took on a new name, the Biblical Research Institute. In addition to commissioning scholarly papers on various topics, including the role of **women** in the church and hermeneutics, the organization has sponsored seminars and Bible conferences. In response to the controversy surrounding the ideas of **Desmond Ford**, it published the 7-volume Daniel and Revelation Series (1982-1992).

BLACK, BARRY CLAYTON (1948-). Seventh-day Adventist **minister** and naval chaplain. Black received his B.A. from **Oakwood College** (1970), M.Div. (1973) from **Andrews University,** M.A. from United States International University, and D.Min. from Eastern Baptist Seminary. Commissioned as a Navy chaplain in 1976, in 2000 Black became the first African American and first Seventh-day Adventist to serve as chief of Navy chaplains. While a naval chaplain Black became known to the general public for officiating at John Kennedy, Jr.'s burial at sea and for his participation in the September 11 memorial services at the Pentagon in 2001 and 2002. After his retirement from the Navy, the **United States** Senate elected Black as its 62nd chaplain, the first African American and former military chaplain to hold that position.

BOLIVIA. Bolivia was the last South American country in which Seventh-day Adventists became established. **Literature evangelists** entered the country in 1897 and again in 1902, but it was not until 1907 that Edward Thomann and his wife arrived as the first Adventist missionaries, working among both the Spanish and Indian populations. **Ferdinand Stahl** and his wife Ana arrived in 1909 and were later joined by colporteurs and other missionaries. Despite difficulties, including violence and health problems, missionaries established a station among the Indians at Collana in 1924. Five years later the Bolivia Training School opened at Collana, but it later moved several times. In 1929 Dr. H. E. Butka arrived and developed the Adventist Hospital of Chulumani. The Bolivia **Union Mission** organized in 1996 as part of the South-American **Division.** As of 2003 it had 250 **churches** with a membership of about 105,000, and operated Andes Adventist **Academy,** Bolivia Adventist University, and Bolivia Union Printing.

BOSNIA-HERZEGOVINA. As of 2003 Seventh-day Adventists in Bosnia-Herzegovina were organized as the West **Conference** of the South-East **European Union Conference,** which was part of the Trans-European **Division.** The conference had 22 **churches** with a membership of about 650. *See* SERBIA.

BOTSWANA. William H. Anderson received permission in 1921 to establish a hospital in Botswana on the condition that there be no evangelizing. In the following year, however, J. R. Campbell was allowed to conduct meetings and in 1927 H. Walker established a **mission** station at Kanye. The Botswana **Field** organized in 1959 and three years later the first Adventist school opened. As of 2003 the denomination in Botswana was organized into the North and South Botswana Fields, which were attached fields of the **Zimbabwe Union Conference** of the Southern **Africa**-Indian Ocean **Division**. The two fields had 59 **churches** with a membership of over 21,000. Kanye Hospital and two clinics were located in Botswana.

BOURDEAU, AUGUSTINE CORNELIUS (1834-1916). Seventh-day Adventist **minister**. Born in **Canada**, Bordeau was working as a Baptist preacher when he converted to sabbatarian Adventism in 1856, along with his brother **Daniel T. Bourdeau**. Baptized and **ordained** to the Adventist ministry the following year, he worked along with his brother as a **self-supporting** preacher for several years among the French-speaking people of Quebec and Vermont. In 1862 he helped organize the Vermont **Conference**; later he worked in the American Midwest and in Quebec, where he served as president of the Quebec Conference. Bourdeau went to **Europe** in 1884, returning to the **United States** in 1888, where he carried out **evangelism** in several states as well as Canada.

BOURDEAU, DANIEL T. (1835-1905). Seventh-day Adventist **minister**. Born in **Canada** and a member of the Baptist church, Bourdeau with his brother **Augustine C. Bourdeau** converted to Adventism in 1856. **Ordained** to the Adventist ministry in 1858, he subsequently worked as a **self-supporting** minister with his brother among the French-speaking people of Quebec and Vermont. In 1858 he went to California where he worked with **John N. Loughborough** until 1870. Evangelizing French-speakers, he established **churches** in Wisconsin and Illinois in 1873. In 1876 he joined **John Nevins Andrews** for a year in **Switzerland** where he edited papers and carried out **evangelism** in Switzerland, **Italy**, and **France**. In 1882 he returned to **Europe**, where he was joined by his brother two years later, and worked in France, Switzerland, and Italy. He came back to the **United States** in 1888, continuing his work as an evangelist.

BRADFORD, CHARLES E. (1925-). African American Seventh-day Adventist **minister** and church administrator. Educated at **Oakwood College**, Bradford served as a minister in Texas from 1946 to 1952 and then worked as an administrator and pastor in the Central States **Conference** from 1952 to 1957 and as an administrator in the Northeastern Conference between 1957 and

1959. In 1961 he became president of the Lake **Region Conference** and nine years later joined the **General Conference** (GC) as an associate secretary. Between 1979 and 1990 Bradford served as president of the North American **Division**, the most significant denominational administrative position held by an African American. While division president, he began the process of ending North America's "special relationship" to the GC, in which Americans both largely funded and controlled the central administration of the church, and gave the division a more independent role similar to that of other world divisions. Among his books were *Preaching to the Times* (1975), *The God Between* (1984), *Find Out About Prayer* (1993), and *Sabbath Roots: The African Connection* (1999).

BRANCH DAVIDIANS. *See* DAVIDIAN SEVENTH-DAY ADVENTISTS.

BRANSON, WILLIAM HENRY (1887-1961). Seventh-day Adventist **minister** and church administrator. After education at **Battle Creek College** and **Emmanuel Missionary College,** Branson worked as a **literature evangelist, evangelist,** and minister in the American South, receiving **ordination** in 1910. Assuming the presidency of the South Carolina **Conference** in 1911, he served in a succession of administrative positions: president of the Cumberland Conference (1913-1915), Southeastern **Union Conference** (1915-1920), and African **Division** (1920-1930); vice president of the **General Conference** (GC, 1930-38); and president of the **China** Division (1938-40). After returning to China to serve as division president from 1946 to 1949, Branson was president of the GC from 1950 to 1954. Among his books were *Missionary Adventures in Africa* (1925), *In Defense of the Faith* (1933), and *The Drama of the Ages* (1950).

BRAZIL. Seventh-day Adventism first entered Brazil through papers sent to **German** immigrants. Beginning in 1893, Albert B. Stauffer, a **literature evangelist,** sold German and English books and was soon joined by other booksellers. By 1895 they had baptized 35 individuals, all German, into the Seventh-day Adventist Church. They also made their first Portuguese convert that same year. Meanwhile, W. H. Thurston arrived in the country in 1894 and worked as a **self-supporting** missionary in Rio de Janeiro until 1900. Late in 1895 Huldreich F. von Graf came to the country and the following year organized the first **church**, located at Gaspar

Alto, Santa Catarina; the congregation constructed a church building in 1898. Graf and other missionaries continued to expand their efforts, creating a school, Curitiba International College, in 1896 and establishing a paper, *The Herald of Truth*, in 1900. Two years later they organized the Brazilian **Conference** with 15 churches and more than 850 members. In 1920 the church **ordained** the first Brazilian Adventist **minister. Leo B.** Halliwell established a medical-missionary boat ministry among the Indians of the Amazon with the *Luzeiro* in 1931, and the first Adventist hospital opened in 1942. In the following year, a Portuguese version of the *Voice of Prophecy* began radio broadcasts. Through the influence of German **evangelist Walter Schubert**, new evangelistic techniques emerged. Using these methods, Alcides Campolongo began conducting evangelistic campaigns in São Paulo in 1961 that brought about the explosive growth of Adventism in that city. As of 2003 Adventists in Brazil, part of the South American **Division**, were organized into three **Union Conferences** and two Union **Missions** with 4,223 churches and more than one million members. Adventist institutions in Brazil included **Brazil Adventist University**, Northeast Brazil College, Latin-American Adventist Theological Seminary, 23 secondary schools, eight hospitals, numerous clinics and orphanages, Brazil Food Factory, Adventist Media Center-Brazil, and **Brazil Publishing House**.

BRAZIL ADVENTIST UNIVERSITY. Seventh-day Adventist **educational** institution located in São Paulo and Engenheiro Coelho, SP, Brazil. The Adventist Seminary of the Brazilian **Union Conference** of Seventh-day Adventists opened in 1915 to train workers for the denomination and graduated its first class in 1922. Over time the school operated under a number of names: Adventist Seminary (1919), Adventist College (1923), Brazilian Adventist College (1942), and Adventist Training Institute (1961), although it became popularly known as "Brazil College." By the early 1920s the school had more than 200 students and was supplying personnel for the church. Out of the 29 individuals who had graduated by 1927, for instance, 27 became denominational employees. Through the mid-1930s the available courses were almost entirely at the secondary level, but beginning in 1936 the school began emphasizing post-secondary work and by 1941 had become a junior college. Over the next decade the school introduced professional programs in business, education, and theology. By

1950 the institution had a total enrollment of over 600, with 145 students at the post-secondary level.

After extensive upgrading and expansion of the physical facilities at the institution, the denomination in 1959 granted permission for the school to offer a theology degree. By the early 1970s the institution had gained government approval for a secondary teaching program and schools of music and nursing. New programs brought increasing numbers of students. With over 700 individuals enrolled by 1980, the school had become the largest post-secondary Adventist institution in **Latin America**. Graduate education in theology arrived with the development of the **Latin American Theological Seminary**, which began offering courses on the Brazil and **River Plate College** campuses in 1981. After the government expropriated part of the land of the São Paulo campus, the institution in 1983 established a second campus in a rural area about 90 miles northwest of the city. As of 2003 the São Paulo campus was divided into nine schools: Biology, Education, Mathematics, Music and Arts, Nursing, Nutrition, Physical Education, Physical Therapy, and Science of Computing. The Engenheiro Coelho campus had eight schools: Business Administration, Education, Engineering, Language, Music and Arts, Social Communication, Graduate Studies, and the Theological Seminary.

BRAZIL PUBLISHING HOUSE. Seventh-day Adventist **publishing** house located in Tatui, São Paulo, **Brazil**. After W. H. Thurston, an American missionary, and Guilherme Stein began publishing *The Herald of Truth* in 1900 they searched for funds to purchase a printing press. By 1905 they had set up a press and issued their first papers; soon the publishing house was established as a branch of the International **Tract and Missionary Society**. **Frank H. Westphal** wanted the press to more effectively provide Portuguese language publications for the denomination and therefore helped it move in 1908-09 to Estaçã de São Bernardo, which was located in a more heavily populated area. By 1914-15 the press was publishing eight books, nine tracts, German and Portuguese monthly papers, and editions of the **Union Conference** paper. With financial help from the **United States**, the press expanded its production capacity in the 1920s and trained **literature evangelists** to sell its publications. By 1926 there were 85 such sales people. Because investment in plant and machinery came from elsewhere, the publishing house was able to devote its profits to various projects in the 1930s, including a school in São Paulo and a launch for the Amazon. A Brazilian law requiring that all periodicals be published by nationals led to nationalization of the publishing house board in 1941 and the appointment of Brazilian magazine editors by early the following year. Despite these political problems, sales continued to increase, with the publishing house in the 1940s becoming the most productive Adventist press outside North America. By the 1990s Brazil Publishing House was supplying more than 2,600 literature evangelists with books and other materials. Since being established, it had published about 450 different book titles, which had sold over 30 million copies. As of 2003 the house was publishing seven periodicals plus nine quarterly Bible Study Guides for the **Sabbath schools**.

BREATH OF LIFE. Seventh-day Adventist television program for an African American audience. Established in 1974, under the leadership of Charles D. Brooks, *Breath of Life* aired in specific cities for several weeks prior to an evangelistic campaign. Subsequently it became a weekly program that appeared on the Black Entertainment and other cable and satellite networks. After Brooks's retirement in 1997, Walter L. Pearson took his place.

BRINSMEAD, ROBERT DAVID (1933-). Australian critic of Adventism. After discovering the writings of **Alonzo T. Jones** and **Ellet J. Waggoner** while a student at **Avondale College**, Brinsmead developed a form of perfectionism which, with his brother John, he promoted among Adventists in **Australia** and the **United States** in the 1950s and 1960s. After their membership in the Seventh-day Adventist Church was revoked in 1961, the Brinsmeads organized the "Sanctuary Awakening Fellowship," based in the United States, through which they expanded their influence into **Asia** and **Africa**. In 1968 they began publishing a magazine, *Present Truth*. Largely through the influence of **Desmond Ford**, by the mid-1970s Robert abandoned his perfectionism in favor of **righteousness by faith** and began directing *Present Truth* to both Adventists and other Christians. Soon, however, he rejected the Adventist doctrines of the seventh-day **Sabbath,** the **sanctuary**, and the inspiration of **Ellen G. White**. In 1978 he changed the name of his magazine to *Verdict* and in 1980 published his criticisms of Adventism in a book entitled *Judged by the Gospel*.

BROWNSBERGER, SIDNEY (1845-1930). Seventh-day Adventist **educator**. Brownsberger converted to Seventh-day Adventism in 1866 while a student at the University of Michigan. After graduating with a bachelor's degree in classical studies in 1869 he served successively as superintendent of schools in Maumee and Delta, Ohio. In 1874 he became principal of **Battle Creek College** where he struggled to combine a traditional academic curriculum with Adventist concerns for such elements as student behavior and manual labor. While leading the college he also received a master's degree from the University of Michigan. He left the college in 1881 to engage in farming for a short time before becoming principal of Healdsburg College (later **Pacific Union College**) in California, a position he held until 1887. He then farmed and performed **self-supporting** ministerial and educational work. In 1909 he and Arthur W. Spalding established the Asheville Agricultural School and Mountain **Sanitarium** near Fletcher, North Carolina.

BUENOS AIRES PUBLISHING HOUSE. Seventh-day Adventist **publishing** house located in Florida, Buenos Aires, **Argentina**. In 1897 Adventist missionaries in Argentina began publishing *The Lighthouse* and seven years later organized the South American Editorial House. The house used commercial printers until Joseph W. Westphal in 1905 established the Present Truth Printing Office at **River Plate College**; two years later the printing office moved to Florida, Buenos Aires. Desiring to have one publishing house produce Spanish-language materials for all of South America, in 1910 Westphal merged the **Chile** Publishing House, which had been founded in 1900, with the Argentinian house. In 1913 the new entity adopted as its name the South American Union Editorial House. Meanwhile, in 1911 it had begun publishing a missionary paper, *The Signs of the Times*, for all the Spanish-speaking countries in the **union conference**. In addition to importing Spanish books from **Pacific Press** in the **United States** and the denomination's publishing house in **Spain**, the Buenos Aires house produced *The World's Crisis* and *Armageddon* during World War I. With financial assistance from the **General Conference** the house moved into new facilities in 1925. At the same time, it emphasized the development of **literature evangelists**, increasing the number selling its publications from 57 in 1920 to 83 in 1926.

Although its sales fluctuated, affected by such elements as the economic depression of the 1930s and legal restrictions on importing publications into Chile, the Buenos Aires house grew significantly; between 1940 and 1950, for instance, its sales increased from \$US151,000 to \$US239,000. By 1950 it was the sixth largest of the 39 Adventist publishing houses outside North America. In the mid-1950s the house acquired new printing equipment, which helped it keep up with a growing demand for publications and in 1965 it established a branch in Chile. Total book sales in the **division**, including both the Brazil and Buenos Aires publishing houses, expanded from more than $US1,000,000 in 1953 to $US17,000,000 in 1980. In 1973, however, the publishing house suffered a fire, which destroyed its library, archives, and editorial offices, but did not seriously damage the printing equipment. A reconstructed and newly designed plant officially opened in 1978, although it had begun operating some time earlier. As of 2003 the Buenos Aires Publishing House published, in addition to books, six periodicals and six Bible Study Guides for **Sabbath schools**.

BULGARIA. In the 1890s a group of **German** immigrants from **Russia**, who had settled near the **Romanian**-Bulgarian border, first introduced Seventh-day Adventism into Bulgaria. E. S. Popoff, a Bulgarian from the **United States**, arrived in the country in 1897, receiving help the following year from **Ludvig R. Conradi**, who conducted the first Adventist **baptisms**. In 1899 **Ellen G. White's** book, *Steps to Christ*, was translated into Bulgarian. C. Motzer, from **Germany**, organized the Bulgarian **Mission** by 1913. In 1915 a European denominational leader reported that Bulgaria had three **churches** with 56 members. Five years later there were nine churches with 205 members and the Bulgarian Publishing House operated at the mission headquarters in Sofia. By 1937 there were 730 members and the denomination had acquired two church buildings, but World War II brought organized efforts to an end. After years of struggle with the government to control its own affairs, the denomination received official recognition in 1990. As of 2003 the Bulgarian Union of Churches, part of the Euro-**Africa Division**, had 103 churches with a membership of over 7,000. The Bulgarian Publishing House was located in Sofia.

BURGESS, GEORGIA ANNA (BURRUS) (1866-1948). Seventh-day Adventist missionary. Converted to Adventism at age sixteen, Georgia Burrus attended Healdsburg College (later **Pacific Union College**) and subsequently taught at a Bible training school held in Oakland, California. In 1895, as the first Mission Board appointee, she went to **India** as a **self-supporting** missionary. At first studying Bengali and making contact with Indian women, she soon received money from a South African donor and with Mae Taylor opened a school for Hindu girls in 1896. In 1903 she married Luther J. Burgess, secretary-treasurer of the Indian **Mission**, and together they **evangelized** the Bengali-, Hindi-, Urdu-, and Khasi-speaking peoples. In 1935 they returned to the **United States**.

BURKINA FASO. Henri Kempf, a French Seventh-day Adventist missionary who had worked in **Togo**, arrived in Burkina Faso in 1971 and held his first **evangelistic** campaign two years later, at which time the Burkina Faso **Mission** was organized. As of 2003 the mission, part of the Sahel **Union Mission** of the Western **Africa Division**, had six **churches** with a membership of nearly 2,000. Bazeka Horticultural **Adventist Development and Relief Agency** Center and two clinics and dispensaries were located in Burkina Faso.

BURUNDI. David E. Delhove, who arrived from **Rwanda**, established the Buganda **mission** station in 1925. A second mission station, Ndora, opened in 1937, by which time 39 schools and churches had been established. As of 2003 the Burundi Association was an Attached **Field** of the East-Central **Africa Division**, with 155 **churches** and nearly 75,000 members. Two secondary schools and seven dispensaries and health centers were located in Burundi.

BUTLER, GEORGE IDE (1834-1918). Seventh-day Adventist **minister** and church administrator. In 1839 Butler's family accepted the teaching of **William Miller** that Jesus would return about 1843. Through contacts with **Joseph Bates** and **Ellen G. White** the Butlers by 1850 had become part of the sabbatarian Adventist movement. In 1853 Butler's father moved the family from their native Vermont to join other Adventists in Waukon, Iowa. After a period of skepticism, George adopted the sabbatarian Adventist faith in 1856, taught school for two years, and in 1859 married and purchased a farm.

When B. F. Snook and William H. Brinkerhoff, respectively president and secretary-treasurer of the Iowa **Conference**, became critical of the **General Conference** (GC) and Ellen G. White, Butler replaced Snook as president of the conference in 1865 and was **ordained** to the ministry two years later. Serving in this office until 1872, he battled the influence of the critics, who became known as the "Marion party" (which became the **Church of God**), eventually stabilizing the Iowa Conference and impressing others with his administrative abilities.

Becoming GC president in 1872, Butler moved to Battle Creek, where he oversaw establishment of **Battle Creek College**. In the face of criticism of **James** and **Ellen G. White**, Butler wrote an essay on *Leadership* in which he argued that all Adventists must defer to the Whites in regard to church policy. After Ellen White responded by telling him that his theory gave her husband and herself too much authority and influence, Butler resigned the presidency in 1874 (to be succeeded by James White), went to California to work for a short time at **Pacific Press,** and then in 1876 was again elected president of the Iowa Conference, in which position he oversaw the **evangelization** of Missouri and Kansas.

In 1880 Butler once more became president of the GC and in that position dealt with a crisis that led to the temporary closure of Battle Creek College. In 1884 he traveled to **Europe** to gather information and offer advice regarding the development of Adventist **mission** work, including the establishment of publishing houses in **Switzerland, Norway,** and **Great Britain.** On his return to the **United States** he encountered the emerging issue of **righteousness by faith** promoted by **Alonzo T. Jones** and **Ellet J. Waggoner.** Opposing the new views, which he believed ultimately threatened the doctrine of the seventh-day **Sabbath,** Butler wrote a tract, *The Law in the Book of Galatians,* in 1886. Ill with malaria and unable to attend the **General Conference session of 1888,** he telegraphed his supporters to "stand by the old landmarks." When it became apparent that Ellen G. White was supporting Waggoner and Jones, Butler sent his resignation as president.

Shortly thereafter, Butler moved to a farm in Bowling Green, Florida, where he cared for his wife, Lentha, who had suffered a stroke, and occasionally conducted evangelistic meetings. In 1901, after his wife died, the Florida Conference elected him president and the following year the newly formed Southern **Union Conference** called him to a similar position. Replicating Seventh-day Adventist work in the Midwest and the West, he encouraged the development of schools and **sanitariums** throughout the South and the creation of the **Southern Publishing Association.** Between 1902 and his retirement in 1908 he also served on the GC Executive Committee.

In 1907 Butler had remarried and after retirement he and his new wife, Elizabeth Work Grainger, returned to his Florida farm. He spoke at Adventist **camp meetings** and carried on extensive correspondence with church leaders. In 1918 he was diagnosed with a brain tumor and died shortly thereafter.

BYINGTON, JOHN (1798-1887). Seventh-day Adventist **minister** and first president of the **General Conference.** A Methodist preacher and farmer in Buck's Bridge, New York, Byington encountered **Millerism** in 1844 but did not become a believer. In 1852, however, he read a copy of the *Review and Herald* and accepted sabbatarian Adventism. Three years later he built an Adventist church near his home. At the request of **James White**, Byington moved to Michigan in 1858 and spent the next 15 years as a **self-supporting** preacher in that state. Working to establish the movement as a denomination, Byington became president when the **General Conference of Seventh-day Adventists** was organized in 1863. He served two one-year terms in this position.

C

CAMBODIA. Fred L. Pickett, the first Seventh-day Adventist missionary to enter Cambodia, arrived in 1930. Refused permission to build a church, he established a congregation of 32 Cambodian members at Tinh Bien, a village in neighboring Cochin **China**. Other missionaries came during the next several years, among them Robert Bentz and his wife, who oversaw a Bible school and maternity clinic in Phnom Penh from 1939 to 1941. World War II, however, forced all foreign missionaries to leave. Ralph E. Neall, the first post-war Adventist missionary, arrived in 1957, followed by other workers. The first Adventist **church** building opened in 1962 in Phnom Penh. Political developments, however, closed organized Adventist efforts from 1965 until 1972, when the church opened an English-language school. After the Khmer Rouge gained power in 1975, denominational work again came to a halt. Beginning around 1980, however, the **Adventist Development and Relief Agency** and **Adventist Frontier Missions** worked in the refugee camps located in Thailand to which many Cambodians had fled. In the early 1990s Adventist missionaries once more entered Cambodia and the church received official recognition from the government in 1993. As of 2003 the Cambodia Adventist **Mission**, part of the Southeast Asia **Union Mission** of the Southern **Asia**-Pacific **Division**, had four churches and a membership of about 4,000.

CAMEROON. After **William H. Anderson** chose a **mission** site at Nanga-Eboko in 1926, Robert L. Jones organized a **Sabbath school** and primary school two years later. Marius Raspal conducted the first **baptism** in 1929 and the first Seventh-day Adventist **church** organized in 1930 with about 16 members. As additional missionaries arrived and native **evangelists** emerged, Adventism spread to several areas of the country. In 1955 the first contact with the Pygmy population took place. Primary schools and, after 1950, secondary schools became an important part of Adventist efforts. The first hospital opened in the mid-1950s. As of 2003 the Seventh-day Adventist Church in Cameroon was divided into two **conferences** and two missions, part of the Central African **Union Mission** of the Western **Africa Division**, with 780 churches and nearly 100,000 members. Adventist University Cosendai, Central African Publishing House, Koza Adventist Hospital, Batouri Adventist Hospital, six clinics and dispensaries, and four secondary schools were located in Cameroon.

CAMP MEETINGS. Religious gatherings, usually in rural areas, where those attending live in tents or other temporary accommodations. The **Millerites** held their first camp meeting in Quebec in 1842 and another a few days later in East Kingston, New Hampshire. They held an additional 29 meetings that year, 40 in 1843, and 55 in 1844. Generally, these meetings followed the Methodist pattern with three open-air preaching services each day interspersed by social and prayer meetings. After the sabbatarian Adventists organized the Seventh-day Adventist Church in 1863, they avoided holding camp meetings because they feared the possibility of unruly crowds. But as local **churches** began to gather in four-day quarterly meetings, the Illinois-Wisconsin **Conference** in September 1867 organized a conference-wide "convocation meeting" at Johnstown Center, Wisconsin, which drew some 300 campers. A short time later, a similar meeting took place at Pilot Grove, Iowa. The success of these meetings led the **General Conference** (GC) to call the first "official" camp meeting at Wright, Michigan, in September 1868. Other regional meetings also took place that year. In 1869 the GC recommended that state conferences organize all future camp meetings. From that time on camp meetings grew in popularity, becoming a staple of Adventist life in both North America and elsewhere. The first camp meeting in **Europe** took place at Moss, **Norway**, in 1887 and the first in **Australia** at Brighton, Victoria, in 1893. Although camp meetings remained popular in North America throughout the 20th century, with many conferences developing permanent campground facilities, by the 21st century most such meetings lasted only a weekend rather than the one to two weeks that had previously prevailed.

CANADA. Seventh-day Adventism first entered eastern Canada when **Joseph Bates** and **James** and **Ellen G. White** visited former

Millerites in 1850. During the next two decades, S. Hutchins, L. W. Sperry, and **Augustine** and **Daniel Bourdeau** evangelized the area, organizing in 1862 the Potton/Troy **church**, whose congregation included people from both Vermont and Canada. Two years later the first all-Canadian Adventist church organized with members from Westbury and Easton. In 1876 the first church in Ontario organized at Wyoming after John Fulton conducted meetings there. In 1880 the Quebec **Conference** organized, followed in 1890 by the Ontario Conference, and in 1902 by the Maritime Conference. Meanwhile, Adventist **evangelists** moved into British Columbia in 1886, organizing their first church four years later. In 1895 **literature evangelists** began working in Alberta, making possible the organization of a church at Leduc in 1898. Manitoba saw its first organized Adventist church congregation in 1893 and Saskatchewan in 1906. The British Columbia Conference organized in 1902, Manitoba in 1903, Alberta in 1906, and Saskatchewan in 1912. Many of the early converts in western Canada came from the **German** and **Ukrainian** immigrant populations. In 1907 the Alberta Conference established the Alberta Industrial Academy in Leduc; in 1909 the conference moved the school to Lacombe where it later developed into Canadian University College. The Ontario Conference in 1903 established Lornedale Academy in Oshawa; it is now Kingsway College, which offers two years of tertiary education. As of 2003 the Seventh-day Adventist Church in Canada, also known as the Canadian **Union Conference**, was part of the North American **Division**, having 328 churches with a membership of over 50,000. In addition to Canadian University College and Kingsway College, it operated eight secondary schools and the Canadian Adventist Media Center.

CANRIGHT, DUDLEY MARVIN (1840-1919). Seventh-day Adventist **minister** and later critic of Adventism. Converted to Adventism while in his teens, Canright began preaching at age 19 and received **ordination** five years later in 1865. In 1873 he evangelized with **Merritt E. Cornell** in California but, after a dispute with **James** and **Ellen G. White**, left the ministry for a short time. In 1876 he became a member of the **General Conference** Executive Committee and subsequently president of the **Sabbath School** Association and the Ohio **Conference**. After receiving formal training in elocution, in 1880 he left the ministry again for four months to conduct speaking classes in Michigan and Wisconsin. In 1882 Canright ended his work as an Adventist minister and became a farmer in Otsego, Michigan. Five years later he informed **George I. Butler**, president of the General Conference, that he no longer accepted Adventism's distinctive beliefs. Shortly after resigning his Adventist church membership in February 1887, he joined the Baptist congregation in Otsego and was ordained the minister of that church in April, a position he held for about two years. He wrote *Seventh-day Adventism Renounced* (1888), which became a major source for critics of Adventism, and *Life of Mrs. E. G. White* (1919), which criticized the Adventist leader for plagiarism and inconsistency, among other issues.

CAPE VERDE. In 1935 A. F. Raposo arrived in Cape Verde as the first Seventh-day Adventist missionary to the country, **baptizing** 15 individuals the following year. Antonio J. Gomes built the first Adventist building, which contained a school, church, and residence, at Nossa Senhora do Monte, in 1938. As of 2003 the Cape Verde **Mission** was part of the Sahel **Union Mission** of the Western **Africa Division** with 15 **churches** and a membership of over 4,000.

CARIBBEAN. *See* ANTIGUA AND BARBUDA; BAHAMAS; BARBADOS; CAYMAN ISLANDS; DOMINICAN REPUBLIC; GRENADA; GUADELOUPE; HAITI; JAMAICA; LEEWARD AND WINDWARD ISLANDS; MARTINIQUE; NETH-ERLANDS ANTILLES; PUERTO RICO; TRINIDAD AND TOBAGO; VIRGIN ISLANDS.

CAYMAN ISLANDS. Gilbert McLaughlin, a layman, introduced Seventh-day Adventism to the Cayman Islands in the mid-1890s. **Literature evangelists** arrived about the same time and W. W. Eastman conducted **evangelistic** meetings between 1895 and 1897. In 1929 the Caymans organized as a separate **Mission** with two churches and 33 members but later transferred to the **Jamaica Conference**. In 1944 they again became a separate mission. As of 2003 the Cayman Islands Mission was part of the West Indies **Union Conference** in the Inter-American **Division**, with nine **churches** and a membership of over 2,200.

CENTRAL AFRICAN REPUBLIC. Jean Kempf established a school and **mission** headquarters in Bangui in 1960 and three years later conducted his first **baptism**. By 1971 missionaries had established three mission stations and in 1974 built the first Adventist church building in the country. In 1989 the denomination placed an **evangelistic** center and book center in Bangui. As of 2003 the Central African Republic **Mission** was part of the Central African **Union Mission** in the Western **Africa Division**, with 46 **churches** and a membership of about 7,000.

CHAD. Seventh-day Adventists began work in Chad in 1967 and organized the Chad **Mission** in 1973. As of 2003 it was part of the Central African **Union Mission** in the Western **Africa Division**, with 40 **churches** and a membership of over 2,200. The Bere Health Centre was located in Chad.

CHAPEL MUSIC. Recording subsidiary of **Pacific Press Publishing Association**. Producing and distributing recordings for the Seventh-day Adventist market, although including **musical** artists of other faiths, Chapel Records—later Chapel Music—formed in 1955 and concentrated on popular styles, from gospel songs as represented by the **King's Heralds** and **Del Delker** in the 1950s to more contemporary approaches introduced by the **Wedgwood Trio** in the 1960s and the **Heritage Singers** in the 1970s and 1980s.

CHERIAN, MALIAKAL EAPEN (1926-1998). Seventh-day Adventist **educator** and church administrator. A native of **India**, Cherian earned a B. A. from Spicer Memorial College, M.A. degrees from **Andrews University** and the University of Maryland, and a Ph.D. from the University of Pune. Meanwhile joining the staff at Spicer in 1944, he served in a variety of positions as a teacher and administrator prior to becoming president of the institution in 1963. As president he strengthened the undergraduate academic programs, worked with the University of Pune to have Spicer students accepted as graduate students despite the college's unaccredited status, and instituted a D.Min. program. In 1990 he became president of the Southern Asia **Division**, where he established centers for the study of Islam and Hinduism and increased the involvement of lay people in the organization's decision making. Cherian retired in 1997.

CHICAGO MEDICAL MISSION. Seventh-day Adventist social welfare agency. Promoted by **John Harvey Kellogg** and partly funded by the Medical Missionary and Benevolent Association, the Chicago Medical Mission opened in 1893, using facilities of the Pacific Garden Mission. In this location it offered several services:

a medical dispensary and visiting nurse program, free baths, free laundry, and a one-cent lunch. In 1896 the mission purchased an old church, which it established as a "Workingmen's Home" that provided sleeping accommodations, bath and laundry facilities, and meals. Temporary work, including rug weaving and broom making, was available to the unemployed so that they could cover their expenses at the home. About the same time Kellogg also acquired another building that provided a classroom and dormitory for **American Medical Missionary College** students who gained clinical experience working at the mission. The building also served as a settlement house, which offered such services as a free kindergarten and day care for the children of working mothers, classes in cooking and sewing, health lectures, and a maternity home for unwed mothers. The nonsectarian character of the mission caused friction with Adventist leaders and the project became increasingly dependent on funds raised outside the denomination. As Kellogg came into direct conflict with the church and the American Medical Missionary College went into decline, he found it increasingly difficult to fund the mission. Gradually dropping services until only the dispensary was left, the mission closed in 1913.

CHILE. Seventh-day Adventist **literature evangelists** first arrived in Chile in 1894, obtaining their first convert—an Englishman—two years later. In 1895 Granville H. Baber began missionary work as superintendent of the newly organized Chile **Mission**, which also included **Bolivia, Peru**, and **Ecuador**. By the following year there were about 70 Adventists in the country. In 1900 the first issue of *The Signs of the Times* appeared, followed the next year by the *Adventist Review*, which in 1904 became the official paper of the South American **Union Mission**. In 1907 Chile organized as a **conference**. Meanwhile, Adventists had established their first school, which later developed into Chile Adventist University. By 1930 the conference had 29 churches and over 1,700 members and was operating eight schools. A hospital opened in 1958 and a secondary school in 1963. As membership in the church grew, the territory of Chile went through several reorganizations. As of 2003 the Chile Union Mission, organized in 1966 and part of the South American **Division**, had 490 churches with a membership of over 100,000. It operated the Chile Adventist University, 11 secondary schools, and the Los Angeles Adventist Clinic. A branch of the **Buenos Aires Publishing House** was located in Chile.

CHINA, PEOPLE'S REPUBLIC OF. Abram La Rue, a Seventh-day Adventist layman, sold denominational **publications** to English-speaking people in **Hong Kong** and Shanghai in the late 1880s and subsequently had two tracts translated into Chinese. In 1902 the **General Conference** (GC) sent Jacob N. Anderson, his wife, and sister-in-law to Hong Kong where they opened a school for English-speaking Chinese children. Later that same year, Edwin H. Wilbur and his wife went to Canton. Eric Pilquist arrived a short time later and in 1903 Adventists conducted their first **baptism** in the country and organized their first **church** with eight members. Timothy Tay, who had been baptized in **Singapore**, became the first Chinese missionary to his native people in 1904. That same year Adventists opened their first Chinese-language schools and began printing tracts in Chinese. Law Keem, a Chinese physician from the **United States**, began medical work in south China in 1905 and Dr. **Harry Miller**, who had begun similar efforts in central China two years earlier, started publishing *The Gospel Herald* that same year. In 1906 the missionaries **ordained** their first Chinese **minister**, Nga Pit Keh. After the China **Union Mission** organized in 1909 it opened a school the following year in central China. The institution moved several times and eventually settled in Shanghai, where mission leaders had built a publishing house in 1908, and became known as the China Union Training School. By this point the Adventist church in China had established its institutional base and continued to expand during subsequent years, despite political and economic upheaval, leading the GC in 1930 to organize it as a separate **Division**.

By the end of World War II China had nearly 23,000 members in 261 churches, ten medical institutions, and one publishing house. With the establishment of the People's Republic of China in 1949, however, Seventh-day Adventism as an organized work, along with other Christian organizations, experienced severe repression and went underground. The China Division dissolved in 1952 and other organizations soon after, but many individuals maintained their faith. Beginning in 1979 Adventist leaders began to make contact with these believers and Adventist literature made its way into the country from **Hong Kong**. As of 2003 the Seventh-day Adventist Church in China, which did not have an organizational structure, reported 898 churches and a membership of about 311,000.

CHINA, REPUBLIC OF (TAIWAN). T. S. Yang, a **literature evangelist** from mainland **China**, sold Seventh-day Adventist

publications in Taiwan between 1907 and 1912, but there was no organized Adventist presence on the island for many years thereafter. After Taiwan became part of the Japan **Union Mission** in the early 1930s, Nagao Wachi arrived to work in the city of Tainan. When World War II stopped Adventist missionary efforts, Taiwan had a membership of 14. After the war ended Taiwan came under the South China Union Mission, which in 1947 sent two representatives to Taiwan to survey the situation, but they could find only one Adventist. The following year three Chinese missionaries arrived and began **evangelistic** efforts. Meanwhile, several Adventists were among the increasing numbers of refugees from mainland China who fled to Taiwan. With about 20 members at the end of 1948, the Taiwan Mission organized in December.

In January 1949 the first American Adventist missionaries arrived and formed at Taipei the first Adventist **church.** Because of the political situation in the People's Republic of China, in 1950 Taiwan became part of the South China Island Union Mission under the **General Conference**. Missionaries from mainland China came to Taiwan in 1951 where they established a training school and other facilities. The Taiwan Theological Institute opened in 1952 and within a year began offering college-level work; in 1962 it became Taiwan Missionary College. With more missionaries in Taiwan, Adventists in 1953 began working among the native tribal peoples in Ta She. By the early 1960s about half of the Adventist membership in Taiwan came from the indigenous people. **Harry W. Miller**, who had worked in China for many years, opened Taiwan Adventist Hospital in 1955; it moved into more adequate facilities in 1987. Beginning in 1958 Adventists broadcast the *Voice of Prophecy* in Mandarin and in 1968 a program in Taiwanese. Six years later the denomination started television programming. As of 2003 the Taiwan Mission, part of the Chinese **Union Mission** of the Northern **Asia**-Pacific **Division**, had 48 churches with a membership of over 4,000. Taiwan Adventist Academy, Taiwan Adventist College, Taiwan Adventist Hospital, and Signs of the Times Publishing Association were located on the island.

CHRISTIAN CONNECTION. Nineteenth-century restorationist movement. In New England, the Christian Connection (originally spelled "Connexion") developed around Abner Jones and Elias Smith, calling for the restoration of New Testament Christianity. The movement was revivalistic and opposed Calvinism and **trinitarianism**. The **Millerite** publicist, **Joshua V. Himes**, led a

Christian Connection church in Boston, and two of the founders of sabbatarian Adventism, **James White** and **Joseph Bates,** had a Christian Connection background and carried its anti-trinitarianism into the new movement.

CHRISTIAN RECORD SERVICES INTERNATIONAL, INC. Seventh-day Adventist organization that provides materials for the blind. Although the International **Tract and Missionary Society** purchased a stereotype machine in 1897 or 1898 to produce some Braille tracts, Austin Wilson, a blind student at **Battle Creek College,** sought to convince church leaders that a more sustained program was needed. They decided to publish a monthly journal and asked Wilson to print it; the first issue of the *Christian Record* appeared in January 1900. When the **Review and Herald Publishing Association** building burned in 1902, destroying all the equipment, the Christian Record moved to College View, Nebraska. Over time other services developed, including a Bible correspondence program, a lending library, summer camps for blind children, and additional magazines. Unlike many Adventist organizations, Christian Record provided services for other Christian groups in addition to its sponsoring denomination. It drew funds from the Seventh-day Adventist Church to support all of its services and from other donors for nonsectarian projects.

CHRISTOLOGY. Theology of the nature and mission of Jesus. In addition to the issue of the **Trinity,** Seventh-day Adventist Christological discussion has revolved around whether Jesus had a pre-fall or post-fall nature and the implications of this issue for Christian living. While she asserted that Jesus was both fully God and fully human, **Ellen G. White** believed that in his humanity he had a post-fall nature. Nonetheless, she stated, Jesus was sinless and without corruption. Ultimately, in works such as *The Desire of Ages* (1898), she emphasized Christ's role as a mediator between God and man, with his divinity connecting him with God and his humanity with human beings.

Ellet J. Waggoner, who was a leading figure in Adventist discussion of **righteousness by faith** in the late 1880s, understood that Jesus had the same sinful tendencies as all humanity but because of his divinity could not sin. Waggoner increasingly stressed Christ's immanence within the human heart, an indwelling that will ultimately produce sinless living. This belief that through the power of Jesus humanity can achieve victory over sin subsequently became a major theme in Adventism, represented in such movements as the Victorious Life emphasis of the 1920s and the influence of **Robert Brinsmead** in the 1950s and 1960s.

Responding to this emphasis, **Edward Heppenstall**, who upheld a clear doctrine of righteousness by faith, argued that Jesus' nature was sinless and differed from that of fallen human beings. Humanity's salvation, in Heppenstall's view, is a gift of grace that is realized by faith in the **atoning** death and resurrection of Jesus, rather than upon what an indwelling Christ accomplishes in our lives.

While views such as Heppenstall's grew to prominence in the denomination during the post-World War II years, reflected in books such as *Seventh-day Adventists Answer Questions on Doctrine* (1957), the earlier stress on Christ's sinful nature did not disappear. This view came to the fore once again in the writing of Herbert Douglass, who served as assistant editor of the *Review and Herald* from 1970 to 1976. Douglass believed that Christ had a sinful human nature but, through dependence on God, did not succumb to sin. Consequently, all humanity can gain victory over sin just as he did. Indeed, according to Douglass, the **Second Advent** is waiting upon a generation of Christians to gain this victory. Heppenstall and Douglass, as well as two other writers, summarized their views in essays contributed to *Perfection, the Impossible Possibility* (1975). Views such as those of Waggoner and Douglass attracted Adventists because they seemed to offer a means of fulfilling God's law, while that of Heppenstall appealed because it offered the hope of salvation to those who regarded such fulfillment as beyond normal human achievement. Both sides in the debate drew liberally on the voluminous writings of Ellen G. White, who never developed a systematic view of the issue. Several critics of Adventism understood references to Jesus' sinful nature as meaning that he sinned, but those Adventist writers who believed that Jesus inherited a post-fall nature have consistently argued that he never succumbed to temptation. The article on "Christ: His Person and Work" in the *Handbook of Seventh-day Adventist Theology* (2000) presented the traditional Christian view of the nature of Christ as being both fully divine and fully human, yet without sin.

CHURCH. The basic organizational unit of the Seventh-day Adventist Church. The Seventh-day Adventist Church took the position by 1883 that local churches should be organized only with the oversight of a state **conference.** The president of a conference or **mission** or a **minister** designated by the president presides over the organizational process. If there are potential members of the proposed church who have been members of another local Adventist church or the conference church (in which individuals hold membership when there is no local church), they bring letters of transfer of membership to the organizing session and, under the presiding officer, vote those who are newly joining the denomination into local church membership. In cases where there are no individuals with previous Adventist church membership, the presiding minister chooses three newly baptized individuals who then vote on an additional individual. As individual names are voted into membership, they join the group to vote on subsequent names. Once individuals have been voted into local church membership, the presiding minister chairs a nominating committee that fills such local church offices as **elder** and **deacon**. After elders and deacons have been ordained, the church may request the conference to receive it into membership at its next constituency meeting. Churches may disband in consultation with the conference or, in cases of apostasy, by vote of the conference constituency meeting. The procedure for organizing a church and conducting its business are delineated in the *Church Manual*.

CHURCH MANUAL. Official Seventh-day Adventist handbook for local **churches**. Although in 1882 a committee prepared a church manual that was published in the *Review and Herald* the following year, the **General Conference session** of 1883, because of the denomination's historic opposition to creeds, decided not to officially adopt the document. While other publications appeared regarding the local church and its officers, **John N. Loughborough's** *The Church, Its Organization, Order and Discipline* (1907) functioned unofficially as a manual in the early 20th century. In 1932 the **General Conference** (GC) issued the first edition of the *Church Manual*, but a GC session took its first action on the document when in 1946 it voted that such sessions must approve all future revisions. The *Manual* covers such matters as local church organization, responsibilities of church officers, and the relationship of the local church to the **conference** and its officers.

CHURCH OF GOD (ADVENTIST). *See* CHURCH OF GOD (SEVENTH-DAY).

CHURCH OF GOD GENERAL CONFERENCE. Denomination that arose out of the **Millerite** movement. Popularly called "Age to

Come Adventists," this group congregated around Joseph Marsh's *Advent Harbinger and Bible Advocate.* In 1849 Marsh introduced the idea that "the end" meant the closing of the millennium and that those who had not accepted Christ would have a second chance to do so during "the age to come." Although uncomfortable with church organization, the group formed the North Western Christian Conference of the Church of God in 1855 in Indiana and subsequently other state conferences. In 1888 these conferences came together as the short-lived Church of Jesus Christ in Philadelphia. They developed a permanent organization when in 1921 they organized the Church of God of the Abrahamic Faith with headquarters in Oregon, Illinois. The organization is now known as the Church of God General Conference and has its headquarters in Morrow, Georgia. As of 1995 it had about 5,000 members.

CHURCH OF GOD (SEVENTH-DAY). Adventist group that traces its origins back to the original sabbatarian Adventist movement. After H. S. Case and C. P. Russell came into conflict with **Ellen G. White** in Jackson, Michigan, in 1853, they began publishing *The Messenger of Truth* and two years later formed an alliance with J. M. Stephenson and D. P. Hall in Wisconsin, who were advocating the belief that during the millennium individuals would receive a second chance to accept Christ. *The Messenger*, however, stopped publication in 1858. Meanwhile, Gilbert Cranmer, who had broken from the main sabbatarian Adventist movement, formed his own group, including several individuals who had supported *The Messenger*, and began publishing *The Hope of Israel* in 1863, which was printed on the former *Messenger* press. After this latest paper went out of existence in 1865, Henry Carver of Marion, Iowa, purchased the press and moved it from Michigan to his home state. He was a member of a group in Iowa that had rejected the inspiration of Ellen G. White and by the mid-1860s was known as the Church of Jesus Christ, although Seventh-day Adventists called them the "Marion Party." Reviving *The Hope of Israel*, Carver's group moved toward church organization, forming the General Conference of the Church of God in 1869. Two years later they renamed their paper the *Advent and Sabbath Advocate and Hope of Israel*, a title that they reduced to *Advent and Sabbath Advocate* in 1874.

As the church brought in other sabbatarian Adventists who rejected the inspiration and authority of Ellen G. White, it developed a more formal church structure, forming conferences in

Michigan, Iowa, and Missouri (where its headquarters were located), all of which adopted the name "Church of God." A conflict in 1933, largely over organizational issues, resulted in the establishment of the Church of God (7th Day), led by A. N. Dugger, which chose Salem, West Virginia, for its headquarters. Although the two groups reunited in 1949, establishing new headquarters in Denver, Colorado, Dugger formed a new Church of God (7th Day) and other divisions developed in subsequent years. As of 1995, the Church of God (Seventh-day) had a membership of 125,000 while the Church of God (7th Day) had a membership of about 1,000.

CITY MISSIONS. Seventh-day Adventist **evangelistic** program. Concerned with evangelizing the cities, **Stephen N. Haskell** proposed using the **tract and missionary societies** to establish permanent missions in urban areas. The missions were to provide living quarters for workers, a storage area for the books and tracts that the workers would distribute throughout the city, and a reading room. Some missions also contained a hall for public meetings. Beginning in 1883, the denomination by 1886 was operating missions in 25 cities, among them New York, Chicago, San Francisco, and Washington, D.C. Although the missions helped establish Adventism in urban areas, they proved too expensive to operate and few lasted into the 1890s.

CLARK, HAROLD WILLARD (1891-1986). Seventh-day Adventist scientist and **creationist** writer. Clark studied under **George McCready Price** while a student at **Pacific Union College** from 1920-22. After graduation he replaced Price and in 1933 became the first Adventist to obtain a master's degree in biology, which he earned at the University of California. After studying glaciation in the West, he rejected Price's view that glaciers had never covered much of North America. He also parted from Price in concluding that there is a definite sequence in the geological column. Continuing to hold to a literal reading of Genesis, including Price's view that the Flood could explain most geological phenomena, Clark developed a theory of "ecological zonation." He argued that the fossil record corresponded to the ecological zones of the Noachian world. He also accepted limited evolution through natural selection. Even before publication of Clark's book, *Genes and Genesis* (1940), Price was accusing him of heresy and in 1941 forced a formal hearing before a church-appointed committee of **ministers**, but he was unable to gain a condemnation of Clark's views. The "ecological zonation" theory subsequently had considerable influence on Adventist creationism. Among other books, Clark also published *The New Diluvialism* (1946) and *Fossils, Flood, and Fire* (1968).

CLEMENT, LORA E. (1890-1958). Seventh-day Adventist editor. Clement attended **Union College** and after graduation in 1908 began working as secretary to M. E. Kern, who was heading the recently established **Missionary Volunteer** Department. In 1911 she joined the staff of *The Youth's Instructor*, becoming associate editor in 1918 and editor in 1923, holding the latter position until 1952. As editor Clement increased the magazine's circulation from about 25,000 to 50,000, wrote a weekly column entitled "Let's Talk it Over," and in 1929 instituted "Pen League," an annual writing contest. After leaving *The Youth's Instructor*, Clement became librarian for the **Review and Herald Publishing Association**. Her books included *Learning to Live* (1940), *Let's Talk it Over* (1940), and *Managing Yourself* (1945).

CLEVELAND, EDWARD EARL (1921-). African American Seventh-day Adventist **evangelist**. Educated at **Oakwood College**, Cleveland served as a pastor and evangelist in the South Atlantic **Conference** from 1946 to 1950 and as an evangelist in the Southern **Union Conference** from 1950 to 1954. In 1954 he joined the **General Conference** as associate director of ministerial training in the **Ministerial Association**. He became especially well known for his evangelistic crusades in large cities around the globe, among them Chicago, New York, Port of Spain, Warsaw, Dar es Salaam, Johannesburg, Melbourne, and Sydney. Among his books were *Ask the Prophets* (1970), *Free at Last* (1970), and *The Exodus* (1986).

COGGIN, CHARLOTTE JOAN (1928-). Seventh-Day Adventist cardiologist and medical **educator**. Coggin received her B.A. (1948) from **Columbia Union College**, M.D. (1952) from the College of Medical Evangelists, and subsequently pursued postgraduate training at several other institutions, including Children's Hospital in Los Angeles, Hammersmith Hospital in London, and the Hospital for Sick Children in Toronto. She joined the staff of **Loma Linda University** (LLU) in 1961 as a cardiologist and co-director of the heart surgery team. After performing successful surgery on a three-year-old Pakistani girl in 1961 at the White Memorial Hospital in Los Angeles, Coggin received a request from

U.S. Vice President Lyndon B. Johnson to export medical services to **Pakistan**. In 1963 she and two other surgeons plus an anesthesiologist, a nurse, and a heart-lung technician traveled to Karachi, where during the next six weeks they performed 44 operations. Subsequently, under her direction the heart team provided open-heart surgery services in many countries, including **Greece**, Saudi Arabia, **Kenya**, and the People's Republic of **China**. In 1973 she became assistant dean, and later associate dean, in the LLU School of Medicine with responsibility for international programs. Coggin also provided consultation to the television and film industries on medically-oriented productions.

COLLEGE OF MEDICAL EVANGELISTS (CME). *See* LOMA LINDA UNIVERSITY.

COLOMBIA. Although at least one Seventh-day Adventist **minister** and several **literature evangelists** had entered Colombia previously, E. Max Trummer held the first public meetings in the country in 1921. He became superintendent of the Colombia **Mission** when it organized the following year and formed a **church** in Bogotá in 1923. A second church organized at Barranquilla in 1924. After division into four missions in 1925, the denomination in Colombia became part of the Colombia-Venezuela **Union Mission**. As of 2003 the Colombian **Union Conference**, established as a separate organization in 1989, was part of the Inter-American **Division**, with 841 churches and a membership of about 197,000. In addition to 10 secondary schools, the Union Conference operated Colombia Adventist University and five clinics and dispensaries.

COLPORTEUR. *See* LITERATURE EVANGELISTS.

COLUMBIA UNION COLLEGE (CUC). Seventh-day Adventist **educational** institution located in Takoma Park, Maryland. Shortly after the **General Conference** moved its headquarters to the Washington, D.C. area, denominational leaders opened Washington Training College in 1904. Three years later, as the church sought to expand its **missions** emphasis, the school changed its name to Washington Foreign Mission Seminary and focused on the training of missionaries. By 1913 it had sent 90 individuals to various locations around the world. In 1914, however, the institution introduced a liberal arts program and adopted the name Washington Missionary College (WMC); it awarded its first B.A.

degrees the following year. As the need for accreditation grew, in 1933 the college divided into two parts, Washington Junior College—which soon received accreditation from the Middle States Association of Colleges and Schools—and WMC. After WMC achieved accreditation in 1942 it dissolved the junior college. In 1959 the school sent the first Adventist **student missionary**, starting a program that became an important part of denominational life. The institution changed its name to Columbia Union College in 1961 and in 1983 introduced an Adult Evening Program that emphasized business and health care related curricula. As of 2003 the school offered 37 undergraduate majors and had an enrollment of about 1,100, including students in the Adult Evening Program.

COMMISSION ON RURAL LIVING. Seventh-day Adventist agency to encourage church members to move to small towns and rural areas. Seventh-day Adventists had never been comfortable with urban areas, which they believed had powerful non-Christian influences, including entertainment, commercialism, and general secularization. As the cities became increasingly industrialized and the industries unionized after passage of the National Labor Relations (Wagner) Act in 1935, church leaders believed that by moving away from cities church members could avoid both many evil influences and difficulties with unions. Furthermore, after atomic bombs fell on Hiroshima and Nagasaki in 1945, it appeared that cities would be increasingly unsafe. In 1946, following an invitation from the **General Conference, Edward A. Sutherland** helped establish the North American Commission for **Self-supporting** Missionary Work, which sought to encourage families to move to rural communities. A few months later, the commission merged with the previously established Committee on Country Living to form the Commission on Rural Living. Sutherland served as secretary and **Carlyle B. Haynes** as assistant secretary. Haynes collected and distributed information regarding rural employment opportunities; the commission sponsored several conferences in 1949; and various individuals wrote articles for denominational publications promoting country living. In addition, the commission collected relevant **Ellen G. White** comments into a booklet, *Country Living* (1946), and published a companion "how-to" booklet under the title *From City to Country Living* (1950). In 1950 the Commission for Self-Supporting Missionary Enterprises succeeded the Commission on Rural Living.

CONDITIONAL IMMORTALITY. Doctrine that denies the natural immortality of the soul, positing instead that at death the person becomes nonexistent until the resurrection of the dead at the time of Christ's coming. **George Storrs**, a Methodist minister and anti-slavery activist, published tracts in 1841 and 1842 arguing that immortality comes only through faith in Jesus (conditionalism) and that the wicked will be completely destroyed rather than burn in hell forever (annihilationism). After becoming a **Millerite**, he began publishing the *Bible Examiner* in 1843, which introduced these views to the rapidly growing movement and brought him into conflict with most of its leaders, of whom only **Charles Fitch** adopted conditionalism. Nonetheless, Storrs had considerable influence on the Millerite movement, which at its 1844 general conference passed a statement that issues regarding the state of the dead were not essential points of doctrine. After Christ did not come in 1844, the Millerites who met at the Mutual Conference of Adventists in Albany in 1855 eventually split on the issues of conditionalism and annihilationism. The dominant *Advent Herald* group, which later formed the **American Evangelical Adventist Conference**, advocated the traditional view that each person has an immortal soul, while the *Bible Advocate* and *Second Advent Watchman* adopted the conditionalist position. After the *World's Crisis* began publication in the early 1850s it became the principal vehicle for conditionalist views and eventually played a leading role in the development of the **Advent Christian Church**. In 1863 Storrs and others who now took the view that the wicked would never be resurrected formed the Life and Advent Union.

Sabbatarian Adventist leaders also adopted conditionalism. **Ellen G. White** rejected the doctrine of immortality of the soul in 1843 and **James White** and **Joseph Bates**, both of whom had been members of the conditionalist **Christian Connection**, alluded to a belief in conditionalism in early publications. **Roswell F. Cottrell** made the first clear sabbatarian Adventist statement of the doctrine in an 1853 *Review and Herald* article, and in 1854 James White wrote another series in the same publication on the "Destruction of the Wicked." That same year D. P. Hall published articles in the *Review* that were republished as a book with the title *Man Not Immortal* (1854). Similarly, **John N. Loughborough** wrote an additional series of articles, also published as a book, under the title *Is the Soul Immortal?* (1856). It appears that conditionalism had become an established doctrine among sabbatarian Adventists by the mid-1850s.

After organizing as a church, Seventh-day Adventists continued to publish books advocating conditionalism, among them **Dudley M. Canright's** *History of the Doctrine of the Immortality of the Soul* (1871) and **Uriah Smith's** *Man's Nature and Destiny* (1884). In the 20th century, **Leroy Edwin Froom** wrote an historical apologetic for the doctrine in *The Conditionalist Faith of our Fathers* (1965-66). The major Adventist statements of **Fundamental Beliefs** in 1872, 1931, and 1980 also affirmed conditionalism. A recent unofficial explanation of conditionalism appeared in the *Handbook of Seventh-day Adventist Theology* (2000).

CONFERENCE. A unit of Seventh-day Adventist church organization composed of the individual **churches** within a given geographical area. Apparently following the Methodist model, sabbatarian Adventists in Michigan organized a state conference of churches in 1862. Six other conferences formed shortly thereafter. In 1863 representatives from all but one conference met to organize the **General Conference.** The organizational procedures followed in 1861-62 largely remain in practice. The churches send delegates to a conference constituency meeting at which they elect officers, including a president and a treasurer, all of whom are usually **ministers.** Among its functions, the conference assigns ministers to churches, operates secondary schools, and pays the salaries of pastors, evangelists, and teachers within its territory. The conference is part of a **union conference**, an association of conferences created in 1901, to whose constituency meeting it sends delegates.

CONGO, DEMOCRATIC REPUBLIC OF (FORMERLY ZA-IRE). Christopher Robinson established Songa **Mission** Station some 400 miles northwest of Lubumbashi in 1920 and was followed by A. C. Le Butt who started the Katanga Mission Station near Lubumbashi two years later. By 1932 there were 11 mission stations, all of them having a school and most a dispensary. During the political turmoil that followed independence in 1960, most of the missionaries left and African leaders attempted to protect the stations and continue their work, but contact with the organized denomination was broken in several locations. In the mid-1960s Adventists began broadcasting radio programs and reopening some mission stations. The Kasai Project, started in 1972, focused on mission work among the Kasai people who were seeking refuge under the umbrella of the recognized churches after the gov-

ernment declared the Independent Churches illegal. Some of the
Kasai remained with the Adventists even after restrictions on the
Independent Churches eased. Despite continued political and social
instability in the Congo, the Seventh-day Adventist Church grew
rapidly. As of 2003 the Seventh-day Adventist Church in the
Democratic Republic of Congo was divided into the East Congo
Union Mission with 855 churches and over 220,000 members, and
the West Congo Union Mission with 419 churches and a
membership of over 220,000. The missions were part of the East-
Central Africa Division. Adventist University at Lukanga, three
secondary schools, Songa Adventist Hospital, and numerous
clinics and dispensaries were located within the two union
missions.

CONGO, REPUBLIC OF. The Seventh-day Adventist Church
established the Republic of Congo Attached **Mission** Station in
1972. As of 2003 it was under the Central African Union Mission,
part of the Western **Africa Division**, with eight **churches** and a
membership of 375.

CONRADI, LUDVIG RICHARD (1856-1939). Seventh-day
Adventist **minister** and church administrator. Born in **Germany**,
Conradi, whose first name is usually anglicized as Louis,
immigrated to the **United States** at age 17. In 1878, through the
influence of an Iowa family with whom he was boarding, Conradi
converted to Seventh-day Adventism. He then attended **Battle
Creek College**, where he completed the four-year course in little
more than a year. In 1881 he went to the Dakota territory to
evangelize the Russian and German Mennonite population and
later worked in Nebraska, Kansas, and Pennsylvania. He was
ordained to the ministry in 1882.

The **General Conference** (GC) sent Conradi to **Europe** in
1886 where he worked in **Switzerland**, **Germany**, and **Russia**.
Accused of teaching Jewish heresy while in the Crimea, he and his
associate, **Gerhard Perk**, were imprisoned for 40 days. In 1889
Conradi moved to Hamburg, Germany, where he established the
headquarters of the German Seventh-day Adventist Church. Two
years later, the GC separated Germany and Russia from the Central
European **Conference**, organizing the territory as a separate
mission, and appointed Conradi to oversee it. By 1900 there were
nearly 2,000 Adventists in Germany, triple the number in **France**,
Switzerland, and **Italy** combined. In 1901 Conradi became the first
president of the General European Conference and two years later

a vice-president of the GC. He traveled extensively to **Africa**, the **Middle East**, and **Latin America**, where Adventism was impacting the German population. In 1913 the European conferences formed the European **Division** Conference with Conradi serving as president until 1922. Throughout this time he wrote tracts and books in German and both revised and enlarged an English edition of **John Nevins Andrews's** *History of the Sabbath* (1912) and translated it into German.

Conflict emerged in the German church during World War I after German leaders, who were under intense government pressure, consented to allow members to bear arms and also perform essential services on the **Sabbath** while in the military. A German Reform Movement emerged that criticized the leaders for subordinating themselves to the government. In 1920 **Arthur G. Daniells**, president of the GC, led a delegation to Europe to settle the issues. After Conradi continued to defend the actions of the German denominational leaders and the Reform Movement pressed for a change in leadership, the **General Conference session** of 1922 moved him to the position of GC field secretary.

For some time Conradi had been questioning certain Adventist positions, including the **Sanctuary Doctrine** and the inspiration and authority of **Ellen G. White**. In 1931 church leaders called him before a 35-person committee to defend his views, after which they removed his ministerial credentials. Upon returning to Germany, he joined the Seventh Day Baptists and subsequently brought about 500 Adventists into that denomination. He offered a critical account of Adventism in *The Founders of the Seventh-day Adventist Denomination* (1939).

COOK ISLANDS. The *Pitcairn* visited several of the Cook islands in 1891 and Seventh-day Adventist missionaries arrived in 1894. From that time on most of the missionaries came from **Australia**. An interesting situation developed when in 1899 the government ordered that two Christmas days be observed in order to move the island's calendar from an eastern to a western hemisphere day sequence. Under the old calendar, Christians had worshiped on Saturday; under the new they had to move their day of worship to Sunday. A number of them, not wanting to make the change, approached the Adventist missionaries asking to learn about the **Sabbath** doctrine and several individuals joined the church. Between 1916 and 1923 the Cook Islands were part of the Eastern Polynesian **Mission**; after that time they were a separate mission. As of 2003 the Cook Islands Mission, part of the **New Zealand-**

Pacific **Union Conference** of the **South Pacific Division,** had 15
churches with a membership of nearly 800. Papaaroa College was
located on the islands.

CORNELL, MERRITT E. (1827-1893). Seventh-day Adventist
minister and **evangelist.** A **Millerite** who was a member of the
group that eventually became the **Church of God General
Conference,** Cornell converted to sabbatarian Adventism in 1852
through the influence of **Joseph Bates.** He quickly began
evangelistic work. In 1854 he and **John N. Loughborough**
conducted tent meetings in Battle Creek, Michigan, the first tent
evangelism conducted by sabbatarian Adventists. Cornell also
evangelized in Iowa and elsewhere in the Midwest. In 1871 he
went to California where he worked again with Loughborough
conducting tent meetings in San Francisco. In 1874 he and **Dudley
M. Canright** held meetings in Oakland. After evangelistic
meetings in Dallas, Texas, the following year, he left the ministry,
although he occasionally preached. He returned to the Adventist
ministry in 1890 and remained active until his death.

COSTA RICA. The first Adventist contacts with Costa Rica occurred
around 1900 when Frank J. Hutchins visited the country several
times in his missionary schooner. Several **literature evangelists**
entered the area in 1902 and the first **baptisms** and organization of
a **church** took place in 1903. Missionaries established a primary
school in 1921 and in 1927 organized both a secondary school and
the Costa Rica-**Nicaragua Mission.** The following year they
established Costa Rica as a separate mission with four **churches**
and 148 members. As of 2003 the Costa Rica Mission, part of the
Central American **Union Conference** of the Inter-American
Division, had 90 churches and a membership of over 41,000.
Three secondary schools and Central American Adventist
University were located in the country.

CÔTE D'IVOIRE. Seventh-day Adventism first came into the Ivory
Coast in the 1920s when two European traders from **Ghana** settled
in Tiemelekro, and about the same time two members of the Dida
tribe converted to Adventism in Ghana and brought their new faith
to the southern Ivory Coast. Although the Ghana **Mission** sent J.
K. Garbrah to the Ivory Coast to **baptize** those who had become
interested in Adventism, no sustained effort in the region took
place until after World War II. American missionaries arrived for
the first time in 1946. As of 2003 the Côte D'Ivoire/Guinea

Mission, part of the Sahel **Union Mission** of the Western **Africa Division**, had 46 **churches** with a membership of nearly 8,500. The mission operated Bouake Adventist Secondary School. The division offices were located in Abidjan.

COTTRELL, ROSWELL F. (1814-1892). Seventh-day Adventist **minister.** Born into a Seventh Day Baptist family, Cottrell converted to sabbatarian Adventism about 1851 through reading the *Review and Herald.* In addition to poems and articles that he published in Adventist periodicals, he wrote a series of Bible lessons for young people that in 1854 were published in the *Youth's Instructor* and the following year appeared as a book, *The Bible Class* (1855). After the *Review and Herald* moved to Battle Creek, Michigan, in 1855, he served as a member of the editorial committee. As a minister he worked with **John N. Loughborough** and W. S. Ingraham in New York and Pennsylvania. Although he opposed the move to organize the Seventh-day Adventist Church, writing letters to the *Review and Herald* expressing his views, Cottrell ultimately reconciled himself to the new denomination and continued to serve as an Adventist minister. Set to music, two of his poems appeared in the *Seventh-day Adventist Hymnal* (1985).

COUNCIL ON INDUSTRIAL RELATIONS. Seventh-day Adventist agency for dealing with labor unions. Because of **Ellen G. White's** counsel to avoid belonging to organizations such as labor unions, Seventh-day Adventists experienced growing problems as American industry became increasingly unionized after passage of the National Labor Relations (Wagner) Act in 1935. Ten years later the **General Conference** created the Council on Industrial Relations to negotiate accommodations from labor unions for church members. **Carlyle B. Haynes** developed a document entitled "Basis of Agreement" which pledged that although not becoming union members, Adventists would neither work nor picket during strikes, would comply with workplace regulations, and would pay to charity an amount equivalent to union dues. The United Auto Workers accepted the document in 1948 as well as many union locals, but other unions rejected it. As the labor situation in the **United States** changed, particularly with the development of "Right to Work" laws, the General Conference discontinued the Council on Industrial Relations in 1954 and in 1961 officially abandoned the "Basis of Agreement" as the "exclusive" Seventh-day Adventist policy regarding organized labor.

CREATIONISM. Belief that the world was created in six 24-hour days about 6,000 years ago and that the biblical flood accounts for most geological phenomena. Nineteenth-century Adventists rejected Charles Darwin's theory of evolution because they believed that it was incompatible with the Genesis account of creation. In the early 20th century **George McCready Price**, a Seventh-day Adventist schoolteacher, began developing what he believed were scientific arguments against evolutionary theory and in support of what has come to be known as creationism. He rejected the existence of the geological column and argued that the biblical flood could explain most geological data, a position now called "flood geology." Through his books and articles, Price became well known in conservative Christian circles and was the primary intellectual influence on Henry W. Morris and John C. Whitcomb, Jr., authors of *The Genesis Flood* (1961), which is the founding document of the modern creationist movement. Other significant Adventist creationist authors included **Harold W. Clark** and **Frank L. Marsh**. In 1958 the denomination established the **Geoscience Research Institute** to help it address issues in science and religion. Although the Seventh-day Adventist Church still holds strongly to creationism, recent surveys have suggested that increasing numbers of its scientists accept some form of evolutionary theory and the view that earth history extends over a long period of time. To promote dialogue between the scientists, theologians, and church administrators, the denomination sponsored a series of three annual Faith and Science Conferences beginning in 2002.

CROATIA. Robert Schillinger, later aided by Albin Mocnik, first took Seventh-day Adventism into Croatia about 1908. The Adreatic **Conference** formed four years later. As of 2003 the Croatian Conference, established in 1925, belonged to the Adriatic **Union Conference**, part of the Trans-**European Division**, with 83 churches and a membership of 3,241. Adriatic Union College-Croatia, a secondary school, and Adriatic Union Publishing House were located in Croatia. *See also* YUGOSLAVIA.

CROSIER, OWEN R. L. (1820-1912). Millerite preacher and editor. Along with **Hiram Edson** and Franklin B. Hahn, Crosier (later spelled Crozier) published the *Day-Dawn*, a Millerite paper in which he first proclaimed the view that on October 22, 1844, Jesus had moved from the Holy to the Most Holy Place of the heavenly **sanctuary**. This view eventually influenced **Joseph Bates** and

James and **Ellen G. White** and became a central doctrine of the Seventh-day Adventist Church. Although Crosier accepted the doctrine of the seventh-day **Sabbath** for a time, he soon abandoned both the Sabbath and sanctuary doctrines. He worked with Joseph Marsh on the *Advent Harbinger* from 1847 to 1853, from which developed the **Church of God General Conference** and in 1858 was an evangelist for the **Advent Christian Church**.

CUBA. Seventh-day Adventists organized the Cuban **Mission** in 1905, little more than a year after the first **literature evangelists** had entered the country, and established their first **church** that same year. From six members in 1905, the Adventist Church grew to over 1,000 members by the mid-1930s. In 1922 the mission began a secondary school near Bartle in Oriente Province, later moving it to Santa Clara, where it gradually expanded its offerings, in 1958 becoming a senior college under the name Antillian Union College. Meanwhile, in 1935 the Cuban Mission reorganized as the Cuban **Conference**. In that same year the conference began a radio program entitled "The Voice of the Watchman." By the mid-1940s Cuba was the headquarters of the Inter-American **Division**. But the Fidel Castro revolution of 1959, when Adventist church membership was about 5,500, brought an end to radio broadcasts, evangelistic meetings, and the operation of private schools; one result was that Antillian Union College moved to **Puerto Rico**. The Cuban Adventist church was largely isolated from Adventists elsewhere until the late 1970s when limited contacts began to occur. Meanwhile, in 1969 Cuban Adventist leaders started offering an educational program for church workers that eventually developed into an affiliation with the **Montemorelos University** in **Mexico** through which bachelors degrees in religion became available. In 1990 the first class graduated and in 1996 the Cuba Adventist Seminary moved into new facilities. As the political situation became more open, Adventists in the 1990s began conducting public **evangelism** and distributing religious literature. As of 2003 the Cuban **Union Conference**, part of the Inter-American Division, had 238 churches with a membership of over 23,000.

CYPRUS. Moses Boursalian, an Adventist from **Armenia**, arrived in Cyprus as a refugee from **Turkey** about 1912. Together with his son, who later worked as a **literature evangelist** on the island, a group of about 10 believers had developed by 1930. R. S. Greaves, who had worked in **Greece**, arrived in 1932 and other missionaries came after World War II. The Cyprus **Mission** organized in 1953 and the first Adventist church building was built three years later. Political problems created difficulties for the denomination in the 1960s and 1970s, but a Greek **evangelistic** campaign took place in 1992. As of 2003 the Cyprus Section of the **Middle East Union Mission**, part of the Trans-**European Division**, had one **church** with a membership of 76.

CZECHOWSKI, MICHAEL BELINA (1818-1876). Seventh-day Adventist missionary to **Europe**. Born in **Poland** and a Roman Catholic priest, Czechowski, whose middle name is sometimes stated as Bonaventura, renounced the priesthood and came to North America some time after the revolutions of 1848. Converted to Protestantism while living in Canada, he joined the sabbatarian Adventists after attending a tent meeting in Findlay, Ohio, in 1857. Afterwards he began working with **Daniel T. Bourdeau** among the French-speaking people of Canada and New England. In 1860 he settled in New York, establishing an Adventist congregation in Brooklyn. During this time he published an account of his experience in Europe under the title *Thrilling and Instructive Developments* (1862).

Wanting to spread the Adventist message to Europe, he asked **John N. Loughborough** to convince the **General Conference** to send him as a missionary to Europe. Not fully trusting Czechowski, church leaders turned down his request. He then obtained support from the **Advent Christian Church,** sailing to Europe in 1864. First preaching in the Piedmont valleys of **Italy**, he moved to **Switzerland** because of opposition from both Catholic and Protestant leaders. Despite his Advent Christian sponsorship, Czechowski taught the seventh-day **Sabbath** as well as Seventh-day Adventist interpretations of the prophecies of Daniel and Revelation. He also published tracts, a prophetic chart, and a paper, *L'Evangile Eternel*. In the Swiss village of Tramelan he formed a congregation of nearly 60 members but did not tell the group about either the Advent Christian or Seventh-day Adventist churches.

When Albert Vuilleumier, a member of the congregation, discovered a copy of the *Review and Herald* in a room that Czechowski had used, he learned about Seventh-day Adventists, a discovery that led to contact with General Conference leaders and ultimately the decision to send **John Nevins Andrews** to Europe as the denomination's first official missionary. When he learned of the contacts between the Swiss and Adventist leaders in Battle

Creek, Czechowski became upset and, also beset by financial and personal problems, moved to **Germany** and then to **Hungary**. Finally, he settled in **Romania**, where he established a congregation in Pitesti. Czechowski died in Vienna in 1876.

CZECH REPUBLIC. Antonin Simon, a Czech who was living in Hamburg, **Germany**, converted to Seventh-day Adventism in the early 1890s after reading some tracts. He soon returned to his home country and gradually developed a group of believers, with whom **Ludvig R. Conradi** met in 1894. John P. Lorenz, an **ordained minister**, arrived in 1901 and the following year organized an Adventist **church** with a membership of 20. In 1906 the Hamburg Publishing House began publishing a Czech paper, *Herald of Truth*, with one of these original church members serving as editor. Five years later two **missions** formed, the Bohemian Mission with 114 members and the Moravian-Silesian Mission with 135 members. After the end of World War I the denomination organized the Czechoslovakian **Union Conference** and established the Czechoslovakian Publishing House and a training school. By 1939 there were 97 churches with over 3,000 members in Czechoslovakia. World War II greatly disrupted the church, however, forcing the closure of the publishing house and school. Although efforts were made to reestablish these institutions after the war, the government in 1951 dissolved the **conferences** and shortly thereafter closed the churches. In 1956 the churches opened once again, followed by the conferences, publishing house, and school by 1968. In 1993, following Czechoslovakia's division into two countries, the union conference took the name Czecho-Slovakian Union Conference. As of 2003 the Bohemian Conference, part of the Czecho-Slovakian Union Conference of the Euro-**Africa Division**, had 69 churches and a membership of about 3,000. Sazava Theological Seminary, Czech Publishing House, and Adventist World Radio-Czech Republic were located in the Czech Republic.

D

DANIELLS, ARTHUR GROSVENOR (1858-1935). Seventh-day Adventist **minister** and church administrator. Converted to Adventism at age ten, Daniells later attended **Battle Creek College** for one year and taught public school for another year before entering the ministry in 1878. Subsequently he worked as an **evangelist** in Texas and Iowa and served for a year as secretary for **James** and **Ellen G. White**. In 1886 the **General Conference** (GC) sent him as a missionary to **New Zealand**, where he became president of the New Zealand **Conference** in 1889, a position he held until 1891. The following year he became president of the **Australian** Conference, working closely with Ellen White, who had arrived in Australia in 1891, and in 1895 president of the Central Australian Conference when the Australian conference was split into two parts. Meanwhile, the Australasian **Union Conference** had formed in 1894; Daniells became president three years later.

In 1901 Daniells returned to the **United States** for the **General Conference session** and, drawing on his experience with union conference organization in Australia and supported by Ellen G. White, led the reorganization of the Seventh-day Adventist Church. Among other things, the 1901 session abolished the office of president, replacing it with a 25-person GC Executive Committee. For the next two years Daniells served as chairman of the executive committee, becoming president of the GC when that position was restored in 1903. During his presidency Daniells oversaw a number of major developments. The GC moved its offices from Battle Creek, Michigan, to the Washington, D.C. area in 1903. After fire burned the **Battle Creek Sanitarium** in 1902, Daniells and **John Harvey Kellogg** engaged in a prolonged struggle over control of the denomination's medical work that ended with Kellogg's dismissal from the church in 1907. That same year **Alonzo T. Jones**, who was closely associated with Kellogg and accused Daniells of being dictatorial, lost his ministerial credentials. Meanwhile, **Albion F. Ballenger** raised questions regarding the **sanctuary doctrine** and also lost his ministerial credentials in 1905. After publishing a book explaining his views, Ballenger raised public debate in the church for several years beginning about 1910.

In addition to addressing these organizational and doctrinal conflicts, Daniells also strongly supported **missions**, significantly increasing the number of missionaries each year until the outbreak of World War I. Consequently, the number of Adventists outside North America outnumbered those within by 1921. Also, with the development of **division** conferences in 1913 and their reorganization into divisions in 1918, Daniells established the organizational structure that the Seventh-day Adventist Church maintained into the early 21st century.

A strong leader, Daniells inspired opposition over both theological and administrative issues during his long presidency;

these opponents blocked his renomination as president at the 1922 GC session, which chose **William A. Spicer** instead. Daniells became head of the newly created Ministerial Commission (later renamed **Ministerial Association**). Long concerned about the quality of the Adventist ministry, Daniells led ministerial institutes in North America between 1923 and 1925 and in Australia, the **South Pacific** islands, and South America between 1928 and 1930. He also established a journal, *The Ministry*, edited by **LeRoy Edwin Froom**, which began publication in 1928. Emphasizing during these years the need for a personal relationship with Jesus, Daniells published *Christ Our Righteousness* in 1926. He retired in 1931.

DAVIDIAN SEVENTH-DAY ADVENTISTS. Religious group that split from the Seventh-day Adventist Church. In the late 1920s, Victor T. Houteff, a **Bulgarian** immigrant to the **United States** and member of a Los Angeles Seventh-day Adventist **church**, began teaching that the Adventist Church was "fallen" and that, among other things, those who followed his warnings would constitute the 144,000 of Revelation 7:4 and 14:1. He began publishing his views in 1930 in a paper entitled *The Shepherd's Rod*, which became the name by which his followers were popularly known. Five years later he and 11 followers moved to Waco, Texas, where they established the Mount Carmel Center, intended to be the gathering place for the 144,000. Although Houteff preferred that his followers remain within the Seventh-day Adventist Church, in 1942 he organized the Davidian Seventh-day Adventist Church so that those followers who had lost their church membership could obtain **noncombatant** status. Prior to Houteff's death in 1955 it appears that as many as 125 people lived at one point in the Mount Carmel Center. By provision of Houteff's will leadership of the group passed to his wife, Florence Houteff, who later announced that on April 22, 1959, God would remove the Jews and Arabs from Palestine and establish a new "Davidic" kingdom. Reportedly, several hundred people gathered at the center on that date; when nothing special happened, disillusionment set in and the movement broke apart.

After the Davidians formally dissolved in 1962, a struggle took place to control the Mount Carmel Center and the movement's religious legacy. One portion of the Davidians reorganized in California as the Branch Davidians; they returned to Waco, where Ben and Lois Roden led the group in the late 1960s and the 1970s. Vernon Howell, a former Seventh-day Adventist who had changed his name to David Koresh, gained control of the organization in the 1980s and actively evangelized near Adventist college campuses, attracting several young Adventists to join the Branch Davidians. Rumors that he was hoarding arms at Mount Carmel led to a raid on February 23, 1993, by the Bureau of Alcohol, Tobacco, and Firearms. The Branch Davidians resisted, killing four agents. The Federal Bureau of Investigation (FBI) then took over the case, instituting a siege that lasted until April 19, when it attacked the Mount Carmel site. Fire, the origin of which has been blamed on both Koresh and the FBI, destroyed the buildings, killing 78 Branch Davidians including Koresh.

This Waco incident had repercussions two years later. Timothy McVeigh, a Gulf War veteran, had no connection with the Branch Davidians but regarded the government action at Waco as evidence that it was the enemy of the American people. On the second anniversary of the Waco disaster, April 19, 1995, he bombed the Alfred P. Murrah Federal Building in Oklahoma City, Oklahoma, killing 168.

DEACON. A local **church** officer, next in rank to an **elder**. The Washington, New Hampshire, church possibly appointed the first Adventist deacons in 1851. Reference to the **ordination** of deacons through the laying on of hands first appeared in an 1853 report from Massachusetts. While at first it seems that deacons provided leadership for all of the functions of the local church, as the office of **elder** gained acceptance the deacons' responsibility became limited to such matters as the care of church property, assistance at the Communion service, and visitation of the sick and poor. **Women** hold a corresponding office entitled deaconess; in addition to visitation they do such things as prepare the Communion table and assist women **baptismal** candidates. Deacons and deaconesses are elected for one-year terms.

DELKER, ARDELLA V. (1924-). Seventh-day Adventist gospel singer. Converted to Adventism in 1947 through Julius L. Tucker's **Quiet Hour** meetings in Oakland, California, Delker soon began singing on the evangelist's radio broadcasts. Later that same year she joined the **Voice of Prophecy** (VOP) staff as a secretary and occasionally performed on its programs. In 1950 she began singing regularly on the broadcasts and the following year the VOP released her first records on its own label. With the establishment of **Chapel Records** in 1955 her many recordings spread widely among the Adventist membership. She regularly participated in

VOP **evangelistic** campaigns both in North America and, beginning in 1968, internationally. Delker retired in 1990 but continued
to occasionally participate in VOP evangelism and, with Ken
Wade, wrote her autobiography, *Del Delker: Her Story* (2002).

DENMARK. John G. Matteson, a native of Denmark, sent his
Danish-language paper, *Advent Tidings*, from the **United States** to
Denmark beginning in 1872. As interest in Adventist doctrines
developed, he requested that the **General Conference** send him as
a missionary to his home country, where he arrived in 1877. The
following year he organized the first Seventh-day Adventist
church in northern **Europe.** In 1880 the Denmark **Conference,** the
first Adventist conference outside North America, organized with
seven churches and 91 members. By 1906 there were 18 churches
with 746 members. Health care became an important part of
Adventist efforts in Denmark, with the **Sködsborg Sanitarium,**
founded by Dr. Carl J. Ottosen in 1898, becoming the best-known
Adventist institution in Europe until its sale in 1992. In the 20th
century, Adventism grew slowly in Denmark. As of 2003 the
Danish Union of Churches, organized in 1992 as part of the Trans-
European **Division,** had 47 churches and a membership of about
2,700. It operated Danish Junior College and the Danish
Publishing House.

DICK, EVERETT NEWFON (1898-1989). Seventh-day Adventist
historian and founder of the **Medical Cadet Corps.** In 1934 Dick,
a professor of history at **Union College,** founded the College
Medical Corps on his campus to prepare Adventist young men for
noncombatant military service. After he made a presentation at a
meeting of Adventist **educators** in 1937, several other Adventist
colleges adopted similar programs. In 1939 the **General
Conference** approved the program, renaming it the Medical Cadet
Corps. Dick was also a noted historian, pioneering research in
Adventist history with his University of Wisconsins doctoral
dissertation, which was eventually published as *William Miller and
the Advent Crisis* (1994), but becoming most well-known for his
work on the history of the American West. Among his books were
The Sod House Frontier (1937) and *The Dixie Frontier* (1948).

DIVISION. Administrative unit of the **General Conference** (GC) of
Seventh-day Adventists. In the early 20th century Seventh-day
Adventist leaders in **Europe** increasingly felt the need for a formal
administrative unit that would coordinate the **union conferences** in

their region. In 1912 they proposed the development of a division conference, an administrative unit whose officers would be chosen by delegates from the union conferences. Although **Arthur G. Daniells**, president of the GC, at first opposed this concept, he changed his mind by the time of the 1913 **General Conference session**. This session created a European Division Conference and, despite Daniells's objections, a North American Division Conference, each with its electing constituency. Because of problems that developed in **Germany** during World War I and the policies of **Ludvig R. Conradi**, president of the European Division Conference, the GC session of 1918 disbanded the existing division conferences. In their place it created the "division." Despite the similarity in name, the division was a very different entity from the division conference, for it was part of the GC administrative structure, headed by a GC vice president (the title was later changed to division president) who was chosen at a GC session, rather than by a meeting of regional union conference delegates. Church leaders believed that by making divisions part of the GC structure they would preserve church unity throughout the world. The European, North American, Asiatic, and South American Divisions were the first entities under this new structure. Over time, as church membership expanded, the denomination modified existing divisions and created new ones but maintained divisional organization.

As they developed, the divisions acquired their own budgets and administrative structures and developed policies for their regions. The one exception was the North American Division, which GC officials described as having a "special relationship" to the central organization. Although there was a vice president for North America, there were no other specified officers for the region. Administrators justified this arrangement on the basis that GC operations depended on North American funds. North Americans, however, desired greater independence from the GC, and other divisions objected to the fact that North Americans largely controlled the GC. Changes began to take place in the early 1980s. In 1982 GC personnel assigned to North America for the first time held a year-end meeting similar to that held by the other divisions. Other developments took place, including the writing of a mission statement and the creation of a budget, until in 1990 the GC session voted to establish the North American Division on the same basis as other world divisions. Although part of the GC structure and despite the concern for unity among GC officials, the divisions have developed much of the independence that division conferences had acquired during their short life from 1913 to 1918.

DOMINICAN REPUBLIC. Seven individuals were already observing the seventh-day **Sabbath** when Charles Moulton, a **literature evangelist** from **Jamaica**, arrived in the Dominican Republic in 1907. Although Moulton organized several **Sabbath schools**, it was not until Homer D. Casebeer came in 1917 that the first **church** was organized. The Dominican **Mission** formed in 1924 with two churches and 147 members; by 1962 membership had reached nearly 6,000 members. In 1963 the mission became the Dominican **Conference**, after which membership increased almost exponentially. As of 2003 the Dominican **Union Mission**, part of the Inter-American **Division**, had 536 churches and a membership of nearly 175,000. The Union Mission operated Dominican Adventist University, eleven secondary schools, and a radio station.

DORCAS WELFARE SOCIETIES. Seventh-day Adventist local **church** organization for providing disaster aid and help to the needy. Several Adventist **women** in 1880 formed the "Battle Creek Church Maternal Association" to help students at **Battle Creek College**. As their activities expanded to include providing clothing and food for needy families and giving attention to widows and their children and to the sick, the organization changed its name to "Dorcas and Benevolent Association," named after the woman referred to in Acts 9:36. This organization established the pattern for the "Dorcas Welfare Societies" that developed in many other local churches. When the Home Missionary Department of the **General Conference** formed in 1913, its responsibilities included the development of these local church organizations. In 1934 churches in the Chicago area formed the first Dorcas Welfare Federation to coordinate the activities of the local church societies within a given region. Three years later the Home Missionary Department published *The Dorcas Society Handbook* (1937). To encourage further activity along these lines, the **Ellen G. White Estate** compiled **Ellen White's** statements on the subject of social aid in a book entitled *Welfare Ministry* (1952). In the 1950s churches also developed Health and Welfare Centers, which stored supplies, taught classes in such things as first aid and home nursing, and provided services to those in need. The denomination published a manual for these organizations in 1958. By the late 1960s, churches began using the term "Community Services" to describe both the Dorcas Welfare Society and Health and Welfare Center activities, a usage reflected in the *Community Services Manual* published in 1978, and the former names gradually disappeared.

E

ECUADOR. Political difficulties and health problems of church workers plagued the early years of Seventh-day Adventism in Ecuador. Thomas A. Davis began selling Adventist books in the country in 1904. The following year George A. Casebeer became the first Adventist **minister** to enter the territory and a short time later the Adventist church in Ecuador formed separate **mission**. In 1907 Joseph W. Westphal **baptized** the first Adventist convert. That same year, however, Davis's wife died, political unrest occurred, and both Davis and Westphal left the country. Over the next few years other workers arrived, probably organizing the first **church** in 1912, but several fell victim to tropical diseases and had to leave. Although there were 23 Seventh-day Adventists in Ecuador by 1916, that number had dropped to 17 by 1924, at which time only two missionaries remained. In 1927, however, G. A. Schwerin entered the country to begin **evangelistic** work and Adventist membership started to increase significantly, rising from 31 in 1927 to 65 the following year then to 269 by 1949. **Walter Schubert's** evangelism in 1950 brought the total number of Adventists in Ecuador to 395 at the end of the year. By the late 1950s there were more than 1,000 members and in 1961 Adventists opened Ecuador Mission **Academy** in Guayaquil. As of 2003 the Ecuador **Union Mission**, part of the South American **Division**, had 84 churches and approximately 43,000 members. The union mission operated three secondary schools and the Quito Adventist Clinic.

ECUMENISM. Cooperative movement among Christian churches. When the Federal Council of Churches (FCC) in Christ was founded in 1908, Seventh-day Adventists did not join, in part because of concern that such an organization might support Sunday legislation and lead to a union of church and state. Adventists expressed similar worries when the World Council of Churches (WCC) formed in 1948. Beyond the issue of **religious liberty**, Adventists were also unwilling to join the ecumenical movement because they wanted to preach their message to all people in all places rather than accept being restricted to assigned territories. While not a member of these organizations, however, the Seventh-day Adventist Church participated in some of their subsidiary organizations, such as the Broadcasting and Film Commission and the Church World Service Commission of the National Council of Churches (formerly the FCC) and the Faith and Order Commission of the WCC, with **Bert Beverly Beach** playing a significant role in bringing contact between the latter organization and the Seventh-day Adventist Church. The discussion between Faith and Order and the Adventists resulted in publication of *So Much in Common* (1973). Conferences between Adventist and Lutheran ministers that took place in **Europe** between 1994 and 1998 led to a joint report that outlined similarities and differences between the two groups and recommended that the Lutheran World Federation regard Seventh-day Adventists as a genuinely Christian church. *See also* EVANGELICAL-ADVENTIST DIALOGUES.

EDSON, HIRAM (1806-1882). Seventh-day Adventist **minister** and contributor to the **sanctuary doctrine**. A Methodist farmer in Port Gibson, New York, in 1839 Hiram Edson accepted **William Miller's** teaching that Jesus would return about 1843. After later adopting **Samuel Snow's** view that this event would occur on October 22, 1844, Edson began holding evening meetings at his home until the day on which Christ's second coming was expected. When Christ did not return, most of the discouraged people attending the meeting left and Edson and those remaining went to his barn to pray. The next morning, as Edson and a companion were walking across a field, he experienced a strong impression that rather than coming to earth, Jesus on October 22 had moved from the Holy to the Most Holy Place of the heavenly sanctuary described in Hebrews 8 and 9. Although some have interpreted this event as a vision, it most likely was a vivid thought or realization. In the following weeks Edson, **O. R. L. Crosier**, and Dr. Franklin B. Hahn together studied biblical passages relating to the heavenly sanctuary. Crosier published their conclusion that the sanctuary to be cleansed, which Miller had interpreted as being the earth, was in fact the sanctuary in heaven in an 1845 issue of the *Day-Dawn*, which he edited, and the following year in the *Day-Star*, published by Enoch Jacobs.

As this new interpretation of what had occurred on October 22, 1844 spread, it attracted the attention of **Joseph Bates** and **James** and **Ellen G. White**, who began corresponding with Edson. In 1846 Bates met with Edson and soon convinced him of the

Sabbath doctrine, while Bates in turn accepted Edson's views on the heavenly sanctuary. When the **Sabbath conferences** began in 1848, Edson participated, the third of these meetings taking place on his farm, and played a major role in developing the sabbatarian Adventist movement. After James White began publishing his papers, Edson sold his Port Gibson farm in 1850 to help defray expenses. Two years later he sold another farm in Port Byron so that White could purchase a printing press. Although later **ordained**, Edson made his living as a farmer.

EDUCATION. Because they expected the imminent return of Jesus, early sabbatarian Adventists had little interest in providing education for their children. During the 1850s, however, **James** and **Ellen G. White** urged parents to provide home schooling to their children so that they could acquire necessary skills. After moving to Battle Creek in 1855, Adventist leaders made several short-lived attempts to establish a primary school. In 1868 **Goodloe Harper Bell**, a recent convert, opened a private school for Adventist students in Battle Creek, which eventually became known as the "Select School." The **General Conference** (GC) acquired this school in 1872 and in 1874 transformed it into **Battle Creek College** operated by the Seventh-day Adventist Educational Society. In 1882 Adventists in California established Healdsburg College (later **Pacific Union College**) while their co-religionists in Massachusetts opened that same year the "New England School," soon renamed **South Lancaster Academy**. From this point on educational institutions became, along with **publishing** and **health care**, an essential element in Adventist expansion. After arriving in **Australia** in 1884, for instance, Adventist missionaries established in 1897 the **Avondale** School for Christian Workers, the first Adventist educational institution outside North America.

Adventists established these early schools to train workers for their young denomination, but prior to the 1890s they gave little attention to elementary education. Following calls from Ellen White for local **churches** to develop schools and the influence of such people as **Edward A. Sutherland** and **Frederick Griggs** at Battle Creek College, however, the number of church schools increased rapidly after 1897, reaching 220 by 1900. Subsequently **Alma McKibben** and **Sarah Peck** developed textbooks for teaching Bible and reading. The emergence of Adventist elementary schools also forced a clearer definition of secondary education. Although **academies** had previously functioned as training schools little different from the colleges, by the 1920s they had become well-defined secondary schools, equivalent to the American public high school.

While Adventist elementary education was becoming well established in the **United States**, schools also emerged as an important element of the denomination's **evangelistic** thrust, particularly in **Latin America, Africa**, and **China**. In the Lake Titicaca region of **Peru**, Ana and **Ferdinand Stahl** established a school at La Plateria about 1911 that spawned 26 additional schools by 1918, a number that increased to 113 by 1951. Somewhat similarly, **Solusi Mission**, founded in 1894 in present-day **Zimbabwe**, trained teachers who then established numerous schools throughout the region and made education the chief means of Adventist evangelism in Africa. In China, beginning with Ida Thompson's Bethel Girl's School, which opened in 1904, by 1916 the denomination was operating 118 elementary and mission schools with an enrollment of about 5,000.

From these beginnings an extensive Adventist educational system developed that by the early 21st century included over 4,500 primary schools with nearly 750,000 students, approximately 1,100 secondary schools with about 240,000 students, and 95 tertiary institutions with more than 62,000 students. In the **United States** local **churches** typically operated primary schools, while **conferences** sponsored secondary institutions and **Union Conferences** supported the colleges and universities. **Andrews University, Loma Linda University**, and **Oakwood College** received support from the GC and North American **Division**. This pattern generally holds for other parts of the world as well, although there were variations.

Throughout their history Seventh-day Adventists endeavored to implement a philosophy of education enunciated by Ellen G. White that called for a balance of spiritual, mental, and physical activity. Both Battle Creek and Healdsburg Colleges had trouble finding a way to incorporate physical labor into the school program. After the Avondale school included agriculture, carpentry, printing, and sewing in its curriculum, other Adventist schools followed suit, with both secondary schools and colleges developing industries in which students not only learned practical skills but also earned money with which to pay for their education. Economic and technological changes in the last half of the 20th century, however, undermined the viability of campus industries in the United States and few schools continued to operate such programs. Student labor continued to play an important role in many schools in developing countries, however. *The Journal of*

Adventist Education (formerly *The Journal of True Education*, begun in 1939), published by the GC Department of Education, provided Adventist educators the opportunity to discuss the issues they faced.

As Adventists sought to put their educational philosophy into practice, they felt no need to gain approval from the outside world. But their commitment to health care ultimately led them to obtain accreditation for their institutions. In 1915 the GC decided to pursue American Medical Association (AMA) approval of the **College of Medical Evangelists** so that its graduates would receive general recognition as qualified physicians. In 1922 the institution received an "A" rating from the AMA but soon learned that in order to maintain that rating it must accept only students who had graduated from an accredited college. This brought about an intense debate within the church leadership during the 1920s over the issue of whether denominational colleges should seek accreditation. Many individuals feared that such accreditation would force Adventist institutions to discard their unique features and become similar to "worldly" schools. In 1928 the church formed the Seventh-day Adventist Board of Regents and the following year the Association of Seventh-day Adventist Colleges and Secondary Schools, with the hope that they could function as the necessary accrediting agencies. When it became clear that these agencies would not be recognized by such organizations as the AMA, Adventist schools began to seek accreditation from their regional associations. **Pacific Union College** in California became in 1932 the first Adventist college to receive senior college accreditation and by 1936 the GC rescinded all restrictions on accreditation. After they became accredited, Adventist institutions began gradually changing their function from one of training workers for the church to that of offering a broad array of programs to its members, most of whom would work in the secular world.

Prior to World War II the major institutions that Adventists established outside the United States functioned as training schools for ministers, teachers, and other denominational workers. With the exception of Philippine Union College (later **Adventist University of the Philippines**), which conferred its first baccalaureate degrees in 1935, they did not grant degrees. Between 1944 and 1973, however, all of the major institutions became four-year tertiary schools. Adventist colleges in the United States aided several of them in this process. Beginning in the 1950s schools outside North America entered into affiliation agreements with American institutions that oversaw their educational programs and awarded degrees to their graduates. Avondale College, for instance, had such an affiliation with Pacific Union College. In the 1970s, national governments began granting approval to Adventist schools, often for specific degree programs, thereby enabling them to reduce or eliminate their dependence on American institutions. Although not all of them acquired such recognition, by 2000 there were 79 postsecondary Adventist institutions outside North America.

Meanwhile, the denomination developed its own accreditation process. The Board of Regents, which had its origins in the accreditation debates of the 1920s and 1930s, through the influence of **Charles Hirsch** while secretary of the GC Department of Education, extended its accreditation process beyond the United States, beginning with **Newbold College** in 1970. Twenty years later the Accrediting Association of Seventh-day Adventist Schools, Colleges, and Universities replaced the Board of Regents. It currently operates side-by-side with other accrediting associations or government ministries, examining schools from a church perspective that complements what the other agencies are doing.

Another major development in Adventist education was the emergence of graduate education, which began in the 1950s. Although a few colleges offered the M.A. degree, the GC's decision to move the **Seventh-day Adventist Theological Seminary** and the graduate programs of Potomac University to **Andrews University** in 1959 laid the basis for a large-scale graduate enterprise. In the 1970s and 1980s Andrews developed doctoral programs in theology, biblical studies, ministry, and education. In 1987 Adventist doctoral education became international with the establishment in the Philippines of the **Adventist International Institute of Advanced Studies**.

EGYPT. In 1877 Seventh-day Adventists in Naples sent the *Signs of the Times* to fellow Italians in Alexandria. The next year Romualdo Bartola, a businessman and **self-supporting** missionary from **Italy**, **baptized** seven individuals. In 1879 Dr. Herbert Ribton, who had been baptized in Italy and had carried out missionary work there for several years, arrived in Alexandria, where he opened a school. He and two of his converts were killed, however, in an 1882 anti-foreign uprising. Near the end of the 19th century several more Adventists arrived in Egypt and in 1902 the

Oriental **Union Mission** organized, although by 1912 there were only 18 Adventists in the country, most of them **Europeans** or **Armenians**. **George D. Keough**, who had come to Egypt in 1908, organized the first all-Egyptian **church** in 1913. In 1923 Adventists published *The Sure Word of Prophecy* in Arabic in an effort to attract the Arab population. When the Egypto-Syrian **Mission** formed that year, Egypt had 70 Adventists. In 1946 the mission opened the Egypt Training School. Church growth, however, was slow. As of 2003 the Egypt **Field**, part of the **Middle East** Union Mission under the Trans-European **Division**, had 17 **churches** with a membership of about 700. Nile Union **Academy** and a food factory were Union Mission institutions.

ELDER. Apart from the **minister**, the highest local **church** officer. Although **deacons** were the first officers appointed in Adventist churches, discussion of the appointment of elders had arisen by 1854. A *Review and Herald* article in 1861 clearly told the churches that they should have both elders and deacons. While at first it was understood that the elder guided a church in an advisory capacity, by the mid-1870s the office's functions included **baptisms**, officiating at the communion service, conducting business meetings, and visiting members. Elders received **ordination** that, according to an 1885 **General Conference session** action, was to be recognized by other local churches. With a few exceptions, only men were elected as elders until 1975 when the General Conference session approved ordination of **women** for the position. Elders are elected for a one-year term.

ELLEN G. WHITE ESTATE, INC. Seventh-day Adventist organization that holds custody of the writings of Ellen G. White. In her will, dated February 9, 1912, **Ellen G. White** designated five individuals, four of them members of the Executive Committee of the **General Conference** (GC), to serve as a self-perpetuating board of trustees to oversee her manuscripts, copyrights, and the publishing of her work. Ellen White's son, **William C. White**, served as secretary of the board from 1916 to 1937. The estate formally incorporated in 1933, and four years later, after W. C. White's death, moved from Ellen White's former home near St. Helena, California, to the GC headquarters in Takoma Park, Maryland. Family involvement in the estate continued as **Arthur L. White** succeeded his father as secretary, serving in that position until 1978, after which time leadership passed to non–family members. Although incorporated as an independent organization, the White Estate received an annual appropriation from the GC and most board members were also members of the GC Executive Committee.

In addition to maintaining Ellen White's manuscripts and responding to inquiries regarding her and her writings, the estate published compilations of her statements on a variety of topics, prepared two indexes (1927, 1962-92), and supervised the translation of most of her books. In addition, it promoted the reading of White's works through local **church** programs such as "Testimony Countdown," begun in 1969. In 1961 the organization established a branch office with copies of her manuscripts at **Andrews University** when the **Seventh-day Adventist Theological Seminary** moved to Berrien Springs, Michigan. In 1974 the first Ellen G. White Research Center, essentially a new name for a branch office, opened at **Newbold College** in **Great Britain**; by the early 21st century research centers existed in every world **division**. Ellen White's published works also became available to a wider public through CD-ROMs and the World Wide Web.

EL SALVADOR. John L. Brown arrived in 1915 as the first Seventh-day Adventist missionary in El Salvador and began selling books. In 1916 he held his first public meetings, **baptizing** 14 individuals and organizing a **church** in San Salvador. By 1918 there were 50 Adventists. As of 2003 the El Salvador **Conference** and the East El Salvador **Mission** were part of the Central American **Union Conference**, which was under the Inter-American **Division**. El Salvador had 337 churches with a membership of about 114,000. The Adventist Training School of El Salvador and one secondary school were located in the country.

EMMANUEL MISSIONARY COLLEGE (EMC). Former name of Seventh-day Adventist **educational** institution located in Berrien Springs, Michigan. After **Edward A. Sutherland** and **Percy T. Magan** gained approval to move **Battle Creek College**, they purchased farmland near Berrien Springs, Michigan, in the southwestern corner of the state. In 1901 they opened Emmanuel Missionary College (EMC), which was chartered as a benevolent rather than an educational institution because Sutherland opposed the awarding of degrees. After using various facilities within the village during its first year of operation, EMC in 1902-03 moved into four wooden buildings, constructed with student labor. Ever a reformer, Sutherland introduced several unique features to the school program, among them a plan whereby students took only one intensive course at a time and performed eight hours of manual labor during the day in combination with a three-hour class at night. Financial problems dogged the Sutherland administration and controversy surrounded his curricular innovations. In 1904 Nelson W. Kauble became president. He ended the "one-study" plan but continued to emphasize practical experience, particularly in agriculture. With the coming of Otto J. Graf as president in 1908, the school in 1910 acquired a new charter which enabled it to offer academic degrees and officially established it as a Lake **Union Conference** rather than **General Conference** (GC) institution. Gradually EMC developed a stronger financial position and a recognizable college curriculum, although concern for practical education remained, as represented by expansion of the farm and development of a wood products manufacturing enterprise. In 1922 the school received junior-college accreditation from the North Central Association of Colleges, although it took until 1939 to obtain senior college accreditation. Brick buildings began to replace wooden structures in 1937. Meanwhile, enrollment increased from 138 in 1908 to 503 in 1941. With the return of veterans after World War II enrollment moved from 502 in 1944 to 1,093 in 1947, the curriculum and faculty expanded, and new buildings were constructed. By 1959 EMC was the second largest Seventh-day Adventist college in North America, with an enrollment of 1,043. In that year the GC voted to move the **Seventh-day Adventist Theological Seminary** and graduate programs of Potomac University to the EMC campus, which in 1960 became **Andrews University**, named after **John Nevins Andrews**. The new university achieved a fully integrated administration in 1962.

EQUATORIAL GUINEA. Although two Seventh-day Adventist families had lived on the island of Bioko for some time, the first missionary, José Lopez, arrived on the island in 1960 and **baptized** his first converts in 1962. Political instability forced foreign missionaries to leave in 1972, after which individuals native to the country carried on the denomination's work. In 1974 one of these persons went to Bata, thereby becoming the first Adventist to enter continental Equatorial Guinea. As of 2003 the Equatorial Guinea **Mission**, part of the Central African **Union Mission** of the Western **Africa Division**, had 17 **churches** with a membership of nearly 1,300.

ESTONIA. Gerhard Perk and Heinrich J. Loebsack entered Estonia in 1897 and, after **baptizing** three individuals, organized the first Seventh-day Adventist **church** that same year. The following year the first Adventist tract in the Estonian language appeared in print. In 1920 the Estonian **Conference** organized with a membership of about 1,000. Between 1937 and 1940 the conference sponsored a theological school but after Estonia became part of the Soviet Union in 1940 all church institutions closed. As of 2003 the Estonian Conference, reestablished in 1989 after the fall of the Soviet Union, was part of the Baltic **Union Conference** under the Trans-**European Division**. The conference had 19 churches with a membership of about 1,800.

ETHIOPIA. The Scandinavian **Union Conference** sent two missionaries to neighboring Eritrea in 1907. One of those individuals, Valdemar E. Toppenberg, moved to Addis Ababa in 1921 where he established a **mission** headquarters. The Ethiopian **Union Mission** organized two years later. Dr. George C. Bergman arrived in 1927, opening the Taffari Makonnen Hospital in 1928 and the Empress Zauditu Memorial Hospital in 1934. The Italian invasion of 1935, however, resulted in the expropriation of all Protestant property. After Italy was forced out of the territory, the Zaudito Hospital opened again and in 1947 Toppenberg established the Ethiopian Adventist Training School. As of 2003 the Ethiopian Union Mission, part of the East-Central **Africa Division**, had 599 churches with about 123,000 members. Ethiopian Adventist College, three secondary schools, Gimbie Hospital, 14 clinics and dispensaries, and the Ethiopian Advent Press were located in the country.

EUROPE. *See* ALBANIA; BELGIUM; BOSNIA-HERZEGOVINA; BULGARIA; CROATIA; CZECH REPUBLIC; DENMARK; ESTONIA; FINLAND; FRANCE; GEORGIA; GERMANY; GREAT BRITAIN; GREECE; GREENLAND; HUNGARY; ICELAND; IRELAND; ITALY; LATVIA; LITHUANIA; LUXEMBOURG; MADEIRA ISLANDS; MALTA; MOLDAVIA; NETHERLANDS; NORWAY; POLAND; PORTUGAL; ROMANIA; RUSSIA; SLOVAK REPUBLIC; SLOVENIA; SPAIN; SWEDEN; SWITZERLAND; UKRAINE; YUGOSLAVIA.

EVANGELICAL-ADVENTIST DIALOGUES. Series of meetings that took place in 1955 and 1956 between evangelical and

Adventist leaders. From their beginnings, Seventh-day Adventists had faced the criticism that they were a non-Christian cult, largely because of their alleged legalism, adherence to the **sanctuary doctrine**, and apparent dependence on a non-biblical authority in the person of **Ellen G. White**. After its publication, **Dudley M. Canright's** *Seventh-day Adventism Renounced* (1889) became a standard source for most critics of Adventist theology. In the mid-1950s Walter R. Martin was asked by the Zondervan Publishing Company, an evangelical publisher, to write a book exposing Adventism as a non-Christian cult. From Donald Grey Barnhouse, editor of *Eternity* magazine, Martin obtained the name of T. Edgar Unruh, president of the East Pennsylvania **Conference**, and contacted him, asking for representative books and an opportunity to talk directly with Adventists qualified to answer his questions. A short time later a series of dialogues began which over time involved **R. Allan Anderson, LeRoy Edwin Froom**, Walter E. Read, and Unruh on the Adventist side and Martin, George E. Cannon, Donald Grey Barnhouse, Donald Grey Barnhouse, Jr., and Russell Hitt on the evangelical side. The evangelicals presented the Adventists with a series of formal questions. The Adventists prepared written responses to these questions and, before submitting them to Martin and his colleagues, sent them out to more than 200 Adventist scholars, **ministers**, and church administrators for comment. After making final revisions and giving the answers to Martin, church leaders used them as the basis for the book *Seventh-day Adventists Answer Questions on Doctrine* (1957).

Meanwhile, Martin had concluded that Adventists were indeed Christians, although he disagreed strongly with some of their doctrinal positions, and announced this conclusion in a series of highly controversial articles published in *Eternity* in 1956 and again in *The Truth About Seventh-day Adventists* (1960). Not all Adventists were happy with Martin's conclusion, however, for they believed that *Questions on Doctrine* revised some traditional Adventist positions. **Milian L. Andreasen**, who published *Letters to the Churches* (1959), was probably the most vocal critic. The **General Conference** responded to Martin's criticism of Adventist theology with *Doctrinal Discussions* (n.d.). Not all evangelicals changed their minds about Adventists; Anthony Hoekema, for instance, included them among *The Four Major Cults* (1963). Nonetheless, Martin's work contributed significantly to better relations between Adventists and other Christians. *See also* ECUMENISM.

EVANGELISM. Believing that they have a message that must be preached prior to Christ's **Second Advent**, Seventh-day Adventists have emphasized evangelism throughout their history. In the 19th century the denomination regarded its **ministers** primarily as evangelists rather than church pastors. Thus individuals such as **Joseph Bates, John Loughborough, Stephen Haskell**, and **James White** itinerated constantly in their search for new believers. They conducted their meetings in a variety of venues, including homes, schools, churches, and tents. When the denomination began holding **camp meetings** in 1868, it used these sessions for both revival among its members and evangelism of others. The development of **publishing**, which included tracts, papers, and books, and beginning in 1869 the organization of **tract and missionary societies**, went hand-in-hand with evangelism, for often the ministers organized their itineraries in response to inquiries from readers. The introduction of **literature evangelism** in the 1880s, through which subscription books were sold to the public, further opened up opportunities for ministers to expand their activities. Outside of North America, such literature evangelism was often the primary means of spreading the Adventist message.

Nearly all Adventist evangelism in North America prior to the 1880s concentrated on rural areas. Recognizing that the church must reach the burgeoning population of the cities, Haskell developed a plan for the tract and missionary societies to establish **city missions**; by 1886 such missions were operating in 25 cities, among them New York, Chicago, San Francisco, and Washington, D.C. Although these missions successfully created an Adventist presence in several cities, their expense led the church to close most them by the early 1890s.

Meanwhile, Adventists were attempting to penetrate another difficult area, the American South. **Robert M. Kilgore** began working in Texas in 1877 and an African American, **Charles M. Kinney**, began to evangelize the Upper South in 1889. A few years later, **James Edson White** and Will Palmer had a steamship built, which they took down the Mississippi River in 1895. First holding an evening school for African Americans, they soon built a small church in Vicksburg. Two years later White used similar methods in Yazoo City and began publishing a small paper. The efforts of both Kinney and White enabled Adventism to establish a base among Southern African Americans.

With the ascendancy of **Arthur G. Daniells** to denominational leadership, after 1901 the denomination placed a new emphasis on evangelism. Haskell once again emphasized the need to evangelize the cities, this time using door-to-door book sales and Bible studies and, beginning in 1902, health-education classes. That same year he began publishing an evangelistic paper, the *Bible Training School*, which was sold in the city streets. During the next few years several prominent city evangelists emerged, including Otto O. Bernstein, **James K. Humphrey**, Elmer L. Cardey, and K. C. Russell. Because some of the techniques used by these men were controversial, Daniells convened a meeting of about 50 evangelists in 1912 in which he and other church leaders emphasized that the speakers must avoid sensational advertising and theatrical methods and preach only "salvation through Jesus Christ." Partly as a result of this meeting, evangelists soon supplemented their public speaking with personal visitation and incorporated health and temperance subjects into their programs. Evangelists experimented with other techniques as well. A. V. Cotton used steriopticon pictures; Judson S. Washburn introduced a Bible correspondence course; and **Carlyle B. Haynes** and E. L. Cardy learned how to work effectively with newspapers to gain coverage of their meetings. Music became an increasingly prominent element, most significantly in the work of Henry de Fluiter, who worked with evangelist R. E. Harter and composed many songs, including "Over Yonder" and "Tell It to Every Kindred and Nation," that became popular with Adventist audiences.

The outbreak of World War I in 1914 further spurred Adventist evangelistic efforts but at the same time renewed the temptation toward sensationalism. **General Conference** president Daniells applied Adventist prophetic interpretation to world events before large crowds in Portland and Pittsburgh in 1916. Across the country other Adventist evangelists focused on the events of the war. Some of them predicted that Turkey would fall, an event that they believed would probably lead to the great final battle of history known as Armageddon These assertions led *Review and Herald* editor **Francis Wilcox** to caution that no one knew how the European conflict would end. To the chagrin of some evangelists, Turkey did not fall. As Wilcox had noted, a proper approach to prophecy required considerable humility.

By the 1920s the denomination was changing its approach to evangelism. Increasingly it distinguished between the functions of the pastor and the evangelist and devoted more funds to the support of the local **church**. **Conferences** also began to employ **Bible Instructors**, usually **women** who were paid less than ministers, to conduct Bible studies with families and other small groups. The denomination also encouraged lay people to become more active in evangelizing and prepared a variety of materials to support their efforts. While important in North America, lay evangelism played a more significant role in spreading Adventism in **Latin America**, **Asia**, and **Africa**, particularly in the last half of the 20th century.

Those individuals who became professional evangelists continued to explore new techniques. Charles T. Everson and Taylor G. Bunch, influenced by Protestant evangelist Billy Sunday, constructed temporary wooden tabernacles in which they held their meetings. Philip Knox incorporated slides of astronomical photography into his presentations. And J. H. Tindall developed "medical missionary evangelism" that sought to coherently address both the physical and spiritual needs of his listeners.

As evangelists experimented with techniques and evangelism became a distinct profession, it became apparent that special training was needed. In 1937 **John L. Shuler**, with the support of the Southern **Union Conference**, introduced a field school in conjunction with an evangelistic campaign in Greensboro, North Carolina. Similar field schools took place elsewhere and Shuler published a textbook, *Public Evangelism* (1939). Spurred by the field schools, the colleges appointed instructors in evangelism, starting with **R. Allan Anderson** at **La Sierrra College** in 1938. The most important development in Adventist evangelism between World Wars I and II, however, was the use of radio. **H. M. S. Richards** began radio broadcasts in Southern California in 1926. Other evangelists followed, including John Ford, Fordyce Detamore, Shuler, and Anderson. Richards's broadcasts developed into the *Voice of Prophecy* radio program, which by 1942 was broadcasting nationally. That same year **Braulio Perez** began a Spanish *Voice of Prophecy* program for Latin America. Eventually a version of the program, in some places entitled *Voice of Hope*, was being broadcast in every world division of the denomination. Success with radio led to early adoption of television, with the creation of **William A. Fagal's** *Faith for Today*, which began broadcasting weekly in 1950. In 1958 **George Vandeman** introduced *It Is Written*. Although originally designed as a series of programs that would be broadcast regionally in conjunction with an evangelistic campaign, *It Is Written* soon developed into a regular weekly broadcast. In 1974 the denomination established a third television program, *Breath of Life*, directed toward an African American audience.

After World War II North American Adventist evangelism appears to have become less sectarian. One study has found, for example, that whereas earlier preachers had emphasized prophecy and the **Sabbath**, in the 1950s they were giving more attention to

the home and Christian life. Having to compete with television and
other activities, evangelists worked to find effective methods for
post-war society. Short two-week campaigns, introduced by Detamore in 1953, replaced the three-month and longer efforts of an
earlier era. And the **Missionary Volunteer Department** of the
General Conference in 1954 involved the denomination's young
people in "Voice of Youth" evangelistic programs, usually conducted in local **churches**. Leo R. Van Dolson and William Love-
lace, among others, experimented with a variety of audience participation formats, out of which eventually developed the **Revelation Seminars** that are now a major means of Adventist evangelism. In **Latin America Walter Schubert** developed a highly successful approach to evangelism in Roman Catholic societies that
focused on family and social issues rather than the prophecies of
Daniel and Revelation.

Finally, always alert to the possibilities of new technology, the
denomination telecast over satellite a **Mark Finley** evangelistic series, called Net '95, to nearly 4,000 churches in the North American **Division**. The following year, Net '96 sent its telecast to approximately 1900 sites in Latin America, **Europe**, and **Africa**,
with simultaneous translation of the program into 12 languages. In
1997 the South American **Division** presented a similar program in
Spanish, directed particularly to some 450 Spanish congregations
in North America but available throughout Latin America as well.
This was followed in 1998 by Pentecost '98, sponsored by the Africa-Indian Ocean Division and sent to about 500 sites throughout
Africa. Net '98, featuring Dwight Nelson, was the first of these
programs to be telecast throughout the world. Satellite evangelism
has since become a standard Adventist method, using such outlets
as the independent **Three Angels Broadcasting Network** and the
denomination-owned Adventist Television Network.

F

FAGAL, WILLIAM A. (1919-1989). Seventh-day Adventist television **evangelist**. After graduating from **Atlantic Union College** in
1939, Fagal pastored several **churches** in the New York **Conference** and in the late 1940s began live radio broadcasting of services from his Brooklyn church. The **General Conference** in 1950
asked Fagal to develop a television program. *Faith for Today*,
which first appeared on a New York station on May 21, 1950 and
became a network program the following December. Rather than
presenting sermons, Fagal developed a format that emphasized re-

ligious drama, followed by a short talk. Desiring to connect his television program with personal contact, Fagal introduced "decision meetings" in 1965 and soon provided materials for other Adventist **ministers** and evangelists to conduct similar meetings, particularly in places where *Faith for Today* was televised. He also wrote several books, among them *By Faith I Live* (1965) and *Three Hours to Live* (1967), and a weekly column for the *Signs of the Times*. Fagal retired as executive director of *Faith for Today* in 1980.

FAITH FOR TODAY. Seventh-day Adventist television program. **William A. Fagal**, a Seventh-day Adventist **minister**, founded *Faith for Today* in New York City in 1950 and expanded the **General Conference** sponsored program to several other American cities by the end of the year. The half-hour program included a short drama, a brief sermon, music by a male quartet, and an invitation for viewers to enroll in a Bible correspondence course. By the late 1950s the program was appearing on 130 stations nationwide with an estimated viewing audience of four million. Beginning in the mid-1950s the program also appeared outside the **United States**, first broadcasting in the **Philippines**, **Australia**, and on United States armed forces television stations, and later in **Nigeria** and South America. In 1956 the program moved from kinescope to film and in 1963 began recording in color. In 1972 *Faith for Today* relocated from New York to the **Adventist Media Center** in Thousand Oaks, California, and soon changed its format to that of a hospital drama, *Westbrook Hospital*. Daniel G. Matthews replaced Fagal as head of *Faith for Today* in 1980 and five years later introduced a talk-show/magazine format under the title *Christian Lifestyle Magazine*, shortening the name to *Lifestyle Magazine* in 1991.

FIELD. An organizational unit of the Seventh-day Adventist church. A field is similar to a **conference** in form and function except that it does not usually support itself financially and the next higher organizational unit elects its officers. The term field is essentially equivalant to **mission**.

FIGUHR, REUBEN R. (1896-1983). Seventh-day Adventist **minister** and church administrator. Educated at **Pacific Union College** and **Walla Walla College**, Figuhr began working as an **evangelist**, pastor, and teacher in the Western Oregon **Conference** in 1915. **Ordained** to the ministry in 1918, a short time later he entered the

U.S. Army. After returning to denominational employment, in 1923 he went to the **Philippines**, where he served in a number of positions until he became president of the South American **Division** in 1941. Nine years later he joined the **General Conference** as a vice president and was elected president in 1954, serving in that position until his retirement in 1966. During his presidency, Figuhr promoted the development of graduate education, which ultimately led to the establishment of **Andrews University**, and the organization of the **Geoscience Research Institute**.

FIJI. Although **John I. Tay** arrived in Fiji in 1891 as the first Seventh-day Adventist missionary, he died soon thereafter. Four years later the Fiji **Mission** organized with John M. Cole working in the capital, Levuka. In 1896 John E. Fulton opened Adventist work first in Tamavua and then in Suva Vou. Fulton made sufficient progress among the native population that in 1908 a Fijian went as a missionary to **New Guinea**. Meanwhile, Adventists established their first school in Fiji in 1904, one of several schools that in 1940 were consolidated into Fulton College, and in 1949 established Suva as the headquarters of the Central Pacific **Union Mission**. As of 2003 the Fiji Mission was part of the Trans-Pacific Union Mission of the **South Pacific Division**. It had 140 churches with a membership of over 22,000. Fulton College and Navesau Junior Secondary School were located on Fiji.

FINLAND. Through the request of A. F. Lundqvist, a sea captain who had converted to Seventh-day Adventism in England, a **literature evangelist**, Emil Lind, entered Finland in 1891. Olof Johnson, president of the Swedish **Conference**, and two women helpers arrived in 1902 and soon made their first converts. The following year they published **Ellet J. Waggoner's** *Christ and His Righteousness* in Finnish. By 1894 they had converted between 50 and 60 individuals and that year organized in Helsinki the first Adventist **church**. Three years later they began publishing a paper, *Watchman of the Times*. In 1909 the Finnish churches established the Finland Conference and in 1917 began a "Missionary School." The government of Finland gave the Adventist church official recognition in 1943. The Seventh-day Adventist Church in Finland went through several organizational changes, ultimately becoming the Finland **Union Conference** in 1955 with a membership of over 4,500. It established the Lapland **Mission** in 1983. As of 2003 the Finland Union Conference, part of the Trans-**European Division**, had 73 **churches** and a membership of about 5,500. It operated

Finland Junior College, Hopeaniemi Health and Rehabilitation Centre, and the Finland Seventh-day Adventist Publishing House.

FINLEY, MARK (1945-). Seventh-day Adventist television **evangelist.** After receiving his B.A. from **Atlantic Union College** in 1967, Finley served as a pastor in the Southern New England and Georgia-Cumberland **Conferences** from 1967 to 1974. In 1974 he became the ministerial secretary and conference evangelist for the New England Conference, moving from that position in 1979 to establish the North American **Division** Evangelism Institute, located in Illinois, through which he conducted numerous field schools to train Adventist pastors in evangelistic techniques. While directing the institute, he completed an M.A. at **Andrews University** in 1985. He joined the Trans-**European** Division in 1985, where he served as ministerial secretary, again holding numerous evangelism field schools for European **ministers**, returning to the **United States** in 1990 to become vice president for evangelism in the Michigan Conference. The following year he joined the staff of the television program *It Is Written* and became speaker/director in 1992. As part of the program's activities, he conducted evangelistic campaigns in major cities, including London, Budapest, Belgrade, Karachi, and Seoul. Among his books were *The Almost Forgotten Day* (1988), *The Cross and the Kremlin* (1992), and *Solid Ground* (2003).

FITCH, CHARLES (1805-1844). Millerite preacher. First a Congregationalist and later a Presbyterian **minister**, Charles Fitch was active in reform causes and published *Slaveholding Weighed in the Balance of Truth* (1837). After reading **William Miller's** lectures, in 1838 he accepted the belief that Christ would return about 1843 but, because of opposition from his fellow ministers, soon abandoned his new views. In 1839 he adopted the understanding of perfection taught at Oberlin College and published *Views of Sanctification* (1839), which resulted in his resignation from the Presbyterian ministry because of the denomination's opposition to his ideas. In 1841, through the influence of **Josiah Litch**, he restudied Miller's prophetic interpretation and once again adopted the belief that Christ's coming was very near. With the help of Apollos Hale, he designed a prophetic chart that he presented to the 1842 Millerite general conference in Boston. Known as the "1843 chart" (because that was the year of Christ's expected return), Millerite preachers used it extensively. In 1842 Fitch went to Ohio where he preached on the imminent advent of Jesus at

Oberlin College in September 1842. He returned to Oberlin about a year later and publicly debated his beliefs. Also in 1843 he began editing the *Second Advent of Christ*, a weekly Millerite journal published in Cleveland, and in July published his call for the Millerite believers to leave the Protestant churches which, he argued, by their rejection of the new understanding of the Advent had become part of Babylon. This sermon later appeared as a pamphlet and was reprinted in other Millerite papers. In 1844 he adopted **conditionalism** and the practice of **baptism** by immersion. While traveling from Cleveland to Rochester in September 1844, he stopped in Buffalo where he conducted baptisms in Lake Erie on a cold day and shortly thereafter fell ill. While sick, he accepted the **seventh-month** teaching of **Samuel S. Snow**. Fitch died on October 14, about a week before the day on which he expected Christ to return.

FIVE-DAY PLAN TO STOP SMOKING. Seventh-day Adventist anti-smoking program. J. Wayne McFarland, a physician, and Elman J. Folkenberg, a **minister**, developed over several years the Five-Day Plan to Stop Smoking. As ultimately formulated, the program involved a series of five consecutive evening meetings in which the leaders presented information regarding the dangers of smoking, established a support group for those desiring to quit the habit, and invoked the spiritual resources of Bible reading and prayer. Adopted by the **General Conference** in 1962, the program became one of the most successful health efforts sponsored by the Adventist church. The American Cancer Society frequently co-sponsored the program and the U.S. Navy contracted with the church to present the program on its bases. Adventist **evangelists** in many countries found it a useful supplement to their preaching. In 1974 an average of 60 Five-Day Plan series took place each week. After conducting studies of the effectiveness of the Five-Day Plan in 1980 and 1984, the denomination in 1985 introduced a revised program, the Breathe-Free Plan, which it further revised and released in 1993. *See also* TEMPERANCE.

FOLKENBERG, ROBERT S. (1941-). Seventh-day Adventist **minister** and church administrator. Born into a missionary family in **Puerto Rico**, Folkenberg received his B.A. (1962) and M.A. (1963) from **Andrews University**. After serving a pastoral internship in Michigan and working as an **evangelist** in the Columbia **Union Conference**, he went as a missionary to **Panama** in 1966. In 1970 he became president of the **Honduras Mission**. Four years later Folkenberg joined the Central American Union Conference as secretary, becoming president of the organization in 1975. In 1980 he began serving as assistant to the president of the Inter-American **Division**. He returned to the **United States** in 1985 to become president of the Carolina **Conference** and in 1990 was elected president of the **General Conference** (GC). While in Central America Folkenberg strongly emphasized **evangelism**, developed several radio stations, built an acute care hospital in Honduras, and established the denomination's first orphanage in the region. As GC president he strongly promoted the **Global Mission** program. A 1998 civil lawsuit over financial issues against Folkenberg and several denominational entities with which he had been associated led to his resignation from the GC presidency in 1999, although the suit was settled out of court. In cooperation with the Carolina Conference and *The Quiet Hour* Folkenberg subsequently developed Global Evangelism, a program that organized lay people to conduct evangelistic meetings in various parts of the world.

FOOT WASHING. Ceremony in remembrance of Christ's action before his last supper. The practice of foot washing was controversial in early Adventism, when some associated it with fanaticism, but became established by the early 1850s. The ceremony is practiced prior to and in conjunction with the **Lord's Supper**.

FORD, DESMOND (1929-). Seventh-day Adventist theologian and biblical scholar. A native of **Australia**, Desmond Ford converted to Seventh-day Adventism while in his teens. He served in the **ministry** before competing his B.A. at **Avondale College** (1958). He then earned an M.A. degree from the **Seventh-day Adventist Theological Seminary**, a Ph.D. in speech from Michigan State University (1961), and, while teaching at Avondale, a Ph.D. in New Testament from the University of Manchester in Great Britain (1972). Ford influenced **Robert Brinsmead** to reject the perfectionism he had been teaching in favor of **righteousness by faith**. Brinsmead then began arguing that Adventists were mistaken in including both justification and sanctification within righteousness by faith and about 1970 provoked a major debate among Australian Adventists over this distinction. Many church members believed that Brinsmead's new views would ultimately undermine the **Sabbath** doctrine.

At this time Ford was chair of the theology department at Avondale and, because of his connection with Brinsmead, was caught up in the controversy. He participated in a 1976 conference at Palmdale, California, which was arranged by the **General Conference** to settle the issue but ended up spreading it to the **United States**. Ford later joined the religion department at **Pacific Union College** (PUC) as a visiting professor where in 1979 he made a public presentation in which he argued that the denomination's **sanctuary doctrine** was not biblical, thereby stirring up another storm of controversy. PUC gave Ford a leave of absence to more fully develop his ideas and present them to a group of scholars and church administrators. The "Sanctuary Review Committee" examined his document, subsequently published as *Daniel 8:14, The Day of Atonement and the Investigative Judgment* (1980), and at a meeting in Colorado in the summer of 1980 issued statements on the sanctuary doctrine and the role of **Ellen G. White** in doctrinal issues.

Although many participants in the Colorado meeting believed that the statements were broad enough to include both Ford and his critics, the Australasian **Division** removed Ford's ministerial credentials a few weeks later. This action produced further controversy in both Australia and the United States, with significant numbers of both lay people and ministers severing their ties with the Adventist denomination. Ford, however, remained a practicing Seventh-day Adventist and developed a radio and preaching ministry, *Good News Unlimited*. Among his books were *Daniel* (1978), *The Forgotten Day* (1981), *Jesus and the Last Days* (1984), and *Right with God Right Now* (1999).

FOREIGN MISSION SEMINARY. *See* COLUMBIA UNION COLLEGE.

FOY, WILLIAM ELLIS (1818-1893). African American **Millerite** preacher and visionary. At age 17 William Foy, a resident of Maine, converted to Christianity through the preaching of Silas Curtis, a Free Will Baptist. Soon after his baptism, Foy married and moved to Boston where he sought training to enter the Episcopal ministry. In 1842 Foy experienced a vision in which he saw scenes of the righteous entering heaven. A few weeks later he had another vision, this time concerning the final judgment. After being asked to tell what he had seen in these visions to a Boston Methodist Episcopal Church, from March through May 1844 Foy traveled extensively, speaking to churches of various denominations. When he spoke at Beethoven Hall in Portland, Maine, the young **Ellen** Harmon (later **White**) was in attendance. Although Foy left full-time preaching so that he could earn a living, he experienced a third vision, probably occurring in 1844, concerning the experience of true Christians just before Christ's second coming. In early 1845 Foy talked with Ellen Harmon and heard her publicly present her visionary experiences, which, according to her account, he confirmed as being similar to his own. **John N. Loughborough** later regarded this similarity as evidence that Ellen Harmon's visions were divinely inspired. Foy wrote an account of his visions in *The Christian Experience of William E. Foy* (1845), published by John and Henry Pearson who had been active in the Millerite movement. He subsequently served as a pastor in northern Maine.

FRANCE. After arriving in **Switzerland** in 1874, **John N. Andrews** began **evangelizing** French-speaking people in the country. **Daniel T. Bourdeau** joined him in 1876 and shortly thereafter spent three weeks in Alsace, at the time part of **Germany**, where he made a few converts. Soon he and Andrews were publishing a French-language *Signs of the Times*, which, because of difficulties in holding public meetings, became an important medium for communicating Adventist beliefs. Adventism grew slowly, however. In 1907 the French **Mission** became a **conference** with 227 members in 16 **churches** and companies. The Life and Health Publishing House formed in 1922 and the denomination began broadcasting various radio broadcasts in the late 1940s. As of 2003 the Seventh-day Adventist Church in France was divided into the North France and South France Conferences, part of the Franco-Belgian **Union Conference** of the Euro-**Africa Division**. The conferences had 111 churches with a membership of approximately 10,000. The Union Conference operated several radio stations and production centers in France. The Life and Health Publishing House and Salève Adventist University, founded in 1921, were located in France but operated under the Euro-Africa Division.

FRENCH GUIANA. R. T. Colthurst entered French Guiana about 1940 and conducted house-to-house **evangelism**. A. H. Linzau followed in 1946 and by the late 1940s had organized the first Seventh-day Adventist **church**. Marcel Perau and Paul Joseph began selling books in 1952 in St. Laurent du Maroni and began working among the Carib Indians who lived in the area. In 1958 S. B. Jean-Elie **baptized** the first Carib converts. As of 2003 the French Guiana **Mission**, part of the French Antilles-Guiana **Union Mission** of the Inter-American **Division**, had six churches with a membership of over 1,700.

FRENCH POLYNESIA. A. J. Read introduced Seventh-day Adventism to French Polynesia in 1891 on the first voyage of the *Pitcairn*. Two years later Benjamin J. Cady established a school on Raiatea. In 1906 he became superintendent of the newly formed Eastern Polynesian **Mission**, which included French Polynesia, the **Cook islands**, Easter Island, and Pitcairn. By 1914 the mission had 43 church members; in 1916 French Polynesia became a separate mission. As of 2003 the French Polynesia Mission was part of the New Zealand-Pacific **Union Conference** of the **South Pacific Division**. It had 29 churches with a membership of over 4,400. Tiarema Adventist College was located on Tahiti.

FRIEDENSAU UNIVERSITY. A Seventh-day Adventist **educational** institution located near Magdeburg, **Germany**. Through the influence of **Ludvig R. Conradi**, the **German Conference** opened the first training school for Adventist **ministers** in Europe in 1899 near Magdeburg. By the 1912-13 school year about 250 students from throughout **Europe** were attending the school, but World War I forced the institution to close in 1917. Although it reopened in 1919, the establishment of other schools in Europe impacted its enrollment, which dropped to less than 100 by the mid-1930s, by which time Friedensau served only the East German **Union Conference**. In 1939 the school became the ministerial training institution for all of Germany but closed in 1943 because of World War II. The school opened again in 1947 but the political division of Germany generally limited its source of students to the German Democratic Republic and Communist nations of Eastern Europe.

    With the reunification of Germany, Friedensau once again began serving German-speakers from throughout Europe. In 1990 the theological seminary received government recognition and began offering a degree program in theology in 1992. The following year the institution established a Christian social science faculty that developed programs in social work and social education. Other offerings included an undergraduate religion program and courses in music and German as a foreign language. As of 2003 about 200 students were enrolled at the school.

FROOM, LEROY EDWIN (1890-1974). Seventh-day Adventist **minister**, teacher, and writer. In 1915 Froom entered the Seventh-day Adventist ministry in Maryland and two years later took an editorial position at **Pacific Press Publishing Association**. In 1918 he went to **China** where he edited the Chinese language *Signs of the Times*, returning to the **United States** to edit *The Watchman* from

1922 to 1925. He became associate secretary of the **Ministerial Association** in 1926 and served as secretary from 1941 to 1950. In the early years of the association he helped **Arthur G. Daniells** complete *Christ Our Righteousness* (1926), prepared nine Bible studies on the importance of one's spiritual life, and wrote *The Coming of the Comforter* (1928), which was based on lectures that he had presented at ministerial institutes in 1927. Froom became the first editor of *The Ministry* in 1928, a position he filled until 1950. Seeking to establish a historical base for Seventh-day Adventist beliefs, he wrote *The Prophetic Faith of Our Fathers* (1950-54) and *The Conditionalist Faith of Our Fathers* (1965-66). Froom also participated in the **evangelical-Adventist dialogues** that took place in 1955-56 and contributed to *Seventh-day Adventists Answer Questions on Doctrine* (1957). He later argued in *Movement of Destiny* (1971) that belief in the full deity of Jesus and **righteousness by faith** had deep roots in Adventist history. Froom also frequently taught courses in historical theology at the **Seventh-day Adventist Theological Seminary**.

FUNDAMENTAL BELIEFS. Official statements of Adventist doctrines. From their beginnings in the 1840s Adventists opposed adoption of a statement of beliefs, arguing that the Bible was their only creed. When **Uriah Smith** wrote his 25 *Fundamental Principles* in 1872 he clearly stated that the document was intended to provide information to inquirers and was not to be viewed as a creed or used as a basis for discipline. Following requests from Adventist missionaries in **Africa**, who needed to provide information to other mission agencies, the **General Conference** (GC) Executive Committee requested **Charles H. Watson**, GC president, to appoint a committee for the purpose of writing a statement of beliefs. *Review and Herald* editor **Francis Wilcox** wrote the statement of 22 *Fundamental Beliefs* that was accepted by the committee and first appeared in the 1931 *Yearbook* and then in the 1932 *Church Manual*; subsequent editions of both books also included the statement. Interestingly, no **General Conference session** took a vote on the statement, although the 1946 meeting voted that only such sessions could make changes in the *Church Manual*, thereby giving indirect approval to the *Fundamental Beliefs*. After the denomination experienced a number of theological controversies in the 1970s, the 1980 GC session voted to approve a revised statement of 27 *Fundamental Beliefs*. The preamble to the statement asserted that for Adventists the Bible was the only creed and that the following articles of belief expressed the church's current understanding of Scripture and were subject to further revision. *Seventh-day Adventists Believe . . .* (1988) provided extended commentary on the 1980 doctrinal statement.

G

GABON. Although Seventh-day Adventists began working in Gabon in 1975 and organized a **Mission** three years later, they attracted few members. In 1981 the denomination received recognition from the government and Daniel Cordas began Seventh-day Adventist efforts in Libreville and Port Gentil. In the 1990s Max Pierre's **evangelism** brought increasing numbers of converts. As of 2003 the Gabon Mission, part of the Central African **Union Mission** of the Westerm **Africa Division**, had 11 churches and a membership of 2,200.

GAMBIA, THE. Seventh-day Adventist **literature evangelists** first entered The Gambia in 1973 and, despite much opposition, the first public **evangelistic** meetings took place in 1975. With 22 church members in the country by 1980, Louis C. Nielsen arrived in 1981 to establish a **mission** station; he opened an elementary school two years later. As of 2003 The Gambia Mission Station of the West African **Union Mission**, part of the **Africa**-Indian Ocean **Division**, had three **churches** with a membership of about 550.

GENERAL CONFERENCE OF SEVENTH-DAY ADVENTISTS (GC). The central administrative organization of the Seventh-day Adventist Church. As originally formed in 1863, **conferences** were the constituent element of the General Conference. Delegates from six state conferences met on May 20-23 in Battle Creek, Michigan, where they wrote a constitution and elected officers and a three-person executive committee that was soon expanded to five individuals. As described in the constitution, the GC supervised all **ministers**, promoted missionary work, and raised funds. Delegates convened annually in a **General Conference session**. With the geographical growth of Adventism and its move into new areas of endeavor, the original organizational structure became strained. Independent organizations, tied to the GC through interlocking directorates, oversaw many of the activities of the church. These organizations included the International **Tract and Missionary Society**, the **Sabbath School** Association, the Seventh-day Adventist **Publishing** Association, the Seventh-day Adventist **Educational**

Society, the **Health Reform Institute**, and the American Health and **Temperance** Society.

Beginning in 1886, denominational leaders began to make changes in the organizational structure. In that year they expanded the executive committee from five to seven persons and created the GC Association as the legal entity that would hold property and finances for the church. In 1887 the GC president acquired an administrative assistant, and secretaries for **education**, foreign **missions**, and home missions joined the central administration. The position of foreign mission secretary disappeared in 1889 when the GC session created the Foreign Mission Board. In that same year, the session voted to have biannual rather than annual meetings. Four years later the denomination created another independent agency, the Medical Missionary and Benevolent Association. In 1892 and 1897 GC presidents attempted, with little success, to create intermediate administrative districts between the conferences in the **United States** and the GC. Instead, the GC session of 1897 expanded the executive committee to 13 people. By the end of the century it was widely apparent that the denomination's organizational structure was unwieldy.

Meanwhile, **Asa T. Robinson** in **Africa** developed the concept of having conference departments rather than independent agencies control activities such as education and publishing. In **Australia, Arthur G. Danniells** helped establish a **union conference** structure that brought individual conferences into an associated framework. After Robinson moved to Australia in the mid-1890s, he in-troduced departments into its conference and union conference structure. Drawing upon this experience under the leadership of Daniells and with the support of **Ellen G. White**, delegates to the 1901 GC session addressed the long-standing organizational issues. They voted several significant changes. First, following the Australian model, they decided to group the conferences into regional union conferences and made these entities the constituent element of the GC. In the future, union conferences, rather than conferences, would choose the delegates to the GC sessions. Second, they established a 25-member GC Executive Committee to replace the existing boards and committees. The chairman of the executive committee would act as chief executive of the church but the title of president was discarded. Third, the session established departments to replace the former Sabbath School and Religious Liberty Associations. At the next session, which took place in 1903, the delegates restored the position of president.

In 1912 **European** denominational leaders proposed to group regional union conferences together into division conferences. The 1913 GC session adopted this proposal and created the European and North American Division Conferences. But the behavior of European leaders during World War I created concern among GC officers that the division conferences had the potential of becoming too independent. The 1918 GC session, therefore, voted to disband the division conferences and replace them with **divisions**. Despite the similarity in name, this new organizational entity was different in that it was part of the GC itself. Rather than having officers voted on by delegates from the union conferences, GC sessions would choose the officers of the divisions and a vice president of the GC would preside over each division. Although the denomination would rearrange departments and divisions many times in ensuing years, with this decision the GC session established the basic organizational structure of the General Conference of Seventh-day Adventists that continues to the present.

GENERAL CONFERENCE SESSION. A meeting of delegates from the worldwide Seventh-day Adventist Church. Seventh-day Adventists commonly use the term **General Conference** (GC) to refer to both the central administrative structure of the church and the periodic sessions that constitute the ultimate organizational authority in the denomination. GC sessions took place annually from 1863 to 1889 and biannually from 1891 to 1905. Between 1905 and 1970 sessions occurred every four years, with the exceptions of 1913-18 and 1930-36, and since 1970 every five years. The GC Constitution and Bylaws define the membership of a GC session. The delegates to the sessions come from two groups. Regular delegates, 25 percent of whom must be lay members, represent **union conferences**, **union missions**, and similar organizations. Delegates at large represent the GC and its **divisions** and organizations. These delegates choose the officers of the GC, revise the constitution and bylaws, and address organizational issues.

GENERAL CONFERENCE SESSION OF 1888. Seventh-day Adventist meeting in Minneapolis that debated **righteousness by faith**. In the mid-1880s two young Adventist **ministers, Ellet J. Waggoner** and **Alonzo T. Jones**, began writing articles in the *Signs of the Times* advocating the position that "righteousness by faith" must become a personal experience in the lives of believers. In particular, they interpreted Paul's reference to the "schoolmaster" law in Galations 3 as including the entire moral law, rather than only the Old Testament ceremonial and sacrificial laws, which was the prevailing Adventist view. **George I. Butler**, president of the **General Conference** (GC), and **Uriah Smith**, editor of the *Review and Herald*, strongly opposed Waggoner and Jones because they feared that the new view of the law would undermine the **Sabbath** doctrine. A GC committee studied the issue in 1886 but was unable to settle the controversy.

During the next several months **Ellen G. White** refused to take a position, despite Butler's appeals, but urged the church to fully and openly discuss the issues. As delegates met at Minneapolis, Minnesota, in October 1888 for the **General Conference session**, Butler—who was unable to attend—wired his supporters to "stand by the old landmarks." Many of the delegates opposed Jones and Waggoner because the young men had not deferred to senior authority. Jones did not help matters when, after making presentations on interpretation of prophecy that challenged some of Smith's interpretations, he made some caustic remarks regarding the esteemed editor. Waggoner then gave a series of studies on Romans and Galatians in which he argued that the law only establishes man's sinfulness. Salvation comes through Jesus, he said, not through obedience to the law. J. H. Morrison, a close associate of Butler, responded that Adventists had always accepted righteousness by faith. Nonetheless, he asserted, Waggoner's position undercut the church's unique message that the **Sabbath** must be obeyed as earth's history drew to an end.

Despite Ellen White's sermons supporting Waggoner, the session generally turned against the new view, although it took no formal vote. During the next several years, however, attitudes began to change. In 1889 White, Waggoner, and Jones spoke throughout the nation at Adventist **camp meetings** and ministerial institutes. Waggoner again spoke on Romans several times at the 1891 GC session and both he and Jones continued to write articles for the *Signs of the Times*. The leaders who had opposed the new view started to change their minds. Near the end of 1890 Smith stated that he had been wrong in opposing Jones and Waggoner. Morrison, Butler, and others made similar statements in 1893. Pockets of opposition remained, however, until the generation represented by such people as Butler and Morrison had largely passed away.

Interpretation of what happened at Minneapolis became a controversial issue within Adventism when ministers Robert J. Wieland and Donald K. Short began arguing in the 1950s that the Seventh-day Adventist Church must corporately repent for rejecting the 1888 message of righteousness by faith so that the final outpouring of the Holy Spirit could take place. Among Wieland's books were *The 1888 Message* (1980), *1888 Re-examined* (1987), and *Let History Speak* (2001). The "1888 Message Study Committee" formed in 1985 to promote the Wieland-Short view by publishing a newsletter, books, and other materials, and holding meetings. The issues involved the meaning of righteousness by faith as well as the question of corporate repentance. In response, the denomination issued many publications of its own on the Minneapolis conference and the theology of righteousness by faith, including A. V. Olson's *Through Crisis to Victory, 1888-1901* (1966) and George R. Knight's *A User-Friendly Guide to the 1888 Message* (1998).

GEORGIA. Dr. Vagan Pampanjan began **evangelizing** among Armenians in Tbilisi in 1904 and two years later Dr. Albert Ozel worked among the **German** and Lett populations. Although Ozel organized a **church**, he was exiled to Narinsky about 1914. As of 2003 the Georgian Mission, part of the Caucasus **Union Mission** of the Euro-**Asia Division**, had four **churches** with over 300 members.

GEOSCIENCE RESEARCH INSTITUTE (GRI). Seventh-day Adventist organization for the study of issues related to creationism and science. Because Adventist science teachers were concerned about the lack of trained geologists and paleontologists in the church, the Fall Council of the **General Conference** (GC) Executive Committee in 1957 established a Committee on the Teaching of Geology and Paleontology and allocated money to provide appropriate graduate training for selected individuals. The committee became the Geoscience Research Institute the following year. The original members of the institute, which was located on the campus of **Andrews University**, included **Frank L. Marsh**, P. Edgar Hare, and Richard Ritland.

Divisions over purpose and methodology characterized the institute's first 15 years of existence. Marsh, who headed the institute, approached the issues from the standpoint of religious authority and wanted the organization to concentrate on criticism of evolutionary theory. In contrast, Ritland sought to have it engage in open investigation and discussion of both the scientific and religious issues. Hare soon left to join the Carnegie Institution and Marsh in 1964 joined the Biology Department at Andrews University. At that point, Ritland became the head of the GRI and brought in a number of young scientists. The group performed several functions, including conducting field tours for church administrators and teachers, writing articles for denominational journals, and giving lectures at Adventist institutions and churches. Differences in outlook continued, however, represented by Harold G. Coffin's book *Creation—Accident or Design?* (1969), which advocated a slightly revised form of the flood geology proposed by **George McCready Price,** and Ritland's *A Search for Meaning in Nature* (1970), which emphasized design and accepted some degree of evolution.

But the election of Robert H. Pierson as GC president in 1966 led to a change of direction at the GRI, for his administration wanted the institute to emphasize apologetics and defend the flood geology position. In 1971 Ritland left the GRI to join the Andrews University Biology Department and, with physicist Robert H. Brown, who became director in 1973, the institute advocated flood geology and a 10,000 year-old earth. Some of the scientists that Ritland had brought into the institute soon departed, to be replaced by individuals more sympathetic to defense of traditional positions. Under Brown, nonetheless, the GRI sought to establish a stronger scientific base for flood geology, often severely criticizing the scientific evidence and methodology used by popular creationists. It began publishing *Origins*, a semiannual professional journal, in 1974 and *Geoscience Reports*, a publication for elementary and secondary teachers, in 1981. When Ariel Roth became director in 1980, the GRI moved to **Loma Linda University** in California and in 1991 established branch offices at Salève Adventist Institute in **France** and **River Plate Adventist University** in **Argentina**. After his retirement in 1994 and replacement by L. James Gibson, Roth published *Origins: Linking Science and Scripture* (1998).

GERMANY. After writing to a group of **Sabbath**-observers in the Rhineland and receiving an invitation to visit, James Erzberger and **John Nevins Andrews** entered Germany from **Switzerland** in 1875. Erzberger stayed until the late 1870s, during which time he **baptized** the first Seventh-day Adventists and organized two **churches. Ludvig R. Conradi** arrived in 1886 and two years later **Gerhard Perk** and Emil Frauchiger came to sell books. In 1889 Conradi chose Hamburg as the location for the Adventist headquarters in Germany and established a publishing agency. Two years later a **mission**, including both Germany and **Russia**, organized with Conradi as president; at the time the Adventist church in

Germany had about 100 members. In 1894 the mission opened a school to train **ministers**.

With more than 1,000 members in Germany, in 1898 the mission reorganized as the German **Conference**, which included **Austria, Hungary, The Netherlands, Romania, Bulgaria,** and **Serbia** as well as Germany. The next year the conference opened the **Friedensau** training school near Magdeburg. By 1901 the German Conference had nearly 4,000 members, the largest conference in **Europe,** and reorganized as a **Union Conference.** Adventism in Germany had become financially self-supporting and as early as 1895 was sending missionaries to **Latin America** and soon thereafter to **Tanzania** and elsewhere. Despite the emergence of the German Reform Movement during World War I and Conradi's departure soon after the war, Adventism in Germany continued to grow, reaching 36,000 members by 1927.

Increasing political and social problems in Germany, however, led the denomination in 1928 to create the Central European **Division,** which continued until 1971, to accommodate the situation. The advent of National Socialism brought futher difficulties to the church. At times the government confiscated denominational property and observance of the Sabbath proved difficult in the Labor Corps and the military. Adventists leaders attempted to avoid Jewish connections by calling the Sabbath a "rest day" and **Sabbath school** "Bible School." Church papers also frequently praised Hitler and supported German military actions in Austria, the Sudetenland, and Czechoslovakia. Nevertheless, the church faced increasing restrictions on the selling of books and the sending of missionaries. The outbreak of war forced the closure of the publishing house and the Friedensau school and destroyed many homes and churches. Furthermore, more than 3,000 German Adventists died as a result of the war. Once the conflict was over, the **General Conference** sent relief aid to Germany, schools reopened, and publishing resumed.

The creation of the German Democratic Republic in 1949 necessitated the organization of a separate Union of Seventh-day Adventists, which received recognition from the East German government. Adventists in the Federal Republic of Germany organized into the West and South German Union Conferences. When Germany reunited in 1990, a consolidated North German Conference formed and Friedensau became the ministerial seminary for all of Germany. More significant than organizational changes, Adventism had difficulty coping with the increasingly secularized postwar Germany, with the result that its membership largely stagnated. As of 2003 the South and North German Union Conferences, part of the Euro-**Africa** Division, had 572 churches with over 35,000 members. Denominational institutions in Germany included Friedensau Adventist University, Marienhoehe College, the German Health Food Factory, Berlin Hospital, Voice of Hope media center, and the German Seventh-day Adventist Publishing House.

GHANA. Francis I. U. Dolphijn adopted the seventh-day **Sabbath** in 1888 as a result of reading Seventh-day Adventist publications. He taught others his new beliefs and requested that the **General Conference** send a missionary. Lawrence C. Chadwick visited these new believers in 1892 but the first permanent missionaries did not arrive until 1894. Although illness caused great problems for the missionaries, they made their first **baptisms** in 1897. Several other missionaries arrived in subsequent years, eventually establishing a mission station and school at Agona. In 1918 they organized the West African Combined **Mission**, which included **Sierra Leone**, **Liberia**, and the Gold Coast. In 1945 the mission opened a two-year teacher training college in Bekwai, which had been made the headquarters of the reorganized Gold Coast Mission in 1933. Dr. John A. Hyde established Kwahu Hospital in 1955 and soon began a School of Nursing; the government nationalized the hospital in 1973. In 1962 the Asokore-Koforidua Teacher Training College opened. Meanwhile, the Gold Coast Mission became the Ghana Mission in 1957 and, with continual growth in membership, the first Black **conference** in **Africa** in 1970. As of 2003 the Ghana **Union Conference,** part of the Western Africa **Division,** had 777 **churches** and nearly 270,000 members. Valley View University and Advent Press were located in Ghana.

GLOBAL MISSION. A strategic program to establish new Adventist **churches** within population segments of one million where there was no Adventist presence. Originally proposed in 1986 by **Neal C. Wilson**, president of the **General Conference**, the **General Conference session** of 1990 adopted the plan and created the Office of Global Mission. The office established study centers in various parts of the world to develop and test methods for reaching Islamic, Hindu, Buddhist, Judaic, and secular populations, which were particularly difficult to penetrate. It also developed the Center for International Relations to help place lay members in government or business positions in countries where traditional missionaries were forbidden. The Global Mission program also identified specific cities, language, ethnic, and socio-economic groups that had no Adventist presence. Between 1990 and 2000 the Office of Global Mission reported a number of successes, including doubling the number of Adventists in **Bangladesh**, moving membership from zero to 3,200 in **Cambodia**, and increasing church membership in **Russia** by 43 percent.

GREAT BRITAIN. William Ings, a native of England who had lived in the **United States**, began selling Seventh-day Adventist books in England in 1878. A short time later **John N. Loughborough** arrived to help him and in 1880 **baptized** six converts. Three years later he organized the first British Adventist **church** at Southampton. The following year Milton C. Wilcox began publishing the *Present Truth*. The British population was slow to accept this imported religion, however, as there were only about 100 Adventists by 1883. Nonetheless, various individuals endeavored to take Adventism to different parts of Great Britain. Dores A. Robinson organized the first church in **Ireland** in 1891, but it took 10 years until Harry E. Armstrong was able to do the same in Scotland in 1901 and another two years before William H. Meredith established a church in Wales. The South England Conference organized in 1898, followed by the North England Conference, and Irish, Scottish, and Welsh **Missions** in 1902. Also in 1902, these organizations joined as the British **Union Conference**. Church leaders founded Duncombe Hall Missionary College in North London in 1902; after several moves it located in Binfield, near Bracknell, Berkshire, in 1946, where it took the name **Newbold College**. Despite these efforts, by 1953 there were only 7,000 Adventists in Great Britain. Some 25 years later that number had grown to 13,000, almost entirely the result of immigration from former British colonies in the West Indies.

As the number of Black Adventists increased, they sought to establish their influence in the church organization. In 1973 they organized the London Laymen's Forum and the following year began publishing a paper, *Comment*, that drew attention to the situation of Blacks in a Caucasian-dominated church organization. In 1976 the church defeated a proposal to establish **regional conferences** similar to those in the **United States**. **General Conference** officers came to Great Britain in 1978 and recommended that the conferences and union conferences place Blacks in leadership positions. A short time later both conferences elected their first Black officers. In 1985 Cecil R. Perry, a Black, became president of the South England Conference and in 1991 president of the British Union Conference. By the mid-1990s the Adventist church in Great Britain had become a largely Black denomination. Ironically, the new Black leadership found it necessary to appoint a Caucasian director of **evangelism** so that the church could reach beyond the immigrant community. As of 2003 the British Union Conference, part of the Trans-**European Division**, had 218 churches with a membership of about 21,000. The division operated Newbold College while the union conference held the Stanborough Press, the Roundelwood Centre and Nursing Home, and two secondary schools.

GREAT CONTROVERSY. Phrase used by Seventh-day Adventists to refer to the cosmic conflict between God and Satan. In the second edition of his pamphlet *The Seventh-day Sabbath, A Perpetual Sign* (1846), **Joseph Bates** introduced the basic sabbatarian Adventist understanding of history when he argued that God's faithful remnant, who keep the seventh-day Sabbath, are at war with the beast whose mark or sign is Sunday observance. **Ellen G. White** gradually developed this concept into a theological perspective that encompassed all existence, both physical and spiritual. Based on a vision she experienced on March 14, 1858, she began describing her understanding of history in *Spiritual Gifts*, vol. 1, *The Great Controversy Between Christ and His Angels and Satan and His Angels* (1858), which covered events from the fall of Lucifer in heaven to the recreation of the new earth. In *Spiritual Gifts*, vol. 3, *Important Facts of Faith in Connection With the History of Holy Men of Old* (1864) she discussed biblical history from the Creation to the giving of the Ten Commandments; volume 4, *Important Facts of Faith: Laws of Health and Testimonies* (1864), continued her account to the time of Solomon and briefly examined the first advent of Jesus. She later expanded these works in *The Spirit of Prophecy*, 4 vols. (1870-84), each volume of which carried the phrase "Great Controversy" in its subtitle. Her final reworking of this material appeared in the "Conflict of the Ages Series," which included *Patriarchs and Prophets* (1890), *The Story of Prophets and Kings* (1917), *The Desire of Ages* (1898), *The Acts of the Apostles* (1911), and *The Great Controversy Between Christ and Satan* (1888).

As her ideas ultimately developed, White explained history as a trial in which Satan charges that God is unfit to rule the universe. Fallen human beings, as well as unfallen angels and inhabitants of other worlds, comprise the jury that observes how the consequences of Satan's rebellion work themselves out within earthly history. As a result of Satan's challenge, God has initiated a plan in which he seeks to save the human race from the sin into which it has fallen. While the key elements in this plan are the incarnation, death, and resurrection of Jesus and the **Second Advent**, White believed that as history moved toward its end, God's truth—which humans had corrupted—would be restored, beginning with the Protestant Reformation and culminating in the preaching of the seventh-day Sabbath doctrine. This restoration would produce increasing conflict between those who are truly faithful to God and those who follow Satan and thereby demonstrate to the universe the destructive nature of Satan's principles. As human history reaches its final crisis, however, Jesus will intervene by returning to take the faithful of all ages to heaven where they will spend the **millennium**, at the end of which Satan and his followers will be completely destroyed. With God vindicated, the saints will return to the new earth where Christ reigns and sin will arise no more.

GREAT DISAPPOINTMENT. Term commonly used by Seventh-day Adventists to refer to the mistaken expectation of the **Millerites** that the second coming of Jesus would take place on October 22, 1844. *See also* MILLER, WILLIAM; MILLERITE MOVEMENT; SANCTUARY DOCTRINE.

GREECE. Although H. A. Henderson went to Greece for about two years in 1899-1900 and **Warren E. Howell** arrived in 1907 to work for another two years, they won no converts to Seventh-day Adventism. The first Greek convert appears to have been George Brakas, who had come into contact with a **Sabbath**-observing group, but apparently not Adventist, in Constantinople in 1908. The following year R. S. Greaves of the Turkish **Mission** met Brakas and **baptized** him and three other members of his family. In 1910 Greaves baptized another man in Athens who had accepted Adventism as a result of reading publications that had been sent to him from America. Greaves established the Greek Mission that same year and stayed in the country until World War I, returning again in 1921. Meanwhile, political difficulties caused many Greeks to flee **Turkey** for Greece. Among these refugees were some Adventists who in Thessaloniki formed the first Adventist **church** in 1923. Churches also organized in Athens and Berea in the 1920s. Adventist progress in this Orthodox country was very slow, however. As of 2003 the Greek Mission, an attached **field** of the Trans-**European Division**, had six churches with a membership of 277.

GREEN, WILLIAM HAWKINS (1871-1928). African American Seventh-day Adventist **minister** and church administrator. Green earned a degree in law from Shaw University and practiced the legal profession in Washington, D.C. and North Carolina before becoming a Seventh-day Adventist in 1901. Entering the ministry, he pastored churches in Pittsburgh, Atlanta, Washington, D.C., and Detroit between 1905 and 1918. In 1918 he became the first African American secretary of the Negro **Department** of the **General Conference**, serving in that position until his death in 1928.

GREENLAND. Andreas Nielsen from **Denmark** arrived in Greenland in 1954 to begin **evangelism, baptizing** his first convert that same year. The church operated the Sködsborg Clinic in Gödthaab between 1959 and 1992. The *Adventist Encyclopedia* (1996) reported that there were 13 church members in 1993. As of 2003 Greenland was part of the Danish Union of Churches of the Trans-**European Division**.

GRENADA. As of 2003 the Grenada **Mission**, organized in 1983 as part of the Caribbean **Union Conference** of the Inter-American **Division**, had 33 **churches** and over 9,500 members. *See also* LEEWARD AND WINDWARD ISLANDS.

GRIGGS, FREDERICK (1867-1952). Seventh-day Adventist educator. After graduating from high school, Frederick Griggs successfully passed the examination for a teaching certificate and took a position for the 1887-88 academic year at the Swan Creek School in Michigan. After teaching for a year, he attended **Battle Creek College** in 1888-89 before returning to the Swan Creek School for the following year. In 1890 Griggs became principal of the preparatory school at Battle Creek College. In 1896-97 he attended the University of Buffalo, returning to Battle Creek College to establish a one-year teacher's training course. After becoming principal of **South Lancaster Academy** in 1899, Griggs served as secretary of the **General Conference** Department of **Education**, a position he held from 1903 until 1910 and again between 1915 and 1918.

During his first term as education secretary, Griggs guided the development of a system of clearly defined Adventist elementary, secondary, and tertiary schools. He also helped denominational schools pull back from the radical reforms instituted by **Edward A. Sutherland** at Battle Creek College in favor of a more moderate approach that sought to combine academic quality with spiritual concern and practical experience. Between 1910 and 1914 Griggs served as president of **Union College**, where he reorganized the curriculum and restored the school to financial health. After another stint at the Department of Education, he became president of **Emmanuel Missionary College**, which achieved junior college accreditation during his administration and increased its enrollment.

In 1925 Griggs became field secretary of the General Conference and in 1931 president of the Far Eastern **Division**, followed by the presidency of the **China** Division from 1936 to 1938. After returning to the **United States**, he served as a field secretary of the General Conference, with the responsibility of serving as chairman of the boards of the **Pacific Press Publishing Association** and the **College of Medical Evangelists**. He retired in 1949.

GUADELOUPE. Seventh-day Adventist missionary Philip Giddings opened the first Protestant **mission** on Guadeloupe in 1914, working on the island until 1924. During that time he **baptized** about 12 individuals, most of them of British descent, but a hurricane in 1928 forced most of these converts to leave the island. Two **literature evangelists** from **Martinique** arrived in 1932; the first **church** organized three years later. Adventists opened their first school on the island in 1947 and organized the Guadeloupe **Conference** in 1965. As of 2003 the Guadeloupe Conference (which includes several dependencies of Guadeloupe), part of the French Antilles-Guiana **Union Mission** of the Inter-American **Division**, had 53 **churches** and a membership of over 10,000. It operated two secondary schools.

GUAM AND MICRONESIA. James G. Gibbon, a sailor who had accepted Seventh-day Adventist beliefs after reading tracts given to him by **Abram La Rue**, settled in the Western Carolines sometime after the turn of the century. In response to a letter from Gibbon's son William, Adventist missionaries **evangelized** the island in 1930 and 1932, **baptizing** more than 20 persons. Other baptisms soon followed. Andrew N. Nelson and F. R. Millard stopped in Guam in 1945 while on their way to **Japan**. During their short stay they met with the family of Congressman Manuel Ulloa, who had had contact with an Adventist member of the United States Navy during World War II, and baptized several individuals before leaving. Robert E. Dunton arrived on the island in 1948 and organized a **church**. The Guam-Micronesia **Mission** organized that same year. Limited Adventist efforts took place on Saipan where a dental-medical clinic opened in 1970 and the denomination erected a church building on Pohnpei in 1966. As of 2003 the Guam-Micronesia Mission of Seventh-day Adventists was an attached field of the Southern Asia-Pacific Division with 19 churches and a membership of over 3,600. Four secondary schools and a radio station were located within the mission.

GUATEMALA. Elmer L. Cardey and Claire A. Nowlen established the Guatemala English School in 1908. Five years later J. B. Stuyvesant arrived to head the school and that same year organized the Guatemala **Mission.** In 1927 J. E. Boehme established mission work among the Indians at Solala. Much of subsequent Adventist efforts took place among the Indians. Adventists opened their first medical clinic in 1962. As of 2003 Guatemala was organized into the Central Guatemala Conference and the East and West Guatemala Missions, which were part of the Central American **Union Conference** of the Inter-American **Division.** The conference and missions had 343 **churches** with a membership of over 98,000. The Progreso Adventist Co-Educational School was located in Guatemala City.

GUINEA. A lay couple introduced Seventh-day Adventism into Guinea in 1987 and in 1992 refugees from **Liberia,** including an Adventist **minister,** arrived. **Adventist Frontier Missions** began working in the area in the 1990s. As of 2003 Guinea was combined with **Côte d'Ivoire** as a **mission,** part of the Sahel **Union Mission** of the Western **Africa Division.** The mission had 46 **churches** and a membership of nearly 8,400.

GUINEA-BISSAU. The first two Adventists on Guinea-Bissau converted in 1955 after reading a book that had probably been sold by a visiting **literature evangelist.** Permanent Adventist work began in 1973 with the arrival of Francisco Cordas from Portugal. The first **church** organized the following year and the Guinea-Bissau **Mission** formed in 1985. As of 2003 the mission was part of the Sahel Union Mission of the Western **Africa Division.** It had two churches with a membership of over 1,600.

GUYANA. According to early reports, Seventh-day Adventism first entered British Guyana in 1883 when a sea captain, who had been asked to take Adventist publications to Georgetown, scattered papers on the wharf. Some individuals who read those papers contacted the International **Tract and Missionary Society,** which arranged for a **literature evangelist** who visited the country in 1886. The following year the **General Conference** sent G. G. Rupert who, during his short stay, baptized 30 individuals and organized a **church**. By 1892 there were 41 Adventists and in 1895 a second church organized. In 1897 the West Indian **Mission Field** formed, followed by the East Caribbean **Conference** in 1903 and the British Guiana Conference in 1906. In 1924 British Guiana joined with French and Dutch Guiana to create the Guiana Mission, which became the Guiana **Conference** two years later. Meanwhile, in 1910-11 Ovid E. Davis began working among the Indians in the interior but died soon thereafter. When A. W. Cott reached these people in 1927 he found them still singing hymns that they had learned from Davis. Although an Adventist physician worked in British Guiana for a time beginning in 1908, the denomination did not establish significant medical work until the 1950s. As of 2003 the Guyana Conference, part of the Caribbean **Union Conference** of the Inter-American **Division**, had 121 churches with a membership of about 41,000. The Davis Memorial Clinic and Hospital was located in Georgetown.

H

HAITI. The first Seventh-day Adventist converts in Haiti resulted from exposure to denominational **publications**. Henry Williams and his wife began observing the **Sabbath** in 1879 and Michel Nord Isaac, a Methodist minister, adopted the doctrine in 1904 or 1905 and made other converts. W. Jay Tanner, an Adventist **evangelist**, arrived in Haiti in December 1905 and **baptized** more than 40 individuals. The Haitian **Mission** organized that same year. E. Fawer, an Adventist **minister** from **Europe**, arrived in 1907 and organized the first Seventh-day Adventist **church**. By the end of that year there were over 80 Adventists in Haiti. As other workers arrived, membership continued to increase, reaching more than 600 by 1920. In 1921 Adventists began their **educational** work with the opening of the Haitian Seminary and by 1924 there were Adventist churches in all parts of the country. In 1959 the denomination divided the mission into the North and South Haiti Missions; two years later the southern mission began Adventist medical work with the opening of a small clinic. As of 2003 the Haitian Union Mission, established in 1989, was part of the Inter-American **Division**, and had 351 **churches** with a membership of over 260,000. It operated the Haitian Adventist University, two secondary schools, and the Adventist Hospital of Haiti.

HALLIWELL, LEO BLAIR (1891-1967). Seventh-day Adventist missionary. Converted to Adventism while a young man, Halliwell and his wife Jessie went to **Brazil** in 1921 to serve as missionaries. Concerned with the health conditions of the people living along the Amazon, Halliwell took a course in the treatment of tropical diseases, raised money to build a river launch, and designed and built the boat. In 1931 he launched the *Luzeiro* (Lightbearer). With his wife, who was a nurse, for the next 25 years he traveled the Amazon, treating people for disease and **evangelizing**. In 1958 the Brazilian government honored the Halliwells with the National Order of the Southern Cross. The Halliwells inspired others to follow their example; by 1979 there was a fleet of 14 launches with nine doctors and 17 nurses as well as other workers. Halliwell wrote about his experiences in *Light Bearer to the Amazon* (1945) and *Light in the Jungle* (1959).

HAMMILL, RICHARD (1913-1997). Seventh-day Adventist **educator** and church administrator. After graduating from **Walla Walla College** in 1936 Hammill served in various **evangelistic** and pastoral capacities until going as a missionary to **Vietnam** in 1940. When Japanese forces invaded that country in August 1941, Hammill and his family moved to the **Philippines** where a few months later he was arrested by the Japanese and placed in an internment camp. Released from the camp in 1945, Hammill returned to the **United States** and earned an M.A. in biblical languages from the **Seventh-day Adventist Theological Seminary**. In 1946 he began teaching at Southern Missionary College (SMC); two years later he attended the University of Chicago, where he completed a Ph.D. in Old Testament Studies in 1950. Returning to SMC, he became academic dean in 1952. Three years later he joined the Department of Education of the **General Conference** (GC) as associate secretary. Among other responsibilities he served as editor of the *Journal of True Education* (later the *Journal of Adventist Education*) and played a key role in the discussions that led to the establishment of the **Geoscience Research Institute** and **Andrews University** (AU). In 1963 Hammill became president of AU, helping stabilize the new institution and expanding its offerings to include doctoral level education and a program of international academic affiliations, beginning with **Helderberg College** in **South Africa**. Elected a vice president of the GC in 1976, he helped establish the **University of Eastern Africa, Baraton** and Adventist University of Central Africa. Hammill retired in 1980 and subsequently published his autobiography, entitled *Pilgrimage* (1992).

HARE, ROBERT (1858-1953). Seventh-day Adventist **evangelist** and editor. A native of **New Zealand,** Hare was a boat-builder when he converted to Adventism in 1885 as a result of the preaching of **Stephen N. Haskell.** He then attended Healdsburg College (later **Pacific Union College**) in the **United States,** graduating and receiving **ordination** in 1888. He returned to New Zealand that same year to work with **Arthur G. Daniells** in evangelism; two years later he went to **Australia** where he served as an evangelist until his retirement in 1929. During this time he also edited the *Bible Echo* (1898-1902), the Australian **Union Conference** paper, and taught Bible at **Avondale College** (1908-11, 1916-19). Between 1924 and 1929 he worked in **New Zealand, Fiji,** and Pitcairn as well as Australia. He wrote several hundred poems that appeared in denominational periodicals, some of which were collected in *Along Life's Journey* (1948), and published two children's books, *Tales of Grit for Boys and Girls* (1938) and *Stories that Inspire* (1939).

HARTLAND INSTITUTE OF HEALTH AND EDUCATION. **Self-supporting** Seventh-day Adventist **educational** organization located in Rapidan, Virginia. Opened in 1983, Hartland Institute operates an unaccredited "Christian missionary college" and a wellness center, publishes books and the *Last Generation* magazine, and sponsors conferences and **evangelistic** campaigns. Increasingly critical of the alleged departure of the Seventh-day Adventist Church from historic Adventist beliefs and practices, by the end of the 20th century the institute was largely estranged from the denominational leadership.

HASKELL, STEPHEN NELSON (1833-1922). Seventh-day Adventist **minister** and church administrator. A soap manufacturer and part-time Adventist preacher, Haskell accepted the **Sabbath** doctrine in 1853 and a few months later converted to sabbatarian Adventism through the influence of **Joseph Bates.** After working as a **self-supporting** minister in New England, Haskell received **ordination** in 1870 and that same year became president of the New England **Conference,** a position he held until 1887 except for 1876-77. He also simultaneously served as president of the Maine Conference from 1884 to 1886 and the California Conference from 1877 to 1887. Long concerned with the distribution of Adventist

literature, in 1869 he helped his wife Hetty and other Adventist **women** in South Lancaster, Massachusetts, form the Vigilant Missionary Society. The following year, after being elected New England Conference president, he created the New England **Tract and Missionary Society**, which sought to establish local missionary societies in every Adventist **church** within its territory. This organization established a model that the **General Conference** followed in 1874 when it created the International Tract and Missionary Society, an organization that Haskell headed from 1876 to 1885.

Haskell went as a missionary to **Australia** and **New Zealand** in 1885 and to **England** in 1887. In 1889-1890 he traveled the world to investigate **mission** possibilities. Upon his return he again served as president of the California Conference (1891-94) until going back to Australia where he taught at the **Avondale** school and conducted evangelism (1896-99). Once again in the **United States** in 1900, Haskell evangelized in New York, Tennessee, and California, conducted Bible training institutes for church workers, and became president of the California Conference for a third time (1908-11). During the remainder of his life, he engaged in a variety of activities, including **temperance** advocacy, printing books for the blind, helping develop the White Memorial Hospital in Los Angeles, and speaking at various Adventist gatherings. Among his books were *The Story of Daniel the Prophet* (1901), *The Story of the Seer of Patmos* (1905), and *The Cross and Its Shadow* (1914).

HAWAII. Abram La Rue and L. A. Scott arrived on Oahu by 1885 and sold denominational **publications**. In 1886 **evangelist** William M. Healey began holding meetings in Honolulu and **baptized** nine individuals. Two years later A. J. Cudney stopped at Oahu on his way to Pitcairn and organized a **church**. Although later missionaries operated schools that existed for short periods of time, the Bethel Grammar School, opened in 1914, was the first permanent Adventist **educational** institution, becoming the Hawaiian **Mission Academy** in 1921. In the 1920s the denomination spread to other islands with churches organized on Hilo (1921) and Maui (1929). As of 2003 the Hawaii **Conference**, part of the Pacific **Union Conference** of the North American **Division**, had 25 churches with a membership of over 5,000. Hawaiian Mission Academy and Castle Medical Center were located on the islands.

HAYNES, CARLYLE BOYNTON (1882-1958). Seventh-day Adventist **minister** and church administrator. Converted to Adventism at age 18, Haynes received **ordination** in 1908 and actively engaged in **evangelism** from 1908 until 1922, at which time he became president of the Greater New York **Conference**. Meanwhile, he had also served as the secretary of the War Service Commission in 1918, working to maintain the rights of Adventist soldiers as **noncombatants** and **Sabbath** observers. Between 1926 and 1930 he was president of the South American **Division**, where he sought to have nationals move into leadership positions, and from 1934 to 1940 he served as president of the Michigan Conference. With the outbreak of World War II the **General Conference** reestablished the War Service Commission and once again called Haynes to be the director, a position he held until his retirement in 1955. During this time he also served as a member of the **Council on Industrial Relations**, where he developed the "Basis of Agreement" adopted by some labor unions, and as a member of the **Commission on Rural Living**. Among his books were *The Other Side of Death* (1916), *Christianity at the Crossroads* (1924), and *From Sabbath to Sunday* (1928).

HEALDSBURG COLLEGE. *See* PACIFIC UNION COLLEGE.

HEALTH CARE. After experiencing a vision in 1863 that taught her to regard concern with health as a sacred duty, **Ellen G. White** began advocating vegetarianism and the use of natural remedies in the place of drugs to treat illness. She visited **James Caleb Jackson's** water cure establishment in Dansville, New York, the following year and returned in 1865 with her husband, **James White**, to have him treated for a recent stroke. Dissatisfied with some of the treatments prescribed for James and objecting to various social activities at the water cure, she removed her husband to treat him herself. In 1866 she urged the **General Conference** to develop its own health institution; it responded by opening the **Health Reform Institute** in Battle Creek, Michigan, in 1867.

Just another struggling water cure during its first several years, the institute entered a new era when **John Harvey Kellogg**, a graduate of Bellevue Medical College in New York, became director in 1877. Indicating a new direction for the institution, Kellogg renamed the institution the Medical and Surgical **Sanitarium**, although it became generally known as the **Battle Creek Sanitarium**. Also in 1877 he established the School of Hygiene, through which he sought to train **ministers** and **missionaries** in the hydropathic methods and vegetarian diet he advocated. Although this school operated for only a few years, Kellogg reactivated it in 1889 under the name Sanitarium Training School of Medical Missionaries. Meanwhile, in 1883 he introduced a three-month nursing course that expanded to two years in 1884 and three years in 1893. In this program nurses learned Kellogg's system of diet, hydropathy, and Swedish massage as well as Adventist doctrine and the nature of **mission** service. Kellogg also established the **American Medical Missionary College** in 1895 to prepare physicians who were trained in his philosophy.

The Battle Creek Sanitarium became a model for the creation of other Adventist sanitariums. The Rural Health Retreat, later renamed St. Helena Sanitarium, opened in northern California in 1878, but rapid expansion of Adventist health care took place after the formation of the Medical Missionary and Benevolent Association (MMBA) in 1893, with Kellogg as its president. Promoting the establishment of sanitariums and training schools for medical-missionary workers, which would be affiliates of the organization, the MMBA initiated a period of growth. In 1896 the association listed 17 sanitariums, 12 of which were located outside the **United States**. By 1901 the total number had increased to 27 and in 1908 it stood at 78, of which 40 were operated by the denomination while the others were private enterprises. The size of these institutions ranged from less than 15 to more than 100 beds but most of them were between 30 and 50 beds. Nearly all of the sanitariums, both denominational and private, operated training schools for missionary nurses. Financial pressures on the smaller institutions and the conflict between Kellogg and denominational leaders, which resulted in the dismantling of the MMBA in 1904 and the dropping of the doctor's church membership three years later, led to the closure of several sanitariums and the American Medical Missionary College.

Despite these problems Seventh-day Adventists continued to regard health care as an important part of their mission, often calling it the "right arm of the message," for it provided an entering wedge for missionary work. They opened a sanitarium and nursing program in Loma Linda, California, in 1906, naming the institution the **College of Medical Evangelists** in 1909. The following year the school began offering a full medical course. By 1921 the church was operating 20 sanitariums in North America and 14 elsewhere. By 1940 the number of sanitariums in North America had dropped to 15 while those abroad had increased to 51, **Asia** and **Africa** having 36. The largest of all Adventist medical institutions was **Sködsborg Sanitarium** in **Denmark**, which had 315 beds in 1940, but three sanitariums in **China** and another three also outside North America had a bed capacity over 100. The total bed capacity in North America was 1,800; elsewhere it was over 5,800, two-thirds of which was in **Latin America**, Africa, and Asia. Particularly notable institutions included **Sydney Sanitarium and Hospital (Australia)**, Mwami Mission Hospital (Nyasaland/**Zimbabwe**), Shanghai Sanitarium (**China**), and River Plate Sanitarium (**Argentina**).

Treatment rooms that provided outpatient services also became significant during this period, their number increasing from 10 in 1921 to 68 in 1940, three-quarters of which were located in Africa and Asia, not including China. Operated by physicians or nurses, they offered a flexible and relatively inexpensive means of providing medical care. Perhaps the foremost example of this flexibility was **Leo Halliwell's** use of a boat, beginning in 1931, to provide medical services to the people along the Amazon. In 1940 these various small enterprises treated over 200,000 patients.

Although World War II and nationalization of hospitals in some countries closed several Adventist medical facilities, the total number of all types continued to grow, reaching over 400 by 1975 and 500 in 1995; during that same 20 year period the number of patients treated increased from 4,500,000 to over 7,000,000. New hospitals, a term that increasingly replaced sanitarium because of the emphasis on acute care, opened in such places as **Mexico, Nicaragua, Jamaica, Puerto Rico, Brazil, Pakistan, Tanganyika**, and **Uganda**, among others. While hospitals were larger and therefore received more attention, dispensaries, medical and dental clinics, and medical boats were an equally important component of Adventist health care. Although used previously in a limited way, beginning in the 1960s airplanes became an important means of reaching remote locations. To support its expanding health care system, particularly in Latin America, the church opened medical schools at **Montemorelos University** (1975) and **River Plate University** (1994). Many of its colleges and universities also continued to offer nursing programs.

New treatments also emerged. In the 1940s Adventist physicians developed a treatment for *fogo selvagem* or "savage fire," a previously untreatable skin disease common in Brazil. In 1978 the denomination received the Indigenous Medal of Merit from the Brazilian government for this and other medical work. More notoriously, in 1984 Dr. Leonard Bailey of Loma Linda University gained worldwide attention when he transplanted a baboon's heart into two-week-old "Baby Fae." Although this infant died, Bailey continued to transplant human hearts into babies, performing over

200 such surgeries by 1996 and becoming a leading physician in
the procedure. Meanwhile, in 1990 the Loma Linda Medical Center opened the Proton Treatment Center, the first such hospital-
based program in the world, treating some 2,000 patients by 1996.
This high-technology approach to medicine symbolized the dramatic transformation of Adventist health care from its humble water cure beginnings.

HEALTH REFORM. Promotion of healthful eating, **temperance**, and
drugless medicine. Seventh-day Adventism emerged during a period when a number of health reformers, including Sylvester Graham, **James C. Jackson**, and Dio Lewis, were advocating such
practices as vegetarianism and hydrotherapy. Influenced by these
ideas, by the 1850s several sabbatarian Adventists had adopted a
variety of health reform practices. No systematic approach to the
issue of health developed, however, until after **Ellen G. White** experienced a vision at Otsego, Michigan, in 1863, which influenced
her to promote temperance, vegetarianism, and the use of natural
remedies as a part of Adventist religious practice. In 1864 she included a chapter on health in *Spiritual Gifts*, vol. 4, in which she
condemned the use of pork by Adventists who continued to eat
meat, advocated a vegetarian diet, and opposed the use of drugs.
Later that year, Ellen and **James White** visited Dr. James C. Jackson's "Our Home Hygienic Institute," a water-cure in Dansville,
New York, where they learned first-hand about drugless treatments. Returning to Battle Creek, Ellen prepared a series of pamphlets entitled *Health, or How to Live*, each of them including an
article by her as well as excerpts from major health reform writers.
When James suffered a stroke in 1865, Ellen took him to Dr.
Jackson's establishment but, not fully agreeing with the doctor's
treatment program and concerned about the social activities at the
institution, after three months she brought her husband back to
Battle Creek. At this point, Ellen White recommended that the
General Conference establish a health reform institution of its
own. In 1866 the **Health Reform Institute** opened in Battle Creek
but struggled to maintain its existence until **John Harvey Kellogg**
became superintendent in 1876. Under his leadership, the institute
became known as the **Battle Creek Sanitarium** and during the
next decade developed into a model for Adventist **sanitariums
and hospitals** elsewhere.

In addition to establishing a health reform institution, the Adventists in 1866 also began publishing a journal, *The Health Reformer*, edited by Dr. Horatio S. Lay, who had served on Dr. Jack-

son's staff. When subscriptions began to decline, largely because columnist Russell B. Trall opposed the use of such things as salt, butter, and eggs, James White took over the editorship in 1871; in 1874 Kellogg became editor and four years later changed the magazine's name to *Good Health*. As the denomination spread geographically, it started up other magazines including *Good Health* (London), *Australasian Good Health*, and *Pacific Health Journal* (California). In 1904, partly because *Good Health* was entirely under Kellogg's control, the **Review and Herald Publishing Association** took over the *Pacific Health Journal*, which was published by the Pacific **Union Conference**. In July the magazine appeared as *Life and Health*, the name under which it was published—except for a few months in 1915—until 1981 when it was renamed *Your Life and Health*. In 1985 the magazine took the name *Vibrant Health*. Although this journal remained the denomination's chief health publication in the **United States**, by the end of the 20th century the church was publishing more than 20 other health-related journals worldwide in a variety of languages. Like the early Adventist health reformers, these publications continued to emphasize healthful living, including vegetarianism, exercise, and temperance. But unlike their mid-19th century predecessors, they accepted standard medical practice for treating diseases.

In addition to institutions and magazines, Adventists developed food factories, beginning at the Battle Creek Sanitarium in the 1880s, to produce meat substitutes, cereals, and other products. In the United States **Loma Linda Foods** and **Worthington Foods** became important enterprises, while **Sanitarium Health Foods** in Australia reached well beyond the Adventist market. The denomination also published numerous cookbooks, which in recent years have included vegan as well as vegetarian cuisine.

While the phrase "health reform" was no longer prominent in the Adventist vocabulary by the late 20th century, the concern with healthful living has remained an important element of the denomination's outlook. Numerous studies have examined Adventist populations to determine the relationship between diet and heart disease and cancer, among other issues. Some of these studies have suggested that Adventists in the United States have a life span that averages six years longer than the average of the general population. There is considerable variation in Adventist practice, however. Although temperance, including the avoidance of alcoholic beverages, tobacco, and drugs, is expected behavior for church members, vegetarianism has always been an individual decision

and has no bearing on denominational membership. *See also*
HEALTH CARE; SANITARIUMS AND HOSPITALS.

HEALTH REFORM INSTITUTE. *See* BATTLE CREEK SANI-
TARIUM.

HELDERBERG COLLEGE. Seventh-day Adventist educational institution located in Somerset West, Cape, **South Africa**. With
funds provided primarily by **Pieter Wessels**, a South African layman, the school opened as Claremont Union College at Claremont
in 1893. The first Adventist college to be established outside North
America, the institution offered an educational program extending
from primary through tertiary levels. Its college subjects included
Greek, Latin, trigonometry, geometry, chemistry, physics, logic,
and moral science; most of the school's 31 graduates became
teachers. Because of the encroaching suburbs of Cape Town, the
denomination closed the school in 1918 and reopened it the following year as South African Training School (renamed Spion Kop
College in 1922) on the Spion Kop Mission Farm near Ladysmith,
Natal. At this location the school emphasized training courses, all
of which had become two-year programs by 1923, for **ministers**
and **Bible Instructors**, and graduated 30 students. Finding the Natal location too isolated, in 1928 the college moved to Somerset
West, where it was called African Missionary College but soon
took the name Helderberg College. During the first few years at its
new location the college continued the programs it had offered in Natal, but by the early 1930s it had developed three-year
programs in theology and domestic science and started a
commercial program in 1946. In 1951 the institution became a
senior college and began offering degree courses of the University
of South Africa as part of its four-year diploma programs.
Helderberg entered into an affiliation agreement in 1976 with
Andrews University to offer B.T. and B.B.A. degrees; in time
additional B.A. programs became available through this program.
The institution entered into another affiliation agreement in 1997
with **Southern Adventist University** for B.B.A. degrees in
accounting and management. While these affiliations made
American degrees available to its students, Helderberg sought
accreditation from the South African government to offer its own
degrees. In 2001 it received this approval. As of 2003 the
institution offered the B.A. degree in six areas and the B.B.A. in
two areas. With the racial integration of the South African **Union
Conference**, which began in 1991, the student body at Helderberg

College shifted from Caucasian to a Black majority. As of 2003 the institution had nearly 400 students.

HENRY, SAREPTA MYRENDA (IRISH) (1839-1900). Woman's Christian **Temperance** Union (WCTU) leader and Seventh-day Adventist writer and speaker. When her husband died in 1871, Henry, the daughter of a Methodist minister, supported herself and her three children through teaching and writing. Beginning in 1874 she organized women in Rockford, Illinois, to promote temperance and soon became active in the recently organized WCTU, for which she became a national evangelist. The WCTU later published a book of her poems, *The Marble Cross; and Other Poems* (1886). Plagued with ill-health in the late 1880s, she had become an invalid by 1895 as a result of a heart ailment. While a patient at the **Battle Creek Sanitarium**, in 1896 she converted to Seventh-day Adventism and shortly thereafter recovered her health. She resumed her work for the WCTU and in 1898 and 1899, having received a **ministerial** license from the **General Conference**, traveled the Adventist **camp meeting** circuit as part of the Holiness revival sweeping through the denomination. Her book, *The Abiding Spirit* (1899), drew from stenographic notes of her presentations. She also developed a plan for "**woman** ministry" and lectured widely to Adventists on the mother's role in the moral education of her children. Henry's books from her Adventist period also included *Studies in Home and Child Life* (1898) and *Good Form and Christian Etiquette* (1900).

HEPPENSTALL, EDWARD (1901-1994). Seventh-day Adventist theologian. Born in **Great Britain**, Heppenstall was an agnostic prior to converting to Seventh-day Adventism at about age 22. After studying at Stanborough College (later **Newbold College**), in 1931 he entered **Emmanuel Missionary College**, from which he received a B.A., and then attended the University of Michigan, where he earned an M.A. in history. After working as a pastor in Michigan for several years, in 1940 he became a member of the religion faculty at **La Sierra College** and while teaching there earned a Ph.D. in religious education from the University of Southern California. In 1955 he joined the **Seventh-day Adventist Theological Seminary**, staying there until 1967, when he left for the Division of Religion at **Loma Linda University**, from which he retired in 1970. Noted for his Christocentric emphasis, through his teaching he influenced many Adventist pastors and religion teachers. A contributor to the *Seventh-day Adventist Bible Com-*

mentary (1953-57) and *Seventh-day Adventists Answer Questions on Doctrine* (1957), he produced his major works after retirement. His books included *Our High Priest* (1972), *Salvation Unlimited* (1974), and *The Man Who Is God* (1977). *See also* CHRISTOLOGY.

HERITAGE SINGERS. Seventh-day Adventist singing group. Founded in 1971 in Portland, Oregon, by Max and Lucy Mace, the Heritage Singers became one of the denomination's most popular musical organizations. Drawing on both country and various pop styles, the group toured widely in both the **United States** and abroad and released many recordings. Along with the **Wedgwood Trio**, the Heritage Singers helped transform popular Adventist **music**, moving it from the traditional gospel songs performed by *a cappella* quartets and singers accompanied by piano or organ to contemporary songs that incorporated both acoustic and electronic instruments as well as percussion.

HIMES, JOSHUA VAUGHAN (1805-1895). Minister and **Millerite** publicist. Born in Rhode Island, Himes became a full-time **Christian Connection** minister in 1827. After working as a revivalist in Massachusetts for three years, in 1830 he became pastor of the First Christian Church in Boston, staying there until 1837. During this time he was active in reform causes, helping found both the New England Anti-Slavery Society and the New England Nonresistance Society. These activities caused friction within his congregation that led to the establishment in 1837 of the Second Christian Church, which asked Himes to be its pastor. The new group built the Chardon Street Chapel the following year. This church building became the center for many reform activities.

Himes met **William Miller** at a Christian Connection conference in November 1839, and invited him to present his views regarding the second coming of Jesus at the Chardon Street Chapel. Miller's two series of lectures, his first in Boston, took place in December and January. After Miller returned to Boston for a third time in February 1840 to speak at another church, Himes decided to help him further publicize his message and began publishing the *Signs of the Times* in March. By the summer of 1840 Himes was emerging as the leader of the Millerite movement, organizing lecture tours and establishing temporary papers in locations where Miller or other speakers were conducting meetings. He published tracts and books, including the *Second Advent Library* and a hymnbook entitled *The Millennial Harp*, and planned general conferences. Without Himes's effort, it is unlikely that Miller's views would have sparked a movement.

Although strongly promoting Miller's message that Christ was coming soon, Himes did not accept the predicted date of "about 1843" until 1842. He also was slow accepting the **seventh-month movement's** belief, which emerged in the summer of 1844, that Christ would come on October 22, 1844, not publicly supporting that predicted date until October 6. It appears that for Himes the nearness of Christ's coming was more important than identifying the specific time of the event.

After Jesus did not return on October 22, Himes both resumed publishing papers and worked to help the Millerite believers. He admitted that the October date was simply wrong and, with the appearance of radical new interpretations and practices among the Millerites, he organized a meeting that took place in Albany, New York, in April 1845. The Mutual Conference of Adventists consolidated the moderate Millerites and rejected the radicals; out of it eventually came the Evangelical Adventists, the **Advent Christians**, and the Church of God of the Abrahamic Faith (later **Church of God General Conference**).

Himes went to England in 1846 where he held meetings and established the *European Advent Herald*. Returning to America, he edited *The Advent Herald*, the publication around which the Evangelical Adventists were forming. In 1855 he went to California for a time and three years later sold his paper to the Evangelical Adventists. He then adopted the view that Christ would return between 1866 and 1868 and for three years published *The Voice of the Prophet* to promote his ideas. In the early 1860s he adopted **conditionalism**, which he had previously opposed, and soon moved to Michigan where he edited *The Voice of the West and the Second Advent Pioneer* for the Advent Christians and served as a minister. Conflict with Advent Christian leaders and charges of immoral behavior, however, led to his dismissal from the paper and the Advent Christian ministry in the early 1870s. In 1874 Himes began publishing the *Himes' Journal* to defend himself, but Miles Grant, an Advent Christian leader, put out *A Statement of Facts Relating to Elder Joshua V. Himes* in 1875, which virtually destroyed Himes's influence in the Adventist community. Joining the Episcopal Church in 1878 and ordained as a minister the following year, Himes spent the remainder of his life as rector of the St. Andrews Church in Elk Point, South Dakota.

HIRSCH, CHARLES B. (1919-2003). Seventh-day Adventist **educator** and church administrator. After military service in Europe between 1941 and 1945, Hirsch completed his B.A. (1948) at **Atlantic Union College** and M.A. (1949) and Ph.D. (1954) at Indiana University. After working at Teacher's College in Connecticut in 1950-51, he became chair of the history department at **La Sierra College**, serving from 1951 to 1955. In 1955 he accepted a similar position at Washington Missionary College (later **Columbia Union College**); four years later he became president of the institution. Between 1965 and 1967 he was vice president of academic administration at **Andrews University** and then moved to the **General Conference** (GC) to become secretary of the Department of Education. In this position he developed a denomination-wide system of school accreditation, transforming the Board of Regents from a North American to an international agency. In 1981 he was elected general vice president of the GC, serving in that position until his retirement in 1985.

HOLY FLESH MOVEMENT. Radical late 19th-century Holiness movement within Seventh-day Adventism. Beginning in 1892, Holiness influences began appearing in the preaching of **Alonzo T. Jones** and **William W. Prescott,** who taught that the Holy Spirit was about to descend and promoted physical healing as a manifestation of the Spirit's work. Although their revival was largely limited to Adventists in the Battle Creek area and died out in 1894, **Albion F. Ballenger** and others again picked up Holiness themes in the "Receive Ye the Holy Ghost" revival of 1897-1900. Ballenger, Jones, and **S. M. I. Henry** preached at **camp meetings** and **churches** throughout the **United States** that baptism by the Holy Spirit would bring both victory over sin and "salvation from sickness." In Indiana, R. S. Donnell and S. S. Davis, respectively president and **evangelist** of the **conference,** radicalized these ideas by teaching that true conversion replaces corruptible earthly flesh with incorruptible "translation flesh," thereby producing "born" sons of God who would live to see Christ's reappearing. Christians who did not have this experience were "adopted sons" who would die and be resurrected at the **second advent.** Accompanied by highly emotional meetings, these concepts spread quickly among Indiana Adventists in 1899 and 1900. Opposition from denominational leaders and **Ellen G. White** brought the movement to a halt by early 1901. More significantly, the experience with what it regarded as fanaticism also led the **General Conference** to stop supporting Ballenger's speaking tours, in the process also ending the Adventist Holiness revival.

HOME STUDY INTERNATIONAL. Seventh-day Adventist correspondence school. While serving as secretary of the **General Conference** Department of Education, **Frederick Griggs** in 1909 launched what was called the "Correspondence School" (soon renamed "Fireside Correspondence School"), with **Warren E. Howell** as president. In that year more than 62 students registered and by 1916 it was offering 11 secondary and nine college courses. The program incorporated in 1931 as "Home Study Institute." In 1990, now calling itself "Home Study International," the organization named its three academic divisions: "Home Study Elementary School," "Home Study High School," and "Griggs University." The following year Griggs University began offering degrees to international students who had no access to an Adventist college. As of 2003 Home Study International was accredited by several agencies and held affiliations with **Columbia Union College, Oakwood College,** and **Andrews University.**

HONDURAS. Some time prior to 1887, Mrs. E. Gauterau, who had converted to Seventh-day Adventism while in California, returned to her home in the Bay Islands and shared with relatives and friends the many denominational **publications** she had brought with her. In 1887 T. H. Gibbs, a **minister** from New Orleans, distributed more Adventist papers and books in the area. Thus when L. C. Chadwick arrived in 1891, he found several people already knowledgeable regarding Adventist beliefs and **baptized** about 20 individuals. That same year Frank H. Hutchins came to the islands to serve as a pastor and established a congregation on Roatan. Two additional ministers arrived in 1893 and by the end of the year church membership had climbed to over 100. The missionaries opened a school that same year and in 1897 launched a mission boat, the *Herald*. By 1905 there were five **churches** and a membership, mostly in the Bay Islands, of 160. In 1918 the Honduras **Mission** organized, covering the territory of both Honduras and British Honduras; by 1937 it had 624 members. In the latter half of the 20th century Adventists accelerated their work in Honduras, including radio broadcasts, translation of books into Indian languages, establishment of schools, and major **evangelistic** campaigns. As part of the **Global Mission** program of the 1990s, church workers emphasized establishing new churches in areas of Honduras without a previous Adventist presence. As of 2003

Seventh-day Adventism in Honduras was divided into three missions, part of the Central American **Union Conference** of the Inter-American **Division**, and had 187 churches and a membership of over 123,000. The Adventist Educational Center and Valley of the Angels Hospital were located in Honduras.

HONG KONG. Abram La Rue, a layman, arrived in Hong Kong in 1888 and began **evangelizing** the seamen who came to the city's ports. An acquaintance at the colonial court translated into Chinese a chapter from **Ellen G. White's** *Steps to Christ*, which La Rue had printed as a tract for distribution to the native population. J. N. Thompson arrived as a missionary in 1902 and **baptized** seven individuals whom La Rue had converted. Although the Seventh-day Adventist Church established its South China headquarters in Hong Kong in 1916, by 1920 there were only two Adventists besides the missionaries in the colony. In 1937 the denomination opened a school and purchased land for the South China Training Institute, which it transferred from Canton to Hong Kong in 1939. After World War II Adventists carried out evangelistic campaigns and in 1949 transferred to Hong Kong staff members from the China **Division** office and the China Training School in the **People's Republic of China**. By 1958 Hong Kong had about 1,600 church members. Adventists opened their first hospital in the colony in 1964. As of 2003 the Hong Kong-Macao **Conference**, part of the Chinese **Union Mission** of the Northern **Asia**-Pacific Division, had 18 **churches** with a membership of about 3,900. Hong Kong Adventist College, three secondary schools, and two hospitals were located within the mission.

HOPE INTERNATIONAL. Independent Seventh-day Adventist organization located in Knoxville, Illinois. Lay Adventists in the Seattle, Washington, area founded Hope International in 1964 because they were concerned about the doctrinal direction of Adventism following the **evangelical-Adventist dialogues** of the mid-1950s and the publication of *Seventh-day Adventists Answer Questions on Doctrine* (1957). Although the organization purchased property near Eatonville and sponsored a variety of activities, it had no real impact on Adventism until Ron Spear, a retired Adventist **minister**, became actively involved in its leadership in 1985. He introduced a bimonthly magazine, *Our Firm Foundation*, organized annual **camp meetings**, and published several books, all of which took the position that the Seventh-day Adventist Church was abandoning its historic beliefs on such matters as the human

nature of Christ, the authority of **Ellen G. White**, and the necessity
of a simple lifestyle. In 2003 the organization moved its headquarters from Washington State to Knoxville, Illinois. The Seventh-day
Adventist leadership issued reports in 1992 and 2000 condemning
Hope International's allegedly disruptive activities, particularly its
acceptance of tithe funds from church members.

HORN, SIEGFRIED H. (1908-1993). Seventh-day Adventist **educator** and **archaeologist**. Born in **Germany**, Horn began serving as a
minister in **The Netherlands** in 1930 before going as a missionary
to Java and Sumatra in 1932. Interned by the Japanese during
World War II, he began studying ancient languages and, upon his
release, took up graduate education at the **Seventh-day Adventist
Theological Seminary**, Johns Hopkins University, and the University of Chicago, receiving his Ph.D. in Egyptology from the latter in 1951. He became chair of the Department of Archaeology
and History of Antiquity at the theological seminary that same
year. Subsequently, in addition to his teaching duties, he led tours
through the **Middle East** for **ministers** and religion teachers and,
beginning in 1960, served as a staff member of the Drew-
McCormick archaeological expedition in Jordan. In 1962 he
founded *Andrews University Seminary Studies*, which he edited
until 1974. From 1968 to 1973 he directed the Andrews University
archaeological excavation at Tell Hesbon, also in Jordan. He also
served as dean of the theological seminary from 1972 to 1974.
Among his publications were *Light from the Dustheaps* (1955),
The Spade Confirms the Book (1957), and *Records of the Past Il-
luminate the Bible* (1963).

HOSPITALS. *See* HEALTH CARE; SANITARIUMS AND HOSPI-
TALS.

HOWELL, WARREN EUGENE (1869-1943). Seventh-day Adventist **educator** and church administrator. After teaching and serving
as an administrator at several schools, including **Emmanuel Missionary College** and **Healdsburg College**, between 1894 and
1906, Howell went as a missionary to **Greece** in 1907. Returning
to the **United States** in 1909, he became the first president of the
Fireside Correspondence School (later **Home Study International**). In 1914 he became assistant secretary of the **General Conference** (GC) Department of Education and from 1918 to 1930
served as secretary of the department. Very concerned with im-
plementing **Ellen G. White's** philosophy of education and main-

taining the distinctiveness of Adventist education, he opposed the move toward accreditation of Adventist colleges in the 1920s. After 1930 he served as secretary to the president of the GC.

HULL, MOSES (1836-1907). Seventh-day Adventist **minister** who converted to spiritualism. Hull converted to sabbatarian Adventism in 1857, probably during an **evangelistic** meeting in Illinois. Soon he began preaching in Iowa and was **ordained** in 1858. During the next few years he evangelized the American Midwest and Northeast, becoming known as a forceful preacher. In addition to tracts, he wrote *The Bible from Heaven* (1863), in which he presented evidence that he believed established the truth of Christianity. In 1862 he began challenging spiritualists to debate, but after one encounter in Paw Paw, Michigan, he admitted becoming confused during the debate. Denominational leaders then sent him to work with **John N. Loughborough** in New England, but in September 1863, he quit preaching for the Seventh-day Adventist Church. Joining the spiritualists, he became a prominent lecturer and writer. Among his books were *The Contrast: Evangelicalism and Spiritualism Compared* (1873) and *Encyclopedia of Biblical Spiritualism* (1895). He also wrote a pamphlet, *The Devil and the Adventists* (1899).

HUMPHREY, JAMES K. (?-1952). Seventh-day Adventist **minister** and founder of the Sabbath Day Adventist Church. An ordained Baptist minister from Jamaica, Humphrey converted to Seventh-day Adventism in 1902. Soon thereafter Humphrey founded the Harlem Seventh-day Adventist **Church**, which by 1920 had a membership of approximately 600. In 1924 he established the Second Harlem Adventist Church, which resulted in the other congregation becoming known as the "First Harlem" church. Increasingly concerned about the position of African Americans in a Caucasian-dominated denomination, at the 1929 Spring Council of the **General Conference** Executive Committee Humphrey proposed the organization of Black **conferences**, an idea that was referred to a study committee where it died. Ironically, denominational leaders later picked up the concept and formed **regional conferences** in 1945. Humphrey, meanwhile, developed a plan for an African American owned and operated community that he called "Utopia Park," which was to include an orphanage, old-age home, and school, among other things. As he raised money for this project in 1929, denominational leaders learned of his activities and asked Humphrey to abandon the program because it allegedly involved the Seventh-day Adventist Church in a private enterprise over which the denomination had no control. When Humphrey refused to do so, the Greater New York Conference removed his ministerial credentials on November 31, 1929. Two days later **William A. Spicer** and several other denominational representatives met with the First Harlem congregation. When it became clear that the congregation fully supported their pastor, the Greater New York Conference on January 14, 1930 voted to drop the First Harlem Church from "its sisterhood of churches."

Subsequently, under Humphrey's leadership, the congregation reorganized itself as the "United Sabbath Day Adventist Church" and, after a short time, began meeting in their former church building which they rented from a Baptist group who had bought it from the Seventh-day Adventists. Three years after Humphrey's death in 1952, the Sabbath Day Adventists moved into their own church building and the following year combined with another Adventist group to form the Unification Association of Christian Sabbath-keepers. Although racial and administrative issues had led to the formation of this group, by the 1950s they differed theologically from Seventh-day Adventists, primarily in their refusal to regard **Ellen G. White** as divinely inspired.

HUNGARY. Although **Michael B. Czechowski** may have introduced Seventh-day Adventist beliefs into Hungary in the late 1860s, he seems to have left no permanent effect. When John F. Huenergardt visited Budapest briefly in 1898, he met Anna Nagy, an Adventist woman who had moved there from Transylvania some time before. In 1901 Michael B. Osz began **evangelizing** in Budapest, where Huenergardt joined him in 1903. That same year, the first Adventist **church** organized in Bekescsaba. In 1907 the Hungarian **conference** organized; by 1925 it had a membership of about 1,000 and reorganized into a **union conference** with two local conferences. Meanwhile, the Hamburg Publishing House had established a branch in Hungary in 1911 that later became an independent institution, operating until the government took it over in 1949. In 1940 the government dissolved the Seventh-day Adventist Church but allowed it to open the following year under the name "Church of the Bible Followers." As political restrictions lifted beginning in the 1960s, two **conferences** organized in 1967 and in 1989 the denomination opened the Advent Publishing House. As of 2003 the Hungarian Union Conference of the Trans-**European Division** had 111 churches with a membership of about

4,000. It operated the Hungarian Theological Seminary and the Advent Publishing House.

HYMNODY. James White compiled the first sabbatarian Adventist hymnal in 1849 under the title *Hymns for God's Peculiar People that Keep the Commandments of God and the Faith of Jesus* and published several other hymnals during the next decade. White's *Hymns for Those Who Keep the Commandments of God and the Faith of Jesus* (1855) was the first sabbatarian Adventist hymnal to include tunes. Most of the **music** in these early hymnals drew from psalm tunes, folk hymns published in **Joshua V. Himes's** *Millennial Harp,* and the genteel classical-style hymns of Lowell Mason and his followers. About five percent of the hymns came from Adventist writers, **Roswell F. Cottrell** and **Annie R. Smith** being the most prominent.

The **General Conference** (GC) published the first official hymnal, *Hymns and Tunes for Those Who Keep the Commandments of God and the Faith of Jesus* in 1869, which was later replaced by *Hymns and Tunes: The Seventh-day Adventist Hymn and Tune Book for Use in Divine Worship* (1886). Gospel songs appeared in **James Edson White's** *Hymns of Praise for Use at Lectures and Revival Meetings* (1878) and more extensively in his *The Song Anchor: A Choice Collection of Favorites for **Sabbath School** and Praise Service* (1878). This latter volume contained the first published songs of **Frank E. Belden,** who produced his own *Christ in Song* (1900, 1908), which served as the denomination's unofficial hymnal until the mid-20th century. Although the GC published *The Church Hymnal: Official Hymnal of the Seventh-day Adventist Church* in 1941, it took about 10 years before the new hymnal replaced Beldon's volume. This new book included classic hymns of the Protestant tradition, gospel songs, and about thirty new hymns composed by Adventists. It remained the standard Adventist hymnal until the publication of *The Seventh-day Adventist Hymnal* (1981). The new hymnal drew many hymns from its predecessor, but also added African American spirituals, German chorales, psalm tunes, a few contemporary popular Christian songs, and new Adventist compositions. The committee that compiled the hymnal sometimes revised traditional texts in an attempt to reduce archaic and exclusive language.

In the 20th century a variety of books appeared for use in **evangelistic** meetings and Sabbath schools. *The Junior Song Book* (1931) was the first Adventist compilation to include spirituals. *Gospel Melodies and Evangelistic Hymns* (1944), a revision of

Roy Allen Anderson's *Gospel Melodies* (1931), offered a popular alternative to the more formal official hymnal. Most of the pieces in *Sabbath School Songs* (1952) came from the second edition of *Christ in Song* while *Singing Youth* (1953) included more recent compositions. *Advent Youth Sing* (1977) was oriented to contemporary songs and printed guitar chords along with the usual musical score.

I

ICELAND. In 1897 the Denmark **Conference** sent David Ostlund as the first Seventh-day Adventist missionary to Iceland. The following year Ostlund printed and distributed books by **James** and **Ellen G. White** and in 1900 began publishing a paper, *The Seed*. Nils Anderson, a **literature evangelist**, joined Ostlund in 1903. In 1906 Adventists organized their first **church** on the island and in 1914 the Iceland **Conference**. The church operated schools and private treatment rooms at various times and places. As of 2003 the Iceland Conference, an attached **field** of the Trans-**European Division**, had six churches with a membership of 537 and operated the Iceland Publishing House.

INDIA. Seventh-day Adventist **literature evangelists** entered India in 1893 and successfully sold their books. **Georgia** Burrus (later **Burgess**) arrived in Calcutta as a **self-supporting** missionary in 1895, preparing the way for Dores A. Robinson and Martha May Taylor, who came later that year. The Adventists were very active in 1896. Burrus and Taylor opened a school for Hindu girls that year, while Robinson held **evangelistic** meetings and published tracts under the auspices of the International **Tract and Missionary Society**. Olney G. Place, a physician, and three nurses also arrived in 1896 to open treatment rooms and train Indian assistants and nurses; within a few years these limited efforts developed into the Calcutta **Sanitarium**. The denomination also opened a second school and an orphanage. By 1898 the missionaries were reporting that four European families and four or five Bengali families had converted to Adventism. When **William A. Spicer** arrived in 1898 he established a paper, *The Oriental Watchman*, which literature evangelists sold in India and several surrounding areas, including Ceylon, Burma, and the **Malay** States. Spicer returned to the **United States** in 1901 and was replaced by John L. Shaw, who oversaw the establishment of the Watchman Press in 1903 and, about the same time, the organization in Calcutta of the first Adventist **church.** By 1904 there were 130 Seventh-day Adventists in India.

During the next several years, Adventist missionaries moved out from Calcutta into other areas of India. They entered the Bombay region in 1905, but did not establish a permanent presence until George F. Enoch arrived in 1908. By 1911 he was operating a girl's school in Panvel, northeast of Bombay, and was translating tracts and books into the Marathi language. In 1907 several Adventist missionaries met with a group of Tamil **Sabbath**-observers in extreme southern India and by 1909 had established a mission station there. And, in 1906 Luther H. Burgess and his wife, the former Georgia Burrus, began working near the Nepal border and four years later opened a school near Dehra Dun. Meanwhile, in 1907 the Calcutta Sanitarium moved to Mussoorie, above Dehra Dun.

During the first half of the 20th century, Adventism grew most rapidly in southern India, which had been strongly influenced by Christianity, where it opened several schools and medical facilities. The denomination in 1921 established the headquarters of the Southern Asia **Division** in Pune and three years later relocated the Oriental Watchman Publishing House nearby. George A. Nelson opened a small clinic in Surat in 1936 that by 1942 had become Surat Hospital. About the same time, Spicer Junior College moved its college operations to Kirkee, near Pune.

Adventist efforts in northern India centered on Lucknow, where the Indian Christian Training School opened in 1915 and a girls' school four years later. Around the same time, the North India Boys' School began operating at Hapur and an English language school in Mussoorie, opened in 1911, provided education for the children of missionaries.

As of 2003 the Seventh-day Adventist Church in India was divided into four Union "Sections," which together formed most of the Southern Asia Division, and three Attached **Fields**. It had 1776 **churches** with a membership of nearly 630,000. Adventist College of Professional Studies, Flaiz Adventist College, Northeast Adventist College, Seventh-day Adventist College—Bangalore, Seventh-day Adventist Community College, Spicer Memorial College, and 15 secondary schools were located in India. Adventists in India also sponsored 11 hospitals and the Oriental Watchman Publishing House.

INDONESIA. The first Seventh-day Adventist missionary to Sumatra, Ralph W. Munson, established a mission station at Padang in 1900.

Five years later one of Munson's converts, Immanuel Siregar, introduced Adventism to the Bataks in northern Sumatra. During the next few years other missionaries, including Sim Gee Nio from **Singapore**, arrived in Sumatra and Java and in 1910 began publishing the *Malay Messenger of Truth*. The first Adventist **baptism** in Java occurred in 1911 and the following year **Griffeths F. Jones** organized the first Adventist **church** on the island. In 1913 the missions in the East Indies, including those in Sumatra and East and West Java organized as the Malaysian Union **Mission**. During the 1920s Adventism spread to other islands in the region. As a result of the work of Samuel Rantung, in 1921 a church organized in the Celebes; other Adventist groups formed on Sabang and Ambon and a training school opened near Bandung, Java. When the territory reorganized as the Netherlands East Indies **Union Mission** in 1929, it reported having over 1,700 members in 48 churches and companies. Despite the disruption caused by World War II, including the internment by the Dutch government of all **German** missionaries, Adventism continued to expand. By 1952 church membership had reached 10,000, a number that doubled during the next decade. As of 2003 the Seventh-day Adventist Church in Indonesia was divided into the East Indonesia **Union Conference** and the West Indonesia Union Mission, which were part of the Southern **Asia**-Pacific **Division**. The denomination had over 1,100 churches with nearly 200,000 members. Indonesian Adventist University, Mount Klabat Callege, Surya Nusantara Adventist College, 10 secondary schools, 18 clinics, and Indonesia Publishing House were located in the country.

INGATHERING. Annual appeal for funds by Seventh-day Adventists to the general public. Jasper Wayne, who lived in Iowa, initiated the program in 1903 when he erroneously received some denominational papers and began to distribute them in return for a donation that he dedicated to **missions**. Receiving a favorable response, Wayne the following year talked about his experience with the president of the Nebraska **Conference;** after **Ellen G. White** endorsed the idea, Nebraska developed a conference-wide plan of solicitation. In 1908 the **General Conference** Executive Committee recommended that all churches adopt the program, called "Harvest Ingathering," which was to take place during the last week of November. For several years the denomination published special issues of the *Signs of the Times* and *The Watchman* (later *These Times*) for distribution in the campaigns. By the early 1960s Ingathering, as it was called after 1942, had collected $136 million, which the church applied to a wide variety of projects throughout the world, including North America. In the 1980s, however, the practice of seeking donations from the public declined, partly because people were uncomfortable asking for money and also because of increased concern about the safety of the young people who played a major role in the solicitation program.

INGS, WILLIAM (?-1897). Seventh-day Adventist **minister** and missionary. Born in England but growing up in the **United States**, Ings went to **Switzerland** in 1877 to help **John Nevins Andrews**. The following year he visited England for two weeks, during which time he converted two individuals to Adventism. He told Andrews about the conversions after returning to Switzerland, with the result that Andrews sent him back to England where, within about three months, he reported 10 **Sabbath**-observers. In response to his calls for a more experienced worker, the **General Conference** in 1878 sent **John Loughborough** to superintend Adventist efforts in **Great Britain**. Ings thereafter concentrated on distribution of Adventist **literature** until returning to the United States in 1882. He served as a minister in the California **Conference**, which **ordained** him in 1884. In 1886 he went back to England where he helped establish a publishing house, returning to the California Conference in 1897.

INSTITUTE OF WORLD MISSION. Seventh-day Adventist program for training missionaries. In 1956 the Annual Council of the **General Conference** Executive Committee voted that a six-week training program for missionaries be established. It took 10 years, however, before Myrl O. Manley and Gottfried Oosterwal conducted a four-week training institute at **Andrews University** for 21 **mission** appointees and missionaries on furlough in which they sought to prepare these individuals to work cross-culturally. Known as the "Summer Institute of World Mission," the program expanded to five weeks in 1971 and six weeks the following year. In 1972 the program's name also changed to "Institute of World Mission." Beginning with one summer institute, the leaders soon added additional sessions that took place in the autumn and winter, and, because an increasing number of missionaries were coming from outside the **United States**, **Europe** and **Australia** developed their own institutes in the 1980s. By 2003 the Institute of World Mission was conducting several programs, including two-week institutes for outgoing missionaries, retreats for missionaries returning to their homelands, retreats for the children of missionaries returning to the United States for schooling, a "Passport to Mission" self-study course, and a training program entitled "Global Partnerships" for lay people who would be working for business or government in areas where traditional missionaries were not allowed to enter. The institute also sponsored "Go" conferences to develop interest in mission service.

INVESTIGATIVE JUDGMENT. Seventh-day Adventist doctrine of God's judgment that takes place prior to the **Second Advent** of Jesus. Based on his study of Daniel 8:14, **William Miller** concluded that the "cleansing of the sanctuary" referred to the purification of the earth by fire at the time of the second coming of Jesus, which he at first believed would take place about 1843 but later more precisely identified as occurring between March 21, 1843 and March 21, 1844. **Samuel S. Snow** subsequently interpreted the date to be October 22, 1844, the view adopted by those who became sabbatarian Adventists. When Christ did not return as expected, **O. R. L. Crosier** in 1845 and 1846 put forward the idea that the sanctuary to be cleansed was the heavenly sanctuary referred to in the biblical book of Hebrews. Drawing an analogy between the sanctuary services of the ancient Israelites and the sanctuary in heaven, Crosier argued that on October 22, 1844 Jesus had moved from the Holy to the Most Holy Place, but he did not explain the nature of the cleansing of the heavenly sanctuary.

Over time, however, the sabbatarian Adventists connected the cleansing of the sanctuary with the concept of a pre-Advent judgment. As early as 1841 **Josiah Litch** had suggested that judgment must take place prior to Christ's return. Miller also posited a similar idea in a March 1845 letter. More significantly, in January 1845 Apollos Hale and Joseph Turner wrote in the *Advent Mirror* that the judgment had commenced on October 22 and that the time of probation had ended, an interpretation that became known as the **shut door theory**. This shut door interpretation was accepted by most sabbatarian Adventists until the early 1850s and probably shaped their thinking about the judgment. Nonetheless, only a few hints of what became the investigative judgment doctrine appeared in sabbatarian Adventist writing prior to 1854 when **John Loughborough** was the first to clearly identify the cleansing of the sanctuary with the judgment of Revelation 14. The following year **Uriah Smith**, drawing primarily on Daniel 10 and Revelation 14 and 20, further developed the concept, arguing that in 1844 Jesus began the process of examining the books that recorded the acts of all men. Finally, in 1857 **James White** gave the emerging doctrine a name when he spoke of an "investigative judgment" that will take place prior to Christ's second coming to determine who will be saved.

As part of the larger **sanctuary doctrine**, the investigative judgment has had a history of controversy within Adventism, with prominent individuals such as **Dudley M. Canright, Albion F. Ballenger, Ludvig R. Conradi**, and **Desmond Ford** criticizing it in various ways. In recent years, Adventist theologians have favored the term "Pre-Advent Judgment" over the traditional "Investigative Judgment."

IRAN. Frank F. Oster and Henry Dirksen worked among Christian groups in northwestern Iran, beginning in 1911. In 1914 Oster gained his first converts, a Russian family, and in 1923 **baptized** his first Iranians and organized the first Adventist **church**. In 1924 he opened two schools, one for Assyrian and the other for **Armenian** children, and by 1926 reported that there were about 150 members in the country. Henry E. Hargreaves, a physician, came to Iran in 1925 to begin medical work; Arsen Arzoo joined him a year later. Although the denomination opened several more schools in the late 1920s and early 1930s, the government had closed all of them by 1940. In 1946, however, the Iran Training School opened and in 1963 received authorization from the government to offer a high school curriculum under the name Iran Adventist **Academy**. After the revolution of 1979, Adventist efforts largely closed down, symbolized by the government appropriation of the academy in 1990. As of 2003 the "Iran **Field**" was an attached field of the Euro-**Africa Division**. It had two churches with a membership of 32.

IRAQ. Bashir Hasso, a native of Mosul, converted to Seventh-day Adventism while living in Beirut, **Lebanon**. Soon thereafter he returned to Iraq and by 1923 had seven persons ready for **baptism** when Walter K. Issing, an Adventist missionary in Beirut, visited Mosul in 1923 and organized the first Adventist **church** in Iraq. That same year Adventists formed the Mesopotamian **Mission**. Other missionaries followed, opening their first school in 1931. In 1946 Adventists opened Dar es Salaam Hospital and the Iraq Training School, both located in Baghdad; the school eventually developed into a secondary institution. The government later nationalized both institutions. The mission elected its first Iraqi as president in 1957 and in 1959 received official recognition from the government. As of 2003 the Iraq **Field** (the name by which it has been known since 1970) was part of the **Middle East Union Mission** of the Trans-European **Division**. It had three churches with a membership of about 200.

IRELAND. As early as 1861 the *Review and Herald* published reports of individuals in Ireland who had become **Sabbath**-observers as a result of reading Adventist literature. In 1885 R. F. Andrews briefly visited Ireland and won one convert. He returned the next year with Sands H. Lane and was followed in 1888 by **Stephen N. Haskell** and J. H. Durland. None of these Adventist missionaries stayed for more than a few weeks, however. M. A. Altman in 1898 and William Hutchinson in 1902 began more sustained efforts and in the latter year the Irish **Mission** organized. By 1933 the denomination reported 33 members in the mission. Toward the end of the 20th century, the denomination sent some lay people to work in Ireland, but membership remained small. As of 2003 the Irish Mission, which included both the Republic of Ireland and Northern Ireland, was part of the British **Union Conference** of the Trans-**European Division**. It had six **churches** with a membership of about 300.

IRWIN, GEORGE A. (1844-1913). Seventh-day Adventist **minister** and church administrator. Converted to Christianity while held at the Andersonville prison during the American Civil War, Irwin was a member of the Congregational and Methodist churches before adopting Seventh-day Adventism during the winter of 1884-85. He soon began working as a minister and served in various administrative positions in the Ohio **Conference** prior to becoming conference president in 1889. In 1895 he became president of District No. 2, an organizational entity that had been created in 1893 to coordinate the state conferences in the Midwest. After his election as president of the **General Conference** (GC) two years later, Irwin unsuccessfully sought to transform the district organizations into effective administrative units. After leaving the GC presidency in 1901, he served as president of the Australasian **Union Conference** until 1905 and then held several administrative positions in the **United States**, including the presidency of the Pacific **Union Conference** between 1910 and 1912.

ISRAEL. Although a few Seventh-day Adventists had visited Palestine prior to 1898, John H. Krum, a **German** Adventist from the **United States**, arrived in Jaffa that year to sell denominational books. Over the next two years two nurses arrived, who opened treatment rooms in Jaffa. In 1901 Krum moved his activities to Jerusalem. **Ludvig R. Conradi** visited Palestine in 1904 and organized the Jaffa-Jerusalem **church**, made up mostly of missionary families and German converts. By 1908 the missionaries were reporting about 20 members. Although World War I interrupted Adventist efforts in Palestine, in 1929 Bror Farnstrom reopened treatment rooms in Jerusalem and about five years later the Arabic **Union Mission** moved its headquarters from Beirut, **Lebanon**, to Haifa, where additional treatment rooms opened. With the advent of World War II and the creation of the state of Israel in 1948, Adventists experienced considerable difficulty, although the Farnstroms stayed until 1952, at which time the denomination had about 12 members in the country. Since that time the church has grown slowly, largely the result of immigration. As of 2003 the Israel **Field**, organized in 1931, was an attached field of the Trans-European Division. It had 13 churches with a membership of about 1,000.

ITALY. An unofficial missionary, **Michael B. Czechowski**, preached Adventist doctrines in Italy in 1864 and made some converts, particularly in Torre Pellice, who later joined the Seventh-day Adventist Church. In 1877 **John Nevins Andrews** visited Naples where he baptized Dr. Herbert P. Ribton, who continued Adventist **evangelistic** efforts. Among the 22 Adventist converts who had been won by 1878 was Romualdo Bertola, a commercial traveler who carried Adventism to several Mediterranean countries and formed an Adventist group in Alexandria, **Egypt. Daniel T. Bourdeau** organized an Adventist **church** in Naples in 1884 and then located for a time in Torre Pellice. Charles T. Everson established an Adventist presence in Rome in 1902 and G. L. Lippolis began working in Florence in 1910 and Pisa in 1912. The first Adventists entered Sicily in 1916; five years later the first Adventist Church on the island organized. Having now spread to several locations in the country, in 1926 the denomination established the Italian Publishing House in Florence and two years later created the Italian **Union Mission**, with 19 churches and 410 members. Although World War II isolated the Italian Seventh-day Adventist Church, membership grew from 845 members in 1939 to about 1,200 in 1945. Also, because of the war, Adventists established a training school in Florence, which opened in 1940 and developed into Italian Junior College. After the war, Adventists began broadcasting programs over local radio stations. As of 2003 the Italian Union of Churches of the Euro-**Africa Division** had 92

churches with a membership of about 6,000. It operated Italian
Theological Seminary, the Italian Publishing House, and several
radio stations and production centers.

IT IS WRITTEN. Seventh-day Adventist television program. **Evangelist George Vandeman** developed a plan for a series of television
programs targeting urban audiences that in 1955 won the approval
of the Autumn Council of the **General Conference** (GC) Executive Committee. First broadcast in 1958 in California, *It Is Written*
addressed doctrinal issues but, unlike *Faith for Today*, used little
music. Originally planned for regional broadcast in conjunction
with evangelistic campaigns, *It Is Written*'s success led Vandeman
to transform it into a permanent weekly program. Although the
first few films were made in California, *It Is Written* program production soon moved to the GC headquarters in Takoma Park,
Maryland. In 1971 it relocated to the **Adventist Media Center** in
Thousand Oaks, California. With Vandeman's retirement, Mark
Finley became the director of the program and principal speaker in
1992. Broadcasts are dubbed into a number of languages, including
Russian and Portuguese. Between 1974 and 1990 a French version
of the program with George Hermans as speaker was broadcast in
eastern Canada.

J

JACKSON, JAMES CALEB (1811-1895). American physician and
health reformer. Previously active as an abolitionist, Jackson became interested in hydrotherapy after an illness in 1847. Soon
thereafter he and Dr. S. O. Gleason opened the "Glen Haven Water
Cure" at the south end of Skaneateles Lake in New York. After
Gleason left the establishment about two years later, Jackson took
a short course at a health reform medical school and operated
"Glen Haven" with the help of Dr. Harriet Austin until a fire
destroyed the building in 1858. Jackson and Austin then moved to
Dansville, New York, where they opened "Our Home Hygienic
Institute." In 1879 Jackson's son, Dr. James H. Jackson, took over
management of the institute. James C. Jackson wrote extensively
for the *Water Cure Journal* and in 1858 began publishing his own
health paper, first entitled the *Letter Box* and later *Laws of Life*. He
also wrote *How to Treat the Sick Without Medicine* (1868). An
article he wrote in 1863 on the treatment of diphtheria, however,
was perhaps the most influential, for it brought him to the attention
of **Ellen G. White**, who soon made health a major concern of

Seventh-day Adventists. After taking her husband to "Our Home" for treatment in 1865, she proposed that Adventists develop their own water-cure institution. Modeled on "Our Home," the Health Reform Institute eventually became world famous as the **Battle Creek Sanitarium**.

JAMAICA. James Palmer, a Jamaican who had received a Seventh-day Adventist book from his father, contacted the International **Tract and Missionary Society** about 1890 and received additional publications, which he distributed in Kingston. Out of these efforts a small group of **Sabbath**-observers emerged. After L. C. Chadwick of the Tract Society visited the group, two individuals began working as **literature evangelists**. Another member of the group, Margaret Harrison, went to the **Battle Creek Sanitarium** in 1893 and while there attended the **General Conference session**, at which she appealed for a missionary to be sent to Jamaica. Albert J. Haysmer arrived on the island that same year and in 1894 organized 37 members into the first Adventist **church**. Largely because a number of young people worked as literature evangelists, church membership grew quickly, reaching 300 by 1896. The following year the West Indian **Mission** organized and in 1903, when membership had reached 1,200, the Jamaica **Conference** formed. The following year the conference sent a missionary to **Puerto Rico**, the first of several missionaries from Jamaica who worked in the region. The first Jamaican **ministers** received **ordination** in 1908.

Wanting to prepare more national workers, Adventists established the West Indian Training School at Willowdean in 1906 and moved it the following year to Riversdale. Although this institution closed in 1913, it reopened at Mandeville in 1919 and eventually became Northern **Caribbean** University. It took longer for Adventist medical work to become established. D. E. Wellman opened treatment rooms in Kingston in 1913, but shortage of funds forced closure five years later. In 1945, however, the denomination opened Andrews Memorial Hospital, also in Kingston. The *Voice of Prophecy* began broadcasting in 1947, which, along with the distribution of Adventist books and the work of lay members in **evangelism**, resulted in Adventism's rapid growth. By the early 1990s, one out of 15 Jamaicans was a Seventh-day Adventist. As of 2003 the Seventh-day Adventist Church in Jamaica was divided into three conferences and was part of the West Indies **Union Conference** of the Inter-American **Division**. Jamaica had 574 churches with over 192,000 members. Eight Adventist secondary schools were located on the island as well as Northern Caribbean University, Andrews Memorial Hospital, and four clinics.

JAPAN. The first Seventh-day Adventist contact with Japan occurred when **Abram La Rue** in 1889 distributed denominational publications in Yokohama and Kobe. When **Stephen N. Haskell** visited Japan the following year he found several individuals interested in the issue of the **Sabbath** and **baptized** one person. In 1896 W. C. Grainger and Teruhiko H. Okohira, a native of Japan who had lived in the **United States**, arrived as missionaries and opened the Shiba Bible School in Tokyo. Other missionaries soon followed and in 1899 a Seventh-day Adventist **church** organized with a membership of 25 and a **publishing** house started operations. The missionaries operated a **sanitarium** in Kobe from 1903 to 1909 while in 1908 Japanese Adventist physicians opened a privately owned medical facility. Harry F. Benson started a training school in Tokyo in 1908 but because of government restrictions, Adventists were not able to develop regular schools in Japan until 1949. The Japan **Conference** formed in 1917 but reorganized as the Japan **Union Mission** two years later, at which time it had 14 churches and 305 members. In 1926 the training school moved from Tokyo to Naraha where it took the name The Japan Threefold Educational School. While the Naraha school accepted only males as students, a similar school for females opened at the same time in Tokyo.

Because of the denomination's ties with the United States and conflicts with official ideology, the Japanese government dissolved the Seventh-day Adventist Church in 1943 and confiscated its properties, which were returned after World War II ended. The Naraha school, which was closed between 1943 and 1947, reopened as a coeducational institution and in 1953 became a senior college. Also, beginning in 1949 the church developed an elementary through secondary educational system. The *Voice of Prophecy* began broadcasting in 1947 and public **evangelistic** campaigns started that same year. As of 2003 the Japan **Union Conference**, part of the Northern **Asia**-Pacific **Division**, had 115 churches with a membership of over 14,000. It operated one secondary school, Japan Missionary College, three hospitals and sanitariums, the Japan Publishing House, and the Japan Food Factory.

JONES, ALONZO TREVIÉR (1850-1923). Seventh-day Adventist **minister** and later critic of the church. While a U.S. Army officer stationed at Fort Walla Walla, Jones attended **evangelistic** meetings conducted by Isaac Van Horn and converted to Seventh-day Adventism in 1874. Upon receiving his discharge from the army, he entered the Adventist ministry and in 1877 became the first president of the North Pacific **Conference**, one month before receiving **ordination**. In 1884 Jones moved to northern California where the following year he became assistant editor of the *Signs of the Times*. Two years later he and **Ellet J. Waggoner** were co-editing the magazine. Based on their study of the biblical books of Romans and Galations, Jones and Waggoner concluded that the Seventh-day Adventist Church wrongly emphasized the law of God. They wrote numerous articles, taught classes at **Healdsburg College**, and preached in surrounding churches that true Christians must rely on Jesus Christ for their salvation, a teaching that they described as **righteousness by faith**. Conflict with the church leadership, including **George I. Butler** and **Uriah Smith,** led to an inconclusive committee examination of their theology in 1886 and a stormy **General Conference session of 1888**. At that conference, Jones presented some interpretations of prophecy that differed from those of **Uriah Smith**, the authoritative prophetic interpreter within Adventism, and made some caustic remarks regarding Smith that helped create a negative atmosphere even before Waggoner began presenting his ideas on righteousness by faith. Although most of those attending the conference appear to have rejected the righteousness by faith ideas of Waggoner and Jones, **Ellen G. White** supported them and during the next three years traveled the country with them speaking in behalf of righteousness by faith.

Jones meanwhile fought in behalf of **religious liberty**. He became editor of the *American Sentinel*, serving that journal from 1887 to 1897. He appeared before the United States Senate Committee on Education and Labor in 1888 and 1889 to oppose the national Sunday law proposed by H. W. Blair. In 1890 he went before the House Committee on the District of Columbia, arguing against W. C. P. Breckinridge's bill outlawing labor on Sunday within the district. And, according to one witness, he attempted to convince President Benjamin Harrison to veto an 1893 law stipulating that the Chicago World's Fair close on Sunday if it was to receive a federal appropriation. Whether appearing before Congress, writing in Adventist periodicals, or speaking publicly, Jones maintained a position of strict separation of church and state.

Influenced by Holiness theology, from 1892 to 1894 Jones and **William W. Prescott** actively promoted a revival in the Battle

Creek area that emphasized reception of the Holy Spirit and physical healing. As part of the revival, the two men advocated the divine inspiration of the visions of a young woman, Anna Rice. But when **Ellen G. White**, who was living in **Australia**, wrote to say that Miss Rice's visions did not come from God, Jones and Prescott admitted that they had been wrong and the revival came to an end. When Jones became editor of the *Review and Herald*, a position he held from 1897 to 1901, he was a strong advocate of the "Receive Ye the Holy Ghost" movement, a second Holiness revival within Adventism, this time led by **Albion F. Ballenger**.

Also, in 1897 Jones became a member of the **General Conference** (GC) Executive Committee and very quickly emerged as a reformer. During that first year he headed a committee that investigated the management of the **Review and Herald Publishing Association** and issued a report that criticized royalty policies and treatment of employees. He called for reform of Adventist **education** and played a significant role in bringing **Edward A. Sutherland** to the presidency of **Battle Creek College**. He also repeatedly called for organizational reform, arguing that the church placed too much power in the hands of a few. Although the GC session of 1901 replaced the position of GC president with an executive committee, **Arthur G. Daniells**, who served as chairman, soon began identifying himself as president of the church. When Daniells pushed through a revision of the constitution in 1903 that restored the presidential office, Jones fought him bitterly. At the same time that he was opposing the concept of a GC president, however, Jones held the position of president of the California Conference from 1901 to 1903.

In 1903 Jones returned to Battle Creek to serve as president of **John Harvey Kellogg's** newly opened Battle Creek College, a rival to the former college which had moved to Berrien Springs to become **Emmanuel Missionary College**. Almost inevitably, he became intimately involved with the growing estrangement between Kellogg and the Seventh-day Adventist Church. Already alienated from Daniells, Jones regarded the GC president as a power-hungry administrator who was departing from the principles of both Scripture and Ellen G. White. In 1906 he strongly attacked the GC leadership in a talk later printed as *Some History, Some Experiences, and Some Facts* (1906). In 1907 the GC asked Jones to return his ministerial credentials; in 1909 Jones requested and received a hearing before a committee, but the committee reaffirmed the 1907 decision. Shortly thereafter, the Berkeley, California, **church**, where he held membership dropped him from its rolls. Although Jones never abandoned Seventh-day Adventist beliefs, he remained estranged from the denomination and associated with individuals and groups that existed on the edges of Adventism, among them **Albion F. Ballenger** and the **Seventh-day Adventist Reform Movement**. He published a journal, *American Sentinel of Religious Liberty,* from 1915 to 1923. Becoming ill in early 1923 he entered the Adventist Washington **Sanitarium and Hospital**, later transferring to the Battle Creek Sanitarium where he died of a cerebral hemorrhage. Among his books were *Civil Government and Religion* (1890), *The Empires of the Bible* (1897), and *The Great Empires of Prophecy* (1898).

JONES, GRIFFITHS FRANCIS (1864-1940). Seventh-day Adventist missionary. A Welsh mariner who qualified as a Master of the Mercantile Marine, Jones converted to Seventh-day Adventism in 1893. After working in health **evangelism** with Drs. Daniel and Lauretta Kress in England, he completed a **Bible instructor's** course at Keene **Academy** in the **United States**. Departing for the **South Pacific**, he and his wife carried out missionary work in French Polynesia, **Singapore**, Java, Borneo, and the **Malay** States. In 1914 he began using a small mission launch, the *Advent Herald*, to **evangelize** the **Solomon Islands**, where he established a school. He later evangelized New Guinea and New Caledonia before returning to England where he engaged in city mission work in London. Leaving his homeland again, he pursued missionary efforts in Algiers, **Spain**, Gibraltar, and **South Africa**. During his life he worked in 38 different countries or islands among people speaking 34 languages.

JORDAN. The first Seventh-day Adventists to move east of the Jordan River were Tigran Zacharian, a **literature evangelist**, in 1912 and Ibrahim el-Khalil, who held **evangelistic** meetings at Es-Salt. **George D. Keough baptized** 12 individuals at Es-Salt in 1926 and organized a **church**. In the 1950s most of the members of this church moved to Amman. Adventists operated schools at various times and places in Jordan, beginning in the 1930s. As of 2003 the Seventh-day Adventist Church in Jordan—along with **Lebanon** and Syria—was part of the East Mediterranean **Field**, which in turn was under the **Middle East Union Mission** of the Trans-European **Division**. This field had six **churches** with a membership of 690. Amman Adventist Secondary School and an orphanage, Amman Care Home, were located in Jordan.

K

KAZAKHSTAN. Andrei Lubchenko brought Seventh-day Adventism to the village of Chernigovka after World War I and soon thereafter several families converted to the new faith. During the 1920s some Adventist **ministers** worked in the Kustanai region and established **churches** in other villages, but when political and religious oppression began many converts left the area and those who remained were not allowed to hold worship services. With the loosening of repression in the 1950s, open religious practice could again take place. Michael Kulakov, exiled in Kazakhstan, reorganized the Adventist church in Alma-Ata and restored contact between the separated Adventist families. Repression again disrupted the churches in the late 1950s but in the mid-1960s Adventists were once again able to hold public worship and began erecting church buildings and establishing new congregations. Beginning in 1968, the churches in Kazakhstan started receiving visits from **General Conference** representatives. The independence of Kazakhstan in 1991 brought increased **religious liberty**. As of 2003 the Seventh-day Adventist Church in Kazakhstan was divided into two **Conferences** and was part of the Southern **Union Conference** of the Euro-**Asia Division**. The denomination had 60 churches with a membership of nearly 3,500.

KELLOGG, JOHN HARVEY (1852-1943). Seventh-day Adventist **health reformer,** physician, and director of the **Battle Creek Sanitarium**. A few months after Kellogg's birth, his family converted to Seventh-day Adventism and when he was four moved from Jackson, Michigan, to Battle Creek. While a teenager Kellogg worked as a typesetter at the **Review and Herald Publishing Association**, where he prepared **Ellen G. White's** *Health, or How to Live* and the magazine *The Health Reformer* for publication. He became interested in the health principles that appeared in these works and in the journals that the Review and Herald office was receiving. He soon decided to become a vegetarian. Meanwhile, he was also working closely with **James White**, who in 1872 encouraged him to accompany his brother **Merritt G. Kellogg** and three other Adventists to attend Dr. Russell T. Trall's Hygieo-Therapeutic College in New Jersey. After completing Trall's six-month course, Kellogg then attended the University of Michigan Medical School but left in 1874 without receiving a degree. With money loaned by James White, Kellogg next matriculated at Bellevue Hospital Medical School in New York, from which he received the M.D. in 1875. While attending medical school, Kellogg began serving in 1874 as editor of *The Health Reformer*, the title of which he changed to *Good Health*. In 1876 he became superintendent of the Health Reform Institute. He soon renamed this institution the Medical and Surgical **Sanitarium**, but as it developed over the next two decades it became famous as the **Battle Creek Sanitarium**.

In addition to broadening the work of the sanitarium, Kellogg implemented his philosophy of health, which he referred to as "biologic living," in the institution's dining rooms. A strict vegetarian, he also opposed the use of eggs, cheese, butter, salt, condiments, and, until late in life, milk. In place of these foods, he advocated a diet of whole grains, fruit, nuts, and legumes and further recommended the consumption of two meals a day and thorough mastication of food. To aid people in adopting his dietary reforms, Kellogg developed a baked multigrain cereal that he called "Granola," peanut butter, and meat substitutes made from nuts and wheat gluten, many of which were sold through the Sanitarium Food Company and the Sanitas Food Company. Further experimentation in the 1890s led to the invention of a flaked wheat product, which he called "Granose Flakes." When the commercial possibilities of these flakes became apparent, Kellogg's brother, Will Keith, established the independent Toasted Corn Flake Company that helped make flaked grains a standard American breakfast food. Unfortunately, conflicts over naming rights for their companies and products that occurred between 1910 and 1921 estranged the brothers.

Kellogg lectured widely to both Adventist and general audiences and frequently presented his views to such professional meetings as the Pan-American Medical Congress, the Mississippi Valley Medical Association, and the New York Academy of Medicine. In addition to editing *Good Health*, he prepared a health almanac that sold as many as 200,000 copies annually. Among his books were *The Uses of Water in Health and Disease* (1876), *The Home Handbook of Domestic Hygiene and Rational Medicine* (1880), *First Book in Physiology and* Hygiene (1888), *Plain Facts for Young and Old* (1901), and *Rational Hydropathy* (1901).

Interested in addressing social as well as health problems, Kellogg took needy children, eventually totaling 42 in number, into his home and with his wife Ella sought to establish an environment that incorporated contemporary theories of child development and psychology. Under the auspices of the Seventh-day Adventist Medical Missionary and Benevolent Association (MMBA), of which Kellogg served as president, he opened the **Chicago Medical Mission** in 1893 and the Haskell Home for Orphans in Battle Creek in 1894. In addition to these activities, he also promoted a number of educational ventures, some of them short-lived, in conjunction with the sanitarium. These included the School of Hygiene (1878), Training School for Nurses (1883), Training School for Medical Missionaries (1889), School of Domestic Economy (1888), American Medical Missionary College (1895), and Normal School of Physical Education (1909).

Toward the end of the 19th century Kellogg came into increasing tension with Seventh-day Adventist leaders, in part because he criticized Adventist **ministers** for not fully adopting vegetarianism and other health reform practices and because he sought, through the MMBA, to control all of the denomination's medical efforts. In the 1890s he also began espousing theological ideas that were regarded as pantheistic. These issues came to a head after the sanitarium burned down in 1902. To raise money for erecting a new building Kellogg wrote *The Living Temple* (1903), which the denomination refused to print because of its alleged aberrant theology. About the same time, he became increasingly critical of Ellen G. White, who had reproved him for some of his actions, and was on a collision course with **Arthur G. Daniells**, the newly elected **General Conference** president who was determined to establish ministerial control over all institutions. Kellogg also attempted to establish a new Battle Creek College, something that did not take place until 1923, which was regarded by denominational leaders as an effort to undermine the newly created **Emanuel Missionary College**. Also, in 1904 he dissolved the MMBA and, in the perception of church leaders, transferred its assets to other organizations he controlled while leaving its debts to the church. All of these tensions led to the decision by the Battle Creek Tabernacle Seventh-day Adventist **Church** to drop him from membership in 1907.

Kellogg continued to direct the sanitarium, which probably experienced its best days in the 1920s, until the Great Depression forced it into receivership in 1931. Kellogg also became active in the eugenics movement, establishing the Race Betterment Foundation which sponsored major conferences in 1913, 1914, and 1928. Beginning in 1911 he served on the Michigan State Board of Health, on which he had previously served in the 1880s, and worked actively to promote health consciousness in the state. In 1930 he opened the Miami-Battle Creek Sanitarium in Florida, concentrating most of his attention on this new institution during the next decade. At the time of his death, he was involved in legal struggles over control of the Battle Creek Sanitarium's assets.

KELLOGG, MERRITT GARDNER (1832-1922). Seventh-day Adventist physician and missionary. Stepbrother of **John Harvey Kellogg**, Merritt Kellogg converted to Seventh-day Adventism at age 20. He moved to California as a **self-supporting** missionary in 1859 and by 1864 had converted more than 12 individuals to Adventism. In 1867 he returned to the East where he took a short medical course at Russell T. Trall's Hygeio-Therapeutic College in New Jersey. On his way back to California he stopped at the 1868 **General Conference session** and pleaded for the church to send **evangelists** to the West Coast. A short time later, **John N. Loughborough** and **Daniel T. Bourdeau** arrived in California, where Kellogg assisted them in evangelistic meetings. In 1878 and 1879 he helped create the Rural Health Retreat, just above the Napa Valley, and in 1893 went as a missionary to the **South Pacific**. In **Australia** he helped design and build **Sydney Sanitarium**. He returned to California in 1903 and, because of health problems, lived in retirement.

KENYA. Arthur A. Carscallen, a Canadian, and A. C. Enns, a German, with the assistance of Peter Nyambo of **Malawi**, established the first Seventh-day Adventist mission station at Gendia near Kendu Bay of Lake Victoria in 1906. With the arrival of other missionaries another station opened in 1909 about 15 miles away at Wire Hill. Four years later the missionaries **baptized** their first Luo converts. Before World War I ended their work, other Adventist missionaries established four additional stations in areas east of Lake Victoria, engaging in **evangelism** and starting schools. Because of destruction by the German army during the war, when missionaries returned in 1920 and 1921 they spent much of their time in rebuilding. Expansion occurred as well, however. Grace Clark established a boarding school for girls at the Kamagambo station in 1922, which, combined with another small school operating at the station, developed into Kamagambo Training School a few years later. Significant medical efforts in Kenya began when Dr. George A. S. Madgwick opened Kendu Hospital in 1925. After 1930 Adventist efforts spread beyond Lake Victoria as stations opened near Nairobi and Mombasa. With the help of government grants-in-aid, Adventist schools multiplied throughout the region, but after the denomination decided in 1956 to relinquish these funds because of church-state concerns many of the schools passed out of denominational control. Church membership grew significantly after World War II and in 1972 D. K. Bazarra became the first African to serve as president of the East African **Union Mission**, which had been organized in 1921. As of 2003 this mission, which included both Somalia and Kenya, was part of the Eastern-**Africa Division** and had 2,882 **churches** and a membership of more than 625,000. **University of Eastern Africa Baraton**, six secondary schools including Kamagambo High School and Teachers' College, two hospitals, many clinics and dispensaries, and the Africa Herald Publishing House were located in Kenya.

KEOUGH, GEORGE D. (1882-1971). Seventh-day Adventist missionary and **educator**. Born in Scotland, Keough worked as an Adventist **minister** in southern **England** for three years, beginning in 1905. He then went to **Egypt** in 1908, where he learned the Arabic language and became head of the Upper Egypt **Mission**. In 1913 he organized the first indigenous Adventist **church** in Egypt and 10 years later became president of the newly established Egypto-Syrian Mission. Keough left Egypt in 1929 to teach Bible at **Newbold College** in England, staying there until 1937, when he returned to the **Middle East**. In 1942 he joined the **Seventh-day Adventist Theological Seminary**, teaching Arabic and Bible until 1946. He then moved to Beirut, **Lebanon**, where he established the Voice of Prophecy Bible Correspondence School in 1948. In 1955 Keough returned to England to teach at Newbold until his retirement in 1965.

KERN, MILTON EARL (1875-1961). Seventh-day Adventist **educator** and church administrator. After serving between 1900 and 1904 as head of the Bible and History departments at **Union College**, Kern became secretary of the Young People's Department at the Central **Union Conference**. This was the first department for young people within the Seventh-day Adventist Church. At his urging, a **General Conference** (GC) council in 1907 recommended that a GC Young People's Department be established, something that was accomplished within the next few months and Kern became departmental secretary. He held that position from 1907 to 1930. Between 1910 and 1914 he also served as dean of the Foreign Mission Seminary (later **Columbia Union College**) in Washington, D. C., and later as associate secretary (1930) and secretary (1933) of the GC. Appointed dean of the **Advanced Bible School** in 1933, he became president of the institution when it became the **Seventh-day Adventist Theological Seminary** four years later, serving in that position until 1943. From that year until his retirement in 1950, he worked as a field secretary of the GC.

KILGORE, ROBERT MEAD (1839-1912). Seventh-day Adventist **minister** and church administrator. When he returned home in 1865 from serving as a captain in the Union army, Kilgore discovered that his parents had converted to Seventh-day Adventism. After adopting their new faith, in 1868 he began working as a tentmaster with **George I. Butler** and **Merritt E. Cornell** in their **evangelistic** campaigns and was **ordained** to the ministry shortly thereafter. At the request of the **General Conference**, he went to Texas in 1877 where, despite difficulties, he organized **churches** in three towns. The following year, the Texas **Conference** formed with about 200 members and elected him president. After establishing Adventism in Texas, he went to the Illinois Conference where he served as president from 1885 to 1891 and subsequently held a number of administrative posts elsewhere as well as continuing to work as an evangelist. He opposed **Alonzo T. Jones** and **Ellet J. Waggoner** when they presented **righteousness by faith** at the **General Conference session of 1888** but later changed his position. In 1890, in the face of racial prejudice and persecution in the American South, he advocated the establishment of separate churches for African Americans, a policy that the denomination later adopted.

KING, GEORGE ALBERT (1847-1906). Seventh-day Adventist **literature evangelist** and founder of subscription book sales. A native of Canada who had converted to Adventism, King at first wanted to be a **minister** but **James White** advised him against it. Instead, at the suggestion of an Adventist layman, he began selling denominational magazines and tracts, including *Signs of the Times*, *Good Health*, and **John Harvey Kellogg's** *Home Handbook of Domestic Hygiene and Rational Medicine*. Encouraged by his success at selling publications, King in the early 1880s urged the **General Conference** to combine **Uriah Smith's** *Thoughts on Daniel* and *Thoughts on Revelation* into an illustrated book that canvassers could sell to the public. In response, the **Review and Herald Publishing Association** bound together several copies of the current editions of Smith's books. When King demonstrated that he could sell this volume, the publishing house in 1882 produced the illustrated edition that he had requested. The volume proved to be a success and King sold books, recruited **literature**

evangelists, and promoted denominational subscription book sales for the remainder of his life.

KING'S HERALDS. Seventh-day Adventist male gospel quartet. Originating as the "Lone Star Quartet" at Southwestern Junior College in 1927, the group joined the *Tabernacle of the Air* radio broadcast in 1936. When the program changed its title the following year to *The Voice of Prophecy*, the quartet became known as "The King's Heralds." An *a cappella* quartet, it became popular in Adventist circles, working in **evangelistic** and **camp meetings**, presenting concerts, and recording on **Chapel Records**. As a result of financial pressures at the **Adventist Media Center**, in 1982 the quartet became an independent ministry and shortened its name to "The Heralds." By 2003 a total of 26 individuals had sung in the quartet, which now described itself as "trans-denominational."

KINNEY, CHARLES M. (1855-1951). African American Seventh-day Adventist **evangelist**. Converted to Adventism by **John N. Loughborough** during meetings in Reno, Nevada, in 1878, Kinney attended **Healdsburg College** from 1883 to 1885. After he served as a **literature evangelist** in Kansas, in 1889 the **General Conference** assigned Kinney to work in Louisville, Kentucky, where he was **ordained** a short time later. He seems to have been the first African American Adventist to receive ordination. For more than 20 years and working mostly alone, Kinney conducted evangelism in the American South. Developing a strategy of working in oneplace for at least six months, Kinney organized his first **church** at Bowling Green, Kentucky, in 1891; many others followed. Because of his wife's illness, he retired from the **ministry** in 1911.

KNIGHT, ANNA (1874-1972). African American Seventh-day Adventist **educator** and missionary. Converted to Adventism through reading **Ellen G. White's** *Steps to Christ*, Knight attended Mount Vernon **Academy** in 1894 and graduated from **Battle Creek College** four years later. After operating a **self-supporting** school in her native Mississippi, she went to **India** as a missionary in 1901. In 1909 Knight returned to the **United States** to work as a teacher, nurse, and **Bible instructor** in the American South. At the age of 98, she served as president of the National Colored Teachers' Association. She told her life story in *Mississippi Girl* (1952).

KNIGHT, GEORGE R. (1941-). Seventh-day Adventist **educator** and author. Knight received his B.A. (1965) from **Pacific Union**

College and M.A. (1966) and B.D. (1967) from **Andrews University**. After serving as a pastor in Texas from 1967 to 1969, he taught at Houston Junior **Academy** for one year; he then worked as principal of the same school from 1972 to 1976. Receiving an Ed.D. (1976) from the University of Houston, Knight joined the faculty of the School of Education at Andrews University, where he taught from 1976 to 1985. He transferred to the Church History Department of the **Seventh-day Adventist Theological Seminary** in 1985 where he continued to teach as of 2003. A popular speaker and prolific author, Knight addressed issues in education, history, and theology. His books included *Philosophy and Education* (1980), *Myths in Adventism* (1985), *From 1888 to Apostasy* (1987), *Angry Saints* (1989), *The Pharisee's Guide to Perfect Holiness* (1992), *Millennial Fever and the End of the World* (1993), *The Fat Lady and the Kingdom* (1995), *Organizing to Beat the Devil* (2001), and *Walking with Paul through the Book of Romans* (2002).

KOREA. While visiting **Japan**, Son Heung Cho converted to Seventh-day Adventism in 1904 through the influence of **evangelist** Hide Kuniya. On the ship that he took back to Korea, Cho in turn converted Im Ki Pan. Once arriving in Korea these men aroused interest in Adventism among Korean Christians, who requested that Kuniya come to their country. Kuniya arrived in August 1904 and soon baptized 70 persons and organized four **churches**. William R. Smith arrived in 1905 and Mimi Scharffenberg in 1907 and together they established a school at Sunan. Additional missionaries, including Dr. Riley Russell, came to Korea in 1908. That same year the Korean **Mission** organized with five **churches** and over 100 members. The missionaries established a publishing house and began printing tracts in 1909 and in 1911 started a paper entitled *Three Angels' Message*; in 1917 they changed the title to *Signs of the Times*. In 1912 the missionaries established their headquarters in Seoul and formed the Chosen **Conference** in 1917. Two years later the conference reorganized as the Chosen **Union Mission**. Meanwhile, in 1911 the denomination established the Chosen Industrial School in Sunan that six years later introduced a two-year **ministerial** course. In 1919 this institution became the Chosen Union Training School. The ministerial training program later moved to Seoul and in 1937 became the Chosen Union Workers' Training Institute. After establishing a clinic in Seoul in 1931, the denomination opened the Seoul **Sanitarium** in 1936, which Dr. George H. Rue directed for many years. With the outbreak of World War II all American missionaries left Korea in early 1941 and two years later the Japanese police arrested the Korean leaders who were directing the church.

Shortly after the war ended, Korean Adventists met together and chose temporary leaders, as several of those who had been imprisoned had died or were in poor health. The first missionaries, including Dr. Rue, returned in 1947. The outbreak of the Korean War in 1950, however, once more forced the missionaries to leave. Nonetheless, the Korean Union Training School opened in 1951; three years later it received authorization to offer a college program and took the name Korean Union College. The military and political upheavals brought native Koreans to church leadership more quickly than in many other countries. Perhaps as a result, the denomination grew rapidly, often increasing by 25 percent annually. By 1968 Korea was itself sending missionaries abroad, going to such places as **Libya** and **Brazil**. In 1969 Adventists opened their first school for teaching English. Staffed largely by **student missionaries** from the **United States**, the school eventually had more than 1,400 students and by 2003 the denomination was operating 33 other such schools in the country. As of 2003 the Korean **Union Conference**, part of the Northern **Asia-Pacific Division**, had 688 churches with a membership of over 167,000. It operated **Sahmyook University** and Sahmyook Nursing and Health College, seven secondary schools, three food companies, five hospitals, and the Korean Publishing House.

KYRGYZ REPUBLIC. Combined with **Tajikistan, Turkmenistan,** and **Uzbekistan,** as of 2003 the Kyrgyz Republic was part of the Central **Asia Conference**, which in turn was part of the Southern **Union Conference** of the Euro-Asia **Division**. The conference had 42 **churches** and a membership of about 3,500.

L

LAOS. Richard C. Hall opened the first Seventh-day Adventist **mission** station in Laos in 1957. By 1961 he and the other missionaries who joined him had organized a **church** with 44 members, most of them from the Maeo tribe. War forced the evacuation of all missionaries in 1962. Five years later new missionaries began arriving and by 1974 they had organized two churches with 87 members. Again war stopped missionary work in 1975 and there was no contact between Laotian Adventists and the denomination until 1984. Although two churches remained active, because of government prohibitions they did not receive a **minister** until 1991. As of 2003 Laos was an Attached Church of the Southeast Asia **Union Mission**, part of the Southern **Asia Division**. It had two churches and a membership of 522.

LA RUE, ABRAM (1822-1903). Seventh-day Adventist lay missionary. A former gold miner, La Rue converted to Seventh-day Adventism while working as a sheepherder in California in the early 1880s. After briefly attending **Healdsburg College**, he went to **Hawaii** about 1883 and sold Adventist publications. His work opened the way for an Adventist missionary who arrived in 1885. La Rue then traveled to **Hong Kong** where he established a mission for seamen and sold Adventist literature. Although working primarily among Europeans, La Rue also distributed two tracts that a friend had translated into Chinese. In addition to his work in Hong Kong, La Rue also distributed Adventist literature in other areas of **Asia**, including **China**, **Japan**, and **Indonesia**.

LA SIERRA UNIVERSITY (LSU). Seventh-day Adventist **educational** institution in Riverside, California. In 1922 the Southeastern California **Conference** of Seventh-day Adventists opened La Sierra **Academy** near Riverside. In 1927 the academy became Southern California Junior College. Twelve years later it received a unique three-year accreditation, primarily for the pre-medical curriculum, from the Northwest Association of Colleges and Secondary Schools. Although World War II delayed implementation of the school's plans to become a four-year college, the school obtained authorization from the **General Conference** in 1944 to offer a full college program and acquired accreditation as a four-year college two years later from the Northwest Association. By the mid-1960s it was offering master's degrees in several fields. Partly because of its geographical proximity to **Loma Linda University**, La Sierra merged with the university in 1967 but continued operating as a separate campus. Organizational difficulties led to a decision to separate the institutions in 1990. The following year the Riverside campus adopted the name La Sierra University. As of 2003 the university was composed of four schools: College of Arts and Sciences, School of Business and Management, School of Education, and School of Religion.

LATIN AMERICA. *See* ARGENTINA; BELIZE; BOLIVIA; BRAZIL; CHILE; COLOMBIA; COSTA RICA; CUBA; ECUADOR; EL SALVADOR; FRENCH GUIANA; GUATEMALA; GUY-

ANA; HONDURAS; MEXICO; NICARAGUA; PANAMA; PARAGUAY; PERU; SURINAME; URUGUAY; VENEZUELA.

LATIN-AMERICAN THEOLOGICAL SEMINARY. Seventh-day Adventist theological program, administered by the South American **Division** office, located in Brasilia, DF, **Brazil**. Established in 1979, the seminary has no campus or faculty of its own but through summer courses offers degree programs on several Adventist campuses throughout South America utilizing faculty from schools in the division who teach intensive courses at a variety of locations. As of 2003 it provided undergraduate programs (including the B.A. in religion and theology as well as other courses of study) on campuses in **Argentina, Bolivia, Brazil, Chile,** and **Peru** and several graduate programs (M.A. in religion and theology—Argentina, Brazil, and Peru; D.Min.—Brazil and Peru; and D.Th.—Argentina).

LATVIA. Gerhard Perk and some Seventh-day Adventist **literature evangelists** entered Latvia in the mid-1890s and in May 1896 **Ludvig R. Conradi** organized a **church** of 12 members in Riga. Because government regulations did not allow public **evangelism,** the growth of Adventism, which reached more than 300 by 1912, occurred largely because of book sales and personal contacts. When Latvia gained independence after World War I and established **religious liberty,** the denomination organized the Latvian **Conference,** established a publishing house and training school, and pursued evangelism vigorously. By 1934 it had over 2,000 members. Religious freedom largely ended in 1935 and when the Soviet Union took over the country in 1940 the church entered a period of further repression. With the loosening of restrictions in the 1970s, the Latvian Conference reorganized in 1979 and, after Latvian independence, again in 1994. As of 2003 the conference, which was part of the Baltic **Union Conference** of the Trans-**European Division,** had 46 churches with a membership of over 3,800.

LAY, HORATIO S. (1828-1900). Seventh-day Adventist **health reformer,** physician, and **minister.** After an apprenticeship with a physician in Pennsylvania, Lay was practicing allopathic medicine in Allegan, Michigan, when he converted to sabbatarian Adventism about 1856. In the early 1860s he took his wife to **Dr. James C. Jackson's** Our Home Hygienic Institute, where he also worked on the staff. In 1865 he became vice president of the National Health

Reform Association. Although Lay returned to his medical practice in Allegan about 1865, the following year he agreed to superintend the newly established Health Reform Institute, later **Battle Creek Sanitarium,** and edit *The Health Reformer.* Disagreements over how both the magazine and the institute should be run led in 1868 to Lay's dismissal from *The Health Reformer* and two years later from the institute's management. He returned to private practice and later obtained an M.D. from the Detroit College of Medicine. In 1884 he became a minister in the Michigan **Conference.**

LEBANON. The first Seventh-day Adventist contact with Lebanon occurred about 1897 when **Abram La Rue** briefly visited the area and left some denominational **publications.** Henry P. Holser from the Central European **Conference** spent a short time in the country the following year. The denomination's long-term presence in the country began when Elias Zarub, a Presbyterian minister, con-verted to Adventism in 1902 as a result of contact with a Syrian who had lived in the **United States.** After spending a short time at **Emmanuel Missionary College,** Zarub returned to Lebanon in 1903 and **evangelized** the area for a time but apparently left the Adventist church in 1908. Meanwhile, W. H. Wakeham, from the Egyptian **Mission,** came to Lebanon in 1905 and **baptized** a few individuals. When Walter K. Issing from **Germany** arrived in 1908 he organized the Syrian-**Egyptian** Mission with headquarters in Beirut. By 1915 the **church** in Beirut had 10 members, but over the next few years the mission had no director and the membership decreased. Revitalization of Adventism in the area occurred when 10 Adventist **Armenian** refugees from **Turkey** came to Beirut in 1923 and established a church. There were both Armenian and Arabic congregations from this time forward.

Soon thereafter Adventists began establishing institutions. They started their first school in 1929; it became a 12-grade school in 1967. In 1939 the Adventist College of Beirut opened to offer a two-year training program for church workers; it became **Middle East** College in 1947. Middle East Press began operating in 1947. In 1959 the denomination established an evangelistic center in Bei-rut, which at various times operated a Bible correspondence school and a physical therapy clinic and conducted evangelistic meetings. Meanwhile, from the organization of the first mission in 1908, the denomination's efforts in Lebanon went through several reorgani-zations. In 1970, along with Jordan and Syria, Lebanon became the East Mediterranean **Field.** The civil war that took place between 1975 and 1991 forced both Middle East College and Middle East

Press to move to **Cyprus**, although they returned to Lebanon when peace was reestablished. As of 2003 the East Mediterranean Field, part of the Middle East **Union Mission** of the Trans-**European Division**, had six churches and a membership of nearly 700. Middle East University and two secondary schools were located in Lebanon.

LEEWARD AND WINDWARD ISLANDS. As was the case in many other places in the **Caribbean**, Seventh-day Adventism first entered the Leeward and Windward Islands through informal contacts and **literature evangelism**. In 1888 Mrs. A. Roskruge became an Adventist while visiting **Great Britain** and on returning to Antigua aroused interest among her acquaintances. About the same time a literature evangelist, William Arnold, came through the area selling books. Between 1890 and 1892, Dexter A. Ball preached on the islands and established a small group of believers on Antigua. Other booksellers and **ministers** worked on the islands during the next few years and in 1897 the area organized as the West Indian **Mission**. By 1903 there had been sufficient growth of the denomination to enable the **churches** of the Lesser Antilles to organize into the East Caribbean **Conference**. By 1907, when the West Indian Union Conference formed, there was a significant Adventist presence on Antigua, Dominica, St. Lucia, St. Vincent, Grenada, Tortola, St. Kitts, and Nevis. In 1910 the mission was operating a small boat in the Virgin Islands and the following year opened efforts in the Grenadines. By the early 1930s the Leeward Islands had 25 organized churches with nearly 1,500 members. Adventists later began efforts on Virgin Gorda and Saba. One out of every 25 people on the island of Antigua were Seventh-day Adventists by the 1990s.

As of 2003 the East Caribbean Conference, part of the Caribbean **Union Conference** of the Inter-American **Division**, included **Barbados**, Dominica, St. Vincent, and the Grenadines. It had 101 **churches** with a membership of over 32,000. The Grenada Mission, which included Carriacou, Grenada, and Petit Martinique, had 33 churches and a membership of over 9,500. The North Caribbean Conference included Anguilla, Antigua, Barbuda, British Virgin Islands, Montserrat, St. Kitts-Nevis, U.S. Virgin Islands, Saba, St. Eustatius, and St. Maarten. It had 63 churches with a membership of over 21,000. The St. Lucia Mission had 33 churches with a membership of more than 11,500. Two secondary schools and several medical clinics were located on these islands.

LESOTHO. David Kalaka, who served as a guide for **Stephen N. Haskell** on a trip to what was then called Basutoland in 1896, became the first Seventh-day Adventist in the country. Three years later he and J. M. Freeman established an Adventist mission station at Kolo. Other missionaries constructed a second mission in 1910. As of 2003 the Lesotho **Conference** was part of the Southern **Africa Union Conference**, which belonged to the Southern Africa-Indian Ocean **Division**. The conference had 25 churches and a membership of over 4,500. Two secondary schools, Maluti Adventist Hospital, and four clinics and dispensaries were located in Lesotho.

LIBERIA. The first Seventh-day Adventist missionaries, R. Helbig and E. Flammer of **Germany**, arrived in Liberia in 1926. The following year they established a **church**, school, and dispensary at Seahn. The first Adventist converts received **baptism** in 1930. In 1935 K. Noltze, who had come to Liberia in 1927 about the time the Liberian **Mission** organized, established the Konola Mission Station in 1935 and two years later opened a boarding school for boys that eventually developed into a secondary school. When the missionaries had to leave Liberia during World War II, an African, I. W. Harding, became the president of the Liberian Mission. In 1945 African American missionaries came from the **United States** to Liberia and took over leadership of the mission. With the start of political and military conflict in 1989 many church members became refugees and the denomination's efforts in the country were disrupted. As of 2003 the Liberia Mission, part of the West African **Union Mission** of the Western Africa **Division**, had 38 churches and a membership of over 18,000. It operated Konola Academy and Seventh-day Adventist Cooper Hospital.

LIBERTY. Seventh-day Adventist **religious liberty** magazine. *Liberty*, a successor to *Sentinel of Christian Liberty*, began publication as a quarterly in 1906. Now a bimonthly, it is published by the North American **Division** of Seventh-day Adventists.

LIBYA. In 1956, after receiving government permission three years earlier, Dr. Roy S. Cornell opened a hospital in Benghazi. In 1968 the hospital moved into a new building, but the following year it was nationalized. Meanwhile, 17 members of the hospital staff organized a **church** in 1960. With the nationalization of the hospital, nearly all Adventists left Libya. As of 2003 Libya was part of the

Trans-Mediterranean Territories, an Attached **Field** of the Euro-Africa **Division**. There were no membership statistics for Libya.

LINDSAY, KATHERINE (1842-1923). Seventh-day Adventist physician and nursing educator. Graduating from the University of Michigan Medical College in 1875, Lindsay joined the staff of the **Battle Creek Sanitarium** and established a School of Nursing in 1883. In 1895 she went to **South Africa** to work at the Claremont **Sanitarium.** While in **Africa** she traveled to a number of **mission** stations in the interior of the continent. Returning to the **United States** in 1900, she became superintendent of the Colorado Sanitarium in 1902, where she concentrated her efforts on the School of Nursing until retiring in 1920.

LISTEN. Seventh-day Adventist **temperance** magazine. Established as a quarterly in 1948, *Listen* became a bimonthly in 1957 and a monthly in 1966. Published primarily for young people, the magazine features prominent personalities from such fields as sports and entertainment who advocate temperance. It also includes informational articles on alcohol-, tobacco-, and drug-free living.

LITCH, JOSIAH (1809-1886). Millerite preacher. A Methodist minister, Litch read **William Miller's** *Evidence From Scripture and History of the Second Coming of Christ* in 1838 and accepted its argument that Christ would return about the year 1843. Soon thereafter the young minister wrote a synopsis of Miller's views entitled *The Midnight Cry.* Later in 1838 Litch wrote *The Probability of the Second Coming of Christ About A.D. 1843* in which he not only accepted the 1843 date but also predicted that the Ottoman Empire would collapse in August 1840. Turkey's response to an ultimatum from European powers on August 11, 1840 was subsequently widely regarded by Millerites as a fulfillment of the prophecy and evidence of the truth of their interpretive system.

In 1841 Litch took a leave of absence from the Methodist ministry to become a full-time advocate of belief in the expected **Second Advent** of Christ. It was about this time that he influenced **Charles Fitch** to once again adopt the Millerite views. He also argued in *Address to the Clergy* (1841) that a judgment would take place before the second advent, a view that probably later influenced the sabbatarian Adventist concept of the **investigative judgment**. The following year, Litch organized the first Millerite **camp meeting** at Stanstead in eastern Canada in June 1842. In

1842 and 1843 he worked in Philadelphia and the surrounding area, establishing a paper entitled *The Philadelphia Alarm*. While in Philadelphia, Litch opposed the influence of **George Storrs** and his theology of annihilationism and **conditionalism**, publishing *The Anti-Annihilationist* for a time in 1844. After **Samuel S. Snow** started the **Seventh-month Movement** by predicting that Jesus would return on October 22, 1844, Litch strongly rejected the idea in August 1844. Nonetheless, by October he had changed his mind and was perhaps the last major Millerite leader to accept the new date.

After Jesus did not return on October 22, Litch participated in the Mutual Conference of Adventists that took place in Albany in 1845. While he rejected such prophetic reinterpretations as the **shut door theory**, Litch maintained his interest in prophecy. Although concluding in 1848 that the Jews would return to Palestine, he increasingly moved toward a futurist interpretation of prophecy, represented by his publication in 1873 of *A Complete Harmony of Daniel and the Apocalypse*. Joining the **American Evangelical Adventist Conference** in 1848, he strongly opposed Seventh-day Adventists, debating **Daniel T. Bourdeau** in 1880.

LITERATURE. Seventh-day Adventist attitudes toward literature have been strongly influenced by **Ellen G. White's** comments condemning the reading of fiction. She believed that such reading promoted immoral principles, excited the imagination, and encouraged light reading and love of entertainment. As a result of these comments, many of which were compiled in *Counsels to Parents, Teachers, and Students Regarding Christian Education* (1913), Adventists often opposed the use of novels and short stories in their schools. This negative view of fiction found its fullest expression in Leon William Cobb's *Give Attendance to Reading* (1966), where the retired English teacher categorically rejected the reading of novels and short stories on the basis of a literal interpretation of Ellen White's statements.

Despite the dominance of this strongly negative view, Adventists revealed some flexibility. Ellen White herself recommended John Bunyan's *Pilgrim's Progress* and compiled religious stories, many of which were fictional, into a volume entitled *Sabbath Readings for the Home Circle* (1878). In "A List of Good Books for Young Folks," published in the *Review and Herald* in 1886, **Dudley M. Canright** included *Pilgrim's Progress*, *Robinson Crusoe*, *Aesop's Fables*, and *Uncle Tom's Cabin* among his recommendations. **Goodloe Harper Bell**, who had taught at both **Battle**

Creek College and **South Lancaster Academy**, advocated a moral stance toward literature and emphasized poetry in *Studies in British and American Literature* (1900). Nonetheless, he included fictional selections, although not identified as such, from Nathaniel Hawthorne, Charles Dickens, and other novelists. This moral stance and emphasis on poetry also characterized George Washington Rine's series of articles on literature that appeared in *The Youth's Instructor* in 1898 and 1899. Rine, who taught English at Healdsburg College and **Pacific Union College**, used the fictional device of a high school classroom dialogue to discuss literary themes, recommending 13 writers that all students should read, among them Washington Irving and Nathaniel Hawthorne. Some 40 years later, John D. Snider published *I Love Books: Why, What, How, and When We Should Read* (1942), a work that went through three editions. Although the subtitle of the first edition, which was subsequently changed to "A Guide Through Bookland," reflected traditional Adventist moral concerns regarding literature, the author took a largely positive view of what he called "imaginative literature." His reading recommendations included *Pilgrim's Progress*, *Robinson Crusoe*, *Hamlet*, and *David Copperfield*, among other works.

After World War II Adventist English teachers began exploring the cultural background for Ellen White's condemnation of fiction and analyzed how terms such as "fiction," and "novel" had developed over time. In 1949 Harry W. Tippett, a former English teacher who was then serving as an editor at the **Review and Herald Publishing Association** (RHPA), presented a paper to college teachers in which he argued that fiction and truth were not incompatible and urged that fiction should not be rejected on the basis of its form alone. Twelve years later, Paul T. Gibbs, chair of the English department at **Andrews University**, examined Ellen White's comments, concluding that when she used the term "fiction," she was referring to cheap, popular stories rather than serious literature. In 1965 John O. Waller, who succeeded Gibbs at Andrews University, examined Ellen White's Methodist background, the popularity of 19th-century magazine fiction, and White's own practice in *Sabbath Readings for the Home Circle*. Waller concluded that critical reading of fiction would meet White's approval.

By the late 1960s increased use of fiction in Adventist classrooms prompted considerable debate which led to the establishment of a **General Conference** Department of Education study committee and the subsequent publication of a *Guide to the Teaching of Literature in Seventh-day Adventist Schools* (1971), much of which Waller drafted. This pamphlet argued that when Ellen White used the term "fiction" she was referring to literature that was "addictive," "trashy," and "escapist" and cautiously recommended that some "non-factual" works could be studied in the Adventist classroom. The debate over the teaching of fiction largely died in the 1970s, although occasionally articles on the subject continued to appear in Adventist publications. While discussing the history of Adventist attitudes toward fiction, Delmer Davis's *Teaching Literature* (2002) moved beyond that issue to engage contemporary literary theory and tentatively explore the implications of Adventist theology for literary criticism.

With a negative view of fiction dominating Adventism throughout much of its history, it is not surprising that Adventist **publishing** houses were slow to adopt the genre. Possibly the first denominational book—apart from the *Sabbath Readings* compilation—to use a fictional device was Charles L. Taylor's *The Marked Bible* (c. 1919), which presented a biblical argument for the seventh-day Sabbath through the story of a sailor who reads an underlined Bible that his mother had placed in his trunk. But books for children and adolescents seem to have most freely used the techniques of fiction. Neal Wayne Northey's four-volume *Old Homestead Tales* (1930-31), a collection of animal stories for grade school children, incorporated dialogue between the various birds, beavers, and other creatures within what appear to have been fictional settings.

Beginning in the late 1940s fictional works for a young audience, though never labeled as novels, appeared more frequently. Adventist publishers regarded as "non-factual" such works as R. E. Finney, Jr.'s *Judy Steps Out* (1948), **Arthur S. Maxwell's** *The Secret of the Cave* (1951), Mabel Earp Cason's *Spotted Boy and the Comanches* (1963), and June Strong's *Project Sunlight* (1980). By the 1990s, paralleling the increasing popularity of religious fiction produced by evangelical publishers, **Pacific Press Publishing Association** (PPPA) and RHPA frequently published novels—though still never identified as such—for an adult audience. Works such as June Strong's *Mindy* (1977), the story of a Christian wife married to an unconverted husband, Kay Rizzo's *She Said No* (1994), which dealt with rape, and Ken Wade's apocalyptic *The Orion Conspiracy* (1994) achieved considerable popularity. More recently Adventist publishers have also explored the possibilities of biblical fiction with Terri L. Fivash's *Joseph: A Story* (2002) and Daniel J. Drazen's *Samuel: One Small Light* (2002). As the 20th century gave way to the 21st, it was apparent that fiction had carved out a place in the Adventist subculture, even if the subculture remained unwilling to use the common terminology.

With the uncertain place of fiction throughout most of Adventist history, church members contributed little to the literary culture of the larger society. A few writers who had childhood Adventist backgrounds, however, did emerge to literary prominence. Arna Bontemps published poetry and novels, including *God Sends Sunday* (1931) and *Black Thunder* (1936) as well as nonfiction about the African American experience. Probably the best known of African American novelists during the first half of the 20th century, Richard Wright wrote about his experiences living in his Adventist grandmother's home in *Black Boy* (1945) and achieved considerable fame and critical acclaim with *Native Son* (1940). In recent years, David James Duncan, a writer from the American Pacific Northwest, extensively drew upon his Adventist background in *The Brothers K* (1992), his second novel.

In contrast to fiction, poetry seems to have been accepted by Adventists, though the denomination placed little emphasis on the genre. The *Review and Herald* published Uriah Smith's lengthy "The Warning Voice of Time and Prophecy" and "A Word for the Sabbath" in 1853, both of which subsequently appeared as booklets. Smith ultimately published about 35 poems in the *Review and Herald* and additional verse in *The Youth's Instructor*. Smith's sister, **Annie**, who had published a few poems in a New York literary magazine, published 45 poems in the *Review and Herald* between 1851 and her death in 1855. *Home Here and Home in Heaven* (1855) collected Annie's poems and some by her brother.

Although the *Review and Herald* and *The Youth's Instructor*, as well as other denominational publications, continued to print poems, most of them of a didactic nature, no individual poets rose to prominence in the church until Adlai Esteb, whose *Driftwood and Other Poems* was published by the PPPA in 1947. During the next few years the RHPA published some books of poetry, including **Robert Hare's** *Along Life's Journey* (1948), Marjorie Lewis Lloyd's *Crosses and Crowns* (1949), and Minnie Embree Parker's *Poems from Daily Life* (1953). Subsequently only a few such books have appeared from Adventist presses. *Spectrum*, an independent journal founded by the Association of Adventist Forums in 1969, has frequently published poetry by Adventist writers that is more self-consciously artful than the verse appearing in other Adventist publications. Outside the **United States**, Adventist **Lithuanian** poet Zita Kirsnauskaite has achieved considerable acclaim.

Because of negative attitudes toward the theatre, similar to their views of fiction, Adventists have written little drama. One exception was Ken Greenman's "The Waiting," a play about the **Millerites** that won a Washington, D.C. New Playwrights Theatre award and was later published in *Spectrum* (1981).

LITERATURE EVANGELIST. An individual, traditionally called a colporteur, who sells Seventh-day Adventist publications to the public, often through door-to-door solicitation. Although some individuals sold Adventist books in **Europe** in the 1860s, the denomination did not officially develop a program until the 1880s. **George King**, who had successfully sold **John Harvey Kellogg's** *Home Handbook of Domestic Hygiene and Rational Medicine*, urged the church to develop a subscription edition of **Uriah Smith's** *Thoughts on Daniel* and *Thoughts on Revelation*. The **Review and Herald Publishing Association** bound the existing editions into a single volume and, after King demonstrated that these could be sold, produced an enlarged illustrated edition and thereby began a significant line of denominational endeavor. Although literature evangelists entered many areas of the world before Adventist **ministers** arrived, by the late 1890s such activity had largely disappeared in the **United States**. As an administrative assistant to **General Conference** president **Arthur G. Daniells, Edwin R. Palmer** revitalized literature evangelism in the early 1900s, including reviving **conference** tract societies, instituting periodic literature evangelism conventions, and instituting a scholarship program for student booksellers. Since that time, literature evangelism has remained an important part of the denomination's mission strategy although the literature sold has changed over time. In the 1930s literature evangelists sold *Bible Readings for the Home Circle* and some of **Ellen G. White's** books. **Arthur S. Maxwell's** books for children, *Bedtime Stories* (a series of 48 annual volumes which began publication in the 1924) and *The Bible Story* (1951-58), and an adult volume, *Your Bible and You* (1959), later became staples of literature evangelism. In recent years, students have sold magazine-style works, including both doctrinal and health publications.

LITHUANIA. Prior to World War I Seventh-day Adventist congregations developed in Memel and other cities of the territory that would become Lithuania. In 1919 W. Strohl, a native of **Latvia**, worked in Lithuania as a **self-supporting evangelist** but reported that outside of groups in Memel and Zagare, no Adventist congregations existed in the country. In 1921 Lithuania became a **mission** field of the Baltic **Conference**. About that same time Strohl left Lithuania to take ministerial training at **Friedensau** Missionary Seminary and then returned in 1923 to work in Siauliai. By 1924 the mission had 130 members. The denomination began publishing Lithuanian papers in 1925 and two years later received government recognition. World War II forced foreign missionaries to leave and persecution after the war caused many members to flee the country as well. With few pastors and mostly older members, Adventism made little progress until the political situation began to loosen in the 1980s. With the coming of independence to Lithuania in 1990, the denomination engaged once more in public evangelism, attracting new members and developing a younger generation of **ministers**. As of 2003 the Lithuanian **Field**, part of the Baltic Union Conference of the Trans-European **Division**, had 13 **churches** and a membership of about 900.

LOMA LINDA FOODS. Seventh-day Adventist health food company. Loma Linda Foods had its origins in the Sanitarium Food Company at Loma Linda, California, which started making breads and crackers in 1905 but gradually added other health foods. In 1933 the manufacturer adopted the name Loma Linda Food Company and opened a new factory near Riverside. At first its principal product was a cereal named Ruskets, but it later produced numerous meat substitutes and other products. In 1989 the company sold its name and baby formula business and renamed itself La Loma Foods. The following year **Worthington Foods** purchased La Loma Foods. *See* HEALTH REFORM.

LOMA LINDA UNIVERSITY (LLU). Seventh-day Adventist **educational** institution in Loma Linda, California. After her return to the **United States** in 1900, **Ellen G. White** began urging the establishment of Seventh-day Adventist **sanitariums** in southern California and asked John A. Burden, a **minister**, to look for suitable locations. Among the properties that he found, Burden negotiated the purchase of a resort hotel in Loma Linda in 1905. Later that year the Southern California **Conference** took over ownership of the property and instruction in nursing began early in 1906. That same year a committee comprised of representatives of both the Pacific **Union Conference** and Southern California Conference named the school the Loma Linda College of Evangelists and stated that the new institution would offer nursing, general college programs, and an evangelistic-medical curriculum. After a period of uncertainty regarding its purpose and curriculum, in 1909 the institution took a new name, **College of Medical Evangelists** (CME), and received a charter authorizing it to offer both academic and professional degrees. The following year the Pacific Union Conference recommended that CME offer a full medical course, a decision confirmed by the **General Conference** (GC) a short time later.

Although the first medical class graduated in 1914, the institution faced a period of uncertainty, for it was both in debt and had received the lowest possible rating from the American Medical Association (AMA). Under the leadership of Newton G. Evans, M.D., and financial help from the GC, which took over ownership of the institution, the school improved its performance, finally reaching the desired "A" rating in 1922. The AMA's insistence that to keep this rating CME should only accept graduates from accredited schools led Seventh-day Adventist colleges to work for accreditation during the next several years. Meanwhile, CME gained ownership of Loma Linda Sanitarium in 1910 and opened a clinic, which became White Memorial Hospital, in 1913 in Los Angeles where students could spend the last two years of their program in clinical instruction. The medical school program, however, eventually ran into difficulties because it was split between two campuses, a problem that was resolved by construction of the Loma Linda Medical Center, completed in 1967. Ownership of White Memorial Hospital passed to the Southern California Conference that same year. Students thereafter spent their entire four-year program at Loma Linda.

In addition to the schools of Medicine and Nursing, the institution established schools of Public Health (1948), Dentistry (1953), and Allied Health Professions (1966). Meanwhile it also created a Division of Religion (1953), later renamed the School of Religion and then Faculty of Religion, and a Graduate School (1961). The institution changed its name to Loma Linda University in 1961. In 1967 La Sierra College merged with Loma Linda University but maintained its separate campus in Riverside; in 1990 it separated from LLU to become **La Sierra University**. Apart from its educational programs, the university became well known for sending heart-surgery teams to other countries, beginning with **Pakistan** in 1961, and for its heart transplant operations, most famously in the "Baby Fae" case of 1984, when Dr. Leonard Bailey transplanted a baboon's heart into a human. Most importantly, throughout its history, the institution enabled Adventists to both envision and develop a worldwide medical missionary program. *See also* HEALTH CARE.

LONGACRE, CHARLES SMULL (1871-1958). Seventh-day Adventist **minister** and **temperance** and **religious liberty** advocate. Longacre had graduated from State Teachers College in Kutztown, Pennsylvania, and was teaching public school when he converted to Adventism in 1895. After selling denominational books during the summer of 1896 he attended **Battle Creek College** where he completed the ministerial course in 1898. For the next several years he served as a minister and, for nine years, as religious liberty secretary in the Pennsylvania **Conference**. In 1908 he began teaching at **South Lancaster Academy**, where he became principal the following year. Longacre joined the **General Conference** in 1913, becoming associate secretary and, within a few months, secretary of the Religious Liberty Association (later the Religious Liberty Department) until 1936, at which time he again became associate secretary. The following year he also became editor of *Liberty*, working in that position until 1942. In addition, between 1932 and 1941 he served as secretary of the American Temperance Society. While fulfilling these tasks Longacre earned an M.A. degree from George Washington University in 1916, and completed a three-year correspondence law program offered by La Salle Extension University.

Longacre played a significant role in representing Adventists to the larger society. During World War I he sought both to educate Adventist draftees regarding what they must do to obtain **noncombatant** classification and to encourage the War Department to rectify the problems Adventist soldiers were having with maintaining their noncombatant status and observing the **Sabbath**. He actively participated in the political effort to establish and then maintain prohibition, representing the Seventh-day Adventist Church at Anti-Saloon League national conventions, three of which he chaired. When the League of Nations began studying reform of the calendar, which would result in changing the weekly cycle of the **Sabbath**, Adventists and others protested. Longacre and a group of Adventists, including **Jean Nussbaum**, traveled to Geneva in 1931 to present the denomination's position. In the following decade, he was involved in preliminary discussions that led to the founding of Protestants and Other Americans United for the Separation of Church and State in 1948. Among his publications were *Freedom: Civil and Religious*

(1920), *The Church in Politics* (1927), and *Roger Williams—His Life, Work, and Ideals* (1939).

LORD'S SUPPER. Celebration in remembrance of Christ's last meal with his disciples prior to this death. As early as one of the 1848 **Sabbath** conferences, Adventists were celebrating the Lord's Supper. When the denomination organized in the 1860s, the celebration became part of the quarterly meeting to which members would come from a wide geographical area. Preceded by the practice of **foot washing**, the Lord's Supper, also called the Communion Service, uses unleavened bread and unfermented grape juice, which are understood as symbolic of the flesh and blood of Jesus. The ceremony is performed quarterly and is open to **baptized** Adventists and other Christians.

LOUGHBOROUGH, JOHN NORTON (1832-1924). Seventh-day Adventist **minister**, church administrator, and denominational historian. A house painter who also preached to groups who had come out of the **Millerite** movement, Loughborough converted to sabbatarian Adventism in 1852 through the preaching of **John Nevins Andrews**. Soon thereafter he went with **Hiram Edson** on a tour of sabbatarian Adventist groups in western New York and Pennsylvania and received **ordination** to the ministry in 1854. After spending the summer of 1856 conducting **evangelistic** meetings in New York state but receiving very little financial support, Loughborough became discouraged and joined the Adventist community in Waukon, Iowa, where he planned to do carpentry work and preach as time and finances permitted. Late that year **James** and **Ellen G. White** visited Waukon and strongly encouraged Loughborough to join them in active ministry, which he did.

Loughborough served as president of the Michigan **Conference** (1865-68) and treasurer of the **General Conference** (GC) (1868-69). Also in 1868 he traveled to California with **Daniel T. Bourdeau**, where he established several Adventist **churches** in the northern part of the state and also worked in Nevada before becoming the first president of the California Conference (1873-78). The GC sent Loughborough in 1878 to **Great Britain**, where he worked for five years, **baptizing** 37 individuals and forming a church in Southampton. Returning to the **United States** in 1883, Loughborough traveled throughout the country on behalf of the GC, speaking at **camp meetings** and churches. He also again served as president of several conferences: Upper Columbia Conference (1884-85), California Conference (1887-90), and Illinois Conference (1891-95). While working in California, Loughborough edited the *Pacific Health Journal* (1887-90). The pioneer minister made a world tour for the church in 1908 and then retired. Among his books were *The Hope of the Gospel* (1860), *The Prophetic Gift in the Gospel Church* (1901), *The Church, Its Organization, Order, and Discipline* (1907), and *The Great Second Advent Movement* (1905).

LUXEMBOURG. Charles Kamm, a Seventh-day Adventist **minister** from France, worked in Luxembourg from 1926 to 1929 and **baptized** several individuals but did not organize a **church.** A few attempts at **evangelism** took place in the late 1940s and early 1950s with no tangible results, partly because of legal restrictions. Adventists broadcast a series of programs over Radio-Luxembourg in 1968, followed by evangelistic meetings in 1969. In 1971 Marc Cools, who came from **Belgium,** organized a church of 13 members and worked in Luxembourg for 10 years. In 1993, according to the *Seventh-day Adventist Encyclopedia* (1996), there were 55 members in Luxembourg. As of 2003 the Belgian-Luxembourg **conference,** part of the Franco-Belgian **Union Conference** of the Euro-**Africa Division,** had a total of 25 churches and a membership of over 1,600, but there were no specific statistics for Luxembourg itself.

M

MACAO. Abram La Rue distributed Seventh-day Adventist **literature** in Macao in the 1880s and Adventist missionaries in **China** used the city as a summer residence in the early 20th century. But the first sustained Adventist effort began with the arrival in 1922 of H. B. Parker and Ho Wai Yu from Canton. The denomination established a kindergarten and elementary school in Macao in 1953 and a secondary school in 1961 but these closed in 1967 when the government reclaimed the land. About 25 years later the church built Macao Sam Yuk Middle School. In 1993, according to the *Seventh-day Adventist Encyclopedia* (1996), Macao had one church with 26 members. As of 2003 the Hong Kong-Macao Conference, part of the Chinese **Union Mission** of the Northern **Asia-**Pacific **Division,** had 18 **churches** and a membership of over 3,900. There were no specific statistics for Macao.

MCELHANY, JAMES LAMAR (1880-1959). Seventh-day Adventist
minister and church administrator. A native of California, McElhany attended Healdsburg College (later **Pacific Union College**)
before beginning work for the denomination in 1901 distributing
tracts and giving Bible studies. Between 1903 and 1906 he conducted **evangelism** in **Australia**, during which time he was **ordained** to the **ministry**. He then served in the **Philippines** and
New Zealand before returning to the **United States** in 1910. After
working as a **sanitarium** chaplain and church pastor, in 1913 he
became president of the Greater New York **Conference** and subsequently served as the president of several other conferences until
becoming general vice-president of the **General Conference** (GC)
in 1930 and president in 1936. In this latter capacity McElhany
supported the organization in 1944 of black regional conferences
and oversaw the development of relief work after the end of World
War II. He served as a general field secretary of the GC from 1950
until his death.

MCKIBBEN, ALMA (1871-1974). Seventh-day Adventist teacher
and textbook author. Shortly after Alma's birth in Iowa, her family
moved to California where her mother and father converted to Seventh-day Adventism, although they do not appear to have been
baptized at this time. After making further moves, the family settled in Colorado about 1878. A few years later Alma, along with
her mother and grandmother, was baptized into the Adventist
church. She attended Healdsburg College (later **Pacific Union
College**) from 1889 to 1892, completing the Normal Course, and
married Edwin McKibben, a teacher at the school, shortly after her
graduation. After Edwin's death four years later, she taught a home
school in the San Pasqual Valley in 1897 and in 1898-99 served as
the first teacher at the Centralia **church** school, one of the the
earliest church-sponsored Adventist elementary schools.

In 1899 McKibben moved back to Healdsburg where she
taught at a summer institute for teachers and then instructed the in-
termediate grades at Healdsburg Preparatory School until 1902.
Between 1902 and 1908 she held several different positions at
Healdsburg College. During this time she wrote *Bible Lessons*,
Books 1-3, for grades 4-6 (1903), the first Bible textbooks for the
denomination, and contributed sections to the first *Church School
Manual* (1906). In 1908 McKibben taught at the Western Normal
School in Lodi and between 1909 and 1911 she worked for the
California **Conference**, primarily in the Young People's **Mission-
ary Volunteer** department. From 1911 to 1919 she taught at the

Pacific Union College preparatory school, during which time she
wrote *Bible Lessons*, Book 4, for grades 7 and 8 (1912) and *Bible
Lesson Manual for Parents and Teachers* (1914, 1918), contributed to a new *Church School Manual* (1918), and frequently
helped direct teacher institutes and conventions. After convales-
cence from influenza, McKibben taught at Mountain View **Academy** from 1921 until retiring in 1932. Throughout her teaching career she prepared new editions of her various textbooks.

MADAGASCAR. Seventh-day Adventism entered Madagascar beginning in 1917 through contacts with André Rasamoelina, an inspector of Protestant schools. Rasamoelina subsequently translated
Ellen G. White's *Steps to Christ* into Malagasy, which was published in 1925. Marius Raspal, an Adventist missionary on Mauritius, went to Madagascar the following year and **baptized** four individuals, including Rasamoelina, in 1927. In 1929 the Madagascar
Mission organized with 102 church members. The Malagasy Publishing House opened in 1930 and a primary school, headed by
Rasamoelina, began shortly thereafter. In 1938 the Indian Ocean
Union Training School held its first classes. Adventists began
broadcasting radio programs in French in 1946 and Malagasy two
years later; they opened their first dispensary in 1969. As of 2003
the Seventh-day Adventist Church in Madagascar was organized
into one **conference** and two missions, which were part of the
Indian Ocean **Union Mission** of the Southern **Africa**-Indian Ocean
Division. The island had 340 **churches** with a membership of over
73,000. Adventist University Zurcher, two secondary schools,
Andapa Adventist Hospital, 12 clinics and dispensaries, and
Adventist Printing House were located on Madagascar.

MADEIRA ISLANDS. Stephen N. Haskell in 1889 and **Warren E.
Howell** in 1922 visited the Madeira Islands, but it was the latter's
article in the *Review and Herald* that sparked the interest of Joa-
quim Gomes da Silva, a native of Madeira who was living in **Hawaii**. In the mid-1920s he began selling Adventist publications in
Madeira. The first missionaries arrived in 1931 and **baptized** 14
individuals the following year. As of 2003 the Madeira Islands
were part of the **Portuguese** Union of Churches of the Euro-**Africa
Division**. There were no specific statistics for the islands.

MADISON COLLEGE. Self-supporting Seventh-day Adventist **educational** institution in Madison, Tennessee. In 1904 **Edward A.
Sutherland** and **Percy T. Magan** resigned their positions at **Em-**

manuel **Missionary College** and, with the encouragement of **Ellen G. White**, purchased land in Tennessee for a self-supporting school. Opening that same year as Nashville Agricultural Normal Institute, the school offered short courses and practical training for the preparation of missionaries. With the establishment of the Madison Rural **Sanitarium** in 1907, nursing soon became the most popular educational program. From its beginning, the school offered work opportunities, among them the sanitarium, a food factory, and a farm, through which students could earn all of their expenses. It received accreditation as a junior college in 1928 and as a four-year college five years later. In 1937 it took the name Madison College. Almost from its beginning the Madison school sought to encourage its graduates to establish similar self-supporting institutions. Eventually nearly 40 small schools, sanitariums, and other facilities were scattered throughout the American South, much of their work funded by the Layman Foundation established in 1924 by Lida Funk Scott. Sutherland served as president of the college from the institution's founding until 1946. In the 1950s and early 1960s Madison College and Madison Sanitarium faced increasing financial and accreditation problems. Ownership of the institutions passed in 1963 to the Southern **Union Conference,** which closed the college the following year.

MAGAN, PERCY TILSON (1867-1947). Seventh-day Adventist **educational** administrator. Emigrating from Ireland to the **United States** in 1886 and converting to Seventh-day Adventism soon thereafter, Magan worked briefly as a **minister** in Nebraska and then entered **Battle Creek College** in 1888. In 1889-90 he traveled around the world with **Stephen N. Haskell** to examine **mission** possibilities and wrote reports in the *Youth's Instructor* that helped raise interest in missions. After serving for a year as associate secretary of the Foreign Mission Board, Magan began teaching Bible and history at Battle Creek College in 1891 and became dean in 1897 as part of **Edward A. Sutherland's** reform administration. After moving the college in 1901 to Berrien Springs, Michigan, where it was renamed **Emmanuel Missionary College**, he left with Sutherland in 1904 to found the Nashville Agricultural and Normal Institute (later **Madison College**). While working at this institution Magan earned an M.D. degree from the University of Tennessee in 1914 and left the following year to become dean of the College of Medical Evangelists (CME; later **Loma Linda University**). Under Magan's leadership, the CME attained an "A" rating from the American Medical Association in 1922. To maintain this rating, Magan pushed hard in the 1920s for the denomination to seek accreditation for its colleges; although **Pacific Union College** received accreditation in 1932, the **General Conference** did not allow all senior colleges to seek accreditation until four years later. Meanwhile, Magan became president of the CME, serving in that position until 1942.

MALAWI. George James, an Englishman who had attended **Battle Creek College**, visited Malawi, at the time known as Nyasaland, in 1893 but soon died from malaria. In 1902 the Seventh-day Adventist Church purchased a former Seventh Day Baptist mission station that they later named Malamulo, the Chichewa word for "commandments." Thomas Branch and his daughter Mabel opened a school at the **mission** and in 1905 **baptized** their first converts. In 1925 the school introduced a teacher-training course and in the late 1940s secondary and ministerial-training programs. In 1963 it changed its name from Malamulo Training Institute to Malamulo College. Missionaries established Malamulo Press in 1926 by printing tracts and other materials on a small hand press. In the 1930s the press moved to a larger building and added commercial printing to its activities; it adopted the name Malamulo **Publishing** House in 1965. Meanwhile, the first clinic opened at Malamulo in 1915 and, after the arrival of Dr. Carl Birkenstock from **South Africa** and the erection of a new building, began offering more advanced **health care** services in 1927. In subsequent years the hospital became a major treatment facility for leprosy, established training programs in nursing, midwifery, and medical assistance, and sponsored clinics in various parts of Malawi. Although Malamulo was the center of Seventh-day Adventist efforts in Malawi, other missions formed beginning in the 1920s and the Seventh-day Adventist Church grew rapidly. As of 2003 the Malawi **Union Mission**, part of the Eastern **Africa Division**, had 742 **churches** with a membership of over 213,000. Lake View Seminary and Training Center, three secondary schools, three hospitals, 17 clinics and dispensaries, and Malamulo Publishing House were located in Malawi.

MALAYSIA. The first Seventh-day Adventist missionaries arrived at Kuala Lumpur in 1911 and three years later organized the first **church** and the Federated Malay States **Mission**. By 1931 the mission had five churches and about 250 members, most of them of non-Malayan ancestry. A clinic, established in Penang in 1925, eventually developed into Penang Adventist Hospital.

Although **Abram La Rue** visited Sabah, or North Borneo as it was then known, sometime between 1888 and 1903 and a Chinese **literature evangelist** came to the area in 1909, the first permanent Adventist missionaries did not arrive until 1913. In the mid-1920s Indonesian missionaries entered the interior and **baptized** several individuals, but these efforts lapsed until the 1960s. By 1942 Sabah had eight churches and 337 members. After World War II Adventism began to grow significantly in Sabah and in the 1960s missionaries from the **Philippines**, **Indonesia**, and the **United States** came into the area, but government policy changed in the 1970s and thereafter, with some exceptions, Malaysians led the denomination's efforts.

Abram La Rue visited Sarawak about the same time that he arrived at Sabah and a Chinese literature evangelist sold books there in 1915. After the government refused to allow a missionary to stay in Sarawak, two Chinese Adventist laymen from **Singapore** settled in Kuching and began **evangelizing**. When **religious liberty** was proclaimed in 1925, the Adventists became more publicly active, renting a building for meetings and establishing a school. In 1931 Gustavus B. Youngberg and E. Sinaga began working among the Dayak people and in 1933 the Ayer Manis Training School began operating in the Dayak region. After the disruption of World War II, missionaries returned to Sarawak and reestablished their work among the Dayaks.

As of 2003 the Seventh-day Adventist Church in Malaysia was organized into three missions. The Peninsular Malaysia Mission had 26 churches and a membership of over 4,000. The Sabah Mission had 126 churches and a membership of more than 24,000. The Sarawak Mission, which also included Brunei, had 82 churches and a membership of about 14,500. These missions were part of the Southeast **Asia Union Mission** of the Southern Asia-Pacific **Division**. Three secondary schools, Penang Adventist Hospital, and Southeast Asia Publishing House were located in Malaysia.

MALINKI, K. MORRISON (c. 1852-1957). Seventh-day Adventist **evangelist** and teacher. Educated at the Church of Scotland Mission, located near Blantyre, Nyasaland (now **Malawi**), Malinki obtained a teaching certificate in 1890. Although the time is uncertain, a few years later he began observing the seventh-day **Sabbath**, perhaps influenced by Joseph Booth, a Seventh Day Baptist who had established a mission at Matsidi on the Zambesi River. Hired by Booth about 1900, Malinki started teaching at the Zambezi Industrial Mission about two miles away and during the next few years established additional schools. Meanwhile, Booth converted to Seventh-day Adventism and the denomination purchased his mission. Subsequently, Malinki also converted to Adventism and, after being invited by Thomas Branch, an African American Adventist missionary, began teaching for the Malamulo Mission in 1904. Malinki placed the schools he had established under the mission, which in turn appointed him as the inspector of all Seventh-day Adventist village schools in southern Nyasaland. In 1920 Malinki left **education** to become an evangelist in the Cileka area and was **ordained** to the ministry in 1927. Although he retired in 1930, Malinki continued to participate in **camp meetings** and evangelism.

MALTA. Seventh-day Adventist **literature evangelists** first entered Malta in 1957 and the following year received governmental permission for a three-month annual bookselling campaign. In the 1990s additional **evangelistic** efforts began. As of 2003 the Seventh-day Adventist Church in Malta was part of the Italian Union of Churches, which belong to the Euro-**Africa Division**. There were no statistics specifically for Malta.

MARANATHA VOLUNTEERS INTERNATIONAL. Seventh-day Adventist volunteer organization. Maranatha Flights International, founded in 1969 by commercial photographer John Freeman of Michigan, organized lay people for short-term projects to construct church and school buildings in areas ranging from **Canada's** Northwest Territories to **Sierra Leone** and Borneo. After merging with Volunteers International in 1989, the organization adopted the name Maranatha Volunteers International and established its headquarters in Sacramento, California. As of 2003 Maranatha published *The Volunteer*, a quarterly magazine.

MARION PARTY. *See* CHURCH OF GOD (SEVENTH-DAY).

MARSH, FRANK LEWIS (1899-1992). Seventh-day Adventist biologist and advocate of **creationism**. Marsh studied geology under **George McCready Price** at **Emmanuel Missionary College** (EMC) in the late 1920s and greatly admired his mentor. After graduating from EMC he taught at a Seventh-day Adventist secondary school; while in that position he also earned an M.S. in Zoology from Northwestern University in 1935. Soon thereafter he joined the **Union College** faculty and earned a Ph.D. in botany from the University of Nebraska in 1940, the first Adventist to acquire a doctoral degree in biology. In 1941 Marsh published *Fundamental Biology* in which he argued that the Genesis statement "after their kind" asserted a natural law that placed limits on cross-hybridization. Three years later *Evolution, Creation, and Science* developed this concept further by attributing the diversity in the natural world to changes that had taken place within the original "kinds," or what Marsh called "baramins," of creation. The book prompted an exchange of letters between the Columbia University geneticist Theodosius Dobzhansky and Marsh. In 1957 Marsh joined the newly established **Geoscience Research Institute** where he took the position that scientific interpretation must be subordinate to theology. Interpretive conflicts with other members of the staff led to Marsh's appointment in 1964 to the Department of Biology at **Andrews University**; he retired about seven years later. Marsh's additional publications included *Studies in Creationism* (1950), *Life, Man, and Time* (1957), *Evolution or Special Creation?* (1963), *Variation and Fixity in Nature* (1976), and *Prairie Tree: Early Days on the Northern Illinois Prairie* (1978).

MARSH, JOSEPH (1802-1863). Millerite preacher and editor. Marsh was the pastor of a **Christian Connection** church in Union Mills, New York, and editor of a Connection journal, *The Christian Palladium*, prior to accepting **William Miller's** teaching that Jesus would return about the year 1843. Forced out of his editorial position because of his Millerite belief, he began publishing the *Voice of Truth* in January 1844. In 1843 Marsh supported **Charles Fitch's** call for the Millerites to leave the established churches and in September 1844 he supported the **seventh-month movement**. After the **Great Disappointment**, Marsh's journal was open to the **shut door theory** but opposed many of the other radical ideas that were circulating among the Millerites. He did not participate in the Mutual Conference of Adventists held in Albany in 1845 and criticized its actions because he interpreted them as moving toward establishment of a creed and a church organization. He soon began advocating the "Age-to-Come" doctrine and renamed his paper the *Advent Harbinger and Bible Advocate*. The group that formed around these beliefs eventually developed into the **Church of God General Conference**. Age-to-Come ideas also influenced some sabbatarian Adventists who, together with others, established the **Church of God (Seventh-day)**. Around 1850 Marsh published in the *Advent Harbinger* criticisms of the seventh-day **Sabbath** doctrine.

MARTINIQUE. Philip Giddings, a Seventh-day Adventist missionary in **British Guiana**, visited Martinique in 1919 before settling on the island in 1924. Michel Nord Isaac, who came from **Haiti**, replaced him in 1928 and, after conducting **evangelistic** meetings, organized the first Adventist **church**. In 1929 Adventist churches in Martinique and **Guadeloupe** organized as the West Indian **Mission**. Although membership grew rapidly, the denomination did not establish its first school until 1954. The Martinique **Conference** organized in 1974. As of 2003 the conference, part of the French Antilles-Guiana **Union Mission** of the Inter-American **Division**, had 57 churches and more than 13,000 members. Antilles Guyane Adventist Secondary School and Radio of Hope were located on Martinique.

MATTESON, JOHN GOTTLIEB (1835-1896). Seventh-day Adventist **minister** and missionary. Born in **Denmark**, Matteson immigrated to the **United States** with his family in 1854. In 1862 he was ordained to the Baptist ministry but the following year converted to Seventh-day Adventism and within a few months had in turn converted to his new faith all but one of the families in his Wisconsin church. During the next several years he **evangelized** among the Scandinavian immigrants who had settled in the American Midwest and in 1872 began a Danish-language paper, the *Advent Herald*. Matteson's work was the first significant effort by an Adventist to attract immigrant converts. Some of Matteson's converts sent copies of his paper to relatives and friends in Denmark; these recipients then sent requests to the **General Conference** (GC) for an Adventist minister to come to their country. At the GC's request, Matteson went to Denmark in 1877 and the following year established his headquarters in Christiania, **Norway**. He organized a **church** and in 1879 began publishing the *Signs of the Times* and two years later a health periodical. In 1882 he established the Scandinavian Publishing House, often called Christiania Publishing House, which printed books and magazines for Denmark, **Sweden**, and Norway. After establishing Adventism in Scandinavia, Matteson returned to the United States in 1888 and taught at **Union College** in Lincoln, Nebraska.

MAXWELL, ARTHUR STANLEY (1896-1970). Seventh-day Adventist editor and author. Shortly after graduating in 1915 from Stanborough College (later **Newbold College**), Maxwell began working as a copyreader for the Stanborough Press. In 1920 he became editor of the British *Present Truth* and the *Missionary*

Worker, positions he held until 1936. He also served as a pastor and between 1925 and 1932 as manager of the Stanborough Press. In 1937 Maxwell went to the **United States** to become editor of the *Signs of the Times*, staying in that position until 1970. In addition to editing magazines, Maxwell wrote books for both children and adults. Beginning in 1924 he published for 48 years an annual volume entitled *Uncle Arthur's Bedtime Stories*, which as subscription books sold more than 37 million copies. Between 1951 and 1958 he published *The Bible Story*, a 10-volume work that, again through subscription sales, sold more than 1.5 million copies. An adult book, *Your Bible and You* (1959) reached similar sales figures. Maxwell wrote a total of 79 books for children and 33 for adults.

MEDIA. *See* ADVENTIST MEDIA CENTER; ADVENTIST WORLD RADIO; *AMAZING FACTS*; *BREATH OF LIFE*; EVANGELISM; *FAITH FOR TODAY*; *IT IS WRITTEN*; *QUIET HOUR*; THREE ANGELS BROADCASTING NETWORK; *VOICE OF PROPHECY*; *YOUR STORY HOUR.*

MEDICAL CADET CORPS (MCC). Seventh-day Adventist organization that prepared young men for military service. In 1934 **Everett N. Dick** established the College Medical Corps at **Union College** to train males for military service as **noncombatant** medics. Two years later Cyril B. Courville, a major in the Army Reserve, created the Medical Cadet Corps for students at the College of Medical Evangelists (later **Loma Linda University**). Other Adventist colleges implemented similar programs and in 1939 the Fall Council of the **General Conference** Executive Committee gave official approval and centralized direction under the title Medical Cadet Corps. A **Women's** Cadette Corps also operated in some places. Active during World War II, the MCC largely went out of existence after the war until the **United States** again introduced the draft in 1950. Reestablished at that time, the MCC training program continued in the United States until the draft was abolished in 1972. In other countries that have a draft or mandatory military service, however, the denomination has instituted similar military training programs.

MELASHENKO, ELORIE LONNIE (1947-). Seventh-day Adventist **minister** and radio/television **evangelist**. Melashinko received his B.A. (1968) from **La Sierra University** and M.Div. (1970) from **Andrews University**. He served as a pastor in California from 1972 to 1977, receiving ordination in 1974. After joining *It is Written* as associate director-speaker in 1977, he conducted **Revelation Seminars** with **George Vandeman**. In 1981 Melashenko became pastor of the Adventist church in Paradise, California, where he adapted his worship services into a radio program entitled "Sounds of Praise." He began working as an announcer with the *Voice of Prophecy* radio program in 1989 while continuing to serve as a pastor, but by 1993 was working full-time as director-speaker. In addition to broadcasting over radio, Melashenko was actively involved in evangelistic campaigns in such places as **Brazil**, the **Philippines**, **Russia**, **Ukraine**, **Venezuela**, and **Zambia**; many of the meetings were transmitted by satellite. Among Melashenko's books are (with David B. Smith) *A Suitcase Full of Faith,* (with John Thomas McLarty) *Stand at the Cross and Be Change*d (1997), and *Amazing Grace* (2003).

MESSAGE. Seventh-day Adventist **evangelistic** magazine for African Americans. *Message* was the successor to two earlier denominational papers established by **James Edson White**, *Gospel Herald* (1898-1903) and the similarly entitled but separate *Gospel Herald* (1904-1923). Beginning as a quarterly in 1935, as of 2003 it was a bimonthly published by the **Review and Herald Publishing Association**.

MEXICO. A group of Seventh-day Adventist missionaries arrived in Guadalajara in 1893 to start a school and a medical clinic. About a year later they organized an Adventist **church** and in 1896 began publishing a missionary magazine. In 1899 George W. Caviness and two assistants established an English-language school in Mexico City and in 1903 organized the Mexican **Mission**. A short time later, the missionaries formed a publishing house in Mexico City and transferred the missionary magazine to that location. **Literature evangelism** was an important part of Adventist efforts; Spanish-language editions of *Steps to Christ* appeared as early as 1899 and by 1915 booksellers were working as far away as the Yucatán and Monterrey.

The Mexican revolution forced American missionaries out of Mexico for a short time in 1914 and the following year publication of the magazine, now named *Signs of the Times*, moved to the **Review and Herald Publishing Association** in the **United States**. Despite the difficulties, the Mexican Mission in 1923 reported 17 churches and 505 members. After reorganization into several separate missions in the intervening years, in 1926 the Mexican Union

Mission formed with 29 churches and 656 members. **Self-supporting** clinics started in various parts of Mexico, beginning in 1929, although many of them were short-lived. The church made several efforts to establish schools but this proved difficult because of government regulations. Finally, the Mexican Agricultural and Industrial School began in 1942 near Montemorelos. A secondary school, by 1951 it had become Montemorelos Vocational and Professional College, which offered some postsecondary education in nursing and ministerial training. In 1973 the institution became **Montemorelos University**. Meanwhile, a **sanitarium** opened at Montemorelos in 1947; it eventually became Montemorelos University Hospital. The denomination also established elementary schools for Indians beginning in the 1930s.

As of 2003 the Seventh-day Adventist Church in Mexico was divided into two **union conferences** and one mission, which were part of the Inter-American **Division**. The union conferences had 1,112 churches and a membership of more than 380,000, about two-thirds of the membership being in southern Mexico. Linda Vista University, Montemorelos University, Navojoa University, six secondary schools, Adventist Sanitorium, Montemorelos University Hospital, Southeast Hospital, and three clinics and dispensaries were located in Mexico.

MIDDLE EAST. *See* ALGERIA; ARMENIA; CYPRUS; EGYPT; IRAN; IRAQ; ISRAEL; JORDAN; LEBANON; LIBYA; MALTA; TUNISIA; TURKEY.

MILLENNIUM. Term referring to the 1,000-year period mentioned in Revelation 20. Most Second Great Awakening preachers believed that Jesus would return after the millennial reign of God's spirit on earth, a position known as postmillennialism. In contrast, **William Miller** taught a version of premillennialism, saying that Jesus' return would bring the present age of the world to an end and initiate the reign of the saints on a renewed earth for a thousand years. Apparently as early as 1845 some Adventists were taking the position that the restored earth would not come into being until after the millennium. How widespread this latter view was is unclear, but it appears to have provided the starting point for the sabbatarian Adventists, who during the late 1840s developed a distinctive understanding of the millennium. In 1846 **Joseph Bates** stated in his tract *The Opening Heavens* that the only place to be renewed at the Second Advent would be the spot on which the Holy City was to come down.

The following year **Ellen G. White** wrote a letter to Bates, later published in *A Word to the "Little Flock,"* saying that the resurrected and living saints would return with Jesus to heaven and later told another individual that the new heavens and new earth would emerge when the wicked had been destroyed after the millennium. These views appeared in more systematic form in a *Present Truth* article, published in April 1850, in which White stated that the resurrected saints would live in heaven for a thousand years, after which the Holy City would descend to earth and would be attacked by the newly resurrected wicked. After destroying the wicked, God would restore the earth. **James White**, in an *Advent Review* article of September 1850, added another element when he stated that during the millennium the saints in heaven would participate in judging both the wicked angels and humanity, after which the punishment would be executed. Ellen White put forward a similar view in a November 1850 *Present Truth* article. It appears, therefore, that by the end of 1850, the sabbatarian Adventists had developed a view of the millennium that included the following: Christ would take the resurrected and living saints to heaven at the beginning of the millennium; the earth, to which Satan would be confined, would be desolate for a thousand years; the saints would participate in judging the wicked angels and humans; at the end of the millennium the Holy City would descend to earth where Satan and the resurrected wicked would unsuccessfully attack it; and after fire destroyed the wicked and the old earth, a new earth would arise.

MILLER, HARRY WILLIS (1879-1977). Seventh-day Adventist physician and missionary. A 1902 graduate of the **American Medical Missionary College**, Miller also studied at Rush Medical College and published an article on blastomycetes in the *Journal of Dermatology* before going to **China** in 1903. After he and his wife Maude—also a physician—had studied the Chinese language and operated dispensaries in Hsintsai and Shantsai, she died of what was later learned to be sprue, a vitamin deficiency disease. In 1908 Miller briefly returned to the **United States** where he married again and taught at the Washington **Sanitarium** nursing school and the Foreign Mission Seminary (later **Columbia Union College**), before returning to China that same year. Serving as superintendent of the China **Mission** in Shanghai from 1908 to 1909, Miller then went to Chouchiakou, where he started a school, which eventually became the China Training Institute, and practiced medicine. Becoming ill with sprue in 1911, Miller once again returned to the United States.

After living in Ohio caring for an elderly relative and teaching for a short time at Mount Vernon **Academy**, Miller became **General Conference** medical secretary and medical director of Washington Sanitarium in 1913, serving until 1925. In addition to bringing financial stability to the sanitarium, he also developed a reputation as an excellent thyroid surgeon during this period. Returning to China in 1925, he managed the new Shanghai Hospital and Sanitarium and also made frequent visits to the **Philippines**, where he conducted surgeries; during this time he began experimenting with the production of soy milk and published an article in 1936 in the *Chinese Medical Journal* on a soy infant formula. Miller also served as the first president of the China **Division** from 1931 to 1936.

The Japanese invasion of China forced the closure of the Shanghai Hospital and Sanitarium in 1937; Miller then moved to a clinic at Hankow until leaving for the United States in 1939. While in America he served as the medical director of Mount Vernon Hospital and formed the International Nutrition Laboratory to produce soy milk and other products. He sold his company to **Loma Linda Foods** before returning to China in 1949. Evacuated from China in 1950, he returned to the United States where his wife soon died. In 1953, after remarrying, he went to the **Republic of China** (Taiwan) to oversee the development of a new sanitarium. After being awarded the Blue Star of China by Chiang Kai-Shek in 1956 for meritorious service to the people of China, he returned to the United States three years later. In subsequent years Miller worked in **Trinidad, Libya,** and **Japan** and served as a consultant to the World Health Organization and the United Nations. His books included *The Way to Health* (1920) and *Tuberculosis, A Curable Disease* (c. 1947).

MILLER, WILLIAM (1782-1849). American farmer and Baptist preacher who predicted that Jesus would return about the year 1843. Raised a Baptist in upstate New York, Miller became a deist some time after moving to Poultney, Vermont, in 1803. He was politically active and filled several local offices, including sheriff, constable, and justice of the peace. Elected a lieutenant of the Vermont militia in 1810, he participated in the War of 1812 and rose to the rank of captain in the regular army. His experience in the war, particularly at the Battle of Plattsburg in 1814, pushed him to reconsider his deistic beliefs and, after moving his family back to his boyhood home in Low Hampton, he began attending church services. In 1816 he converted to Christianity. Challenged by his deist friends to harmonize the apparent contradictions of the Bible, Miller began an intense study of Scripture.

Especially interested in the 2,300-day prophecy of Daniel 8:14, in which he understood that a prophetic "day" represented an actual year, by 1818 Miller had reached the conclusion that the **Second Advent** of Jesus would occur about the year 1843. Reluctant to present his conclusions publicly, Miller continued to study for several more years until in 1831 he received an invitation to preach in a nearby town, where he prompted a revival. The following year he published a series of 16 articles in the *Vermont Telegraph*, combined the following year into a pamphlet entitled *Evidences from Scripture & History of the Second Coming of Christ About the Year A.D. 1843, and of His Personal Reign of 1,000 Years*. Three years later he expanded this pamphlet into a book with the same title. Increasingly invited to speak at churches, he acquired a preaching license from his local Baptist church in 1833 and by the end of 1834 was engaged full-time in promoting his views. Over the next few years Miller became a noted revivalist in upstate New York, Maine, and Vermont, giving some 800 "lectures" between 1834 and 1839. Most of the ministers who invited him to their churches were probably more interested in the conversions he made than in the specifics of his prophetic interpretation.

In 1839 Miller received invitations to preach in several Massachusetts churches. While speaking in Exeter he met **Joshua V. Himes**, a **Christian Connection** minister in Boston, who invited him to speak at his church, which Miller did in late 1839 and early 1840. By March 1840 Himes was publishing a paper, the *Signs of the Times*, to promote Miller's views and pushed Miller to speak in other large cities such as New York and Philadelphia. In addition to publications, Himes organized conferences, beginning in 1840, but Miller could not attend these meetings until the fifth conference took place near his home in 1841. As the movement grew, pressure built upon Miller to more precisely fix the date of the Advent. Finally, in January 1843 he wrote that, based on his analyisis of the Jewish calendar, Jesus would come some time between March 21, 1843 and March 21, 1844.

Despite the radical nature of his own prediction, Miller took a conservative approach to other concepts that appeared in the movement he had spawned. After **Charles Fitch** preached his "Come out of Babylon" sermon in July 1843, Miller objected to separation from the existing churches but could do little to halt the separatist impulse. Miller also opposed the **conditionalist** views of **George Storrs** that were gaining influence. When Christ did not come in March 1844, or in April as some **Millerites** suggested would happen, Miller admitted his error regarding the date but expressed confidence that Jesus would return soon. After **Samuel S. Snow** began presenting in August his new interpretation that Jesus would come on October 22, 1844, prompting what became known as the **seventh-month movement**, Miller took until October 6 to accept the new view. Although deeply disappointed that Christ did not come as expected, Miller for several weeks after October 22 expressed belief that Christ would come very soon, probably before the year's end. But by late December he was suggesting that his calculations could be off by as much as five years. Pressed by Himes, who was concerned about the extremist positions that some of the Millerites were taking, Miller by March 1845 rejected the **shut door theory** which said that probation had closed for Christians on October 22. He signed the call for and participated in the Mutual Conference of Adventists that opened in Albany on April 29, 1845. Following Miller's address, in which he warned against the adoption of new theories, the conference drew a dividing line between the moderate and radical Adventists.

Miller continued to believe that Christ's coming was near, but beginning in 1846 physical disability prevented him from playing an active role in Adventist developments. He maintained contact with Himes, who came to be with him during his last few days, expressing objections to doctrinal conflict but holding no regrets regarding his mistaken interpretations.

MILLERITE MOVEMENT. Millennialist religious movement of the 1840s based on the ideas of **William Miller**. Although Miller had concluded as early as 1818 that the **Second Advent** of Jesus would occur around the year 1843 and publicly preached that view in the 1830s, it was not until **Joshua V. Himes** began publishing *The Signs of the Times* in Boston in March 1840 that a movement developed. Himes organized the first general conference, held the following October, at which a number of prominent clergymen, including Henry Dana Ward, Henry Jones, and **Josiah Litch**, spoke about their expectation that Christ would return soon. As the movement formed, many other clergymen and lay people **evangelized** in its behalf. In addition to Himes, several leaders emerged, among them **Charles Fitch**, Josiah Litch, **Joseph Marsh**, Elon Galusha, and Nathaniel Southard. Although the believers referred to themselves as "Adventists," observers called them "Millerites," the name by which they are generally known historically.

The general conferences proved to be an effective means for planning strategy and about a dozen took place over the next few years. The conference held in May 1842 was particularly important, for it was the first to specifically support the 1843 date. About 120 local conferences also occurred between 1840 and 1844. In addition to conferences, the Millerite leadership organized **camp meetings**, the first one taking place in eastern Canada in June 1842. A short time later, they purchased a large tent—reportedly the biggest one in the United States—that the Millerite leaders transported from place to place for the larger camp meetings. Between 1842 and 1844 more than 125 Millerite camp meetings were held with an estimated attendance of one-half million. Nearly all of this activity occurred in the northeastern and midwestern United States; Millerism had only minor impact on the American South.

To publicize both their teachings and their meetings, the Millerite leaders published numerous papers, tracts, and books. In conjunction with a series of meetings in New York in 1842, Himes published *The Midnight Cry*. While intended to be only a temporary publication, it had such success that it continued publication through 1845. Other important papers included *Trumpet of Alarm* (Philadelphia), *Second Advent of Christ* (Cleveland), *Voice of Elijah* (Montreal), and *Western Midnight Cry* (Cincinnati). *The Advent Shield* was a scholarly quarterly and *The Advent Message to the Daughters of Zion* addressed a female audience. A second *Midnight Cry* and the *Second Advent Harbinger* appeared in **Great Britain**. Himes also published a hymnbook, the *Millennial Harp*, a 50-volume (some were only tracts) Second Advent Library, and a prophetic chart designed by Apollos Hale and Charles Fitch that Millerite preachers used extensively.

As the movement developed, it met considerable criticism from both clergymen and the secular press. By 1842 some Millerites were losing their church memberships as a result of their new belief and a few denominational groups took actions stating that their ministers could not teach Millerite doctrine. Responding to this situation, in July 1843 Charles Fitch preached a sermon calling on Millerite believers to "Come out of Babylon," which appeared in several papers and shaped a separationist trajectory for what had previously been an interchurch movement. Some of the movement's commentators estimated that as many as 50,000 people had left their churches by the fall of 1844.

While at first Miller had stated that Christ would return "about" the year 1843, his followers pressured him to more precisely identify the date of the second coming. In January 1843, after studying the Jewish calendar, Miller stated that Jesus would return between March 21, 1843 and March 21, 1844. After the 1844 date had passed, some Millerites, using a different Jewish calendar, identified April 18 of that same year as the correct ending date. That prediction also proved wrong. During the early summer of 1844 the Millerite movement experienced considerable confusion, though it continued to hold conferences and camp meetings. At the Exeter, Massachusetts, camp meeting, however, **Samuel S. Snow** presented his belief, based on a typological analysis of the Day of Atonement and other Old Testament Jewish festivals and ceremonies, that Jesus would return on October 22, 1844. Although most of the principal Millerite leaders did not at first accept this interpretation, it quickly swept through the ranks, becoming known as the **seventh-month movement**, when Snow publicized his views in a new paper, *The True Midnight Cry*. As October 22 approached a large number of Americans, estimates ran from 50,000 to 250,000, anxiously awaited their Lord's return. When nothing extraordinary happened on the expected momentous day, true believers were crushed and afterwards referred to their experience as "the **Great Disappointment**."

In the aftermath of October 22, the Millerites went in several directions. Probably most returned to their former churches while some gave up Christian belief entirely. Fanaticism of various kinds and spiritual interpretations of what had happened on October 22 also appeared in Millerite circles. To gain control over the movement, Himes and other leaders called the Mutual Conference of Adventists which met in Albany in April 1845 and sought to separate mainstream Millerites from the radicals. Out of those who met at Albany, three principal Adventist churches eventually developed: the **American Evangelical Adventist Conference**, the **Advent Christian Church**, and the Church of God of the Abrahamic Faith (later **Church of God General Conference**). From the radicals not invited to the Albany conference, the sabbatarian Adventists, who in the 1860s formed the Seventh-day Adventist Church, emerged as the largest of all the groups with Millerite roots.

MINISTER. An individual authorized to conduct pastoral work within the Seventh-day Adventist Church. There are three types of ministers within the denomination. An **ordained** minister is authorized to perform all pastoral functions. Licensed ministers are similar to those who are ordained except that **divisions** determine their specific responsibilities. In the North American Division, for example, licensed ministers are excluded from organizing **churches** and ordaining local church officers. A third category is the commissioned minister. Again, divisions determine to whom the commissioned minister credential is given. In North America, **Bible Instructors**, hospital chaplains, and various denominational administrative officers receive this credential.

MINISTERIAL ASSOCIATION. General Conference (GC) department responsible for supporting and developing the **ministers** of the Seventh-day Adventist Church. Through the late 19th and early 20th centuries, denominational leaders repeatedly expressed concern regarding the quality of their ministers. To rectify the situation, during his presidency (1888-97) of the GC **Ole A. Olsen** introduced "ministerial institutes" that varied in duration from a few weeks to a few months. Later **Arthur G. Daniells** worked with the GC **Education** Department to develop an annual reading course for ministers. But Albert W. Anderson's organization of a ministerial association in **Australia** in 1920 led the **General Conference Session** of 1922 to establish a Ministerial Commission, soon renamed Ministerial Association, and appoint Daniels to head the new department. Rather than being an administrative department, the Ministerial Association collected and distributed information regarding the profession and encouraged young men to become ministers. Beginning in 1923 it conducted institutes in various parts of the **United States** and in 1928 launched a magazine, *The Ministry*, edited by **LeRoy Edwin Froom**. In the 1940s the association placed increasing emphasis on **evangelism** and, after the establishment of the **Seventh-day Adventist Theological Seminary** in 1937, several of its officers became involved in the formal education of ministers. Since that time, among other activities it has conducted continuing education seminars and sent copies of *Ministry* to all clergy in the **United States**. Beginning in 1983 it initiated a program, which became known as **Shepherdess International**, to support the wives of ministers.

MISSION. An organizational unit of the Seventh-day Adventist Church. A mission is similar to a **conference** in form and function except that it does not usually support itself financially and the next higher organizational unit elects its officers.

MISSIONARY. *See* MISSIONS.

MISSIONARY VOLUNTEER SOCIETY (MV). Seventh-day Adventist youth organization. The early Seventh-day Adventist Church gave little specific attention to young people beyond the **Sabbath school** and **Battle Creek College**. Recognizing a need in their local church, in 1879 Luther Warren and Harry Fenner of Hazelton, Michigan, organized what appears to have been the first Adventist youth organization, which sponsored social activities and distributed denominational literature. This effort remained only a local affair, however, and it was not until the 1890s that other groups, encouraged by **Ellen G. White**, formed in such places as Adelaide in **Australia** and **Union College** in Nebraska. A **conference**-wide youth group, calling itself the "Christian Volunteers" organized at the Ohio **camp meeting** in 1899 and the following year a similar group formed in **Germany**.

Seeing the success of these organizations and partly inspired by the interchurch Student Volunteer Movement that was developing at the time, the **General Conference** (GC) asked the Sabbath School Department in 1901 to encourage the development of such groups elsewhere; by 1903 the department reported that 186 organizations were active. In 1907 the GC created the Young People's Department and appointed Milton E. Kern, who had organized the youth group at Union College, to be chairman of the new entity. Later that year a convention in Ohio chose the name "Young People's Society of Missionary Volunteers" for the youth organizations. Because these "MV Societies," as they were called, targeted older youth, in 1909 the **General Conference session** developed plans for young people between the ages of 10 and 15, calling this organization the "Junior Missionary Volunteer Society" (JMV). During the next several years the Youth Department developed a number of programs for the JMV and MV societies, including a Young People's Day, reading courses, daily devotional materials called the "Morning Watch," a year-long Bible reading plan, and a progressive series of classes leading to certificates (and later, pins). The types of church-sponsored activities began broadening when conferences started organizing summer camps, starting with Michigan in 1926, and Germany held the first youth congress in 1928. Meanwhile, local Adventist organizations modeled on the Boy Scouts began appearing as early as 1911; in the 1930s groups in California adopted the name **Pathfinder Club.** In 1950 these clubs became a recognized denominational program that worked in conjunction with the MV societies. After World War II youth congresses also became a significant activity, with North America holding its first congress in 1947 and **Europe**

holding congresses in **Czechoslovakia** and **Great Britain** the
following year. Other congresses followed in the 1950s and 1960s.
In 1979 the denomination changed the names of the youth
organizations to Adventist Youth (AY) and Adventist Junior Youth
(AJY) and renamed the classes Pathfinder/AJY classes. Six years
later the Youth Department became part of the Church Ministries
Department.

MISSIONS. Early Seventh-day Adventists had little interest in spreading their teachings beyond North America, largely because they
were small in number and had few financial resources. When **Michael B. Czechowski**, a Polish immigrant convert, asked the **General Conference** (GC) to send him to **Europe** the denomination's
leaders turned him down. In 1864, however, Czechowski went to
Europe anyway under the auspices of the **Advent Christian
Church**. He nonetheless taught Seventh-day Adventist doctrines in
Italy, **Switzerland**, and elsewhere but did not tell his converts
about the Seventh-day Adventist Church. One of his Swiss believers, Albert Vuilleumier, found a copy of the *Review and Herald*
and initiated correspondence with the American church. In 1869
another member of the Swiss Adventist group, James Erzberger,
traveled to America and met with denominational leaders. These
contacts led to the decision in 1874 to send **John Nevins Andrews**
to Europe as the first official Seventh-day Adventist missionary.
Three years later, in response to pleas by Scandinavians who had
read Adventist literature received from relatives in the **United
States**, the GC sent **John G. Matteson** to **Denmark**. In 1878
William Ings began working in **Great Britain**, where **John N.
Loughborough** joined him later that year. During this first,
European, stage of Adventist mission development, the missionaries in several places set up publishing houses and began
producing missionary papers, thereby establishing a pattern that
would be used by Adventist missionaries throughout the world.

The second stage of Adventist missions took place in the
1880s and 1890s, as missionaries moved into all of the major continents of the world, though in most cases they first **evangelized**
the European populations of these regions. In 1885 the first Adventist missionaries, including **Stephen N. Haskell**, went to **Australia**. Shortly thereafter, **John I. Tay** arrived on Pitcairn Island; in
1890 the denomination launched the schooner *Pitcairn*, with Tay
and other missionaries aboard, to work throughout the **South Pacific**. In 1886, in response to requests from Dutch residents of
South Africa who had learned about Adventism, the denomination

sent D. A. Robinson and several other missionaries. Although some lay Adventists had preceded them, the first **literature evangelists** arrived in South America in 1891; **Frank A. Westphal, a minister,** joined them in 1894. About the same time, Dan T. Jones established a mission in **Mexico. Georgia Burrus Burgess** went to **India** in 1895, followed in 1898 by **William A. Spicer. Abram La Rue,** a layman, began evangelizing in **Hong Kong** and elsewhere in East **Asia** in 1887; in 1896 W. C. Grainger arrived as the first Adventist missionary in **Japan.**

Meanwhile, after Cecil Rhodes's British South Africa Company granted the Adventists land in present-day **Zimbabwe,** several missionaries moved from South Africa to establish **Solusi Mission** in 1894, the first significant effort by Adventists among indigenous peoples. Under the leadership of GC presidents **Arthur G. Daniells** and William A. Spicer, the denomination in the first three decades of the 20th century entered what one historian has called the "golden age of Adventist missions." During Daniells's administration (1901-22), the number of missionaries going out averaged about 100 annually and under Spicer (1922-30) the average climbed to more than 160. With such an emphasis on missions, it is not surprising that by 1921 the number of Adventists outside North America was greater than that in the denomination's homeland.

Although two World Wars and numerous revolutions frequently disrupted the denomination's missionary efforts, the church continued to grow, particularly in **Africa,** the **Philippines, New Guinea, Korea,** and **Latin America,** and the leadership of the church in these areas increasingly passed from American, European, or Australian missionaries to national leaders. As a result, the function of the missionary often changed from a leadership to a support role. In addition to producing their own national leaders, Asia, Africa, and Latin America increasingly sent out their own missionaries. The denomination sought to better prepare its missionaries to work cross-culturally by establishing the **Institute of World Mission** in 1966. It also used the insights of the social sciences to develop a **Global Mission** strategy, beginning in 1990, that focused on reaching population groups and geographical regions without an Adventist presence. The development of the parachurch **Adventist Frontier Missions** provided additional support.

MOLDOVA. As of 2003, the Moldova **Union Conference,** part of the Euro-**Asia Division,** had 134 **churches** with a membership of over 11,000. *See also* ROMANIA.

MONGOLIA. Russian missionaries, working out of **China**, printed some tracts in Mongolian about 1926. In 1931 Otto Christensen established a **mission** station at Kalgan and soon began printing various tracts and other materials while Russian missionaries maintained two smaller mission stations in the region. The advent of war in the late 1930s halted Adventist mission efforts in Mongolia until **Adventist Frontier Missions** began working there in the 1990s. As of 2003 the Mongolian **Mission Field**, an attached field of the Northern **Asia-Pacific Division**, had one **church** and a membership of 369.

MONNIER, HENRI (1896-1944). Seventh-day Adventist missionary. Born in **Switzerland**, Monnier was working in England when he was convinced by David E. Delhove to join him in **mission** work in **Africa**. In 1921 they established the Gitwe Mission in present-day **Rwanda** and the following year the Rwankeri Mission about 100 miles further north. Monnier's wife had died shortly after arriving in Africa; after three years of working alone, in 1924 Monnier went back to **Europe** where he remarried and returned to Africa the following year, working there until the advent of World War II. His efforts inspired what missiologists have described as something like a "people movement" that brought thousands of Hutu and Tutsi people into the denomination in the early 1930s. While working in Africa, Monnier was a member of a translation group that produced the Kinyarwanda language New Testament, published by the British and Foreign Bible Society in 1931. In addition, he also wrote a Kinyarwanda grammar for the use of English-speaking missionaries and several pamphlets in the Kinyarwanda language. After leaving Africa, he worked in **Lebanon** and **Syria**.

MONTEMORELOS UNIVERSITY. Seventh-day Adventist **educational** institution in Montemorelos, Nuevo León, **Mexico**. A secondary school, Mexican Agricultural and Industrial School, and the Seventh-day Adventist Theological Seminary, which offered two years of post-secondary theology, opened near Montemorelos in 1942. By 1944 the institution had won state recognition for both primary and secondary programs. Three years later Montemorelos Hospital opened and in 1948 started a school of nursing. The school administration also directed the hospital, although it was otherwise a separate institution. In 1951 the Agricultural and Industrial School took the name Montemorelos Vocational and Professional College. A normal school opened in 1957 and achieved official recognition four years later. "Licientura" programs in theology and public accountancy were instituted in 1967; at the same time the school of nursing moved from the hospital to the college. The state of Nuevo León granted a charter in 1973 creating the University of Montemorelos, and authorized it to establish a number of new programs. Montemorelos Hospital merged with the university in 1974 and the following year, with help from **Loma Linda University**, a medical school began conducting classes. In 1981 **Andrews University** began an extension program for the M.A. in religion, followed six years later by an M.S. in administration. Montemorelos offered its first graduate degrees in 1989 with the M.Ed. and M.P.H. The school established a **music** conservatory in 1990 and added various graduate programs in subsequent years, including a Ph.D. in education in 1993. As of 2003 the university was organized into several professional schools: Business Administration, Chemistry, Dental Technology, Education, Engineering and Technology, Fine Arts, Medicine, Music, Nursing, Nutrition, and Theology.

MOOKERJEE, LAL GOPAL (1882-1952). Seventh-day Adventist **evangelist**. A member of a Calcutta family that had converted to Seventh-day Adventism, Mookerjee established in 1906 the Gopalganj mission in present-day **Bangladesh**. After attending Washington Missionary College (later **Columbia Union College**), in the **United States**, he returned to **India**, where he worked as an evangelist in Calcutta until 1913. He subsequently held a number of administrative positions, edited the Bengali *Signs of the Times*, and taught at the insitution later named Spicer Memorial College.

MORE, HANNAH (1808-1868). Missionary to **Liberia**. More was a Christian missionary in **Africa** who met **Stephen N. Haskell** while visiting the **United States** in 1861 or 1862. Haskell gave her **John N. Andrews**'s *History of the Sabbath* and other Seventh-day Adventist **literature**, which led her to convert to Adventism, probably in 1863. She returned to Africa where she superintended an orphanage, operated by a British missionary society, at Cape Palmas, Liberia. While in Liberia, More shared her new beliefs with a missionary colleague, Alexander Dickson, who later introduced Adventism into **Australia**. After losing her position at the orphanage because of her Adventist beliefs, in 1866 More went to Battle Creek, Michigan, where she unsuccessfully sought employment with the Seventh-day Adventist Church. Eventually a former missionary colleague living in northern Michigan offered her a job but she died a few months later. **Ellen G. White**, who had been away from Battle Creek when More visited the area, later told the Adventists that they had missed an important opportunity by not being more receptive to the former missionary.

MOROCCO. The first Seventh-day Adventists entered Morocco in 1925 when a lay member started a **Sabbath school** and Jean Reynaud began conducting **evangelism**. When a missionary family arrived in 1928 they organized a **mission**. In 1932 and 1933 two physicians from the **United States** began working among the indigenous population. Although by 1964 there were five churches with 165 members, the government later prohibited mission work. The *Adventist Encyclopedia* (1996) reported that in 1993 there were about 12 members who met in private homes. As of 2003 Morocco was part of the Trans-Mediterranean Territories, an attached **field** of the Euro-**Africa Division**. There were no statistics available for Morocco.

MOZAMBIQUE. Two students from the Malamulo **mission** station in present-day **Malawi** introduced Seventh-day Adventism into Mozambique, then Portuguese East **Africa**, in 1931. Adventist missionaries visited the country in 1933 and two years later Max Webster established the Munguluni mission station. Webster **baptized** his first converts in 1939 and in 1940 the first Adventist school opened; by the 1950s it was offering a preparatory course for teachers. Also in the 1940s the denomination began publishing materials locally, although it did not establish a publishing house until 1963. In the 1950s and 1960s missionaries created several new mission stations. Dispensaries opened at Munguluni in 1958 and Marrucia in 1963. Civil war in the late 20th century forced many Adventists to flee to Malawi, but they began returning in the mid-1990s. As of 2003 the Mozambique **Union Mission**, part of the Euro-**Africa Division**, had over 900 **churches** and a membership of about 170,000. The Union Mission operated Mozambique Adventist Seminary and Mozambique Publishing House.

MUSIC. Probably because of its direct connection with worship, Seventh-day Adventists have given much more attention to music than to the other **arts**. Music was an important part of the **Millerite camp meetings**, for which **Joshua V. Himes** published the *Millennial Harp* in 1842. In 1848 **James White** drew on Himes's **hymnal** for many of the songs that he included in *Hymns for God's Peculiar People*, the first sabbatarian Adventist hymnal. Six years after the organization of the **General Conference**, the denomination published its first official hymnal, *Hymns and Tunes for Those Who Keep the Commandments of God and the Faith of Jesus*. New official hymnals appeared in 1886, 1941, and 1985.

During their first three decades of existence Adventists sang their hymns without instrumentation. In 1877, however, James White used a reed pump organ at a California camp meeting. Despite the misgivings of some, instrumental accompaniment soon became acceptable. About 1881 the Battle Creek Seventh-day Adventist **Church** purchased a two-manual organ and Edwin E. Barnes emigrated from England to become the church organist and teach students from **Battle Creek College.**

Much of the musical life of the denomination revolved around its schools, which began to place importance on music in the 1890s despite an often utilitarian approach to education. **South Lancaster Academy** started offering lessons in voice, piano, and organ in 1890 and in 1904 established a music department headed by pianist Edna S. Farnsworth. Meanwhile, **Union College** (UC) in Nebraska organized one of the first choral groups in the denomination for the dedication of the College View Church in 1894. Soon after Battle Creek College's 1901 move to Berrien Springs, where it became **Emmanuel Missionary College** (EMC), it provided a reed organ and a two-manual vocalion on which students could practice, which suggests the availability of lessons. When Washington Training College, later renamed Washington Missionary College (WMC) and then Columbia Union College (CUC), opened in 1904 it offered voice and organ lessons and two years later introduced a program for the study of sacred music, all taught by Walton John. **Walla Walla College** (WWC), which had a music department as of 1892, and **Pacific Union College** (PUC) installed their first pipe organs in 1910 and 1912, respectively. PUC established its music department in 1914 under the leadership of violinist Noah Paulin. During the inter-war years choirs became a firmly established part of the denomination's colleges. George W. Greer began teaching at PUC in 1926 and soon thereafter organized the denomination's first *a cappella* choir, with which he toured. At WMC Victor Johnson, who joined the faculty in 1929, organized both a choir and a traveling glee club. About the same time, Harry Hadley Schyde organized choirs at **Atlantic Union College** (AUC), formerly South Lancaster Academy, which achieved considerable local renown. When Greer moved from PUC to WMC in 1937 he established an *a cappella* choir and presented a new challenge to the previously existing oratorio chorus when he scheduled a performance of Handel's *The Messiah*, something that had never been done before at the school. By 1940 performances of *The Messiah* and *Elijah* had become annual affairs. Somewhat similarly, Harold A. Miller, who joined the faculty of Southern Junior College, later Southern Missionary College (SMC) and then **Southern Adventist University** (SAU), in 1935, had his choir participate in annual performances of *The Messiah* with Chattanooga's civic chorus and orchestra.

Instrumental groups also developed about the same time. Noah Paulin directed concert bands and orchestras from the beginning of his tenure at PUC. At EMC Louis Thorpe, who formerly had played in John Philip Sousa's Navy Band, led both band and orchestra in the 1920s and would do so later at WWC. In 1937 George Wargo, principal violist for the National Symphony Orchestra and a teacher at the Peabody Conservatory of Music, began working part-time for WMC as conductor of the orchestra. In 1942 he became chair of the school's music department. Bela Urbanowsky, a student of violin teacher Eugene Ysaye, joined the faculty of AUC in 1937, where he directed the orchestra for the next four years.

With their musical groups maturing, the colleges also began to offer degrees in music. WWC, for instance, awarded an unaccredited Bachelor of Music, beginning in 1914, and an accredited B.A. in music in 1937. As other Adventist colleges became accredited, starting with PUC in 1932, they soon introduced music degree programs.

As they acquired more highly trained musicians, the college academic programs and musical organizations emphasized classical music. In the Adventist churches at large, however, gospel music dominated. In 1878 the denomination published a gospel music collection, *The Song Anchor*, which included works by **Frank E. Belden**, a young Adventist songwriter. In the early 20th century Belden compiled *Christ in Song*, which included many gospel songs; its 1908 edition became so popular in the churches that it was sometimes described as the denomination's "unofficial hymnal." Focusing on popular gospel songs useful in **evangelistic** meetings, **Roy Allan Anderson** published *Gospel Melodies* in 1931; revised as *Gospel Melodies and Evangelistic Hymns* in 1944, it became a staple of **Sabbath school** and youth meetings. Meanwhile, at the Adventist colleges male students frequently organized gospel quartets, a form popular in conservative Protestant circles. One group, which came together at Southwestern Junior College, later **Southwestern Adventist University** (SWAU), joined the

Tabernacle of the Air radio broadcast in 1936; the following year the program took the name *Voice of Prophecy* while the quartet became known as the **King's Heralds**. This *a cappella* group achieved enormous popularity in Adventist circles. After **Del Delker** began singing for *Voice of Prophecy* in 1947 she also became a fixture in Adventist music. As recordings of the *Voice of Prophecy* performers became available in the 1950s, they were common possessions in Adventist homes. When the television programs *Faith for Today* and *Breath of Life* formed, they also organized male quartets, although they never gained the popularity of the *King's Heralds*.

While there was some tension between the classically oriented college music teachers and the gospel music interests of the typical Adventist church member, nearly all Adventist music leaders were agreed that such forms of popular music as jazz, swing, and rock and roll were inappropriate for the Christian. Because Adventist young people were exposed to this music through radio, television, and recordings, the church fought a constant battle to limit its influence. While control of private tastes and habits was not possible, school and college administrators, teachers, and church pastors set rules governing what could be performed at social functions and concerts. The problems became particularly significant in the late 1960s as the **Wedgwood Trio**, a folk trio from SMC, achieved widespread popularity in the denomination and thereby introduced contemporary sounds into popular Adventist music. Drawing the line between acceptable and unacceptable music seemed increasingly difficult. Therefore, after considerable study the 1972 Autumn Council of the **General Conference** Executive Committee voted "Guidelines Toward An SDA Philosophy of Music." Among other things, this document emphasized that music should be uplifting, compatible with Scripture, and give precedence to the text, observing that jazz, rock, and their derivatives were incompatible with these principles.

These guidelines, however, appear not to have had the impact desired, for they were written at the very time that the contemporary Christian music movement was taking form. By the 1990s students and professional groups were performing this music on Adventist campuses throughout the **United States** and recordings of groups ranging from the country-oriented **Heritage Singers** to the rock sounds of Big Face Grace sold widely. In addition, the rapid expansion of Adventism outside North America introduced world music into the church; when African rhythms and Caribbean steel drums, for instance, resounded at the 2000 **General Confer-**

ence Session in Toronto, they caused considerable consternation in some sectors of the denomination.

Not all was controversy, however. Beginning in the 1960s several music departments at Adventist colleges achieved accreditation from the National Association of Schools of Music, beginning with WWC in 1963. Starting about the same time, a number of college churches, including those at WWC, AU, and **Loma Linda University** installed major organs. Within the next two decades PUC, UC, and SAU also installed major organs; as the largest tracker-action organ in the United States, the SAU instrument gained recognition internationally as a major achievement. In 1976 the Seventh-day Adventist Church Musicians' Guild organized under the leadership of Oliver S. Beltz and Albert E. Mayes for the purpose of promoting high quality sacred music. Although this organization disbanded in 1989, its endowment of the Oliver S. Beltz Chair of Sacred Music left a lasting legacy at the **Seventh-day Adventist Theological Seminary**. In 1982 another organization, the International Adventist Musicians Association, formed for the purpose of discussing and bringing attention to all types of Adventist music. Among Adventist musical groups, Virginia-Gene Rittenhouse's *New England Youth Ensemble*, first organized at AUC in 1972, probably received the greatest recognition, traveling internationally many times and performing frequently in such places as Carnegie Hall in New York City. Rittenhouse moved the ensemble in 1993 to CUC, where it often performed with the college's choral groups conducted by James Bingham. In March 2004 Bingham conducted Ritthenhouse's oratorio, *The Vision of the Apocalypse*, at Carnegie Hall.

Also, individual Adventist musicians achieved renown, among them Herbert Blomstedt, conductor of the San Francisco Symphony from 1985 to 1995, and the black gospel group Take Six. Country music singer Roy Drusky successfully continued his career after his conversion to Adventism. "Little Richard" Penniman, a rhythm and blues singer, has had an intermittent relationship with the church. Although not members of the denomination as adults, pop musician "Prince" Rogers Nelson and classical singers Shirley Verrett and Thomas Hampson had Adventist backgrounds.

MYANMAR (FORMERLY BURMA). In 1902 two **literature evangelists**, Herbert B. Meyers and A. G. Watson, entered Burma, as Myanmar was then known. Meyers stayed for several years and developed a group of Seventh-day Adventist believers. In response to their request for a **minister**, Heber H. Votaw arrived in 1905 and established the Burma **Mission**. Ollie Oberholtzer, a physician, came two years later. As other missionaries came to the country they established schools, beginning with the Meiktila Industrial School in 1909. In 1915 missionary work began among the Karen people and in 1924 among the Taungthu. By 1922 Seventh-day Adventists had six **churches** with 182 members, about which time it began publishing materials in the Burmese and Karen languages. World War II forced the missionaries to leave the country but on their return they established a hospital and press at Rangoon and reopened many schools. When a revolutionary government came to power, foreign missionaries had to leave Myanmar and leadership of the church passed to national leaders. At the same time, the government nationalized the hospital and several schools. As of 2003 the Myanmar **Union Mission**, part of the Southern **Asia-**Pacific **Division**, had 189 churches and a membership of over 23,000. The Union Mission operated Myanmar Union Adventist Seminary and Kinsaung Publishing House.

N

NAMIBIA. The first Seventh-day Adventist **evangelistic** campaign in South-West **Africa**, as Namibia was then called, took place in 1937-38 at Windhoek and resulted in five **baptisms**. Except for two **literature evangelists** who worked in the area, however, no further evangelistic efforts took place until 1954 when the South-West Africa **Field** organized. The church grew slowly and most converts came from the European population until the 1960s when the first Black and mixed-race **churches** organized. As of 2003 the Namibia Field, part of the Southern Africa **Union Conference** of the Southern Africa-Indian Ocean **Division**, had 55 churches with a membership of about 13,000.

NELSON, KATHRYN JENSEN (1891-1970). Seventh-day Adventist nursing **educator**. After receiving a teaching certificate from Waupaca County Junior College in Wisconsin, Nelson completed the nursing program at the College of Medical Evangelists (CME; later **Loma Linda University**), in 1917. She then worked as a supervisor at Loma Linda **Sanitarium** and the School of Nursing at the Washington Sanitarium and Hospital and served as a school nurse at the Danish-Norwegian Seminary in Hutchinson, Minnesota. Appointed in 1921 as assistant secretary in the Medical Department of the **General Conference**, she had the responsibility of overseeing the training of nurses in the denomination. She began an annual

statistical survey of the denomination's nursing schools and, recognizing the need for nurses to acquire further education, developed in 1924 a five-year pilot B.S. curriculum between Washington Missionary College (later **Columbia Union College**), and the
Washington Sanitarium and Hospital nursing program. This affiliation helped prepare the way for the establishment of baccalaureate
nursing programs at other Adventist colleges. In addition, she introduced a Nurses Institute in 1923 and a more formal summer
school, beginning in 1924, to provide continuing education for
working nurses.

Jensen (she was not yet married) also promoted the development of standards of nursing education, serving on the Committee
on Standards and Qualifications of the Adventist Board of Regents
that was established in 1928, and in the late 1930s pushed for accreditation of denominational nursing schools by the National
League of Nursing Education. She traveled widely in the **United
States** and **Europe**, assessing Adventist sanitariums and nursing
programs. Appointed associate secretary of the Medical Department in 1932, she completed an M.A. in Nursing Education at
Catholic University of America in 1936. She resigned from the
Medical Department in 1940 to marry Nels Nelson, an Adventist
minister in Minnesota.

After her husband accepted the position of chaplain at the
Boulder Sanitarium in Colorado, Nelson, as she was now known,
worked as clinical coordinator of the institution's School of Nursing and helped integrate its curriculum with that of **Union College**.
In 1948 she became the first dean of the School of Nursing at the
CME in Loma Linda, California, where she combined the White
Memorial Hospital School of Nursing in Glendale with the CME's
nursing program. Before retiring in 1956 she also developed a
graduate program in nursing. Nelson's books included *The Mother
and the Child* (1927), *Fundamentals in Massage for Students of
Nursing* (1932), *Kate Lindsay, M.D.* (1963), and, with Harold M.
Walton, *Historical Sketches of the Medical Work of Seventh-day
Adventists from 1866 to 1896* (1948). With George Knapp Abbott
and Fred B. Moor, she also wrote *Physical Therapy in Nursing
Care* (1945).

NETHERLANDS, THE. Ludvig R. Conradi organized a **church** of
five members, probably at Winschoten, in 1887 but within the next
two years most of these individuals moved to the **United States**. In
1889 Conradi established another church, this time with nine
members. Four years later Reinhold G. Klingbeil began **evangelis-**

tic efforts in Rotterdam, **baptizing** six individuals in 1895, and in 1897 Joseph Wintzen started **publishing** the *Signs of the Times*. The denomination organized the Holland **Mission** Field in 1901 and began publishing *The Advent Messenger*. By 1912 there were about 250 Adventists in the country. The Hamburg Publishing House established a branch in the Netherlands in 1929 that ten years later became a separate institution. The Netherlands **Union Conference** formed in 1938 and after World War II opened a junior college. As of 2003 the Netherlands Union Conference, which belonged to the Trans-European **Division**, had 50 churches with a membership of about 4,000.

NETHERLANDS ANTILLES. The first Seventh-day Adventist missionaries arrived in the Netherlands Antilles in 1926 and in 1934 organized a **church** of 16 members in San Nicolas, Aruba. The denomination printed its first tracts in the Papiamento language in 1941 and established its first school in 1955. As of 2003 the Netherlands Antilles **Conference**, part of the Venezuela-Antilles **Union Mission** of the Inter-American **Division**, had 26 churches with a membership of over 5,000. Antillean Adventist Hospital was located in Curacao.

NEWBOLD COLLEGE. Seventh-day Adventist **educational** institution located near London, England. Originally established as Duncombe Hall Missionary College in North London in 1901, the school moved six years later to Watford, where it became Stanborough Missionary College. In 1931 it moved again to an estate near Rugby and took the name Newbold College. After World War II ended in 1945, it moved to its present location in Binfield, near Bracknell, Berkshire. The North European **Division** chose Newbold in 1954 as its advanced training center. In 1958 the school negotiated an affiliation with **Columbia Union College** through which students on the Newbold campus could earn bachelor's degrees from the American institution. A similar affiliation with **Andrews University** began in 1983. The Council for National Academic Awards (later called the Open University Validation Services, United Kingdom) accredited Newbold in 1992. As of 2003 the school offered six baccalaureate programs.

NEW CALEDONIA AND LOYALTY ISLANDS. Griffeths F. Jones first carried Seventh-day Adventism to New Caledonia in 1925 and visited the Loyalty Islands the following year. Because the Adventists had not received official permission to work in the islands, Jones had to leave New Caledonia in 1927 after **baptizing** 10 individuals. Miss C. F. Guiot, a French citizen who had arrived in 1926, remained on the islands until 1950. In 1954 the New Caledonian **Mission** organized. As of 2003 the mission, part of the **New Zealand**-Pacific **Union Conference** of the **South Pacific Division**, had five **churches** and a membership of over 300.

NEW ZEALAND. In 1885 **Stephen N. Haskell** arrived in Auckland from **Australia** and in 1886 **baptized** 15 individuals. **Arthur G. Daniells** came to New Zealand in 1886 to conduct **evangelism** and organized the first Adventist **church** in 1887 at Kaeo. **Robert Hare**, one of Haskell's first converts, meanwhile studied for the ministry at Healdsburg College (later **Pacific Union College**), returning in 1888 to conduct evangelism with Daniells. In 1889 the New Zealand **Conference** organized with 155 members. By 1905 the conference had 13 churches with a membership of over 500 and in 1908 opened a secondary school that eventually developed into Longburn Adventist College. As of 2003 the denomination in New Zealand was organized into two conferences, and was part of the New Zealand-Pacific **Union Conference** of the **South Pacific Division**. The conferences had 85 churches with a membership of about 11,000. Longburn Adventist College and two secondary schools were located in New Zealand.

NICARAGUA. A **literature evangelist**, Frank J. Hutchins, began selling books in Nicaragua in 1892. C. F. Brooks accepted Adventist beliefs in 1898 and, as a layperson, established a group of believers at Yulu that later organized into a **church**. By the time the Nicaragua **Mission** organized in 1929 there were four English-speaking churches with, reportedly, only one Spanish-speaking member. Dr. N. M. Brayshaw began medical work in 1920, but no hospital opened until 1948 when C. J. McCleary created the **self-supporting** Adventist Clinic and Hospital in Puerto Cabezas. Operation of the hospital passed to the Central American **Union Conference** in 1954, after which the institution moved to La Trinidad. The government nationalized the facility in 1980. As of 2003 the Nicaragua Mission, part of the Central American Union Conference of the Inter-American **Division**, had 135 churches and a membership of over 55,000. The union conference operated Adventist Vocational School of Nicaragua.

NICHOL, FRANCIS DAVID (1897-1966). Seventh-day Adventist editor. Born in **Australia**, at age eight Nichol moved to Loma

Linda, California, with his parents, who had converted to Adventism. After briefly serving as a pastor, in 1921 he became associate editor of the *Signs of the Times*. While at this magazine he and another of the journal's editors, Alonzo Baker, held a well-publicized series of debates with Maynard Shipley, an advocate of evolutionary theory. In 1927 he joined the staff of the *Review and Herald* and in 1945 became editor, serving in that position for the rest of his life. Also, between 1934 and 1945 he edited *Life and Health* and later served as chief editor of the *Seventh-day Adventist Bible Commentary* (1953-57). Among his books were *Answers to Objections* (1932), *The Midnight Cry* (1944), and *Ellen G. White and Her Critics* (1951).

NIGERIA. In 1914 David C. Babcock, who had worked in **Sierra Leone**, entered Nigeria with two assistants. By the end of the year they had established a mission station at Erunmu in the Western Region, were operating three schools, and reported having made seven converts. As other missionaries arrived, they pushed into the Eastern Region in the 1920s. The East and West Nigerian **Missions** organized in 1930 and in 1931 a dispensary opened in the Northern Region. In 1932 the missionaries started a teacher training school at Ibadan, transferring it to Ihie in 1947, where it was named Nigerian Training College. The North Nigeria Mission organized in 1952 and three years later Adventist Training College started offering classes at Otun. About the same time, medical missionaries established hospitals at Ahoada and North Ngwa. The Adventist College of West Africa, now Babcock University, opened at Ede in 1960. The Nigerian Civil War that took place from 1967 to 1970 resulted in the nationalization of the Nigerian Training College, a secondary school at Ihie, and the hospitals in Ahoada and Ngwa. Despite the political difficulties, church membership continued to grow and Nigerians rose to church leadership. As of 2003 the Nigeria **Union Mission,** part of the Western **Africa Division**, had **691 churches** and a membership of nearly 200,000. Babcock University, one secondary school, four hospitals, and 18 clinics and dispensaries were located in Nigeria.

NONCOMBATANCY. A willingness to serve in the military but not bear arms. After the start of the American Civil War, three viewpoints arose within the newly organized Seventh-day Adventist Church: active participation in the war effort, pacifism, and willingness to serve in the military but not bear arms. As the nation moved toward conscription, adopted in 1863, Adventists gradually

came to a consensus around the third position; they would accept
being drafted but would not bear arms. The conscription law, however, had no provisions for conscientious objectors or noncombatants. Most Adventists, therefore, took advantage of an element of
the law that allowed them to purchase an exemption for $300. In
February 1864 Congress amended the conscription law to allow
conscientious objectors to work in hospitals or care for liberated
slaves. But Adventists continued to use the exemption provision
until Congress in July restricted it to officially recognized conscientious objectors. The following month **John Nevins Andrews**
met with Provost Marshal General James B. Fry and presented him
with a recent Adventist publication entitled *The Draft*, which explained the church's noncombatant position. Fry subsequently as-
sured Andrews that he would order the Army to recognize Adventists as noncombatants. Adventist soldiers, however, had considerable difficulty gaining recognition from local commanders. On the
other hand, during the last few months of the war the Seventh-day Adventist church dropped from membership soldiers who
voluntarily enlisted.

With the outbreak of World War I in 1914, the Seventh-day
Adventist Church again had difficulty defining its position, a situation exacerbated by the fact that it was now an international body.
Under intense governmental pressure a number of **German** Adventist leaders said that conscripted church members would bear
arms and perform essential military services on the **Sabbath**. Other
German leaders arranged noncombatant service in the medical
corps for draftees, while some supported a pacifist position and
recommended that members refuse to participate in the military. In
Great Britain and **Australia** Adventists were able to gain recognition as noncombatants, although British soldiers had considerable
difficulty with Sabbath observance. In the **United States** church
leaders did little until April 1917 when they debated in the Spring
Council of the **General Conference** (GC) Executive Committee
whether to reaffirm the noncombatant position or move toward
pacifism, ultimately coming down on the side of noncombatancy,
although their decision applied only to the church in the United
States. Because of the difficulties Adventist draftees experienced
in gaining recognition as noncombatants from their local draft
boards and with Sabbath observance in the military, the church established the War Service Commission in 1918 to address these
problems.

Responding to questions posed by students at **Walla Walla
College** in 1930, the **General Conference session** of that year es-

tablished a committee to study the issue of military service. The committee, however, was unable to reach a consensus. In 1934 the Spring Council of the GC Executive Committee revised and then approved a pamphlet entitled *Our Youth in Time of War*, which had been written by an officer of the Columbia **Union Conference**. This pamphlet strongly rejected all forms of pacifism in favor of noncombatancy. That same year **Everett N. Dick** started a College Medical Corps at **Union College** to train young men for medical service in the military. In 1939 the denomination adopted this program, renaming it the **Medical Cadet Corps**, and recommended that all Adventist colleges in the United States put the program in place. In 1940 the GC reinstituted the War Service Commision under the leadership of **Carlyle B. Haynes**, who had also headed it during World War I. Most American Adventist soldiers in World War II adopted the noncombatancy position and had relatively few problems with either their refusal to bear arms or their observance of the Sabbath. One soldier, Desmond T. Doss, was awarded the Medal of Honor for his actions during the battle of Okinawa, when he lowered 75 wounded men over a cliff to safety.

Noncombatancy remained the church's official position in the 1950s and 1960s, although unlike during the Civil War it never again became a matter of membership. Beginning in the mid-1950s the denomination cooperated with the United States Army in Project Whitecoat, a program that used Adventist noncombatants to allegedly test defenses against biological warfare. In the late 1960s this program came under considerable criticism, particularly in an article by Seymour Hersh published in *Ramparts*, a radical political journal. The **Vietnam** War, however, provoked many Adventist young people to question the church's noncombatant position and, after considerable controversy, the Autumn Council of the GC Executive Committee voted in 1969 to support those Adventists who sought to gain recognition as conscientious objectors. With the end of the draft in the United States in 1972, the church organization, while favoring noncombatancy as its historic policy, essentially left the issue of military service to individual conscience.

NORWAY. Responding to requests from people in **Europe** who had read his Danish-language paper published in the **United States**, **John G. Matteson** went to **Denmark** in 1877 and the following year arrived in Norway. By early 1879 he had organized a **church** in Christiania (now Oslo) and later that year established a publishing house in the city that began putting out a Norwegian *Signs of* *the Times*. In 1886 three additional missionaries arrived from the United States. The following year they organized the Norwegian **Conference** and held what appears to have been the first Seventh-day Adventist **camp meeting** in **Europe**. By 1901 Norway had over 600 members. As elsewhere in much of Europe, Adventist growth was slow in the 20th century. As of 2003 the Norwegian **Union Conference**, part of the Trans-European **Division**, had 70 churches and a membership of nearly 5,000. The Union Conference operated Norwegian Junior College, Skogli Health and Rehabilitation Center, and Norwegian Publishing House.

NUSSBAUM, JEAN (1888-1967). Seventh-day Adventist physician and **religious liberty** advocate. After graduation from a medical school in Lyons, in 1914 Nussbaum worked for the Serbian government to fight a typhus epidemic until political conditions forced him to leave the country the following year. After working in Dieppe and Le Havre, he established a medical practice in Paris. In 1931 the Southern European **Division** asked Nussbaum to join **Charles S. Longacre, Arthur S. Maxwell,** and **Roy Allan Anderson**, who were to attend the League of Nations meeting in Geneva which had on its agenda the subject of calendar reform. Adventists were concerned about this reform proposal because it would result in a "floating" **Sabbath** that could occur any time during the week. The denomination requested Nussbaum's help because none of their representatives spoke French and the physician had contacts with high-level officials. When the proposal came before the League, Nussbaum gave a speech that apparently turned opinion against it. A short time later the Southern European Division appointed him religious liberty secretary and in subsequent years he met several times with Pope Pius XII and sought to establish religious freedom in **Romania** and **Bulgaria**. After World War II he attended the 1945 meeting of the United Nations in San Francisco and developed an acquaintance with Eleanor Roosevelt. Later he successfully gained the reopening of Adventist churches in **Spain** and obtained freedom of worship for Adventists in **Colombia**. Still a practicing physician, he was active in the French Anti-Tobacco Society and served as president of the Institute Curie, an organization of Protestant doctors.

O

OAKWOOD COLLEGE (OC). Seventh-day Adventist African American **educational** institution located in Huntsville, Alabama.

In 1895 a committee appointed by the **General Conference** purchased land near Huntsville, Alabama, where it planned to establish an industrial school for African Americans. After land was cleared and some existing buildings repaired, Oakwood Industrial School opened in November 1896. Accommodating both boarding and day students, the school taught basic secondary subjects as well as agriculture, masonry, and carpentry for the boys and cooking, sewing, laundering, and gardening for the girls. In 1899 it began offering a two-year diploma. After two name changes—Huntsville Training School and Oakwood Manual Training School—the institution became Oakwood Junior College in 1917, eventually offering programs in theology, teacher training, music, secretarial science, and pre-nursing. In 1918 it graduated its first two junior college students. Becoming a four-year college in 1943 and awarding its first baccalaureate degrees in 1945, Oakwood College gained accreditation from the Southern Association of Colleges and Schools in stages between 1958 and 1963. In 1964 it became a member of the United Negro College Fund. By 2003 the school had about 1,700 students from 38 countries and offered liberal arts and professional degrees.

OLSEN, OLE ANDRES (1845-1915). Seventh-day Adventist church administrator. Born in **Norway**, at age five Olsen immigrated with his parents to the **United States**, where they settled in Wisconsin. About four years later his family converted to sabbatarian Adventism. In 1869 he began working as a licensed **minister** in the Wisconsin **Conference**. After receiving **ordination** in 1873, he became president of the Wisconsin Conference the following year, staying in that position until 1876 when he left to **evangelize** among the Scandinavian-American population. After serving as president of several conferences, including Wisconsin (1880-81), Dakota (1882-83), Minnesota (1883-85), and Iowa (1884-85), in 1886 he went to Norway, where he became the first president of the Norway Conference the following year. The controversy-filled **General Conference session of 1888**, which he did not attend, elected him **General Conference** (GC) president. Holding that office until 1897, Olsen struggled with financial and organizational issues, taking the first steps toward establishing a GC budget and encouraging the development of the **Union Conference** concept in **Australia**. After leaving the denomination's presidency, he worked in **South Africa** and **Europe** before successively becoming president of the British Union Conference in 1902 and the Australian Union Conference in 1905. He returned to the United States in 1909 where he served as secretary of the North American Foreign Department of the GC and as vice president of the North American **Division** Conference, beginning in 1913.

ORDINATION. The ceremony of setting an individual apart from other church members for particular roles in the church. Although several of the leaders of the sabbatarian Adventist movement had been ordained as **ministers** in their previous denominations, the issue of ordination emerged in the early 1850s. Many Adventists regarded ordination as a move in the direction of church **organization**, which they opposed. Nonetheless, **James White** and other leaders believed that ordination was necessary so that the small Adventist congregations would know which traveling preachers they could trust. It appears that the first ordination to the Adventist ministry took place at New Haven, Vermont, in the fall of 1853. In December of that year White wrote an article in the *Review and Herald* in which he argued for the necessity of ordination. About the same time that they began ordaining ministers, the sabbatarian Adventists ordained **deacons** in their local congregations. By 1854 the *Review and Herald* was reporting several such ordination services. That same year, **Joseph Bates** suggested that sabbatarian Adventists institute the office of **elder** to supervise local congregations between visits by an ordained minister. This position appears to have become established by 1856.

From the beginning of the practice within Adventism, only males received ordination. In the 1970s, however, pressure began to build for female ordination, thereby provoking a debate in which North American and **European** Adventists generally supported ordination of **women** while those from many other parts of the world, particularly **Latin America** and **Africa**, opposed such ordination. In 1974 the Annual Council of the **General Conference** (GC) Executive Committee authorized the **divisions** in exceptional cases to allow the ordination of women as local elders. Ten years later the GC Executive Committee's Annual Council voted that divisions were free to determine their own policies regarding the ordination of women as local elders. Meanwhile, a debate over ordination of women to the ministry had developed and in the mid-1980s the GC appointed study commissions to examine the issue, but the church achieved no real consensus.

At the **General Conference session** of 1990, delegates voted down a proposal to permit the ordination of women to the ministry but accepted another proposal that allowed licensed and commissioned ministers, categories of authorized ministers who were not ordained and which included women as well as men, to conduct weddings and **baptisms**. In 1995 the GC session voted down by a three to one margin, similar to the 1990 vote, a North American proposal to have divisions determine their own policies regarding the ordination of women as ministers. Many of those supporting ordination of women argued that it was a matter of male and female equality while others saw female ordination as contrary to the Bible. After the 1995 rejection of female ministerial ordination, a few local congregations in North America ordained women to the ministry but these actions carried no authority beyond the **church** that performed the ceremonies.

ORGANIZATION, SEVENTH-DAY ADVENTIST. Like other groups that arose out of the **Millerite movement**, early sabbatarian Adventists opposed church organization. Much of this opposition arose from the experience of being forced out of their original churches because they had adopted Millerite beliefs. Leading sabbatarian Adventists, particularly **James White**, developed a comprehensive view of the movement, however, which recognized that its survival depended upon some degree of organization. As early as 1851 White began urging the need for "Gospel Order" and published a series of editorials on the subject in the *Review and Herald* in December 1853. About that same time, local congregations began accepting and dismissing members and **ordaining deacons**, and White and other leaders started the practice of ordaining **ministers**.

The issue of property ownership, however, pushed the sabbatarian Adventists into more formal church organization. Because local congregations were not legal entities they could not hold property. In one notable case, when the member who owned the land on which the Adventists had built a small church left the group, he claimed ownership of the building and turned it into a vinegar factory. Because of the potential of more problems of this kind, local congregations began to adopt formal organization. The first of these groups appears to have been the Parkville Church of Christ's Second Advent, organized in Michigan in 1860. That same year, White called a conference to meet in Battle Creek to address the legal status of the **Review and Herald publishing office**, which was technically under his ownership. This conference established a committee to apply to the state legislature for authorization to establish an Advent Review Publishing Association. Perhaps more significantly, the conference also decided to adopt the name Seventh-day Adventist. When the committee incorporated the publishing office in May 1861, it decided to use the new name in establishing the Seventh-day Adventist Publishing Association. The 1860 conference also produced a lengthy article on church organization that the *Review and Herald* published in June, urging formal organization of local **churches, conferences** of churches, and a **General Conference** (GC).

The next steps in church organization took place rather quickly and generally followed the proposals made by the 1860 conference. In 1861 delegates from the Michigan churches recommended formation of a conference, a term adopted from the Methodists, and held its first official conference meeting the following year. During the next several months, additional conferences formed in New York, Ohio, Wisconsin, Iowa, Minnesota, and Vermont. In 1863 delegates from all of the conferences except Vermont met in Battle Creek, Michigan, where they organized the GC, electing a president, secretary, and treasurer. It is important to note that these early Adventists adopted a form of indirect, hierarchical representation. Delegates from local churches elected the officers and determined the policies of the conference; delegates from the conferences, not individual churches, elected the officers and determined the policies of the General Conference. Although some individuals separated from the Seventh-day Adventist Church in the early 1860s over the issue of organization, most members accepted the new formalized structure.

As the new denomination entered additional lines of endeavor, it followed the pattern, inaugurated by the Seventh-day Adventist Publishing Association, of establishing new legal entities that were tied to the GC through interlocking directorates. These organizations included the Health Reform Institute (1866, later **Battle Creek Sanitarium**), Seventh-day Adventist **Educational** Society (1874), International **Tract and Missionary Society** (1874), **Sabbath School** Association (1878), and the American Health and **Temperance** Association (1879). The General Conference Association, the legal corporation which held denominational property, formed in 1886. Although in the late 1880s discussion began focusing on bringing these various associations into the conference/GC structure, in 1889 the denomination created an additional entity, the Foreign Mission Board, and in 1893 the Seventh-day Adventist Medical Missionary and Benevolent Association replaced the Health Reform Institute.

With the expansion of the denomination geographically in the late 19th century, leaders in other parts of the world began to experiment with new organizational structures. In **South Africa** Asa

T. Robinson organized a conference in 1891 with departments rather than separate associations to oversee such activities as publishing and tract distribution. When Robinson moved to **Australia** in 1898, he again established a departmental structure within the conferences. Meanwhile, Australia in 1894 formed a union of conferences called the Australasian **Union Conference**. In 1901 the **General Conference session**, under the leadership of **Arthur G. Daniells**, who had worked in Australia, reorganized the denomination. It recommended the formation of union conferences, which would now replace conferences as the constituent parts of the GC and it began the process of dissolving the various associations and replacing them with departments. The next major structural change took place in 1913, when the GC session of that year created the division conferences, which would be formed by delegates from the union conferences in a given geographical region. The **European** Division Conference and the North American Division Conference organized that same year. Experiences during World War I, however, created fear that these large entities might become too independent and in 1918 the GC session dissolved the division conferences and replaced them with **divisions**. The new divisions, rather than having officers and policies determined by delegates from the union conferences in their region, were part of the GC and overseen by its officers. Union conferences remained the basic constituent element of the GC. Although departments and divisions have changed since 1918, the basic organizational structure of the denomination has remained the same. In actual practice, however, in the late 20th century the divisions became increasingly responsive to their regional interests and concerns and less dependent on the GC.

P

PACIFIC PRESS PUBLISHING ASSOCIATION (PPPA). Seventh-day Adventist **publishing** house located in Nampa, Idaho. After appealing for funds in 1874 to establish a publishing house in California, **James White** helped organize the Pacific Seventh-day Adventist Publishing Association the following year. Located in Oakland, the publishing house produced the *Signs of the Times*, which had been founded in 1874, and Adventist books and tracts. In addition to these religious materials, the association—which owned its printing equipment—developed a commercial printing business and by the end of the 1870s was perhaps the best-equipped and largest printer in the American West. In 1879

Charles H. Jones, who had worked at the **Review and Herald Publishing Association**, became manager of the publishing house and subsequently served as vice president and president during his 50 years with the institution.

In 1888 the publishing house changed its name to Pacific Press Publishing Company and began establishing branch offices elsewhere, among them New York (1888-1903), London (1889-1893), Kansas City, Missouri (1893-1924), Portland, Oregon (1904-1963), and Cristobal, Canal Zone, **Panama** (1917-1955). Starting in 1904 when the Pacific Press Publishing Association formed, the press moved from being a stock company to a non-profit enterprise, a process that was completed in 1909. Because the demands of its commercial printing business often impinged on the production of less-profitable denominational publications, the press's board in 1902 voted to reduce the amount of commercial work. Two years later the institution moved to Mountain View, where the San Francisco earthquake of 1906 severely damaged its building. After a quickly constructed replacement building burned to the ground that same year, the board decided to erect a new structure and, similar to a recent action of the Review and Herald Publishing Association, also discontinued its commercial business so that it could concentrate on denominational printing in the future.

In 1915 the press took over the International Publishing Association, which had been organized in 1903 in College View, Nebraska, to publish Adventist works in languages other than English. After several transfers of operation, by 1959 the press had consolidated all foreign-language publication at Mountain View. The press acquired in 1955 a music recording business that had been operated by the Pacific **Union Conference** and three years later organized **Chapel** Records as a separate department. Also, Maracle Press Limited and Kingsway Publishing Association, located in Oshawa, Ontario, **Canada** became part of the press in 1970. Although Maracle Press was sold in 1992, the Kingsway office continued to operate as the press's Canadian branch.

Between 1973 and 1983 the press was the defendant in a series of three related lawsuits, the first initiated by Merikay Silver, revolving around the issue of gender discrimination. In the end, Silver settled her case out of court and the press paid over $600,000 in back pay to its **women** workers. Beyond these results, the suits had significance because they pushed the denomination, at least in the **United States**, to adopt a policy of equal pay for men and women in place of its previous policy of paying the "head of household," usually men, at a higher rate than women or single employees.

Responding to the changing economic conditions in the San Francisco Bay Area, in 1994-95 the press moved its operations to Nampa, Idaho. As of 2003 in addition to producing books and distributing recordings, the press published several denominational periodicals, including *Our Little Friend*, *Primary Treasure*, **Sabbath School** *Bible Study Guide*, and *Signs of the Times*. It also published periodicals in Spanish and French.

PACIFIC UNION COLLEGE (PUC). Seventh-day Adventist **educational** institution located in Angwin, California. At their 1881 **camp meeting**, Adventists in California decided to establish a school and soon brought **Sidney Brownsberger**, former principal of **Battle Creek College**, from Michigan to head the new institution. Healdsburg **Academy** opened in April 1882 with 33 students. Responding to pressure from the local community, 12 weeks later the school changed its name to Healdsburg College, although it did not graduate a college student until 1889. Learning from his negative experiences at Battle Creek College and attempting to follow the educational philosophy of **Ellen G. White**, Brownsberger established dormitories and instituted manual labor, including carpentry, printing, and tentmaking. Partly because the school charged low prices for board, room, and tuition, it experienced continuing economic problems. Although enrollment by 1902 reached 298, of whom 185 were college students, the school industries experienced losses and the institution was acquiring a significant debt that it attempted to alleviate by selling portions of its property. By 1907 it changed its name to Pacific Union College (PUC) and ended operations in Healdsburg the following year.

After the purchase of a resort on Howell Mountain, near St. Helena in the Napa Valley, Pacific College—as it was called for a short time—reopened in the fall of 1909, with Charles W. Irwin as president. Gradually the institution erected new buildings and formalized its academic programs in the early 1920s. In the midst of the accreditation debate that took place in Adventist educational circles, PUC in 1932 received senior college accreditation from the Northwest Association, the first denominational college to achieve such recognition. The Advanced Bible School, precursor to the **Seventh-day Adventist Theological Seminary**, operated on the college campus during the summers of 1934 to 1936. After World War II enrollment doubled with the arrival of veterans, reaching over 1,000 students by 1948 and stretching the campus's physical resources. During the 1960s, under the leadership of President Floyd O. Rittenhouse, the institution embarked on an extensive building campaign that essentially remade the campus. Although enrollment reached a peak of nearly 2,300 in 1975-76, it had dropped to around 1,400 by the early 1990s and has stayed at approximately that level since then.

PAKISTAN. Beginning in 1901 various Seventh-day Adventist **literature evangelists** and missionaries visited the area now known as Pakistan. In 1914 F. H. Loasby and Dr. Victor L. Mann established the Northwest India **Mission** and began working in Lahore, relocating to Chuharkana two years later. Their first **baptisms** took place in 1917 and Loasby moved to Chichoki Mallian that same year and **evangelized** the villages of the region while his wife operated a dispensary. About 1921 or 1922 the hospital that had been established at Chuharkana closed and the building subsequently provided facilities for the Punjab Boys' School, which opened in 1923. Six years later the Punjab Seventh-day Adventist Mission Girls' School opened at Chichoki Mallian. In 1937 the two schools combined as Chuharkana Mandi Elementary School. After several other changes, this institution became Pakistan Union School and College in 1964, graduating its first college class in 1970, and finally Pakistan Adventist Seminary in 1973. Meanwhile, Adventists had established a hospital at Chichoki that operated between 1930 and 1936 and a clinic at Karachi in 1947 that by 1951 had become Karachi Seventh-day Adventist Hospital. As these institutions were developing, Adventist evangelism continued.

Shortly after Pakistan obtained independence in 1947, the denomination reorganized the mission efforts in its territory. The West Pakistan **Union** Mission formed in 1949 with 12 **churches** and about 900 members, while the Pakistan Union Mission, organized at the same time, had 36 churches with approximately 1,700 members. Political changes brought further reorganization in the early 1970s with the East Pakistan Section, part of the Pakistan Union Mission, becoming the **Bangladesh** Section. About the same time, the hospital and seminary became the responsibility of the Southern **Asia Division**. As of 2003 the Pakistan Union Section, part of the Trans-**European** Division, had 68 **churches** with a membership of over 7,000. Pakistan Adventist Seminary, one secondary school, Karachi Adventist Hospital, Peshawar Dental Clinic, Qasid Publishing House of Seventh-day Adventists, and the

Voice of Hope radio-television production center were located in Pakistan.

PALMER, EDWIN R. (1869-1931). Seventh-day Adventist **publishing** administrator. Palmer served in a variety of administrative positions in the **United States** and **Australia** before returning to America in 1901. Palmer then worked with the Lake **Union Conference** to revive **literature evangelism** within its region. Adventist subscription book selling had gone into decline in the 1890s, largely because of the depression that began in 1893. **Conferences** had responded to the situation by laying off book agents and closing the **tract and missionary societies**, actions that further disrupted sales. Consequently, the publishing houses became increasingly responsible for distributing denominational books and papers. By 1903 Palmer had become an administrative assistant to **Arthur G. Daniells**, president of the **General Conference** (GC), and continued to focus on literature evangelism. He opposed turning sales over to the publishing houses, which he believed were more concerned with commercial than spiritual matters, and fought with individuals such as Charles H. Jones, manager of the **Pacific Press**, over whether the conferences or publishers would control the sale of books. The death of Palmer's wife in 1903 and his own health problems created personal difficulties for a time, during which he worked at the Paradise Valley **Sanitarium** (1904) and the Pacific Press (1904-05). In 1905 Palmer returned to the GC where he served as secretary of the Publishing Department until 1913. During that time he reactivated the state tract societies, increased the number of literature evanagelists, held literature evangelism meetings, and developed a scholarship plan for students who sold Adventist literature during the summers. Fundamentally, however, he reestablished for the denomination as a whole the principle of local conference responsibility and control of literature evangelism. In 1912 he became general manager of the **Review and Herald Publishing Association**, staying in that position until 1931.

PANAMA. In the 1890s Seventh-day Adventist missionaries from the Bay Islands of **Honduras** visited the part of **Colombia** now known as Panama and, beginning in 1897, Frank J. Hutchins stopped at various places along the coast with his mission schooner, *The Herald*. The Panama **Mission** organized in 1903 with three **churches** and a membership of 129; three years later the territory came under the direction of the West Caribbean **Conference**. In 1906 the denomination erected its first church building at Mount Hope, near Colón and established the conference headquarters at Cristóbal. Between 1917 and 1955 the **Pacific Press Publishing Association** operated a branch at Cristóbal, Canal Zone, and from 1921 to 1931 the West Caribbean Training School functioned at Las Cascadas. In addition, the Canal Zone provided the first headquarters for the Inter-American **Division** beginning in 1922; with the advent of World War II, in 1942 the offices moved to **Cuba** because of security concerns.

In 1928 Adventists in Panama, along those in the Canal Zone, the Talamanca Valley of **Costa Rica**, and the San Andrés and Old Providence Islands, organized as the Panama **Conference**. Ismail Ellis began working among the Guaymi Indians of Cerro Iglesia in the late 1920s and organized the first church in 1930. José Chavanz entered the area the following year and soon started a school. By 1963 there were 571 members among the Guaymi Indians. In 1962 Claudio Hernandez started efforts among the Cuna Indians of the Mulatas Islands and two years later Obed Quiroz established contact with Indians in the Darien region near the Colombia border. As of 2003 the Seventh-day Adventists Church in Panama was organized as the East Panama Conference and the West Panama Mission, part of the Central American **Union Conference** of the Inter-American **Division**. The conferences had 165 churches and over 50,000 members. Metropolitan Adventist **Academy** and Panama Adventist Institute were located in the country.

PAPUA NEW GUINEA. Unlike their work in many other areas of the world, from the beginning of their efforts American and **European** Seventh-day Adventist missionaries in Papua New Guinea operated hand-in-hand with missionaries from nearby areas. Septimus W. Carr and Peni Tavodi, a **Fijian** teacher, established the first Adventist **mission** in Papua in 1908. The first Adventist missionaries on Bougainville were R. H. Tutty and Nano and Rongapitu, from the Solomon Islands, who arrived in 1924. With several helpers from the Solomons, **Griffeths F. Jones** established a mission station and school on Matupi Island in New Britain's Rabaul Harbour in 1929. The following year Gilbert McLaren, who captained the mission boat *Veilomani* with a Fijian crew, established a station at Raboul. Later that same year he visited several islands in the vicinity of New Ireland and in 1931 placed missionaries from the **Solomons** on Emira and Mussau. Three years later McLaren established a mission station in northeast New Guinea with the help of ten individuals from Mussau and Matupi. In 1935 he created a station on Tong Island of the Admiralty Group and gave responsibility for the mission to Robert Salau of the Solomons. Probably because Pacific islanders were such an indispensable part of Adventist mission efforts, the denomination continued to develop after the European and American missionaries left in 1941 as World War II descended. With the restoration of peace in 1945, American and European missionaries returned and established schools, placed island missionaries in new locations, and began using aircraft to reach remote areas. After numerous reorganizations of the mission efforts, beginning with the Papua **Mission** in 1908, the Papua New Guinea **Union Mission** organized in 1971. By the late 20th century, this Union Mission was the largest in the South Pacific **Division**. As of 2003 it had 816 **churches** with a membership of nearly 214,000. Pacific Adventist University, Sonoma Adventist College, three secondary schools, Sopas Adventist Hospital, and numerous clinics and dispensaries were located in Papua New Guinea.

PARAGUAY. Literature evangelists first entered Paraguay in 1892 but no Seventh-day Adventist missionaries arrived until 1900, when E. W. Snyder came from the **United States**. Making contact with German colonists who had become interested in Adventism as a result of reading the denomination's literature, Snyder **baptized** five individuals in 1901. After Snyder left in 1903, there were no resident missionaries in the country until 1904 when Luis Ernst moved from Argentina to Paraguay. In 1907 the first Adventist **church** organized with 12 members. By 1912 there were seven churches with nearly 200 members, but progress was slow. The Chaco War between Paraguay and **Bolivia** disrupted the denomination's efforts and appears to have reduced the membership to about 100 people. After the Paraguay **Mission** organized in 1948 membership continued to grow gradually, reaching about 500 by 1959. Medical efforts began with the opening of treatment rooms in Asunción in 1945, which were absorbed by the Paraguay Adventist **Sanitarium** when it opened in 1959. Four years later the Hohenau Adventist Sanitarium and Hospital opened near Encarnación. After a decline in the membership in the early 1960s, the denomination began to advance steadily. As of 2003 the Paraguay Mission, part of the Austral **Union Conference** of the South American **Division**, had 45 churches with a membership of nearly 11,000. Two secondary schools, Asunción Adventist Sanitarium and Hohenau Adventist Sanitarium were located in Paraguay.

PATHFINDER CLUB. Seventh-day Adventist organization for young people between the ages of 10 and 15. After the Boy Scouts were founded in 1910, some Seventh-day Adventist young people wanted to join but were unable to do so because of activities on the **Sabbath** and other issues. Responding to this situation, beginning in 1911 local **church** leaders started organizing clubs with such names as the Woodland Clan, Takoma Indians, and Pals, which engaged in learning crafts, hiking, and camping. Arthur W. Spalding, editor of *The Watchman*, started the Mission Scouts in Madison, Tennessee, in 1919 for which he wrote a pledge and law that would have significant influence several years later. By the early 1920s the Missionary Volunteer (MV) Department of the **General Conference** (GC) had established classes in which young people could earn awards, and in 1928 C. Lester Bond, the department's associate secretary, received permission from the Boy Scouts to incorporate some of their Merit Badge ideas and materials into an MV honors program. Also in the 1920s, the denomination began organizing its own summer camps for young people, the first of which took place in Michigan in 1926.

Around 1929-1930, John McKim and Dr. Theron Johnston organized clubs in Santa Ana, California, that used the name Pathfinder and continued in existence until 1936. When the Southeastern California **Conference** established a summer camp in 1930 it adopted the name JMV (the "J" stood for "Junior") Pathfinder Camp, probably because of the involvement of the Santa Ana clubs. In 1937 another Pathfinder Club took form in Glendale, California, which incorporated the military drill used in the emerging **Medical Cadet Corps** in addition to the now traditional crafts and outdoor activities. Although denominational leaders generally opposed the development of these clubs, which they feared shifted interest from missionary to secular activities, Pathfinder Clubs began emerging elsewhere in California and the Pacific Northwest in the early 1940s. In 1946 John Hancock, youth director of the Southeastern California Conference, organized the first conference-sponsored Pathfinder Club in Riverside.

With this official denominational involvement, interest in Pathfinder Clubs moved quickly to the GC, which in 1950 officially recognized the program and published guidelines for organizing local clubs and, among other things, adopted a pledge and law similar to that prepared by Spalding some 30 years earlier. The following year the Oregon Conference hosted the first Pathfinder Fair and the GC published the *Pathfinder Staff Training Course*. In 1953 members of several clubs in New England joined together for a weekend "Camporee," an idea that soon spread elsewhere in the **United States**. By 1957 there were 717 clubs in North America with a membership of over 14,000 and involving more than 3,500 adult leaders. Apparently having lost all reservations about the program, the GC established "Pathfinder Day," an annual Sabbath event in which club members conducted the worship services in local churches. By the early 1990s Pathfinder Clubs had spread among Adventists around the world and had developed a membership of over 900,000.

PAULSEN, JAN (1935-). Seventh-day Adventist **minister, educator,** and church administrator. Born in **Norway**, Paulsen attended Danish Junior College and worked as a ministerial intern before going to the **United States**, where he received his B.A. (1957) from **Emmanuel Missionary College** and M.A. (1958) from the **Seventh-day Adventist Theological Seminary**. Returning to Norway he served as ministerial director of the West Norway **Conference** from 1959 to 1961. He then went to **Ghana** where he taught Bible at Bekwai Teachers Training College from 1962 to 1964. He was **ordained** to the ministry in 1963. In 1964 he became head of the religion department of the Adventist Seminary of West Africa in **Nigeria** and in 1967 president of the institution. Paulsen then joined the staff of **Newbold College** in **Great Britain** in 1968, where he chaired the religion department until becoming the school's president in 1976. Meanwhile, Paulsen had earned a D.Th. in New Testament studies from Tòbingen University in 1972. In 1980 he entered church administration when he became secretary of the Trans-**European Division**, serving in that position until his election as division president in 1983. Elected a vice president of the **General Conference** in 1995, Paulsen became president of the denomination in 1999 after the resignation of **Robert S. Folkenberg**. Paulsen's books include *When the Spirit Descends* (1977) and *Let Your Life So Shine* (2003).

PECK, SARAH ELIZABETH (1868-1968). Seventh-day Adventist **educator**. After graduating from public high school in Menominee, Wisconsin, Peck taught in the city school system until she attended **Battle Creek College** in 1886. Completing the English course in 1888, she helped establish the Minnesota **Conference** School in Minneapolis in 1888. Two years later she returned to Battle Creek College, graduating in 1892. She then took a teaching position at Claremont College (later **Helderberg College**) in **South Africa** in 1892 and while in **Africa** also taught at an Ad-

ventist school in the diamond country near Kimberly. In 1897 she
joined **Ellen G. White** in **Australia** to work as an editorial assistant and continued in that capacity upon returning to the **United
States** in 1901. From 1906 to 1907 she was a member of the **General Conference** (GC) Department of Education Committee on
Textbooks, for which she prepared the third through sixth grade
True Education Readers. She eventually revised the entire eight-
volume series three times. Peck became director of the Normal
Department at **Union College** in 1907, where she also taught flori-
culture and manual training, serving until 1914. She then worked
as superintendent of education in the California Conference between 1915 and 1917, after which she served in the GC Department of Education from 1918 to 1923, overseeing development of
the denomination's elementary education and teacher training programs. During this time she also served as assistant editor of the
Journal of True Education (1919; later *Journal of Adventist Education*), and wrote *Elementary Curriculum for Seventh-day Adventist Schools* (1920) and *God's Great Plan* (1922), the latter a Bible
textbook. Upon her retirement in 1924 she moved to Angwin,
California.

PEREZ, BRAULIO MARCIO (1904-1974). Seventh-day Adventist
radio **evangelist**. Perez's family moved in 1908 from **Spain** to
South America, where he received his **education**, concluding with
his graduation from **River Plate College** in 1930. He joined the
faculty of the Central American College of Seventh-day Adventists
in **Costa Rica** in 1936, but a successful series of evangelistic meetings in **Cuba** in 1940 moved him into a public speaking career. In
1942 he began a radio program that was broadcast over a chain of
Cuban stations and soon thereafter became the speaker for the
Spanish version of *Voice of Prophecy*, later known as *Voice of
Hope*, a position he held until his death. In 1945 he represented the
International **Religious Liberty** Association at the organizational
meeting of the United Nations in San Francisco. Helping coordinate the development of Adventist radio throughout the continent,
he became associate director of the South American **Division's**
Radio Commission in 1946. Known for his polished mastery of the
Spanish language, Perez engaged in frequent evangelistic campaigns, among them tours of **Mexico** in 1959 and South America
in 1962 with the **King's Heralds**.

PERK, GERHARD (1859-1930). Seventh-day Adventist **literature
evangelist, minister,** and church administrator. A Mennonite liv-

ing in **Russia**, Perk converted to Adventism around 1882 as a result of reading denominational **publications**. While Perk was working in Russia as an agent for the British Bible Society, **Ludvig R. Conradi** asked him in 1886 to begin selling Adventist publications. The two men worked together in Russia beginning in July 1886 but while in the Crimea were arrested for proselytizing and put in jail for 40 days. Upon his release, Perk continued his literature evangelism but after another arrest left Russia to work in **Germany** and **Switzerland**. In 1897 he again visited Russia, this time working in the region around St. Petersburg where he established some congregations. After returning to Germany, Perk received **ordination** in 1899. In 1902 he became superintendent of the **Romanian Mission**, but after being expelled from the country he returned to Germany. From that point until his retirement in 1921, Perk served in Germany at various times as the president of two **conferences** and the superintendent of a mission.

PERU. Seventh-day Adventism first entered Peru when church members from **Chile** arrived in Mollendo and Lima in 1898. Four years later Enrique Balada, a Chilean **literature evangelist**, worked briefly in Lima. These efforts resulted in a few converts, who then requested that a missionary be sent to their country. In 1904 Herman F. Ketring came from Chile and **baptized** seven individuals. The following year, Franklin L. Perry arrived from the **United States** and established the Peru **Mission**; in 1907 he organized the Adventist believers in Lima into a **church**. Twelve years later, in 1919, Harry B. Lundquist established the Lima Training School in Miraflores, a suburb of Lima. Meanwhile, denominational **publications** preceded the arrival of Adventist missionaries in the Lake Titicaca region. Thus, when Fernando Osorio arrived in Puno in 1910 he found that four families had already accepted Adventist doctrines.

Soon Osorio also began working among the Aymara Indians in Plateria, preparing the way for Joseph W. Westphal, who baptized 29 in 1911. About this time Ana and **Ferdinand Stahl** arrived in Plateria and established a school. In 1916 the Lake Titicaca Indian Mission organized; four years later the mission dropped the word "Indian" from its name. The Adventist missionaries had considerable success in the Lake Titicaca area, with 10 churches by 1921 and a membership of over 3,000. Titicaca Adventist **Academy**, established near Juliaca in 1922, prepared teachers for the many schools, which by 1951 numbered 113, that the mission operated on the Peruvian side of the lake. From Lake Titicaca Stahl moved in 1921 into central Peru where he established a mission station on the Perené River. Six years later Adventists in this territory organized into the Upper Amazon Mission with Stahl as superintendent. During the 1930s Stahl used a steam launch to navigate the rivers of the region as he pursued his missionary endeavors.

Most of Adventism's growth in Peru up to the 1950s took place among the Indians of Lake Titicaca and central Peru, but after the Lima Training School—which was now called Lima Industrial Academy—moved to Naña in 1945 and a medical clinic opened the following year in Miraflores, new churches developed in several suburbs of the capital city. In 1950 the denomination began broadcasting the *Voice of Prophecy* over the radio. Economic changes in the Lake Titicaca region during the latter half of the 20th century forced many Indians to move to urban areas, resulting in a membership loss in their home territory. As of 2003 the Peru **Union Mission**, part of the South American **Division**, had 1,310 churches with a membership of about 543,000. Peruvian Union University, four secondary schools, and three clinics were located in Peru.

PETERSON, FRANK LORIS (1893-1969). African American Seventh-day Adventist church administrator. Converted to Seventh-day Adventism at age 14, Peterson studied at **Pacific Union College** where in 1916 he became its first African American graduate. He then taught at Oakwood Junior College (later **Oakwood College**) until 1926 when he became an administrator in the Southern **Union Conference**. In 1930 he served for a short time as **minister** of an African American church in Boston before becoming secretary of the North American Negro Department of the **General Conference** (GC). From 1941 to 1945 he served as a pastor in California. He then became president of Oakwood College, holding that position until 1954, at which time he began working as an associate secretary of the GC. In 1962 he became the first African American to be elected as a general vice president of the General Conference, a position he held until his retirement in 1966.

PHILIPPINES. The first Seventh-day Adventist **literature evangelist** arrived in the Philippines in 1905, followed in 1906 by **James L. McElhany**, who worked primarily among the Americans living in Manila. When L. V. Finster came in 1908 he focused on the native population and three years later **baptized** his first converts and organized a **church** in Santa Ana. Gradually Adventism spread beyond Manila. Between 1911 and 1915 E. M. Adams sold books in the southern islands, including Panay and Guimaras, and in 1921 Roy E. Hay began working in northern Luzon. Meanwhile, a **publishing** house began operating in 1914. Beginning with Finster, the Adventist missionaries trained national people as booksellers and evangelists and these individuals contributed significantly to the early spread of the denomination. In 1916 the denomination established the Central Southern Luzon **Conference**, the West Visayan **Mission**, the Cebuan Mission, and the Northern Luzon Mission. At that time there were 11 churches with 846 members. The following year the Philippine Seventh-day Adventist **Academy** opened near Manila; by 1926 it had become Philippine Junior College. Adventist medical efforts began with the establishment of a dispensary in 1928; Manila **Sanitarium and Hospital** opened the following year. Three secondary schools started during the 1930s and in 1936 the junior college became Philippine Union College. By 1939 church membership had reached over 20,000 but World War II brought the internment of foreign missionaries and created severe difficulties for Filipino **ministers** and literature evangelists. Nonetheless, more than 5,000 baptisms took place between 1942 and 1945.

After the war, the denomination repaired and rebuilt facilities and reestablished its organization. With continued growth, which reached 35,000 members by 1951 and 70,000 by 1962, Adventists in the territory reorganized several times. New hospitals opened, including Mindanao Sanitarium and Hospital (1953), Miller Sanitarium, in Cebu City (1955), and the Cagayan Valley Sanitarium and Hospital (1959). In the 1960s the church established evangelistic centers in Manila, Cebu, and Davao City and started broadcasting radio programs in several languages and dialects. The demand for trained workers led in the late 1950s to the creation of graduate programs at Philippine Union College; the school later took the name **Adventist University of the Philippines**. Other colleges were also opened in the Philippines and in 1987 the **Adventist International Institute of Advanced Studies** began offering master's and doctoral education for students from throughout Southeast **Asia**. As of 2003, the denomination in the Philippines was divided into the Central and South Philippine Union Conferences and the North Philippine Union Mission, which were part of the Southern Asia-Pacific **Division**, with over 3,947 churches and nearly 920,000 members. Seven colleges and universities and a graduate school, 21 secondary schools, 11 hospitals, and the Philippine Publishing House were located in the Philippines.

PIERSON, ROBERT HOWARD (1911-1989). Seventh-day Adventist **minister** and church administrator. After attending Southern
Junior College between 1931 and 1933, Pierson worked simultaneously as a pastor and teacher in Georgia and then became secretary of the Home Missionary and **Sabbath School** Department of
the Georgia-Cumberland **Conference**. In 1935 he went as a missionary to **India**, where he was **ordained**, serving there until his
return to the **United States** in 1942. During the next several years
he filled various administrative positions in the Inter-American **Division** until his election as president of the Southern **Asia** Division
in 1950. In this position, Pierson emphasized the preparation of nationals for leadership positions in the denomination. Returning to
the **United States** in 1954, Pierson became president successively
of the Kentucky-Tennessee and Texas conferences before assuming the presidency of the Southern **Africa** Division in 1958.
Elected president of the **General Conference** in 1966, he served in
that position until his retirement in 1979. During his presidency
Pierson repeatedly called for revival and reformation, which he
believed must take place in the church before Jesus could return.
Among his books were *Faith on Tiptoe* (1967), *Angels over
Elisabethville* (1975), *Goodbye, Planet Earth* (1976), and *How to
be a Successful Christian Leader* (1978).

PITCAIRN. Seventh-day Adventist **mission** vessel. Funded by **Sabbath school** offerings, the *Pitcairn* in 1890 sailed to Pitcairn Island, where most the inhabitants had converted to Adventism in
the mid-1880s. Between 1890 and 1899 the *Pitcairn* made six missionary voyages to the **South Pacific**. The product of increasing
Adventist interest in **missions**, the *Pitcairn* further inspired the denomination's enthusiasm. It also helped establish the Sabbath
school as the point of contact between missions and the local
church. The expense of maintaining the ship and the increasing re-
liability of commercial steamship transportation in the region convinced denominational leaders to sell the ship in 1900.

PLUMMER, LORENA FLORENCE (FAIT) (1862-1945). Seventh-
day Adventist church administrator. A teacher in the Iowa public
schools when she and her husband converted to Adventism in
1886, Plummer soon joined the Iowa **Conference Sabbath School**
Department, followed by a similar position in the Minnesota Conference four years later. Throughout her career she went by the
name L. Flora. In 1901 she became corresponding secretary of the
newly organized Sabbath School Department of the **General Con-**

ference, rising to secretary of the department in 1913 and serving in that position until 1936. During her tenure, she sought to make the **Sabbath school** a primary means of converting children and helping adults maintain their religious convictions and practice. She edited the *Sabbath School Worker*, a quarterly aid for leaders and teachers, and wrote *From Acorn to Oak* (1922), *The Soul Winning Teacher* (1934), and *The Spirit of the Teacher* (1935).

POLAND. In 1888 J. Laubhan and H. Szkubowicz came from the Crimea to what was then eastern Poland, now part of **Russia**, and three years later established a Seventh-day Adventist **church** in Zarnówka. From that city, K. Fendel and J. Szledzinski went to Łódź in1893 and won some converts. Over the next several years Adventist churches formed in Poznán, Bielsko, and Warsaw and in 1912 the Warsaw and Moravian-Silesian **Missions** organized. With the creation of Poland as a national state after World War I, the "Seventh-day Adventist Union in Poland" organized in 1921 with a membership of nearly 1,100. Despite legal restrictions on its activities, the denomination established the Polyglot **Publishing** House in 1921 and a training school for **ministers** in 1925. After **Germany** invaded Poland in 1939, it dissolved the Polish Union, confiscated property, and outlawed Adventist public meetings and **literature evangelism**. With the end of World War II, the Seventh-day Adventist Church recovered its properties, reestablished its organization and institutions, and in 1946 received full legal recognition for the first time, which enabled it to conduct public **evangelism**. In 1960 the denomination established a home for the elderly and the following year renamed itself the Seventh-day Adventist Church in Poland. When Communist rule of Poland ended in 1989, the Adventist church upgraded its seminary to a junior college, established the Polish **Religious Liberty** Association, changed its name to the Polish **Union Conference**, and increased its evangelistic activities. As of 2003 this conference, part of the Trans-**European Division**, had 121 churches with a membership of about 5,600. The Polish Spiritual Seminary, Polish Old People's Home, and Polish Publishing House were located in the country.

PORTUGAL. Clarence E. Rentfro, a Seventh-day Adventist missionary from the **United States**, settled in Caxias in 1904. Two years later Ernesto Schwantes from **Brazil** joined him, **baptizing** the first Adventist converts and opening a meeting hall in Lisbon that same year. In 1907 Schwantes and Rentfro traveled north to Porto where they established another congregation. By 1912 the Lisbon and Porto **churches** had 53 members. In 1913 the Portuguese **Mission** organized, followed by the establishment of the Portuguese **Publishing** House in 1924. In 1935 the mission, which by this time had Portuguese leadership, became a **conference**. In 1982 the conference took the name "The Portuguese Union of Churches" and, as of 2003, was part of the Euro-**Africa Division**. It had 89 churches with a membership of over 8,000. Two secondary schools, a retirement home, and the Portuguese Publishing House were located in Portugal.

PREBLE, THOMAS M. (1810-1907). Freewill Baptist minister and **Millerite** preacher. Preble was pastor of the Nashua, New Hampshire, Freewill Baptist Church when he accepted **William Miller's** teaching that Jesus would return about the year 1843. He subsequently preached on behalf of the Millerites and, on at least one occasion, traveled with Miller. In 1844, possibly because of contact with the Washington, New Hampshire, Millerite congregation of which **Rachel Oakes Preston** was a member, Preble began observing the seventh-day **Sabbath.** In February 1845 he published an article on the Sabbath in a Millerite paper, the *Hope of Israel,* thereby becoming the first Adventist to advocate this doctrine in print. The following month he published an enlarged version of his article as *Tract, Showing That the Seventh Day Should Be Observed As the Sabbath* which influenced several Millerites, notably **Joseph Bates**, to adopt the doctrine. Preble, however, observed the seventh-day Sabbath only until 1847 and later published articles criticizing the doctrine in the *Advent Herald* and *World's Crisis,* both published by those who would eventually organize the **Advent Christian Church**. He also wrote articles, published in the *Advent Christian Times,* opposing **Ellen G. White** and Seventh-day Adventists. In 1867 he published a book entitled *The First-Day Sabbath: Clearly Proved by Showing that the Old Covenant, or Ten Commandments, Have Been Changed, or Made Complete, in the Christian Dispensation.*

PRESCOTT, WILLIAM WARREN (1855-1944). Seventh-day Adventist church administrator, editor, and **educator**. Prescott's parents, who were associated with those **Millerites** who eventually formed the **Advent Christian Church**, adopted sabbatarian Adventism in 1858. Graduating from Dartmouth College in 1877, Prescott taught and served as a public school administrator in Vermont from 1877 to 1880 and then with his brother published

The Biddeford Weekly Journal from 1880 to 1882. In 1882 he purchased the *Vermont Watchman and State Journal*, which he published and edited until asked to be president of **Battle Creek College** in 1885. As he expanded the college's physical facilities and enrollment, Prescott after 1888 also began taking on responsibilities, including that of education secretary, for the **General Conference** (GC). While still president of Battle Creek College (1885-94), he helped found and served as president of **Union College** (1891-93) and **Walla Walla College** (1892-94). He became a full-time education secretary in 1894, serving in that position until 1897 and again in 1902-03. In 1895 he traveled to **Australia** where he helped establish **Avondale College**. Two years later the denomination sent him to **Great Britain** to superintend its efforts there; in 1898 he became president of the newly organized British **Conference** of Seventh-day Adventists.

Returning to the **United States**, Prescott became secretary of the Foreign **Mission** Board in 1901, editor of the *Review and Herald* in 1902, and vice president of the GC in 1903. During the controversy with **John Harvey Kellogg** he was a vocal critic of the physician's alleged pantheism, although some individuals argued that a few years earlier Prescott himself had been advocating similar views. In 1909 he left the *Review and Herald* to edit the *Protestant Magazine*, an Adventist publication that opposed many of the activities of the Roman Catholic Church in the United States. After six years with this publication, in 1915 Prescott became a field secretary of the GC and, among his various responsibilities, served as an educational trouble-shooter while president of Avondale College in 1922 and Union College in 1924-25. Following his brief stint as Union's president, he stayed at the school to serve as chairman of the Bible Department from 1925 to 1928. In 1932 he took on a similar position at **Emmanuel Missionary College**, staying there until 1934 but continuing to serve as GC field secretary for three more years. Throughout his career as an editor, administrator, and educator Prescott was involved in theological controversy regarding his advocacy of **righteousness by faith** and revisions of Adventist prophetic interpretation. Among his books were *The Doctrine of Christ* (1920), *The Savior of the World* (1923), and *The Spade and the Bible* (1933).

PRESTON, RACHEL (HARRIS) OAKES (1809-1868). Seventh Day Baptist lay person who influenced some **Millerites** to adopt the seventh-day **Sabbath**. Converted to Methodism at age 17, Preston accepted the seventh-day Sabbath doctrine about 11 years later and joined the Seventh Day Baptist church in Vernon, New York. Shortly thereafter she moved to Washington, New Hampshire, with her daughter Delight, who had obtained a teaching position there. In Washington, Preston (whose name was Oakes at the time) came in contact with a congregation of Millerites, who were known as the "Christian Brethren" and whose pastor was Frederick Wheeler. She convinced Wheeler of the truth of the Sabbath doctrine, which he accepted in March 1844. Later that year several families in his church also began observing the Sabbath, thereby becoming the first sabbatarian Adventists. Preston accepted Millerite beliefs some time in 1844 but did not become a Seventh-day Adventist until near the end of her life.

PRICE, GEORGE (EDWARD) MCCREADY (1870-1963). Seventh-day Adventist **creationist** writer. Born in New Brunswick, **Canada**, Price at about age 14 converted to Adventism with his brother and widowed mother. After working as a **literature evangelist** for several years, he attended **Battle Creek College** from 1891 to 1893, returned to selling books for a time, and then took a one-year teacher-training course at Provincial Normal School of New Brunswick. Beginning in 1897 he taught school in several small towns.

While in Trecadie, New Brunswick, Price became acquainted with a physician, Dr. Alfred Corbett Smith, who roused his interest in the apparent conflict between the theory of evolution and the story of creation recorded in Genesis. In response to the questions raised by evolutionary theory, Price wrote *Outlines of Modern Christianity and Modern Science* (1902), in which he argued that geology should be understood in terms of a recent creation and a worldwide flood.

After a series of jobs in Canada, New York, and Maryland, Price moved to California, where he first served as principal of an Adventist school in Oakland and then worked on construction at a church-owned **sanitarium**. Although he had little formal training in science and never studied geological phenomena in the field, Price continued to write, publishing *Illogical Geology: The Weakest Point in the Evolution Theory* (1906), in which he denied that there was any order to the geological strata. Several years later he put out a revised and expanded version of this book entitled *The Fundamentals of Geology* (1913). Beginning in 1907, Price held a series of teaching positions at Adventist schools: **College of Medical Evangelists** (1906-12), San Fernando **Academy** (1912-13), Lodi Academy (1914-20), **Pacific Union College** (1920-22),

Union College (1922-24), Stanborough College, later renamed **Newbold College** (1924-28), **Emmanuel Missionary College**, (1929-33), and **Walla Walla College** (1933-38). Meanwhile, he published *The New Geology* (1923), a college-level textbook which proposed a "new catastrophism" to replace uniformatarian geology.

With *Q.E.D.: or, New Light on the Doctrine of Creation*, published by the Fleming H. Revell Company, Price came to the attention of Christian fundamentalists outside the Adventist church. In the 1920s and 1930s he wrote for a variety of conservative Christian journals and magazines, among them *Moody Monthly, Sunday School Times, Defender, Bible Champion, Christian Faith and Life, Catholic World, Princeton Theological Review*, and *Bibliotheca Sacra*. Although most fundamentalists did not yet accept his flood geology, preferring instead alternative harmonizations of Genesis and geology, Price's influence continued to grow. When John C. Whitcomb, Jr., and Henry M. Morris published *The Genesis Flood* (1961), however, the situation changed dramatically. Their work, which drew heavily on Price's theories, brought flood geology to the fore among conservative Christians and strongly shaped modern creationism.

While his influence was growing elsewhere, Price sought to maintain the primacy of his views within Adventism. In the 1940s he strongly criticized one of his former students, **Harold W. Clark**, for accepting the validity of the geological column, and unsuccessfully sought to have the church try him for heresy. In an undated work, he referred to the ideas of men such as Clark as *Theories of Satanic Origin*. Price's works also included *God's Two Books* (1911), *Back to the Bible* (1916), *Evolutionary Geology and the New Catastrophism* (1926), *Genesis Vindicated* (1941), *Common-Sense Geology* (1946), and *The Greatest of the Prophets* (1955).

PUBLISHING. Seventh-day Adventist publishing houses trace their origin to **James White**, who began publishing *Present Truth* in 1849 and the *Advent Herald* in 1850, combining the two papers into the *Advent Review and Sabbath Herald* (later *Adventist Review*) in 1850. In 1852 he added *The Youth's Instructor*. He also published hymnbooks, tracts, and books prior to official organization of the Seventh-day Adventist Publishing Association in 1861, which was located in Battle Creek, Michigan. When the organization moved to Washington, D.C., in 1903 it reorganized and adopted the name **Review and Herald Publishing Association**.

The success of the Review and Herald publishing enterprise, which by 1873 had annual sales of $15,000, led James White to establish the Pacific Seventh-day Adventist Publishing Association in Oakland, California, in 1875. This organization published *Signs of the Times*, which White had begun the previous year, as well as books. In 1888 the name changed to **Pacific Press** Publishing Company and in 1904 to Pacific Press Publishing Association.

With publishing playing a major role in Adventist progress in North America, **John Nevins Andrews** began publishing a French-language paper in **Switzerland** in 1876, which led to the establishment of Imprimerie Polyglotte in Basel in 1885. About the same time, Adventist missionaries in **Australia** established the Bible Echo Publishing House in Melbourne. From these beginnings, Adventist missionaries came to regard publishing houses as an essential element of their strategy. By 1921 the denomination operated 25 publishing houses, a number that increased to 61 by 1940. During these same years the houses outside North America increased their production from about 30 percent to 40 percent of all denominational publications. Prior to 1940 the Hamburg Publishing Association, a descendent of Imprimerie Polyglotte, was the largest Adventist publishing house outside North America, although Stanborough Press (**Great Britain**), Signs Publishing Company (Australia), Scandinavian Publishing House (**Norway**), **Buenos Aires Publishing House (Argentina)**, and **Brazil Publishing House** had become significant as well. These large publishing houses printed books and papers in a variety of languages and then shipped them internationally.

A major element in the expansion of Adventist publishing was the development of door-to-door book sales by **literature evangelists**, originally called colporteurs. Probably the first book to be systematically sold in this manner was **John Harvey Kellogg's** *Home Hand Book of Domestic Hygiene and Rational Medicine* (1880). Through the efforts of **George A. King**, who successfully sold the Kellogg volume, the Seventh-day Adventist Publishing Association produced a one-volume edition of **Uriah Smith's** *Thoughts on Daniel and The Revelation* in 1882, which became the first Adventist subscription doctrinal book. By the 1890s literature evangelists were active in **Latin America** and the following decade in Southeast Asia, thereby establishing another element of Adventist expansion. Meanwhile, recognizing the need for central direction of denominational publishing and distribution of printed material, the **General Conference** established a Publishing Department in 1902.

In addition to books and tracts, Adventist publishers have produced a large variety of magazines. While the *Review and Herald* functioned as the general church paper, the *Signs of the Times* became the chief **evangelistic** magazine in the **United States** after *These Times*, begun in 1891, was merged with it in 1984. *Message*, begun in 1930, was an evangelistic magazine directed at African Americans. Beginning with the *Youth's Instructor* in 1852, publishers produced several magazines that were distributed primarily through the **Sabbath school** for children and young people, including *Our Little Friend* (1890), *Primary Treasure* (1957), *Guide* (1952), and *Insight* (which replaced the *Youth's Instructor* in 1970). Denominational health magazines began with *The Health Reformer* in 1866; *Vibrant Life*, the latest title of a magazine that dates back to 1885, is now the major popular health journal. *Liberty*, established in 1906, succeeded other religious liberty papers established in the 1880s, and addressed a largely non-Adventist audience. As of 2003 Adventist publishers were producing 99 English-language periodicals, and 222 other periodicals in a total of 74 languages. In addition, there were 8 **Division** and 35 **Union Conference** papers.

From total sales of over $1.5 million in 1910, the sales of Adventist publications of all types had climbed to over $90 million by 1992. By 2003 there were 57 publishing houses producing material in 338 languages with nearly 7,000 literature evangelists credentialed or licensed to sell these publications.

PUERTO RICO. A. M. Fischer and his wife began **evangelizing** the **Jamaican** population of Puerto Rico in 1901. After her husband died of typhoid fever a year later, Mrs. Fischer continued working until Brenton E. Connerly arrived in 1903. Connerly soon began **publishing** *The Sentinel of the Truth*, production of which moved to the Canal Zone in 1909. In 1920 missionaries established a training school that operated until 1928. Nine years later, a primary school in Santurce started to offer secondary education, becoming Puerto Rico **Academy** in 1946. In 1957 the school moved to Mayagüez, where in 1961 Antillian College was located after moving from **Cuba**. Meanwhile, Adventist membership in Puerto Rico grew to about 2,600 by 1948 and Bella Vista Hospital opened near Mayagüez in 1954. As of 2003 the Puerto Rican **Union Conference**, part of the Inter-American **Division**, had 269 **churches** with a membership of nearly 33,000. Antillian Adventist University, five secondary schools, Bella Vista Hospital, and four clinics were located on the island.

Q

QUIET HOUR, THE. **Self-supporting** Seventh-day Adventist radio and television program. Julius L. Tucker, a pastor in Portland, Oregon, began running a 15-minute broadcast in 1937 that soon became known as *The Quiet Hour*. Upon becoming pastor of the Berkeley, California, **church** in 1943, Tucker reestablished his program in Oakland and six years later broadcast it as a live television program, the first Adventist program in the new electronic medium. When Tucker became the minister of the **Emmanuel Missionary College** church in 1954, he relocated the program again and incorporated it as a nonprofit religious corporation. The program later sponsored various **mission** projects, beginning with the purchase of an airplane for use in **Papua New Guinea.** Leadership of *The Quiet Hour*, which as of 2003 was headquartered in Redlands, California, has remained within the Tucker family. Upon J. L. Tucker's retirement in 1985, his son LaVerne became the director and speaker, serving in that position until 1992, when his son Bill in turn assumed the program's leadership.

R

RANGOSO, KATA (1902-64). Seventh-day Adventist **minister** and church administrator. A native of the **Solomon Islands**, Rangoso attended Adventist mission schools and then worked as a teacher and as an assistant to various **mission** superintendents. He was **ordained** as a minister about 1936. With the evacuation of foreign missionaries during World War II, Rangoso took over the leadership of Adventist missions in the Solomons. In addition to preserving denominational properties, he also organized rescue efforts for downed Allied aviators. He served as president of the Western Solomon Islands **Mission** from 1953 to 1957 and also aided in the translation of the Bible into the Marovo language.

RATZLAFF, DALE (1936-). Seventh-day Adventist **minister** and **educator** and later critic of the denomination. Ratzlaff received a B.A. (1967) from **Pacific Union College** and B.D. (1969) from the **Seventh-day Adventist Theological Seminary**, taught Bible at Monterey Bay **Academy** between 1972 and 1979, and pastored Seventh-day Adventist **churches** in California. During the controversy over **Desmond Ford's** criticisms of the **sanctuary doctrine**, Ratzlaff left the denomination in 1981 because of his own disagreement with the Adventist doctrine of the **investigative judg-**

ment and later served as pastor of two evangelical churches in Arizona. He established Life Assurance Ministries Publications in 1989 and Life Assurance Ministries, Inc. (LAM) in 2000 to address the concerns of former and "inquiring" Seventh-day Adventists, among others. From 2000 to 2004 Ratzlaff edited *Proclamation*, a bimonthly journal published by LAM. Among his books were *Sabbath in Crisis* (1990), *The Cultic Doctrine of Seventh-day Adventists* (1996), *The Truth About Seventh-day Adventist "Truth"* (2000), and *Sabbath in Christ* (2003).

REFORMED SEVENTH-DAY ADVENTIST CHURCH. Short-lived movement formed under the leadership of Margaret Rowen. Converted to Adventism in 1912, Rowen claimed to have received visions beginning in 1916, the year following **Ellen G. White's** death. Sharing her experiences with a prayer group at her South Side Los Angeles **Church**, Rowen developed a small following. At first responding cautiously to her claims, after studying her writings the **General Conference** leaders announced in 1918 that her visions were not of divine origin. By 1919 the denomination had dismissed at least three **ministers**, a physician, and Rowen herself from church membership because of their continued advocacy of her cause. At Rowen's direction, Dr. B. E. Fullmer, the publisher of the movement's *The Reform Advocate and Prayer Band Appeal*, placed in the **Ellen G. White Estate** files a letter allegedly written by **Ellen G. White** stating that Rowen would be the denomination's next prophetess. After Fullmer revealed the fraud in 1925, Rowen attempted to have him murdered two years later and subsequently served a one-year sentence in San Quentin. By that point the Reformed Seventh-day Adventist Church had disintegrated.

REGIONAL CONFERENCE. African American organizational unit of the Seventh-day Adventist Church. As African American Seventh-day Adventists increased in number they became frustrated over their lack of influence on denominational policies. To address this problem, at the 1929 Spring Council of the **General Conference** (GC) Executive Committee **James K. Humphrey** and other Black **ministers** unsuccessfully proposed the organization of separate **conferences** for African Americans. Continued difficulties in the 1930s and 1940s, including the Negro Department's creation of an **evangelistic** magazine, *Message*, edited by a Caucasian, and the refusal of the Washington **Sanitarium** to accept Lucy Byard, an African American who died as a result of this action, prompted the organization in Washington, D.C., of the National Association for the Advancement of Worldwide Work Among Colored Seventh-day Adventists.

With growing pressure from African American members and ministers, the Spring Council of the GC Executive Committee in 1944 adopted a proposal to establish African American conferences. These Regional Conferences, as they were called, would include all of the African American **churches** within a **Union Conference** and would have all of the powers and responsibilities of the other conferences, usually organized by state, within the union. Although six regional conferences organized between 1945 and 1947, and another one formed in 1952, they were a controversial issue among African American Adventists, who in the Canadian, North Pacific, and Pacific Union Conferences rejected their creation. In the Pacific Union Conference, for instance, African Americans between 1945 and 2000 voted down six proposals to form a regional conference. On the other hand, because regional conferences offered greater opportunities for African Americans to attain positions of influence and shape their own church policies, as when they established their own retirement system in 2000, they were unlikely to dissolve in favor of a completely integrated denominational organization.

RELIGIOUS LIBERTY. Principle of freedom of conscience in religious matters. Seventh-day Adventists first addressed religious liberty issues when in 1864 they drafted a statement on participation in military service, which **John Nevins Andrews** presented to the **United States** government. After the National Reform Association, founded in 1863, began actively promoting legislation supporting Sunday as a national rest day, the **General Conference** (GC) in 1883 recommended the publication of a paper opposing the Sunday law movement. The denomination published the *Sabbath Sentinel*, a four-page monthly, in 1884 and, after a hiatus of two years, the *American Sentinel* in 1886. This paper, which carried the name *The Sentinel of Liberty* in 1900-01, continued until 1904. When the Blair Sunday Bill came before the United States Congress in 1888, the GC established a "Press Committee" to develop a strategy for opposing the bill. **Alonzo T. Jones** and John O. Corliss testified against the bill before congressional committees and the denomination sent a pamphlet entitled *Civil Government and Religion* to all members of Congress. During these years, Seventh-day Adventists developed an ideology of the absolute separation of church and state.

After the Blair Bill was defeated, the Press Committee organized the National Religious Liberty Association in 1889. This organization gathered signatures to oppose various pieces of religiously-oriented legislation, prepared and distributed tracts and pamphlets, and published a collection of documents dealing with religious liberty entitled *American State Papers* (1890). In 1893 the association adopted the name International Religious Liberty Association and two years later became the sponsor of the *American Sentinel*. In 1901 the **General Conference session** created the Religious Liberty Department, which began publishing *Liberty* in 1906. The department actively opposed Sunday legislation introduced into the United States Congress and state legislatures and assisted Adventists who were prosecuted for Sunday law violations. While Sunday legislation was a continuing concern, in the 1920s the department also fought efforts in Oregon, Michigan, and Washington to close all private schools and during the following decade sent representatives, including **Charles S. Longacre** and **Jean Nussbaum**, to the League of Nations to oppose calendar reform. Also, by the 1930s denominationally sponsored religious liberty associations had formed in **Australia, Canada, Great Britain**, and the **Philippines**. In the United States, Seventh-day Adventists were involved in a number of important court cases, including *Girouard v. United States* (1946), which declared that **noncombatancy** could not prevent naturalization, and *Hobie v. State of Florida* (1987), which stated that unwillingness to work on the **Sabbath** could not interfere with the right to receive unemployment benefits.

In 1959 the Religious Liberty Department merged with the Bureau of Public Relations to form the Department of Public Affairs. Three years later religious liberty matters became the responsibility of the newly created Department of Public Affairs and Religious Liberty (PARL). Under the leadership of **Bert Beverly Beach** this department appointed individuals as liaisons to the United States Congress and the United Nations and also became active in interchurch relations. As the North American **Division** became an independent entity in the 1990s, it took over some of the functions of the PARL, including publication of *Liberty* in 1993. Meanwhile, the PARL sponsored international and regional conferences on religious liberty and worked with other organizations, including the International Academy for Freedom of Religion and Belief and the Council on Religious Freedom. Among other activities, it opposed the establishment of American diplomatic relations with the Vatican and worked for the rights of minority religions in **Russia** and other former Soviet states. Although the denomination continued to support the separation of church and state, its opposition to government aid for private education moderated in the 1990s, leading the denomination to withdraw its representatives from Americans United for Separation of Church and State, which it had helped found in 1947-48.

REVELATION SEMINAR. Seventh-day Adventist **evangelistic** program. George Knowles at the New Gallery Centre in London introduced in 1969 an interactive, small-group seminar to follow up interests developed during public evangelistic meetings. Two years later Knowles again successfully used the seminar approach in Montreal, Quebec. Subsequently joining the staff of *It Is Written*, he and **George Vandeman** planned a one-day seminar program, at which Vandeman would speak, followed by local pastors conducting a series of 18 evening seminars. By 1975 this approach had developed into the *It Is Written Revelation Seminar*. Within a few years both pastors and lay people began to conduct Revelation Seminars as well. Harry Robinson, a Texas **Conference** administrator, established a resource center for the seminars in 1980 that six years later took the name Seminars Unlimited. Working with the **General Conference**, by the early 1990s this organization was providing a wide range of evangelistic materials to both pastors and lay people throughout the world.

REVIEW AND HERALD. See ADVENTIST REVIEW.

REVIEW AND HERALD PUBLISHING ASSOCIATION (RHPA). Seventh-day Adventist publishing house. Sabbatarian Adventist **publishing** began when **James White** had the first issue of *The Present Truth* printed in Middletown, Connecticut, in 1849. The following year he also began publishing *The Advent Review* and within a few months combined these publications into the *Second Advent Review and Sabbath Herald*. Over the next few years White moved his publishing efforts to several different places until settling in Battle Creek, Michigan, in 1855. Although the sabbatarian Adventists regarded the publishing activity to be a church responsibility, because of their opposition to denominational **organization** the enterprise actually belonged to White. Addressing this problem, a conference in 1860 decided to adopt the name Seventh-day Adventist (SDA) and began the legal steps that led in the following year to incorporation of the SDA Publishing Association, in which shareholders owned non-dividend stock.

During the next several decades the SDA Publishing Association expanded significantly as it conducted a commercial printing business as well as published denominational books and papers. Sales of books and periodicals increased from $15,000 in 1873 to $500,000 in 1890, for example, and the press established branch offices in **Canada** (1889-1902) and Georgia (1889-1901). But because the lucrative commercial printing business frequently gained priority over denominational publications and sometimes resulted in the printing of objectionable items, **Ellen G. White** increasingly called for the press to end its nondenominational business. In 1902 a fire destroyed the publishing house, including both its buildings and printing equipment. Less than a week later, the Publishing Association board, viewing the fire as a judgment of God, voted to discontinue commercial printing as it sought to put the operation back together. Shortly thereafter the **General Conference** decided to relocate to the Washington, D.C., area. Because some of the shareholders objected to this move, the denomination bought their shares.

The **General Conference session** of 1903 voted to dissolve the Seventh-day Adventist Publishing Association and transfer its assets to a new organization, which was incorporated as the Review and Herald Publishing Association under the laws of the District of Columbia in August of that year. The publishing house completed a new building in 1906 and expanded it several times thereafter. As with the Battle Creek operation, the new publishing house created several branch offices, including South Bend, Indiana (1906-38), New York City (1907-22), Peekskill, New York (1922-38), and Winnepeg, Canada (1919-20). In 1970 the RHPA began a lease arrangement with Stanborough Press, Ltd. in Great Britain, under which it provided general oversight and helped pay for equipment upgrades while Stanborough's board remained responsible for daily operations. **Southern Publishing Association** merged with the RHPA in 1980, which three years later moved into a new facility in Hagerstown, Maryland. In addition to books, as of 2003 the RHPA published several magazines for the denomination, including *Guide, Insight, **Listen**, **Message**, Vibrant Life, **Liberty***, and the ***Adventist Review***, in addition to various **Sabbath school** materials.

RICHARDS, HAROLD MARSHALL SYLVESTER (1894-1985). Seventh-day Adventist **evangelist** and radio speaker. The son of an Adventist **minister**, Richards graduated from Washington Missionary College (later **Columbia Union College**) in 1919 and began serving as a pastor in Ottawa, **Canada**. After going to California, where he conducted evangelistic campaigns, in 1926 Richards began experimenting with radio broadcasting. In 1930 he occasionally contributed programs to the *Family Worship* series on KNX in Los Angeles, and soon thereafter began broadcasting his own *Tabernacle of the Air*, financed entirely by contributions. In 1937 the Pacific **Union Conference** began sponsoring the program, which now was appearing on the Don Lee Broadcasting System, and changed its name to *Voice of Prophecy*. By 1942 the Mutual Broadcasting System was broadcasting the program nationwide under **General Conference** sponsorship. Joined by his son, H. M. S. Richards, Jr., as an associate speaker in 1969, Richards continued to be active in the radio program until 1982. The National Religious Broadcasters awarded him Honor Citations in 1967 and 1970. In addition to his radio broadcasts, Richards also spoke frequently at **camp meetings** and evangelistic campaigns and wrote several books, among them *The Indispensable Man* (1927), *Day After Tomorrow* (1956), and *Why I am A Seventh-day Adventist* (1965).

RIGHTEOUSNESS BY FAITH. Christian doctrine that salvation comes through the individual's faith in the sufficiency of Christ's righteousness, death, and resurrection. Because of Seventh-day Adventism's traditional emphasis on the necessity of obeying God's law as embodied in the Ten Commandments, the doctrine of righteousness by faith has had a controversial history within the denomination. In **Uriah Smith's** unofficial 1872 summary of Adventist beliefs, he stated that the Christian was dependent on Christ both for justification and for the grace by which he or she could obey God's law. Nonetheless, Smith followed these assertions with discussion of one's duty to obey the Ten Commandments. Not surprisingly, many critics of Adventism accused the denomination of advocating legalism.

In the 1880s **Ellet J. Waggoner** and **Alonzo T. Jones**, two young **ministers** who worked together on the *Signs of the Times*, began advocating what they called "righteousness by faith," namely that the believer must have a personal encounter with Christ that would in turn transform his or her personal life. In theological terms, Waggoner and Jones included both justification and sanctification, or gospel and law, within their concept of righteousness by faith. Adventist traditionalists, including **General Conference** (GC) president **George I. Butler** and *Review and Herald* editor Uriah Smith, reacted negatively to Jones's and

Waggoner's ideas because they feared that these concepts would undermine the doctrine of the **Sabbath**. After a committee established by the **General Conference session** of 1886 was unable to reach a consensus on the issue, Waggoner and Jones presented their ideas to the **General Conference session of 1888**, where they stirred up considerable opposition. Nonetheless, after **Ellen G. White** threw her support behind the two ministers and traveled with them to **camp meetings** and ministerial institutes over the next two years, the Adventist traditionalists gradually abandoned their opposition and the new ideas regarding righteousness by faith began to pervade the denomination. The "Receive Ye the Holy Ghost" movement of the late 1890s, led by Jones and **Albion F. Ballenger**, saw itself as an extension of the "1888 message," because it emphasized baptism by the Holy Spirit and other Holiness themes as the means by which obedience to the law would occur.

The tension between understandings of justification and sanctification, however, continued to produce discussion and sometimes controversy within Adventism. In 1919 **William W. Prescott** published *The Doctrine of Christ* in which he argued that justification not only freed the sinner from guilt but also brought deliverance from the power of sin. He followed this concept with discussion of "The Victorious Life," a concept borrowed from the Victorious Life Conferences that had started in the United States in 1913. During the 1920s many leading Adventist ministers, including Meade McGuire, Taylor Bunch, and **LeRoy E. Froom**, picked up the idea of the Victorious Life, identifying it with righteousness by faith and arguing that it offered the means of reconciling justification and sanctification by its teaching that Christ provides power for victory over sin.

Although the Victorious Life teaching of the 1920s raised little controversy, righteousness by faith again became an issue in the 1970s. This debate had several roots. In the 1950s Seventh-day Adventism began to move closer to the theology of American evangelicalism with the publication of *Seventh-day Adventists Answer Questions on Doctrine* in 1957, a product of the **evangelical-Adventist dialogue** that took place in 1955-56. Also, Adventist theologians such as **Edward Heppenstall** and Norval Pease began producing articles and books in the 1960s that denied the possibility of perfection, an issue that had long haunted Adventism. In part, these theologians were responding to **Robert Brinsmead**, an **Australian** who in the mid-1950s had started promoting a unique version of perfectionism rooted in the **sanctuary doctrine**. Also in the 1950s, two Adventist ministers, Robert J. Wieland and Donald

K. Short, circulated a manuscript in which they argued that the church must corporately repent for not accepting the "1888 message." About 1970 **Desmond Ford**, chair of the religion department at **Avondale College**, convinced Brinsmead that his perfectionism was wrong. But Brinsmead did not stop there, for he was soon arguing that the Adventist understanding that righteousness by faith included both justification and sanctification was incorrect as well. He stirred up controversy over the issue in Australia and established a magazine, *Present Truth*, which promoted his view that sanctification was not a necessary prerequisite to salvation.

Meanwhile, the editors of the **Review and Herald**, Kenneth Wood and Herbert Douglass, were presenting in its pages their view that mainstream Adventist theology had taken the wrong path since publication of *Questions on Doctrine*, that Jesus had given an example of how to live the sanctified life, and that his **Second Advent** was waiting upon a generation of Christians—i.e., Adventists—who overcame all sin. Responding to the controversy, the GC organized a conference that took place in Palmdale, California, in 1976. This meeting issued the "Palmdale Statement" on righteousness by faith that sought to address the issue in broad enough terms that all sides could identify with it. Nothing was resolved, however, and the controversy became more heated. After several high-level consultations, GC president **Neal C. Wilson** called in 1979 for an end to public debate and appointed a committee to study the issue.

Critics of the so-called "new theology" of Ford and others were not satisfied and established their own publications and institutions, including *Our Firm Foundation*, published by **Hope International** and edited by Ronald Spear, and **Hartland Institute**, which published the works of Colin D. and Russell R. Standish. Wieland and Short in 1985 helped establish the 1888 Study Committee which held meetings and issued publications alleging that Seventh-day Adventists had still not accepted the teaching of Waggoner and Jones. Meanwhile, what might be called mainstream Adventism continued to hold to a concept of righteousness by faith that included both justification and sanctification but avoided the perfectionism that seemed to characterize many of the denomination's traditionalist critics. Others, most prominently including Brinsmead and American minister **Dale Ratzlaff**, left Adventism because they believed that its theology, among other issues, had an incorrect understanding of righteousness by faith.

RIVER PLATE ADVENTIST UNIVERSITY. Seventh-day Adventist **educational** institution located in Entre Rios, **Argentina**. Beginning as a **mission** school with six students taught by Nelson Z. Town at his home in Las Tunas, the school erected its first building at its current location toward the end of 1899 and classes began the following April. Between 1908 and 1912 Walton C. John reorganized the curriculum into six primary and four secondary grades; in 1926 the institution added a two-year teacher-training program. Reorganization of the curriculum in 1946 established a seven-grade primary school, five-year secondary school, and a two- year college program. In 1958 the school expanded to a senior college, with the college in 1962 named The School of Theology and Education. Gradually broadening its offerings over the next three decades, the institution became River Plate Adventist University in 1990, organized into four schools: School of Business Administration, School of Humanities, Education, and Social Sciences, School of Health Sciences, and School of Theology. In 1994 it opened a medical school, the third to be established by the church. Beginning with the teacher-training course in 1954, at several points in its history River Plate received government accreditation of various programs. This process culminated with full government accreditation in 2002. As of 2003 the university had an enrollment of about 1,800 students.

ROBINSON, ASA T. (1850-1949). Seventh-day Adventist **minister** and church administrator. Converted to Adventism at the age of 20, at the urging of **Stephen N. Haskell** Robinson worked as a **literature evangelist** from 1882 to 1884 and then in **city missions** from 1884 to 1886. **Ordained** as a minister in 1886, Robinson became president of the New England **Conference** the following year. In 1891 he went to **South Africa**, where he organized the **churches** into a **conference**. Believing that the membership in South Africa was too small to support separate organizations for such activities as **publishing** and **education**, as was the pattern in the **United States**, he incorporated departments into the conference. Also while in South Africa, he oversaw the establishment of **Solusi Mission**, the first Adventist **mission** for Black Africans. In 1898 Robinson moved to **Australia** where as a conference president he once again incorporated departments into the denominational organization. When the **General Conference** reorganized in 1901 it followed Robinson's organizational pattern by establishing its own departments. Returning to the **United States** in 1904, Robinson served successively as the president of several conferences, including Nebraska, Colorado, and Southern New England. Before retiring at age 80, he worked for several years as the chaplain of the New England **Sanitarium**.

ROMANIA. In 1868-69 **Michael B. Czechowski** introduced Seventh-day Adventist doctrines into Romania. Among the approximately 12 people he converted was Thomas G. Aslan, who later made contact with **John Nevins Andrews** and helped him prepare a Romanian-language paper. Visits in the mid-1880s from **George I. Butler**, president of the **General Conference**, and **Augustine C. Bourdeau**, an **evangelist**, followed these initial contacts. In 1890 **Ludvig R. Conradi** entered Transylvania, then part of **Hungary**, in search of sabbatarians. As a result of Conradi's efforts, by the mid-1890s several individuals in Cluz had converted to Adventism. Meanwhile, in 1892 Conradi organized several **German** Adventists who had recently moved from **Russia** to Romania into a **church**. Eventually these Adventists settled in Viile Noi. Johann F. Ginter, an **evangelist** from Russia, moved to Bucharest in 1904 and soon converted several individuals, among them Peter Paulini and Stefan Demetrescu, who then attended the Adventist training school in **Friedensau**, Germany. By the time that Paulini and Demetrescu returned to Romania, the government had expelled Ginter, but the newly trained Romanian Adventists were ready to take his place. **Conferences** organized beginning in 1907 and the Romanian **Union Conference** formed in 1919 with about 2,000 members. Starting in 1908 Romanian Adventists had their publications printed by the Hamburg press in Germany, but in 1920 they established the Adventist **Publishing** House in Bucharest. Three years later the Romanian Union Training School opened in Bucharest but moved to Dicio-San-Martin in 1926 and then Brasov in 1931.

With the advent of World War II, by which time there were about 13,000 members in Romania, the German military confiscated the training school building in 1941 and completely closed the institution the next year. It opened again in 1944 and beginning in 1950 operated under the name Romanian Theological Seminary. Meanwhile, the publishing house closed in 1942, opening again in 1944 until taken over by the government three years later. With the collapse of the Communist government, a new publishing house opened in 1990 and the Romanian Adventist College of Health in 1991. Despite the difficulties caused by two world wars and a Communist dictatorship, Adventism grew faster in Romania than elsewhere in Europe. As of 2003 the Romanian **Union Confer-**

ence, part of the Euro-Africa **Division**, had a membership of nearly 73,000 and 1,075 **churches**. The Romanian Adventist College of Health, Romanian Adventist Theological Institute, Romanian Adventist Publishing House, and a radio station and production center were located in the country.

RUSSIAN FEDERATION. Seventh-day Adventism first entered Russia when **German** settlers who had immigrated to the **United States** and there converted to Adventism began sending denominational publications to their relatives still living in the land of the Czar. As some of these individuals became interested in Adventist doctrines, they requested that a **minister** visit with them. In 1886 **Ludvig R. Conradi** and **Gerhard Perk** traveled to the Crimea where they organized a **church**. Arrested for proselytizing, they spent 40 days in jail at Perekop but upon release continued their **evangelistic** efforts. Conradi and Perk worked almost entirely among the German population, but when Theofil Babienco, who had been a sabbatarian for several years, accepted Adventism as a result of contact with the Germans, the development of the denomination among the Russians began in Stavropol, where a church organized in 1890. That same year, with about 350 Adventists in Russia, a general meeting took place at Eigenheim, attended by more than 100 persons. Within a year, however, the Russian government arrested and exiled several of the Russian and German converts who had attended that meeting. Babienco, who was exiled to the Herusy area, nonetheless converted more than 200 individuals in his new location.

By the mid-1890s Adventists began entering urban areas. Perk worked in Riga and St. Petersburg, his brother Johann in Vilnius, and other evangelists in Kiev. By 1900 there were 28 churches with more than 1,000 members in Russia; these members formed a **Union Conference** seven years later. In 1905 Adventists began **publishing** books in the Russian language and in 1908 started an **evangelistic** magazine, *Olive Tree*, most of whose issues were printed by the Hamburg Publishing House in Germany. On the eve of World War I the Russian Union Conference had a membership of nearly 6,000 in 240 churches and was financially self-sufficient.

Despite the war and the Russian Revolution, Seventh-day Adventism continued to grow, reaching a membership of over 8,000 by 1920. With Protestants having more freedom during the 1920s, Adventist membership increased to about 13,000 during the decade. But new laws in 1928 greatly restricted church activity and growth slowed considerably, with about 3,000 members added by

1940. During this decade, the government dissolved the local **conferences**, leaving only the **Union Conference**, and sent many **ministers** into exile. By the late 1930s reports from Russia indicated that the government had stopped public worship services and Adventists were meeting in private homes. Although the government lifted some restrictions in the early 1950s, difficulties continued and the church grew slowly, reaching a membership of about 18,000 in the 187 churches registered with the government; in addition, about another 3,000 members did not belong to officially organized churches. Many members of this latter group formed an alternative Adventist church, the True and Free Adventists. This movement, which had a strong Mennonite peace church background, refused to cooperate with a government that sought to rule their consciences. In 1960 the government dissolved the Seventh-day Adventist All-Union Council, which had earlier replaced the Union Conference; as a result, there was no official organization until 1975, when a gradual process of organization began under the leadership of Michael P. Kulakov. Many True and Free Adventists opposed these developments and did not reconcile with the official church until after the fall of the Soviet Union in 1991.

The Seventh-day Adventist Church in Russia had no training facility for ministers, virtually all of whom learned their profession from older pastors. During the glasnost period of the 1980s when the Soviet Union was granting greater freedoms, however, the denomination received permission to establish a seminary at **Zaokski**, near Moscow, which opened in 1988. Four years later, Adventists established a publishing house and about the same time a radio and television production facility. After the fall of Communism, Adventism—similar to other conservative Protestant churches—grew rapidly, virtually tripling its membership in the 1990s, a situation that greatly strained the resources of the newly freed denomination. As of 2003 the denomination in Russia was organized into the East Russian Union **Mission** and the West Russian Union Conference, parts of the Euro-Asia **Division**, with 605 churches and about 52,000 members. Zaokski Theological Seminary, Russian Sahmyook University, five language schools, Adventist Health Center, Source of Life Publishing House, and the Voice of Hope Media Center were located in Russia.

RWANDA. While serving with the **Belgian** military in German East **Africa** during World War I, Daniel E. Delhove concluded that Rwanda-Urundi would be a good place to introduce Seventh-day Adventist **missions**. While in **Great Britain** after the war, he convinced **Henri Monnier** to return with him as a missionary to what was now a Belgian mandated territory. After first occupying three abandoned mission stations, Monnier established the Buganza **mission** station near Lake Muhazi in 1920 and Delhove began the Gitwe station, a few miles from Nyanza, in 1921. In 1923 the Buganza mission moved to a site close to Ruhengeri, where it was called the Rwankeri Mission Station. The first **baptisms** took place in 1924 and a school opened at Gitwe the following year. Alfred Matter, a missionary from **Germany** who had taken a course in tropical medicine, opened a dispensary at Rwankeri in 1923 and with Dr. J. H. Sturges established the Ngoma Mission and Hospital in 1931, located south of Kibuye. The first baptisms at Ngoma took place in 1933 but about the same time, in response to Monnier's efforts, thousands were joining the church in the area around the Rwankeri mission. This growth has been described by missiologists as resembling a people movement that transcended ethnic differences. By the time a new Central African **Union Mission** formed in 1961, church membership in Rwanda had grown so large that the territory around each of the mission stations organized into a separate mission field, with Gitwe becoming the South Rwanda Mission, Ngoma the West Rwanda Mission, and Rwankeri the North Rwanda **Field**. By the time the Rwanda Union Mission formed in 1984, the Seventh-day Adventist Church may have been the largest Protestant denomination in the country. The 1994 civil war between the Hutus and Tutsis forced many individuals to flee the country, however, and disrupted the denomination's work. The International Criminal Tribunal for Rwanda in 2003 convicted Elizaphan Ntakirutimana, an Adventist church administrator, and his son, Dr. Gérard Ntakirutimana, of genocide for the massacre of perhaps 3,000 people inside the Adventist church at Mugonero on April 12, 1994. Despite the conviction, both men continued to proclaim their innocence. As of 2003 the Rwanda Union Mission, part of the East-Central Africa **Division**, had over 1,173 **churches** with a membership of over 340,000. Adventist University of Central Africa, two secondary schools, Mugonero School of Nursing, Mugonero Hospital, nine clinics and dispensaries, and a radio-television production center were located in Rwanda.

S

SABBATH, SEVENTH-DAY. Based on the fourth commandment, doctrine that the Sabbath is to be observed on the seventh day of the week. The Sabbath doctrine came into the **Millerite Movement** through contact between **Rachel Oakes Preston**, a Seventh Day Baptist laywoman, and Frederick Wheeler, pastor of a Millerite congregation in Washington, New Hampshire. Wheeler began observing the seventh-day Sabbath in the spring of 1844 and, possibly toward the end of that year, several members of his congregation also adopted the doctrine. Meanwhile, **Thomas M. Preble**, a Millerite preacher, began observing the Sabbath during the summer of 1844, though it is not known whether he had direct contact with the Washington church. In February 1845 Preble published an article on the Sabbath in Joseph Turner's *Hope of Israel*, a Millerite paper, and a short time later expanded his article in a publication entitled *Tract, Showing that the Seventh Day Should Be Observed as the Sabbath, Instead of the First Day; "According to the Commandment."*

Although Preble ceased observing the Sabbath about two years later and subsequently wrote articles and a book against the doctrine, his tract came to the attention of **Joseph Bates**, a former sea captain and Millerite preacher, who began observing the Sabbath in 1845 and visited Wheeler and his Washington congregation in 1846. That same year Bates published two tracts entitled *The Opening of the Heavens* and *The Seventh Day Sabbath, a Perpetual Sign*. **James** and **Ellen White**, who had met Bates in early 1846, studied the second of these tracts in the fall of that year and, after initial resistance, soon adopted the doctrine and presented it to the small groups of Adventists with whom they were meeting. As the sabbatarian Adventists coalesced, questions arose regarding the proper time for beginning and ending the Sabbath. Bates believed that observance should begin at 6:00 p.m. on Friday and continue to 6:00 p.m. on Saturday, but others argued that it should extend from sundown to sundown. After being asked to research the issue, **John Nevins Andrews**, who had converted to sabbatarianism as a result of reading Preble's tract in 1846, concluded that sundown should mark the hours of the Sabbath and presented his interpretation to a conference of sabbatarian Adventists in 1855. Although Bates and Ellen White both continued to argue for the 6:00 position, at the close of the conference White experienced a vision that confirmed Andrews's views and from that time on Adventists observed the Sabbath from sundown Friday to sundown Saturday. Not surprisingly, given their New England origins, the Adventists followed the Puritan, rather than continental, practice of Sabbath observance, largely restricting the day's activities to worship, Bible study, prayer, and lay **evangelism**.

With his tract *The Seventh Day Sabbath, a Perpetual Sign*, and later publications, Bates interpreted the Sabbath within a prophetic context, ultimately seeing it as the basic element in the **investigative judgment** and as the symbol of faithfulness in the final struggle between God's people and the beastly power referred to in Revelation 13. Seventh-day Adventist historian **George R. Knight** argued in *Millennial Fever* (1994) that it was this prophetic interpretation of the Sabbath that gave the sabbatarian Adventists their distinctive dynamism. In 1859 Andrews examined the doctrine in his *History of the Sabbath and First Day of the Week: Showing the Bible Record of the Sabbath and the Manner in Which it Has Been Supplanted by the Heathen Festival of the Sun*, later enlarged and published in several editions. Drawing upon Seventh Day Baptist arguments as well as reexamination of significant documents, Andrews argued that the Christian church had abandoned the Sabbath largely because of its hostility to Judaism.

Seventh-day Adventist understanding of the Sabbath has remained largely consistent with the concepts developed by the early sabbatarian Adventists, though in recent years there has been greater emphasis on the personal meaning of the observance. Significant works by Adventist scholars included **Samuelle Bacchiocchi**, *From Sabbath to Sunday* (1977) and *Divine Rest for Human Restlessness* (1980), **Desmond Ford**, *The Forgotten Day* (1981), and Kenneth A. Strand, ed., *The Sabbath in Scripture and History* (1982). **Dale Ratzlaff**, a former Adventist minister, critiqued the doctrine in *Sabbath in Crisis* (1990), to which Bacchiocchi responded with *The Sabbath Under Crossfire* (1999).

SABBATH SCHOOL. Patterned after Sunday schools but held for all age groups, a program of worship and study on Saturday mornings in addition to the worship service. When **James White** introduced the *Youth's Instructor* in 1852, he included a series of Bible lessons for young people to study with their parents. There appears to have been no organized Sabbath school, however, until the next year, when White established one in Rochester, New York. Adventist congregations in Buck's Bridge, New York (1854), and Battle Creek, Michigan (1855), also subsequently formed Sabbaath schools. These early Sabbath schools were divided into two divisions, adult and children's, and perhaps drew practices from the Methodist class groups with which many Adventists were familiar. In 1863 **Uriah Smith** wrote the first series of Bible lessons for adults, which were published in the *Review and Herald*. Through the 1860s there was little general organization of Sabbath schools, however, and each local **church** did what it saw best.

Addressing this situation, **Goodloe H. Bell**, who became editor of the *Youth's Instructor* in 1869, began publishing organizational materials for Sabbath school leaders, introduced separate sets of lessons for children and youth, and visited churches where he helped organize Sabbath schools. He also wrote a series of eight Bible-study books for Sabbath school use. Further organization came when Adventists in California organized a Sabbath School Association in 1877, a pattern soon followed by several other states, culminating with the formation of the **General Conference** Sabbath School Association in 1878. These associations attempted to improve children's and young people's programs in the local churches by conducting model Sabbath schools at **camp meetings**, where they introduced a new song book—*The Song Anchor*—and urged the adoption of weekly offerings so that necessary supplies and other materials could be purchased. Battle Creek, Michigan, organized the first Sabbath school for small children in 1878, which eight years later became the kindergarten division. In 1885 the Sabbath School Association began publishing the *Sabbath School Worker*, which contained articles to aid leaders in the organization and teaching of the schools. The *Senior Sabbath School Lesson Quarterly* for adults began publication in 1889, followed the next year by *Our Little Friend*, a magazine that included lessons for kindergarten and primary children.

In 1885 a Sabbath school in Oakland, California, decided to give its weekly offering to support the Adventist missionaries who were going to **Australia**. Shortly thereafter, in 1889-90 Sabbath schools raised about $12,000 to build the missionary ship *Pitcairn*. Soon the Sabbath school became the primary place for promoting the support of **missions**; beginning in 1913 the denomination used all of the regular Sabbath school offerings to fund missions while a separate offering provided for local expenses.

The reorganization of the denomination in 1901 dissolved the Sabbath School Association and replaced it with the Sabbath School Department. Under the leadership of **L. Flora Plummer**, who began as corresponding secretary of the department in 1901 and became secretary in 1913, the organization created a wide array of materials for children, including lessons for more narrowly defined age groups and visual aids for teaching younger children. This process continued into the latter half of the 20th century as the department introduced *Junior Guide* (1953), *Primary Treasure* (1957), *Earliteen Sabbath School Quarterly* (1962), and *Corner-*

stone Connections (1982). In 1970 *Insight* replaced the venerable *Youth's Instructor*, which ceased publication. In 1992 the Sabbath School Department merged into the newly created Church Ministries Department. Although within the Seventh-day Adventist Church the Sabbath School involved all age groups, it was clear that most of the denomination's attention focused on children and teenagers.

SACRAMENTS. Sacred religious rituals of the church. Although Seventh-day Adventists do not normally use the term "sacraments," they regard **baptism** and the **Lord's Supper** as outward signs of the believer's experience of grace, rather than being themselves avenues of grace. Therefore, Adventists practice believer's baptism, which it limits to those who have reached an "age of accountability," usually about 12 years. The Lord's Supper, often referred to as the "Communion Service," is open to baptized Adventists and other believing Christians. Preceded by **foot washing**, often called the "ordinance of humility," this service uses only unfermented grape juice and unleavened bread. Adventists view marriage, ordination, and anointing of the sick as sacred ceremonies but do not include them as signs of the reception of God's grace.

SAHMYOOK UNIVERSITY. Seventh-day Adventist **educational** institution located in Seoul, **Korea**. In 1917 the Chosen Industrial School in Sunan, established in 1907, began offering a two-year **ministerial** course to provide trained personnel for the Chosen **Conference**. Two years later the institution took the name Chosen **Union** Training School; it offered primarily secondary level education. In 1931 the ministerial training program moved to the **union mission** headquarters in Seoul but because of financial problems did not function from 1932 to 1937, at which time it reopened as the Chosen Union Workers' Training Institute. The Japanese invasion forced closure of the school in 1942. Reopened in 1947 as the Korean Union Seminary, the school moved to its present site in 1949. Closed by the Korean War in 1950, the school opened again in 1951, this time under the name Korean Union Training School. At the same time, the Seoul Junior Training Institute, a secondary institution established in the 1930s, transferred to the seminary's campus. After receiving a government permit in 1954 to operate as a college, the institution became known as Korean Union College. In 1961 the college gained permission from the government to grant bachelor's degrees in theology and to establish junior college programs in agriculture and home economics. Between 1966 and 1973 the school dropped its junior college programs while it broadened its senior college curriculum. In 1974 it established a four-year nursing program and in 1981 created a graduate school that over the next few years introduced master's programs in theology, religious education, pharmacy, and chemistry, and a Ph.D. in theology. As of 2003 the university was divided into four schools: Sahmyook College, School of Graduate Studies, Graduate School of Theology, Graduate School of Business Administration, and Graduate School of Health Science and Social Welfare. By this time it had become the largest Adventist educational institution in the world, with approximately 5,000 undergraduate and 500 graduate students.

SAMOA AND TOKELAU ISLANDS. Although Seventh-day Adventist missionaries began working in the Samoan Islands in 1895, and established a school in 1901, they did not win their first converts among the Samoan people until 1915. Six years later they organized the Samoa **Mission** and in 1934 Iiga Kuresa became the first native Samoan to be **ordained** an Adventist **minister.** The *Voice of Prophecy* began broadcasting in the vernacular in 1964. As of 2003 the Samoa Mission, part of the **South Pacific Division**, had 29 **churches** with a membership of nearly 5,000. Samoa Adventist College, a secondary school, was located on Samoa.

SANCTUARY DOCTRINE. Seventh-day Adventist doctrine stating that Jesus entered the Most Holy Place of the heavenly sanctuary on October 22, 1844. Daniel 8:14 states, "Unto two thousand and three hundred days; then shall the sanctuary be cleansed." Believing that in biblical prophecy a "day" stood for an actual year and that the sanctuary must refer to the earth, **William Miller** linked this time prophecy with the 1260 day prophecy of Daniel 7:25 and concluded that the second coming of Jesus would take place about the year 1843. Miller later refined his prediction, based on his study of the Jewish calendar, stating that Christ would return between March 21, 1843, and March 21, 1844. After the **Second Advent** did not take place as expected, **Samuel S. Snow** put forward his interpretation, based upon typological interpretation of the Old and New Testaments, that Jesus would come on the Day of Atonement, which according to his interpretation of the Jewish Karaite calendar fell on October 22. When again the expected event failed to occur, **Hiram Edson**, a **Millerite** farmer in New York, concluded that the sanctuary of Daniel 8:14 did not mean the earth but rather the heavenly sanctuary referred to in Hebrews 8 and 9. Therefore, rather than returning to earth on October 22, 1844, Jesus had moved from the Holy Place to the Most Holy Place, or second apartment, of the heavenly sanctuary. With Dr. Franklin B. Hahn and **O. R. L. Crosier**, Edson studied the issue further and Crosier wrote out their conclusions in articles published in the *Day Dawn* (1845) and the *Day-Star Extra* (1846), both Millerite papers.

Although Crosier later rejected this new interpretation of the sanctuary, his ideas came to the attention of **Joseph Bates**, a former sea captain and Millerite preacher who had recently adopted the doctrine of the seventh-day **Sabbath**. Bates soon met with Edson and, believing that the heavenly sanctuary corresponded with the Old Testament earthly sanctuary, saw a relationship between it and the Sabbath, for the ark—located in the second apartment—contained the Ten Commandments. Bates concluded that when Christ entered the Most Holy Place he had initiated a period of renewed emphasis on the fourth commandment, obedience to which would become an essential element in the judgment. About this same time, the sabbatarian Adventists adopted the **shut door theory** put forward by Apollos Hale and Joseph Turner, which argued that the judgment had begun on October 22 and probation had closed for Christians. Beginning with a series of conferences in 1848 and 1849, Bates, Edson, and **James** and **Ellen White** further developed their understanding of Christ's ministry in the heavenly sanctuary and by the 1850s had linked it with the idea that the judgment had already begun, a concept that they came to call the **investigative judgment**, although they abandoned the belief that the time of probation was over. As the sabbatarian Adventist movement took form, it regarded this sanctuary doctrine, supported by the visions of Ellen G. White, as an essential belief. **Uriah Smith's** unofficial statement of Seventh-day Adventist **fundamental beliefs** in 1872 as well as the official statements of 1931 and 1980 included the doctrine. **Milian L. Andreasen's** *The Sanctuary Service* (1937) and *The Book of Hebrews* (1948) and **Edward Heppenstall's** *Our High Priest* (1973) were important expositions of Adventist sanctuary belief.

Despite its historic significance for Seventh-day Adventists, the sanctuary doctrine has had a controversial history. **Dudley M. Canright** argued in *Seventh-day Adventism Renounced* (1888) that Christ had entered the second apartment of the heavenly sanctuary immediately on his ascension to heaven, a view developed further by **Albion F. Ballenger** in *Cast Out for the Cross of Christ* (c. 1909). Since that time other denominational leaders, including

Ludvig R. Conradi, William W. Fletcher, and R. A. Grieve separated from the church in part because of the sanctuary doctrine. Probably the most significant criticism of the sanctuary doctrine, however, came from **Desmond Ford**, who was already controversial because of his connection with the discussion that took place in the 1970s over **righteousness by faith**. When debate erupted after he had made a speech critical of the doctrine in 1979 at **Pacific Union College**, the **General Conference** (GC) asked Ford to develop his views more extensively and present them to a review committee. At a subsequent conference in Colorado, the committee issued a statement, "Christ in the Heavenly Sanctuary," that seemed to be broad enough to include the interpretations of both Ford and his traditionalist critics. Shortly thereafter, however, the Australasian **Division**, for which Ford worked, removed his ministerial credentials. Ford soon published his interpretation in *Daniel 8:14, The Day of Atonement, and The Investigative Judgment* (1980). Although Ford remained a practicing Adventist, the storm of controversy that developed around his views resulted in the departure from the church of many **ministers** and lay people. Among those who left was **Dale Ratzlaff**, who later wrote *The Cultic Doctrine of Seventh-day Adventists* (1996). In response to the controversy, the GC **Biblical Research Institute** produced several scholarly examinations of the sanctuary doctrine, including Arnold V. Wallenkampf and W. Richard Lesher, eds., *The Sanctuary and the Atonement* (1981) and Frank B. Holbrook, ed., *Doctrine of the Sanctuary* (1989).

SANITARIUM HEALTH FOOD COMPANY. Seventh-day Adventist food company in **Australia** and **New Zealand**. While living in Australia in the 1890s, **Ellen G. White** urged Adventist leaders to begin manufacturing health foods. In 1898 they established a small factory near Melbourne, under the name Sanitas Supply Company, where they produced granola, caramel cereal, and peanut butter. About a year later production moved to Cooranbong, location of the **Avondale** School for Christian Workers, where the firm adopted the name Sanitarium Health Food Company. During its first several years the business developed a considerable debt, but with the arrival in 1904 of G. S. Fisher as manager business improved and two years later the company made its first contribution for **South Pacific** island **missions**. After 1907 the company began opening shops and cafés and in 1928 started selling directly to retail grocery stores. About that same time, it purchased two competing breakfast cereal companies, which further strengthened its market position. By the 1970s the company had 12 factories, eight wholesale distribution agencies, 68 retail stores, and four vegetarian restaurants in Australia and New Zealand. In the 1990s its products included breakfast cereals, peanut butter, vegetarian meat substitutes, and soy milk. Unlike most other denominational health food companies, it marketed its products to nonvegetarians and established itself as a major factor in the Australian and New Zealand food industry. A significant portion of its profits helped support the South Pacific **Division**.

SANITARIUMS AND HOSPITALS. Health care institutions. After **John Harvey Kellogg** became the director of the **Health Reform** Institute in 1876, he soon changed the name to the Medical and Surgical Sanitarium, though it was popularly known as the **Battle Creek Sanitarium**. Using a variant of "sanitorium," Kellogg stated that "sanitarium" would become recognized as meaning a "place where people learn to stay well." This educational function, he believed, distinguished the sanitarium from other medical facilities. Seventh-day Adventists emphasized the sanitarium concept for their in-patient medical facilities until the 1940s, when discussions took place at both the **General Conference** and medical personnel meetings about whether to transform the sanitariums in the **United States** into hospitals emphasizing acute care. Three major elements influenced the transformation: the increasing role of medical insurance in determining health care, the growing specialization of the medical profession, and the rising number of physicians, nurses, and other staff members working within the institutions who were not Seventh-day Adventists. In part, this employment situation resulted from the fact that the institutions were moving away from the practice of hiring their own medical staffs and instead increasingly served private-practice physicians, a policy change that was determined by individual institutions beginning in the 1940s. These changes in the **United States** eventually influenced Adventist health institutions around the world. By 2003 only 13 of the 148 Adventist in-patient medical institutions included "sanitarium" in their names, 10 of them combining the term with "hospital."

The introduction of Medicare in the United States in the 1960s and the increasingly pervasive influence of private health insurance brought about a second major change in the 1970s. To achieve greater economic efficiency, denominational health care institutions began organizing into regional systems that in turn combined into the **Adventist Health System**/United States in 1982. Continuing economic changes in health care, however, forced further reorganization that in 1991 resulted in the reestablishment of regional systems.

SCHARFFENBERG, WILLIAM AUGUST (1896-1973). Seventh-day Adventist **temperance** leader. After graduation from Washington Missionary College (later **Columbia Union College**) in 1918, Scharffenberg went to **China**, where he headed the Shanghai Language School and a branch of the **Home Study** Institute. Returning to the **United States** in 1940, he served as the secretary of the Lay Activities Department of the Central **Union Conference** and then held a similar position at the **General Conference**. In 1946 he became executive secretary of the American Temperance Society and in that position brought high visibility to the temperance cause. In 1948 he established *Listen*, a temperance magazine directed at young people. Two years later, he organized the National Committee for the Prevention of Alcoholism and in 1954 expanded it to an international program. This organization involved both Adventists and others in public temperance education. He helped create the Institute of Scientific Studies for the Prevention of Alcoholism, which held annual educational institutes for members of professions such as teaching, law enforcement, and medicine. Scharffenberg also developed the anti-tobacco film, *One in Twenty Thousand* (1954) and, after becoming the first secretary of the new Temperance Department in 1960, helped introduce the **Five-Day Plan to Stop Smoking** in 1962.

SCHUBERT, WALTER (1896-1980). Seventh-day Adventist **evangelist**. Born in **Germany**, the son of Adventist church administrator George W. Schubert, Walter Schubert began his career as a **ministerial** intern in **Chile** in the 1920s. After becoming president of the Buenos Aires **Conference** in 1935, he developed new techniques of urban evangelism. These methods included beginning an evangelistic series with discussion of family and social issues rather than the traditional Adventist emphasis on prophetic interpretation and avoiding Protestant-style singing and prayers. After gaining the confidence of his audience, he then gradually introduced doctrinal subjects and elements of Protestant worship services. As these techniques brought him considerable success, Schubert became the ministerial secretary for the South American **Division** in 1947 and taught his techniques to other evangelists, particularly through the field schools that he introduced in the early 1950s. In large part due to his influence, Adventist growth in South

America increased rapidly. In 1954 Schubert joined the **General Conference** Ministerial Department.

SECOND ADVENT. Christian doctrine that Jesus will return to earth. In early Adventism the issue of the time of Christ's Second Advent became increasingly important, especially by early 1843. **William Miller** introduced in the 1830s his belief, based on his study of the biblical book of Daniel, that Jesus would physically return to earth about the year 1843. He later refined his understanding of the time of Christ's return, stating that it would occur between March 21, 1843, and March 21, 1844. **Joshua V. Himes**, **Josiah Litch**, Apollos Hale, and Sylvester Bliss set the beginning and ending dates as April 18, based upon their study of the Jewish Karaite calendar. After these dates had passed and Christ did not return, **Samuel S. Snow** brought to prominence his view, based on typological interpretations of the Old and New Testaments, that Jesus would return on the Day of Atonement, which according to his interpretation of the Karaite calendar would occur on October 22, 1844. Again, Christ did not appear as expected.

In the wake of this **Great Disappointment** the former **Millerites** moved in a number of directions, some of them setting new dates for Christ's return. Among those who would become sabbatarians, **James White** for a time adopted the belief that the Second Advent would take place in the fall of 1845. And, in a typological interpretation of the sprinkling of the blood in the ancient sanctuary service, **Joseph Bates** concluded that the event would occur in 1850. But by November 1850 **Ellen G. White** was stating in *Present Truth* that belief in the time of Christ's coming would never again be a test of loyalty to God and discouraged her sabbatarian readers from setting new dates. Although a few individuals continued to set dates for Christ's return, they had little general influence on sabbatarian Adventism, which by the early 1850s largely rejected specific time predictions in favor of an emphasis on the fact that the event would occur "soon," whenever that might be. In addition to abandoning date setting, also by the 1850s the sabbatarian Adventists had moved away from Miller's belief that at the Second Advent Jesus would return to reign during the **millennium** with his saints on earth. The sabbatarians developed an alternative view, asserting that the resurrected and living saints would return with Jesus to heaven where they would spend the millennium participating in the judgment of the wicked angels and humanity. The earth would be desolate during this time, awaiting the descent of the New Jerusalem.

SELF-SUPPORTING WORK. Phrase referring to independent Seventh-day Adventist institutions. Probably the first significant self-financed Seventh-day Adventist enterprise was **Edson White's** *Morning Star* evangelistic effort in the American South in the late 1890s. But the first independent self-supporting Adventist institution developed when, with the encouragement of **Ellen G. White**, **Edward A. Sutherland** and **Percy T. Magan** established the Nashville Agricultural and Normal Institute (later **Madison College**, 1904-1964) in Tennessee. Madison in turn trained its students to establish schools of their own; 39 such schools were located in Tennessee, Alabama, and North Carolina by 1915. In 1914 Lida Scott, daughter of the founder of the Funk and Wagnalls Publishing Company, was a patient at the Madison **Sanitarium** and, impressed by her experience, soon established the Layman Foundation to provide funds for new projects. The institutions financed by this foundation included Little Creek School and Sanitarium (Tennessee), Fletcher Academy and Hospital (North Carolina), and Pine Forest Academy and Sanitarium-Hospital (Mississippi).

Seventh-day Adventist Church officials were often uncomfortable with institutions that described themselves as Adventist but were outside denominational control. Consequently, the 1945 Fall Council of the **General Conference** (GC) Executive Committee proposed the organization of a church sponsored association of self-supporting institutions. In 1946 the GC created the **Commission on Rural Living** and convinced Sutherland to leave Madison to become its secretary. The following year, Sutherland brought together representatives of several self-supporting institutions who formed the Association of Seventh-day Adventist Self-Supporting Institutions (ASI), whose board included representatives of both the GC and the association's members. In subsequent years the nature of the organization changed considerably, as Adventist-owned businesses and other organizations became members. Consequently, the ASI later changed its name to Association of Privately Owned Seventh-day Adventist Services and Industries and then Adventist-Laymen's Services and Industries, though still known by the initials ASI. Several of the traditional self-supporting institutions remained in existence by the turn of the 21st century and new organizations, such as **Maranatha Volunteers International** and **Adventist Frontier Missions**, discovered alternative ways of applying the self-supporting philosophy.

SENEGAL. Robert Erdman introduced Seventh-day Adventism into Senegal in 1953. Working in Dakar, Erdman **baptized** his initial convert from Islam that first year and opened an elementary school in 1959. In 1962 the denomination began broadcasting programs over the radio and in 1972 transformed the mission school into a training school for church workers. As of 2003 Senegal was part of the Senegal/Mauritania **Mission**, which belonged to the Sahel **Union** Mission of the Western Africa **Division**. The mission had three churches with a membership of 344, but there were no statistics specific to Senegal. A radio-television production center was located in Senegal.

SERBIA. *See* YUGOSLAVIA.

SEVENTH-DAY ADVENTIST KINSHIP INTERNATIONAL. Independent organization for support of Adventist and former Adventist gays, lesbians, bisexuals, and transgendered individuals. After contacts between both Adventist and former Adventist gays had been established through magazine advertisements in the early 1970s, several individuals met in Palm Desert, California, in January 1977, where they established a rudimentary organization. At first centered in southern California, Kinship soon had a chapter in Chicago, Illinois, and was joined by a New York group that had been meeting since 1974. In 1980 it sponsored its first annual meeting, attended by 35 members. Three professors from the **Seventh-day Adventist Theological Seminary** and two pastors also attended the meeting as unofficial delegates from the **General Conference** (GC). In 1981 the organization incorporated as Seventh-day Adventist Kinship International, Inc. Six years later the GC sued Kinship over use of the name Seventh-day Adventist, but a federal judge ruled in 1991 that Kinship was not infringing on the denomination's title. In 1990 Kinship participated in the first Adventist-sponsored HIV/AIDS conference and has since frequently sent information packets on the disease to local Adventist **churches**. As of 2003 Kinship sponsored Kinship Online and an annual "Kampmeeting"; it also published a newsletter entitled *Connections*. Regional organizations in the **United States** and elsewhere also held a variety of activities.

SEVENTH-DAY ADVENTIST REFORM MOVEMENT. Originating among Seventh-day Adventists in **Germany**, a movement that believed the Adventist church to be "fallen." The outbreak of World War I introduced conscription in Germany and placed great pressure upon the church to cooperate with the government. In consequence, several Seventh-day Adventist leaders in the country informed German military authorities that Adventists would both bear arms and engage in essential military services on the **Sabbath**. A number of Adventists in Germany and other countries under German church leadership disagreed with what they regarded as compromise and gradually linked together to protest the policy. In response, the German church disfellowshipped about two percent of its membership. Some historians have also linked Johann Wieck, a visionary, with the German dissenters, but the movement has consistently denied the connection. By the time **Arthur G. Daniells**, president of the **General Conference**, met with leaders of the dissenting movement in 1920, the latter had developed a negative attitude toward the church leadership because it had not publicly disavowed the German church's actions, and Daniells regarded the movement as separatist. Consequently, the talks failed to bring about reconciliation. Further talks in 1922 accomplished little. In 1925 the Seventh-day Adventist Reform movement organized at Gotha, Germany, establishing a denominational structure similar to that of the Seventh-day Adventist Church. In 1929 it registered with the German government but in 1936, after Adolf Hitler's government dissolved their organization, the church reestablished its headquarters in **Switzerland**. After World War II ended, the church in 1949 moved its headquarters to the **United States**.

The Seventh-day Adventist Reform Movement holds a theology very similar to that of Seventh-day Adventism, but regards its parent church as "backslidden" or "fallen." *The Reformation Herald* is the church's official journal. Active in many parts of the world, the church has established **publishing** houses, missionary schools, and Bible courses, among other things. In 1952, the International Missionary Society split off from the Reform Church, largely because it took a somewhat more liberal position on divorce and remarriage. As of 2003 the Seventh-day Adventist Reform Movement had about 28,000 members, most of them in the United States, **Australia**, and **Brazil**. Its headquarters were located in Roanoke, Virginia. The General Conference of the International Missionary Society, which was strongest in **Europe**, was located in Mosbach/Baden, Germany, with a membership of about 15,000.

SEVENTH-DAY ADVENTIST THEOLOGICAL SEMINARY. Part of **Andrews University**, Seventh-day Adventist institution for the training of **ministers** and religion teachers. Since at least the

1880s Adventist leaders had expressed concern about the quality of the denomination's ministers and had sought to address the issue through ministerial institutes, reading programs, and the establishment of the **Ministerial Association**. In the late 1920s they began talking about creating a postgraduate theological school, but nothing was done until the 1932 Fall Council of the **General Conference** (GC) Executive Committee, which voted to establish such a program at one of the Adventist colleges in North America. The following year, the council approved a different proposal, this one stipulating the initiation of a 12-week program for Bible teachers in **academies** and colleges in the summer of 1934 at **Pacific Union College** (PUC). This Advanced Bible School, which drew faculty from several colleges, took place at PUC from 1934 to 1936.

The GC Executive Committee in 1936 decided to establish a theological seminary that would be independent of any of the colleges and located close to the denomination's headquarters in Takoma Park, Maryland. When the school opened in temporary quarters in the summer of 1937 it offered majors in Bible and Christian Church history and minors in Greek and Hebrew.

At first operating for only two three-month sessions (summer and winter quarters) annually and awarding no degrees, the new institution gradually expanded its offerings. Moving into a new building in 1941, the seminary received authorization the following year to award the M.A. in religion. At the same time, it introduced a spring quarter. In 1943 the school added a division of Missions and Christian Leadership, which continued until 1947, and in 1945 added a fall quarter, thereby becoming a year-round program. By that point, the seminary was offering 95 courses and had departments of Archaeology and History of Antiquity, Bible and Systematic Theology, Biblical Languages, Church History, and Practical Theology. In the 1950s the seminary, which was essentially operating a graduate rather than professional program, began placing more emphasis on training in pastoral practice by introducing classes in pastoral counseling and biblical preaching. Meanwhile, in an attempt to have all Adventist ministers receive seminary training, the Fall Council of the GC Executive Committee in 1953 voted to require that all ministerial students attend the theological seminary for one year immediately after graduation from college. Although numerous changes were made to this plan in subsequent years, the denomination continued to encourage its ministers in North America to complete seminary training.

In 1956 the GC Executive Committee decided to establish a university that would include the theological seminary and a school of graduate studies combined with Washington Missionary College (later **Columbia Union College**) as its undergraduate division, the whole to be called Potomac University. Although the two postgraduate entities were formed into the new university in 1957, the merger with the college encountered difficulties, particularly because no adequate site could be found for the new institution. In 1958 the GC Executive Committee voted to abandon its original plan and instead merge the seminary and graduate school with **Emmanuel Missionary College** in Michigan. During the 1959-60 academic year, the seminary taught classes in both Maryland and Michigan but completed its move by the following year, at which time the new institution—including the seminary, graduate school, and undergraduate college—acquired the name **Andrews University**. After becoming integrated into the university, the seminary in 1963 initiated *Andrews University Seminary Studies* and in 1968 began organizing **archaeological** digs in **Jordan**, both projects led by **Siegfried Horn**.

Receiving accreditation from the American Association of Theological Schools (AATS) in 1970, the seminary began offering new degrees. Responding to a revision adopted by AATS for all seminaries, it changed the B.D. to an M.Div. in 1971. The seminary then introduced programs for the D.Min. in 1973 and D.Th. in 1974. That same year it developed a joint M.Div./M.S. in Public Health curriculum with **Loma Linda University** and in the 1980s established various institutes and centers for Archaeology, Church Ministry, Continuing Education for Ministry, Youth Resources, and Hispanic Ministry. In 1984 it created the Adventist Center in Jerusalem, **Israel**, which provided the opportunity for students to pursue on-location study.

As the Seventh-day Adventist Church grew rapidly, particularly in **Latin America**, **Africa**, and **Asia**, it became clear that the denomination needed to provide seminary education outside of North America. In the 1950s the seminary introduced extension schools to provide postgraduate training for ministers; by 1995 it was offering masters degrees in religion and pastoral ministry on 11 campuses. Increasingly, however, the North American seminary was providing a supporting role as other areas of the world developed their own programs for the professional training of ministers.

SEVENTH-MONTH MOVEMENT. **Millerite** movement that formed around the belief that Jesus would return on October 22, 1844. In February 1844 **Samuel S. Snow** published in the *Midnight Cry* his argument that Jesus would return in the fall of 1844, rather than in the spring of that year as **William Miller** believed. Following a suggestion made by Miller in 1843, Snow believed that the Old Testament ceremonial Sabbaths had been types of which Christ's earthly ministry was the antitype. Those Old Testament types that took place in the seventh month of the Jewish year, particularly the Day of Atonement, were yet to fulfilled, he argued. Combining this view with the Millerite expectation that Jesus would return in 1844, Snow concluded that the **Second Advent** would take place on the tenth day of the seventh month, which, according to his interpretation of the Jewish Karaite calendar, was October 22. Snow's February article received little attention, but when he presented his views at the Exeter, New Hampshire, **camp meeting** in August he stirred up great enthusiasm. A few days later, Snow published his views as *The True Midnight Cry* and his interpretation swept through the Millerite ranks.

The Millerite leaders, including Miller, **Joshua V. Himes**, and **Josiah Litch**, reacted cautiously to the Seventh-month movement, over which they seemed to have no control. The pressure built, however, and by late September these individuals began to adopt the October 22 date. **Joseph Marsh's** *Voice of Truth* supported the new interpretation in its September 25 issue, while Nathaniel Southard adopted it in the next day's edition of the *Midnight Cry*. Sylvester Bliss wrote a letter on September 30 indicating his acceptance, while Himes publicly expressed his belief at a meeting at the Boston Tabernacle on October 6. On that same day, Miller wrote to Himes saying that he had accepted the date. Litch, who announced his acceptance on October 12, may have been the last of the major Millerite leaders to accede to Snow's views. When Christ did not return on October 22, most Millerites abandoned giving any prophetic significance to the date. The major exception was the small sabbatarian Adventist movement, which argued that the Millerites had been mistaken only about the nature of the event, not the time. Rather than returning to earth, they said, Christ on October 22 had moved from the Holy to the Most Holy Place of the heavenly **sanctuary** as described in Hebrews 8 and 9. Subsequently, they developed their distinctive related doctrines of the sanctuary and the **investigative judgment**.

SEYCHELLES. Daniel Ignace, a Seventh-day Adventist **evangelist** from Mauritius, arrived in the Seychelles in 1930 and the following year a **church** with 23 members organized. In 1936 Karl Sturzenegger, a missionary from **Switzerland**, started a school that continued in operation until taken over by the government in 1979.

Meanwhile, the denomination organized the Seychelles **Mission** in 1947. As of 2003 the Seychelles Mission, part of the Indian Ocean **Union Mission** of the Southern **Africa**-Indian Ocean **Division**, had four churches with a membership of 700.

SHEPHERDESS INTERNATIONAL (SI). Seventh-day Adventist organization for the support of ministers' wives. Following up interest that had developed during meetings of ministers' wives at recent **General Conference sessions**, in 1984 the **General Conference** Executive Committee Annual Council authorized Shepherdess International as a pilot program under the direction of Marie Spangler and Ellen Bresee; in 1987 it became an official organization of the Ministerial Department. Among its activities, SI provides guidance for the organization of regional chapters, publishes *Shepherdess International Journal*, and prepares and distributes a variety of resource materials.

SHULER, JOHN LEWIS (1887-1984). Seventh-day Adventist **evangelist**. Shuler served as a **conference** president in the 1920s but emerged in the following decade as an influential evangelist, conducting several successful campaigns in the American South. Among his techniques, he developed effective advertising, created Bible marking classes, and introduced a progressive series of opportunities for decisions by those in his audience rather than waiting for a single big decision at the end of his campaign. In 1937 he began communicating these techniques to young pastors and evangelists in a field school, held in conjunction with an evangelistic series in Greensboro, North Carolina, followed by similar schools in other locations. Two years later he joined the **Seventh-day Adventist Theological Seminary** where he introduced a course on evangelistic philosophy and methods. He also published *Public Evangelism* (1939), which became the standard textbook on evangelism in Adventist colleges in the 1940s. Shuler remained active as an evangelist, conducting major urban campaigns through the 1940s, culminating with a series of field schools in **Great Britain, Fiji, New Zealand**, and **Australia** in 1950.

SHUT DOOR THEORY. Belief that probation had closed for Christians and the judgment had begun on October 22, 1844. After Jesus failed to physically return on October 22, 1844, many **Millerites** sought to explain what had happened. Influenced by some earlier comments by Miller and believing that Christ had come in a spiritual sense on October 22, Apollos Hale of the *Advent Herald* and

Joseph Turner of *The Hope of Israel* proposed in January 1845 that the eternal fate of each individual Christian had been settled on that day and that God's judgment had begun. Therefore, drawing on imagery in the parable of the ten virgins in Matthew 25, they argued that the door of salvation was now shut. Himes and other Millerite leaders opposed this "shut door" explanation, although it took Himes some time to wean Miller away from it, and strongly condemned it at the Mutual Conference of Adventists in 1845. Meanwhile, **Samuel S. Snow** and others who had led the **Seventh-month movement** adopted the shut door theory and called those who rejected their views "apostate Adventists." **Joseph Bates** and **James White**, among other leaders of the developing sabbatarian Adventist movement, both accepted the shut door theory, and **Ellen G. White** experienced a vision in December 1844 that appeared to support this understanding. In 1849, however, she had another vision that portrayed Jesus shutting the door to the Holy Place of the heavenly **sanctuary** and opening the door to the Most Holy Place, where light shone on the Ten Commandments. Soon some sabbatarian Adventists were speaking of both a shut door, referring to those who had rejected the gospel message, and an open door that was available to certain individuals despite the fact that they had not believed Christ was coming in 1844. As the sabbatarian Adventist movement increasingly attracted individuals who had no previous connection with the Millerite movement, James White and Joseph Bates concluded that their shut door views were wrong and by 1854 had largely abandoned shut door/open door language. Hale's and Turner's belief that the judgment had begun on October 22, 1844, however, appears to have influenced the sabbatarian Adventist doctrine of the **investigative judgment**.

SIERRA LEONE. An African American Seventh-day Adventist dentist and his wife with the last name of Hyatt arrived in Freetown in 1905 and were joined later that year by David C. Babcock, a **minister**. Babcock and his wife soon constructed a church building and established a **sanitarium** and school. When Thomas M. French arrived in 1907 he began a ministerial training school at Waterloo. In 1912 Adventist **evangelists** moved both north and south. R. P. Dauphin, one of the first African converts in Sierra Leone, began working in Matotoka while I. W. Harding went to Gbangbama. Shortly after the Sierra Leone **Mission** organized in 1913, it became an important source for denominational workers in West **Africa**. Dauphin, for example, helped introduce Adventism into Ni-

geria in 1914. After World War II disrupted Adventist efforts in the country—the military took over the training school, among other things—the church moved its mission headquarters from Waterloo to Bo, where it established a secondary school in 1961. In 1965 it organized another secondary school at Magburaka and began operating the Masanga Leprosy Hospital under contract with the government. In the early 1970s *Voice of Prophecy* and *Faith for Today* began broadcasts over radio and television. As of 2003 the Sierra Leone Mission, part of the West African **Union Mission** of the West Africa **Division**, had 52 **churches** with a membership of over 13,000. Peninsula Secondary School, Yele Seventh-day Adventist Secondary School, and Masanga Leprosy Hospital were located in Sierra Leone.

SIGNS OF THE TIMES. Seventh-day Adventist **evangelistic** magazine. **James White** began publishing the *Signs of the Times* weekly in Oakland, California, in June 1874 and within a year had established the Pacific Seventh-day Adventist Publishing Association (later **Pacific Press**). Planned to be a West Coast version of the *Review and Herald*, the weekly magazine addressed Adventist readers. As national mail service improved, however, making it possible for all Adventists to receive the *Review and Herald* in a timely fashion, the *Signs of the Times* developed into an evangelistic magazine for the territory west of the Mississippi River, subscriptions to which were sponsored by **church** members. Beginning in 1909 the *Signs* published a monthly as well as the weekly version but reverted to a weekly edition in 1922. In 1957 it introduced color and began producing the magazine only as a monthly publication. Although circulation reached as high as 340,000 in 1947, falling subscriptions by the 1970s led to several changes, most significantly the dropping of an agreed-on territorial division with *These Times*—the evangelistic magazine that was distributed east of the Mississippi—which in 1984 led to a merger of the two magazines. Although denominational publications elsewhere in the world frequently used the title *Signs of the Times*, their publications had no editorial connection with the North American magazine.

SINGAPORE, REPUBLIC OF. Although various Seventh-day Adventists, including **Abram La Rue**, had earlier visited Singapore, **Griffeths F. Jones** and Robert Caldwell established a permanent mission station in 1904. Two years later the efforts in Singapore organized as part of the **Malaysian Mission**. Membership growth was slow, reaching about 50 in 1909 and 332 in 1932. During this same time missionaries started a small school in 1905 that developed into the Singapore Training School by 1915, and in 1919 they established the Malaysian **Publishing** House. World War II closed the publishing house; when it reopened after the war it received in 1950 some of the equipment of the Signs of the Times Publishing House in **China**. The training school meanwhile continued to expand its programs, becoming Southeast **Asia** Union College in 1958, and in 1984 it began an affiliation with **Walla Walla College**. The institution closed in 1997, however, when the government appropriated the property through the right of eminent domain. As of 2003 the Singapore Mission, part of the Southeast Asia **Union Mission** of the Southern Asia-Pacific **Division**, had seven **churches** with a membership of about 2,200. San Yu Adventist School was located in Singapore. *See also* MALAYSIA.

SKÖDSBORG SANITARIUM. Seventh-day Adventist medical institution located near Copenhagen, **Denmark**. Strongly influenced by **John Harvey Kellogg's Battle Creek Sanitarium**, Carl Ottosen, M.D., a graduate of the University of Copenhagen, established Sködsborg **Sanitarium** in 1898 where he combined hydrotherapy with massage, exercise, and diet. Beginning with 20 beds, by 1921 it had more than 375 beds and had become the largest medical institution in the denomination. It also inspired the development of at least 10 additional sanitariums and hospitals in northern **Europe** and through its Physiotherapy School trained some 2,000 physiotherapists, who served as missionaries, established private clinics, and worked in public hospitals. From its beginning, the sanitarium also operated a School of Nursing. The denomination sold the sanitarium in 1992, but the Physiotherapy School continued operating as a separate **self-supporting** Adventist institution at the facility.

SLOVAK REPUBLIC. Seventh-day Adventism entered Slovakia in 1904 when several Slovaks, who had converted to Adventism in the **United States**, returned to their native country. In 1919 the denomination organized the Slovakian **Mission**; in 1968 the mission became the Slovakian **Conference**. As of 2003 the Slovakian Conference, part of the Czecho-Slovakian **Union Conference** of the Euro-**Africa Division**, had 42 churches with a membership of about 2,200. The Slovakian **Publishing** House was located in the Slovak Republic. *See also* CZECH REPUBLIC.

SLOVENIA. As of 2003 the Slovenian **Conference**, part of the Adriatic **Union Conference** of the Trans-**European Division**, had 13 churches with a membership of about 500. *See also* CROATIA.

SMITH, ANNIE REBEKAH (1828-1855). Seventh-day Adventist poet and sister of **Uriah Smith**. Converted as a Baptist at age 10, Smith adopted **Millerite** beliefs in 1844. During the next six years she alternated between teaching in various schools and attending Charlestown Female Seminary in Massachusetts. Interested in **literature** and **art**, she published several poems in *The Ladies' Wreath*, a New York literary magazine, between 1850 and 1852. At her mother's urging, Smith attended a meeting conducted by **Joseph Bates** in 1851 and a month later sent a poem to the *Review and Herald*. **James White** published her poem and invited her to move to New York State and help with the paper, which she did until 1854. During that time she contributed 45 poems to the *Review and Herald* and the *Youth's Instructor*. Ill with tuberculosis, she returned to Massachusetts, where she died at age 27. *Home Here and Home in Heaven* (1855) collected her poems and others by her brother Uriah. Several of Smith's poems were set to music; three appeared in the *Seventh-day Adventist Hymnal* (1981).

SMITH, URIAH (1832-1903). Seventh-day Adventist editor, author, and inventor. Although he had accepted **Millerite** beliefs while a young boy, Smith had relatively little interest in religion when he attended Phillips Exeter Academy from 1848 to 1851. Perhaps persuaded by his sister, **Annie Smith**, he participated in a sabbatarian Adventist conference in 1852 and, after several weeks of study, was **baptized** into the movement. Shortly thereafter he contributed a long poem, "The Warning Voice of Time and Prophecy," to the *Review and Herald* and in May 1853 joined the paper's staff. In 1855 Smith became editor of the *Review and Herald*, a position he was to hold for most of his life, though sometimes he alternated as associate editor. In 1869 he left the paper for a year for health reasons and in 1873, because of a disagreement with **James White**, he departed Battle Creek to work as an engraver, but returned after a few months.

Smith played a significant role in systematizing Seventh-day Adventist doctrinal understanding, particularly with his 1872 summary of Adventist **fundamental beliefs**. Nonetheless, he took theological positions that were sometimes controversial. Smith regarded the doctrine of the **Trinity** as unscriptural (a view held by

most 19th-century Seventh-day Adventists but later largely abandoned), occasionally questioned the authority of **Ellen G. White**,
and for several years opposed the teaching of **righteousness by
faith** promoted by **Ellet J. Waggoner** and **Alonzo T. Jones**. But
he had long-lasting influence on the denomination's understanding
of prophecy with his books *Thoughts, Critical and Practical, on
the Book of Revelation* (1867) and *Thoughts, Critical and Practical, on the Book of Daniel* (1873). Through the urging of **George
King**, the **Review and Herald Publishing Association** combined
these books into a single illustrated volume in 1882 that became a
highly successful subscription book. Among Smith's other books
were *The Bible Student's Assistant* (1858), *The Biblical Institute*
(1877), *The United States in Prophecy* 1876), *Modern Spiritualism*
(1896), *Looking Unto Jesus* (1898), and *Here and Hereafter*
(1897).

In addition to his writing, Smith spoke at **camp meetings** and
other gatherings and was active in denominational **organization**.
In 1861 he became treasurer of the Seventh-day Adventist Publishing Association, the first legally chartered Adventist organization,
and in 1863 assumed the presidency of the Michigan **Conference**.
Later that same year he was elected secretary of the **General Conference** (GC), a position he was to hold many times in subsequent
years, and in 1876-77 he served as GC treasurer. When the Seventh-day Adventist Educational Society formed in 1875 he became
secretary and seven years later assumed the position of chairman of
the board of **Battle Creek College** and served as a lecturer on religion at the school. Perhaps reflecting this organizational experience, he published *Key to Smith's Diagram and Parliamentary
Rules* (1881).

Smith, who had lost a leg due to infection at about the age of
13, patented in 1863 an improved artificial limb, which sold widely
in the wake of the American Civil War. He also invented a school
desk with a folding seat in 1874 that was manufactured by the Union School Furniture Company and used extensively throughout
the United States.

SNOW, SAMUEL SHEFFIELD (1806-1870). **Millerite** preacher and
initiator of the **Seventh-month movement**. After having been a
skeptic for some time, Snow converted to Christianity as a result of
reading **William Miller's** lectures in 1839. At the East Kingston,
New Hampshire, **camp meeting** of 1842 Snow committed himself
to full-time service as a preacher of Miller's message and the following year received **ordination** to the ministry from the Mil-

lerites. In February 1844 he published an article in the *Midnight Cry* arguing that the Old Testament festivals were types to which Christ's ministry was the antitype. Because the seventh-month festivals, particularly the Day of Atonement (which he believed represented the **Second Advent** of Jesus), had not yet been fulfilled, he calculated on the basis of the Jewish Karaite calendar that Jesus would return on October 22, 1844. Snow preached this interpretation in several places, including New York, Philadelphia, and Boston, in the spring and early summer of 1844 but his message attracted little attention until he presented it at the Exeter, New Hampshire, camp meeting in August. Several individuals reported that it swept through the meeting like a wild fire. A few days later Snow began publishing the *True Midnight Cry*, which spread his views among the Millerite rank and file during the next several weeks, although leaders such as **Joshua V. Himes** and Miller resisted it until late September and early October.

After Jesus did not physically return in October as expected, Snow accepted in early 1845 Joseph Turner's **shut door theory**, which argued that the judgment had begun on October 22; the door of probation had shut and Jesus would return when the judgment was completed. Snow soon identified himself as the prophet Elijah preparing the way for Christ's coming and began publishing the *Jubilee Standard* while some of his followers put out *The True Day Star*. In 1848 he issued *A Proclamation to All People, Nations, Tongues, and Kings* in which he claimed to be Jesus' prime minister and called on all political authorities to surrender power to him. Snow may have continued serving as pastor of his Church of Mount Zion in New York City until his death, although some sources state that he became insane.

SOLOMON ISLANDS. Griffeths F. Jones began Seventh-day Adventist **mission** efforts in the Solomon Islands in 1914 when he established a mission station, including a school, on New Georgia. As other missionaries arrived, mission work spread to other islands, including Gatukai (1915), Telina (1917), Rendova (1917), and Vella Lavella (1918). Indigenous islanders took Adventism to Rononogo (1920) and Choiseul (1921). In 1922 the Signs Publishing Company of **Australia** donated printing equipment to help establish a press at Batuna, on the island of Vagunu; it soon **published** the Gospel of John and a collection of **hymns** in the Marovo language. About 1924 the Batuna Training School opened nearby. During the 1920s and 1930s, Adventist missions expanded to Guadalcanal (1926), Kolombangara (1937), and San Cristobal (1940).

Also, Solomon Islanders went as missionaries to Bougainville (1924) and New Britain (1929). Although the Japanese invasions of 1942 forced out all foreign missionaries, **Kata Rangoso** took over the leadership until their return after World War II. In 1950 Adventist missionaries began working on Buka and in 1966 established a hospital on Malaita. Adventist mission work on the islands went through several organizational changes until in 1972 it became the responsibility of the Western Pacific **Union Mission**. As of 2003 the Solomon Islands, organized as the Eastern and Western Solomon Islands Missions, part of the Western Pacific Union Mission of the **South Pacific Division**, had 134 **churches** with about 24,000 members. Four secondary schools, Atoifi Adventist Hospital, and 14 clinics were located on the islands.

SOLUSI MISSION. First permanent Seventh-day Adventist **mission** for Black Africans. In 1894 Cecil Rhodes's **South Africa** Company granted 12,000 acres of land, located in present-day **Zimbabwe**, to the Seventh-day Adventist Church. In July of that year a group of American and South African missionaries arrived in Bulawayo from South Africa and built a rudimentary mission station, leaving Fred Sparrow to develop it further. About a year later **William H. Anderson** and other missionaries arrived and began constructing buildings and planting crops. During this time the station was known as the Matabele Mission; within a few years it changed its name to Solusi, after a local chief who had aided the missionaries. Although the Matabele rebellion of 1896 and a severe famine disrupted their work, the missionaries developed a school, starting with 30 Matabele famine survivors, and in 1902 organized a **church**. Farming became a significant element of the mission and by 1912 it was able to support itself from agricultural income. Meanwhile, in 1910 it returned about 4,000 acres to the government in exchange for land near Umtali (now Mutare), where the missionaries established Inyazura (now Nyazura) Mission Station. By 1933 the school was offering a teacher-training program and acquired the name Solusi Training School. It began offering a secondary program in 1948 and six years later became known as Solusi Missionary College. In 1958 it introduced a four-year theological curriculum and in 1969 a two-year business course. Beginning in 1981 the secondary program, known as Solusi Adventist Secondary School, came under the direction of a separate administration. In 1992 it moved to its own campus, though located on college property, at which time it took the name Solusi Adventist Vocational Secondary School. The college developed in 1984 an affiliation program with **Andrews University**, which oversaw its curriculum and faculty and granted degrees. The school is now known as Solusi University.

SOUTH AFRICA. William Hunt, a diamond prospector who had become a Seventh-day Adventist in California, arrived at the Kimberly diamond fields in South Africa in the mid-1870s and by 1878 had converted several Europeans to Adventist doctrines. In 1885 **Pieter Wessels**, who lived near Kimberly but apparently had had no contact with Hunt, began observing the **Sabbath** as a result of his study of the Bible. Some time later G. J. Van Druten of Beaconsfield, one of Hunt's converts, introduced Wessels to the diamond miner who in turn told Wessels about the Seventh-day Ad ventist Church. In 1886 Van Druten and Wessels wrote to the **General Conference** requesting that a missionary be sent to South Africa. Dores A. Robinson, Charles L. Boyd, and other missionaries arrived at Cape Town in 1887. Leaving the others behind, Boyd traveled on to Kimberly where he conducted **baptisms** and organized a **church** with 21 members. When **Asa T. Robinson** arrived in 1892 he organized five churches with 138 members into the South African **Conference**. After the discovery of diamonds on his farm in 1891, Johannes Wessels, Pieter's father, sold the property to the de Beers Mining Company and gave a large amount of money to the denomination. Following the Battle Creek model, a college, **publishing** house, orphanage, and **sanitarium** soon opened. Because of financial difficulties resulting from the Anglo-Boer War (1899-1902) and conflicts that developed between some of the American missionaries and members of the Wessels family, church income from the Wessels decreased. The small membership in South Africa could not sustain so many institutions, with the result that the orphanage and sanitarium closed in the early 20th century.

Although most of the early Adventist efforts in South Africa occurred among the European population, in the 1890s both Coloured and African individuals converted to the new religion. The South African **Union Conference**, organized in 1902, oversaw all Adventist organizations in the country, but the conferences and **missions** that developed under its umbrella formed along ethnic lines, with Europeans and Coloureds in one set of organizations and Africans in another. The coming of apartheid in 1948 made the situation more difficult and in 1966 the **Union Conference** divided. Subsequently, the South African Union Conference served as the White and Coloured organization and the newly formed

Southern Union functioned as the Black African entity. With the exception of **Lesotho** and **Swaziland**, which belonged to the Southern Union Conference, both union conference organizations covered the same geographical area. As international pressure mounted for South Africa to end apartheid, the Adventists increasingly recognized that their own version of apartheid was unjustifiable. The **General Conference** appointed study commissions to examine the problem in 1981 and again in 1990; the latter commission recommended that the union conferences merge by December 1991 and that the conferences unify by December 1993. After considerable debate, a newly organized Southern Africa Union Conference took form by the recommended deadline, but some of the conferences were still working on unification in the early 21st century. As of 2003 the five conferences in South Africa, part of the Southern **Africa** Union Conference of the Southern Africa-Indian Ocean **Division**, had 642 churches with over 66,000 members. Helderberg College, Bethel College, six secondary schools, Adventist Professional Health Services, and Southern Publishing Association were located in South Africa.

SOUTHERN ADVENTIST UNIVERSITY (SAU). Seventh-day Adventist **educational** institution located in Collegedale, Tennessee. At the invitation of pastor **Robert M. Kilgore**, George W. Colcord and his wife Asenath opened Graysville **Academy** in 1892. After four years of **self-supporting** operation, in 1896 it became a **General Conference** (GC) institution. The following year the academy became Southern Industrial School and in 1901 took the name Southern Training School. In 1903 Graysville **Sanitarium** opened; it was closely associated with the school and offered work opportunities for students. After fire destroyed the girl's dormitory in 1915, the board, which for some time had been discussing relocation of the school, found property near Chattanooga and in 1916 opened Southern Junior College. About this same time ownership of the institution transferred from the GC to the Southern **Union Conference**. Beginning with 57 students, the junior college reached an enrollment of more than 100 by 1934-35 and in 1936 received accreditation. In 1944 it received permission from the General Conference to become a senior college and adopted the name Southern Missionary College, receiving accreditation from the Southern Association of Colleges and Schools in 1950. As the institution continued to develop it again changed its name in 1982, when it became known as Southern College of Seventh-day Adventists. In 1996 it began offering graduate classes and adopted the name Southern Adventist University (SAU). As of 2003 SAU had over 2,200 undergraduate students, the most of any Adventist college or university in North America. In addition to its 50 baccalaureate degrees, it also offered graduate degrees in business, education, psychology, nursing, computing, and religion.

SOUTHERN PUBLISHING ASSOCIATION (SPA). Former Seventh-day Adventist **publishing** house located in Nashville, Tennessee. **Edson White** had established the Gospel Herald Publishing Company in Nashville in late 1900 or early 1901 as a **self-supporting** venture but within a short time it combined with the Atlanta branch of the **Review and Herald Publishing Association** and incorporated as Southern Publishing Association (SPA) in June 1901. After a period of financial difficulties, the publishing house became more prosperous and began building a new plant in 1905. That same year it opened its first branch office in Fort Worth, Texas (1905-32), followed by others in Hickory, North Carolina (1906-08), New Orleans, Louisiana (1907-11), and Atlanta, Georgia (1909-32). In its early years the SPA published several works in simple language for the often poorly educated people of the American South. These books included *The New Testament Primer*, *Best Stories from the Best Book*, and *Christ Our Saviour*, the latter an adaptation for children of **Ellen G. White's** *Desire of Ages*. During its existence, the SPA also published several magazines, among them *The Southern Watchman* (later *These Times*), *Message*, and *Adventist Home*. Although it moved into a new plant in 1973, during the 1970s SPA met increasing financial difficulties and in 1980 merged with the Review and Herald Publishing Association.

SOUTH LANCASTER ACADEMY. First Seventh-day Adventist **academy.** Opened in South Lancaster, Massachusetts, without a name in 1882, the "New England School" incorporated in 1883 as South Lancaster Academy. **Stephen N. Haskell,** who was serving as president of the New England **Conference,** helped establish the school and **Goodloe H. Bell** became its first principal. More a training school for denominational workers than a well-defined secondary institution, the academy introduced teacher training in 1886. As its functions became clearer, in 1918 the school took the name Lancaster Junior College and four years later became **Atlantic Union College.** Meanwhile, the secondary program became a separate entity under the name South Lancaster Academy. Although the academy gradually developed a separate staff and administration, it did not completely separate from the college until it moved to its own campus in 1968.

SOUTH PACIFIC. *See* AUSTRALIA; FIJI; FRENCH POLYNESIA; GUAM AND MICRONESIA; HAWAII; NEW CALEDONIA AND LOYALTY ISLANDS; NEW ZEALAND; PAPUA NEW GUINEA; SAMOA AND TOKELAU ISLANDS; SOLOMON ISLANDS; TUVALU; VANUATU.

SOUTHWESTERN ADVENTIST UNIVERSITY (SWAU). Seventh-day Adventist **educational** institution located in Keene, Texas. In 1894, through the effort of W. S. Greer, president of the Texas **Conference**, the Texas School opened near Dallas. Renamed Keene Industrial **Academy** in 1897, it became Southwestern Junior College in 1916. In 1963 it became a senior college, adopting the name Southwestern Union College, which it changed to Southwestern Adventist College in 1977. In 1995 the institution's enrollment passed 1,000 and the following year it adopted the name Southwestern Adventist University. As of 2003 it offered baccalaureate degrees in 28 fields and a master's degree in elementary education.

SPAIN. Two Seventh-day Adventist brothers, Frank and Walter Bond, left California in 1903 as missionaries to Spain, soon settling in Sabadell. The following year they **baptized** three individuals, a number that reached 27 by 1907. In 1915 the Barcelona **Publishing** House organized and published *The Signs of the Times* until the Spanish Civil War erupted in 1936. After the difficulties of the Civil War and World War II, the denomination established the Safeliz Publishing House in 1952 and a seminary, which became Sagunto Adventist College, in 1967. When the government granted full **religious liberty** in 1978, Adventists increased their **evangelistic** activity and in 1992 signed an Agreement of Cooperation with the State of Spain, which gave the denomination official recognition. As of 2003 the Spanish Union of Churches, part of the Euro-**Africa Division**, had 77 churches with a membership of nearly 9,000. Sagunto Adventist College, one secondary school, Safeliz Publishing House, Spanish Food Factory, and a retirement home were located in Spain.

SPECTRUM. Quarterly journal published by the **Association of Adventist Forums** (AAF). Beginning publication in 1969, *Spectrum* addressed a wide variety of subjects, including the relationship of science and religion, **education**, denominational **organization** and finance, theology, and the role of **Ellen G. White** in Adventist thought and practice. Occasionally these articles criticized established Adventist perspectives and as a result raised tensions between denominational leaders and AAF. At first modeled largely on scholarly journals and drawing authors primarily from Adventist colleges and universities, the journal gradually developed a more popular style and published a broader range of authors. In addition to publishing news reports and analytical essays, the journal also addressed the arts, frequently featuring poetry, painting, sculpture, photography, and an occasional short story.

SPICER, WILLIAM AMBROSE (1865-1952). Seventh-day Adventist missionary and church administrator. Spicer worked in **Great Britain**, beginning in 1887, as secretary to **Stephen N. Haskell** and as a member of the editorial staff of *Present Truth.* Returning to the **United States** in 1892, he served as secretary of the Foreign **Mission** Board, which had been established in 1889, until going to **India** in 1898, where he became editor of the *Oriental Watchman.* In 1901 he returned to the United States to again become secretary of the Foreign Mission Board, serving until 1903 when missions became a responsibility of the **General Conference** (GC) Executive Committee, at which time Spicer became secretary of the GC, staying in that position until 1922. During these years Spicer shaped the foreign mission program of the Seventh-day Adventist Church, an influence that continued during his tenure as president of the GC from 1922 to 1930. He then served as a general field secretary of the GC until 1940, traveling widely to advise and encourage the **churches**. Among Spicer's books were *The Hand of God in History* (1913), *Our Day in the Light of Prophecy* (1917), *Miracles of Modern Missions* (1926), *Beacon Lights of Prophecy* (1935), and *Pioneer Days of the Advent Movement* (1941).

SRI LANKA. In 1904 Harry Armstrong and G. K. Owen introduced Seventh-day Adventism into Colombo and about the same time R. W. Yeoman sold denominational **publications** on the island. In 1916 an **Indian evangelist**, T. S. Nayagampillai, **baptized** the first converts, a proctor of the Supreme Court and his wife. H. A. Hansen organized the first Adventist **church** in 1922 and soon baptized the first Sinhalese converts. That same year he organized the Ceylon **Mission** and the following year opened a school that by 1952 had become Lakpahana Training School. In 1953 the Adventist churches on the island formed a **union mission**. A clinic opened in

1964 and about the same time the training school acquired a printing press to provide work for students; by the early 1970s a **publishing** house had formed. As of 2003 the Sri Lanka Mission of Seventh-day Adventists, an Attached **Field** of the Southern **Asia**-Pacific **Division**, had 31 churches and a membership of about 3,600. Lakpahana Adventist College and Seminary, Lakeside Adventist Hospital, and Lakpahana Publishing House of Seventh-day Adventists were located in Sri Lanka.

STAHL, FERDINAND ANTHONY (1874-1950). Seventh-day Adventist missionary to South America. Stahl and his wife Ana converted to Seventh-day Adventism in 1902 and soon thereafter took the nursing course at the **Battle Creek Sanitarium**. Afterwards they operated treatment rooms in Cleveland, Ohio, and a **sanitarium** in Akron. Sent by the **General Conference** in 1909 as missionaries, they began **evangelizing** the Indians in the area around La Paz, **Bolivia**. In 1911 they moved to the **Peruvian** side of Lake Titicaca where they worked among the Aymara and Quechua Indians. Influenced by Manuel Comacho, an experienced social reform advocate and recent convert to Adventism, the Stahls established schools, eventually reaching more than 100 in number, that by teaching the Indians to read and write enabled them to challenge the established political and economic order. Not surprisingly, the Stahls aroused considerable opposition that reached a peak in 1913 when some 200 men, led by Puno Bishop Monsignor Valentin Ampuero, attacked the Adventist believers and forced them to march some 21 miles to jail. Several scholars have concluded that the **educational** work begun by the Stahls reordered the social and political structure of the Peruvian highlands. The schools also provided a model for educating the native peoples that influenced other Peruvian educational programs. Also, in part because of the Stahls' work among the Indians, Peru in 1913 revised its constitution to eliminate reference to an official religion. In 1920 the Stahls moved from Lake Titicaca to the headwaters of the Amazon, where they established Metraro Mission Station and used a steam launch to ply the rivers of the region.

STORRS, GEORGE (1796-1879). Millerite preacher and advocate of **conditionalism**. Raised a Congregationalist, Storrs became a Methodist minister in 1825. Increasingly involved in the antislavery cause, with LeRoy Sunderland he began publishing *Zion's Watchman* in 1836 in an effort to bring the Methodist Church into the antislavery movement. Increasing conflict with his denomination over the issue of slavery led to his withdrawal from Methodism in 1840 and rejection of any kind of church organization. In 1841, influenced by a book written by Henry Grew, Storrs published *An Enquiry: Are the Souls of the Wicked Immortal? In Three Letters*, expanded in a second edition the following year. Strongly shaped by eschatological concerns, this work argued that only the saved would receive immortality and that the wicked would ultimately experience complete destruction rather than burn eternally in Hell.

Through the influence of **Charles Fitch,** Storrs accepted in 1842 **William Miller's** teaching that Jesus would return about the year 1843. He worked in the fall of 1843 with **Joshua V. Himes** in Cincinnati and stayed in that city to edit the *Western Midnight Cry.* In 1844 he moved to Albany, New York, where he established the *Bible Examiner*, which combined his conditionalism with Millerite prophetic interpretation. Storrs convinced Fitch to accept conditionalism in 1844 but came into conflict with Himes and **Josiah Litch** over his continued advocacy of the doctrine. When **Samuel S. Snow** began advocating his **seventh-month** interpretation in 1844, Storrs became a strong voice in behalf of the belief that Jesus would return on October 22, going so far as to tell people to close their businesses as they awaited their Savior. After Jesus did not return as expected, Storrs began taking the position that the Bible did not teach anything regarding the time of the **Second Advent** and in 1845 said that the seventh-month movement had been a delusion. In the early 1850s he adopted the age-to-come beliefs of **Joseph Marsh** but eventually sided with those who rejected these views, many of whom formed the **Advent Christian Church.** Soon, however, he accepted the view of John T. Walsh, an Advent Christian preacher, that the wicked dead would never be resurrected. In 1863 the Life and Advent Union coalesced around this view and elected Storrs as their president. He then edited a paper, *Herald of Life and of the Coming Kingdom*, to promote belief in the nonresurrection of the wicked but, according to early Adventist historian Isaac C. Wellcome, later abandoned this view.

STUDENT MISSIONARY. *See* ADVENTIST YOUTH SERVICE.

SUDAN. Although some Seventh-day Adventist missionaries worked briefly in Sudan prior to World War II, Farris Basta Bishai, who moved from **Egypt** to Khartoum, established the first permanent

Adventist presence in 1953. By 1961 three individuals had been converted but the church lost contact with them as a result of civil turmoil. In 1974 the denomination reestablished its organization in the North and in 1979 began working in the South, but it continued to experience tensions between the peoples of the two regions. As of 2003 the Seventh-day Adventist Church in Northern Sudan was organized as the Sudan **Field** and had 14 **churches** with a membership of nearly 5,000 while the South Sudan Field had 16 churches with a membership of over 5,000. These fields were part of the Middle East **Union Mission** of the Trans-**European Division**.

SURINAME. A Seventh-day Adventist group developed in Suriname as early as 1894 but seems to have disbanded within a few years. One of its members, however, organized a **Sabbath school** in Paramaribo in 1931. After two **literature evangelists** worked with this group, Arthur A. Carscallen **baptized** 13 individuals in 1932. In 1940 the first **church** organized, followed by formation of the Suriname **Mission** in 1945 and governmental recognition of the denomination in 1953. Beginning in 1956 Adventist missionaries worked among Indian groups in the interior. As of 2003 the Suriname Mission, part of the Carribbean **Union Conference** of the Inter-American **Division**, had 17 churches with over three thousand members.

SUTHERLAND, EDWARD ALEXANDER (1865-1955). Seventh-day Adventist **educator** and promoter of **self-supporting** institutions. After teaching public school in Iowa for three years, Sutherland entered **Battle Creek College** in 1887 and graduated three years later. He then served as principal of an Adventist school in Minnesota before returning to Battle Creek College to serve as dean of men and Bible teacher in 1891; under his influence some 150 students signed a petition requesting that meat be removed from the dining room menu, a foretaste of his reformist tendencies. In 1892 he went to **Walla Walla College**, where as principal he established a vegetarian menu in the dining hall and introduced a flexible academic program so that individuals could prepare for denominational work in as little as a year. Becoming president of Battle Creek College in 1897, he dropped the classical course, introduced short courses similar to those at Walla Walla, and stopped giving degrees, which he regarded as contrary to biblical principles. Unable to fulfill his vision of a work-study program in Battle Creek, Sutherland, with dean **Percy T. Magan**, moved the school

to Berrien Springs, Michigan, in 1901 where it took the name
Emmanuel Missionary College. Here he established his radical
reform program, including the equal division of each weekday between classes and physical labor, the introduction of the "one-
study" plan whereby students took only one course at a time, and
inclusion of students as voting members of the committees that ran
the school.

Financial and enrollment difficulties, however, led Sutherland
and Magan to leave in 1904 for Nashville, Tennessee, where they
established the **self-supporting** Nashville Agricultural and Normal
Institute (later **Madison College**). Here Sutherland was able to
more fully establish his work-study curriculum and other reforms.
After starting a **sanitarium** on the grounds of his institute,
Sutherland attended the medical school at the University of
Tennessee, graduating in 1914. He served as president of Madison
College until 1946 and as medical superintendent of the sanitarium
from 1914 to 1940. In 1946 he returned to denominational
employment to serve as secretary of the **Commission on Rural
Living** and helped organize the Association of Seventh-day
Adventist Self-supporting Institutions in 1947. Sutherland
explained his educational philosophy in *Living Fountains or
Broken Cisterns* (1900) and *Studies in Christian Education* (1952).

SWAZILAND. Joseph N. Hlubi, a Swazi who lived in the Transvaal
and had converted to Seventh-day Adventism in 1918, moved to
Swaziland in 1920 at the urging of Joel C. Rogers, an American
missionary in Nyasaland. Hlubi's wife started a school at Ma-
hamba two years later; by the mid-1960s it had grown into a six-
level institution. In addition to developing at least three other primary schools, Adventists operated a dental clinic at Mbabne from
1977 to 1991 and opened an eye clinic at Manzini in 1984. A
unique element of Adventist mission efforts in Swaziland was the
conversion of several members of the royal family, which resulted
in the organization of a **church** at the Lozitha Royal Residence. As
of 2003 the Swaziland **Conference**, part of the Southern Africa
Union Conference of the Southern **Africa**-Indian Ocean **Division**,
had 11 churches with a membership of over 3,000. One secondary
school and Swaziland Eye Services were located in the country.

SWEDEN. After the Seventh-day Adventist Church in 1874 began
publishing the *Swedish Advent Herald* for Swedish immigrants to
the **United States**, some of these individuals sent copies of the paper to their relatives in Sweden. Soon requests for an Adventist

missionary came from that country. The **General Conference** responded to requests from throughout Scandinavia in 1877 by sending **John G. Matteson** to **Denmark**. By 1880 Matteson had established his headquarters in **Norway**, where among his converts was a Swede by the name of Jonas Pehrson Rosquist. Encouraged by Matteson, Rosquist moved back to Sweden in 1880 and soon developed a group of believers at the village of Grythyttan. Later that year Matteson organized a **church** of 45 members. Two more churches and the Swedish **Conference** organized in 1882. Despite the emigration of several converts to the **United States** and legal restrictions on its activities in Sweden, Adventism continued to develop, reaching about 250 members by 1886, by which time it had introduced a missionary magazine, organized the Scandinavian **Sabbath School** Society, and established a publishing house. In 1892 the conference sent missionaries to **Finland** and in 1902 to **Iceland**. It opened its first church schools in 1895, when membership had reached about 600, and in 1898 established a training school which 10 years later became the Swedish Missionary School. As of 2003 the Swedish **Union Conference**, part of the Trans-**European Division**, had 44 churches and a membership of nearly 3,000. Swedish Junior College, Swedish Nutana Food Company, and the Swedish Union Publishing Service were located in Sweden.

SWITZERLAND. Michael B. Czechowski entered Switzerland as an unofficial Seventh-day Adventist missionary in 1865 and the following year conducted his first **baptisms** in Lake Neuchâtel and started a missionary paper. In 1867 he developed a group of believers in Tramelan who, after Czechowski left, discovered in his room a copy of the *Review and Herald*, which for the first time introduced them to the existence of the Seventh-day Adventist Church. They corresponded with **General Conference** leaders and sent James Erzberger, a former theology student, to Battle Creek, Michigan, in 1869. Erzberger was soon **ordained** and returned to Switzerland the following year. In 1874 **John Nevins Andrews** arrived in Switzerland as the first official Adventist missionary and two years later was joined by **Daniel T. Bourdeau**. These two men in 1886 began publishing a French-language *Signs of the Times* for distribution in both Switzerland and France, where Bourdeau settled later that year. Buel L. Whitney arrived in 1883 and the following year helped organize the Swiss **Conference**, which established its headquarters, including a **publishing** house, in Basel. By 1885 Switzerland had ten Adventist **churches** with a membership of 224. When **Ludvig R. Conradi** came to Switzerland in 1886 he began working in the German-speaking area of the country, establishing a paper and organizing a church in Zurich in 1887. Legal restrictions led to the closing of the publishing house in 1895; its building then provided facilities for a **sanitarium**. Also, between 1896 and 1901 a boarding school operated at Perles but no church schools started up until the 1920s. The denomination in Switzerland went through several organizational changes, ultimately resulting in the formation of the Swiss **Union Conference** in 1929, at which time there were 50 churches with about 2,000 members. As of 2003 this union conference (which also included Liechtenstein), part of the Euro-**Africa Division**, had 54 churches and a membership of about 4,000. One secondary school, Lake Geneva Sanitarium, two retirement homes, and Advent Publishers were located in Switzerland.

SYDNEY ADVENTIST HOSPITAL. Seventh-day Adventist **health care** institution located at Wahroonga, New South Wales, **Australia**. In 1896 Alfred W. Semmens, who had received training at the **Battle Creek Santarium**, opened a hydropathic treatment facility in Ashford, near Sydney. Because of an increasing number of patients, Semmens transferred his work to Summer Hill where, after the arrival of Dr. E. R. Caro as director, it became the Sydney Medical and Surgical **Sanitarium** in 1897. When the leaders developed plans to build a new sanitarium building, they moved the patients to a health retreat at **Avondale** in 1901, where they stayed until the new Sydney Sanitarium and Hospital opened in 1903. The institution continued to expand, adding new wings to the building in 1920 and 1933. In 1927 the sanitarium received government authorization to offer nurse's training; over the years many of its nursing students served the denomination as missionaries in the **South Pacific** and in other capacities. In 1973 the sanitarium moved into new facilities and took the name Sydney Adventist Hospital. Five years later the Australian Council on Healthcare Standards gave it accreditation, the first private hospital in New South Wales to receive such recognition. With 320 beds by 1995, the institution was the largest private hospital in the state. Meanwhile, in 1980 Avondale College took responsibility for the nursing program, although the students continued to gain most of their clinical experience at the hospital. In 1994 the hospital affiliated with the Faculty of Medicine at the University of Sydney to provide clinical experience for medical students. In addition to its on-site activities, the hospital also sent volunteer surgical teams to such places as **China** and many islands of the South Pacific.

T

TAIWAN. *See* CHINA, REPUBLIC OF.

TAJIKISTAN. The first Seventh-day Adventists arrived in Tajikistan when two Molokan brothers, Ivan and Vasily Kosmjinin, entered the country as immigrants in 1929. Several **evangelists** worked in the territory in the 1950s but the political situation made progress difficult. As of 2003 Tajikistan belonged to the Central **Asia Conference** (which also included **Kyrgyz Republic, Turkmenistan, and Uzbekistan**), which was part of the Southern **Union Conference** of the Euro-Asia **Division**. This conference had 42 **churches** with a membership of about 3,500; there were no specific statistics for Tajikistan.

TANZANIA. Negotiations between **Ludvig R. Conradi** and colonial officials opened the way for Johan Ehlers and A. C. Enns, Seventh-day Adventist missionaries from **Germany**, to enter German East **Africa** in 1903 where they established the Friedenstal Station in the northeast area of the colony. As other missionaries arrived, mostly from Germany, the first **baptisms** took place in 1908 and the church grew rapidly with the establishment of new mission stations in the west near Lake Victoria. Among the new missionaries were two **Friedensau** students, Bruno Ohme and Ernst Kotz, whom Conradi had sent for language study at the Oriental Seminar of the University of Berlin. Kotz subsequently reduced the Chasu language to writing and published a grammar and a translation of the book of Matthew. When British military forces entered the colony in 1914 the German missionaries left, although Valdemar E. Toppenberg from **Denmark** and Dr. F. W. Vasenius from **Finland** were able to stay for the duration of the war. Nonetheless, African converts kept four schools in operation. After World War I, with the area under **Great Britain** and renamed Tanganyika, British missionaries arrived in 1921 and reopened several mission stations and established headquarters at Ikizu. In 1953 Heri Adventist Hospital opened, near Lake Tanganyika. Meanwhile, **literature evangelists** began working in Zanzibar, a coastal island, in the 1930s but Adventists did not establish a permanent presence until they opened a dispensary in 1987. With Adventist membership in Tanganyika reaching over 13,000 in 1960, a **Union Mission** organized.

About the same time African preachers began conducting meetings in urban areas and in 1963 **Edward E. Cleveland**, an African American **evangelist**, conducted a campaign in Dar es Salaam. With Adventism growing rapidly, the Voice of Prophecy Press (later renamed Tanzania Adventist Press) began operations in 1969 and the Tanzania Adventist Seminary at Arusha opened in 1975. The seminary began offering junior college classes in 1979. As of 2003 the Tanzania Union Mission, part of the Eastern Africa **Division**, had 1,282 **churches** with nearly 275,000 members. Tanzania Adventist College, two secondary schools, Heri Adventist Hospital, many clinics and dispensaries, and Tanzania Adventist Press were located in the country.

TAY, JOHN I. (1832-1892). Seventh-day Adventist missionary. Converted to Adventism in 1873, Tay fulfilled a long-standing dream when he worked his passage to Pitcairn Island in 1886. After five weeks on the island he had converted most of the adult inhabitants. When Tay reported his experience to the **General Conference**, its leaders decided to send him and A. J. Cudney back to Pitcairn. After Cudney was lost at sea, however, Tay returned to the **United States**. Soon the denomination built its own mission ship, the *Pitcairn*, on which Tay and his wife and other missionaries sailed to Pitcairn in 1890. During the next two years the ship visited Tahiti, Rarotonga, **Samoa**, **Fiji**, and Norfolk Island. Tay stayed on Fiji to establish mission work but died a few months later.

TEMPERANCE. Abstinence from alcohol, tobacco, and nonmedical drugs. **Ellen G. White** experienced a vision in 1848 that showed her the injurious effects of alcohol and tobacco (as well as coffee) and in 1851 she described tobacco as a "filthy weed." Nonetheless, no sustained effort to discourage sabbatarian Adventists from using tobacco developed until about 1853, when antitobacco articles began appearing in the *Review and Herald*, although they tended to emphasize that tobacco was a waste of money rather than bad for one's health. In 1855 sabbatarian Adventists in Vermont made abstinence from tobacco a requirement for **church** fellowship and similarly strong statements increasingly appeared in the *Review and Herald* during the late 1850s. It seems that by the end of that decade a consensus had developed among sabbatarian Adventists that tobacco usage and Christianity were incompatible. The early Adventists also opposed alcohol consumption except for the use of "domestic wine" for medicinal purposes and the **Lord's Supper**. Complete abstinence seems not to have become the denomination's position until the 1870s. The denomination said little about nonmedical drugs until they became a social issue in post–World War II American society. By that point it had developed a well-established position of abstinence toward alcohol and tobacco that extended naturally to drugs.

As they developed a consistent position of abstinence, Adventist leaders sought to promote this view throughout the church. In 1878 they established the American Health and Temperance Association, with **John Harvey Kellogg** as president. Three years later this organization had nearly 10,000 members. Reflecting the growth of the denomination abroad, in 1881 the organization replaced "American" with "International" in its title and continued in operation until the Medical Missionary and Benevolent Association formed in 1893 and absorbed its activities. Led by **Charles S. Longacre**, Adventists supported the early 20th century movement to establish prohibition in the **United States**. About the time the prohibition experiment (1919-33) ended, Adventists organized the American Temperance Society (ATS) and published a small paper, the *Temperance Bulletin*, but did not give much prominence to temperance activities. This situation changed in 1946 when the **General Conference** (GC) examined the denomination's temperance program and the following year organized the International Temperance Association and gave the ATS a new constitution. Most importantly, it appointed **William A. Scharffenberg** as executive secretary of the ATS. He helped create *Listen* magazine in 1948 to address young people, organized temperance conventions, and established the National Committee for the Prevention of Alcoholism and the Institute of Scientific Studies for the Prevention of Alcoholism—organizations that reached well beyond the Seventh-day Adventist Church. In 1954, also under Scharffenberg's leadership, the denomination produced an antitobacco film, *One in 20,000*, which was followed by several other films dealing with both tobacco and alcohol. In 1962 the denomination introduced the **Five Day Plan to Stop Smoking**, a program that was used widely until the 1980s when it was replaced by the Breathe Free program. Meanwhile, in 1960 the GC created the Temperance Department, appointing Scharffenberg as its first secretary; in 1980 this department combined with the Health Department to form the Health and Temperance Department.

Despite Adventism's strong advocacy of abstinence, social changes, particularly in the United States and **Europe**, appeared to be bringing changes in Adventist behavior by the 1980s. In response, the GC created the Institute of Alcoholism and Drug Dependency to study the situation. In a multiyear study, the institute found that about one-fourth of Adventist college students and about 15 percent of adults and secondary school students drank alcohol to at least some degree. Disturbed by these findings, the church sought to give greater attention to temperance in the curriculum of its schools and established a peer prevention campaign under the title Youth to Youth.

THAILAND. Robert A. Caldwell sold Seventh-day Adventist books in Bangkok in 1906 or 1907 and when **literature evangelists** from **Singapore** arrived more than 10 years later they reported discovering a group of **Sabbath** observers. In response, the denomination sent two missionaries in 1919. About the same time, Tan Thiam Tsua, who had accepted Adventism in **China,** also came to Thailand. The missionaries in 1925 established schools in Bangkok and Ban Pong and by 1926 had developed a church membership of 88. Most of the members were Chinese, although a Thai had been **baptized** in 1925. In 1930 a second **mission** station opened at Ubol, which within a few years included a school and a clinic. By 1936 there were 150 members in Thailand. Ralph F. Waddell opened a clinic in Bangkok in 1937 that grew into Bangkok Adventist Hospital. This institution later sponsored the establishment of clinics in Phuket and Haad Yai. During World War II the school building in Bangkok burned down and was rebuilt in 1947. In 1960 the Thailand Training School for educating **ministers** opened in Bangkok and three years later the Thailand **Publishing** House began operations. Meanwhile, in 1962 the denomination broadcast its first Thai language radio program. As of 2003 the Thailand Mission, part of the Southeast Asia **Union** Mission of the Southern **Asia**-Pacific **Division**, had 39 **churches** with a membership of over 12,000. Chiang Mai Adventist Academy, Mission College, Mission Health Food Company, Mission Hospital Bangkok, Mission Hospital Phuket, and Thailand Publishing House were located in the country.

THEOLOGICAL ORIENTATION, SEVENTH-DAY ADVENTIST. In their early history Seventh-day Adventists developed a system of interrelated beliefs but had little interest in developing a systematic theology. They regarded the Bible as God's authoritative revelation and interpreted it in largely literal terms, although they generally advocated a dynamic view of inspiration that emphasized thoughts rather than specific words. At the same time,

William Miller, who began the movement out of which Adventism arose, and **Uriah Smith**, who served for many years as editor of the *Review and Herald*, were among the many Adventists who used reason to both interpret and supplement Scripture, thereby establishing a heritage that drew extensively from historical and scientific evidences.

This rationalism influenced the antitrinitarian and semi-Arian views of 19th-century Adventism, but beginning in the 1880s Adventism moved toward the orthodox view of the **Trinity** that characterizes the denomination today. The Adventist understanding of salvation is thoroughly Arminian, emphasizing the availability of universal **atonement** but also asserting that acceptance is dependent on individual choice or free will. Following Wesleyan theology, Adventists regard salvation as involving first the conferral of God's grace (justification), which then over time reshapes the life of the believer (sanctification). Whether perfection can be achieved during earthly life has been a matter of considerable debate among believers.

Within this basically Arminian outlook, Adventists also emphasize the law and the covenants in a manner similar to that of Reformed thought. They strongly argue for the perpetuity of the moral law, which provides the standard on which God's judgment will be based. Nonetheless, God's grace through the death of Jesus is the means of salvation. Not surprisingly, this largely Wesleyan synthesis of law and grace has produced extensive discussion over what Adventists call **righteousness by faith**.

Many of Adventism's more distinctive doctrines also have roots outside the movement. Its understanding of **conditional immortality**, which rejects the natural immortality of the soul, came into Adventism from the restorationist **Christian Connection**. The historicist interpretation of Biblical prophecy, which regards the books of Daniel and the Revelation as portraying great historical periods, derived from Miller in particular but was accepted by most premillennialists prior to the failure of Miller's prediction of Christ's second coming in 1844. Also, the Adventist approach to the **Sabbath**, which regards it as a holy time set apart for worship, drew from the Puritans. Adventism also holds two distinctive beliefs, although even these have connections with the broader Christian community. First, it accepts **Ellen G. White** as a divinely inspired messenger of God, but officially it regards her authority as secondary to the Bible, the "lesser light" that leads one to the "greater light" of Scripture. White strongly shaped both the institutional and doctrinal understanding of Adventism. Her Methodist background appeared in the denomination's increasing emphasis on God's grace and the person of Jesus that developed in the late 19th century. Second, the related doctrines of the **sanctuary** and the **investigative judgment**, which posit that since 1844 Jesus has been performing the work of High Priest in the heavenly sanctuary spoken of in Hebrews, build on traditional understandings of the offices of Christ and the final judgment. Interpretations of both Ellen G. White and the sanctuary doctrine have stirred much debate in recent Adventism.

THESE TIMES. Seventh-day Adventist **evangelistic** magazine. In 1901 the **Southern Publishing Association** combined two magazines, *Tennessee River Watchman* and *Southern Review*, to create the *Southern Watchman*, which largely served as a source of news and inspiration for Adventist readers in the American South. After absorbing the *Gospel Herald* in 1903, the journal soon changed its name to *The Watchman* and by 1907 had become an evangelistic publication directed toward those who were not Adventists. In 1909 it switched from weekly to monthly publication and in 1917 took the name *The Watchman Magazine*. In 1946 the magazine title changed to *Our Times*, because of apparent confusion with the Jehovah's Witnesses *Watchtower* publication, but five years later it became *These Times*, after the publishers learned that another periodical used the name *Our Times*. Despite these numerous name changes, *These Times* had become the Adventist evangelistic magazine for the **United States** east of the Mississippi River, while the *Signs of the Times* served the western territory. With both magazines experiencing increased costs and decreasing subscriptions, which were paid for by individual church members, the **General Conference** in 1979 decided that they would compete in an open marketplace, meaning that both could advertise and be distributed nationally. Meanwhile, the Southern Publishing Association was also experiencing financial difficulties and merged with the **Review and Herald Publishing Association** in 1980. After the merger, problems continued to plague *These Times* and in 1984 it merged with the *Signs of the Times*, publishing its last issue in March of that year.

THIRD ANGEL'S MESSAGE. Phrase used by Seventh-day Adventists to refer to the denomination's distinctive doctrinal beliefs. As the sabbatarian Adventist movement emerged from the **Great Disappointment** of 1844, **Joseph Bates** called attention to the three angels' messages of Revelation 14:6-13 in the second edition of his pamphlet, *The Seventh-day Sabbath, A Perpetual Sign* (1847). He applied these passages to recent Adventist history: the first angel (verses 6-7) represented the **Millerite movement**, the second (verse 8) referred to Adventist preachers who preached the fall of Babylon, and the third (verses 9-11) found expression in the Millerite call to come out of Babylon. After the Great Disappointment, he argued, those who came out of Babylon began preaching the Sabbath (verse 12), a doctrine that according to his interpretation of this prophecy would be restored before the end of time. In his paper, *Present Truth*, **James White** revised this interpretation by including both the preaching of the fall of Babylon and the call to come out within verse 8. He applied verses 9-12 to the advocacy of the seventh-day Sabbath, which, he believed, constituted the climactic restoration of God's truth prior to the end of time. As they abandoned their **shut door** beliefs in the early 1850s, Adventists increasingly regarded their movement as preaching the messages of all three angels but used the phrase "Third Angel's Message" as a shorthand reference to both their distinctive beliefs and what they understood to be their unique mission.

THREE ANGELS BROADCASTING NETWORK (3ABN). Self-supporting Seventh-day Adventist television station located in Thompsonville, Illinois. Founded by Danny Shelton, the Three Angels Broadcasting Network began transmitting via satellite in 1986. In 1992, after a series of **evangelistic** meetings by John Carter in Nizhny Novgorod, **Russia**, the network established the 3ABN Russian Evangelism Center, where in 1993 it began producing Russian-language programming. In 1999-2000 3ABN increased its satellite coverage of **Europe**, **Africa**, the **Middle East**, and **Asia**, and added 3ABN radio. 3ABN programming included church services, evangelistic presentations, children's shows, and health discussions, among other types of family and religious broadcasts.

TIBET. John N. Andrews, a physician, established a dispensary in 1919 at Kangding, **China**, close to the Tibetan border. In 1931 two Tibetans received **baptism** into Seventh-day Adventism at Kangding and about the same time H. E. Schultz converted two Tibetan lamas in Gansu, China. In 1938 Feng Yung-seng went from China to Lhasa, where he **evangelized** for a time and returned with requests that the Adventists start a medical institution there. World War II brought these contacts to an end and there is currently no Adventist presence in Tibet.

TITHE. For Seventh-day Adventists, 10 percent of income which is given to the denomination. Early sabbatarian Adventist **ministers** supported themselves through donations and part-time work in various occupations. The economic depression known as the "Panic of 1857," however, drastically reduced contributions and forced the leaders to examine the issue of financial support. In 1859 the Battle Creek **church** adopted the Systematic Benevolence plan and recommended it to other sabbatarian Adventist churches. Based on the first-day offerings of I Corinthians 16:2, the plan encouraged male members aged 18 to 60 to give five to 20 cents weekly, as they were able, and women to give two to 10 cents. It also asked those who owned property to give one to five cents for each $100 of value. Later that year a general conference of Adventist leaders endorsed the systematic benevolence plan. In 1860 and 1861 Adventist publications began speaking of giving ten percent of income on property, the first references to the principle of tithing, and by the mid-1870s the view that members should give 10 percent of all of their income was becoming widespread. In 1876 the **General Conference session** voted that it was the duty of all members to give ten percent of their income from all sources, but church members were slow to respond, probably because the **United States** was in the midst of an economic depression. Two years later the General Conference session again adopted the principle that each member should give 10 percent of all their income and appointed a committee to prepare a pamphlet on the subject, published a short time later under the title *Systematic Benevolence*. Although the denomination strongly promoted tithing and Adventists commonly followed the practice, it never became a requirement for church membership.

From the time the Seventh-day Adventist Church organized, it took the position that funds received through systematic benevolence and then tithing were to be used exclusively for the support of the **ministry** and church administration at the **conference, union conference**, and **General Conference** levels. Economic pressures in the 1970s forced reconsideration of this practice. In 1976 the Fall Council of the GC Executive Committee voted to allow the use of tithes for up to 30 percent of elementary school teachers' salaries and in 1990, amid concerns that the denomination was administratively top-heavy, the executive committee decided that a larger proportion of the tithe could remain with the conferences, with lesser amounts going to the union conferences and GC.

TOGO. George Vaysse, a **literature evangelist**, worked in Togo for two years, beginning in 1956. In 1960 Henri Kempf, a missionary in **Côte d'Ivoire**, met with those who had developed an interest in Seventh-day Adventism and four years later moved to the country to establish a permanent Adventist presence. As of 2003 the Togo **Mission**, part of the Sahel **Union Mission** of the Western **Africa Division**, had 32 **churches** with a membership of about 7,000. Glei Adventist Eye Hospital was located in Togo.

TRACT AND MISSIONARY SOCIETIES. Former organizations that distributed Seventh-day Adventist literature. Tract and missionary societies originated with a group of **women** who began holding prayer meetings in the Massachusetts home of Mary and **Stephen Haskell** in 1868 or 1869. With Stephen's help, these women formed the Vigilant Missionary Society in 1869 and, in addition to visiting those who were poor or sick, began mailing Adventist tracts to people whose addresses they had obtained from a variety of sources. When Haskell became president of the New England **Conference** in 1870, he organized the New England Tract and Missionary Society with the goal of establishing missionary societies in every **church**. After **James White** observed the activities of these societies he began advocating their establishment throughout the denomination's churches. Haskell started traveling to various conferences to help organize societies, and White in 1874 began publishing *The True Missionary* to promote them.

That same year the **General Conference session** created the General Conference Tract and Missionary Society to coordinate the activities of local church and conference societies; in 1882 it changed its name to International Tract and Missionary Society. The local church societies gradually developed the responsibility for collecting payments for denominational journals, purchased bulk subscriptions to the *Signs of the Times* for free distribution, and sometimes paid for periodicals and books that a church member might in turn sell to others and then repay the society. This latter function led in the early 1880s to the development of subscription book **literature evangelism**, particularly through the work of **George King**. As literature evangelism grew, the conference societies acquired the responsibility for recruiting and training the booksellers and distributing books to them.

With the denominational reorganization of 1901, the International Tract and Missionary Society dissolved, with first a publication committee and then the Publishing Department taking its place. This department oversaw what were increasingly called the local church Home Missionary Societies and established in 1913 a separate Home Missionary Branch. Five years later this branch became the Home Missionary Department. In 1966 this department was took the name Lay Activities Department and in 1985 became part of the Church Ministries Department. Meanwhile, in 1924 the conference tract and missionary societies, which were acting as the distributors for the denominational publishing houses, were renamed Book and Bible Houses. In 1972 they adopted the name Adventist Book Centers, although some currently use the title Christian Book Center.

TRINIDAD AND TOBAGO. Seventh-day Adventist **publications** sent from **Great Britain** to Tobago in 1879 prompted the development of a group of believers led by James R. Braithwaite, but the group did not become permanent. In 1891 and 1892 William Arnold, a **literature evangelist** from the **United States**, worked in Trinidad, where he was followed by Charles D. Adamson, a Caribbean, who arrived in 1903 and soon formed several **Sabbath**-observing groups. In 1895 the first Adventist **church** in Trinidad organized at Couva, followed shortly thereafter by a second church in Port of Spain. By 1900 there were three churches with about 160 members. In 1899 literature evangelists had begun working on Tobago, where in 1903 Warren G. Kneeland held **evangelistic** meetings, **baptizing** four individuals. By 1912 there were 12 churches with 632 members on the two islands. Denominational leaders, meanwhile, established a small printing plant in Trinidad in 1906, East Caribbean Training School in 1927, and the Port of Spain Seventh-day Adventist Clinic in 1948. Evangelism by T. J. Warner in the 1930s and **Edward E. Cleveland** in the 1960s, for example, brought continued growth to the Adventist church in the region. As of 2003 Trinidad and Tobago were organized as the South Caribbean **Conference**, part of the Caribbean **Union Conference** of the Inter-American **Division**. The conference had 137 churches with a membership of about 56,000. Caribbean Union College, three secondary schools, Community Hospital of Seventh-day Adventists, two clinics, and the Centre for Health Promotion and Wellness were located on the islands.

TRINITY. Christian doctrine that God exists in three persons: Father, Son, and Holy Spirit. Partly because of the influence of the restorationist **Christian Connection**, most Seventh-day Adventists in the 19th century did not accept the doctrine of the trinity. Leading figures such as **James White, Uriah Smith, Joseph H. Waggoner,**

and **John N. Loughborough** believed that the doctrine was unbiblical and, among other things, that it posited the existence of three gods. Smith's 1872 statement of **fundamental beliefs**, for instance, affirmed belief in "one God" and "one Lord Jesus Christ" but made no statement regarding belief in the trinity. With the emergence of **righteousness by faith** as an issue in the 1880s, however, some individuals began to question the denomination's antitrinitarian stance. In 1892 Daniel T. Spear published a pamphlet entitled *The Bible Doctrine of the Trinity* in which he argued that rather than teaching that there were three gods, the doctrine presented one God acting in three persons. Nonetheless, Smith a few years later wrote *Looking Unto Jesus* (1898), where he abandoned his earlier view that Jesus had been created but still saw God the Father as existing first in time.

But the 1890s was a key period in Adventist thinking regarding the trinity, for **Ellen G. White's** *The Desire of Ages* (1898) took a strong trinitarian position, asserting that Jesus was eternally self-existent and fully equal with the Father and referring to the Holy Spirit, which most Adventists had thought of as an "influence" rather than a person, as the third person of the Godhead. White's view appears to have had considerable influence, for when **Francis M. Wilcox** published a summary of beliefs in the *Review and Herald* in 1913 he stated that Adventists believed in the trinity. When Wilcox wrote another, more official, statement of fundamental beliefs in 1930 he referred to the "Godhead, or Trinity" and said "that Jesus Christ is very God." This statement appeared in the 1931 *Seventh-day Adventist Yearbook* and the following year was included in the *Church Manual*. Although a few individuals, including **religious liberty** leader **Charles S. Longacre** and **Pacific Union College** religion teacher William R. French, continued to hold antitrinitarian views, the doctrine of the trinity dominated Adventist belief after World War II. When the denomination again prepared an official statement of fundamental beliefs in 1980 it reaffirmed the trinity in terms similar to those of the 1930 statement.

Toward the end of the 20th century, however, some Adventists—often called "historic Adventists"—sought to revive the views of the denomination's founders, including their antitrinitarianism. In response, the church published *The Trinity* (2002) by Woodrow Whidden, Jerry Moon, and John W. Reeve, which examined the history of the doctrine in both the Christian Church generally and Adventism in particular and strongly argued that it was biblically grounded and theologically important.

TRUTH, SOJOURNER (ISABELLA BAUMFREE) (c. 1797-1883).
African American abolitionist and women's rights advocate. Born
a slave in Ulster County, New York, Baumfree (as she was then
known) was emancipated in 1827. She worked as a domestic in
New York City for a time and in 1833 joined Elijah Pierson in establishing a short-lived commune. In response to a vision in 1843,
she adopted the name Sojourner Truth and began traveling
throughout the North advocating abolitionism, speaking at least
twice at **Millerite camp meetings**. In 1856 Truth moved to Har-
monia, Michigan, and later to Battle Creek, where she became associated with prominent Seventh-day Adventists, including **Ellen
G. White**, **Uriah Smith**, **John Byington**, and **John Harvey
Kellogg**. After the Civil War ended in 1865 she worked for a time
with the National Freedmen's Relief Association and then with the
Freedmen's Hospital in Washington, D.C. She also lectured widely
in behalf of women's rights and the freed slaves and spoke
frequently at the **Battle Creek Sanitarium**, **Battle Creek College**,
and the Adventist "Dime Tabernacle" in Battle Creek. At her
death, the Battle Creek "Tabernacle" was reported to have held a
memorial service for her, although whether she was ever a member
of the denomination is unclear.

TUNISIA. In 1928 Alphonse Gissler arrived in Tunis to conduct Seventh-day Adventist **evangelistic** work and nine years later the Tunisia **Mission** organized. In 1947 the mission reported having one
church with 60 members but in 1955 it merged with the Algerian
Mission and, because of political changes, all church members
eventually departed from the country. As of 2003 there was no organized Adventist presence in Tunisia, although the country was
included as part of the Trans-Mediterranean Territories, an Attached **Field** of the Euro-**Africa Division**.

TURKEY. Theodore Anthony, a Greek immigrant to the **United
States**, converted to Seventh-day Adventism about 1888 and in
1889 arrived in Turkey where he worked among the Christians in
what was then called Constantinople. Among his converts was
Zadour G. Baharian who **evangelized** widely in the **Middle East**
and in 1894 was **ordained** to the Adventist **ministry**. Several Adventist missionaries arrived in the early 20th century and **church**
membership reached about 350 prior to World War I. The **Armenian** massacres of 1914-15 and the war, however, reduced church
membership by nearly half and by 1923 most of the remaining
missionaries and church members had left the country. Although

there was usually at least one denominational representative continuing evangelistic efforts throughout the remainder of the 20th century, the Seventh-day Adventist Church had a very small presence in the country. As of 2003 the Turkey **Field**, an Attached Field of the Euro-**Africa Division**, had two churches with a membership of 35.

TURKMENISTAN. In 1982 Vjacheslav Chubarov moved to Ashgabat and began **evangelizing**. The *Adventist Encyclopedia* (1996) reported that in 1993 there was one **church** with 26 members. As of 2003 Turkmenistan belonged to the Central **Asia Conference** (which also included **Kyrgyz Republic**, **Tajikistan**, and **Uzbekistan**), which was part of the Southern **Union Conference** of the Euro-**Asia Division.** This conference had 42 churches with a membership of about 3,500; there were no specific statistics for Turkmenistan.

TUVALU. Tavita Niu arrived in Funafuti from **Samoa** in 1946 and established a school two years later. The first Seventh-day Adventist **baptisms** took place in 1949. In 1950 Niu left for Kiribati and local **church** members carried on the Adventist efforts in Tuvalu. In subsequent years Adventism spread to Nui (1959), Niutao (1961), Vaitupu and Nukefetau (1962), and Nanumanga (1991). As of 2003 the Tuvalu Attached **Mission**, part of the Trans-Pacific **Union Mission** of the **South Pacific Division**, had one church and a membership of 170.

U

UGANDA. Although E. C. Enns, a Seventh-day Adventist missionary working in Tanganyika, visited Uganda in 1906, the first permanent missionaries did not arrive until 1936. At that time Spenser G. Maxwell and two African helpers established the Nchwanga mission station about 118 miles northwest of Kampala. In 1929 Rye Andersen joined Maxwell and, after the latter left to superintend the East African **Union Mission**, Valdemar E. Toppenberg came to serve as superintendent in Uganda. In 1932 Andersen established the Kakoro mission station in the eastern section of the country and a few years later M. E. Lind, who had replaced Toppenberg, held **evangelistic** meetings in the northern region. In the 1940s Adventist efforts spread to other areas as missionaries established two more stations. In 1948 the denomination opened the Bugema Training School near Kampala; by 1953 the school had become a senior high school recognized by the government and in 1990 it began offering college level courses, becoming known as Bugema Adventist College. About the time this school opened, Ishaka Mission Hospital began offering **health care** services near Mbarara in 1950. This hospital introduced a nurse's training program in 1977, but because of the nation's political oppression under Uganda president Idi Amin the program closed in 1979; it restarted in 1987. Meanwhile, after Amin's fall in 1986, Samson Kisekka, an Adventist physician, became prime minister and later vice president of Uganda. As of 2003 the Uganda Union Mission, part of the East-Central **Africa Division**, had 714 **churches** with a membership of about 124,000. Bugema University, Bugema Adventist Secondary School, Ishaka Adventist Hospital, 17 clinics and dispensaries, and Upper Nile Press were located in Uganda.

UKRAINE. Ludvig R. Conradi and **Gerhard Perk evangelized** the German population of the Ukraine and organized the first Seventh-day Adventist **church** at Berdibulat in 1886. After the establishment of the Soviet Union and increasing political and religious restrictions, Adventism became an underground movement. As government policies became more flexible, in 1978 the denomination organized several **conferences** and 10 years later formed the Ukrainian **Union Conference**. As of 2003 this union conference had 834 **churches** with a membership of about 60,000. The Ukrainian College of Arts and Sciences, an English language school, Voice of Hope Media Center, and Source of Life **Publishing** House were located in the Ukraine.

UNION COLLEGE (UC). Seventh-day Adventist **educational** institution located in Lincoln, Nebraska. Established by conferences from the area between the Mississippi River and the Rocky Mountains, Union College opened in 1891. To meet the needs of the immigrant populations of the region and encourage the maintenance of their cultures, the college was divided into separate English, German, and Scandinavian departments, each of which had its own classes, dormitory, and dining arrangements. This system lasted until about 1910 when the denomination established foreign language schools in other locations. UC resisted the educational reform movement led by **Edward A. Sutherland** and maintained standard course formats and graduation requirements, although it did emphasize vocational training. The college historian, **Everett N. Dick**, believed that the influence of nearby University of Nebraska helped UC maintain its more traditional approach to education. Perhaps for the same reason, UC was more open to accreditation than other Adventist schools. In 1905 it received accreditation from the New York Board of Regents and the following year the University of Nebraska agreed to recognize the premedical courses students took at the college.

After becoming president in 1914, H. A. Morrison sent faculty for university study to obtain M.A. degrees as he prepared to seek regional accreditation. Denominational leaders in 1922 refused to support an application for senior college accreditation, however; but because students wanting to attend the College of Medical Evangelists (later **Loma Linda University**) needed to have accredited undergraduate courses, they approved application for junior college accreditation, which was received in 1923. After being told in 1930 that it would lose its junior college accreditation because it offered four-year degrees, the school again experienced pressure for full accreditation. In 1937 UC received senior college accreditation from the North Central Association of Schools and Colleges.

As it developed, the school accomplished a number of "firsts" for an Adventist educational institution. In 1946 it introduced the first collegiate nursing program, receiving accreditation from the National Nursing Accreditation Service in 1952, and in 1953 it established the first social work major. And in 1967 its education program was the first to receive accreditation from the National Council for the Accreditation of Teacher Education. During the 1980s and early 1990s the school experienced enrollment problems but by 2003 seemed to have stabilized at about 850 students annually. It offered about 30 undergraduate degree programs.

UNION CONFERENCE. Unit of Seventh-day Adventist **organization.** When the Seventh-day Adventist Church organized between 1861 and 1863 it established three levels of organization. The local **church** was at the base of the structure. Its delegates elected the officers and determined the constitution and bylaws of the **conference,** which usually included all of the churches within a state. The conferences in turn elected delegates who chose the officers and wrote the constitution and bylaws of the **General Conference** (GC), which oversaw the operations of the entire denomination.

As the denomination spread across the **United States** and began to establish itself in such places as **Australia, Great Britain,** and **South Africa** in the 1880s, denominational leaders increasingly recognized they needed some form of organization to bring conferences into a closer working relationship with one another. In

1888 the GC Executive Committee divided North America into four districts and assigned individual committee members to oversee these districts. The following year the committee revised this arrangement and established six districts. Those superintending the districts attended **camp meetings** and conference sessions and served as liaisons between the conferences and the GC. In 1892 **Ole A. Olsen**, president of the GC, suggested that the districts be transformed into formal organizational entities, but no one picked up the idea until two years later when **Australia** united its conferences into the Australian Union Conference. In 1897 **George Irwin**, who that year replaced Olsen as president, proposed without success that North America follow the Australian model.

By 1901 delegates to the **General Conference session** recognized that church reorganization was imperative. With the strong encouragement of **Ellen G. White** and the leadership of **Arthur G. Daniells**, who had served as president of the Australasian Union Conference, the session adopted a proposal to group conferences into regional union conferences and make these new units the constituent elements of the GC. Under this new structure, local churches continued to choose the delegates who determined the constitution and bylaws of the conferences, but now the conferences elected delegates who met to take similar actions regarding the union conference, and the union conferences chose delegates who again had similar responsibilities at the GC sessions. The denomination has retained this form of organization, although between 1913 and 1918 it established **Division** conferences that grouped union conferences together. The term union was also used for regional groupings of **missions**, although they differed from conferences in that GC sessions chose their officers and they were not financially self-sustaining.

UNION MISSION. *See* MISSION; UNION CONFERENCE.

UNITED STATES. Sabbatarian Adventism emerged out of the **Millerite** movement, which was concentrated in the northeastern United States, in the 1840s. **James** and **Ellen White** and **Joseph Bates**, the principal founders of sabbatarian Adventism, were all New Englanders, and **Hiram Edson**, who contributed the **sanctuary doctrine** to the movement, lived in upstate New York. When James White began **publishing** papers in 1849 he distributed them mainly in New England and New York but soon expanded to Michigan, sometimes called the "third New England" as New Englanders migrated first to New York and then to Michigan. Because some Adventists were moving as far west as Iowa and they believed that people outside of their native region would be more responsive to their message, the Whites moved their publishing operation to Battle Creek, Michigan, in 1855. An indication of the geographical distribution of sabbatarian Adventism appears in the fact that by the time the **General Conference** of Seventh-day Adventists formed in 1863, state **conferences** had organized in Iowa, Michigan, Minnesota, New York, Ohio, Vermont, and Wisconsin. The denomination at this point had 3,500 members. While concentrated in the American Midwest, Adventists organized the Seventh-day Adventist Publishing Association (1860), Health Reform Institute (1866, later **Battle Creek Sanitarium**), and **Battle Creek College** (1874), all located in Battle Creek. As they expanded geographically, Adventists replicated around the world this tripartite pattern of **publishing, health care,** and **educational** institutions.

From the Midwest, Adventism hopped to the Pacific Coast when **Merritt Kellogg** moved to California in 1859 and, after he had prepared the way, was followed by **evangelists John N. Loughborough** and **Daniel T. Bourdeau** in 1868. Five years later the California Adventists, who numbered 238, formed a conference and within a short time established the **Pacific Seventh-day Adventist Publishing Association** (1875), the Rural Health Retreat (1878), and Healdsburg College (1882). After some Adventists moved from California to the Walla Walla region in the Pacific Northwest, they were followed by evangelist Isaac Van Horn in 1874; three years later the North Pacific Conference organized.

While Adventism was developing on the West Coast, it began to penetrate the immigrant populations of the Midwest and Great Plains. **John G. Matteson** of Wisconsin in the mid-1860s started **evangelizing Danish, Norwegian,** and **Swedish** immigrants in his home state and Minnesota, Missouri, and Kansas. After a **German** immigrant, **Ludvig R. Conradi**, converted to Adventism in 1878, he worked among the German population of the Dakotas, Nebraska, and Kansas. By 1885 Adventist membership was distributed as follows: Northeast (Maine, Vermont, New Hampshire, Massachusetts, New York, and Pennsylvania), 2,774; Midwest (Michigan, Ohio, Indiana, Wisconsin), 7,927; Trans-Mississippi West (Iowa, Minnesota, Missouri, Dakotas, Kansas, Nebraska, Colorado), 6,007; California, 1,587; and the Pacific Northwest (present-day Oregon, Washington, Idaho, Montana), 255.

With the exception of Texas, which had 300 members, by the mid-1880s Adventism had made little penetration of the American

South, where it had 538 members. Beginning in the 1890s, how-
ever, Adventists established institutions in the region. Graysville
Academy, ancestor of **Southern Adventist University**, first
opened its doors in 1892 in Tennessee. Three years later **Edson
White** began working among the African American population in
Mississippi and Alabama, an effort that led to the establishment of
Oakwood Industrial School in 1896 near Huntsville. **Southern
Publishing Association**, located in Nashville, Tennessee, organ-
ized in 1901 and three years later the **self-supporting** Nashville
Agricultural and Normal Institute (later **Madison College**) started
operation nearby. By 1903 membership in the southern states had
grown to more than 2,500.

    With membership firmly established in all areas of the United
States by the early 20th century, certain trends emerged during the
next few decades. The move of the General Conference from
Michigan to the Washington, D.C., area seems to have sparked development in the Northeast, where membership jumped from about
8,000 in 1903 to 23,000 in 1929. Although the Midwest continued
to hold the largest number of Adventists, membership there grew
very little during the same years, while in the Southwest it grew
ten times, from about 3,000 to nearly 30,000. The South, though
still small compared to the larger membership areas, also experienced significant growth, from about 2,500 to more than 11,000
members. These geographical patterns continued to characterize
the denomination's growth during the 20th century.

    As of 2003 the eight Union Conferences into which the United
States was divided had the following membership figures: Atlantic,
479 churches with a membership of about 91,000; Columbia, 605
churches with a membership of about 111,000; Lake, 494 churches
with a membership of about 75,000; Mid-America, 472 churches
with a membership of about 57,000; North Pacific, 407 churches
with a membership of about 86,000; Pacific, 653 churches with a
membership of about 209,000; Southern, 982 churches with a
membership of about 204,000; and Southwestern, 530 churches
with a membership of about 76,000. The total number of churches
in the United States was 4,622, with a membership of over 910,000.
Although largely Caucasian through the mid-20th century, by 2003
the denomination was 53 percent Caucasian, 31 percent Black, 12
percent Hispanic, and 5 percent Asian. Numerous educational,
health, and publishing institutions existed in the United States.
Also, the Inter-American Division operated the Inter-American Adventist Theological Seminary, Inter-American Division Publishing
Ministry, and Inter-American Health Food Company in Florida.

UNIVERSITY OF EASTERN AFRICA, BARATON. Seventh-day Adventist **educational** institution located in Eldoret, **Kenya**. In 1978 the Kenyan government granted the Seventh-day Adventist Church land on which the Baraton Animal Husbandry Research Station had been located. Two years later the denomination opened at this location the University College of Eastern **Africa**, which graduated its first students in 1983. In 1991 it adopted the name University of Eastern Africa Baraton and became the first private university in Kenya to receive a charter from the government. As of 2003 the university was divided into four schools: Business, Education, Humanities and Social Sciences, and Science and Technology. In addition to a variety of bachelor's degrees, it began offering master's degrees in education (1999) and public health (2000). With about 1200 students as of 2003, the University of Eastern Africa was the largest Adventist educational institution in Africa.

URUGUAY. Seventh-day Adventist **literature evangelists** worked among the European population in Uruguay beginning in 1892. An American, Lucy Post, arrived in 1895 at Nueva Palmira, where an interest in Adventist teachings had developed, and was joined later that year by **Jean Vuilleumier** from **Switzerland**. Meanwhile, Joseph W. Westphal, president of the South American **Mission**, and John McCarthy **evangelized** the Europeans in the region of Nueva Helvecia and organized a **church** in 1896. That same year, the missionaries formed the 48 Adventists in Uruguay into a mission. Otto Heydeker started the first Adventist school in the country at Nueva Helvecia in 1908 and two nurses, Meda Kerr and Francisca Brockman, arrived from the **United States** in 1909 to provide **health care** services. In 1943 the mission opened Uruguay Adventist **Academy** near Montevideo; the school received accreditation in 1954. Membership in Uruguay grew slowly, reaching 802 by 1937 but increased more rapidly after World War II, moving from 1,329 in 1947 to 2,203 in 1957. As of 2003 the Uruguay Mission, part of the Austral **Union Conference** of the South American **Division**, had 46 churches with a membership of about 5,500. Uruguay Adventist Academy, a dispensary, and Uruguay [food] Factory were located in the country.

UZBEKISTAN. Although there is some evidence that Seventh-day Adventist **churches** existed in Uzbekistan in the 1920s, virtually nothing is known about them. Two families in Stalino began observing the **Sabbath** in 1955 and K. A. Korlenko started **evangel-**

istic activities in Tashkent in 1957 but was imprisoned in 1964. Several individuals also worked in Tashkent and the *Adventist Encyclopedia* (1996) reported that in 1993 there were four churches in the city. As of 2003 the Uzbekistan **churches** belonged to the Central **Asia Conference** (which also included **Kyrgyz Republic, Tajikistan,** and **Turkmenistan**), which was part of the Southern **Union Conference** of the Euro-Asia **Division**. This conference had 42 **churches** with a membership of about 3,500; there were no specific statistics for Uzbekistan.

V

VANDEMAN, GEORGE E. (1916-2000). Seventh-day Adventist **evangelist**. Vandeman was a field instructor in evangelism at **Emmanuel Missionary College** prior to joining the **Ministerial Association** of the **General Conference** in 1947. He then conducted evangelistic campaigns in Pittsburgh (1948), Washington, D.C. (1951), and London (1952), among other places. In the mid-1950s he began working on a series of television programs entitled *It Is Written,* which he planned to show in a given area for several weeks prior to starting an evangelistic effort. Starting in Fresno, California, in 1958, he subsequently conducted *It Is Written* campaigns in such places as Washington, D.C., Detroit, and Philadelphia. By the mid-1960s *It Is Written* had become a weekly program, broadcast internationally, for which Vandeman served as principal speaker until his retirement in 1991. Among his books were *Planet in Rebellion* (1960), *The Cry of a Lonely Planet* (1983), and *My Dream: Memoirs of a One-of-a-kind Disciple* (1995).

VANUATU. C. H. Parker from **Australia** arrived in what was then called the New Hebrides in 1912 and settled at Port-Vila. Asked by the government to move to an area not inhabited by Europeans, Parker decided to establish a **mission** station on Atchin. Although no one converted until 1922, missionaries continued to come to the islands, establishing stations on Santo and Ambrym and opening a training school on Aore in 1927. By 1949 Seventh-day Adventist membership had reached about 450. In 1961 a clinic opened on Aore. As of 2003 the Vanuatu **Mission,** part of the Western Pacific **Union** Mission of the South Pacific **Division,** had 52 **churches** with a membership of over 14,000. Aore Adventist **Academy** and six clinics were located in Vanuatu.

VAUCHER, ALFRED-FELIX (1887-1993). Seventh-day Adventist **evangelist, educator,** and author. The grandson of Catherine Revel, perhaps the first Adventist convert in **Europe,** Vaucher was largely self-educated. Although a Swiss citizen, he grew up in **Italy,** where he worked first as a **literature evangelist** and then as a **Bible instructor** from 1903 to 1907. Between 1907 and 1910 he served as an evangelist in **Switzerland,** after which he continued similar work in Italy. Between 1913 and 1920 he carried various responsibilities in **France,** including being a pastor, editing the *Signs of the Times,* and serving as a **conference** president and a **union conference** secretary. In 1920-21 he taught Bible at training schools in Nîmes, France, and Gland, Switzerland. He joined the faculty of the newly established Salève Adventist Seminary in France in 1921, serving at this institution as a teacher until 1941, when he became chaplain at Lake Geneva **Sanitarium.** He was president of the French-Swiss conference in 1944-45 until becoming president of the Salève seminary in 1945. Leaving this position in 1951, he continued teaching at the seminary into his mid-eighties. Vaucher published many essays on doctrinal issues and had considerable influence on European Adventism. Among his books were *The History of Salvation* (1921) and *A Forgotten Celebrity: Father Manuel De Lacunza y Diza (1731-1801)* (1941).

VENEZUELA. Brenton E. Connerly, a Seventh-day Adventist **minister,** visited Venezuela in 1907 and distributed denominational **publications.** Three years later F. G. Lane and R. E. Greenidge arrived and began **evangelistic** and medical efforts in Caracas. They achieved their first converts in 1912. S. A. Oberg replaced Lane in 1915; William E. Baxter took Oberg's place two yars later. Despite opposition and illness, the missionaries made gradual progress and in 1919 the Venezuela **Mission** organized; at that time the **church** in Caracas had 19 members. In 1922 Greenidge started the Camaguán Training School, which operated until about 1937 or 1938, and in 1940 the Caracas Adventist Dispensary opened. By 1956 Venezuela had about 1,800 members in 22 churches. In 1963 the Venezuela Secondary School opened in El Limón, a suburb of Maracay, but moved to Nirgua in 1963 where it developed into Venezuelan Adventist University by 1990. As of 2003 Venezuela was divided into two **conferences** and three missions, part of the Venezuela-Antilles **Union** Mission of the Inter-American **Division.** It had 458 churches with a membership of about 113,000. Venezuelan Adventist University, five secondary schools, Venezuela Adventist Hospital, and three clinics and dispensaries were located in the country.

VIETNAM. The first Seventh-day Adventist missionary to what was then French Indo-China, Rankin H. Wentland, arrived in Saigon in 1929. In 1937, by which time there were five **churches** with about 250 members, Roland H. Howlett established a training school in Saigon and soon started a press at the school that eventually became the Vietnam Adventist **Publishing** House. With the advent of World War II, however, the American missionaries evacuated the country, leaving the **mission** efforts in the hands of Robert Bentz, who had recently come from **France**. When American missionaries returned in 1947, they developed several schools and in 1955 opened a hospital in Saigon. With the collapse of the South Vietnam regime in 1975, the new government took over all of the denomination's institutions and all missionaries had to leave the country. Contact between Vietnam and the denomination broke off until 1988 when G. C. Johnson, president of the Southeast Asia **Union Mission**, visited what was now called Ho Chi Minh City and succeeded in restoring communication. As of 2003 the Vietnam Mission, part of the Southeast **Asia** Union Mission of the Southern Asia-Pacific **Division,** had seven churches and a membership of about 6,500.

VINCENT HILL SCHOOL. Seventh-day Adventist **educational** institution located in Mussoorie, **India**. Founded as Mussoorie Intermediate School in 1911, the school functioned under a variety of names until 1922 when it became Vincent Hill School, opening on a new site and offering 12 grades. In the mid-1920s it became Vincent Hill School and Junior College but in 1951 discontinued the junior college curriculum. Prior to 1955, during which time the school prepared students for the Cambridge Senior School Leaving Certificate, it primarily served European and Anglo-Indian Adventists. After it shifted to an American curriculum in 1955, the school largely educated the children of American missionaries and in that capacity was a unique Adventist institution. Changes in the Indian government's visa policy, however, made it increasingly difficult to obtain teachers and reduced the number of American missionaries who needed to have their children educated. The school closed in 1969.

VIRGIN ISLANDS. In 1901 A. Palmquist, a **literature evangelist**, sold books on St. Thomas and the following year worked on other islands. Albert J. Haysmer arrived on St. Thomas in 1901 and, after holding **evangelistic** meetings, **baptized** eight individuals. Lee Wellman began evangelizing Tortola in 1902 and H. C. J. Walleker and James M. Matthews worked on St. Croix and St. John in 1908 and 1909. In the 1930s lay persons from **Puerto Rico** began evangelizing the Spanish-speaking population. As of 2003 the Virgin Islands belonged to the North Caribbean **Conference**, part of the Caribbean **Union Conference** of the Inter-American **Division**, which had 63 churches with a membership of over 21,000. There were no statistics specifically for the Virgin Islands. St. Thomas-St. John Seventh-day Adventist Secondary School was located on St. Thomas.

VOICE OF PROPHECY, THE (VOP). Seventh-day Adventist radio program. After having some experience with radio broadcasting beginning in 1926, evangelist **H. M. S. Richards** introduced the *Adventist Hour and Tabernacle of the Air* on Los Angeles and Long Beach stations in 1934. Two years later he supplemented his preaching with the Lone Star Four male quartet. Essentially a private venture during its first two years of existence, in 1937 the program acquired the Pacific **Union Conference** as its sponsor and changed its name to *The Voice of Prophecy*. At the same time the male quartet took the name **The King's Heralds** and the program began broadcasting along the Pacific Coast over the Don Lee network. In 1942, now under **General Conference** sponsorship, the *VOP* began appearing on the Mutual Broadcasting System, which had 89 stations. That same year the program introduced the Voice of Prophecy Bible Correspondence School, developed by Fordyce Detamore, through which listeners could subscribe to a series of Bible lessons. In 1947 the program added contralto soloist Del Delker. In addition to its broadcasts in the English language, the *VOP* began a Spanish-language program in 1942, with **Braulio Perez** as speaker, and by 1947 was broadcasting internationally in six languages. Richards continued as director and speaker until 1969, when H. M. S. Richards, Jr., took over the program, with his father now assisting. **Lonnie Melashenko** became director and speaker in 1993.

The *VOP* organization also supplemented its regularly broadcast program with additional activities. In 1969 it organized the Voice of Prophecy Evangelistic Association, which established a team of evangelists who conducted preaching campaigns around the world. It also developed several specialized radio programs, including *Way Out* (1969) for youth and *Let's Talk* (1985), a live

call-in show. As of 2003 the *VOP* was broadcasting on more than
400 radio stations in North America and was also presenting a
weekly telecast on a variety of cable channels. Affiliated programs
appeared on more than 1,500 radio stations internationally.

VUILLEUMIER, JEAN (1864-1956). Seventh-day Adventist **minis-
ter** and missionary. The son of Albert Vuilleumier, one of the first
Seventh-day Adventists in **Europe**, Vuilleumier began working at
the Basel Publishing House in 1883 before coming to the **United
States** in 1890, where he translated materials for the International
Tract and Missionary Society and taught Bible at **Battle Creek
College**. In 1895 he went as a missionary to South America, using
his knowledge of languages in preaching and editing *Lighthouse*, a
Spanish-language missionary paper. Around 1900 he returned to
Europe and worked as an **evangelist** and editor of two French-
language papers, *The Messenger of Prophecy* and *The Signs of the
Times*. In 1911 he moved to **Canada** to evangelize among the
French-speaking population and then returned again to Europe
after World War I to edit the French-language *Signs of the Times*
and *Adventist Review*.

W

WAGGONER, ELLET J. (1855-1916). Seventh-day Adventist **min-
ister**, author, and physician. Educated at **Battle Creek College** and
Bellevue Hospital Medical School, where he earned an M.D.,
Waggoner practiced medicine for a while before entering the Sev-
enth-day Adventist ministry. At the invitation of his father, **Joseph
H. Waggoner**, he became assistant editor of the *Signs of the
Times* in 1883 and two years later co-editor along with **Alonzo T.
Jones**. He and Jones also taught occasionally at Healdsburg Col-
lege (later **Pacific Union College**). Inspired by the preaching of
Ellen G. White, Waggoner began studying the biblical books of
Romans and Galations and, with Jones, started writing and speaking about **righteousness by faith**. When several Adventist leaders,
including **George I. Butler** and **Uriah Smith**, objected to
Waggoner's and Jones's interpretations, fearing that they undermined the necessity of observing the **Sabbath,** the issue went to a
committee which was unable to resolve it. Waggoner later explained his views more fully in a tract entitled *The Gospel in the
Book of Galatians* (1888). At the 1888 **General Conference session** Waggoner gave a series of presentations arguing that the law
of God, i.e., the Ten Commandments, demonstrates man's sinful-

ness, but only the acceptance by faith of Jesus' righteousness brings salvation and victory over sin. Waggoner's views stirred great controversy, but during the next several years he spoke at **camp meetings** and ministerial institutes, sometimes with Jones and Ellen White, and gradually much of the denomination accepted his ideas.

In 1892 Waggoner went to **Great Britain** to edit *Present Truth* but while there developed what were alleged to be pantheistic concepts of God and increasingly mystical interpretations of Adventist doctrines regarding the **sanctuary** and the **investigative judgment**. After serving briefly as president of the South England **Conference,** in 1902 he returned to the **United States** and taught for a short time at **Emmanuel Missionary College** before going to Battle Creek, Michigan, to edit the *Medical Missionary* magazine. His 1905 divorce and subsequent marriage to Edith Adams, whom he had met in England, led to his separation from the Seventh-day Adventist Church. After living from 1907 to 1910 in **Denmark,** where he taught English to university students, he returned to America in 1910 to work for **John Harvey Kellogg** at the **Battle Creek Sanitarium**. Waggoner's books included *Fathers of the Catholic Church* (1888), *Christ and His Righteousness* (1890), *The Gospel in Creation* (1895), *The Glad Tidings* (1900), and *The Everlasting Covenant* (1900).

WAGGONER, JOSEPH HARVEY (1820-1889). Seventh-day Adventist **minister** and editor. Originally a Baptist and editor and publisher of a political paper in Baraboo, Wisconsin, Waggoner converted to sabbatarian Adventism in 1852. He almost immediately turned to **evangelism**, traveling throughout the American Midwest. He also began writing books, *The Law of God* (1854), *The Nature and Testimony of Modern Spiritualism* (1857), and *The Kingdom of God* (1859), and served as a corresponding editor of the *Review and Herald*. Although he reluctantly accepted the move toward denominational **organization** that took place between 1860 and 1863, he served on the 1860 committee that chose the name Seventh-day Adventist. In 1875 he accompanied **James White** westward to help establish the Pacific Seventh-day Adventist Publishing Association (later **Pacific Press**) and the *Signs of the Times*; he served as editor of the *Signs* from 1881 to 1886. He also continued to write books, among them *The Spirit of God* (1877) and *The Atonement* (1884), which approached theological issues in a rationalistic and legalistic manner.

WALLA WALLA COLLEGE (WWC). Seventh-day Adventist **educational** institution located in Walla Walla, Washington. Sponsored by the **conferences** in the Pacific Northwest, Walla Walla College opened in 1892. During its first decade the college increasingly emphasized vocational education and short courses that would quickly provide workers for the denomination. Under President Marion E. Cady (1905-11), however, the school introduced four-year baccalaureate programs and improved its teacher education curricula. In 1922 WWC gained approval from the University of Washington for its first two years of college courses and 10 years later received accreditation as a junior college from the Northwest Association of Secondary and Higher Schools. In 1935 it achieved accreditation as a senior college. With the expansion of enrollment after World War II, WWC established a School of Nursing in 1946 and a Department of Engineering the following year. It also introduced master's programs in biology (1949) and education (1950), the first graduate programs in Seventh-day Adventist colleges. In 1988 it added a graduate program in social work. As of 2003 Walla Walla College offered 33 majors, graduate programs in biology, education, and social work, and had an enrollment of about 1,700 students.

WASHINGTON MISSIONARY COLLEGE. *See* COLUMBIA UNION COLLEGE.

WATSON, CHARLES HENRY (1877-1962). Seventh-day Adventist church administrator. An **Australian** businessman who converted to Adventism in 1902, Watson attended the **Avondale** School for Christian Workers between 1907 and 1909. After **ordination** to the **ministry** in 1912, he became president of the Queensland **Conference** and two years later vice president of the Australasian **Union Conference**. Upon becoming president of the union conference in 1916, he emphasized development of the missionary program to the **South Pacific**. In 1922 he became vice president and associate treasurer of the **General Conference** (GC) and president in 1930. During the six years that he served as GC president, Watson effectively drew upon his business experience to help the denomination survive the Great Depression. Through budget cutting, careful international placement of reserves, and streamlining of administration, Watson was able in 1936 to report a balanced budget, despite a one-third reduction in income since 1930. He then returned to Australia to serve as president of the Australasian **Division** from 1936 to 1944.

WEDGWOOD TRIO. Seventh-day Adventist singing group. Begun by Bob Summerour, Don Volmer, and Jerry Hoyle while students at **Newbold College** in 1964-65, the acoustic folk music trio started to perform professionally while attending Southern Missionary College (later **Southern Adventist University**) the following year, recording their first album in 1966. Soon signed by Chapel Records (later **Chapel Music**), they gained great popularity with young Adventists, presenting concerts at colleges and universities, **camp meetings**, and elsewhere. In 1969 the group added keyboards and rhythm instruments as they sought a more contemporary sound, and Gary Evans replaced Volmer. By 1973, however, their music had become too radical for the denomination and Chapel Records withdrew their most recent album, *Dove*, from circulation. Nonetheless, along with the **Heritage Singers**, which organized in 1971, the Wedgwood Trio helped change Adventist popular **music**, opening it to pop, country, gospel, and rock influences. Beginning in 1991, the original trio performed popular reunion concerts.

WEIDNER, JOHN HENRY (1912-1994). Leader of the Dutch-Paris Underground (also called Line) during World War II. The son of a Seventh-day Adventist **minister**, Weidner graduated from Salève Adventist Seminary and then went into the textile business. After failing to escape **France** during the **German** invasion of 1940, he developed a network of about 300 people that helped some 1,000 individuals, most of whom were Jews, escape the Nazis through routes to **Spain** and **Switzerland**. After the war ended, Weidner aided in the prosecution of war criminals and in 1958 moved to the **United States**, where he and his wife developed a health food business in California. For his actions Weidner received honors from many governments, including **The Netherlands**, France, and **Israel**. Herbert Ford's *Flee the Captor* (1966) told Weidner's story.

WEIMAR INSTITUTE. **Self-supporting** Seventh-day Adventist **health care** and **educational** institution located in Weimar, California. Weimar Institute opened in 1978 offering the Newstart Lifestyle Program that addressed various health problems, including heart disease, diabetes, and obesity, through exercise and nutrition. In association with its health program, the institute also began Weimar College in 1978, a non-accredited institution providing programs in pastoral **ministry**, religion, health, English language, and liberal studies. Three years later Weimar **Academy** opened.

Both the academy and the college sought to revive the original Adventist emphasis of providing students with a balanced work-study experience. As of 2003 the institute operated several businesses, including a bakery, market, and inn.

WESSELS, PIETER (1856-1933). Seventh-day Adventist lay person who helped establish the denomination in **South Africa**. Through personal Bible study Wessels, member of a South African farm family living near Kimberly, began observing the seventh-day **Sabbath** in 1885. Later G. J. van Druten introduced him to William Hunt, a Seventh-day Adventist diamond miner, who told him about the Sabbath-observing denomination. After the 1892 arrival of missionaries whom he had requested from the **United States**, Wessels helped them become established in South Africa. In 1891 diamonds were discovered on the farm of Pieter's father, Johannes; after Pieter later visited Battle Creek he used money from the sale of the farm to establish Adventist institutions on the Battle Creek model, including a college, sanitarium, **publishing** house, and orphanage. In 1894 Wessels and **Asa T. Robinson** met with Cecil Rhodes, head of the South Africa Company and premier of South Africa, to request land in the north for a mission. Given the land, Wessels along with other church members took Rhodes's letter detailing the grant to Dr. Leander Starr Jameson in Bulawayo. He then helped with the initial establishment of **Solusi Mission**. In later years Wessels helped **evangelize** the Dutch population of South Africa.

WESTPHAL, FRANK HENRY (1858-1944). Seventh-day Adventist missionary. Converted to Adventism at age 19, Westphal attended **Battle Creek College** and worked as a **literature evangelist** before entering the **ministry**. After being **ordained** in 1883 he superintended a **city mission** in Milwaukee, Wisconsin, and then taught history in the German Department at **Union College**. In 1894 he went to South America as its first ordained Adventist minister. Establishing his headquarters in Buenos Aires, Westphal oversaw the development of Adventist **missions** in **Argentina**, **Uruguay**, and **Brazil**. For health reasons, he returned to the **United States** in 1901 and taught again at Union College until going back to South America in 1904. After working primarily in **Chile**, Westphal returned to the United States in 1920.

WHITE, ARTHUR LACY (1907-1991). Seventh-day Adventist **minister** and secretary of the **Ellen G. White Estate**. Educated at **Pa-**

cific Union College, White worked in 1928-29 as secretary to
Edward A. Sutherland, president of Madison College. He then
returned to California where he assisted his father, William C.
White, the son of Ellen G. White, in administering the Ellen G.
White Estate. After his father's death, White was elected secretary
in 1937 and served in that position until 1978. In this position, he
oversaw the estate's move to Washington, D.C., and integration
into the General Conference, the production of numerous compilations of his grandmother's writings—including *Counsels on Diet
and Foods* (1938), *The Adventist Home* (1952), and *Selected
Messages* (1958), and the establishment of the Ellen G. White
Research Center at Newbold College in 1974. He lectured in many
places and taught courses on Ellen G. White and her writings at the
Seventh-day Adventist Theological Seminary. Among his books
were *Ellen G. White, Messenger to the Remnant* (1956), *The Ellen
G. White Writings* (1973), and the six-volume *Ellen G. White*
(1982-86).

WHITE, ELLEN GOULD (HARMON) (1827-1915). Cofounder of
the Seventh-day Adventist Church, visionary, and author. Growing
up in Portland, Maine, Ellen Harmon received a head injury at age
nine that effectively ended her formal schooling. In 1840 she,
along with her family, accepted William Miller's teaching that Jesus would return about the year 1843. Some two years later she
was baptized, at her request by immersion, into the Methodist
Church to which her family belonged. In 1843, however, this
church dropped her and her family's membership because of their
adherence to Miller's views. After Christ did not return on October
22, 1844, Samuel S. Snow's revised dating of Miller's prediction,
Ellen sought through prayer to understand the Great Disappointment. While having prayer with four other women in December
1844 she experienced a vision in which she saw the Millerites on a
narrow path leading to the New Jerusalem. After experiencing a
second vision about one week later, telling her to report to others
what she had seen, Ellen began speaking to small groups of Millerite believers, telling them that according to her first vision they
were on the right path and must remain faithful. In 1845 Ellen met
James White, a former schoolteacher and Millerite preacher, who
for a time accompanied her on her speaking appointments. In 1846
they married.
    Shortly after their marriage, the Whites studied Joseph
Bates's pamphlet, *The Seventh Day Sabbath, A Perpetual Sign*,
and began observing the Sabbath in the fall of 1846. In April 1847

Ellen experienced a vision that confirmed to her the truth of the Sabbath doctrine. Although her first child, Henry, was born in August 1847, Ellen believed that she must continue her traveling and lodged her son with another family. Meanwhile, she and James met with other Adventists and through a series of conferences in 1848 the sabbatarian Adventist movement took shape around the doctrines of the seventh-day Sabbath and the **sanctuary**. In November 1848 Ellen experienced a vision telling her that James should **publish** a paper; in July of the next year he produced the first issue of *ThePresent Truth*, which was followed in 1850 by the *Advent Review*. In November 1850 James combined the two papers into the *Second Advent Review and Sabbath Herald*. At one point he considered abandoning publication of *Present Truth* but Ellen insisted that he continue. In 1851 the Whites moved to Saratoga Springs, New York, where he published *A Sketch of the Christian Experience and Views of Ellen G. White* (1851). This 64-page pamphlet included Ellen's accounts of several of her visions, which had been previously published as broadsides and articles. The following year the Whites moved to Rochester, New York, and installed a press in their rented house. Joined by Ellen's sister Sarah and her husband Stephen Belden and **Uriah** and **Annie Smith**, all of whom lived in the same house, they continued producing the *Review and Herald* and *The Youth's Instructor*, which James had started in 1852. Meanwhile, Ellen's second and third sons were born, **James Edson** in 1849 and **William Clarence** in 1854.

In addition to publishing their papers, the Whites continued their travels among the sabbatarian Adventists and in 1855 decided to move their publishing operation to Battle Creek, Michigan, where a number of believers had been established. The next year, following a vote by the Battle Creek congregation, a vision of Ellen's was printed as *Testimony for the Church* (1851), the first of a long series of such publications. In 1858 she experienced a vision regarding the conflict between Christ and Satan that she recounted in the first volume of *Spiritual Gifts* (1858); this work introduced the **Great Controversy** theme that she was to develop further throughout her life. A fourth son, John Herbert, was born in 1860 but lived only a few months.

After the Seventh-day Adventist Church **organized** between 1861 and 1863, Ellen's attention turned to issues of health and institution building. In June 1863 she experienced a vision concerning diet and medical practice. Before the year was over, however, two of her sons came down with diphtheria and, following instructions in an article by **James C. Jackson**, she successfully used hydropathic treatments to bring about their recovery, although Henry died from pneumonia that same year. In 1864 James and Ellen visited Jackson's water-cure establishment in Dansville, New York, to observe his methods. Upon returning to Battle Creek James published *Health; or, How to Live* (1865); each volume in this series of six pamphlets included a compilation of writings by various health reformers and an article by Ellen that she said was based on her 1863 vision. After James suffered a stroke in 1865 Ellen took him to Dansville, but left after three months because she disagreed with Jackson's recommendation of complete rest. In December of that year she had a vision telling her that **health reform** was to be integrated into Adventism's religious witness and that the denomination should establish its own health institution. Upon her return to Battle Creek, she urged the **General Conference session** of 1866 to create such an institution. By August Seventh-day Adventists were publishing *The Health Reformer* and shortly thereafter opened the Health Reform Institute (later **Battle Creek Sanitarium**).

After Ellen helped James recover his strength between 1865 and 1868, the Whites once again began traveling, particularly to the Adventist **camp meetings** that began in 1868. Ellen called for Adventists to broaden their ideas of what they might accomplish. In the midst of the developments that were leading to the establishment of **Battle Creek College**, she published a "testimony" in 1872 on "Proper Education," in which she said that correct education should address a balance of physical, mental, moral, and religious concerns. Based on visions that she experienced in 1874 and 1875, she also began calling for the establishment of **missions** abroad, including the creation of publishing houses.

Although James died in 1881, Ellen continued to travel, speak, and write, increasing her influence on the young church. From 1885 to 1887 she traveled in **Europe**, to which Adventists had sent their first missionary in 1874. Upon her return to the **United States** she wrote *The Great Controversy Between Christ and Satan During the Christian Dispensation* (1888), an expansion of the fourth volume of *The Spirit of Prophecy* (1884). At the controversy-filled **General Conference session of 1888** she spoke nine times and then traveled widely in 1889 and 1890 preaching, often with **Ellet J. Waggoner** and **Alonzo T. Jones**, in behalf of **righteousness by faith**. During this same time she wrote *Patriarchs and Prophets* (1890) and *Steps to Christ* (1892), the latter originally published by Fleming H. Revell rather than one of the Adventist publishing houses. In 1891 she went to **Australia**, in part urged by **General**

Conference (GC) leaders who were uncomfortable with her continued support of Waggoner and Jones. Accompanied by her son **William C. White** and several assistants, she helped shape the development of Adventism in Australia and **New Zealand**, particularly the establishment of the Avondale School for Christian Workers (later **Avondale College**). While in Australia she continued the **Christological** emphasis that had begun during the righteousness by faith debate, publishing *Thoughts from the Mount of Blessing* (1896), *The Desire of Ages* (1898), and *Christ's Object Lessons* (1900), works that eventually helped establish the doctrines of **trinitarianism** and righteousness by faith within Adventism.

Returning to America in 1900, White purchased property near St. Helena, California. Asked to attend the **General Conference session** of 1901, she strongly called for reorganization of the denomination and dispersion from Battle Creek. The session, among other things, established **union conferences** and GC departments. That same year, Battle Creek College moved to Berrien Springs, Michigan, where it took the name **Emmanuel Missionary College**, and two years later GC headquarters transferred to Washington, D.C. Back in California, Ellen White urged the further development of the denomination's medical efforts and was personally involved in the establishment of Paradise Valley **Sanitarium** and the medical school that eventually became **Loma Linda University**. She continued to make health a major element in Adventist consciousness through her publication of *The Ministry of Healing* (1905). In 1909 she made her last trip to the East to attend the GC session, speaking at camp meetings along the way. Prior to her death she completed *The Acts of the Apostles* and most of *The Story of Prophets and Kings* (1917). In February 1915 she fell and broke her hip and was confined to her bed and wheelchair for the remaining months of her life.

WHITE, JAMES EDSON (1849-1928). Seventh-day Adventist **publisher** and **evangelist**. The second son of **James** and **Ellen G. White**, Edson from 1877 to about 1880 managed the business affairs of the Pacific Seventh-day Adventist Publishing Association (later **Pacific Press**). Returning to Battle Creek, he worked with the **Sabbath School** Association from 1880 to 1886 in various capacities, during which time he helped begin publication of the *Sabbath School Worker* in 1885 and a Sabbath School songbook, *Joyful Greetings for the Sabbath School* (1886). Also in the 1880s he established the J. E. White Publishing Company, which produced books for subscription sales and set the type for *Hymns and Tunes* (1886), the new Adventist hymnal. Influenced by his mother's "Our Duty to the Colored People" (1891) at a time when he was going through a spiritual crisis, Edson convinced Will Palmer, a former associate, to join with him in a mission effort in the American South. They soon published *The Gospel Primer* (1895), a simple reader that they asked Adventists to both purchase and sell. With the proceeds from this book and donations they contracted for the building of a riverboat, which they named the *Morning Star.* Between 1895 and 1905 Edson and his associates plied the Mississippi River and its tributaries, establishing schools and congregations among the African American population under the auspices of the Southern Missionary Society that White had organized. To inform and gain support for his efforts, he began publishing the *Gospel Herald* in 1898 and that same year produced a compilation of his mother's articles entitled *The Southern Work.* In late 1900 or early 1901 he established the Gospel Herald Publishing Company, ownership of which in 1901 passed to the Southern **Union Conference**, where it became the **Southern Publishing Association**. As the union conference gradually took responsibility for the evangelistic and **educational** activities of the Southern Missionary Society, White concentrated on raising money for missionary work in the South through the publication of subscription books, including *Best Stories from the Best Book* (1900), *The Coming King* (1906), and *Past, Present, and Future* (1909). Because of his wife's failing health, White moved back to Michigan in 1912 and, after her death in 1917, turned his attention to making stereopticon slides for evangelistic use.

WHITE, JAMES [SPRINGER] (1821-1881). Cofounder of the Seventh-day Adventist Church and church administrator. Although most biographical references list White's middle name as Springer, his most recent biographer argues that that there is no evidence supporting this practice. Born in Palmyra, Maine, White for health reasons was unable to attend school until he was 19. Nonetheless, after 12 weeks of schooling he was able to obtain a teaching certificate and taught the following winter. He then attended school for another 17 weeks and taught a second winter but in 1842 accepted **William Miller's** teaching that Jesus would return about the year 1843. For the next two years he worked as a **Millerite** preacher, during which time he was **ordained** as a minister by the **Christian Connection**. Still maintaining his Millerite belief after the **Great Disappointment** of October 22, 1844, White met Ellen

Harmon early in 1845 and soon began accompanying her to speaking appointments. After marrying in 1846, James and **Ellen G. White** studied **Joseph Bates's** *The Seventh Day Sabbath, A Perpetual Sign* and began observing the Sabbath in the fall of that year. Leaving Henry, their son who had been born in 1847, in the care of another family, the Whites traveled extensively among the developing sabbatarian Adventists and published *A Word to the "Little Flock,"* which included Ellen's accounts of her visions and articles by James. In 1848 they participated in a series of conferences, often called "Sabbath Conferences," that forged the movement's distinctive doctrines, particularly the Sabbath and the **sanctuary**.

Strongly encouraged by his wife, in 1849 James began publishing *Present Truth*, which emphasized the Sabbath doctrine. Seeking to show that the sabbatarians were the true Adventists, he introduced the *Advent Herald* the following year. He shortly thereafter combined the two papers into the *Second Advent Review and Sabbath Herald*; White served as editor of this publication from 1851-55 and in 1861-64, 1871-72, 1873-77, and 1880-81. When he was not editor, his name was always on the masthead, usually as associate editor. Also in 1849, he published the first of a series of **hymnbooks**, *Hymns for God's Peculiar People*. After living in several locations, the Whites finally settled in Rochester, New York, in 1852, where James installed a handpress in his home and established what was called the **Review and Herald** Office. During this time White published his wife's *A Sketch of the Christian Experience and Views of Ellen G. White* (1851) and started *The Youth's Instructor* in 1852. As the Whites continued to travel among the sabbatarian Adventists they made several trips to Michigan. As a result, individuals in the Battle Creek area encouraged them to relocate, which they did in 1855. Two years later James was able to purchase a steam press.

As he traveled and pursued his publishing activities, White became increasingly convinced that the sabbatarian Adventists needed to **organize**, and started speaking about "gospel order" as early as 1853. He also believed that his publishing operation, which had been largely financed by donations but technically was his private business, must be incorporated. Despite the objections of many Adventists who regarded church organization as an evil, White succeeded in getting the Seventh-day Adventist Publishing Association incorporated in 1861 and **conferences** and a **General Conference** (GC) organized in 1862 and 1863. He subsequently served as president of the publishing association until his death (except for 1865-68) and as GC president several times: 1865-67, 1869-71, and 1874-90.

With their interest in health issues raised by Ellen's 1863 health vision and the death of their son Henry as well as the illness of their other two sons that same year, the Whites in 1864 visited **James C. Jackson's** water-cure establishment in Dansville, New York, where they observed his methods. In 1865 James published *Health, or How to Live*, a series of six pamphlets that compiled the writings of health reformers and articles by Ellen. In August of that year, however, James suffered a stroke. His wife took him to Dansville for three months but, disagreeing with Jackson's recommendation of total rest, moved her husband back to Michigan where he slowly recovered. In 1870 White was elected president of the board of directors of the Health Reform Institute (later **Battle Creek Sanitarium**), which the church had established during his illness, and the following year he became editor of *The Health Reformer*, a position he held until 1874. Both the institute and the paper were in financial difficulties at the time he acquired these new responsibilities, but White was able to bring them some stability until he turned them over to **John Harvey Kellogg**. During this same time, White was also instrumental in creating the Seventh-day Adventist Educational Society, which established **Battle Creek College** in 1874. White served as the college president until 1880 but **Sidney Brownsberger** ran its day-to-day operations.

At the same time that Battle Creek College was being established, White—always a religious entrepreneur—went to California where he founded *The Signs of the Times* in 1874, a journal intended to provide news and instruction for Adventists on the West Coast of the **United States**. The following year he purchased a press and organized the Pacific Seventh-day Adventist Publishing Association (later **Pacific Press**). White continued as editor of the *Signs* until his death in 1881 and served as president of the publishing association in 1877-78 and 1879-80. Never having fully recovered from his stroke and holding responsibilities in both Michigan and California, White by the late 1870s was clearly worn out but nonetheless had difficulty turning responsibilities over to others. After attending **camp meetings** in the summer of 1881, however, he contracted a serious fever and died on August 6. His books included *Life Incidents in Connection with the Great Advent Movement* (1868), *Sketches of the Christian Life and Public Labors of William Miller* (1875), *The Early Life and Later Experience and Labors of Elder Joseph Bates* (1878), and *Life*

Sketches . . . of Elder James White, and His Wife, Mrs. Ellen G. White (1880).

WHITE, WILLIAM CLARENCE (1854-1937). Seventh-day Adventist **minister** and assistant to his mother, **Ellen G. White**. The third son of **James** and **Ellen G. White**, William attended R. T. Trall's Hygeo-Therapeutic College in New York State during the winter of 1872-73 and studied with **Goodloe H. Bell** in 1873-74. In 1875 he became the acting business manager of the Pacific Seventh-day Adventist **Publishing** Association (later **Pacific Press**) and a few months afterwards was elected treasurer of the California **Conference**. In 1876 he became the president and business manager of the publishing house while his wife Mary served as treasurer. In 1877 he returned to Battle Creek to attend **Battle Creek College** but was soon elected to the institution's board of trustees. About the same time he was also appointed a director of the Health Reform Institute (later **Battle Creek Sanitarium**), vice president of the **Review and Herald Publishing Association**, and a member of the executive committee of the **Sabbath School** Association. In 1879 he was elected acting foreign **missions** secretary for the **General Conference** (GC). That same year he became a vice president of the Pacific Seventh-day Adventist Publishing Association, although he did not move back to California until 1880. In 1881 he was elected president of the Healdsburg College (later **Pacific Union College**) board and in that capacity helped establish the school.

With James White's death in 1881, however, William began giving attention to his mother's affairs. He accompanied her to **camp meetings** on the way to the **General Conference session** in 1883, which elected him to several positions, including the GC Executive Committee, and **ordained** him to the ministry. The following year the GC sent him, along with his mother and family, to **Europe** to help establish a publishing house in Basel. While in Europe William compiled and edited *Historical Sketches of the Foreign Missions of Seventh-day Adventists* (1886) and traveled widely with his mother to visit Adventist congregations. Returning to the **United States** in 1887, White was elected GC foreign mission secretary as well as a member of several committees. After the **General Conference session of 1888** he served as acting president of the GC for about six months until **Ole A. Olsen**, the newly elected president who was still in **Norway**, returned to America. In 1890 White's wife died of tuberculosis contracted in Europe and the following year he accompanied his mother to **Australia** and served as the GC's district superintendent for the region until 1897.

While in Australia, William, along with **Arthur G. Daniells**, developed in 1894 the Australasian **Union Conference**, a new form of denominational organization that drew conferences into a regional unit. Elected president of the new organization, White oversaw the development of the **Avondale** School for Christian Workers and struggled with an ongoing financial crisis. He also married Edith Lacey in 1895. Overwhelmed with his various denominational responsibilities, William resigned as union conference president in 1897; he took the position of vice president and continued to serve on the boards of several Adventist institutions in Australia. Before they left Australia, his mother requested that William give more attention to her affairs and from that point on he played a decreasing role in denominational organizations.

Upon returning to America in 1900, William served as an intermediary between his mother and denominational administrators, working on the 1901 reorganization of the denomination, addressing the **John Harvey Kellogg** crisis of 1902-07, and helping to establish Loma Linda Sanitarium (later **Loma Linda University**) in 1905. He also supervised Ellen's editorial staff, which was helping her complete her book manuscripts, and played a significant role in developing *Testimonies for the Church*, vol. 8 (1904), *The Acts of the Apostles* (1911), *Counsels to Teachers, Parents, and Students Regarding Christian Education* (1913), a revision of *Gospel Workers* (1915), and *Life Sketches of Ellen G. White* (1915). He also supervised the translation of his mother's works into other languages. After Ellen's death in 1915, William became secretary of the **Ellen G. White Estate**, holding that position until his death in 1937. During that time he continued the work he had begun in 1900, overseeing the indexing of her manuscript files, the production of several compilations of her writings, and the compilation of the *Scriptural and Subject Index to the Writings of Mrs. Ellen G. White* (1926). Representing his mother's legacy to the denomination, William increasingly experienced tensions with the GC leaders, who felt that he was too independent. After considerable discussion between these men and William White, the estate incorporated in 1933 and its representatives signed agreements for its relocation to GC headquarters in Takoma Park, Maryland. Although William died before the move was completed, his son **Arthur White**, who succeeded him as secretary, completed the transition in 1938.

WILCOX, FRANCIS MCCLELLAN (1865-1951). Seventh-day Adventist editor. After working in **evangelism** and **city missions** from 1886 to 1890 in the New York **Conference**, Wilcox became editor of the *Sabbath School Worker* and recording secretary of the Sabbath School Association in 1901. From 1893 to 1897 he was secretary of the Foreign **Mission** board and edited the *Home Missionary* magazine. Moving from Michigan to Colorado for health reasons, from 1897 to 1909 he served as a pastor and chaplain of the Colorado **Sanitarium**, and for a time as the sanitarium's business manager. He became an associate editor of the *Review and Herald* in 1909 and two years later the editor, holding that position until 1944. While editor, Wilcox strongly upheld the authority of **Ellen G. White** and during World War I counseled evangelists against predicting that it would lead to Armageddon. He also wrote the statement of **fundamental beliefs** that appeared in the 1931 *Yearbook* and the *Church Manual* (1932). His books included *Facing the Crisis* (1920), *What the Bible Teaches* (1926), *The Coming Crisis* (1933), *The Testimony of Jesus* (1934), *The Gospel of Health* (1935), *Seventh-day Adventists in Time of War* (1936), *The Early and Latter Rain* (1938), and *Heart to Heart Talks* (1948).

WILSON, NEAL C. (1920-). Seventh-day Adventist **minister** and church administrator. The son of Adventist missionaries, Wilson served as accountant of the South **Asia Division** in 1939-40 and as acting treasurer of the Oriental Watchman Publishing House in 1940 before graduating from **Pacific Union College** in 1942. After working as an **evangelist** in the **United States** from 1942 until 1944, at which time he was **ordained**, he joined the **Middle East** Division as a pastor-evangelist in 1944. He then became president of the Egypt **Mission** in 1945 and the Nile **Union Mission** in 1950. Returning to the United States in 1959, he served as a department secretary in the Central California **Conference** and the Columbia **Union Conference** prior to becoming president of the latter organization in 1962. In 1966 he was elected vice president of the **General Conference** (GC) and became president in 1979, serving in that position until his retirement in 1990. As president he publicly put the GC behind efforts in the 1980s to end racial discrimination in the British Union Conference. In 1986 he proposed that the denomination develop a worldwide strategy; the **Global Mission** program grew out of this proposal. The following year he spoke to Soviet leaders at the International Forum for a Nonnuclear world, during which he offered denominational help with

health care in the Soviet Union. At Wilson's invitation, Konstantin Kharchev, chairman of the Soviet Union's Council of Religious Affairs, visited various denominational facilities in the United States in 1987. These exchanges helped improve the situation of the denomination in the Soviet Union. Wilson was also the driving force behind the decision to move the GC headquarters in 1989 from Takoma Park to Silver Spring, Maryland, where a new office building was constructed.

WOMEN. Throughout much of Adventist history women have played an important, though not always recognized, role. Several women, including Lucy Hersey, Oive Maria Rice, and Sarah J. Paine Higgins worked as preachers in the **Millerite Movement**. Emily C. Clemons and Clorinda S. Minor, in addition to preaching, edited a Millerite periodical for women, *The Advent Message to the Daughters of Zion*, which began publication in May 1844. In post-Millerite Adventism, Abigail Mussey and Lauretta Elysian Armstrong Fassett rose to prominence. **Ellen G. White**, however, became the most significant of early Adventist women as she worked with **Joseph Bates** and **James White** to found the Seventh-day Adventist Church. Until her death in 1915, Ellen White encouraged the sabbatarian Adventists to establish **publishing, educational**, and **health care** enterprises, urged them to pursue worldwide missionary activity, and helped shape their theological understanding through her speaking and many articles and books.

Along with Ellen White, several other women helped shape 19th-century Seventh-day Adventism. By 1915 the denomination had licensed—but did not **ordain**—at least 34 women to serve as **ministers**. Among these women, Ellen Lane worked with her minister husband in Michigan, Sarah Lindsay **evangelized** with her husband in western New York and Pennsylvania, and Hetty Hurd Haskell assisted her husband in **England, South Africa**, and **Australia**, as well as the **United States**. In addition to preaching, women also held significant administrative positions in the denomination. Three women served as treasurers of the **General Conference** (GC): Adelia Patten Van Horn (1871-73), Fredricka House Sisley (1875-76), and Minerva Jan Loughborough Chapman (1877-83). It is also apparent that women were active in **conference** leadership; in 1905, for instance, there were 20 female conference treasurers, 20 education department secretaries, and 38 **Sabbath school** department secretaries. Although these numbers continued to increase through 1915, they went into decline thereafter. Two key factors appear to have been involved. First, the 1923 Fall Council of the GC Executive Committee decided that all departmental leaders should be ordained, which effectively limited such positions to men. Second, the advent of the Great Depression in 1929 reduced the number of denominational employees. In making these reductions, the denomination—which generally regarded men as the head of a household—kept males on the payroll while releasing females. Although **L. Flora Plummer** served as secretary of the GC Sabbath School Department from 1913 to 1936, by the mid-1940s women had completely disappeared from denominational administrative positions.

Throughout the 19th century Seventh-day Adventists had been willing to license women as ministers, but they never provided for their ordination. At the 1881 **General Conference Session** a resolution to establish ordination of women to the ministry was introduced but died after being referred to the GC Executive Committee. While in **Australia** Ellen White in 1895 published an article in the *Review and Herald* urging that some women should be consecrated to certain activities through the "laying on of hands," which implied ordination at some level. That same year an Australian **church** ordained women to the local office of **deaconess**. In 1900 the same church again ordained deaconesses and in 1915 a Pacific **Union Conference** church ordained women to a similar position. These services ordaining women to local church offices appear to have been isolated incidents, however.

Beginning in the late 1960s, as a result of both the practical necessity of needing more pastors in certain areas and the influence of the feminist movement in western societies, the Seventh-day Adventist Church began slowly appointing women to both pastoral and administrative positions. In 1968, the Finland Conference, in which women had been serving as pastors for several years, unsuccessfully requested that the GC allow it to ordain females to the ministry. This was followed in 1972 by the Potomac Conference's ordination of Josephine Benton as a local church **elder** and a request from **Germany** for permission to do the same for Margarete Prange, who was serving as a pastor. About the same time, the Far Eastern **Division** asked for advice regarding the ordination of women. A 1973 meeting of church administrators and religion teachers at Camp Mohaven, a denominational facility in Ohio, recommended to the GC that women be ordained as local church elders and as "associates in pastoral care," and that the denomination initiate a program to lead to ordination of women as ministers in 1975. The GC Executive Committee's Annual Councils (as the

Fall Councils were now called) of 1973 and 1974, however, voted only to continue studying these issues. The **Biblical Research Committee**, which had begun examining the role of women in the church in 1972, followed up the Camp Mohaven meeting with a group of 13 research papers in 1975 but did not make these papers generally available until several years later. Meanwhile, in 1975 the GC Executive Committee Spring Council voted to approve the ordination of women as local church deaconesses and elders and to encourage women to serve as **Bible instructors** and assistant pastors. At the same time, however, it voted that women could be granted only missionary licenses, thereby officially ending the 19th-century practice of giving women ministerial licenses. Two years later, the GC Executive Committee Annual Council adopted the term "Associates in Pastoral Care" for members—particularly women—of pastoral staffs who were not in line for ordination.

While these discussions were taking place, another women's issue emerged. Historically, the denomination had paid those employees who were "heads of households" at a higher rate than those—mostly women—who were single. In 1973 Merikay Silver, an editorial assistant at the **Pacific Press**, whose husband had recently lost his job, filed a class-action suit against her employer after her application for head of household status was rejected. Before the suit was settled out of court in 1983 it had spawned two government suits against Pacific Press for retaliation against an employee and violation of the Equal Pay Act. In consequence of these legal challenges, the Seventh-day Adventist Church in the United States adopted the practice of equal pay for equal work, which primarily benefited women.

Although the economic position of women church employees improved as a result of the Merikay Silver case, the place of females in the administrative and pastoral structures of the church changed slowly. Beginning in the early 1970s the conferences and **Union Conferences** began appointing women to administrative positions, particularly in the Sabbath school and education departments. These developments led in 1975 to the appointment of M. Carol Hetzell as director of the GC Communications Department, the first time a woman had held such a position in more than 30 years. In 1979 the GC Executive Committee Annual Council, deciding that it wanted to encourage more women to enter the ministry, established funding to provide internships in North America for Bible instructors and associates in pastoral care. At the same time it also changed the denomination's policy to allow unordained male pastors to conduct **baptisms**.

Momentum toward women's ordination seemed to build during the next few years. Several women, some of them sponsored financially by their conferences, enrolled in the **Seventh-day Adventist Theological Seminary**. The **Association of Adventist Women** (AAW) organized in 1982 and in the following year the North American **Division** Office of Human Relations established a Women's Commission, which included one female representative from each Union Conference and met once a year to examine women's issues. In 1984 the Potomac Conference authorized eight ordained local elders, including three women, to perform baptisms in their churches. After the women had baptized 12 individuals over the next several weeks, GC administrators called the conference leaders to a meeting in which the latter agreed to stop women from baptizing in return for the GC's commitment to begin a new study of women's ordination.

The 1984 GC Executive Committee Annual Council reaffirmed the 1975 decision that women might be ordained as local elders and voted to call a Commission on the Role of Women in the Church, which first met in March 1985. Also in 1984, the Annual Council authorized the establishment of **Shepherdess International**, a pilot program to provide support for minister's wives. The GC session of that year followed the commission's recommendation in urging denominational leaders to include women in all aspects of the church's ministry that did not require ordination. At that same session, Nancy Vyhmeister, who taught at the Seventh-day Adventist Theological Seminary, Far East, presented her research that showed at least 85 women (mostly located in North America, **Europe**, and the Far East) being paid for full-time pastoral or evangelistic work. Also in 1985, the GC established a Women's Ministries Advisory Committee, with Betty Holbrook serving as chair.

New organizations also started forming. The North American Division held the first meeting of Adventist women clergy in 1987, with 23 of 40 such individuals attending. The following year Adventist lay persons formed Time for Equality in Adventist Ministry (TEAM) in Maryland and the Adventist Women's Institute (AWI) on the West Coast. In 1989 the Southeastern California Conference established a Gender Inclusiveness Task Force and the Columbia Union Conference endorsed a woman as a candidate for ordination. When the Commission on the Role of Women in the Church met that same year, the North American Union Conference presidents sent a message endorsing women's ordination to the ministry. The commission did not seek ordination of women, however, recommending instead that divisions authorize qualified women to baptize and perform marriages. The 1990 GC session accepted this recommendation but voted down women's ordination to the ministry. A few months later both the North American Division and the General Conference established departments of Women's Ministries, directed respectively by Elizabeth Sterndale and Rose Otis.

In 1993 TEAM published *Keeping Hope Alive*, a survey of 72 women pastors, chaplains, and religion teachers in the North American Division, in which a majority of the individuals expressed their belief that the church had failed to follow the Holy Spirit when it rejected ordination of women. Further publications appeared, including V. Norskov Olsen's *Myth and Truth: Church, Priesthood and Ordination* (1994) and TEAM's *The Welcome Table* (1995) which supported ordination, and Raymond Holme's *Tip of an Iceberg* (1994) and Samuel Koranteng-Pipim's *Searching the Scriptures* (1995), which opposed such action. In 1994 the GC Executive Committee Annual Council accepted a recommendation from the North American Division that the 1995 GC session consider authorizing divisions to ordain women to the ministry if they wished. Prior to the session the denomination published the Biblical Research Institute's papers on the issue that had been completed 20 years previously. Although the July session gave public recognition to two women from **China**, Zhou Hui-Ying and Wu Lan-Ying, who had brought large churches into existence, it rejected ordination by a vote of 1,481 against and 673 in support. Although much of the debate was theological, most observers agreed that cultural issues were at least as important, with North Americans and Europeans generally supporting ordination and **Latin Americans** and **Africans** taking a leading role in the opposition.

Following this disappointment, in September 1995 the Sligo Church in Takoma Park, Maryland, ordained three women to the ministry, an action which was followed by at least six similar ordinations by 2000. Recognition of these ordinations, however, was limited to the local church where they were performed. In 1996 the North American Division established a President's Commission on Women in Ministry, which was charged with examining the expansion of women's roles but was instructed not to discuss ordination; following the commission's recommendation, the division in 2000 appointed Dúane Schoonard as a part-time associate in its Ministerial Association. Meanwhile, in 1997 **La Sierra University** opened a Women's Resource Center that had among its goals the advocacy and support of women in ministry. **Andrews University** Press published *Women in Ministry* (1998),

edited by Nancy Vyhmeister, in which several Seventh-day
Adventist Theological Seminary professors called on both
historical and biblical evidence to argue for women's ordination.
Two years later the General Conference **Ministerial Association**
began publishing a newsletter, *Contact*, sent to Adventist women
in ministry throughout the world church. That same year the
Southeastern California Conference and the Arizona Conference
adopted equal credentials, which used the words "ordained-
commissioned" for both male and female pastors; in 2002 the
constituency of the Northern California Conference asked its
officers to study adoption of similar equal credentials. Although it
was unclear whether the equal credential approach provided a
workable solution to the issue of women's ordination, it was
apparent that in North America at least, the number of Adventist
women in ministry and related fields was increasing. A report from
the Ministerial Association indicated that as of July 2003 80
women were serving as pastors, 47 as medical chaplains, 60 as
teachers or professors of religion, and 9 as campus chaplains.

WORTHINGTON FOODS, INC. Self-supporting producer of vegetarian foods located in Worthington, Ohio. Founded in 1939, Worthington Foods developed soy- and gluten-based meat substitutes.
After Miles Laboratories purchased the company in 1970, it moved
beyond the Adventist and health food store market by introducing
the Morningstar Farms line of products, which were sold in grocery stores. This new approach quadrupled sales within ten years.
In 1978, however, Bayer AG purchased Miles Laboratories and
four years later a group of Adventist businessmen, including the
original founders of Worthington Foods, purchased the company.
Maintaining the Morningstar brand, the new owners continued to
expand their market, achieving record sales of $139.5 million in
1998. In 1999 the Kellogg Company purchased Worthington
Foods for more than $300 million.

Y

YOUR STORY HOUR. **Self-supporting** radio program for children.
Starting in the mid-1940s as a Saturday afternoon story hour for
children in Eau Claire, Michigan, *Your Story Hour* began broadcasting over a nearby Benton Harbor radio station in 1949. Originally hosted by Irene Lovell (replaced in 1951 by Betty Ahnberg)
as "Aunt Sue" and Stanley Hill as "Uncle Dan," the program pre-

sented reenactments of Bible and other character-affirming stories. In the mid-1980s it established production facilities in Berrien Springs, Michigan, and by 2003 appeared on about 3,000 stations around the world in English, Spanish, and Russian with an estimated weekly audience of 22 million. The program also distributed recordings, workbooks, Bible lessons, and *Clubhouse* (formerly *Good Deeder*) magazine.

YOUTH ACTIVITIES. *See* MISSIONARY VOLUNTEER SOCETY; PATHFINDER CLUB; SABBATH SCHOOL.

YOUTH'S INSTRUCTOR. Former Seventh-day Adventist magazine for young people. Established by James White in 1852, the magazine appeared as a monthly through 1869, when it became a semimonthly publication. It appeared again as a monthly in 1872, continuing until December 1880. Meanwhile, it had also begun appearing as a weekly in January 1879 and continued as such until April 1970 when it was replaced by *Insight*. The magazine's longest serving editor was **Lora E. Clement**, who was an associate editor from 1918 to 1923, after which she served as acting editor and then editor until 1952.

YUGOSLAVIA. A Seventh-day Adventist employee, A. Seefried, of the British and Foreign Bible Society, worked in Macedonia and **Albania** for nine years beginning in 1880. Toward the end of the 19th century an Armenian physician by the name of Dr. Garabet settled in Radoviste, Macedonia, and converted a schoolteacher, Atina Dimeva, who later attended the **American Medical Missionary College**. John F. Huenergardt, who was a minister in Cluj, part of present-day **Romania**, visited Mokrin beginning about 1898 and established a **Sabbath school** there the following year. A few years later, Huenergardt learned of some seventh-day **Sabbath** observers in Kumane and visited them in 1905 and later that year organized a **church**. A few months later another church organized in Mokrin. In 1909 Robert Schillinger established a branch of the Hamburg **Publishing** House in Novi Sad and by the next year **literature evangelists** were selling denominational books throughout the country. The Yugoslavian Publishing House formed as an independent entity in 1925 and continued in existence until political turmoil forced its closure in 1946. It resumed operations in 1968. Meanwhile, in 1932 Huenergardt established a training school in Belgrade that moved to Zagreb the following year and operated there until 1942. In 1955 the school reopened in Rakovica and stayed in that location until 1974 when it moved to Marusevec, where a secondary school had been opened four years earlier. After the political changes of the early 1990s, the schools reorganized with the Adventist Theological Seminary moving to Belgrade while the secondary school stayed at Marusevec. As of 2003 the churches in the Federal Republic of Yugoslavia were organized into the North and South **Conferences**, which belonged to the South-East European **Union Conference** of the Trans-**European Division**. The conferences had 171 churches with over 7,000 members. Belgrade Theological Seminary, Yugoslavia Publishing House, a retirement home, and two radio-television production centers were located in the country. *See also* CROATIA, SLOVAK REPUBLIC, SLOVENIA.

Z

ZAMBIA. In 1905 **William H. Anderson** established what became known as the Rusangu **Mission** Station about 100 miles northeast of Kalomo. Twelve years later, Samuel M. Konigmacher, who was working at Rusangu, left to open the Musofu Mission Station near Ndola. Herbert J. Hurlow started a third station in 1921 near the Mweru and Bangweulu lakes. At the Mwami Station, on land purchased in 1925, Dr. E. G. Marcus established a rudimentary hospital in 1927. That same year Konigmacher opened a school at Liumba Hill in Barotseland in 1928; a small dispensary was added in 1935. With mission stations in all sections of the country by the late 1920s, the Seventh-day Adventist Church grew rapidly. As of 2003 the Zambia **Union Mission**, part of the Southern **Africa-Indian Ocean Division**, had over 1,331 **churches** with nearly 400,000 members. Rusangu Secondary School, Mwami Adventist Hospital, Yuka Adventist Hospital, seven clinics and dispensaries, and Zambia Adventist Press were located in the country.

ZAOKSKI THEOLOGICAL SEMINARY. Seventh-day Adventist educational institution located in the Tula Region, **Russian Federation**. In 1986 **General Conference** president **Neal C. Wilson** requested that the Council on Religious Affairs of the Soviet Union approve the establishment of an Adventist **educational** institution. Particularly as a result of an appeal from Mikhail M. Kulakov, the request received approval in 1987 and the seminary opened the following year. Registered with the government in 1991, the Zaokski seminary was the first Christian institution of higher learning to open in Russia since the 1917 revolution and the first Protestant seminary ever. The school graduated its first class of theology students in 1993. In addition to theology, as of 2003 the seminary offered programs in agriculture, financial management, education, and music.

ZIMBABWE. The Seventh-day Adventist Church in 1894 received a grant of land in Matabeleland from Cecil Rhodes, the prime minister of the Cape Colony and head of the **South Africa** Company. **Pieter Wessels** and others selected a site near Bulawayo on which they established what became known as **Solusi Mission**. From Solusi other stations soon followed. Frank B. Armitage established the Lower Gwelo Station in 1903 and M. C. Sturdevant began the Inyazura Station in 1910. Other stations opened at Hanke, Shangani, and Gunde between 1911 and 1920. As of 2003 the Zimbabwe **Union Conference**, part of the Southern **Africa**-Indian Ocean **Division**, had 678 **churches** with a membership of about 375,000. Solusi University, six secondary schools, and 10 clinics and dispensaries were located in Zimbabwe.

Bibliography

The following bibliography offers an extensive but not exhaustive listing of works in English on Seventh-day Adventism and books expressing Adventist views on theological and other issues. Many of the works, particularly those from denominational publishing houses, are of a popular rather than scholarly nature, but academic studies appear as well. The section of books dealing with Adventist beliefs and practices includes both individually influential books and less significant but representative volumes from the span of the denomination's history. While the bibliography is itself selective, the bibliographical essay that introduces it offers a guide to the most significant works and, except where noted, follows the organization of the bibliography.

Historical Literature

As a movement expecting the imminent return of Jesus, it is not surprising that for many years Adventists took relatively little interest in their history. The first works that appeared defended Adventism against its critics. Responding to alleged misrepresentations of William Miller, Sylvester Bliss produced *Memoirs of William Miller*, published in 1853 (listed below under Autobiographies and Memoirs). To a considerable degree letting Miller speak for himself, Bliss included extracts from his correspondence, sermons, and other sources, thereby preserving primary source material that would prove invaluable to later historians. With a similar purpose but focusing more generally on the movement Miller inspired, Isaac C. Wellcome, an Advent Christian minister, wrote *History of the Second Advent Message* about 20 years later. Like Bliss, Wellcome presented extracts from Millerite publications that, in addition to his own memories, remain useful to the researcher. Significantly, in light of later developments, he regarded Seventh-day Adventism as a mistaken departure from the real Millerites.

Such publications, however, did not prevent later writers from continuing to present the Millerite movement as a fanatical movement in which people gave away their property, donned ascension robes, and sometimes went insane. Clara Endicott Sears pulled all of these elements together in *Days of Delusion*, a volume based on contemporary documents and first- and second-hand recollections. Francis D. Nichol, editor of the Seventh-day Adventist *Review and Herald*, replied to Sears and other critics with his well-researched but strongly apologetic *The Midnight Cry*. The first two-thirds of the volume offered a narrative of the movement while the last third responded one by one to the charges against Millerism.

Meanwhile, professional historians were starting to take an interest in the Millerite movement. Everett N. Dick, a Seventh-day Adventist, was the first to seriously examine Millerite primary sources when he researched his University of Wisconsin doctoral dissertation in the late 1920s. Unfortunately, denominational pressures prevented publication of his work until 1994, by which point the volume was itself an historical document. While Dick gave some attention to the social environment of the Millerites, other historians made such contextualization their primary emphasis. Alice Felt Tyler's *Freedom's Ferment* saw the movement as part of the religious and social reform movements of the antebellum period, but repeated the stories of ascension robes and insanity. A few years later, Whitney R. Cross took a similarly broad approach, but concentrated on *The Burned-Over District* of upstate New York and, influenced by Nichol, rejected many of the stories of fanaticism, arguing instead that the Millerites were very similar to their contemporaries.

Another 20 years passed before historians began to look extensively at Millerism again. Ernest R. Sandeen examined the movement within the context of American millennialism in *The Roots of Fundamentalism* while Vern Carner and Ronald L. Numbers, at the time teachers at the Seventh-day Adventist Loma Linda University, organized a series of lectures that were published as *The Rise of Adventism*, edited by Edwin Scott Gaustad. Despite its title, the latter volume concentrated mostly on the social and religious developments that surrounded the emergence of Adventism rather than the movement itself. Nonetheless, it provided an invaluable bibliographical essay on Millerism and early sabbatarian Adventism. During the next several years a number of works appeared that explored in more detail the American nature of the Millerite movement. Among the more important of these works were David L. Rowe's *Thunder and Trumpets*, Ruth Alden Doan's *The Miller Heresy*, Michael Barkun's *Crucible of the Milen-*

nium, and Ronald L. Numbers and Jonathan Butler's edited volume, *The Disappointed.*

The appearance of these often specialized academic studies raised the need for a synthesis. Although no one wrote a scholarly overview of the Millerites, two popular accounts appeared. An Advent Christian historian, Clyde E. Hewitt, published *Midnight and Morning*, a work that was particularly useful for its balanced account of the emergence of the various Adventist denominations after 1844. Seventh-day Adventist writer George R. Knight celebrated the upcoming 100th anniversary of the "Great Disappointment" with *Millennial Fever*. Although he drew upon the scholarship of the past 50 years, which had emphasized the commonalities between Millerism and American society, Knight highlighted the radical nature of the movement. While the volume addressed an Adventist audience, particularly in the last few chapters, Knight's work provides the best general account of the Millerite movement to date.

The many publications on Millerism that appeared from the 1970s to the 1990s seem to have largely exhausted the interest of professional historians. But perhaps a harbinger of things to come was the appearance in 1999 of David Morgan's *Protestants & Pictures*, which included among other things extensive chapters on Millerite and early Seventh-day Adventist art. Morgan offered an entire new angle of vision through which he examined a now seemingly familiar phenomenon, revealing previously unrecognized connections between the Millerites and 19th-century culture.

While the Millerite movement has caught the interest of historians who have no personal connection with Adventism, the history of the Seventh-day Adventist Church has been written almost entirely by members. John N. Loughborough, one of the denomination's pioneer ministers, published the first general account of the church's history under the title *Rise and Progress of Seventh-day Adventists*, which later appeared in an expanded edition entitled *The Great Second Advent Movement*. Combining personal memoir, extracts from documents, and a strongly apologetic purpose, Loughborough is not always reliable but his work is valuable for revealing the self-understanding of Adventism's first generation. M. Ellsworth Olsen's *A History of the Origin and Progress of Seventh-day Adventists*, in contrast, is surprisingly objective in tone and provides a still useful account of Adventism into the early 20th century. Both Loughborough and Olsen presented Seventh-day Adventism as the true spiritual heir of the Millerite movement, a view that differed greatly from Wellcome's earlier work.

As Adventism continued to develop into the mid-20th century, interest in its history increased. Arthur Whitefield Spalding presented a largely anecdotal history in his *Origin and History of Seventh-day Adventists* while C. Mervyn Maxwell focused on the development of Adventist theology in his apologetic *Tell It to the World*. Both authors emphasized narrative over analysis and Maxwell ended his account in the early 20th century. Gary Land's edited volume, *Adventism in America* (listed below under North America), was the first attempt to present a scholarly general account of the denomination's history, although as the title suggested the volume gave attention only to American Adventism. One of the contributors to Land's volume, Richard W. Schwarz, provided what remains the broadest account of Adventist history in his college level textbook, *Light Bearers to the Remnant*. Although dense with facts and providing few interpretive themes, Schwarz's book was remarkably balanced in tone and examined the worldwide expansion of the church. The second edition of this volume, recently revised by Floyd Greenleaf, develops further the discussion of global Adventism.

Although over 90 percent of Adventists now live outside the United States, the world church has received slight specialized study from historians. Gideon Hagstotz's *Seventh-day Adventists in the British Isles* was the first substantive study of Adventism abroad, but the most thorough work thus far is Floyd Greenleaf's extensively researched *The Seventh-day Adventist Church in Latin America and the Caribbean*. Another useful book on the Caribbean is Eric John Murray's *A History of the Seventh-day Adventist Church in Trinidad and Tobago, 1891-1981*. Adventists in the South Pacific Division have published several collections of papers on their history. Africa, similarly, has been the subject of two collections of papers as well as Kofi Owusu-Mensa's *Saturday God and Adventism in Ghana*. With the exception of R. S. Fernando's *The Isles Shall Not Wait*, Adventist history in Asia has received little attention.

While Adventists have written many topical histories, most are of a highly popular nature, emphasizing narrative over analysis and detailed research. Harold O. McCumber, *Pioneering the Message in the Golden West*, and Doug Johnson, *Adventism on the Northwestern Frontier*, examine aspects of the regional expansion of Adventism in North America. P. Gerard Damsteegt, *Foundations of the Seventh-day Adventist Message and Mission*, offers a detailed account of the development of early Adventist theology while Paul A. Gordon, *The Sanctuary, 1844, and the Pioneers*, provides a useful popular discussion of a specific doctrinal issue. A. V. Olsen presents a positive overview of the 1888 controversy regarding righteousness by faith in *Through Crisis to Victory*, but provides little hint that the issue continued to haunt the denomination in the 20th century. Howard Week's *Adventist Evangel-*

ism in the Twentieth Century remains useful, although it covers little after 1960. Adventist religious liberty advocacy has received thorough examination in Douglas Morgan's *Adventism and the American Republic*. And while it addresses more than Adventist thought, Ronald L. Numbers's *The Creationists* offers a thorough and insightful account of Adventism's significant contribution to this movement. Popularly written accounts of African American and Hispanic Adventist history appear in Louis B. Reynolds's *We Have Tomorrow* and Mauel Vasquez's *The Untold Story*.

As of this writing there is no adequate history of Adventist education, although such a work is forthcoming from Floyd Greenleaf. Nonetheless, Maurice Hodgen's *School Bells & Gospel Trumpets* provides an excellent collection of documents and George R. Knight has edited a good collection of short biographies in *Early Adventist Educators*. Brian E. Strayer has written the only book-length history of an academy in *Where the Pine Trees Softly Whisper* (Union Springs Academy), while useful college histories include Everett N. Dick, *Union: College of the Golden Cords* (Union College), Emmett K. Vande Vere, *The Wisdom Seekers* (Andrews University), Dennis Lynn Pettibone, *A Century of Challenge* (Southern Adventist University), Terrie Dopp Aamodt, *Bold Venture* (Walla Walla College), Walter C. Utt, *A Mountain, A Pickax, A College* (Pacific Union College), and Meredith Jones Gray, *As We Set Forth* (Andrews University).

Denominational publishing houses have published many autobiographies and memoirs, beginning with Joseph Bates's *Autobiography* in 1868, which interestingly devotes only a few pages to his Adventist years. James White's *Life Incidents* and Ellen's *Life Sketches* provide personal accounts of the early years of the Adventist movement. W. B. Hill's *Experiences* offers a unique account of 19th-century Adventist evangelism and ministry. Of the many missionary autobiographies and memoirs W. H. Anderson's *On the Trail of Livingston*, Leo B. Halliwell's *Light in the Jungle*, and F. A. Stahl's *In the Land of the Incas* are notable. George E. Vandeman recounts his experiences in television evangelism in *My Dream* while Richard Hammill recalls his life as a missionary and educational and church administrator in *Pilgrimage*. Useful accounts by those who have become disenchanted with the denomination include Merikay McLeod's *Betrayal* and Jerry Gladson's *A Theologian's Journey from Seventh-day Adventism to Mainstream Christianity*.

There is also a plethora of Adventist biographies, but only a few have scholarly substance. Gerald Wheeler's *James White* provides a popularly written account of one of Seventh-day Adventism's founders. Joseph Bates's life has been researched more thoroughly in Godfrey T.

Anderson's *Outrider of the Apocalypse* and George R. Knight's *Joseph Bates*. Arthur L. White has written a 6-volume biography of his grand-mother, *Ellen G. White*, which provides a detailed chronology of her life but offers virtually no analysis or interpretation. In contrast, Ronald L. Numbers critically examines the development of White's health re-form ideas in *Prophetess of Health*. In *The Shaping of Adventism* Gil-bert M. Valentine thoroughly examines the life of William W. Prescott, an influential Adventist editor and educator. Richard W. Schwarz's *John Harvey Kellogg* is based upon solid research but provides no documentation. Two Adventist dissidents have also received attention. George R. Knight examines Alonzo T. Jones in *From 1888 to Apos-tasy*, a well-researched volume that takes a rather negative view of its subject. Albion F. Ballenger, critic of the sanctuary doctrine, is the sub-ject of Calvin W. Edwards and Gary Land's *Seeker After Light*. Robert E. Edwards has written one of the few substantive biographies of a 20th century Adventist leader in *H. M. S. Edwards*, an account of the radio evangelism pioneer.

Beliefs, Practices, and Polity

While Seventh-day Adventists have produced hundreds of books on doctrinal and theological issues, most of these works have been written for evangelistic purposes and tend to have little theological or intellec-tual profundity. Beneath these works, however, there is a foundation of more substantive and original books that explore these matters in some depth.

Historically significant overviews of Adventist belief include James White's *The Biblical Institute*, Uriah Smith's *Synopsis of the Present Truth*, and Francis M. Wilcox's *What the Bible Teaches*. In addition, *Bible Readings* collects biblical texts on doctrinal issues and was long a staple in Adventist homes. Currently, however, the best overview of Adventist theology is Richard Rice's college-level text-book, *Reign of God. Seventh-day Adventists Believe . . .* provides an exposition of the denomination's 27 fundamental beliefs. Fritz Guy presents a sophisticated analysis of theological method in *Thinking Theologically*, while Raul Dederen's edited work, *Handbook of Sev-enth-day Adventist Theology*, is an indispensable reference work. Ste-ven G. Daily calls for a rethinking of Adventist belief in *Adventism for a New Generation*, though few seem to have pursued his suggestions. Recently Norman Gulley has published the first volume of an Adventist *Systematic Theology*.

The Seventh-day Adventist Bible Commentary provides the most authoritative example of Adventist approaches to the Bible. Since the commentary's publication in the 1950s, issues of interpretation and inspiration have received considerable attention. Gordon Hyde edited *A Symposium on Biblical Hermeneutics* for a series of 1974 Bible conferences held for ministers and teachers. Alden Thompson's *Inspiration*, which examines how God works through human language and culture, provoked controversy, some of which is reflected in the Adventist Theological Society's *Issues in Revelation and Inspiration*, edited by Frank Holbrook and Leo van Dolson. Samuel Koranteng-Pipim also critically responds to Thompson and others in *Receiving the Word*.

Although not officially regarded as an extra-biblical source of doctrine, the writings of Ellen G. White have shaped Adventist understanding of the Bible and theology. Among her many books, the most important are those included in the "Conflict of the Ages" series (*Patriarchs and Prophets, Prophets and Kings, The Desire of Ages, Acts of the Apostles*, and *The Great Controversy*), which presents a comprehensive view of salvation history in light of what she describes as the controversy between Christ and Satan. In addition, *Steps to Christ* examines the stages of Christian experience while *Christ's Object Lessons* and *Thoughts from the Mount of Blessing* discuss the teachings of Jesus. White also applied her understanding of Christian principles to two major Adventist endeavors in *The Ministry of Healing* and *Education*.

Given her foundational role in the formation of the church, Adventists have written a number of books affirming the continuing importance of Ellen G. White. Among the more significant of these are Arthur Gosvenor Daniells, *The Abiding Gift of Prophecy*, William A. Spicer, *The Spirit of Prophecy in the Advent Movement*, and Lewis Harrison Christian, *The Fruitage of the Spiritual Gifts*. *The Spirit of Prophecy in the Remnant Church* collects documents illustrating Adventist understanding of Ellen White's role in its faith. T. Housel Jemison's *A Prophet Among You* and Herbert E. Douglass's *Messenger of the Lord* are college-level textbooks; the latter volume responds to the issues that had emerged in the 1970s, including White's alleged plagiarism and errors and her relationship to 19th-century American culture. Among the few systematic studies of Ellen White's thought are Woodrow Whidden's *Ellen White on Salvation* and *Ellen White on the Humanity of Christ*.

Adventists have written relatively few books on the doctrine of God. J. H. Waggoner's *The Spirit of God* reflects the anti-trinitarian views of 19th-century Adventism, but W. H. Branson's *The Holy Spirit* reveals the degree of change that had taken place by the 1930s. Edward Vick's *Speaking Well of God*, A. Graham Maxwell's *Can God Be*

Trusted, and Alden Thompson's *Who's Afraid of the Old Testament God?* are among the more significant recent works. The multi-author *The Trinity* provides both a historical and theological discussion. Richard Rice's controversial *The Openness of God* criticized traditional notions of God's foreknowledge.

The nature of Christ has been a significant issue for Adventists throughout their history. Uriah Smith's *Looking Unto Jesus* expresses the semi-Arian understanding characteristic of early Adventists. In contrast, W. W. Prescott's *The Doctrine of Christ* reveals the recognition of Christ's full divinity that had developed within Adventism by the 1920s. Recent discussions of Jesus have revolved around whether his human nature was similar to that of Adam before the fall or to humanity's post-fall situation. Edward Heppenstall argues for the orthodox view of Christ's sinless nature in *The Man Who Was God* while Ralph Larson asserts that he had a fallen human nature in *The Word Was Made Flesh*. Excellent analyses of this debate appear in Eric Webster's *Crosscurrents in Adventist Christology* and Roy Adams's *The Nature of Christ*.

The understanding of Christ's human nature directly impacts Adventist conceptions of salvation and sanctification, for if Christ had a fallen human nature and yet lived a perfect life then perfection is within the reach of all true Christians. E. J. Waggoner, who helped move the church away from legalism in the 1880s and 1890s, presented his understanding of righteousness by faith in *Christ and His Righteousness*. By the time Arthur G. Daniells wrote *Christ Our Righteousness* in the 1920s, the doctrine had become well established within Adventism. For Adventists, however, righteousness by faith included sanctification as well as justification and hence debate emerged over their relationship to one another. Many books appeared addressing these issues but the multi-author *Perfection* provides a good entry point into the major viewpoints. Other significant books on salvation include Edward Heppenstall, *Salvation Unlimited*, Hans K. LaRondelle, *Christ Our Salvation*, and Edward W. H. Vick, *Is Salvation Really Free?* Martin Webber addresses the variety of Adventist viewpoints in *Who's Got the Truth?*

Although the Bible, Christology, and salvation are issues central to all Christians, the Sabbath, while not unique, is a distinctive Adventist doctrine. John Nevins Andrews's *History of the Sabbath*, which went through several editions, strongly shaped Adventist understandings of how Christianity had moved from Saturday to Sunday observance. More recent examinations of Sabbath history include Kenneth Strand's edited collection of essays, *The Sabbath in Scripture and History*, and Samuele Bacchiocchi's *From Sabbath to Sunday*. A traditional biblical argument for observing the seventh day appears in M. L. Andreasen's *The Sabbath*, but increasingly Adventists have sought to explain the theological significance of the Sabbath. Among works exploring the meaning of Sabbath observance are Samuele Bacchiocci's *Divine Rest for Human Restlessness*, John Brunt's *A Day for Healing*, and Sakae Kubo's *God Meets Man*.

Largely because Genesis 1-2 portrays the Sabbath as the final day of the creation story, Adventists have strongly argued for the historicity of the biblical account. George McCready Price developed the theory of "flood geology," which lies behind most modern creationism. Of his many books, *The New Geology* is the most comprehensive. Frank Lewis Marsh introduces a genetic component to creationism by attempting to identify the "kinds" of Genesis in *Evolution, Creation, and Science*, while Harold W. Clark modifies Price's flood geology by introducing the theory of ecological zonation in *The New Diluvialism*. Subsequent books, including Harold Coffin's *Accident or Design?* and Leonard Brand's *Faith, Reason, and Earth History*, synthesize and refine these theories. Less traditional approaches to creation appear in Richard Ritland's *A Search for Meaning in Nature* and James Hayward's edited collection of papers presented at a conference organized by the Association of Adventist Forums and published under the title *Creation Reconsidered*.

Another distinctive Adventist belief is conditional immortality, which asserts that immortality comes only at the resurrection. Uriah Smith wrote an early exposition of this view in *The State of the Dead and the Destiny of the Wicked*. A mid-20th century treatment of conditionalism is *Life, Death, and Immortality* by Carlyle B. Haynes. LeRoy Edwin Froom argues that conditionalism had a long tradition within Christianity in his well-researched but difficult to read *The Conditionalist Faith of Our Fathers*. Of more recent works, J. R. Zurcher's *The Nature and Destiny of Man* explores conditionalism's philosophical implications and Samuele Bacchiochi's *Immortality or Resurrection?* reexamines its biblical basis.

Not just distinctive, the closely related doctrines of the sanctuary and investigative or pre-Advent judgment (both usually referred to together as the "sanctuary doctrine") are unique Adventist views that rose directly out of their "Great Disappointment" experience. Although there were previous writings on the topic, E. E. Andross, *A More Excellent Ministry*, and Stephen N. Haskell, *The Cross and Its Shadow*, were important efforts to explain the doctrine in detail. M. L. Andreasen's *The Sanctuary Service* offers a more thorough mid-20th century biblical and theological examination. Edward Heppenstall's *Our High Priest* focuses on the priestly ministry of Jesus in heaven, while Herbert

E. Douglass utilizes the sanctuary doctrine to explain the delay of the Second Advent in *Why Jesus Waits*. When Desmond Ford criticized the traditional Adventist position in *Daniel 8:14, The Day of Atonement and the Investigative Judgment*, he provoked several written responses. Among these, Roy Adams explores the history of the debate over the belief in *The Sanctuary Doctrine* and explores its theological significance in his popularly written *The Sanctuary*. Collections of scholarly papers presented to General Conference Daniel and Revelation Committee offer more technical approaches to the issues involved. From a somewhat different angle, Leslie Hardinge discusses the meaning of the Jewish services in relationship to Christ in *With Jesus in His Sanctuary*. More recently, in *Investigating the Judgment* John T. Anderson focuses on the meaning of a pre-Advent judgment.

Although the sanctuary doctrine has been an issue in itself, it is part of Adventism's interpretation of biblical prophecy and eschatology. Uriah Smith's *Thoughts on the Book of Daniel and the Revelation*, which continued the historicist approach inherited from William Miller, dominated Adventist thinking about prophecy for nearly a century. A recent similar work is C. Mervyn Maxwell's *God Cares*. LeRoy Edwin Froom provides a historical apologetic for Adventist approaches to prophecy in his extensively researched but idiosyncratically written *The Prophetic Faith of Our Fathers*.

Since the 1970s, several Adventist commentaries on the books of Daniel and Revelation have appeared, among them Desmond Ford's *Daniel*, Jacques Doukhan's *Secrets of Daniel* and *Secrets of Revelation*, and Ranko Stefanovic's *Revelation of Jesus Christ*. Kenneth Strand, *Interpreting the Book of Revelation*, and Hans K. LaRondelle, *The Israel of God in Prophecy*, address the methodology of prophetic interpretation, while *The Advent Hope in Scripture and History* collects several scholarly papers on eschatology. More general discussions of eschatology include Herbert E. Douglass, *The End*, Samuele Bacchiocchi, *The Advent Hope for Human Hopelessness*, and Jon Paulien, *What the Bible Says about the End-Time*.

Adventists generally have regarded the church as the means through which they take their message to the world. Much of their writing on the church has consequently dealt with organizational issues. John Loughborough's *The Church* functioned as an unofficial guidebook until the first *Church Manual* appeared in 1932. In recent years some writers have begun to examine the theology of the church, notably Russell L. Staples in *Community of Faith* and Richard Rice in *Believing, Behaving, Belonging*. Gottfried Oosterwall's *Mission Possible* introduced serious reflection on missiology and has been followed most significantly by Jon Dybdahl's edited collection, *Adventist Mission in the 21st Century*. Most Adventist writing on women deals with the issue of ordination, and thus is an aspect of the understanding of ecclesiology. Nancy Vhymeister's edited volume, *Women in Ministry*, provides a representative entry into arguments favoring ordination, while Mercedes Dyer's *Prove All Things*, another collection of essays, offers the opposition view. Laura L. Vance's *Seventh-day Adventism in Crisis* provides an observer's sociological analysis of the status of women in the denomination.

Particularly since the mid-20th century Adventists have written many books on the related themes of the Christian life and spirituality. Taylor G. Bunch was one of the first Adventists to probe these themes in depth; *Secrets of Godly Living* is one of his widely read works. More recently Morris Venden has written numerous books interpreting the implications of theology for personal life; *How to Know God's Will in Your Life* is but one example. Dwight K. Nelson has also had extensive influence through such works as *Outrageous Grace*.

Within the general theme of spirituality Adventists have given much of their attention to prayer. In the 1950s Louis K. Dickson addressed this subject in *Key in the Hand*, while in the following decade Glenn A. Coon attracted considerable attention with his *The ABCs of Bible Prayer*. The emphasis on intercessory prayer continues in the several works of Roger Morneau, including *The Incredible Power of Prayer*. More recently, Carol Shewmake has emphasized personal spiritual growth and sensitivity in *Sanctuary Secrets to Personal Prayer* and other books.

Adventist writers have provided many works to guide Adventist parents and their children. Arthur W. Spalding and Belle Wood-Comstock wrote several books that offered authoritative advice in the 1920s and 1930s; Harold Shyrock's numerous volumes played a similar role in the 1940s and 1950s. Charles E. Wittshiebe introduced a new era of frankness regarding sex in the early 1970s with *God Invented Sex*. Books by Alberta Mazat and Nancy Van Pelt have been particularly influential in subsequent years. In contrast to these advice books, Adventists have also pursued empirical research. Charles C. Crider and Robert C. Kristler wrote the first book-length study of *The Seventh-day Adventist Family*; more recently the ValueGenesis study has produced several volumes of data, analysis, and reflection on the attitudes and behavior of high-school-age Adventists.

Adventist writings on health go back to the early years of the organized denomination. Up through the mid-20th century, the denomination provided several authoritative general guides to health and health care, among them John Harvey Kellogg's *Home Hand-Book*, Newton Evans, et al., *The Home Physician and Guide to Health*, and

Hubert Swartout, et al., *Modern Medical Counselor*. Less encyclopedic
and more inspirational works, such as Lewis R. Walton, et al., *How
You Can Live Six Extra Years*, and David C. Nieman's *The Adventist
Healthstyle* have been typical of recent publications. The most important recent publication, however, is Gary E. Fraser's *Diet, Life Expectancy, and Chronic Disease*, which examines the results of the ongoing
Adventist Health Study. Along with a general interest in health, the
denomination has also strongly advocated abstinence from alcohol,
tobacco, and nonmedical drugs. Francis Nichol's *The Case Against
Liquor* is typical of the temperance literature published in the first half
of the 20th century. More recently denominational writers, such as
Walter E. Kloss in *Addiction*, have recognized that intemperance is a
medical as well as moral issue. In contrast, Samuele Bacchiocchi has
offered a biblical argument for abstention in *Wine in the Bible*.

In *Millennial Dreams and Moral Dilemmas* Michael Pearson has
provided the broadest analysis of Adventist ethical thinking. The various publications of the Loma Linda University Center for Christian
Bioethics address issues faced by Adventist medical practitioners and
institutions. Despite their extensive educational enterprise, Adventists
have written relatively little on educational philosophy or practice. Important exceptions are Raymond S. Moore and Todd C. Murdock's
Adventist Education at the Crossroads, which argued that the denomination's schools had lost their unique vision, and Reuben Hilde's response in *Showdown*, which evaluated Adventist education more positively. The *Christ in the Classroom* volumes provide insight into attempts by Adventist college and university teachers to understand their
disciplines within the perspective of their Christian faith. The works of
Raymond and Dorothy Moore, including *Home Grown Kids*, have
helped inspire and shape the home school movement in the United
States. Traditional Adventist opposition to jazz, rock, and related music
appears in Paul Hamel's *The Christian and His Music* and Samuele
Bacchiocchi's *The Christian and Rock Music*; Ed Christian's *Joyful
Noise* takes a more sympathetic view of Contemporary Christian Music's influence on Adventism. Written for both college teachers and
their students, Delmer Davis's *Teaching Literature* and Gary Land's
Teaching History include useful accounts of the history of Adventist
views of these subjects. Roger Dudley and Edwin I. Hernandez report
their empirical study of American Adventist political attitudes in *Citizens of Two Worlds*, which describes and explains the several significant differences between Adventists and other conservative Christians.
William A. Blakely's *American State Papers*, which has appeared in
several editions, remains a valuable collection of primary documents
for the study of the history of American religious liberty.

Among the several works criticizing Seventh-day Adventism, a few have been particularly influential. Until the mid-20th century, most critics drew upon D. M. Canright's *Seventh-day Adventism Renounced*. Rather than depending on Canright, Anthony Hoekema's *The Four Major Cults*, written from a Reformed perspective, extensively examined Adventist writings. Walter Martin's *The Truth About Seventh-day Adventists* drew upon both Adventist literature and conversations with denominational leaders. When Martin concluded, unlike Hoekema a few years later, that Adventists were indeed Christians, he stirred up considerable controversy in fundamentalist and evangelical circles. In recent years Dale Ratzlaff, a former Adventist minister, has written widely read critiques, including *Sabbath in Crisis* (revised as *Sabbath in Christ*) and *The Cultic Doctrine of Seventh-day Adventists*, the latter largely focused on the sanctuary doctrine. Of Adventist responses to their critics, *Questions on Doctrine*, originally written to provide information for Martin, remains the most thorough and least defensive, although readers would be best served by using the recent edition annotated by George R. Knight. Samuele Bacchiocchi's *Sabbath under Crossfire* responds to Ratzlaff's criticisms of the Sabbath doctrine.

Of the general interpretations of Adventism, Malcolm Bull's and Keith Lockhart's *Seeking a Sanctuary* is the most ambitious, seeing Adventism as an alternative version of the American dream. Russell L. Staples's essay in *The Varieties of Evangelicalism* helpfully sorts out both the similarities and differences between Adventist and evangelical theology and practice.

The following bibliography is subdivided as follows:

General Reference

Neufeld, Don F., et al, eds. *Seventh-day Adventist Encyclopedia*, 2nd rev. ed., Commentary Reference Series, vols. 11-12. Hagerstown, MD: Review and Herald, 1996.

Seventh-day Adventist Yearbook. Office of Archives and Statistics, General Conference of Seventh-day Adventists. Washington, DC, 1883-1894, 1904-.

Primary Source Material

Baker, Delbert, comp. *Telling the Story: An Anthology on the Development of the Black SDA Work.* Loma Linda, CA: Loma Linda University Printing Services, 1996.

Bates, Joseph, et al. *Early S.D.A. Pamphlets.* Payson, AZ: Leaves-of-Autumn Books, 1982.

Hodgen, Maurice, ed. *School Bells & Gospel Trumpets: A Documentary History of Seventh-day Adventist Education in North America.* Loma Linda, CA: Adventist Heritage, 1978.

Knight, George R., ed. *1844 and the Rise of Sabbatarian Adventism.* Hagerstown, MD: Review and Herald, 1994.

Vande Vere, Emmett K., comp. *Windows: Selected Readings in Seventh-day Adventist Church History, 1844-1922.* Nashville: Southern, 1975.

Backgrounds to Seventh-day Adventist History

Arasola, Kai. *The End of Historicism: Millerite Hermeneutic of Time Prophecies in the Old Testament,* rev. ed. Uppsala: n.p., 1990.

Ball, Bryan W. *The English Connection: The Puritan Roots of Seventh-day Adventist Belief.* Cambridge: James Clarke, 1981.

———. *The Seventh-day Men: Sabbatarians and Sabbatarianism in England and Wales, 1600-1800.* Oxford: Clarendon Press, 1994.

Barkun, Michael. *Crucible of the Millennium: The Burned-Over District of New York in the 1840s.* Syracuse, NY: Syracuse University Press, 1986.

Boyer, Paul S. *When Time Shall Be No More: Prophecy Belief in Modern American Culture.* Cambridge, MA: Belknap Press of Harvard University Press, 1992.

Carwardine, Richard. *Transatlantic Revivalism: Popular Evangelicalism in Britain and America, 1790-1865.* Westport, CT: Greenwood Press, 1978.

Clark, Jerome. *1844.* 3 vols. Nashville: Southern, 1968.

Cross, Whitney R. *The Burned-Over District: The Social and Intellectual History of Enthusiastic Religion in Western New York, 1800-1850.* Ithaca: Cornell University Press, 1950.

Dick, Everett N. *William Miller and the Advent Crisis, 1831-1844.* Edited with Foreword and Historiographical Essay by Gary Land. Berrien Springs, MI: Andrews University Press, 1994.

Doan, Ruth Alden. *The Miller Heresy, Millennialism, and American Culture.* Philadelphia: Temple University Press, 1987.

Emmerson, W. L. *The Reformation and the Advent Movement*. Washington, DC: Review and Herald, 1983.

Festinger, Leon, Henry W. Riecken, and Stanley Schachter. *When Prophecy Fails: A Social and Psychological Study of a Modern Group that Predicted the Destruction of the World*. Minneapolis, MN: University of Minnesota, 1956; 2nd ed., New York: Harper & Row, 1964.

Gaustad, Edwin, ed. *The Rise of Adventism: Religion and Society in Mid-Nineteenth Century America*. New York: Harper and Row, 1975.

Hardinge, Leslie. *The Celtic Church in Britain*. London: S.P.C.K. for the Church Historical Society, 1972; reprint, Brushton, NY: TEACH Services, 1995.

Harrison, J. F. C. *The Second Coming: Popular Millenarianism, 1780-1950*. New Brunswick, NJ: Rutgers University Press, 1979.

Hatch, Nathan O. *The Democratization of American Christianity*. New Haven, CT: Yale University Press, 1989.

Hewitt, Clyde E. *Midnight and Morning*. Charlotte, NC: Venture Books, 1983.

Knight, George R. *Millennial Fever and the End of the World: A Study of Millerite Adventism*. Boise, ID: Pacific Press, 1993.

Liechty, Daniel. *Sabbatarianism in the Sixteenth Century: A Page in the History of the Radical Reformation*. Berrien Springs, MI: Andrews University Press, 1993.

Morgan, David. *Protestants and Pictures: Religion, Visual Culture, and the Age of American Mass Production*. New York: Oxford University Press, 1999.

Nichol, Francis D. *The Midnight Cry*. Washington, DC: Review and Herald, 1947.

Numbers, Ronald L., and Jonathan M. Butler, eds. *The Disappointed: Millerism and Millenarianism in the Nineteenth Century*. Bloomington, IN: Indiana University Press, 1987.

Rowe, David L. *Thunder and Trumpets: Millerites and Dissenting Religion in Upstate New York, 1800-1850*. Chico, CA: Scholars Press, 1985.

Sandeen, Ernest R. *The Roots of Fundamentalism: British and American Millenarianism, 1800-1930*. Chicago, IL: University of Chicago Press, 1970.

Sears, Clara Endicott. *Days of Delusion: A Strange Bit of History*. Boston, MA: Houghton Mifflin, 1924.

Thomas, N. Gordon. *The Millennial Impulse in Michigan, 1830-1860: The Second Coming in the Third New England*. Lewiston, NY: Edward Mellen Press, 1989.

Tyler, Alice Felt. *Freedom's Ferment: Phases of American Social History to 1860*. Minneapolis, MN: University of Minnesota Press, 1944.

Weber, Timothy P. *Living in the Shadow of the Second Coming: American Premillennialism (1875-1925)*. New York: Oxford University Press, 1979; 2nd. ed., Grand Rapids, MI: Academie Books, Zondervan Publishing House, 1983.

Wellcome, Isaac C. *History of the Second Advent Message and Mission, Doctrine and People*. Yarmouth, ME: by the author, 1874.

Seventh-day Adventist History

General

Andross, Matilda Erickson. *Story of the Advent Message*. Washington, DC: Review and Herald, 1926.

Balbach, A. *The History of the Seventh-day Adventist Reform Movement*. Roanoke, VA: Reformation Herald, 1999.

Brown, Walton J., comp. *Chronology of Seventh-day Adventist Education*. Washington, DC: Department of Education, General Conference of Seventh-day Adventists, 1972.

———. *Patterns of Seventh-day Adventist Education: Century of Adventist Education 1872-1971*. Washington, DC: Department of Education, General Conference of Seventh-day Adventists, 1972.

Cadwallader, E. M. *A History of Seventh-day Adventist Education*. Lincoln, NE: Union College Press, 1958.

Education Department, General Conference of Seventh-day Adventists. *The Story of Our Church*. Mountain View, CA: Pacific Press, 1956.

Herndon, Booten. *The Seventh Day: The Story of Seventh-day Adventists*. New York: McGraw-Hill, 1960.

Historical Sketches of Foreign Missions. Basel, Switzerland: Imprimerie Polyglotte, 1886.

Howell, Emma E. *The Great Advent Movement*. Washington, DC: Review and Herald, 1935.

Knight, George R. *Anticipating the Advent: A Brief History of Seventh-day Adventists*. Boise, ID: Pacific Press, 1993.

———. *A Brief History of Seventh-day Adventists*. Hagerstown, MD: Review and Herald, 1999.

Loughborough, John N. *The Great Second Advent Movement*. Nashville, TN: Southern, 1905.

———. *Rise and Progress of the Seventh-day Adventists*. Battle Creek, MI: General Conference Association of Seventh-day Adventists, 1892.

Maxwell, C. Mervyn. *Tell It to the World: The Story of Seventh-day Adventists*. Mountain View, CA: Pacific Press, 1976.

Mitchell, David. *Seventh-day Adventists: Faith in Action*. New York: Vantage Press, 1958.

Olsen, M. Ellsworth. *Origin and Progress of Seventh-day Adventists*. Washington, DC: Review and Herald, 1975.

Outline of Mission Fields Entered by Seventh-day Adventists. Washington, DC: Mission Board of Seventh-day Adventists, 1905.

Pöehler, Rolf. *Continuity and Change in Adventist Teaching: A Case Study in Doctrinal Development*. New York: Peter Lang, 2000.

Schwarz, Richard W. *Light Bearers to the Remnant: Denominational History Textbook for Seventh-day Adventist College History Classes*. Mountain View, CA: Pacific Press, 1979; 2nd. ed., Schwarz, Richard W., and Floyd Greenleaf. *Light Bearers: A History of the Seventh-day Adventist Church*. Nampa, ID: Pacific Press, 2000.

Spalding, Arthur W. *Captains of the Host: First Volume of a History of Seventh-day Adventists Covering the Years 1845-1900; Christ's Last Legion: Second Volume of a History of Seventh-day Adventists, Covering the Years, 1901-1948*. Washington, DC: Review and Herald, 1949. Also published as *Origin and History of Seventh-day Adventists*. 4 vols. Washington, DC: Review and Herald, 1961.

Spicer, William A. *After One Hundred Years, 1844-1944; How the Work of Seventh-day Adventists Has Spread to the Ends of the Earth*. Takoma Park, DC: Review and Herald, 1944.

———. *Miracles of Modern Missions: Gathered Out of the Mission Records*. Washington, DC: Review and Herald, 1926.

———. *Our Story of Missions*. Mountain View, CA: Pacific Press, 1921.

Steele, Allen. *Loud Let It Ring: Twenty-five Years of Miracles*. Boise, ID: Pacific Press, 1996.

Africa

Elineema, K. B., ed. *Development of the SDA Church in Eastern Africa*. Dar es Salaam, Tanzania: Dar es Salaam University Press, 1995.

Owusu-Mensa, Kofi. *Saturday God and Adventism in Ghana*. New York: Peter Lang, 1993.

Pfeiffer, Baldur, ed. *Seventh-day Adventist Contributions to East Africa, 1903-1983*. New York: Peter Lang, 1985.

Robinson, Virgil. *The Solusi Story: Times of Peace, Times of Peril*. Washington, DC: Review and Herald, 1979.

Asia

Allen, Sydney. *One Week with a Modern Missionary*. Washington, DC: Review and Herald, 1970.

Fernando, R. S. *The Isles Shall Not Wait: The Story of Seventh-day Adventists in Sri Lanka*. Colombo, Sri Lanka: Associated Newspapers of Ceylon, n.d.

Images 1893-1993: The Seventh-day Adventist Church in Southern Asia. Pune, India: Oriental Watchman, 1993.

Oss, John. *Mission Advance in China*. Nashville, TN: Southern, 1949.

Warren, L. Donald. *Isles of Opportunity; Progress and Possibilities in the Philippine Islands*. Washington, DC: Review and Herald, 1928.

Australia, New Zealand, and South Pacific

Ballis, Peter H., ed. *In and Out of the World: Seventh-day Adventists in New Zealand*. Palmerston North, New Zealand: Dunmore, 1985.

Bryson, John. *Evil Angels*. Ringwood, Victoria, Australia: Viking, 1985; New York: Summit Books, 1987.

Clapham, Noel P., ed. *Seventh-day Adventists in the South Pacific: 1885-1895*. Warburton, Victoria, Australia: Signs, 1985.

Ferch, Arthur J., ed. *Journey of Hope: Seventh-day Adventist History in the South Pacific, 1919-1950*. Warburton, Victoria, Australia: Signs, 1991.

———. *Symposium on Adventist History in the South Pacific, 1885-1918*. Warburton, Victoria, Australia, 1986.

Goldstone, S. Ross. *The Angel Said Australia*. Warburton, Victoria, Australia: Signs, 1980.

Hook, Milton Raymond. *Avondale: Experiment on the Dora*. Cooranbong, New South Wales, Australia: Avondale Academic Press, 1998.

Maxwell, Arthur S. *Under the Southern Cross*. Nashville: Southern, 1966.

Palmer, C. S. *Tales of Tonga*. Nashville, TN: Southern, 1959.

Watson, Charles H. *Cannibals and Head-hunters; Victories of the Gospel in the South Seas*. Washington, DC: Review and Herald, 1926.

Young, Rosalind Amelia. *Mutiny of the Bounty and Story of Pitcairn Island, 1790-1894*. Oakland, CA: Pacific Press, 1894.

Caribbean and Latin America

Amundsen, Wesley. *The Advent Message in Inter-America.* Washington, DC: Review and Herald, 1947.
Enoch, George F. *The Advent Message in the Sunny Caribbean.* Port of Spain, Trinidad: Watchman Publishing Company, 1907.
Greenleaf, Floyd. *The Seventh-day Adventist Church in Latin America and the Caribbean.* 2 vols. Berrien Springs, MI: Andrews University Press, 1992.
Murray, Eric John. *A History of the Seventh-day Adventist Church in Trinidad and Tobago, 1891-1981.* Port-of-Spain, Trinidad: College Press, 1982.
Phillips, Glenn O. *Over a Century of Adventism, 1884-1991.* Barbados: East Caribbean Conference of Seventh-day Adventists, 1991.

Europe, Great Britain, and Russia

Christian, Lewis H. *Pioneers and Builders of the Advent Cause in Europe.* Mountain View, CA: Pacific Press, 1937.
———. *Sons of the North and Their Share in the Advent Movement.* Mountain View, CA: Pacific Press, 1942.
Dunton, Hugh, et al., eds. *Heirs of the Reformation: The Story of the Seventh-day Adventist Church in Europe.* Grantham, Lincolnshire, England: Stanborough Press, Ltd., 1997.
Hagstotz, Gideon D. *The Seventh-day Adventists in the British Isles, 1878-1933.* Lincoln, NE: Union College Press, 1936.
Spiets, Marite. *True Witness: The Story of Seventh-day Adventists in the Soviet Union.* Keston, Kent, England: Keston College, 1990.

North America

Aamodt, Terrie Dopp. *Bold Venture: A History of Walla Walla College.* College Place, WA: Walla Walla College, 1992.
Beach, John G. *Notable Women of Spirit: The Historical Role of Women in the Seventh-day Adventist Church.* Nashville: Southern, 1976.
Brock, Peter. *Pacifism in the United States.* Princeton, NJ: Princeton University Press, 1968.
Covington, Ava Marie. *They Also Served: Stories of Pioneer Women of the Advent Movement.* Washington, DC: Review and Herald, 1940.
Damsteegt, P. Gerard. *Foundations of the Seventh-day Adventist Message and Mission.* Grand Rapids, MI: William B. Eerdmans, 1977.

Dick, Everett N. *Founders of the Message.* Washington, DC: Review and Herald, 1938.

————. *Union: College of the Golden Cords.* Lincoln, NE: Union College Press, 1967.

Dudley, Charles E. *Thou Who Hast Brought Us: The Development of the Seventh-day Adventist Denomination among African-Americans.* 3 vols. Brushton, NY: TEACH Services, 1997.

Ellis, Bob. *A Channel of Blessing.* West Frankfort, IL: New Authors Publications, n.d.

Erickson, Matilda. *Missionary Volunteers and Their Work.* Washington, DC: Review and Herald, n.d.

Fiedler, Dave. *Hindsight: Seventh-day Adventist History in Essays and Extracts.* Harrah, OK: Academy Enterprises, 1996.

Gordon, Paul A. *The Sanctuary, 1844, and the Pioneers.* Washington, DC: Review and Herald, 1983.

Graybill, Ronald. *E. G. White and Church Race Relations.* Washington, DC: Review and Herald, 1970.

————. *Mission to Black America: The True Story of James Edson White and the Riverboat MORNING STAR.* Mountain View, CA: Pacific Press, 1971.

Hansen, Louis. A. *From So Small a Dream.* Nashville, TN: Southern, 1968.

Hetzell, M. Carol. *The Undaunted: The Story of the Publishing Work of Seventh-day Adventists.* Mountain View, CA: Pacific Press, 1967.

Johns, Warren L., and Richard H. Utt, eds. *The Vision Bold: An Illustrated History of the Seventh-day Adventist Philosophy of Health.* Washington, DC: Review and Herald, 1977.

Johnson, Doug R. *Adventism on the Northwestern Frontier.* Foreword by Bruce Johnston. Berrien Springs, MI: Oronoko Books, 1996.

Jones Gray, Meredith. *As We Set Forth: Battle Creek College & Emmanuel Missionary College.* Berrien Springs, MI: Andrews University, 2002.

Justiss, Jacob. *Angels in Ebony.* Holland, OH: by the author, 1975.

Knight, George R., ed., *Early Adventist Educators.* Berrien Springs, MI: Andrews University Press, 1983.

Krum, Nathaniel. *The MV Story.* Washington, DC: Review and Herald, 1959.

Land, Gary, ed. *Adventism in America: A History.* Grand Rapids, MI: William B. Eerdmans Publishing Co., 1986; rev. ed., Berrien Springs, MI: Andrews University Press, 1998.

Lewis, Richard B. *Streams of Light: The Story of the Pacific Press.* Mountain View, CA: Pacific Press, 1958.

Lindén, Ingemar. *The Last Trump: A Historico-Genetical Study of Some Important Chapters in the Making and Development of the Seventh-day Adventist Church.* Frankfurt: Peter Lang, 1978.

McCumber, Harold O. *Pioneering the Message in the Golden West.* Mountain View, CA: Pacific Press, 1946.

Mole, Robert L., and Dale M. Mole. *For God and Country: Operation Whitecoat, 1954-1973.* Brushton, NY: TEACH Services, 1998.

Monteith, J. Ernest. *The Lord Is My Shepherd: A History of the Seventh-day Adventist Church in Canada.* Oshawa, ON: Canadian Union Conference of the Seventh-day Adventist Church, 1983.

Morgan, Douglas. *Adventism and the American Republic: The Public Involvement of a Major Apocalyptic Movement.* Foreword by Martin E. Marty. Knoxville: University of Tennessee Press, 2001.

Mustard, Andrew Gordon. *James White and SDA Organization: Historical Development, 1844-1881.* Andrews University, Seventh-day Adventist Theological Seminary Dissertation Series, vol. 12. Berrien Springs, MI: Andrews University Press, 1988.

Numbers, Ronald L. *The Creationists: The Evolution of Scientific Creationism.* New York: Alfred A. Knopf, 1992.

Ochs, Daniel, and Grace Ochs. *The Past and the Presidents.* Nashville, TN: Southern, 1974.

Oliver, Willie, with Patricia L. Humphrey. *We are the Pathfinders Strong: The First Fifty Years.* Hagerstown, MD: Review and Herald, 2000.

Olson, A. V. *Through Crisis to Victory, 1888-1901: From the Minneapolis Meeting to the Reorganization of the General Conference.* Washington, DC: Review and Herald, 1966.

Pettibone, Dennis Lynn. *A Century of Challenge: The Story of Southern College, 1892-1992.* Collegedale, TN: Board of Trustees, Southern College of Seventh-day Adventists, 1992.

Plummer, L. Flora. *From Acorn to Oak: A History of the Seventh-day Adventist Sabbath School Work.* Washington, DC: Review and Herald, 1910.

Publishing Department, General Conference of Seventh-day Adventists. *On the Trail of the Colporteur Evangelist; A Story of Miracles and Providences in Literature Ministry.* Washington, DC: Review and Herald, n.d.

Purdon, Rowena Elizabeth. *That New England School.* South Lancaster, MA: College Press, 1956.

Reid, George W. *A Sound of Trumpets: Americans, Adventists, and Health Reform.* Washington, DC: Review and Herald, 1982.

Reynolds, Louis B. *We Have Tomorrow: The Story of American Seventh-day Adventists with an African Heritage.* Washington, DC: Review and Herald, 1984.

Robinson, Dores E. *The Story of Our Health Message: The Origin, Character, and Development of Health Education in the Seventh-day Adventist Church.* Nashville, TN: Southern, 1943.

Schaefer, Richard A. *Legacy: Daring to Care, The Heritage of Loma Linda.* Loma Linda, CA: Legacy, 1990.

Spicer, William A. *Pioneer Days of the Advent Movement.* Washington, DC: Review and Herald, 1941.

Strayer, Brian E. *Where the Pine Trees Softly Whisper: The History of Union Springs Academy.* Union Springs, NY: Union Springs Academy Alumni Association, 1993.

Sutton, Arthur E. *The Heart Menders: The Dramatic Story of Open-Heart Surgery at Loma Linda University.* Nashville, TN: Southern, 1965.

Syme, Eric B. *A History of SDA Church-State Relations in the United States.* Mountain View, CA: Pacific Press, 1973.

Town, Nelson Z., et al. *The Publishing Department Story.* Washington, DC: Review and Herald, 1927.

Utt, Walter C. *A Mountain, A Pickax, A College: Walter Utt's History of Pacific Union College,* 3rd. ed., Afterword by Eric Anderson. Angwin, CA: Pacific Union College, 1996.

Vande Vere, Emmett K. *The Wisdom Seekers: The Intriguing Story of the Men and Women Who Made the First Institution for Higher Learning among Seventh-day Adventists.* Nashville, TN: Southern, 1972.

Vasquez, Manuel. *The Untold Story: 100 Years of Hispanic Adventism, 1899-1999.* Nampa, ID: Pacific Press, 2000.

Wall, Frank E., and Ava C. Wall. *Uncertain Journey: Adventist Workers with a Mennonite Heritage.* Washington, DC: Review and Herald, 1974.

Walton, Harold M., and Kathryn Jensen Nelson. *Historical Sketches of the Medical Work of Seventh-day Adventists from 1866 to 1896.* Washington, DC: Review and Herald, 1948.

Weeks, Howard B. *Adventist Evangelism in the Twentieth Century.* Washington, DC: Review and Herald, 1969.

Whetje, Myron F. *And There Was Light: A History of South Lancaster Academy, Lancaster Junior College and Atlantic Union College.* South Lancaster, MA: Atlantic Press, 1982.

Wilcox, Francis M. *Seventh-day Adventists in Time of War.* Washington, DC: Review and Herald, 1936.

Autobiographies, Memoirs, and Biographies

Autobiographies and Memoirs

Aitken, Dorothy. *My Love, The Amazon.* Nashville, TN: Southern, 1968.

Aitken, James J., and Dorothy Aitken. *White Wings, Green Jungle: The Story of the Fernando Stahl, the First Seventh-day Adventist Missionary Plane in South America.* Mountain View, CA: Pacific Press, 1966.

Anderson, Emma. *With Our Missionaries in China.* Mountain View, CA: Pacific Press, 1920.

Anderson, W. H. *On the Trail of Livingstone.* Mountain View, CA: Pacific Press, 1919.

Bates, Joseph. *The Autobiography of Elder Joseph Bates.* Battle Creek, MI: Steam Press of the Seventh-day Adventist Publishing Association, 1868. Reprinted as James White, ed., *The Early Life and Later Experience and Labors of Elder Joseph Bates.* Battle Creek, MI: Steam Press of the Seventh-day Adventist Publishing Association, 1878; *Life of Joseph Bates: An Autobiography,* abridged and edited, C. C. Crisler. Washington, DC: Review and Herald, 1927; *The Autobiography of Elder Joseph Bates.* Nashville, TN: Southern, 1970.

Beitzakhar, Michael Simonivitch. *Light Through the Shadows: The True Life Story of Michael Simonivitch Beitzakhar,* trans. and ed., Daniel V. Kubrock. Washington, DC: Review and Herald, 1953.

Bliss, Sylvester. *Memoirs of William Miller Generally Known as a Lecturer on the Prophecies and the Second Coming of Christ.* Boston: Joshua V. Himes, 1853.

Branson, William H. *Missionary Adventures in Africa.* Washington, DC: Review and Herald, 1925.

Cleveland, Clyde C. *Indonesian Adventure for Christ.* Washington, DC: Review and Herald, 1965.

Cleveland, E. E. *Let the Church Roll On: An Autobiography.* Boise, ID: Pacific Press, 1997.

Cooper, Charles S. *Wilderness Parish.* Mountain View, CA: Pacific Press, 1961.

Cristler, Clarence C. *China's Borderlands and Beyond.* Takoma Park Washington, DC: Review and Herald, 1937.

Davy, Yvonne. *Going with God; On Missions of Mercy in Central Africa.* Washington, DC: Review and Herald, 1959.

Delker, Del. *Del Delker: Her Story.* Nampa, ID: Pacific Press, 2002.

Fagal, William and Virginia. *This is Our Story.* Mountain View, CA: Pacific Press, 1980.

Ford, Mrs. Orley. *In the High Andes.* Nashville, TN: Southern, 1932.

Gates, E. H. *In Coral Isles.* Washington, DC: Review and Herald, 1923.

Gilbert, F. C. *From Judaism to Christianity and Gospel Work Among the Hebrews.* Concord, MA: Good Tidings, 1911.

Gladson, Jerry. *A Theologian's Journey from Seventh-day Adventism to Mainstream Christianity.* Glendale, AZ: Life Assurance Ministries, 2000.

Halliwell, Leo B. *Light Bearer to the Amazon.* Nashville, TN: Southern, 1945.

———. *Light in the Jungle.* New York: David McKay, 1959; reprint, Nashville, TN: Southern, 1968.

Hammill, Richard L. *Pilgrimage: Memoirs of an Adventist Administrator.* Berrien Springs, MI: Andrews University Press, 1992.

Harding, Warren G. *An American Looks at Australia.* Washington, DC: Review and Herald, 1943.

Hawley, D. T. *Pakistan Zindabad!* Mountain View, CA: Pacific Press, 1961.

Hayden, Richard, as told to Gwendolen Lampshire Hayden. *From Football Field to Mission Field.* Washington, DC: Review and Herald, 1951.

Hill, W. B. *Experiences of a Pioneer Evangelist of the Northwest.* n.p.: by the author, 1902.

Ising, W. K. *Among the Arabs in Bible Lands.* Mountain View, CA: Pacific Press, 1924.

Jacques, Oliver and Fredonia. *Africa Called Us.* Washington, DC: Review and Herald, 1952.

Jensen, Iona Clark. *Adventure for God on Okinawa.* Mountain View, CA: Pacific Press, 1960.

Joers, Lawrence E. C. *God is My Captain.* Mountain View, CA: Pacific Press, 1945.

———. *Mercy Rides on Wings.* Nashville, TN: Southern, 1960.

Knight, Anna. *Mississippi Girl: An Autobiography.* Nashville, TN: Southern, 1952.

Konigmacher, S. M. *In the Lion Country, or Twelve Years in the African Jungle.* Washington, DC: Review and Herald, 1925.

Lee, Frederick. *Travel Talks on China.* Washington, DC: Review and Herald, 1926.

McKibbin, Alma E. *Step by Step: An Autobiographical Sketch.* Washington, DC: Review and Herald, 1964.

McLeod, Merikay. *Betrayal: The Shattering Sex Discrimination Case of Silver vs Pacific Press Publishing Association.* Loma Linda, CA: Mars Hill, 1985.

Mundy, Susi Hasel. *A Thousand Shall Fall: The Electrifying Story of a Soldier and His Family Who Dared to Practice Their Faith in Hitler's Germany.* Hagerstown, MD: Review and Herald, 2001.

Nelson, Ruth Kipp. *Treasures of Taiwan.* Washington, DC: Review and Herald, 1964.

Oss, Mrs. John. *Triumphs of Faith; Personal Experiences in Service for the King.* Washington, DC: Review and Herald, 1935.

Palmer, C. S. *Tales of Tonga.* Nashville, TN: Southern, 1959.

Passebois, Louis F. *Adventures of a Modern Huguenot.* Nashville, TN: Southern, 1940.

Ponomarov, Alexander. *Desperate Escape: A True Story of Faith Through Relentless Persecution,* trans. Jacob Volkov and Alex Swiridoff. Hagerstown, MD: Review and Herald, 1999.

Reavis, D. W. *I Remember.* Washington, DC: Review and Herald, n.d.

Russell, Riley, as told to Stella Parker Peterson. *It Came in Handy; The Story of Riley Russell, M.D., Physician Extraordinary to the People of Korea.* Washington, DC: Review and Herald, 1969.

Shepard, Loren Clayton. *I'd Like to Do It Again; Mission Experiences in India.* Washington, DC: Review and Herald, 1965.

Stahl, F. A. *In the Amazon Jungles.* Mountain View, CA: Pacific Press, 1932.

———. *In the Land of the Incas.* Mountain View, CA: Pacific Press, 1920.

Stewart, Andrew G. *Trophies from Cannibal Isles.* Washington, DC: Review and Herald, 1956.

Tavukdjian, Serpouhi. *Exiled: Story of an Armenian Girl.* Washington, DC: Review and Herald, 1933.

Tenney, G. C. *Journeys by Land and Sea: A Visit to Five Continents.* Chicago, IL: International Tract Society, 1895.

Thompson, James J. *Fleeing the Whore of Babylon: A Modern Conversion Story.* Westminster, MD: Christian Classics, 1986.

Thurber, Robert B. *In the Land of Pagodas.* Nashville: Southern, 1921.

Toppenberg, Valdemar E. *Africa Has My Heart.* Mountain View, CA: Pacific Press, 1958.

Vandeman, George E. *My Dream: Memoirs of a One-of-a-Kind Disciple.* Boise, ID: Pacific Press, 1995.

Wangerin, T. S. *God Sent Me to Korea.* Washington, DC: Review and Herald, 1968.

———. *High Adventure in Korea.* Mountain View, CA: Pacific Press, 1960.

Wedgewood Trio with Marilyn Thomsen. *Wedgwood: Their Music, Their Journey.* Boise, ID: Pacific Press, 1996.

Westphal, F. H. *Pioneering in the Neglected Continent.* Nashville, TN: Southern, 1927.

White, Ellen G. *Life Sketches of Ellen G. White.* Mountain View, CA: Pacific Press, 1915.

White, James S. *Life Incidents in Connection with the Great Advent Movement.* Battle Creek, MI: Seventh-day Adventist Publishing Association, 1868; reprint with introduction by Jerry Moon, Adventist Classic Library. Berrien Springs, MI: Andrews University Press, 2003.

Williams, A. H. *Afoot and Afloat in Burma.* Takoma Park, Washington, DC: Review and Herald, 1922.

Wood, Clarence E. *In the Land of the Aztecs.* Washington, DC: Review and Herald, 1939.

Yob, Iris M., and Patti Hansen Tompkins, eds. *In Our Own Words.* Santa Ana, CA: Adventist Women's Institute, 1993.

Biographies

Anderson, Godfrey T. *Outrider of the Apocalypse: Life and Times of Joseph Bates.* Mountain View, CA: Pacific Press, 1972.

———. *Spicer: Leader with the Common Touch.* Washington, DC: Review and Herald, 1983.

Baker, Delbert. *The Unknown Prophet.* Washington, DC: Review and Herald, 1987.

Barger, R. Curtis. *Don't You Know? Haven't You Heard?: The Life Story of Eric B. Hare.* Washington, DC: Review and Herald, 1985.

Benton, Josephine. *Called by God: Stories of Seventh-day Adventist Women Ministers.* Smithsburg, MD: Blackberry Hill Publishers, 1990.

Boucher, Sharon. *Luther Warren, Man of Prayer and Power.* Washington, DC: Review and Herald, 1959.

Clark, Harold W. *Crusader for Creation: The Life and Writings of George McCready Price.* Mountain View, CA: Pacific Press, 1966.

Clough, Caroline L. *His Name Was David: The Remarkable Life of Dr. David Paulson, Man of Faith and Founder of Hinsdale Sanitarium.* Washington, DC: Review and Herald, 1955.

Delafield, D. A. *Ellen G. White in Europe, 1885-1887.* Washington, DC: Review and Herald, 1975.

Durand, Eugene F. *Yours in the Blessed Hope, Uriah Smith.* Washington, DC: Review and Herald, 1980.

Edwards, Calvin W., and Gary Land. *Seeker After Light: A. F. Ballenger, Adventism, and American Christianity*. Berrien Springs, MI: Andrews University Press, 2000.

Edwards, Charles G. *Wacifundo and the Whirlwind: The Story of Lowell and Josephine Cunnington Edwards*. Wenatchee, WA: By the author, 1994.

Edwards, Robert E. *H. M. S. Richards*. Hagerstown, MD: Review and Herald, 1998.

Ford, Herbert. *Flee the Captor*. Nashville, TN: Southern, 1966; Updated ed., Hagerstown, MD: Review and Herald, 1994.

———. *For the Love of China*. Mountain View, CA: Pacific Press, 1971.

Gale, Robert. *The Urgent Voice: The Story of William Miller*. Washington, DC: Review and Herald, 1975.

Gish, Ira, and Harry Christman. *Madison, God's Beautiful Farm: The E. A. Sutherland Story*. Mountain View, CA: Pacific Press, 1979.

Greer, Hazel McElhany, and Norma R. Youngberg. *Hymns at Heaven's Gate: The Story of George Greer, Choirmaster*. Mountain View, CA: Pacific Press, 1974.

Haines, Madge. *Fighting Africa's Black Magic; The Fight of E. G. Marcus, M.D. Against Disease and Superstition in East Africa*. Mountain View, CA: Pacific Press, 1938.

Hare, Eric B. *Fulton's Footprints in Fiji*. Washington, DC: Review and Herald, 1969.

———. *An Irish Boy and God: The Biography of Robert Hare, Irish Immigrant, Pioneer Preacher, and Poet*. Washington, DC: Review and Herald, 1965.

Harley, May Carr, and Ruth Wheeler. *Pastor LaRue: The Pioneer*. Washington, DC: Review and Herald, 1937.

Haussler, Doris Holt. *From Immigrant to Emissary*. Nashville, TN: Southern, 1969.

Herndon, Booton. *The Unlikeliest Hero; The Story of Desmond T. Doss, Conscientious Objector, Who Won His Nation's Highest Military Honor*. Mountain View, CA: Pacific Press, 1967.

Kim, Penny Young Sook, Richard A. Schaefer, and Charles Mills. *Though Bombs May Fall: The Extraordinary Story of George Rue, Missionary Doctor to Korea*. Nampa, ID: Pacific Press, 2003.

Knight, George R. *From 1888 to Apostasy: The Case of A. T. Jones*. Washington, DC: Review and Herald, 1987.

———. *Joseph Bates: The Real Founder of Seventh-day Adventism*. Hagerstown, MD: Review and Herald, 2004.

Knott, Ron. *The Makings of a Philanthropic Fundraiser: The Instructive Example of Milton Murray.* Foreword by Patricia F. Lewis and prologue by Milton Murray. San Francisco: Jossey-Bass, 1992.

Krum, Nathaniel. *Charles A. Longacre: Champion of Religious Liberty.* Washington, DC: Review and Herald, 1959.

Kuhn, May Cole. *Skipper of the Sentinel.* Washington, DC: Review and Herald, 1945.

Lantry, Eileen E. *Mission Pilot: High Adventure in Dangerous Places: The David Gates Story.* Nampa, ID: Pacific Press, 2002.

Leonard, Harry, ed. *J. N. Andrews: The Man and the Mission.* Berrien Springs, MI: Andrews University Press, 1985.

Loewen, Gertrude. *Crusader for Freedom: The Story of Jean Nussbaum.* Nashville: Southern, 1969.

Mansell, Donald E., with Vesta W. Mansell. *Under the Shadow of the Rising Sun: The True Story of a Missionary Family's Survival and Faith in a Japanese Prisoner-of-War Camp During WWII.* Nampa, ID: Pacific Press, 2003.

Mastrapa, Selma Chaij, ed. *Notable Adventist Women of Today.* n.p.: Year of the Adventist Woman, 1995.

Maxwell, Stanley M. *The Man Who Couldn't Be Killed: An Incredible Story of Faith and Courage During China's Cultural Revolution.* Boise, ID: Pacific Press, 1995.

McMahon, David P. *Ellet Joseph Waggoner: The Myth and the Man.* Fallbrook, CA: Verdict, 1979.

Moon, Jerry Allen. *W. C. White and Ellen G. White: The Relationship Between the Prophet and Her Son.* Andrews University, Seventh-day Adventist Theological Seminary Dissertation Series, vol. 19. Berrien Springs, MI: Andrews University Press, 1993.

Moore, Raymond S. *China Doctor: The Life Story of Harry Willis Miller.* New York: Harper Brothers, 1961.

Neff, Merlin L. *For God and C.M.E.: A Biography of Percy Tilson Magan upon the Historical Background of the Educational and Medical Work of Seventh-day Adventists.* Mountain View, CA: Pacific Press, 1964. Also published as *Invincible Irishman: A Biography of Percy T. Magan.* Mountain View, CA: Pacific Press, 1969.

Nelson, Kathryn J. *Kate Lindsay, M.D.* Nashville, TN: Southern, 1963.

Numbers, Ronald L. *Prophetess of Health: A Study of Ellen G. White.* New York: Harper & Row, 1976; 2nd ed., *Prophetess of Health: Ellen G. White and the Origins of Seventh-day Adventist Health Reform.* Introduction by Jonathan M. Butler. Knoxville, TN: University of Tennessee Press, 1992.

Odom, Martha Montgomery. *The Making of a Missionary: Highlights in the Life of Oliver Montogomery.* Washington, DC: Review and Herald, 1985.

Ogle, Mary S. *China Nurse: The Life Story of Elisabeth Redelstein.* Mountain View, CA: Pacific Press, 1974.

Oliphant, C. A. *Sweet Success: O. D. McKee, America's Snack Cake King.* Cleveland, TN: Sundial Press, 1994.

Owens, Fern Royer. *Sky Pilot of Alaska.* Mountain View, CA: Pacific Press, 1949.

Robertson, John J. *A. G. Daniells: The Making of a General Conference President.* Mountain View, CA: Pacific Press, 1977.

Robinson, Ella M. *Lighter of Gospel Fires: John N. Loughborough.* Mountain View, CA: Pacific Press, 1954.

———. *S. N. Haskell: Man of Action.* Washington, DC: Review and Herald, 1967.

Robinson, Virgil. *James White.* Washington, DC: Review and Herald, 1976.

Rochat, Joyce. *Survivor: A Biography of Siegfried Horn.* Berrien Springs, MI: Andrews University Press, 1986.

Schwarz, Richard W. *John Harvey Kellogg, M.D.* Nashville, TN: Southern, 1970; reprint, Berrien Springs, MI: Andrews University Press, 1981.

Swift, Joy. *The Long Road to China: The Story of Dr. Harry Miller.* Boise, ID: Pacific Press, 1990.

Thiele, Margaret White. *The Whirlwind of the Lord: The Story of Mrs. S. M. I. Henry.* Washington, DC: Review and Herald, 1953; reprinted as *The Whirlwind of the Lord: The Fascinating True Story of Sarepta Myrenda Irish Henry.* Hagerstown, MD: Review and Herald, 1998.

Tilstra, Albertine Klingbeil. *A Dutchman Bound for Paradise.* Washington, DC: Review and Herald, 1980.

———. *Fearless Heart: The Story of Reinhold Gustav Klingbeil and Cornelia Knecht Klingbeil.* Hagerstown, MD: Review and Herald, 1990.

Utt, Richard H. *Uncle Charlie: A Biography of Charles Elliott Weniger.* Mountain View, CA: Pacific Press, 1978.

Valentine, Gilbert M. *The Shaping of Adventism: The Case of W. W. Prescott.* Berrien Springs, MI: Andrews University Press, 1992.

Vande Vere, Emmett K. *Rugged Heart: The Story of George I. Butler.* Nashville, TN: Southern, 1979.

Westphal, Barbara. *Ana Stahl of the Andes and Amazon.* Mountain View, CA: Pacific Press, 1960.

———. *These Fords Still Run.* Mountain View, CA: Pacific Press, 1962.

Wheeler, Gerald. *James White: Innovator and Overcomer.* Hagerstown, MD: Review and Herald, 2003.

White, Arthur L. *Ellen G. White.* 6 vols. Washington, DC: Review and Herald, 1981-86.

———. *Ellen White: Woman of Vision.* Hagerstown, MD: Review and Herald, 2000.

Willis, Richard J. B. *The Kellogg Imperative: John Harvey Kellogg's Unique Contribution to Healthful Living.* Grantham, Lincolnshire, England: Stanborough Press, 2003.

Wood, Miriam and Kenneth. *His Initials Were F. D. N.: A Life Story of Elder F. D. Nichol, for Twenty-one Years Editor of the Review and Herald.* Washington, DC: Review and Herald, 1967.

Woolsey, Raymond H. *Flying Doctor of the Philippines.* Washington, DC: Review and Herald, 1972.

——— and Ruth Anderson. *Harry Anderson: The Man Behind the Paintings.* Washington, DC: Review and Herald, 1976.

Beliefs, Practice, and Polity

Apologetics, Doctrine, and Theology

Andreasen, M. L. *A Faith to Live By.* Washington, DC: Review and Herald, 1943.

Bible Readings for the Home Circle. Battle Creek, MI: Review and Herald, 1888; rev. ed., Washington, DC: Review and Herald, 1949.

Branson, W. H. *Drama of the Ages.* Nashville, TN: Southern, 1950.

Brunt, John. *Good News for Troubled Times.* Hagerstown, MD: Review and Herald, 1993.

Bunch, Taylor G. *The Seven Epistles of Christ.* Washington, DC: Review and Herald, 1947.

———. *The Ten Commandments.* Mountain View, CA: Pacific Press, 1944.

Canright, D. M. *The Ministration of Angels: and the Origin, History and Destiny of Satan.* Battle Creek, MI: Steam Press of the Seventh-day Adventist Publishing Assoc., 1870.

———. *The Two Laws: As Set Forth in the Scriptures of the Old and New Testaments.* Battle Creek, MI: Steam Press of the Seventh-day Adventist Publishing Assoc., 1876; 2nd ed. 1882.

Coffen, Richard W. *When God Sheds Tears: A Christian Look at the Mystery of Suffering.* Hagerstown, MD: Review and Herald, 1994.

370 Bibliography

Covert, William. The Story of Redemption: From Paradise Lost to Paradise Restored. Oakland, CA: Pacific Press, 1898.
Daily, Steven G. Adventism for a New Generation. Portland, OR: Better Living, 1992; 2nd. ed. 1993.
Dederen, Raoul, ed. Handbook of Seventh-day Adventist Theology. Commentary Reference Series, vol. 12. Hagerstown, MD: Review and Herald, 2000.
Doukhan, Jacques B. Israel and the Church: Two Voices for the Same God. Peabody, MA: Hendrickson, 2002.
General Conference of Seventh-day Adventists. Our Firm Foundation: A Report of the Seventh-day Adventist Bible Conference Held September 1-13, 1952, in the Sligo Seventh-day Adventist Church, Takoma Park, Maryland. 2 vols. Washington, DC: Review and Herald, 1953.
Goldstein, Clifford. God, Gödel, and Grace: A Philosophy of Faith. Hagerstown, MD: Review and Herald, 2003.
———. The Remnant: Biblical Reality or Wishful Thinking? Boise, ID: Pacific Press, 1994.
Gulley, Norman R. Systematic Theology: Prolegomena. Foreword by Millard J. Erickson. Berrien Springs, MI: Andrews University Press, 2003.
Guy, Fritz. Thinking Theologically: Adventist Christianity and the Interpretation of Faith. Berrien Springs, MI: Andrews University Press, 1999.
Haskell, S. N. Bible Handbook. South Lancaster: MA: Bible Training School, 1919.
Haynes, Carlyle B. Christianity at the Crossroads. Nashville, TN: Southern, 1924.
Hull, Moses. The Bible from Heaven, or a Dissertation on the Evidences of Christianity. Battle Creek, MI: Steam Press of the Seventh-day Adventist Publishing Assoc., 1872.
Knight, George R. Myths in Adventism. Washington, DC: Review and Herald, 1985.
———. A Search for Identity: The Development of Seventh-day Adventist Beliefs. Hagerstown, MD: Review and Herald, 2000.
Knowles, George E. The Message Behind the Movement. Boise, ID: Pacific Press, 1988.
Lewis, Richard, ed. The Living Witness: Significant Articles from the Signs of the Times, 1874-1959. Mountain View, CA: Pacific Press, 1959.
Lickey, Arthur E. God Speaks to Modern Man. Washington, DC: Review and Herald, 1952.

Marshall, David. *The Third Angel's Message: A Thrilling Story, A Glorious Message, the Final Challenge.* Grantham, Lincolnshire, England: Stanborough Press, 1987.

Maxwell, Arthur S. *Courage for the Crisis: Strength for Today, Hope for Tomorrow; How to Find Peace of Mind and Fortitude of Spirit for the Dangerous Days Ahead.* Mountain View, CA: Pacific Press, 1962.

Moore, A. Leroy. *Adventism in Conflict: Resolving Issues That Divide Us.* Hagerstown, MD: Review and Herald, 1995.

Nichol, Francis D. *The Answer to Modern Religious Thinking: A Discussion of Current Religious Trends in Their Relation to the Distinctive Teachings of Seventh-day Adventists.* Washington, DC: Review and Herald, 1936.

———. *Reasons for Our Faith: A Discussion of Questions Vital to the Proper Understanding and Effective Presentation of Certain Seventh-day Adventist Teachings.* Washington, DC: Review and Herald, 1947.

Olsen, V. Norskov. *Man, The Image of God: The Divine Design, the Human Distortion.* Washington, DC: Review and Herald, 1988.

Parr, Robert. *The Gospel According to Paul.* Washington, DC: Review and Herald, 1974.

Pease, Norval F. *The Good News: Thirteen Vital Points of Faith.* Washington, DC: Review and Herald, 1982.

Peterson, Frank Loris. *The Hope of the Race.* Nashville, TN: Southern, 1934.

Pierson, Robert H. *We Still Believe.* Washington, DC: Review and Herald, 1975.

Provonsha, Jack. W. *A Remnant in Crisis.* Hagerstown, MD: Review and Herald, 1993.

Reiner, Edwin W. *The Covenants.* Nashville, TN: Southern, 1967.

Rice, Richard. *The Reign of God: Christian Theology in a Seventh-day Adventist Perspective,* 2nd ed. Berrien Springs, MI: Andrews University Press, 1997.

Richards, H. M. S. *What Jesus Said.* Nashville, TN: Southern, 1957.

Scriven, Charles. *The Demons Have Had It: A Theological ABC.* Nashville, TN: Southern, 1976.

Seton, Bernard E. *These Truths We Hold.* Washington, DC: Review and Herald, 1981.

Seventh-day Adventists Believe. . .: A Biblical Exposition of 27 Fundamental Beliefs. Washington, DC: Ministerial Association, General Conference of Seventh-day Adventists, 1988.

Slade, Edwin Keck. *The Way of Life: The World's Great Drama from Paradise Lost to Paradise Restored.* Washington, DC: Review and Herald, 1929.

Smith, Uriah. *Synopsis of the Present Truth: A Brief Exposition of the Views of S. D. Adventists.* Battle Creek, MI: Seventh-day Adventist Publishing Association, 1884.

Spangler, J. R. *And Remember Jesus Is Coming Soon,* ed. John M. Fowler. Silver Spring, MD: Ministerial Association, General Conference of Seventh-day Adventists, 1997.

Spicer, W. A. *Certainties of the Advent Movement.* Washington, DC: Review and Herald, 1929.

Utt, Charles D. *Answers to 343 Bible Questions.* Mountain View, CA: Pacific Press, 1957.

Vandeman, George E. *Planet in Rebellion.* Nashville, TN: Southern, 1960.

Venden, Morris L. *Common Ground: A Look at the Beliefs Seventh-day Adventists Hold in Common with Other Evangelical Christians.* Boise, ID: Pacific Press, 1984.

———. *Higher Ground: A Look at Additional Beliefs of Seventh-day Adventists.* Boise, ID: Pacific Press, 1984.

———. *The Pillars.* Mountain View, CA: Pacific Press, 1982.

———. *Uncommon Ground: A Look at the Distinctive Beliefs of Seventh-day Adventists.* Boise, ID: Pacific Press, 1984.

Vick, Edward W. H. *The Adventists' Dilemma.* Nottingham, England: Evening, 2001.

Walsh, Mary E. *The Wine of Roman Babylon.* Nashville, TN: Southern, 1945.

Weber, Martin. *Adventist Hot Potatoes.* Boise, ID: Pacific Press, 1991.

———. *More Adventist Hot Potatoes.* Boise, ID: Pacific Press, 1992.

White, James. *The Biblical Institute: A Synopsis of Lectures on the Principal Doctrines of Seventh-day Adventists.* Oakland, CA: Steam Press of the Pacific S. D. A. Publishing House, 1878.

———. *Christ in the Old Testament, and the Sabbath in the New.* Oakland, CA: Pacific Press, 1877.

Wilcox, Francis McLellan. *What the Bible Teaches: A Synopsis of Leading Bible Doctrines Setting Forth the Everlasting Gospel as Revealed in Jesus Christ Our Divine Lord and Only Saviour.* Washington, DC: Review and Herald, 1926.

The Bible

Abundant Life Bible Amplifier. 13 vols. Boise, ID: Pacific Press, 1994-97.

Betz, Charles H. *How to Teach the Bible with Power*. Hagerstown, MD: Review and Herald, 1995.

Blanco, Jack J. *The Clear Word Bible: A Paraphrase to Nurture Faith and Growth*. n.p., 1994.

Bunch, Taylor G. *Bible Paradoxes*. Mountain View, CA: Pacific Press, 1953.

Clark, Douglas R., and John C. Brunt, eds., *Introducing the Bible*. Lanham, MD: University Press of America, 1997.

Committee on Problems in Bible Translation, General Conference of Seventh-day Adventists. *Problems in Bible Translation*. Washington, DC: Review and Herald, 1954.

DeFehr, J. Jennings. *Do Both Bible Testaments Harmonize?* Nashville, TN: Southern, 1964.

Gilbert, F. C. *The Bible, a Twentieth-Century Book*. Mountain View, CA: Pacific Press, 1927.

Gillespie, V. Bailey. *To Make Us Wise: How to Make Bible Study Relevant to Your Life Today*. Boise, ID: Pacific Press, 1995.

Gugliotto, Lee J. *Handbook for Bible Study: A Guide to Understanding, Teaching, and Preaching the Word of God*. Hagerstown, MD: Review and Herald, 1995.

Handbook for Bible Students; Containing Valuable Quotations Relating to the History, Doctrines, and Prophecies of the Scriptures. Washington, DC: Review and Herald, 1922.

Hasel, Gerhard F. *Understanding the Living Word of God*. Mountain View, CA: Pacific Press, 1980.

Haynes, Carlyle B. *God's Book*. Nashville, TN: Southern, 1935; rev. ed., published as *The Book of All Nations*. Nashville, TN: Southern, 1950.

Holbrook, Frank, and Leo van Dolson, eds. *Issues in Revelation and Inspiration*. Berrien Springs, MI: Adventist Theological Society, 1992.

Horn, Siegfried. *The Spade Confirms the Book*. Washington, DC: Review and Herald, 1957; rev. ed., 1980.

Hyde, Gordon M., ed. *A Symposium on Biblical Hermeneutics*. Washington, DC: General Conference of Seventh-day Adventists, 1974.

Knight, George R. *Exploring Hebrews: A Devotional Commentary*. Hagerstown, MD: Review and Herald, 2003.

———. *Exploring Mark: A Devotional Commentary*. Hagerstown, MD: Review and Herald, 2004.

Koranteng-Pipim, Samuel. *Receiving the Word: How New Approaches to the Bible Impact Our Biblical Faith and Lifestyle*. Berrien Springs, MI: Berean, 1996.

Kubo, Sakae, and Walter Specht. *So Many Versions? Twentieth Century English Versions of the Bible.* Grand Rapids, MI: Zondervan, 1975; rev. ed., 1983.

Marshall, David. *The Battle for the Book.* Grantham, Lincolnshire, England: Stanborough Press, 1991.

Maxwell, A. Graham. *You Can Trust the Bible.* Mountain View, CA: Pacific Press, 1967.

Maxwell, Arthur S. *Your Bible and You: Priceless Treasures in the Holy Scriptures.* Nashville, TN: Southern, 1959.

Merling, David, ed. *To Understand the Scriptures: Essays in Honor of William H. Shea.* Berrien Springs, MI: Andrews University Press, 1997.

Neufeld, Don F., ed. *Seventh-day Adventist Bible Dictionary.* Commentary Reference Series, vol. 8. Washington, DC: Review and Herald, 1960; rev. ed, 1979.

Nichol, Francis D., et al. *The Seventh-day Adventist Bible Commentary: The Holy Bible with Exegetical and Expository Comment.* 7 vols. Washington, DC: Review and Herald, 1953-57; rev. ed., 1978-80.

Prescott, W. W. *The Spade and the Bible: Archaeological Discoveries Support the Old Book.* Introduction by George McCready Price. Chicago: Fleming H. Revell, 1933.

Source Book for Bible Students; Containing Valuable Quotations Relating to the History, Doctrines, and Prophecies of the Scriptures. Washington, DC: Review and Herald, 1919.

The Study Bible: Presenting the Old and New Testaments and the E. G. White Scripture Comments. Harrah, OK: Academy Enterprises, 1993.

Thiele, Edwin R. *The Mysterious Numbers of the Hebrew Kings: A Reconstruction of the Chronology of the Kingdoms of Israel and Judah.* Chicago, IL: University of Chicago Press, 1951.

Thompson, Alden. *Inspiration: Hard Questions, Honest Answers.* Hagerstown, MD: Review and Herald, 1991.

Van Dolson, Leo R. *Hidden No Longer: A Guide to Inductive Bible Study.* Mountain View, CA: Pacific Press, 1968.

———. *How to Get the Most Out of Bible Study.* Silver Spring, MD: Ministerial Association, General Conference of Seventh-day Adventists, 1996.

Walsh, Mary E. *The Apocrypha.* Nashville, TN: Southern, 1968.

Watts, Dorothy Eaton. *Never Thirst Again: A Woman's Guide to Creative Bible Study.* Hagerstown, MD: Review and Herald, 1996.

Selected Works of Ellen G. White

The Acts of the Apostles in the Proclamation of the Gospel of Jesus. Mountain View, CA: Pacific Press, 1911.

Christ's Object Lessons. Oakland, CA: Pacific Press, 1900; Battle Creek, MI: Review and Herald, 1900.

Christian Temperance, and *Bible Hygiene* by James White. Battle Creek, MI: Good Health, 1890.

The Desire of Ages. Oakland, CA: Pacific Press, 1898.

Early Writings of Ellen G. White. Oakland, CA: Pacific Press, 1882; Battle Creek, MI: Review and Herald, 1882.

Education. Oakland, CA: Pacific Press, 1903.

Ellen G. White Periodical Resource Collection. 2 vols. Boise, ID: Pacific Press, 1990.

Ellen G. White Present Truth and Review and Herald Articles. 6 vols. Washington, DC: Review and Herald, 1962.

Ellen G. White Signs of the Times Articles. 4 vols. Mountain View, CA: Pacific Press, 1974.

Ellen G. White Youth's Instructor Articles. Washington, DC: Review and Herald, 1986.

Fundamentals of Christian Education. Nashville, TN: Southern, 1923.

The Great Controversy Between Christ and Satan. Oakland, CA: Pacific Press, 1888; Battle Creek, MI: Review and Herald, 1888.

The Ministry of Healing. Mountain View, CA: Pacific Press, 1905.

Patriarchs and Prophets: The Great Conflict Between Good and Evil as Illustrated in the Lives of Holy Men of Old. Oakland, CA: Pacific Press, 1890; Battle Creek, MI: Review and Herald, 1890.

Sermons and Talks. 2 vols. Silver Spring, MD: Ellen G. White Estate, 1990-94.

Sketches From the Life of Paul. Oakland, CA: Pacific Press, 1883; Battle Creek, MI: Review and Herald, 1883.

The Southern Work. n.p., 1898.

Spiritual Gifts. 4 vols. Battle Creek, MI: Steam Press of the Seventh-day Adventist Publishing Association, 1858-64.

Steps to Christ. New York: Fleming H. Revell, 1892.

The Story of Prophets and Kings as Illustrated in the Captivity and Restoration of Israel. Mountain View, CA: Pacific Press, 1917.

Testimonies for the Church. 9 vols. Oakland/Mountain View, CA: Pacific Press, 1885-1909.

Thoughts from the Mount of Blessing. Battle Creek, MI: International Tract Society, 1896.

A Word to the "Little Flock." (By Ellen G. White, James White, and Joseph Bates.) Gorham, ME: by the author, 1847.

Selected Compilations of Ellen G. White

The Adventist Home. Nashville, TN: Southern, 1952.
Child Guidance. Nashville, TN: Southern, 1954.
Christian Service. Washington, DC: Review and Herald, 1925.
Colporteur Ministry. Mountain View, CA: Pacific Press, 1953.
Counsels for the Church. Mountain View, CA: Pacific Press, 1991.
Counsels on Diet and Foods. Washington, DC: Review and Herald, 1938.
Counsels on Health. Mountain View, CA: Pacific Press, 1923.
Counsels on Sabbath School Work. Washington, DC: Review and Herald, 1938.
Counsels on Stewardship. Washington, DC: Review and Herald, 1940.
Counsels to Teachers, Parents, and Students Regarding Christian Education. Mountain View, CA: Pacific Press, 1913.
Counsels to Writers and Editors. Nashville, TN: Southern, 1946.
Country Living. Washington, DC: Review and Herald, 1946.
Ellen G. White 1888 Materials. 4 vols. Washington, DC: Ellen G. White Estate, 1987.
Evangelism. Washington, DC: Review and Herald, 1946.
An Exhaustive Ellen G. White Commentary on Daniel and Revelation: A Verse-by-verse Commentary on Daniel and Revelation from the Published and Unpublished Writings of Ellen G. White, Compiled and Meticulously Keyed to Scripture. Harrah, OK: Academy Enterprises, 1980.
Faith and Works. Washington, DC: Review and Herald, 1979.
Gospel Workers. Washington, DC: Review and Herald, 1915.
Last Day Events: Facing Earth's Final Crisis. Boise, ID: Pacific Press, 1992.
Medical Ministry. Mountain View, CA: Pacific Press, 1932.
Messages to Young People. Nashville, TN: 1930.
Mind, Character, and Personality. 2 vols. Nashville, TN: Southern, 1977.
Pastoral Ministry. Silver Spring, MD: Ministerial Association, General Conference of Seventh-day Adventists, 1995.
The Publishing Ministry. Washington, DC: Review and Herald, 1983.
Selected Messages. 3 vols. Washington, DC: Review and Herald, 1958-80.
Temperance. Mountain View, CA: 1949.
Testimonies to Ministers and Gospel Workers. Mountain View, CA: Pacific Press, 1923.
The Truth about Angels: A Behind-the-scenes View of Supernatural Beings Involved in Human Life. Boise, ID: Pacific Press, 1996.

The Voice in Speech and Song. Boise, ID: Pacific Press, 1988.
Welfare Ministry. Washington, DC: Review and Herald, 1952.

Ellen G. White (As Subject)

Abbott, George Knapp. *The Witness of Science to the Testimonies of the Spirit of Prophecy,* rev. ed. Mountain View, CA: Pacific Press, 1948.
Battistone, Joseph. *The Great Controversy Theme in E. G. White Writings.* Berrien Springs, MI: Andrews University Press, 1978.
Christian, Lewis Harrison. *The Fruitage of the Spiritual Gifts: The Influence and Guidance of Ellen G. White in the Advent Movement.* Washington, DC: Review and Herald, 1947.
Comprehensive Index to the Writings of Ellen G. White. Prepared Under the Direction of the Board of Trustees of the Ellen G. White Estate. 4 vols. Mountain View, CA: Pacific Press, 1962-92.
Coon, Roger W. *The Great Visions of Ellen G. White.* Hagerstown, MD: Review and Herald, 1992.
Daniells, Arthur Grosvenor. *The Abiding Gift of Prophecy.* Mountain View, CA: Pacific Press, 1936.
Douglass, Herbert E. *Messenger of the Lord: The Prophetic Ministry of Ellen G. White.* Nampa, ID: Pacific Press, 1998.
Gordon, Paul A. *My Dear Brother M--: Why Ellen White Wrote the Letters in Testimonies for the Church.* Nampa, ID: Pacific Press, 1997.
Graham, Roy E. *Ellen G. White: Co-founder of the Seventh-day Adventist Church.* New York: Peter Lang, 1985.
Haynes, Carlyle B. *The Gift of Prophecy.* Nashville, TN: Southern, 1931.
Jemison, T. Housel. *A Prophet Among You.* Mountain View, CA: Pacific Press, 1955.
Knight, George R. *Ellen White's World: A Fascinating Look at the Times in Which She Lived.* Hagerstown, MD: Review and Herald, 1998.
———. *Meeting Ellen White: A Fresh Look at Her Life, Writings, and Major Themes.* Hagerstown, MD: Review and Herald, 1996.
———. *Reading Ellen White: How to Understand and Apply Her Writings.* Hagerstown, MD: Review and Herald, 1997.
———. *Walking with Ellen White: The Human Interest Story.* Hagerstown, MD: Review and Herald, 1999.
Moore, Arthur Leroy. *Theology in Crisis or Ellen G. White's Concept of Righteousness by Faith as It Relates to Contemporary SDA Issues.* Corpus Christi, TX: Life Seminars Incorporated, 1980.

Ott, Helmut. *Perfect in Christ: The Mediation of Christ in the Writings of Ellen G. White.* Washington, DC: Review and Herald, 1987.

Read, W. E. *The Bible, the Spirit of Prophecy, and the Church.* Washington, DC: Review and Herald, 1952.

Scriptural and Subject Index to the Writings of Mrs. Ellen G. White. Mountain View, CA: Pacific Press, 1926.

Sepúlveda, Ciro, ed. *Ellen White on the Color Line: The Idea of Race in a Christian Community.* Leominster, MA: Biblos Press, 1997.

Spalding, Arthur W. *There Shines a Light: The Life and Work of Ellen G. White.* Nashville, TN: Southern, 1953.

Spicer, William A. *The Spirit of Prophecy in the Advent Movement: A Gift that Builds Up.* Washington, DC: Review and Herald, 1937.

The Spirit of Prophecy in the Remnant Church: Representative Teaching of the Seventh-day Adventist Church on This Subject. Washington, DC: Review and Herald, n.d.

Whidden, Woodrow W., II. *Ellen White on Salvation: A Chronological Study.* Hagerstown, MD: Review and Herald, 1995.

———. *Ellen White on the Humanity of Christ: A Chronological Study.* Hagerstown, MD: Review and Herald, 1997.

White, Arthur L. *The Ellen G. White Writings.* Washington, DC: Review and Herald, 1973.

Wilcox, Francis McLellan. *The Testimony of Jesus: A Review of the Work and Teachings of Mrs. Ellen Gould White.* Washington, DC: Review and Herald, 1934.

Witness of the Pioneers Concerning the Spirit of Prophecy: A Facsimile Reprint of Periodical and Pamphlet Articles Written by the Contemporaries of Ellen G. White. Washington, DC: Review and Herald, 1981.

God, the Holy Spirit, and the Trinity

Branson, William Henry. *The Holy Spirit: His Office and Work in the World.* Nashville, TN: Southern, 1933.

Christensen, Otto H. *Getting Acquainted with God.* Washington, DC: Review and Herald, 1970.

Coffen, Richard W. *When God Sheds Tears: A Christian Look at the Mystery of Suffering.* Hagerstown, MD: Review and Herald, 1994.

Conklin, Dorothy Whitney. *The Golden Oil: The Nature and Work of the Holy Spirit.* Mountain View, CA: Pacific Press, 1961.

Dybdahl, Jon. *Old Testament Grace.* Boise, ID: Pacific Press, 1990.

Erickson, M. Lloyd. *The Embrace of God.* Minneapolis, MN: Bethany House, 1996.

Froom, LeRoy Edwin. *The Coming of the Comforter: Studies on the Coming and Work of the Third Person of the Godhead*. Washington, DC: Review and Herald, 1928.

Hatton, Max. *Understanding the Trinity*. Grantham, Lincolnshire, England: Autumn Books, 2001.

Haynes, Carlyle B. *On the Throne of the World: An Analysis of the Bible Teaching of the Sovereignty of God and His Providential Supervision of the Affairs of Men and Nations, Particularly as It Is Manifested in the Lives of His Disciples*. Nashville, TN: Southern, 1951.

MacGuire, Meade. *Does God Care?*, 4th ed. Mountain View, CA: Pacific Press, 1942.

Maxwell, A. Graham. *Can God Be Trusted?* Nashville, TN: Southern, 1977.

———. *Servants or Friends? Another Look at God*. Redlands, CA: Pine Knoll Publications, 1992.

Paulsen, Jan. *When the Spirit Descends*. Washington, DC: Review and Herald, 1977.

Provonsha, Jack W. *God Is With Us*. Washington, DC: Review and Herald, 1974.

Rice, Richard. *The Openness of God: The Relationship of Divine Foreknowledge and Human Free Will*. Nashville, TN: Review and Herald, 1980. Also published as *God's Foreknowledge and Man's Free Will*. Minneapolis, MN: Bethany House, 1985.

Rosado, Caleb. *What Is God Like?: A Study of Luke 15*. Washington, DC: Review and Herald, 1988.

Shewmake, Carrol Johnson. *The Many Faces of God: Pictures of the Intimacy God Desires with His Children*. Hagerstown, MD: Review and Herald, 2004.

Thiele, Edwin R. *Knowing God*. Nashville, TN: Southern, 1979.

Thompson, Alden. *Who's Afraid of the Old Testament God?* Grand Rapids, MI: Zondervan, 1989.

Vick, Edward W. H. *Speaking Well of God*. Nashville, TN: Southern, 1979.

Waggoner, J. H. *The Spirit of God: Its Offices and Manifestations to the End of the Christian Age*. Battle Creek, MI: Steam Press of the Seventh-day Adventist Publishing Association, 1877.

Warren, Mervyn A. *God Made Known*. Washington, DC: Review and Herald, 1984.

Whidden, Woodrow W., II, Jerry Moon, and John W. Reeve. *The Trinity: Understanding God's Love, His Plan of Salvation, and Christian Relationships*. Hagerstown, MD: Review and Herald, 2002.

Jesus, Christology, and Atonement

Adams, Roy. *The Nature of Christ: Help for a Church Divided over Perfection.* Hagerstown, MD: Review and Herald, 1994.

Anderson, Roy Allan. *The God-Man, His Nature and Work.* Washington, DC: Review and Herald, 1970.

Bradford, Charles E. *The God Between.* Washington, DC: Review and Herald, 1984.

Breitigam, R. R. *The Teacher Sent from God.* Mountain View, CA: Pacific Press, 1960.

Davis, Thomas A. *Was Jesus Really Like Us?* Washington, DC: Review and Herald, 1979.

Douglass, Herbert E., and Leo Van Dolson. *Jesus, the Benchmark of Humanity.* Nashville, TN: Southern, 1977.

Froom, LeRoy E. *Movement of Destiny.* Washington, DC: Review and Herald, 1971.

Gulley, Norman R. *Christ Our Substitute.* Washington, DC: Review and Herald, 1982.

Heppenstall, Edward. *The Man Who Is God: A Study of the Person and Nature of Jesus, Son of God and Son of Man.* Washington, DC: Review and Herald, 1977.

Knight, George R. *My Gripe with God: A Study in Divine Justice and the Problem of the Cross.* Washington, DC: Review and Herald, 1990.

Larson, Ralph. *The Word Was Made Flesh: One Hundred Years of Seventh-day Adventist Christology, 1852-1952.* Cherry Valley, CA: Cherrystone, 1986.

Nelson, Dwight K. *The God-Forsaken God.* Fallbrook, CA: Hart Research Center, 1993.

Prescott, W. W. *The Doctrine of Christ: A Series of Bible Studies Covering the Doctrines of the Scriptures.* 2 vols. Washington, DC: Review and Herald, n.d.

Reiner, Edwin W. *The Atonement.* Nashville, TN: Southern, 1971.

Rice, George E. *Christ in Collision.* Mountain View, CA: Pacific Press, 1982.

Rock, Calvin B. *Seeing Christ: Windows on His Saving Grace.* Hagerstown, MD: Review and Herald, 1994.

Scragg, Walter R. L. *The God Who Says "Yes": The Gospel of Luke.* Washington, DC: Review and Herald, 1987.

Sequeira, Jack. *Saviour of the World: The Humanity of Christ in the Light of the Everlasting Gospel.* Boise, ID: Pacific Press, 1996.

Shuler, J. L. *Christ, the Divine One.* Washington, DC: Review and Herald, 1922.

Simons, Jay. *In Search of the Messiah: What the Bible Teaches About God, His Son, and His People.* Hagerstown, MD: Review and Herald, 1994.

Smith, Uriah. *Looking Unto Jesus: Or, Christ in Type and Antitype.* Battle Creek, MI: Review and Herald, 1897.

Vick, Edward W. H. *Jesus the Man.* Nashville, TN: Southern, 1979.

Waggoner, Joseph H. *The Atonement: An Examination of a Remedial System in the Light of Nature and Revelation.* Battle Creek, MI: Steam Press of the Seventh-day Adventist Publishing Association, 1868.

Webster, Eric Claude. *Crosscurrents in Adventist Christology.* American University Studies. Series VII, Theology and Religion, vol. 6. New York: Peter Lang, 1984. Reprint, Berrien Springs, MI: Andrews University Press, 1992.

Widmer, R. Rubin. *Jesus, the Light of the World; A Study of Contemporary Views.* Nashville, TN: Southern, 1967.

Zurcher, J. R. *Touched with Our Feelings: A Historical Survey of Adventist Thought on the Human Nature of Christ,* trans., Edward E. White. Hagerstown, MD: Review and Herald, 1999.

Salvation, Justification, and Sanctification

Ballenger, A. F. *Power for Witnessing.* Oakland, CA: Pacific Press, 1900; reprint, Minneapolis, MN: Dimension Books, 1963.

Bourdeau, D. T. *Sanctification; or Living Holiness.* Battle Creek, MI: Steam Press, 1864; reprint, Nashville, TN: Southern, 1970.

Branson, W. H. *The Way to Christ: How a Bad Man Can Become Good.* Washington, DC: Review and Herald, 1948.

Brown, Walton J. *Forgiveness.* Hagerstown, MD: Review and Herald, 1991.

Daniells, Arthur G. *Christ Our Righteousness.* Washington, DC: Review and Herald, 1926.

Douglass, Herbert E., Edward Heppenstall, Hans K. LaRondell, and C. Mervyn Maxwell. *Perfection: The Impossible Possibility.* Nashville, TN: Southern, 1975.

Evans, I. H. *This Is the Way: Meditations Concerning Justification by Faith and Growth in Christian Graces.* Washington, DC: Review and Herald, 1939.

Ferch, Arthur J., ed. *Toward Righteousness by Faith, 1888 in Retrospect.* Warburton, Victoria, Australia: Signs, 1989.

Goldstein, Clifford. *Children of the Promise: You Can Have the Assurance of Salvation.* Boise, ID: Pacific Press, 1997.

Henry, S. M. I. *The Abiding Spirit.* Battle Creek, MI: Review and Herald, 1898.

Heppenstall, Edward. *Salvation Unlimited: Perspectives in Rightousness by Faith.* Washington, DC: Review and Herald, 1974.

Heubach, Paul. *Make It Plain: The Plan of Salvation Made Simple.* Nashville, TN: Southern, 1980.

Hopp, Kenneth Harvey. *A Christian Lawyer Looks at the Judgment.* Mountain View, CA: Pacific Press, 1984.

Jones, Alonzo Trévier. *The Consecrated Way to Christian Perfection.* Mountain View, CA: Pacific Press, 1905.

Knight, George R. *Angry Saints: Tensions and Possibilities in the Adventist Struggle Over Righteousness by Faith.* Washington, DC: Review and Herald, 1989.

———. *I Used to Be Perfect: An Ex-Legalist Looks at Law, Sin and Grace.* Boise, ID: Pacific Press, 1994; 2nd ed. subtitled *A Study of Sin and Salvation.* Berrien Springs, MI: Andrews University Press, 2001.

———. *The Pharisee's Guide to Perfect Holiness: A Study of Sin and Salvation.* Boise, ID: Pacific Press, 1992.

LaRondelle, Hans K. *Christ Our Salvation: What God Does for Us and in Us.* Mountain View, CA: Pacific Press, 1980.

———. *Perfection and Perfectionism: A Dogmatic-Ethical Study of Biblical Perfection and Phenomenal Perfectionism.* Berrien Springs, MI: Andrews University Press, 1971; rev. ed., 1975.

Lowe, Harry W. *Redeeming Grace; A Doctrinal and Devotional Study of Salvation by Grace Through Faith.* Mountain View, CA: Pacific Press, 1968.

MacGuire, Meade. *His Cross and Mine.* Washington, DC: Review and Herald, 1927.

Moore, Marvin. *Conquering the Dragon Within: God's Provision for Assurance and Victory in the End Time.* Boise, ID: Pacific Press, 1995.

Nelson, Dwight K. *Outrageous Grace: Finding a Forever Friendship with God.* Nampa, ID: Pacific Press, 1998.

Pease, Norval F. *By Faith Alone.* Mountain View, CA: Pacific Press, 1962.

Priebe, Dennis E. *Face-to-Face with the Real Gospel.* Boise, ID: Pacific Press, 1985.

Provonsha, Jack W. *You Can Go Home Again.* Washington, DC: Review and Herald, 1983.

Sequiera, Jack. *Beyond Belief: The Promise, the Power, and the Reality of the Everlasting Gospel.* Boise, ID: Pacific Press, 1993.

Shuler, J. L. *The Wonders of Salvation.* Boise, ID: Pacific Press, 1985.

Venden, Morris. *95 Theses on Righteousness by Faith: (Apologies to Martin Luther)*. Boise, ID: Pacific Press, 1987.

———. *Righteousness by Faith and the Three Angels' Messages: A Series of Six Sermons Presented in the La Sierra Seventh-day Adventist Church*. Mountain View, CA: Pacific Press, 1975.

Vick, Edward W. H. *Is Salvation Really Free?* Hagerstown, MD: Review and Herald, 1983.

———. *Let Me Assure You of Grace, of Faith, of Forgiveness, of Freedom, of Fellowship, of Hope*. Mountain View, CA: Pacific Press, 1968.

Waggoner, Ellet J. *Christ and His Righteousness*. Oakland, CA: Pacific Press, 1890; reprint, Nashville, TN: Southern, 1972.

Wallenkampf, Arnold V. *Salvation Comes from the Lord*. Washington, DC: Review and Herald, 1983.

———. *What Every Christian Should Know About Being Justified*. Washington, DC: Review and Herald, 1988.

Weber, Martin. *Who's Got the Truth? Making Sense Out of Five Different Adventist Gospels*. Silver Spring, MD: Home Study International Press, 1994.

Wieland, Robert J. *The 1888 Message: An Introduction*. Foreword by Donald K. Short. Nashville, TN: Southern, 1980; rev. ed, Paris, OH: Glad Tidings, 1997.

Wilcox, M. C. *Studies in Ephesians*. Mountain View, CA: Pacific Press, 1927.

———. *Studies in Romans*. Mountain View, CA: Pacific Press, 1930.

Zurcher, J. R. *Christian Perfection: A Bible and Spirit of Prophecy Teaching*. Washington, DC: Review and Herald, 1967.

———. *What Inspiration Has to Say About Christian Perfection*, trans. Edward E. White. Hagerstown, MD: Review and Herald, 2002.

Sabbath

Andreasen, M. L. *The Sabbath: Which Day and Why?* Washington, DC: Review and Herald, 1942.

Andreasen, Niels-Erik. *The Christian Use of Time*. Nashville, TN: Abingdon, 1978.

———. *The Old Testament Sabbath: A Tradition-Historical Investigation*. Missoula, MT: Society of Biblical Literature, 1972.

———. *Rest and Redemption: A Study of the Biblical Sabbath*. Berrien Springs, MI: Andrews University Press, 1978.

Andrews, John N. *History of the Sabbath and the First Day of the Week*. Battle Creek, MI: Steam Press of the Seventh-day Adventist Publishing Association, 1862.

Appel, Dan M. *A Bridge Across Time.* Hagerstown, MD: Review and Herald, 1996.

Bacchiocchi, Samuele. *Divine Rest for Human Restlessness: A Theological Study of the Good News of the Sabbath for Today.* Berrien Springs, MI: by the author, 1980.

———. *From Sabbath to Sunday: A Historical Investigation of the Rise of Sunday Observance in Early Christianity.* Rome: Pontifical Gregorian University, 1977.

Branson, Roy, ed. *Festival of the Sabbath.* Takoma Park, MD: Association of Adventist Forums, 1985.

Brunt, John C. *A Day for Healing: The Meaning of Jesus' Sabbath Miracles.* Washington, DC: Review and Herald, 1981.

Butler, George I. *The Change of the Sabbath: Was It by Divine or Human Authority?* Battle Creek, MI: Review and Herald, 1894.

Canright, D. M. *The Morality of the Sabbath.* Battle Creek, MI: Steam Press of the Seventh-day Adventist Publishing Assoc., 1875.

Davidson, Richard M. *A Love Song for the Sabbath.* Washington, DC: Review and Herald, 1988.

Ford, Desmond. *The Forgotten Day.* Newcastle, CA: Desmond Ford, 1981.

Goldstein, Clifford. *A Pause for Peace: What God's Gift of the Sabbath Can Mean for You.* Boise, ID: Pacific Press, 1992.

Haynes, Carlyle B. *The Attempt to Change God's Holy Day—From Sabbath to Sunday.* Washington, DC: Review and Herald, 1928.

Kubo, Sakae. *God Meets Man: A Theology of the Sabbath and Second Advent.* Nashville, TN: Southern, 1978.

Lewis, Richard. *The Protestant Dilemma: How to Achieve Unity in a Completed Reformation.* Mountain View, CA: Pacific Press, 1961.

Nelson, Gregory P. *A Touch of Heaven: Finding New Meaning in Sabbath Rest.* Nampa, ID: Pacific Press, 1999.

Odom, Robert L. *The Lord's Day on a Round World.* Nashville, TN: Southern, 1946; rev. ed., 1970.

———. *Sabbath and Sunday in Early Christianity.* Washington, DC: Review and Herald, 1977.

Scriven, Charles. *Jubilee of the World: The Sabbath as a Day of Gladness.* Nashville, TN: Southern, 1978.

Strand, Kenneth, ed. *The Sabbath in Scripture and History.* Washington, DC: Review and Herald, 1982.

Straw, Walter E. *Origin of Sunday Observance in the Christian Church.* Washington, DC: Review and Herald, 1939.

Walker, Allen. *The Law and the Sabbath.* Nashville, TN: Southern, 1953.

Weiss, Herold. *A Day of Gladness: The Sabbath among Jews and Christians in Antiquity*. Columbia, SC: University of South Carolina Press, 2003.

Yost, Frank H. *The Early Christian Sabbath*. Mountain View, CA: Pacific Press, 1947.

Creationism and Science

Baldwin, John Templeton, ed. *Creation, Catastrophe, and Calvary: Why a Global Flood Is Vital to the Doctrine of Atonement*. Hagerstown, MD: Review and Herald, 2000.

Brand, Leonard. *Faith, Reason, and Earth History: A Paradigm of Earth and Biological Origins by Intelligent Design*. Berrien Springs, MI: Andrews University Press, 1997.

Clark, Harold W. *The Battle Over Genesis*. Washington, DC: Review and Herald, 1957.

———. *Genes and Genesis*. Mountain View, CA: Pacific Press, 1940.

———. *The New Diluvialism*. Angwin, CA: Science Publications, 1946.

Clark, Robert E. D. *God Beyond Nature*. Mountain View, CA: Pacific Press, 1978.

———. *Science and Christianity—A Partnership*. Mountain View, CA: Pacific Press, 1972.

Coffin, Harold. *Creation: Accident or Design?* Washington, DC: Review and Herald, 1969.

——— and Robert H. Brown. *Origin by Design*. Washington, DC: Review and Herald, 1983.

Hayward, James L., ed. *Creation Reconsidered: Scientific, Biblical, and Theological Perspectives*. Roseville, CA: Association of Adventist Forums, 2000.

Hoen, Rue Everett. *The Creator and His Workshop*. Mountain View, CA: Pacific Press, 1951.

Marsh, Frank Lewis. *Evolution, Creation, and Science*. Washington, DC: Review and Herald, 1944.

———. *Life, Man, and Time*. Mountain View, CA: Pacific Press, 1957.

———. *Studies in Creationism*. Washington, DC: Review and Herald, 1950.

Mitchell, Colin. *Creationism Revisited*. Foreword by John Walton. Grantham, Lincolnshire, England: Autumn House, 1999.

Price, George McCready. *The Modern Flood Theory of Geology*. New York: Fleming H. Revell, 1935.

———. *The New Geology*. Mountain View, CA: Pacific Press, 1923.

———. *Outlines of Modern Christianity and Modern Science.* Oakland, CA: Pacific Press, 1902.

———. *Q.E.D.; or, New Light on the Doctrine of Creation.* New York: Fleming H. Revell, 1917.

Reed, L. A. *The Scriptural Foundations of Science.* Battle Creek, MI: Review and Herald, 1901.

Ritland, Richard. *A Search for Meaning in Nature: A New Look at Creation and Evolution.* Mountain View, CA: Pacific Press, 1970.

Roth, Ariel. *Origins: Linking Science and Scripture.* Hagerstown, MD: Review and Herald, 1998.

Van Dolson, Leo R., comp. *Our Real Roots: Scientific Support for Creation.* Washington, DC: Review and Herald, 1979.

Vick, Edward W. H. *Quest: An Exploration of Some Problems in Science and Religion.* London, England: Epworth, 1975.

Wheeler, Gerald. *Two-Tailed Dinosaur: Why Science and Religion Conflict Over the Origin of Life.* Nashville, TN: Southern, 1975.

Conditionalism and Spiritualism

Bacchiocchi, Samuele. *Immortality or Resurrection?: A Biblical Study on Human Nature and Destiny.* Foreword by Clark Pinnock. Berrien Springs, MI: Biblical Perspectives, 1997.

Canright, Dudley M. *Matter and Spirit; or, the Problem of Human Thought.* Battle Creek, MI: Review and Herald, 1882.

Froom, LeRoy Edwin. *The Conditionalist Faith of Our Fathers: The Conflict of the Ages Over the Nature and Destiny of Man.* 2 vols. Washington, DC: Review and Herald, 1965-66.

Haynes, Carlyle B. *Life, Death, and Immortality.* Nashville, TN: Southern, 1952.

Kellogg, John H. *Harmony of Science and the Bible on the Nature of the Soul and the Doctrine of the Resurrection.* Battle Creek, MI: Seventh-day Adventist Publishing Association, 1879.

Olson, V. Norskov. *Man the Image of God.* Hagerstown, MD: Review and Herald, 1988.

Provonsha, Jack W. *Is Death for Real? An Examination of Reported Near-Death Experience in the Light of the Resurrection.* Mountain View, CA: Pacific Press, 1981.

Smith, Uriah. *The State of the Dead and the Destiny of the Wicked.* Battle Creek, MI: Steam Press of the Seventh-day Adventist Publishing Association, 1873.

Snow, Charles M. *On the Throne of Sin; Spiritualism and the Nature of Man as Related to Demonism, Witchcraft, and Modern Spiritualism.* Washington, DC: Review and Herald, 1927.

Wheeler, Gerald. *Beyond Life: What God Says About Life, Death, and Immortality.* Hagerstown, MD: Review and Herald, 1998.

Zurcher, J. R. *The Nature and Destiny of Man: Essay on the Problem of the Union of the Soul and the Body in Relation to the Christian Views of Man,* trans. Mabel R. Bartlett. New York: Philosophical Library, 1969.

The Sanctuary

Adams, Roy. *The Sanctuary: Understanding the Heart of Adventist Theology.* Hagerstown, MD: Review and Herald, 1993.

———. *The Sanctuary Doctrine: Three Approaches in the Seventh-day Adventist Church.* Berrien Springs, MI: Andrews University Press, 1981.

Anderson, John T. *Investigating the Judgment: Patterns of Divine Judgment.* Hagerstown, MD: Review and Herald, 2003.

Andreasen, M. L. *The Book of Hebrews.* Washington, DC: Review and Herald, 1948.

———. *The Sanctuary Service.* Washington, DC: Review and Herald, 1947.

Andross, E. E. *A More Excellent Ministry.* Mountain View, CA: Pacific Press, 1912.

Branson, W. H. *The Atonement in the Light of God's Sanctuaries.* Mountain View, CA: Pacific Press, 1935.

Brown, M. H. *Christ Our Advocate; His Ministry in the True Tabernacle.* Oakland, CA: Pacific Press, 1894.

Douglass, Herbert E. *Why Jesus Waits: How the Sanctuary Doctrine Explains the Mission of the Seventh-day Adventist Church.* Washington, DC: Review and Herald, 1976.

Gane, Erwin R. *Heaven's Open Door: The Seven Seals of Revelation and Christ Our Heavenly High Priest.* Boise, ID: Pacific Press, 1989.

Gane, Roy. *Altar Call.* Berrien Springs, MI: Diadem, 1999.

Gilbert, F. C. *Messiah in His Sanctuary: A Series of Bible Studies on the Sanctuary and Its Services, in both Type and Anti-type, with Particular Application to the Church Following the Advent Movement of the Years 1834-1844.* Washington, DC: Review and Herald, 1937.

Goldstein, Clifford. *Between the Lamb and the Lion: A New View of Jesus in the Book of Revelation, from the Cross to His Coming.* Boise, ID: Pacific Press, 1995.

Hardinge, Leslie. *With Jesus in His Sanctuary: A Walk Through the Tabernacle Along His Way.* Harrisburg, PA: American Cassette Ministries, 1991.

Haskell, Stephen N. *The Cross and Its Shadow.* South Lancaster, MA: The Bible Training School, 1914; reprint, Nashville, TN: Southern, 1970.

Heppenstall, Edward. *Our High Priest: Jesus Christ in the Heavenly Sanctuary.* Washington, DC: Review and Herald, 1972.

Holbrook, Frank, ed. *Doctrine of the Sanctuary: A Historical Survey (1845-1863).* Daniel and Revelation Committee Series, vol. 5. Silver Spring, MD: Biblical Research Institute, General Conference of Seventh-day Adventists, 1989.

———. *Issues in the Book of Hebrews.* Daniel and Revelation Committee Series, vol. 4. Silver Spring, MD: Biblical Research Institute, General Conference of Seventh-day Adventists, 1989.

Shuler, John L. *The Great Judgment Day: In the Light of the Sanctuary Service.* Washington, DC: Review and Herald, 1923.

Wallenkampf, Arnold V., and W. Richard Lesher, eds. *The Sanctuary and the Atonement: Biblical, Historical and Theological Studies.* Washington, DC: Review and Herald, 1981.

Watson, C. H. *The Atoning Work of Christ: His Sacrifice and Priestly Ministry.* Washington, DC: Review and Herald, 1934.

Prophetic Interpretation and Eschatology

Anderson, Roy Allan. *Unfolding Daniel's Prophecies.* Mountain View, CA: Pacific Press, 1975.

———. *Unfolding the Revelation: Evangelistic Studies for Public Presentation.* Mountain View: Pacific Press, 1953; reprint, 1961; rev. ed., 1974.

Andrews, John Nevins. *The Three Messages of Revelation XIV, 6-12: Particularly the Third Angel's Message.* Battle Creek, MI: Review and Herald Office, 1860.

Bacchiocchi, Samuele. *The Advent Hope for Human Hopelessness: A Theological Study of the Meaning of the Second Advent for Today.* Foreword by W. Richard Lesher. Berrien Springs, MI: Biblical Perspectives, 1986.

Berg, Orley. *The Restless Land: Israel, Its Place in History and Prophecy.* Washington, DC: Review and Herald, 1974.

Bollman, Calvin P. *Heralds of the King, Our Lord's Great Prophecy of His Second Advent.* Washington, DC: Review and Herald, 1920.

Branson, Roy, ed. *Pilgrimage of Hope.* Takoma Park, MD: Association of Adventist Forums, 1986.

Brunt, John. *Now & Not Yet.* Washington, DC: Review and Herald, 1987.

Burrill, Russell. *Hope When the World Falls Apart: Daniel and Revelation's Message of Hope.* Keene, TX: Seminars Unlimited, 2003.

Chaij, Fernando. *The Impending Drama.* Nashville, TN: Southern, 1979.

Christian, L. H. *Facing the Crisis in the Light of Bible Prophecy.* Washington, DC: Review and Herald, 1937.

Conradi, L. R. *The Mystery Unfolded: or, The Seven Seals Opened.* Stanborough Park, Watford, Hertsford, England: International Tract Society, [1912].

Cottrell, Roy Franklin. *The Dawn of a New Day: The Bible Speaks to Our Age.* Mountain View, CA: Pacific Press, 1934.

———. *The Jews and Palestine.* Mountain View, CA: Pacific Press, 1947.

Daniells, Arthur G. *The World War, Its Relation to the Eastern Question and Armageddon.* Washington, DC: Review and Herald, 1917.

Dickson, Louis K. *A World on the March.* Nashville, TN: Southern, 1928.

Douglass, Herbert E. *The End: The Unique Voice of Adventists About the Return of Jesus.* Mountain View, CA: Pacific Press, 1979.

Doukhan, Jacques B. *Daniel: The Vision of the End.* Berrien Springs, MI: Andrews University Press, 1987.

———. *Secrets of Daniel: Wisdom and Dreams of a Jewish Prince in Exile.* Hagerstown, MD: Review and Herald, 2000.

———. *Secrets of Revelation: The Apocalypse Through Hebrew Eyes.* Hagerstown, MD: Review and Herald, 2002.

Ferch, Arthur J. *Daniel on Solid Ground.* Washington, DC: Review and Herald, 1988.

Ford, Desmond. *Daniel.* Nashville, TN: Southern, 1978.

Froom, LeRoy E. *The Prophetic Faith of Our Fathers: The Historical Development of Prophetic Interpretation.* 4 vols. Washington, DC: Review and Herald, 1950-54.

Goldstein, Clifford. *The Day Evil Dies.* Hagerstown, MD: Review and Herald, 1999.

———. *Day of the Dragon: How Current Events Have Set the Stage for America's Prophetic Destiny: The Great Controversy Vindicated.* Boise, ID: Pacific Press, 1993.

Gulley, Norman R. *Christ Our Refuge: Making It Safely Through the Last Days.* Boise, ID: Pacific Press, 1996.

———. *Final Events on Planet Earth.* Nashville, TN: Southern, 1977.

Hardinge, Leslie. *Jesus Is My Judge: Meditations on the Book of Daniel.* Harrisburg, PA: American Cassette Ministries, 1996.

Haynes, Carlyle B. *Twelve Great Signs of the Return of Jesus.* Washington, DC: Review and Herald, 1925.

Holbrook, Frank B., ed. *The Seventy Weeks, Leviticus, and the Nature of Prophecy.* Daniel and Revelation Committee Series, vol. 3. Washington, DC: Biblical Research Institute, General Conference of Seventh-day Adventists, 1986.

———. *Symposium on Daniel: Introductory and Exegetical Studies.* Daniel and Revelation Committee Series, vol. 2. Washington, DC: Biblical Research Institute, General Conference of Seventh-day Adventists, 1986.

———. *Symposium on Revelation.* Daniel and Revelation Committee Series, vols. 6-7. Silver Spring, MD: Biblical Research Institute, General Conference of Seventh-day Adventists, 1992.

Johns, Varner H. *The Secret Rapture and the Antichrist.* Mountain View, CA: Pacific Press, 1942.

Lane, S. H. *Our Paradise Home: The Earth Made New and the Restoration of All Things.* Washington, DC: Review and Herald, 1903.

LaRondelle, Hans K. *Chariots of Salvation: The Biblical Drama of Armageddon.* Washington, DC: Review and Herald, 1987.

———. *The Israel of God in Prophecy: Principles of Prophetic Interpretation.* Berrien Springs, MI: Andrews University Press, 1983.

Lee, Leonard C. *Clouds over America: The United States in Bible Prophecy.* Washington, DC: Review and Herald, 1948.

Loughborough, J. N. *The Saints' Inheritance: or, The Earth Made New.* Battle Creek, MI: Steam Press of the Seventh-day Adventist Publishing Assoc., 1873.

Mansell, Donald Ernest. *Adventists and Armageddon: Have We Misinterpreted Prophecy?* Boise, ID: Pacific Press, 1999.

———. *The Shape of the Coming Crisis: A Sequence of End-Time Events Based on the Writings of Ellen G. White.* Nampa, ID: Pacific Press, 1998.

Marshall, David. *Apocalypse! Has the Countdown Begun?* Grantham, Lincolnshire, England: Autumn House, 2000.

Maxwell, Arthur S. *The Coming King: Ten Great Signs of Christ's Return.* Mountain View, CA: Pacific Press, 1953.

Maxwell, C. Mervyn. *God Cares:* vol 1: *The Message of Daniel for You and Your Family;* vol. 2: *The Message of Revelation for You and Your Family.* Mountain View, CA: Pacific Press, 1981, 1986.

Moore, Marvin. *The Antichrist and the New World Order.* Boise, ID: Pacific Press, 1993.

———. *The Crisis of the End Time: Keeping Your Relationship with Jesus in Earth's Darkest Hour.* Boise, ID: Pacific Press, 1992.

Naden, Roy C. *The Lamb Among the Beasts: A Christological Commentary on the Revelation of John That Unlocks the Meaning of Its
Many Numbers*. Hagerstown, MD: Review and Herald, 1996.

Neff, Merlin L. *Victory out of Chaos: Messages from the Book of Revelation for Today*. Mountain View, CA: Pacific Press, 1942.

Nelson, Dwight K. *What "Left Behind" Left Behind*. Hagerstown, MD:
Review and Herald, 2001.

Newport, Kenneth G. C. *Apocalypse and Millennium: Studies in Biblical Eisegesis*. Cambridge, UK: Cambridge University Press, 2000.

Nichol, Francis D. *Signs of Christ's Coming: Current Events Fulfilling
Bible Prophecy*. Washington, DC: Review and Herald, 1931.

O'Ffill, Richard W. *Standing Firm: A Practical Guide for Living in the
Last Days*. Hagerstown, MD: Review and Herald, 2003.

Olsen, V. Norskov, ed. *The Advent Hope in Scripture and History*.
Washington, DC: Review and Herald, 1987.

Paulien, Jon. *The Deep Things of God*. Hagerstown, MD: Review and
Herald, 2004.

———. *What the Bible Says About the End-Time*. Hagerstown, MD:
Review and Herald, 1994.

Price, George McCready. *The Greatest of the Prophets: A New Commentary on the Book of Daniel*. Mountain View, CA: Pacific Press,
1955.

———. *The Time of the End*. Nashville, TN: Southern, 1967.

Reid, G. Edward. *Are You Ready or Not: Here He Comes*. Fulton, MD:
Omega Productions, 1997.

Roberts, Randall L. *The End Is Near Again: Being Ready for the Return of Jesus Whenever It Happens*. Nampa, ID: Pacific Press,
2003.

Robinson, H. E. *The Eastern Question in the Light of God's Promises
to Israel: Prophetic and Historic*. Battle Creek, MI: Review and
Herald, 1897.

Shea, William H. *Selected Studies on Prophetic Interpretation*. Daniel
and Revelation Committee Series, vol 1. Washington, DC: General
Conference of Seventh-day Adventists, 1982.

Shuler, John L. *The Coming Conflict*. Nashville, TN: Southern, 1929.

Smith, Uriah. *Our Country, the Marvel of Nations: Its Past, Present,
and Future, and What the Scriptures Say of It*, 3rd ed. Battle
Creek, MI: Review and Herald, 1901.

———. *Thoughts on the Book of Daniel and the Revelation*. Battle
Creek, MI: Review and Herald, 1882.

Spicer, William A. *Beacon Lights of Prophecy*. Washington, DC: Review and Herald, 1935.

Stefanovic, Ranko. *Revelation of Jesus Christ: Commentary on the Book of Revelation.* Berrien Springs, MI: Andrews University Press, 2002.

Strand, Kenneth. *Interpreting the Book of Revelation: Hermeneutical Guidelines, with Brief Introduction to Literary Analysis.* Worthington, OH: Ann Arbor Publishers, 1976; 2nd ed., 1979.

————. *Perspectives in the Book of Revelation.* Worthington, OH: Ann Arbor Publishers, 1975; reprint, 1978.

Tait, Asa Oscar. *Heralds of the Morning: The Meaning of the Social and Political Problems of To-Day and the Significance of the Great Phenomena in Nature.* Oakland, CA: Pacific Press, 1899.

Venden, Morris L. *Here I Come, Ready or Not.* Boise, ID: Pacific Press, 1987.

Walton, Lewis R. *Advent! World Events at the End of Time.* Washington, DC: Review and Herald, 1986.

Weber, Martin. *Millennimania.* Silver Spring, MD: Ministerial Association, General Conference of Seventh-day Adventists, 1998.

Were, Louis F. *The Certainty of the Third Angel's Message.* Berrien Springs, MI: First Impressions, 1979.

White, James. *His Glorious Appearing: An Exposition of Matthew Twenty-four*, rev., 15th ed. Battle Creek, MI: Review and Herald, 1895.

White, James Edson. *The Coming King.* Battle Creek, MI: Review and Herald, 1898.

Wilcox, Francis McLellan. *The Coming Crisis.* Washington, DC: Review and Herald, 1933.

Zurcher, J. R. *Christ of the Revelation: His Message to the Church and the World.* Nashville, TN: Southern, 1980.

Church, Evangelism, Worship, and Mission

Anderson, Roy Allan. *The Shepherd-Evangelist: His Life, Ministry, and Reward.* Washington, DC: Review and Herald, 1950.

Ballis, Peter H. *Leaving the Adventist Ministry: A Study of the Process of Exiting.* Westport, CT: Praeger, 1999.

Battistone, Joseph J. *God's Church in a Hostile World.* Washington, DC: Review and Herald, 1989.

Beach, Bert B. *Ecumenism: Boon or Bane?* Washington, DC: Review and Herald, 1974.

Beach, Walter Raymond, and Bert Beverly Beach. *Pattern for Progress: The Role and Function of Church Organization.* Washington, DC: Review and Herald, 1985.

Berg, Orley. *The Work of the Pastor.* Nashville, TN: Southern, 1966.

Bradford, Charles E. *Preaching to the Times: The Preaching Ministry of the Seventh-day Adventist Church.* Washington, DC: Review and Herald, 1975.

Burill, Russell. *Recovering an Adventist Approach to the Life and Mission of the Local Church.* Fallbrook, CA: Hart Research Center, 1998.

Caslow, D. E. *Winning: Lay Bible Ministry Handbook.* Mountain View, CA: Pacific Press, 1981.

Coon, Glenn A. *Path to the Heart: Informal Talks on Personal Soul Winning.* Washington, DC: Review and Herald, 1958.

Crisler, Clarence. *Organization: Its Character, Purpose, Place, and Development in the Seventh-day Adventist Church.* Washington, DC: Review and Herald, 1938.

Dudley, Roger L., and Des Cummings, Jr. *Adventures in Church Growth.* Washington, DC: Review and Herald, 1983.

Dybdahl, Jon L., ed. *Adventist Mission in the 21st Century.* Hagerstown, MD: Review and Herald, 1999.

Emmerson, Kenneth H. *Financing a World Church.* Washington, DC: Review and Herald, 1969.

Erickson, Matilda. *Missionary Volunteers and Their Work.* Washington, DC: Review and Herald, n.d.

Evans, I. H. *The Preacher and His Preaching.* Washington, DC: Review and Herald, 1938.

General Conference of Seventh-day Adventists. *Church Manual.* Washington, DC: General Conference of Seventh-day Adventists, 1932–.

Halswick, Louis Martin. *Mission Fields at Home.* Brookfield, IL: Pacific Press, [1944].

Haynes, Carlyle B. *The Divine Art of Preaching.* Washington, DC: Review and Herald, 1939.

———. *Living Evangelism.* Introduction by Milton E. Kern. Washington, DC: Review and Herald, 1937.

Holmes, Raymond. *The Last Word: An Eschatological Theology of Preaching.* Berrien Springs, MI: Andrews University Press, 1987.

———. *Sing a New Song: Worship Renewal for Adventists Today.* Berrien Springs, MI: Andrews University Press, 1984.

——— and Douglas Kilcher, eds. *The Adventist Minister.* Berrien Springs, MI: Andrews University Press, 1991.

Home Missionary Department, General Conference of Seventh-day Adventists. *Fishers of Men: Studies in the Principles and Practice of Personal Evangelism.* Washington, DC: Review and Herald, [1938].

————. *The Lay Preacher and His Work: Principles and Methods of Lay Evangelism.* Nashville, TN: Southern, 1940.

Hopkins, Gary L., and Joyce W. Hopp. *It Takes a Church: Every Member's Guide to Keeping Young People Safe and Saved.* Boise, ID: Pacific Press, 2002.

Hunt, Joseph N. *No Higher Calling.* Washington, DC: Review and Herald, 1981.

Johnson, Kurt W. *Small Group Outreach: How to Begin and Lead Outreach Bible Study Groups.* Hagerstown, MD: Review and Herald, 1991.

Johnsson, William G. *The Fragmenting of Adventism: Ten Issues Threatening the Church Today; Why the Next Five Years are Crucial.* Boise, ID: Pacific Press, 1995.

Knight, George R. *The Fat Lady and the Kingdom: Confronting the Challenge of Change and Secularization.* Boise, ID: Pacific Press, 1995.

————. *Organizing to Beat the Devil: The Development of Adventist Church Structure.* Hagerstown, MD: Review and Herald, 2001.

Knowles, George E. *How to Help Your Church Grow.* Washington, DC: Review and Herald, 1981.

Lickey, Arthur E. *The Minister-Layman Movement: 20th Century Progressive World Bible Club Plan.* Washington, DC: Review and Herald, 1949.

Loughborough, J. N. *The Church: Its Organization, Order and Discipline.* Washington, DC: Review and Herald, 1907.

Maynard-Reid, Pedrito. *Diverse Worship: African American, Caribbean, and Hispanic Perspectives.* Downers Grove, IL: InterVarsity, 2000.

Ministerial Association, General Conference of Seventh-day Adventists. *By His Side: A Compilation of Essays by Ministers' Wives on Their Important Role as Pastoral and Evangelistic Assistants.* Washington, DC: Review and Herald, 1970.

————. *Manual for Ministers.* Washington, DC: General Conference of Seventh-day Adventists, 1925—.

————. *Seventh-day Adventist Minister's Handbook.* Silver Spring, MD: Ministerial Association, 1997.

Montgomery, Oliver. *Principles of Church Organization and Administration.* Washington, DC: Review and Herald, 1942.

O'Ffill, Daniel W., and Carrol Johnson Shewmake. *What To Say In a Whole New Way: New Words for Witnessing.* Hagerstown, MD: Review and Herald, 1994.

Oliver, Barry David. *SDA Organizational Structure: Past, Present, and Future.* Andrews University, Seventh-day Adventist Theological

Seminary Dissertation Series, vol. 15. Berrien Springs, MI: Andrews University Press, 1989.

Olsen, V. Norskov. *Myth and Truth about Church, Priesthood and Ordination*. Riverside, CA: Loma Linda University Press, 1990.

Oosterwal, Gottfried. *Mission Possible: The Challenge of Mission Today*. Nashville, TN: Southern, 1972.

Palmer, Edwin R. *The Printing Press and the Gospel*. Washington, DC: Review and Herald, 1912.

Patzer, Jere. *The Road Ahead: A Vision for Spiritual Leadership in the 21st Century*. Nampa, ID: Pacific Press, 2003.

Pease, Norval F. *And Worship Him*. Nashville, TN: Southern, 1967.

Pierson, Robert H. *So, You Want to be a Leader! A Spiritual, Human Relations and Promotional Approach to Church Leadership and Administration*. Mountain View, CA: Pacific Press, 1966.

Provonsha, Jack W. *A Remnant In Crisis*. Hagerstown, MD: Review and Herald, 1993.

Rasmussen, Hans L. *Till He Comes*. Washington, DC: Review and Herald, 1974.

Rhodes, John. *Success Secrets for Pastors*. Mountain View, CA: Pacific Press, 1965.

Rice, Richard. *Believing, Behaving, Belonging: Finding New Love for the Church*. Roseville, CA: Association of Adventist Forums, 2002.

Roy, E. Harold. *In Remembrance of Me: Thoughts on the Communion Service*. Hagerstown, MD: Review and Herald, 1996.

Sabbath School Department, General Conference of Seventh-day Adventists. *The Sabbath School: Its History, Organization, and Objectives*, rev. ed. Washington, DC: Review and Herald, 1938.

Samaan, Philip G. *Christ's Way of Making Disciples*. Hagerstown, MD: Review and Herald, 1999.

———. *Christ's Way of Reaching People*. Hagerstown, MD: Review and Herald, 1990.

Schilt, W. Clarence. *Dynamic Small Groups: How to Make Them Happen*. Hagerstown, MD: Review and Herald, 1992.

Sharpe, Timothy N. *My Feet Need Washing, Too*. Washington, DC: Review and Herald, 1990.

Shuler, J. L. *Public Evangelism: Its Approach and Problems*. Washington, DC: Review and Herald, 1939.

Shultz, J. E. *Fifty-Two Prayer Meetings*. Washington, DC: Review and Herald, 1936.

Staples, Russell L. *Community of Faith: The Seventh-day Adventist Church and the Contemporary World*. Hagerstown, MD: Review and Herald, 1999.

Thompson, George B. *Soul Winning*. Washington, DC: Review and Herald, 1916.

Vitrano, Steven P. *How to Preach: A Practical Guide to Better Sermons*. Hagerstown, MD: Review and Herald, 1991.

Waggoner, E. J. *The Honor Due to God: Thoughts on Tithes and Offerings*, 2nd ed. Oakland, CA: Pacific Press, 1884.

Wearner, Alonzo J. *The Art of Personal Evangelism: Practical Instruction Leading to Efficiency in the Finest Art—Soul Winning*. Washington, DC: Review and Herald, 1934.

White, Robert A. *How to Win a Soul*. Nashville, TN: Southern, 1971.

Women

Bacchiocchi, Samuele. *Women in the Church: A Biblical Study on the Role of Women in the Church*. Forewords by Wayne Grudem and James B. Hurley; essays by Rosalie Haffner Lee and William A. Fagal. Berrien Springs, MI: Biblical Perspectives, 1987.

Banks, Rosa Taylor, ed. *A Woman's Place*. Hagerstown, MD: Review and Herald, 1992.

Dyer, Mercedes H., ed. *Prove All things: A Response to "Women in Ministry."* Berrien Springs, MI: Adventists Affirm, 2000.

Habada, Patricia A., and Rebecca Frost Brillhart, eds. *The Welcome Table: Setting a Place for Ordained Women*. Langley Park, MD: TEAM Press, 1995.

Holmes, C. Raymond. *The Tip of an Iceberg*. Wakefield, MI: Adventists Affirm and Pointer Publications, 1994.

Morales-Gudmundsson, Lourdes E., ed. *Women and the Church: The Feminine Perspective*. Berrien Springs, MI: Andrews University Press, 1995.

Rosado, Caleb. *Women, Church, God*. Riverside, CA: La Sierra University Press, 1990.

Underwood, U. J. *Women in Their Place: Does God Call Women?* Berrien Springs, MI: Biblical Foundations, 1990.

Vance, Laura L. *Seventh-day Adventism in Crisis: Gender and Sectarian Change in an Emerging Religion*. Urbana: University of Illinois Press, 1999.

Vyhmeister, Nancy, ed. *Women in Ministry: Biblical and Historical Perspectives*. Berrien Springs, MI: Andrews University Press, 1998.

Christian Life

Andreasen, M. L. *Following the Master*. Nashville, TN: Southern, 1947.

Andross, Matilda E. *The Life That Wins.* Mountain View, CA: Pacific Press, 1922.

Bacchiocchi, Samuele. *Christian Dress and Adornment.* With essays by Laurel Damsteegt and Hedwig Jemison. Berrien Springs, MI: Biblical Perspectives, 1995.

Batchelor, Doug, with Karen Lifshay. *How to Survive in a Dead Church and Other Congregational Hazards to Your Spiritual Health.* Boise, ID: Pacific Press, 1994.

Beach, Walter Raymond. *Focusing on Fundamentals.* Nashville, TN: Southern, 1966.

Bietz, Arthur L. *Pulling Life Together: Source Book for Physicians, Ministers, Teachers, and Laymen.* Mountain View, CA: Pacific Press, 1952.

Blake, Chris. *Searching for a God to Love.* Nampa, ID: Pacific Press, 1999.

Brown, George W. *The Fruit of the Spirit.* Grantham, Lincolnshire, England: Stanborough Press, 1998.

Bunch, Taylor G. *Secrets of Godly Living.* Washington, DC: Review and Herald, 1953.

Carcich, Theodore. *Principles to Ponder.* Washington, DC: Review and Herald, 1963.

Church, Ginger. *A Woman's Walk with God: Finding Balance for Body and Soul.* Hagerstown, MD: Review and Herald, 2004.

Cooper, Douglas. *Living God's Joy.* Mountain View, CA: Pacific Press, 1979.

———. *Living God's Love.* Mountain View, CA: Pacific Press, 1975.

Davis, Thomas A. *How to Be a Victorious Christian.* Washington, DC: Review and Herald, 1975.

———. *Of Course You Can Walk on Water.* Washington, DC: Review and Herald, 1980.

Desir, Monica. *Thank God for Good and Bad Times.* Boise, ID: Pacific Press, 1985.

Douglass, Herbert E. *Faith: Saying Yes to God.* Nashville, TN: Southern, 1978.

Dudley, Roger L. *Passing on the Torch.* Washington, DC: Review and Herald, 1986.

Evans, I. H. *The Way of Love Divine.* Nashville, TN: Southern, 1940.

Fagal, William A. *By Faith I Live.* Nashville, TN: Southern, 1965.

Geraty, Lawrence T., comp. *God's Hand in My Life.* Nashville, TN: Southern, 1977.

Goldstein, Clifford. *By His Stripes.* Boise, ID: Pacific Press, 1999.

Guild, Daniel R. *We Can Have Peace: Victorious Living in Tumultuous Times.* Mountain View, CA: Pacific Press, 1960.

Hackett, Willis J. *Molding the Christian Mind*. Washington, DC: Review and Herald, 1978.

Haffner, Karl. *Pilgrim's Problems: Turn Your Troubles into Triumphs on the Road to God's Front Door*. Nampa, ID: Pacific Press, 2004.

Hammill, Richard L. *In Full Assurance*. Nashville, TN: Southern, 1959.

Hilde, Reuben. *In the Manner of Jesus*. Mountain View, CA: Pacific Press, 1977.

Hoehn, Edward. *God's Plan for Your Life*. Mountain View, CA: Pacific Press, 1953.

Holbrook, Betty. *I'd Pick More Daisies*. Washington, DC: Review and Herald, 1976.

Kern, Milton E. *The Lighted Way*. Washington, DC: Review and Herald, 1922.

Kuzma, Kay. *Creating Love: Principles That Can Revolutionize Your Relationships and Turn Obnoxious People Into Loveable Ones*. Nampa, ID: Pacific Press, 1997.

Lichtenwalter, Larry L. *Well-Driven Nails: How to Find Contentment in a Disappointing World*. Hagerstown, MD: Review and Herald, 1999.

Lloyd, Marjorie Lewis. *Crowns and Crosses: Thoughts and Poems About Life's Crosses*. Washington, DC: Review and Herald, 1949.

MacCarty, Skip. *Things We Don't Talk About: Help for the Private Struggles of Ordinary Adventists*. Hagerstown, MD: Review and Herald, 1997.

McMillan, Len D. *The Family of God and How to Live with Them*. Boise, ID: Pacific Press, 1988.

Mace, J. W. *Ablaze for God: Devotional Talks*. Washington, DC: Review and Herald, 1938.

Marshall, David. *Joy in Jesus: How to Pin Down, Catch and Keep What Most Christians Miss Out On*. Grantham, Lincolnshire, England: Autumn House, 1998.

Maxwell, Arthur S. *Back to God: The Call and the Way*. Mountain View, CA: Pacific Press, 1935.

Melashenko, E. Lonnie, and David B. Smith. *Rock-Solid Living in a Run-Amok World*. Hagerstown, MD: Review and Herald, 1999.

Mosley, Steven. *Burned Out on Being Good: What to Do If Religion Is Wearing You Out*. Nampa, ID: Pacific Press, 1998.

Neff, Merlin L. *Seeing It Through with God: Spiritual Morale in the Hour of Crisis*. Mountain View, CA: Pacific Press, 1943.

Nelson, Dwight K. *The Claim: Nine Radical Claims of Jesus That Can Revolutionize Your Life*. Boise, ID: Pacific Press, 1994.

———. *Outrageous Grace: Finding a Forever Friendship with God*. Nampa, ID: Pacific Press, 1998.

Ochs, D. A. *Happiness in Christian Living.* Nashville, TN: Southern, 1957.

———. *Life's Realities.* Nashville, TN: Southern, 1965.

Ochs, W. B. *The Christ-Centered Life.* Mountain View, CA: Pacific Press, 1961.

Oswald, Helen K. *The Key to Human Hearts.* Nashville, TN: Southern, 1968.

Paulsen, Jan. *Let Your Life So Shine: The Uncommon Rewards of Living Like Jesus.* Nampa, ID: Pacific Press, 2003.

Rice, M. Leslie. *Live and Help Live.* Washington, DC: Review and Herald, 1947.

Rockey, Nancy and Ron, with Kay Kuzma. *Belonging: Overcoming Rejection and Finding the Freedom of Acceptance.* Nampa, ID: Pacific Press, 1998.

Scragg, Walter R. L. *Directions: A Look at the Paths of Life.* Nashville, TN: Southern, 1977.

Scriven, Chuck, comp. *Into the Arena: Insight Essays on the Christian Life.* Washington, DC: Review and Herald, 1975.

Sequeira, Jack. *Laodicea: Christ's Urgent Counsel to a Lukewarm Church in the Last Days.* Boise, ID: Pacific Press, 1995.

Short, Ruth Gordon. *The Windows of Heaven.* Nashville, TN: Southern, 1960.

Snider, J. D. *The Vision Splendid.* Washington, DC: Review and Herald, 1959.

Sutton, Carolyn. *Staying Vertical: A Spiritual Tool Kit for Christ-Centered Living in an Out-of-Balance World.* Hagerstown, MD: Review and Herald, 2004.

Thompson, G. B. *In His Name.* Washington, DC: Review and Herald, 1918.

Thurber, Robert Bruce. *Personal Power for the New Age.* Oshawa, Ontario, Canada: Signs of the Times, 1946.

———. *Without Doubt: Faith for To-Day and To-Morrow.* Oshawa, Ontario, Canada: Signs of the Times, 1947.

Van Dolson, Leo R. *God's Footprint On My Floor.* Nashville, TN: Southern, 1977.

——— and Thomas A. Davis. *Managing God's Gifts: Three Perspectives on Commitment.* Boise, ID: Pacific Press, 1986.

Venden, Lee. *The Pleasure of His Company: Life-Changing Encounters with Jesus.* Hagerstown, MD: Review and Herald, 1994.

Venden, Morris L. *How to Know God's Will in Your Life.* Boise, ID: Pacific Press, 1987.

———. *Obedience of Faith.* Washington, DC: Review and Herald, 1983.

Wakeham, Irene. *Strictly Confidential*. Mountain View, CA: Pacific Press, 1954.

Wellman, S. A. *Your Stewardship and Mine: Its Blessings and Responsibilities*. Washington, DC: Review and Herald, 1950.

Yeagley, Larry. *Heartache and Healing: Coming to Terms with Grief*. Hagerstown, MD: Review and Herald, 1995.

———. *How to Get Beyond Loneliness*. Hagerstown, MD: Review and Herald, 1998.

Spirituality

Andreasen, M. L. *Prayer*. Mountain View, CA: Pacific Press, 1957.

Bunch, Taylor G. *The Perfect Prayer*. Washington, DC: Review and Herald, 1939.

———. *Prevailing Prayer*. Washington, DC: Review and Herald, 1946.

Coon, Glenn A. *The A,B,C's of Bible Prayer*. Washington, DC: Review and Herald, 1972.

——— and Ethel Coon. *Lovely Lord of the Lord's Day*. Mountain View CA: Pacific Press, 1976.

Cooper, Douglas. *Living the Spirit-filled Life*. Boise, ID: Pacific Press, 1985.

Crosby, Tim, Ruthie Jacobsen, and Lonnie Melashenko. *Passion for Prayer: Finding a New and Deeper Intimacy with God*. Hagerstown, MD: Review and Herald, 1998.

Dauphinee, Minnie E. *Drawing Nigh to God*. Washington, DC: Review and Herald, 1945; reprint, 1956; reprint, Redlands, CA: Quiet Hour, n.d.

Dickson, Louis K. *Key in the Hand*. Mountain View, CA: Pacific Press, 1956.

———. *Portals to Power*. Mountain View, CA: Pacific Press, 1957.

Engelkemier, Joe. *30 Days to a More Powerful Prayer Life: A Plan to Transform Your Heart and Your World*. Nampa, ID: Pacific Press, 1998.

Erickson, Matilda. *Alone with God: Fitting for Service*. Mountain View, CA: Pacific Press, 1917.

Kubo, Sakae. *Calculated Goodness*. Nashville, TN: Southern, 1974.

McKibbin, Alma E. *Half Hours with the Bible*. Mountain View, CA: Pacific Press, 1946.

Morneau, Roger. *The Incredible Power of Prayer*. Hagerstown, MD: Review and Herald, 1997.

Mosley, Steven. *Deepen My Heart*. Hagerstown, MD: Review and Herald, 1998.

———. *If Only God Would Answer*. Hagerstown, MD: Review and Herald, 1997.

O'Ffill, Richard. *If with All Your Heart: A God-Seeker's Guide to Effective Prayer*. Hagerstown, MD: Review and Herald, 2004.

———. *Transforming Prayer: Praying to Become Rather Than to Receive*. Hagerstown, MD: Review and Herald, 1999.

Pate, Don. *Episodes at the Olive Press*. Nashville, TN: Southern, 1980.

Paulien Jon. *Meet God Again for the First Time*. Hagerstown, MD: Review and Herald, 2003.

Pearce, William P. *In Touch with God*. Mountain View, CA: Pacific Press, 1915.

Peeler, Emil Dean. *The Zacchaeus Effect: Sometimes the Only Way to Refresh Your Relationship with Jesus Is to Go Out on a Limb*. Nampa, ID: Pacific Press, 2004.

Pelser, Frederick. *Prayer Made Practical: God at Close Quarters*. Grantham, Lincolnshire, England: Autumn House, 1996.

Rich, J. Walter. *The Shepherd and His Sheep: A Study of the Twenty-third Psalm*. Washington, DC: Review and Herald, 1938.

Rizzo, Kay. *A Place in God's Heart: Finding Joy in His Presence*. Nampa, ID: Pacific Press, 2004.

———. *On Wings of Praise: How I Found Real Joy in a Personal Friendship with God*. Hagerstown, MD: Review and Herald, 1996.

Samaan, Philip G. *Christ's Way to Spiritual Growth*. Hagerstown, MD: Review and Herald, 1995.

Shewmake, Carrol Johnson. *Practical Pointers to Personal Prayer*. Washington, DC: Review and Herald, 1989.

———. *Sanctuary Secrets to Personal Prayer: A Handbook for Sanctuary Prayer*. Washington, DC: Review and Herald, 1990.

———. *Sensing His Presence, Hearing His Voice: How to Cultivate Hearing the Voice of God*. Hagerstown, MD: Review and Herald, 1994.

Stevenson, Kris Coffin. *Delighting in God: Prayer Is Opening the Heart to a Friend*. Boise, ID: Pacific Press, 1996.

Wallenkampf, Arnold Valentin. *New By the Spirit*. Mountain View, CA: Pacific Press, 1978.

Watson, Cecilia M. *Spiritfruit: God's Buffet of Christian Graces*. Boise, ID: Pacific Press, 1986.

Watts, Dorothy Eaton. *Prayer Treasures: Discover the Riches of Prayer*. Boise, ID: Pacific Press, 1995.

Wilcox, Francis McLellan. *Day by Day: A Compilation of Bible Texts and Topics*. Washington, DC: Review and Herald, 1937.

———. *The More Abundant Life*. Washington, DC: Review and Herald, 1939.

Williams, Garrie F. *How to Be Filled With the Holy Spirit and Know It.* Washington, DC: Review and Herald, 1991.
Zackrison, James W. *Practical Spiritual Gifts.* Boise, ID: Pacific Press, 1996.

Attitudes and Practices

Benson, Peter L., and Michael J. Donahue. *Valuegenesis: Reports 1-3: A Study of the Influence of Family, Church and School on the Faith, Values and Commitment of Adventist Youth.* Minneapolis, MN: Search Institute, 1990-91.
Dudley, Roger L. *Why Our Teenagers Leave the Church: Personal Stories from a 10-Year Study.* Hagerstown, MD: Review and Herald, 2000.
———. *Why Teenagers Reject Religion and What to Do About It.* Washington, DC: Review and Herald, 1978.
——— with V. Bailey Gillespie, *ValueGenesis: Faith in the Balance.* Riverside, CA: La Sierra University Press/John Hancock Center for Youth Ministry, 1992.
——— and Janet Leigh Kangas. *The World of the Adventist Teenager.* Washington, DC: Review and Herald, 1990.
Gillespie, V. Bailey, ed. *Project Affirmation: Perspectives on Values.* Riverside, CA: La Sierra University Press, 1993.
Larson, Doris and Roland, with V. Bailey Gillespie. *Project Affirmation: Teaching Values.* Riverside, CA: La Sierra University Press, 1993.
South Pacific Division of Seventh-day Adventists. *Valuegenesis: Study 1: Core Report.* Wahroonga, New South Wales, Australia: South Pacific Division of Seventh-day Adventists, 1993.
Strahan, Bradley J. *Parents, Adolescents and Religion.* Valuegenesis Project Report 2. Wahroonga, New South Wales, Australia: South Pacific Division of Seventh-day Adventists, 1994.

Family, Marriage, and Sexuality

Avery-Stuttle, L. D. *Making Home Happy.* Battle Creek, MI: Review and Herald, 1898.
———. *Making Home Peaceful.* Mountain View, CA: Pacific Press, 1899.
Bacchiocchi, Samuele. *The Marriage Covenant: A Biblical Study on Marriage, Divorce, and Remarriage.* Berrien Springs, MI: Biblical Perspectives, 1991.
Beem, Thelma. *The Dignity of a Child.* Nashville: Southern, 1965.

Brothers, Marjorie Burch. *Are We There Yet?: A Practical Guide to Sane Parenting.* Hagerstown, MD: Review and Herald, 1998.

Brown, Jeffrey O. and Pattijean. *A Guide to Parenting: On the Winning Team with Your Children.* Grantham, Lincolnshire, England: Stanborough Press, 2003.

———. *The Total Marriage: A Guide to Successful Marriage.* Grantham, Lincolnshire, England: Autumn House, 1999.

Brown, Reginald K. *Surviving the Loss of a Loved One: Living Through Grief.* Grantham, Lincolnshire, England: Autumn House, 1999.

Chalmers, Elden M. and Esther L. *Making the Most of Family Living.* Mountain View, CA: Pacific Press, 1979.

Couden, Barbara, ed. *Understanding Intimate Violence.* Hagerstown, MD: Review and Herald, 1999.

Crider, Charles C., and Robert C. Kistler. *The Seventh-day Adventist Family: An Empirical Study.* Berrien Springs, MI: Andrews University Press, 1979.

Doran, Sandra Finley. *Every Time I Say Grace, We Fight: Practical Help for Marriages Divided by Religion but United by Love.* Hagerstown, MD: Review and Herald, 1992.

Dudley, Roger and Peggy. *Married and Glad of It.* Washington, DC: Review and Herald, 1980.

Edwards, Josephine Cunnington. *Children Can Be Taught.* Nashville, TN: Southern, 1960.

Franklin-Springer, Eugenia A. *Girl, It's All About You.* Washington, DC: Review and Herald, 1980.

Habenicht, Donna J. *How to Help Your Child Really Love Jesus: Practical Suggestions for Instilling Spiritual Values.* Hagerstown, MD: Review and Herald, 1994.

Hohnberger, Sally. *Parenting by the Spirit: Yes, You Can Be the Parent God Designed You to Be: Raising Godly Children in a Godless World.* Nampa, ID: Pacific Press, 2004.

Kistler, Robert C. *Marriage, Divorce, and —.* Washington, DC: Review and Herald, 1987.

Knight, John F. *What a Married Couple Should Know About Sex: A Book for Married Couples of Any Age and for Those Approaching Marriage.* Mountain View, CA: Pacific Press, 1979.

———. *What a Young Man Should Know About Sex: Answers to Personal Problems*, rev. ed. Mountain View, CA: Pacific Press, 1977.

———. *What a Young Woman Should Know About Sex: Answers to Personal Problems*, rev. ed. Mountain View, CA: Pacific Press, 1977.

Kubo, Sakae. *Theology and the Ethics of Sex.* Nashville, TN: Southern, 1980.

Kuzma, Kay. *Understanding Children.* Mountain View, CA: Pacific Press, 1978.

——— and Jan. *Building Character.* Mountain View, CA: Pacific Press, 1979.

McLaughlin, Kate. *My Son, Beloved Stranger.* Boise, ID: Pacific Press, 1995.

McMillan, Len D. *Parent Teen: An Adventist Counselor on Living With Teens—and Loving It.* Hagerstown, MD: Review and Herald, 1993.

———. *Why Can't My Mate Be More Like Me?* Boise, ID: Pacific Press, 1986.

——— and Marvin Wray. *First Class Male: The Christian Man's Role in Today's World.* Hagerstown, MD: Review and Herald, 1994.

———. *Putting Up with Mr. Right: How to Build Love, Friendship, and Intimacy.* Hagerstown, MD: Review and Herald, 1996.

Mazat, Alberta. *Questions You've Asked About Sexuality.* Boise, ID: Pacific Press, 1991.

———. *That Friday in Eden: Sharing and Enhancing Sexuality in Marriage.* Mountain View, CA: Pacific Press, 1981.

Olson, V. Norskov. *The New Relatedness for Man and Woman in Christ: A Mirror of the Divine.* Loma Linda, CA: Loma Linda University Center for Christian Bioethics, 1993.

Ritz, O. J. *Reflections on Love and Marriage.* Washington, DC: Review and Herald, 1965.

Robertson, Karen. *Raising Kids Right: Refreshingly Simply Advice to Help Take the Frustration out of Raising Children.* Hagerstown, MD: Review and Herald, 1998.

Schurch, Maylan. *But He Hit Me First! or Life in the Darkest Familia.* Washington, DC: Review and Herald, 1977.

Shryock, Harold. *Happiness for Husbands and Wives.* Washington, DC: Review and Herald, 1949.

———. *On Becoming a Man: A Book for Teenage Boys.* Washington, DC: Review and Herald, 1951.

———. *On Becoming a Woman: A Book for Teenage Girls.* Washington, DC: Review and Herald, 1951.

———. *On Being Married Soon.* Washington, DC: Review and Herald, 1968.

———. *On Being Sweethearts.* Washington, DC: Review and Herald, 1966.

Spalding, Arthur Whitefield. *Makers of the Home.* Mountain View, CA: Pacific Press, 1928.

——— and Belle Wood-Comstock. *The Days of Youth: A Study of the Period of Adolescence*. Mountain View, CA: Pacific Press, 1932.

———. *Growing Boys and Girls: The Training and Culture of the Child in Pre-Adolescence from Ten to Thirteen*. Mountain View, CA: Pacific Press, 1931.

Springett, Ronald M. *Homosexuality in History and the Scriptures: Some Historical and Biblical Perspectives on Homosexuality*. Washington, DC: Biblical Research Institute, 1988.

Van Pelt, Nancy. *The Compleat Courtship*. Nashville, TN: Southern, 1982.

———. *The Compleat Marriage*. Nashville, TN: Southern, 1979.

———. *The Compleat Parent*. Nashville, TN: Southern, 1976.

———. *Smart Love: A Field Guide for Single Adults*. Grand Rapids, MI: Revell, 1977.

Williams, Flora H. *You and Your Child*. Nashville, TN: Southern, 1946.

Wittschiebe, Charles E. *God Invented Sex*. Nashville, TN: Southern, 1974.

———. *Teens and Love and Sex*. Washington, DC: Review and Herald, 1982.

Wolcott, Marilyn A. *Respect in the Family*. Hagerstown, MD: Review and Herald, 1999.

Wood-Comstock, Belle. *Is Love Enough? A Discussion of the Problems of the Home and of Married Life*. Mountain View, CA: Pacific Press, 1940.

Youngberg, John and Millie. *Unbroken Circle: How to Take Your Family through the End Time*. Nampa, ID: Pacific Press, 1997.

Health and Temperance

Abbott, George Knapp. *Principles and Practice of Hydrotherapy for Students and Practitioners of Medicine*. Loma Linda, CA: The College Press, 1914.

———, Fred B. Moor, and Kathryn L. Jensen-Nelson. *Physical Therapy in Nursing Care*. Washington, DC: Review and Herald, 1945.

Almack, John C. *A Clear Case Against Narcotics: Alcohol, Tobacco, Marihuana, Opium, and Cocaine*. Mountain View, CA: Pacific Press, 1939.

Bacchiocchi, Samuele. *Wine in the Bible: A Biblical Study on the Use of Alcoholic Beverages*. Berrien Springs, MI: Biblical Perspectives, 1989.

Chen, Philip Stanley. *The Joy of Being a Vegetarian*. Mountain View, CA: Pacific Press, 1977.

Cheraskin, E., and W. M. Ringsdorf, Jr. *Predictive Medicine: A Study in Strategy.* Mountain View, CA: Pacific Press, 1973.

Donaldson, Arthur N. *Health at Home: How to Obtain It.* Mountain View, CA: Pacific Press, 1938.

Duffie, David. *Psychology and the Christian Religion.* Nashville, TN: Southern, 1968.

Evans, Newton, Percy T. Magan, and George Thomason, eds. *The Home Physician and Guide to Health: A Treatise on the Prevention and Cure of Disease.* Mountain View, CA: Pacific Press, 1923.

Farnsworth, Vesta J. *The House We Live In; or, The Making of the Body; A Book for Home Reading, Intended to Assist Mothers in Teaching Their Children How to Care for Their Bodies.* Oakland, CA: Pacific Press, 1900.

Fort, Lyman M. *Alcohol and You.* Mountain View, CA: Pacific Press, 1954.

Fraser, Gary E. *Diet, Life Expectancy, and Chronic Disease: Studies of Seventh-day Adventists and Other Vegetarians.* New York: Oxford University Press, 2003.

Gill, Mabel K. *Mind, Body and Religion.* Nashville, TN: Southern, 1965.

Hansen, Louis A. *Keeping Well.* Nashville, TN: Southern, 1925.

Hardinge, Mervyn G. *A Physician Explains Ellen White's Counsel on Drugs, Herbs, and Natural Remedies.* Hagerstown, MD: Review and Herald, 2001.

Hawley, Don. *Come Alive!: Feel Fit—Live Longer.* Washington, DC: Review and Herald, 1975.

Hewitt, Donald W. *The Cigarette and You.* Mountain View, CA: Pacific Press, 1953.

———. *Diet Without Danger: A Physician's Guide to Shedding Unwanted Weight with Safety and Sanity.* Mountain View, CA: Pacific Press, 1980.

———. *Escape from Alcohol.* Mountain View, CA: Pacific Press, 1953.

Home and Health: A Household Manual. Washington, DC: Review and Herald, 1907.

Jones, Elton. *The Cup that Cheers.* Mountain View, CA: Pacific Press, 1937.

Kellogg, John Harvey. *The Home Hand-Book of Domestic Hygiene and Rational Medicine.* Battle Creek, MI: Good Health, 1880.

———. *Rational Hydrotherapy, A Manual of the Physiological and Therapeutic Effects of Hydriatic Procedures, and the Technique of Their Application in the Treatment of Disease,* 2nd ed. Philadelphia: F. A. Davis, 1902.

————. *The Uses of Water in Health and Disease: A Practical Treatise on the Bath, Its History and Uses.* Battle Creek, MI: Office of the Health Reformer, 1876.

Kellogg, M. G. *Good Health and How to Preserve It.* Battle Creek, MI: Office of the Health Reformer, 1874.

Kloss, Walter E. *Addiction: How Christians Can Respond Positively to a Growing Crisis.* Washington, DC: Review and Herald, 1987.

Kress, Daniel H. *The Cigarette as a Physician Sees It.* Mountain View, CA: Pacific Press, 1931.

Lantry, Eileen E. *The Vitality Makers: A Turbocharged Life-style in Thirty Days.* Boise, ID: Pacific Press, 1985.

Ludington, Aileen, and Hans Diehl. *Dynamic Living: How to Take Charge of Your Health.* Hagerstown, MD: Review and Herald, 1995.

————. *Health Power: Health by Choice Not Chance.* Hagerstown, MD: Review and Herald, 2000.

Marsh, Alice G., et al. *About Nutrition, by the Seventh-day Adventist Dietetic Association.* Nashville, TN: Southern, 1971.

Medical Department, General Conference of Seventh-day Adventists. *Health and Home Nursing: A Textbook.* Washington, DC: Review and Herald, 1949.

————. *Principles of Healthful Living.* Washington, DC: Review and Herald, 1940.

Miller, H. W. *The Way to Health: Principles of Right Living and Methods of Practical Nursing.* Washington, DC: Review and Herald, 1920.

Moore, Raymond S., and Dorothy N. Moore. *Home Made Health: A Family Guide to Nutrition, Exercise, Stress Control, and Preventive Medicine.* Waco, TX: Word, 1986.

Nelson, Kathryn L. *The Mother and the Child: A Dozen Health Visits.* Washington, DC: Review and Herald, 1927.

Nelson, Rueben E. *Dear Mother-to-be; Prenatal Care of the Expectant Mother.* Mountain View, CA: Pacific Press, 1961.

Nichol, Francis D. *The Case Against Liquor: A Calm Portrayal of the Facts and a Proposed Solution of the Age-Old Problem of Liquor.* Washington, DC: Review and Herald, 1944.

Nieman, David C. *The Adventist Healthstyle.* Hagerstown, MD: Review and Herald, 1992.

Noorbergen, Rene. *Programmed to Live: A Scientific Confirmation of Health Reform.* Mountain View, CA: Pacific Press, 1975.

Osman, Jack D. *Thin from Within.* Washington, DC: Review and Herald, 1981.

Ponder, Timothy. *How to Avoid Burnout.* Mountain View, CA: Pacific Press, 1983.

Ramsey, Ronald W., and Rene Noorbergen. *Living with Loss: A Dramatic New Breakthrough in Grief Therapy.* New York: Morrow, 1981.

Richards, B. Franklin. *Health: How to Find It When It's Lost, How to Keep It When It's Found.* Oakland, CA: Pacific Press, 1899.

Richardson, Frank Howard. *A Christian Doctor Talks with Young Parents.* Washington, DC: Review and Herald, 1962.

Rossiter, Frederick M. *The Practical Guide to Health.* Washington, DC: Review and Herald, 1910.

The Shadow of the Bottle: Published in the Interest of Nation-Wide Prohibition of the Liquor Traffic. Washington, DC: Review and Herald, 1915.

Shryock, Harold. *Happiness and Health.* Mountain View, CA: Pacific Press, 1950.

—— and Hubert O. Swartout. *You and Your Health.* Mountain View, CA: Pacific Press, 1970.

Sutton, Arthur E. *The Heart Menders: The Dramatic Story of Open-Heart Surgery at Loma Linda University.* Nashville, TN: Southern, 1965.

Swartout, Hubert O., et al. *Modern Medical Councilor: A Practical Guide to Health.* Mountain View, CA: Pacific Press, 1943.

Thomason, George, and Alonzo L. Baker. *Science Speaks to Young Men on Liquor, Tobacco, Narcotics, and Marijuana.* Mountain View, CA: Pacific Press, 1938.

Van Dolson, Leo R. *The Golden Eight: Eight Dynamic, Golden Rules That Lead to Total Health.* Washington, DC: Review and Herald, 1977.

—— and J. Robert Spangler. *Healthy, Happy, Holy.* Washington, DC: Review and Herald, 1975.

Vollmer, Marion W. *Food: Health and Efficiency; Lessons in Nutrition and Healthful Food Preparation.* Nashville, TN: Southern, 1954.

Walton, Lewis R., Jo Ellen Walton, and John A. Scharffenberg. *How You Can Live Six Extra Years.* Santa Barbara, CA: Woodbridge Press, 1981.

Wilcox, Francis McLellan. *The Gospel of Health: A Discussion of the Underlying Principles of Healthful Living, Based on the Teaching of the Bible and the Writings of Mrs. E. G. White, with the Confirmatory Evidence of Scientific Research.* Washington, DC: Review and Herald, 1935.

Willis, Richard J. B., et al. *Your Health in Your Hands.* Grantham, Lincolnshire, England: Autumn House, 1994.

Wood-Comstock, Belle. *All About the Baby: The Beginnings of Human Life with Early Needs.* Mountain View, CA: Pacific Press, 1930.

———. *The Home Dietitian; or, Food and Health; Scientific Dietetics Practically Applied,* 2nd ed. Washington, DC: Review and Herald, 1922.

———. *Physiology: The Human Body and How to Keep it in Health.* Mountain View, CA: Pacific Press, 1925.

———. *Questions Girls Have Asked.* Nashville, TN: Southern, 1962.

———. *Three Times a Day.* Washington, DC: Review and Herald, 1937.

——— and Alonzo L. Baker. *Plain Facts for Girls and Young Women on Narcotics, Liquor, and Tobacco.* Mountain View, CA: Pacific Press, 1938.

Zackrison, James W., ed. *The Master's Healing Touch.* Hagerstown, MD: Review and Herald, 1997.

Ethics

Brunt, John. *Decision: How to Use Biblical Guidelines When Making Decisions.* Nashville, TN: Southern, 1979.

Kainer, Gordon. *Faith, Hope and Clarity: A Look at Situation Ethics and Biblical Ethics.* Mountain View, CA: Pacific Press, 1977.

Larson, David R. *Abortion: Ethical Issues and Options.* Loma Linda, CA: Loma Linda University, Center for Christian Bioethics, 1992.

Londis, James. *God's Finger Wrote Freedom.* Washington, DC: Review and Herald, 1978.

Pearson, Michael. *Millennial Dreams and Moral Dilemmas: Seventh-day Adventism and Contemporary Ethics.* Cambridge: Cambridge University Press, 1990.

Plantak, Zdravko. *The Silent Church: Human Rights and Adventist Social Ethics.* Foreword by Sakae Kubo. New York: St. Martin's, 1998.

Scriven, Charles. *The Transformation of Culture: Christian Social Ethics after H. Richard Niebuhr.* Scottdale, PA: Herald Press, 1988.

Teel, Charles W., Jr. *Remnant and Republic: Adventist Themes for Personal and Social Ethics.* Introduction by Martin E. Marty. Loma Linda, CA: Loma Linda University, Center for Christian Bioethics, 1995.

Veatch Robert M., and Roy Branson. *Ethics and Health Policy.* Cambridge, MA: Ballinger, 1976.

Walters, James W. *Bioethics Today—A New Ethical Vision.* Loma Linda, CA: Loma Linda University Press, 1988.

Winslow, Gerald. *Triage and Justice.* Berkeley, CA: University of California Press, 1982.

Education

Cady, Marion E. *Education in the Bible: Principles, Practice, and Product of the Ancient Hebrew System, with Applications to the Problems of Modern Education.* Washington, DC: Review and Herald, 1923.

Hale, Katherine B., Sarah Elizabeth Peck, and Marion Ernest Cady. *True Education Reader Series.* 8 vols. Mountain View: Pacific Press, 1907-26.

Hilde, Reuben. *Showdown: Can Seventh-day Adventist Education Pass the Test?* Washington, DC: Review and Herald, 1980.

Knight, George R. *Philosophy & Education: An Introduction in Christian Perspective.* Berrien Springs, MI: Andrews University Press, 1980; 2nd ed, 1989; 3rd ed. 1998.

Moore, Raymond S. *School Can Wait.* Provo, UT: Brigham Young University Press, 1979.

———— and Dorothy N. Moore. *Better Late Than Early: A New Approach to Your Child's Education.* New York: Reader's Digest, 1975.

————. *Home Grown Kids: A Practical Handbook for Teaching Your Children at Home.* Waco, TX: Word, 1981.

———— and Todd C. Murdoch. *Adventist Education at the Crossroads.* Berrien Springs, MI: Hewitt Research Center, 1975.

Rasi, Humberto M., comp. *Christ in the Classroom: Adventist Approaches to the Integration of Faith and Learning.* 29 vols. Silver Spring, MD: Institute for Christian Teaching, 1991—.

Sutherland, E. A. *Living Fountains or Broken Cisterns: An Educational Problem for Protestants.* Battle Creek, MI: Review and Herald, 1900.

Art, Literature, and Music

Bacchiocchi, Samuele, ed. *The Christian and Rock Music: A Study on Biblical Principles of Music.* Berrien Springs, MI: Biblical Perspectives, 2000.

Bell, G. H. *Studies in English and American Literature.* Chicago: Ainsworth, 1900.

Cobb, L. W. *Give Attendance to Reading.* Portland, OR: by the author, 1966.

Christian, Ed. *Joyful Noise.* Hagerstown, MD: Review and Herald, 2003.

Davis, Delmer. *Teaching Literature: A Seventh-day Adventist Approach.* Berrien Springs, MI: Andrews University Press, 2002.

Dunn, Robert P., ed. *Seventh-day Adventists on Literature.* Riverside, CA: Department of English, Loma Linda University, 1974.

Grauman, Helen G. *Music in My Bible.* Mountain View, CA: Pacific Press, 1956.

Hamel, Paul. *The Christian and His Music.* Washington, DC: Review and Herald, 1973.

Hannum, Harold B. *Christian Search for Beauty: A Review of the Relationship of the Arts, Particularly Music, to the Principles of Christianity.* Nashville, TN: Southern, 1975.

———. *Let the People Sing: A Guide to Singing the Lord's Songs with Understanding.* Washington, DC: Review and Herald, 1981.

———. *Music and Worship.* Nashville, TN: Southern, 1969.

Olsen, M. Ellsworth. *Much-Loved Books.* Washington, DC: Review and Herald, 1952.

Snider, John D. *I Love Books: Why, What, How, and When We Should Read.* Washington, DC: Review and Herald, 1942; rev. ed, 1946. Also published as *Highways to Learning: A Guide through Bookland.* Washington, DC: Review and Herald, 1951.

Wehtje, Verne, ed. *Language Matters: Notes toward an Adventist English Program.* Nashville, TN: Southern, 1978.

History

Jones, Alonzo Trévier. *Ecclesiastical Empire.* Battle Creek, MI: Review and Herald, 1901.

———. *The Empires of the Bible from the Confusion of Tongues to the Babylonian Captivity.* Battle Creek, MI: Review and Herald, 1897.

———. *The Great Empires of Prophecy, from Babylon to the Fall of Rome.* Battle Creek, MI: Review and Herald, 1898.

Land, Gary. *Teaching History: A Seventh-day Adventist Approach.* Berrien Springs, MI: Andrews University Press, 2000.

Schwantes, Siegfried. *The Biblical Meaning of History.* Mountain View, CA: Pacific Press, 1970.

Shankel, George Edgar. *God and Man in History: A Study in the Christian Understanding of History.* Nashville, TN: Southern, 1967.

Spicer, William A. *The Gospel in All the World: The Great Sign that Christ's Coming Is Near.* Washington, DC: Review and Herald, 1926.

Vick, Edward W. H. *History and Christian Faith: An Introduction.* Nottingham, England: Evening Publications, 2003.

Wilkinson, Benjamin George. *Truth Triumphant: The Church in the Wilderness.* Mountain View, CA: Pacific Press, 1944.

Society, Culture, and International Affairs

Beach, Bert Beverly. *Vatican II: Bridging the Abyss.* Washington, DC: Review and Herald, 1968.

Bergherm, William H. *No Greater Glory.* Mountain View, CA: Pacific Press, 1959.

Bethmann, Erich W. *Bridge to Islam: A Study of the Religious Forces of Islam and Christianity in the Near East.* Nashville, TN: Southern, 1950.

Bradford, C. E., et al. *Our Times as I See Them.* Nashville, TN: Southern, 1980.

Bruinsma, Reinder. *Seventh-day Adventist Attitudes Toward Roman Catholicism, 1844-1965.* Berrien Springs, MI: Andrews University Press, 1994.

Cleveland, E. E. *The Middle Wall.* Washington, DC: Review and Herald, 1969.

Doukhan, Jacques. *Drinking at the Sources: An Appeal to the Jew and the Christian to Note Their Common Beginnings,* trans. Walter R. Beach and Robert M. Johnston. Mountain View, CA: Pacific Press, 1981.

Dudley, Roger L. *When Teen-agers Cry, Help!: How to Counsel Effectively.* Washington, DC: Review and Herald, 1981.

———. *The World—Love It or Leave It?* Boise, ID: Pacific Press, 1986.

——— and Edwin I. Hernandez. *Citizens of Two Worlds: Religion and Politics among American Seventh-day Adventists.* Berrien Springs, MI: Andrews University Press, 1992.

Gilbert, F. C. *The Cure for Crime: The Terrible Crime Wave that is Sweeping Over the World, the Reasons for it, and the Only Cure.* Washington, DC: Review and Herald, 1926.

———. *The Jewish Problem.* Washington, DC: Review and Herald, 1940.

Haus, Cari Hoyt, and Madlyn Lewis Hamblin. *In the Wake of Waco: Why Were Adventists Among the Victims?* Hagerstown, MD: Review and Herald, 1993.

Kistler, Robert C. *Adventists and Labor Unions in the United States.* Washington, DC: Review and Herald, 1984.

Magan, Percy T. *The Peril of the Republic of the United States of America.* Chicago: Fleming H. Revell, 1899.

Paulien, Jon. *The Day That Changed the World: Seeking God After September 11.* Hagerstown, MD: Review and Herald, 2002.
———. *Present Truth in the Real World: The Adventist Struggle to Keep and Share Faith in a Secular Society.* Boise, ID: Pacific Press, 1993.
Pollard, Leslie N. *Embracing Diversity: How to Understand and Reach People of All Cultures.* Hagerstown, MD: Review and Herald, 2000.
Rasi, Humberto, and Fritz Guy, eds. *Meeting the Secular Mind: Some Adventist Perspectives,* 2nd ed. Berrien Springs, MI: Andrews University Press, 1987.
Rine, George W., et al. *World Problems.* Mountain View, CA: Pacific Press, 1917.
Russell, E. T. *The Conflict Between Capital and Labor: A Fair, Candid, and Impartial Treatment of the Subject from a Non-partisan and Christian Standpoint.* Mountain View, CA: Pacific Press, 1905.
Samaan, Philip. *Blood Brothers.* Boise, ID: Pacific Press, 1991.
Weber, Martin. *Wrestling with Reality.* Boise, ID: Pacific Press, 1993.

Religious Liberty

Benton, Roy Lee. *America, the Bible, and the Constitution.* Washington, DC: Review and Herald, 1946.
Blakely, William A., ed. *American State Papers Bearing on Sunday Legislation.* New York: National Religious Liberty Association, 1891; rev. ed., Willard Allen Colcord, ed. Washington DC: The Religious Liberty Association, 1911; 3rd rev. ed., 1943; 4th rev. ed., 1979.
Haynes, Carlyle B. *World Calendar Versus World Religion: An Analysis of Proposed Calendar Reform.* Angwin, CA: Pacific Union College Press, 1944.
Hegstad, Roland R., comp. *Baseball, Popcorn, Apple Pie and Liberty.* Washington, DC: Review and Herald, 1979.
Holmes, Claude E. *Imperiled Democracy.* Nashville, TN: Southern, 1938.
International Religious Liberty Association. *Freedom, Civil and Religious: The American Conception of Liberty for Press, Pulpit, and Public, as Guaranteed in the Federal Constitution.* Washington, DC: Review and Herald, 1920.
Johns, Varner J. *Forty Centuries of Law and Liberty: A History of the Development of Religious Liberty.* Mountain View, CA: Pacific Press, 1940.

Johns, Warren L. *Dateline Sunday, U.S.A.: The Story of Three and a Half Centuries of Sunday-Law Battles in America.* Mountain View, CA: Pacific Press, 1967.

Jones, Alonzo Trévier. *Civil Government and Religion: Or, Christianity and the American Constitution.* Oakland, CA: Pacific Press, 1889.

———. *The Struggle of the Ages for Civil and Religious Liberty: The Two Republics, or, Rome and the United States of America.* Battle Creek, MI: Review and Herald, 1891.

Littlejohn, Wolcott H. *The Coming Conflict, or the United States to Become a Persecuting Power. A Series of Papers on the Present Sunday Agitation.* Battle Creek, MI: Review and Herald, 1883.

Longacre, Charles S. *The Church in Politics.* Washington, DC: Review and Herald, 1927.

Magan, Percy T. *The Vatican and the War; A Retrospect and Forecast: Being a Review of the Past Attitude of the Vatican Towards Civil and Religious Government, and an Analysis of Her Latest Utterance Upon These Matters as Related to the European War.* Nashville, TN: Southern, 1915.

Nichol, Francis D. *The Story of a Lost Day.* Mountain View, CA: Pacific Press, 1930.

Religious Liberty Association of North America. *Freedom of Religion: The Heritage of Liberty and the Dangers Facing America Today, A Symposium Prepared by the Religious Liberty Association.* Mountain View, CA: Pacific Press, 1944.

Snow, Charles M. *Religious Liberty in America.* Washington, DC: Review and Herald, 1913.

Votaw, H. H. *Your Freedom and Mine.* Washington, DC: Review and Herald, 1948.

Yost, Frank H. *Let Freedom Ring: The Story of Religious Liberty and the Menaces It Faces Today.* Mountain View, CA: Pacific Press, 1946.

Dissident Movements, Critics, and Adventist Responses

Anderson, Dirk. *White Out: How a Prophetess's Failed Visions, Mistaken Prophecies, and Embarrassing Blunders were Covered Up by Her Followers.* Alvarado, TX: Into All the World Wide Web, 1999.

Andreasen, M. L. *Letters to the Churches.* Series A. Baker, OR: Hudson Printing Company, [1959].

Bacchiocchi, Samuele. *The Sabbath Under Crossfire.* Berrien Springs, MI: Biblical Perspectives, 1999.

Ballenger, Albion F. *Cast Out for the Cross of Christ.* Riverside, CA: n.d.

Bellah, Charles G. *Trying the Spirits: Rowenism Weighed and Wanting.* Topeka, KS: Kansas Conference of Seventh-day Adventists, 1923.

Biblical Research Committee, General Conference of Seventh-day Adventists. *The Brinsmead Agitation.* Washington, DC: Review and Herald, 1969.

Bradford, Graeme. *Prophets Are Human.* Victoria, Australia: Signs, 2004.

Branson, W. H. *In Defense of the Faith: The Truth About Seventh-day Adventists, A Reply to Canright.* Washington, DC: Review and Herald, 1933.

Brinsmead, Robert J. *Judged by the Gospel.* Fallbrook, CA: Verdict, 1980.

Canright, D. M. *Life of Mrs. E. G. White.* Cincinnati: Standard Publishing Co., 1919.

———. *Seventh-day Adventism Renounced After an Experience of Twenty-eight Years.* Kalamazoo, MI: Kalamazoo Publishing Company, 1888.

Cleveland, Sydney. *White-Washed: Uncovering the Myths of Ellen G. White,* rev. ed. Greenwood, IN: by the author, 1999.

Conradi, Ludwig R. *The Founders of the Seventh-day Adventist Denomination.* Plainfield, NJ: American Sabbath Tract Society, 1939.

A Critique of Prophetess of Health. Washington, DC: Ellen G. White Estate, 1976.

Douty, Norman F. *The Case of D. M. Canright.* Grand Rapids, MI: Baker, 1964.

Ford, Desmond. *Daniel 8:14, The Day of Atonement, and the Investigative Judgment.* Casselberry, FL: Euangelian Press, 1980.

Goldstein, Clifford. *Graffiti in the Holy of Holies: An Impassioned Response to Recent Attacks on the Sanctuary and Ellen White.* Hagerstown, MD: Review and Herald, 2003.

Hoekema, Anthony. *The Four Major Cults: Christian Science, Jehovah's Witnesses, Mormonism, Seventh-day Adventism.* Grand Rapids, MI: Eerdmans, 1963.

Houteff, V. T. *The Shepherd's Rod.* 2 vols.. Waco, TX: Universal, 1932.

———. *The Shepherd's Rod Series: Original Writings of V. T. Houteff.* Salem, SC: General Association of Davidian Seventh-Day Adventists, 1990.

Issues: The Seventh-day Adventist Church and Certain Private Minis-tries. Silver Spring, MD: North American Division of Seventh-day Adventists, n.d.

Kramer, Helmut H. *The Seventh-day Adventist Reform Movement (Ger-man Reform).* Silver Spring, MD: Biblical Research Institute, Gen-eral Conference of Seventh-day Adventists, 1988.

Martin, Walter R. *The Truth About Seventh-day Adventists.* Grand Rap-ids, MI: Zondervan, 1960.

Ministerial Association, General Conference of Seventh-day Advent-ists. *Doctrinal Discussions.* Washington, DC: Review and Herald, n.d.

Nichol, Francis D. *Answers to Objections: An Examination of the Ma-jor Objections Raised Against the Teachings of Seventh-day Ad-ventists,* rev. ed. Foreword by W. H. Branson. Washington, DC: Review and Herald, 1952.

———. *Ellen G. White and Her Critics.* Washington, DC: Review and Herald, 1951.

Pacific Union Conference of Seventh-day Adventists. *A Reply to the Shepherd's Rod.* Mountain View, CA: Pacific Press, 1934.

Paxton, Geoffrey J. *The Shaking of Adventism.* Grand Rapids, MI: Baker Book House, 1977.

Pickle, Bob. *A Response to the Video: "Seventh-day Adventism—The Spirit Behind the Church."* Halstad, MN: Decisions, 2002.

Ratzlaff, Dale. *The Cultic Doctrine of Seventh-day Adventists.* Fore-word by Kenneth Samples. Glendale, AZ: Life Assurance Minis-tries, 1996.

———. *Sabbath in Christ.* Glendale, AZ: Life Assurance Ministries, 2003.

———. *Sabbath in Crisis.* Applegate, CA: Life Assurance Ministries, 1990.

Rea, Walter T. *The White Lie.* Turlock, CA: M & R Publications, 1982.

Research and Defense Literature Committee, General Conference of Seventh-day Adventists. *The History and Teachings of Robert Brinsmead.* Washington, DC: Review and Herald, 1961.

Robertson, John J. *The White Truth.* Mountain View, CA: Pacific Press, 1981.

Seventh-day Adventist Defense Literature Committee. *History and Teachings of "The Shepherd's Rod."* Washington, DC: The Com-mittee, 1955.

Seventh-day Adventists Answer Questions on Doctrine: An Explanation of Certain Major Aspects of Seventh-day Adventist Belief, Pre-pared by a Representative Group of Seventh-day Adventist Lead-ers, Bible Teachers, and Editors. Washington, DC: Review and

Herald, 1957; reprint, Annotated Edition with Historical and Theological Introduction by George R. Knight, Adventist Classic Library. Berrien Springs, MI: Andrews University Press, 2003.

Spear, Ron. *Adventism in Crisis*. Eatonville, WA: Hope International, 1987.

———. *The Waymarks of Adventism*. Eatonville, WA: Hope International, 1988.

Standish, Russell R., and Colin B. Standish. *Adventism Challenged: The Storm Breaks*. Brisbane, Australia: Hartland Institute, 1986.

———. *Deceptions of the New Theology*. Hartland, VA: Hartland, 1989.

———. *The Embattled Church*. Rapidan, VA: Hartland, 1995.

Tarling, Lowell. *The Edges of Seventh-day Adventism: A Study of Separatist Groups Emerging from the Seventh-day Adventist Church (1844-1980)*. Barraga Bay, Bermagui South, Australia: Galilee, 1981.

Wieland, Robert J. *1888 Re-examined: 1888-1988, the Story of a Century of Confrontation between God and His People*. Meadow Vista: CA: 1888 Message Study Committee, 1987.

Interpretations of Adventism

Bloom, Harold. *The American Religion*. New York: Simon & Schuster, 1992.

Bull, Malcolm, and Keith Lockhart. *Seeking a Sanctuary: Seventh-day Adventism and the American Dream*. San Francisco: Harper & Row, 1989.

Conkin, Paul K. *American Originals: Homemade Varieties of Christianity*. Chapel Hill, NC: University of North Carolina Press, 1997.

Moore, R. Laurence. *Religious Outsiders and the Making of Americans*. New York: Oxford University Press, 1986.

Schwartz, Gary. *Sect Ideologies and Social Status*. Chicago: University of Chicago Press, 1970.

Staples, Russell L. "Adventism." In *The Variety of American Evangelicalism*, eds. Donald Dayton and Robert Johnston. Downers Grove, IL: InterVarsity Press, 1991.

Wilson, Bryan. *Religious Sects: A Sociological Study*. World University Library. New York: McGraw-Hill, 1970.

Libraries and Archival Depositories

Archives and Museum, Oakwood College. Huntsville, Alabama.

Archives and Special Collections, Del Webb Library, Loma Linda University. Loma Linda, California.
Berkshire Christian College. Lenox, Massachusetts.
Center for Adventist Research, James White Library, Andrews University. Berrien Springs, Michigan.
Daniel T. Taylor Collection, American Antiquarian Society. Worcester, Massachusetts.
Ellen G. White Estate, Inc., General Conference of Seventh-day Adventists. Silver Spring, Maryland.
European Archives for Seventh-day Adventist History. Friedensau University, Friedensau bei Burg/Sachen-Anhalt, Germany.
European Archives for Seventh-day Adventist History. Collonges. Salève Adventist University, Collonges-sous-Salève Cedex, France.
Hon Heritage Room, Library, Avondale College. Cooranbong, New South Wales, Australia.
Jenks Collection, Charles B. Phillips Library, Aurora University. Aurora, Illinois.
Office of Archives and Statistics, General Conference of Seventh-day Adventists. Silver Spring, Maryland.

Web Sites

Denominational

Adventist Organization Directory: adventistdirectory.org
Adventist Resources, James White Library, Andrews University: andrews.edu/library/sda.html
Adventist Review: adventistreview.org
Center for Adventist Research, James White Library, Andrews University: andrews.edu/library/car/index.html
Ellen G. White Estate: whiteestate.org
General Conference of Seventh-day Adventists: adventist.org
North American Division Church Directory: database.tagnet.org/nadChurchLocator.html
SDA Obituary Index: andrews.edu/library/car/sdapiobits.html
SDA Periodical Index: andrews.edu/library/car/sdapiindex.html
SDA *Yearbook*: adventistyearbook.org
Women's Resource Center, La Sierra University: adventistwomenscenter.org

Independent

Adventist Pioneer Library: aplib.org
Adventist Today: atoday.org
Association of Adventist Forums/*Spectrum*: spectrummagazine.org
International Adventist Musicians Association: imaonline.com
SDANet: sdanet.org
Three Angels Global Networking Services: home.tagnet.org

Dissident Movements and Critics

Ellen G. White Research Project: ellenwhite.org
Former Adventist Fellowship Online: formeradventist.com
Hope International: hopeint.org
Life Assurance Ministries/Dale Ratzlaff: ratzlaf.com

About the Author

Gary Land is professor of history and chair of the Department of History and Political Science at Andrews University in Berrien Springs, Michigan. He holds degrees from Pacific Union College (B.A.) and the University of California, Santa Barbara (M.A., Ph.D.), and has taught at Andrews University since 1970. He is a member of the Conference on Faith and History and the Association of Seventh-day Adventist Historians. Land was a founding editor of *Adventist Heritage: A Journal of Adventist History* and currently serves as a consulting editor for *Spectrum: The Journal of the Association of Adventist Forums*. He has edited *Adventism in America: A History* (1986, rev. ed., 1998), *The World of Ellen G. White* (1987), and *Growing Up with Baseball: How We Loved and Played the Game* (2004). Land has also written *Teaching History: A Seventh-day Adventist Approach* (2000) and, with Calvin W. Edwards, *Seeker after Light: A. F. Ballenger, Adventism, and American Christianity* (2000).